International Management Behavior

Dedication

To all the friends who have helped me learn about other cultures, and my own.

Henry W. Lane

To my parents and grandparents, whose combined legacy of deep pride in our Old World roots and openness to New World diversity has provided me with a wonderfully rich cultural life.

Joseph J. DiStefano

To Katie and Juhanna, to help them inspire the next generation.

Martha L. Maznevski

International Management Behavior
Text, Readings and Cases

Fourth Edition

Henry W. Lane
Darla and Frederick Brodsky
Trustee Professor in International Business
Northeastern University

Joseph J. DiStefano
IMD, Lausanne, Switzerland
and Professor Emeritus, Richard Ivey School of Business,
The University of Western Ontario

Martha L. Maznevski
The University of Virginia

BLACKWELL
Business

Copyright © Henry W. Lane, Joseph J. DiStefano and Martha L. Maznevski 2000

The right of Henry W. Lane, Joseph J. DiStefano and Martha L. Maznevski to be identified as authors of this work has been asserted in accordance with the Copyright, Designs and Patents Act 1988.

First published 2000

2 4 6 8 10 9 7 5 3 1

Blackwell Publishers Ltd
108 Cowley Road
Oxford OX4 1JF
UK

Blackwell Publishers Inc.
350 Main Street
Malden, Massachusetts 02148
USA

British Library Cataloguing in Publication Data

A CIP catalogue record for this book is available from the British Library.

Library of Congress Cataloging-in-Publication Data has been applied for

ISBN 0-631-21830-0 (hbk)
ISBN 0-631-21831-9 (pbk)

Typeset in 10 on 12pt Baskerville
by Graphicraft Limited, Hong Kong
Printed in Great Britain by TJ International, Padstow, Cornwall

This book is printed on acid-free paper.

Brief Contents

Contents

List of Contributors

○ ○

Henry W. Lane Darla and Frederick Brodsky Trustee Professor in International Business, Northeastern University, Boston

Joseph J. DiStefano IMD, Lausanne, and Professor Emeritus, Richard Ivey School of Business, The University of Western Ontario

Martha L. Maznevski McIntire School of Commerce, University of Virginia, Charlottesville, VA

Neil Abramson Simon Fraser University, Burnaby, BC

Nancy J. Adler McGill University, Montreal

Nick Athanassiou Northeastern University, Boston

Paul W. Beamish Richard Ivey School of Business, The University of Western Ontario

Iris Berdrow Bentley College, Waltham, MA

J. Stewart Black University of California Irvine, Irvine, CA

R. W. P. Blake Memorial University, St John's, Newfoundland

Daniel Campbell New York City

Archie B. Carroll University of Georgia, Athens, GA

Gail Ellement A. T. Kearney, London, UK

Ann Frost Richard Ivey School of Business, The University of Western Ontario

Michael Geringer California Polytechnical State University, San Luis Obispo, CA

Sumantra Ghoshal London Business School, London, UK

Brian Golden Richard Ivey School of Business, The University of Western Ontario

Hal B. Gregersen Brigham Young University, Utah

Edward T. and Mildred Reed Hall   Santa Fe, New Mexico

Geert Hofstede   Senior Fellow, Institute for Research on Intercultural Cooperation and Fellow, Center for Economic Research, Tilburg University, The Netherlands

Jeanne McNett (Instructor's Manual)   Assumption College, Worcester, MA

Piero Morosini   IMD, Lausanne

Allen J. Morrison   Richard Ivey School of Business, The University of Western Ontario

Chantell Nicholls   Richard Ivey School of Business, The University of Western Ontario

Don G. Simpson   Axia Netmedia, London, Ontario

Kathleen Slaughter   Richard Ivey School of Business, The University of Western Ontario

Chow Hou Wee   National University of Singapore, Singapore

Marc Weinstein   University of Oregon, Eugene, OR

Patricia H. Werhane   Darden Graduate School of Business, University of Virginia, Charlottesville, VA

David Wesley   Northeastern University, Boston

Lorna Wright   Queens University, Kingston, Ontario

Preface

○ ○

Nancy J. Adler

Japanese and American management is 95 percent the same and differs in all important respects.
  – T. Fujisawa, Cofounder of Honda Motor Corporation

Managing the global enterprise and modern business management have become synonymous. "International" can no longer be relegated to a category of organizations or to a division within an organization. Definitions of societal and business success now transcend national boundaries. In fact, the very concept of domestic business may have become anachronistic. As the authors aptly describe, "The modern business enterprise has no place to hide. It has no place to go but everywhere."

To succeed, corporations must use global strategies. The last decade of the twentieth century made the importance of such recognition commonplace, at least among leading firms and management scholars. New approaches to managing research and development (R&D), production, marketing, and finance incorporating today's global dynamics have evolved rapidly. Yet, only recently has an equivalent evolution in managing global human resource systems begun to emerge. Although other functional areas increasingly use strategies that were largely unheard of or that would have been inappropriate only one and two decades ago, many firms still conduct the worldwide management of people as if neither the external economic and technological environment, nor the internal structure and organization of the firm, had changed.

In focusing on global strategies and management approaches from the perspectives of people and culture, this book is an important step in helping us, as managers and scholars, to create effective worldwide human resource systems. *International Management Behavior*, Fourth Edition, allows us to examine the influence of national culture on organizational functioning. Rather than becoming trapped within the more commonly

Nancy J. Adler is Professor of Management at McGill University in Montreal, Canada. She conducts research and consults on global management issues worldwide. She has published numerous articles and books, including *International Dimensions of Organizational Behavior*, 3rd edition (Southwestern, 1997), and *Competitive Frontiers: Women Managers in a Global Economy* (Blackwell, 1994). She revised this preface for this edition.

asked, and unfortunately misleading, question of if organizational dynamics are universal or culturally specific, the authors ask us to focus on the crucially important question of when and how to be sensitive to national culture. They allow us to investigate the implications of global approaches for traditional human resource management decisions, as well as for those decisions that will only make sense from the global perspective of firms in the twenty-first century.

How important are cultural differences to organizational effectiveness? Some observers of corporate behavior say "not at all," while others claim that cultural differences are and will remain extremely important. The first group, those adhering to a cultural convergence perspective, argue that organizational characteristics across nations are free, or are becoming free, from the particularities of specific cultures. Their position suggests that as an outcome of "common industrial logic" – most notably of technological origin – institutional frameworks, patterns and structures of organizations, and management practices across countries are converging (Adler and Doktor, 1986, pp. 300–1). In counterdistinction, other managers and scholars argue that organizations are culturebound, rather than culture free, and are remaining so. These scholars conclude that there is no one best way to manage; that is, the principle of equifinality applies to organizations functioning in different cultures. Their research findings indicate that many equally effective ways to manage exist, with the most effective depending, among other contingencies, on the cultures involved (Adler and Doktor, 1986, p. 301).

Perhaps this dilemma has not been resolved because we have been asking the wrong question. If we ask what the influence of cultural diversity is on multinational firms, we realize that the importance and the extent of the impact of national cultural differences depends on the stage of development of the firm, the industry, and the world economy. Thus, the relevant question to ask is when does culture influence organizational functioning rather than if it does or does not. Using a model for the post-World War II development of multinational firms, one can deduce distinct variations in the relative importance of cultural diversity and, consequently, equally distinct variations in the most appropriate approaches to managing people worldwide.

Immediately after World War II, firms operated primarily from an ethnocentric perspective. Firms produced unique goods and services that they offered almost exclusively to the domestic market. The uniqueness of a product and the lack of international competition negated a firm's need to be sensitive to cultural differences. When organizations exported goods, they did so without altering them for foreign consumption. Any cultural differences were absorbed by the foreign buyers, not by the home country's product design, manufacturing, or marketing teams. In some ways, the implicit message to foreigners was, "We will allow you to buy our product" and, of course, the assumption was that foreigners would want to buy. During this initial phase, home country nationals and philosophies dominated management. Culture and global human resource management were perceived as irrelevant.

International competition ushered in phase two, and with it the beginning of a need to market and to produce abroad. Totally unlike the first phase, sensitivity to cultural differences became critical in implementing effective corporate strategy. The first phase's product orientation shifted to a market orientation, with each country's domestic market needing to be addressed separately and differently. Whereas the unique technology of phase one products fits well with an ethnocentric "one best way" approach, now firms began to assume equifinality; that is, that there were many good ways to manage, with each dependent on the particular nation involved. Successful companies no longer expected foreigners to absorb cultural mismatches between buyers and sellers. Rather, home country representatives had to modify their approach to fit with that of their clients and colleagues in each country's markets. Moreover, while cultural differences became important in designing and marketing culturally appropriate goods and services, they became critical in producing them in factories worldwide. Managers had to learn the culturally appropriate ways to manage their human resource systems in each of the countries in which they operated.

During the 1980s, many industries entered a third phase. The environment for these industries had changed again, and with it the demands for cultural sensitivity. Within phase three industries, a number of companies produced very similar products (almost commodities), with the only significant competition being on price. From this global, price-sensitive perspective, cultural awareness falls again to marginal importance. Price competition among almost identical goods and services produced by numerous multi-national competitors negates the importance of most cultural differences and any advantage gained by cultural sensitivity. The primary product design and marketing assumption is no longer "one best way" or even "many best ways" but rather "one least cost way." The primary market has become worldwide, with little geographic market segmentation. Firms can only gain competitive advantage through process engineering, sourcing critical factors on a worldwide basis, and benefiting from economies of scale. Price competition reduces culture's influence to a negligible level.

While some observers believed that the third phase would be the ultimate phase for all industries, it was not; a fourth phase has emerged. In it, top-quality, least-possible-cost goods and services have become the base line, the minimally acceptable standard. Firms gain competitive advantage from strategic thinking and mass customization. Product ideas are drawn from worldwide sources, as are the factors and locations of production. However, final goods and services and their marketing are tailored to very discrete market niches. One of the critical components of this market segmentation, again, becomes culture. Successful phase four firms need to know how to understand their potential clients' needs, quickly translate them into goods and services, produce those goods and services on a least-cost basis, and deliver them to clients worldwide in a culturally appropriate fashion. By this phase, the product, sales, and price orientations of the past almost completely disappear. They are replaced with a strategic, and culturally responsive, design orientation accompanied by a quick, least-cost production function. Needless to say, culture is critically important to this most advanced stage. Similarly, the ability to manage cross-cultural interaction, multinational teams, and global alliances becomes fundamental to business success. Whereas an effective global human resource management strategy in the past varied from being irrelevant to helpful, by this fourth phase it has become essential, a minimum requirement for organizational survival and success.

This book addresses questions involving people, culture, and the corporation. It allows us to examine the implications of alternative approaches to managing people and to managing cultural diversity. It encourages us to maintain the perspective of the global manager. More than merely being interesting and important, *International Management Behavior*, Fourth Edition, is fundamental to our understanding of management in the twenty-first century.

References

Adler, Nancy J., and Fariborz Ghadar, "Strategic Human Resource Management: A Global Perspective," in Rudiger Pieper (ed.), *Human Resource Management in International Comparison* (Berlin: de Gruyter, 1990), pp. 235–60.

Adler, Nancy J., and R. Doktor (in collaboration with S. G. Redding), "From the Atlantic to the Pacific Century: Cross-Cultural Management Reviewed," *Journal of Management,* 12, no. 2 (1986): 295–318.

Vernon, R., "International Investment and International Trade in the Product Cycle," *Quarterly Journal of Economics* (May 1966).

Acknowledgments

The fourth edition of this book has involved a major revision of many of its elements, including the acknowledgments. Both Professors Lane and DiStefano appreciate the support for their work on international business shown by their colleagues and research associates over the years at the Ivey Business School. Professor Maznevski, who graduated from Ivey's Ph.D. program, also acknowledges the broad support and assistance from the Ivey Business School, financial and otherwise, that contributed to her development and to this book. All of us owe a special debt to our professors, colleagues, and friends who shaped our interests and knowledge. We are grateful to: Deans C. B. Johnston, Adrian Ryans, and Larry Tapp; Professors Jim Hatch, Terry Deutscher, and Ken Hardy; the directors of Research and Publications at the Ivey Business School; and especially the donors of the Donald F. Hunter professorship (a Maclean Hunter endowment) and the Royal Bank professorship, which provided extra time for Professors Lane and DiStefano to undertake much of the work presented in this volume.

Since the third edition Professor DiStefano moved to Hong Kong to launch the Ivey EMBA program there and acknowledges with thanks Ivey alumnus, Alexander Chan, for support in the form of the Shirley Chan Memorial Professorship of International Business. In particular this made possible the addition of new Asian cases. In this regard we must also recognize the Richard and Jean Ivey fund of London, Ontario, for funding the development of Asian case studies, some of which appear in this new edition. In January 2000, Professor DiStefano joined IMD in Lausanne, Switzerland. Professor Lane assumed responsibility for Ivey's Americas Program and is grateful to Ivey for the support that made possible the development of many new Latin American cases, including the ones in this edition. He has since moved to Northeastern University where he is the Darla and Frederick Brodsky Trustee Professor in International Business. Professor Maznevski also thanks Dean Carl Zeithaml and the administration at the McIntire School of Commerce. The commitment of the school, both financial and otherwise, to making its programs global has provided substantial support for Professor Maznevski's involvement in this edition.

To this list of acknowledgments we need to add a large number of people and institutions from around the world who have broadened and informed our experience:

managers in both the public and private sectors; colleagues at other universities and institutes; companies who have provided access to their operations for the purpose of writing cases; and a number of former students and research assistants who worked with us to develop material for this and previous editions. Among the former research assistants, a special note of thanks is due to Professor Bill Blake and to Professor Lorna Wright who have gone on to successful academic careers. We would also like to thank David Ager, Dan Campbell, and David Wesley for their contributions.

The restructuring that has taken place in the publishing industry adds considerably to this list of acknowledgments. A series of acquisitions and reorganizations has led to our experience with six publishers and editors during the writing of the four editions. Our sincere thanks go to Joerg Klauck who was at Methuen, Ric Kitowski who was at Nelson Canada, and Rolf Janke who was at PWS-Kent and then Blackwell. All three were strong believers in, and supporters of, this book. We are delighted to be working with Catriona King now, as well as with Blackwell Publishers. We also express our appreciation to colleagues who have provided the publishers, and us, with helpful critiques. To Bob Moran, Ed Miller, Bob Dennehy, Jerry O'Connell, John Stanbury, Christa Walck, Nick Athanassiou, and Jeanne McNett, we say thanks for their reviews, which shaped this, and earlier, editions. Students and managers who have worked with our materials, and colleagues who have adopted our book and have written to us with thanks and suggestions, all have helped us and others learn. To them we also add our gratitude.

Our assistants, past and present, deserve our appreciation for the multiple tests of patience which they have endured gracefully over the years of our efforts: thanks to Sue O'Driscoll, Linda Minutillo, Beth Sinclair, and Jeannette Weston of the Ivey Business School, and Cindy Hoeffer and the rest of the McIntire support group. Last, but hardly least, we thank our families who have supported our learning and the publishing of what we have learned. This has meant time away from home, time spent alone writing, and time and energy devoted to the many visitors and friends from around the world who have been entertained at home. All have been critical to our development. Our spouses, Anne, Lynne, and Brian, have been more than patient; they have contributed significantly to our understanding and commitment, as have all our children. We thank them all for their love and assistance. Notwithstanding this lengthy list of personal acknowledgments, we close with the usual caveat that we alone remain responsible for the contents of this book.

H. W. Lane
Boston, MA

J. J. DiStefano
Hong Kong and Lausanne, Switzerland

M. L. Maznevski
Charlottesville, VA

January 2000

The publisher and authors would like to thank the following for permission to reproduce material in this book:

Adler, Nancy J., *Competitive Frontiers: Women Managers in a Global Economy* (Copyright © Nancy J. Adler, 1994, Blackwell Publishers, Oxford).

Blake, R. William, "Footwear International". Reproduced with the permission of the author © R. William Blake, Faculty of Business Administration, Memorial University of Newfoundland, St John's, Newfoundland, Canada.

Carroll, Archie B., "In Search of the Moral Manager", *Business Horizons*, March–April 1987, pp. 7–15. Reprinted with permission from *Business Horizons*, March–April 1987. Copyright © 1987 by the Board of Trustees at Indiana University, Kelley School of Business.

Ghoshal, Sumantra, "Andersen Consulting (Europe): entering the business of business integration", 1992, © INSEAD, Fontainebleau, France. All rights reserved.

Gregersen, Hal B., Allan J. Morrison and J. Stewart Black, reprinted from "Developing leaders for the global frontier", *Sloan Management Review*, Fall, 1998, pp. 21–32, by permission of the publisher. Copyright © 1998 by Sloan Management Review Association. All rights reserved.

Hall, Edward T. and Mildred Reed Hall, "Key concepts: underlying structures of culture", from *Understanding Cultural Differences* (Intercultural Press Inc., 1995, Copyright © Edward T. Hall Associates, Santa Fe).

Hofstede, Geert, "Cultural constraints in management theories", *Executive* 7(1), 1993 (Academy of Management, Ada, Ohio).

Hofstede, Geert, "The 40 countries" (table) and "The position of the 40 countries . . ." (figures) from "Motivation, leadership and organization: do American theories apply abroad?", *Organizational Dynamics*, summer 1980.

Hofstede, Geert, and M. H. Bond, "Scores on five dimensions for fifty countries and three regions in IBM's international employee attitude survey", from "The Confucius connection: from cultural roots to economic growth", *Organizational Dynamics* 16(4).

Ivey Management Services for "Grupo Financiero Inverlat", "David Shorter", "Bob Chen", "Maria Mancini – Expatriate Compensation (A)", "Japanese-American Seating Inc. (A)", "Hazelton International", "Dan Simpson – International Project Manager", "Global Multi-products Chile", "ABB Poland", "Five Star Beer: Pay for Performance", "Moscow Aerostar", "Robert Mondavi Corporation: Caliterra (A)", "Ellen Moore (A): Living and Working in Korea", "Marconi Telecommunications Mexico", "Ben & Jerry's Homemade Inc.: Background Note", "Iceverks (A): Ben & Jerry's in Russia", "Valley Farms International (A)", "Building Products International: A Crisis Management Strategy (A)", "Citibank Team Mexico: The Salinas Accounts". One time permission to reproduce granted by Ivey Management Services on May 31, 1999.

Lane, H., and D. Simpson, "Bribery in international business: whose problem is it?", *Journal of Business Ethics*, 3, 1984, with kind permission of Kluwer Academic Publishers, Dordrecht.

Lane, H., and P. Beamish, "Cross-cultural cooperative behavior in joint ventures in LDCs", from *Management International Review*, Special Issue 1990 (reprinted by permission of Management International Review, Stuttgart).

Mendenhall, M. E., E. Dunbar and G. R. Oddou, "Expatriate selection, training and career-pathing: a review and critique" (figure), from *Human Resource Management*, Fall 1987 (Copyright © 1987 John Wiley & Sons, Inc., New York. Reprinted by permission of John Wiley & Sons, Inc.).

Morosini, Piero, "Global Execution: Have you forgotten what 95% of management is about?", *IMD Perspectives for Managers*, Nov. 1998, reprinted by permission of IMD, Lausanne.

Stewart Black, J., and Hal B. Gregersen, reprinted from "Serving two masters: managing the dual allegiance of expartriate employees", *Sloan Management Review*, Summer, 1992, pp. 61–71 by permission of the publisher. Copyright © 1992 by Sloan Management Review Association. All rights reserved.

Wee, Chow Hou, "From battlefields to corporate boardrooms: Lessons from Sun Tzu's *Art of War*" (revised version) reprinted by permission of Chow Hou Wee.

Werhane, Patricia H., "Exporting mental models: global capitalism in the twenty-first century", *Business Ethics Quarterly* (forthcoming), reprinted by permission of Patricia H. Werhane.

INTRODUCTION

○ ○

Global Management, Culture, and This Book

The Influence of Culture on Management Behavior

This book is different. It is not just another book about global business. It is about people who conduct business globally. It illustrates and explores typical situations that managers encounter: the problems and opportunities; the joys and frustrations; the successes and failures; and the decisions they must make. The case studies in this book describe situations that anybody could confront while pursuing an international business career. You don't have to wait until you are the chief executive officer or president of a company to experience these situations.

We focus on the implementation of management decisions and the resulting operating issues and problems – and not just on theory. Our aim is to help you develop an understanding of the practice – the doing – of global business and management. There's a difference between studying a subject from a theoretical perspective and studying it in an applied way. In the first instance, you are able to talk about the subject. In the second instance, you are able to do it. Someone may be extremely knowledgeable about art, music, or drama – a real student of these activities. However, this doesn't mean that he or she is a good artist, musician, or actress. In the same way, knowing and talking about global management are not the same as managing globally. Being a good manager requires knowledge of theory and concepts, but also requires skills and practice. This book provides both knowledge and opportunities for practice to develop important global management skills.

International business is not impersonal, so international business should not be studied solely in an impersonal way. For example, it is useful to understand trade theories; to know how to hedge the future value of currencies in which a corporation is dealing; to be able to weigh the pros and cons of exporting versus licensing; or to understand the advantages of a joint venture versus a wholly-owned subsidiary. Although such knowledge is important, it is not enough. Eventually, the conceptualizing, the strategizing, and debating of alternatives has to give way to action. A manager must leave headquarters to implement a project, sell a product, or negotiate an alliance – in other words, to interact with colleagues, customers, and suppliers from other places, to try to get other people to do things, and to experience what it really means to do business globally. In this book we focus on the interactions, on getting things done with and through other people in a global context.

In this part of the text, we introduce the cultural perspective and describe why it is so central to international management behavior. We then outline and discuss four types of expertise required by global managers, and show how this book aims to help readers develop that expertise. We also describe in more detail some important aspects of the book, including the purpose of the three parts of text, readings, and cases, and we provide some notes on cases in general. We close with some personal observations on the joys and value of developing global management expertise.

The Cultural Perspective

One of our basic premises is that there is a link between successful global business and cultural awareness and sensitivity. Why do we make this the central core of the book? There are many people who might argue that this perspective is misleading. They would assert that cultures around the world are converging, that business is business everywhere, and that people are basically the same all over. Of course, there is some truth to each of these statements. People around the world wear jeans and European designer fashions, eat at McDonald's, and listen to Sony Walkmen. Currencies are traded globally every moment, and there are global infrastructures for conducting business. They would also argue that everyone has the same basic physiological and psychological needs.

However, the meaning of the behaviors and how business is conducted differ dramatically from one culture to another. These differences may not be important on the surface or in a quick interaction, but they deeply affect commitments, relationships, cooperative decision making, and other critical elements of social interaction. Take the McDonald's example. Not only does McDonald's change its menu in different parts of the world – serving beer in Germany, a McLobster sandwich on Canada's east coast, and tropical shakes in Hong Kong – but the meaning of eating at McDonald's changes from one culture to another. As a Malaysian student said to her American peers, "In Kuala Lumpur, we don't eat at McDonald's for convenience like people in the United States do. And we rarely take the food out to eat. We eat at McDonald's when we feel like having a hamburger, the same way you might eat at a Chinese restaurant when you feel like you want Chinese food. To say that we're becoming Westernized because McDonald's does well there is as wrong as saying the United States is becoming Easternized because there are a lot of Chinese restaurants."

We will define culture more specifically in the next part of the book, but for now let us say that culture is an implicit agreement among a group of people concerning what people's actions mean. Most cultures agree on some basic principles, but there is a lot of variation on the details. The agreement on basic principles makes it appear as if cultures are converging. It allows mergers and acquisitions to be negotiated, money and goods to be traded, and employees to stay briefly in foreign countries without too much trouble. It allows us to work together, at least on the surface. However, the differences become apparent when people have to interact more intensively with each other on a day-to-day basis. This is when the synergy anticipated from the mergers and acquisitions is more elusive than anticipated, when the goods traded for the money don't arrive on time or are not in the condition expected, or when the stay in the foreign country is prolonged.

Not surprisingly, research shows clearly that culture influences the practice of management. Many management concepts, techniques, and systems developed and taught in business schools are based on cultural beliefs, values, and assumptions about how managers should behave, and they work well in the countries in which they were developed. However, these concepts, techniques, and systems may not work as intended in other cultures. If they are transferred to another country and used improperly, they can compound managers' problems. For example, management by objectives (MBO), a standard North American management tool, is based on an assumption that subordinates will share their objectives with their superior. This is an unrealistic assumption in many cultures that have strong status differentials and that maintain hierarchies. For example, a recent study showed that in Spain, subordinates strongly prefer that their bosses supervise their work directly, and feel very uncomfortable making their own decisions or telling the boss what the decision should be.[1] Another comparative study of preferences for different performance appraisal practices showed that Taiwanese respondents preferred to focus more on group performance than on individual performance and also preferred less direct and open relations between supervisors and subordinates than did North American respondents.[2] MBO probably would have to be implemented very differently in these countries than in the United States, where it was "invented."

Cultural differences, if not understood, can also pose significant barriers to the implementation and success of a business venture. For example, there tends to be less emphasis on personal relationships between suppliers and customers in the United States or Canada, where business is usually the primary focus and where a personal relationship might develop from the business relationship. In most of the rest of the world, however, people want to establish the personal relationship first, and from that relationship business may develop. Even in the initial negotiations, customers in many countries are at least as interested in personal relationships with the company's after sales service providers as they are in the product itself. These customers want a product and a supplier they trust, and believe it will come only from people they trust. A student once said that this advice only means, "paying attention to the customer's needs and wants is just good business." Most certainly! Understanding your customers and their culture is simply good business practice. However, in our own culture either intuitively or through experience, we tend to know what a customer in our culture needs or wants. The point is, in international business more time must be spent to find out what the customer in his or her own environment wants and needs.

Good business practice, coupled with good intercultural skills, should be an unbeatable combination. One would think that good business practice automatically would include good intercultural skills. Unfortunately, this is not always the case, and therefore both need to be stressed. In this book, we combine knowledge and concepts from the areas of cultural studies and international business so readers can improve their global management skills.

The Global Manager

In this book, we use the terms "international" and "global" interchangeably. It is important, though, to understand the difference that has evolved in their meanings. An international perspective tends to describe interactions between two countries – the home country and one other – or rather straightforward interaction among more countries but in which each country is treated completely separately. Until recently, this has been an adequate model for much of the world's international business activity. However, globalization has come to mean transforming our international perspective to a global perspective, one that does not see national borders as being contiguous with business borders. For example, an international company will have mostly autonomous units in each country or region, but a global company may split the activities of a single product's value chain across several countries and treat the globe as one unit for that product.

In spite of our tendency to use both terms, our philosophy is emphatically global because the most effective businesses are moving this way. And the most effective managers, whatever their company's approach, manage as if the company were global. They make strategic decisions taking into account what is best for the business and for the customer, wherever that customer is, and they implement ideas in the way that is best for the people carrying out the decisions. They select the best people to do the jobs, whoever they are and wherever they're from, and they manage those people in a manner consistent with their values and culture. Percy Barnevik, Chief Executive Officer (CEO) of Asea Brown Boveri (ABB), estimates that his company needs "500 or so global managers [among 30,000 managers worldwide], people who are internationally minded, but are also comfortable with their nation of origin."[3] These are the people who run the global businesses.

What does the emergence of the term global manager really imply? In the broadest terms, it means reorganizing the way one thinks as a manager and as a student of management. As one executive put it, "to think globally really requires an alteration of our mind-set."[4] Thinking globally means extending concepts and models from one-to-one relationships (we to them) to holding multiple realities and relationships in mind simultaneously, and then acting skillfully on this more complex reality. The shift means that even if a manager has a regional responsibility for marketing for Central and South America, she or he will not only have to understand Latin cultures and speak Spanish and Portuguese, but also may have to deal with research and development (R&D) labs in Japan, Europe, and North America to provide customer information and to get updates on emerging new products. The same manager may have to discuss product problems with manufacturers in Southeast Asia late at night, South American time, and then send a fax about the potential solution to an alternative supplier in Eastern Europe.

The global manager must act differently, must organize the complexity of the management task in a new way. The major shift in behavior is that since it is impossible to know and control all aspects of the job, the managers' role must become much more one of facilitating processes, ideas, and behaviors of others. The Board of Governors of the American Society for Training and Development published the following list of skills required by global executives in 1990, and it is still relevant ten years later:[5]

Domestic and International	*Global*
• All-knowing	• Leader as learner
• Domestic vision	• Global vision
• Predicts future from past	• Intuits the future
• Caring for individuals	• Caring for institutions and individuals
• Owns the vision	• Facilitates vision of others
• Uses power	• Uses power and facilitation
• Dictates goals and methods	• Specifies processes
• Alone at the top	• Part of an executive team
• Values order	• Accepts paradox of order amidst chaos
• Monolingual	• Multicultural
• Inspires the trust of boards and shareholders	• Inspires the trust of owners, customers, and employees

This list encompasses many of the particular skills required by global managers and demonstrates the new paradigm well. Reviewing a wide range of literature dealing with global strategy, global marketing, global operations management, and global human resource management, we drew a profile of four major types of expertise demonstrated by effective global managers: *strategic*; *adaptive*; *interpersonal*; and *cross-cultural*.[6] Each type of expertise incorporates a high level of both knowledge and skills. The four types are closely related to each other, but it is useful to focus on each separately for a clearer understanding of their roles in effective global management.

Global Strategic Expertise

A global manager must be both highly knowledgeable about global business, and able to integrate new knowledge into a big picture view of the company, its industry, and its environment. The new global economy is shaped and driven by flows of money, goods, services, and people around the world. Often it is characterized by volatile foreign exchange, changing government policies, resistance to standardized products, and new economies of scale.

Managers who understand these flows and what causes them to change will be better equipped to respond to the changes, predict them, and even influence them. A working knowledge of international relationships and foreign affairs, including global financial markets and exchange rate movements, is critical. Managers who have strong knowledge of and experience with a broad range of strategic responses will be able to implement strategy more effectively. Major players in the new global environment will have a fast response capability and be entrepreneurial and flexible. They will also embrace global responsibilities to take advantage of manufacturing rationalization, mass customization of products, and low-cost, global sourcing. Managers with this global perspective will need to strike a balance between national responsiveness and exploitation of global economies of scale. This is the vaunted ability to "think globally, but act locally."

Global success, therefore, is contingent on striking a balance between capitalizing on resources and needs within national boundaries and the ability to capture a vision of a world without boundaries. One aspect of managing this balance often includes moving decision-making authority as close to the customer as possible to ensure that local requirements are satisfied. Thus the global manager's job, as mentioned earlier, becomes one of facilitating the work of local managers within the context of the overall strategy. But even local managers will perform better if they understand the global strategy, enacting it within the context of their local environment.

Although the purpose of this book is not to focus on building global strategic expertise (other books do that well), the other three types of expertise – which *are* the focus of the book – are best developed within the context and understanding of global strategy. The decision-making situations provided in the cases in this book, as well as examples throughout the text, are intended to help the reader develop this global strategic context.

Adaptive Expertise

Global managers need the expertise to create adaptation, change, and flexibility in two directions: in themselves; and in their organization. First, global managers themselves must be flexible and adaptable. They will be sailing in a sea of change that they must somehow navigate, and the ability to adapt oneself is a fundamental prerequisite. Managers who are globally competent are deeply curious about the world and other people, and they are effective learners. They have broad interests, are open to a variety of experiences, and are willing to experiment and to take risks. Their enthusiasm is contagious, and they share their knowledge and learning with others effectively throughout the organization.

A few years ago, a visiting scholar from the People's Republic of China typified these characteristics for us. She soon knew more people than several other scholars who had been at our school for many months. Although her specialty was finance, she audited classes from all disciplines. She interviewed the old-timers, secretaries, researchers, students, and seasoned teachers. Nor were her interactions confined to work. She learned our humor, visited churches, traveled across the country by air, bus, train, and boat, went to country fairs and even insisted on trying golf! By the end of her year, she understood the institution better than most faculty who had been there for several years; she understood the country almost as well as any native. Then, she transferred her knowledge to her colleagues in China and abroad through an extraordinary report[7] and a series of lectures and seminars. Now she has leveraged her knowledge and skill into a thriving consulting business serving the World Bank and many commercial organizations.

One of the most unexpected personal experiences of global managers is the difficulty of adapting to different cultural environments. Although the figures have decreased somewhat over the last ten years, still fully 25 percent of expatriates return to their home country earlier than anticipated, and the single most frequent reason for early return is failure to adapt to the other culture.[8] Often, when thinking about international business, places like London, Paris, Frankfurt, Geneva, Sydney, Singapore, Hong Kong, Tokyo, New York, and Vancouver come to mind. But business does not always take place in these cities, and living and working in another country is not always glamorous. Nor is it business only conducted in industrialized countries. Corporations pursue business opportunities in remote places and under difficult conditions. Some countries in which large corporations operate and earn substantial revenue have difficult economic, political, and living conditions. Global managers often have to travel to these places, in spite of the increasing use of communications technology, and they and their families often live in these locations. Personal learning, adaptation, and flexibility are critical to developing and sustaining an effective career in global management.

Global managers must also manage their organizations to be flexible and adaptable. An individual manager alone cannot be expected to develop and use all the diverse skills required for successful global management. The organization itself, then, must assist global managers as much as possible, and global managers must design and operate the very organizations that will help them to be more effective. These new organizations are characterized by flexibility and multidimensionality. Networks, alliances, outsourcing, virtual departments are all currently implemented in global organizations with varying degrees of frequency and effectiveness. Managers are creating borderless organizations where the ability to learn, to be responsive, and to be efficient is well established within the firm's administrative heritage. We will describe these new organizations in more detail in Part 2 of the text. For now, the point is that these new structures are operated best, of course, by a cadre of managers with strong personal adaptive expertise.

Not only must global managers build the organizations to be flexible and adaptable, they must also manage them in a dynamic way, constantly changing to respond to and influence the movements in the industry. The shortening of product life cycles, driven by technological change in the products and how they are manufactured and delivered, contributes to the acceleration of change. Managing change in an unstable environment is a constant challenge. Forever fine-tuning the balance between global and local pressures under changing competitive conditions, global managers must frequently reorganize resources, human networks, technology, and marketing and distribution systems.

As difficult as these constant changes are to manage, the overall transition to global operations represents a formidable challenge in itself. Existing international operations, often marked by standardization of products and uniformity of procedures, may be a barrier to effective globalization. There are many mechanisms for making the transition. For example, flexible factories, which can produce "mass customized" products are a potential response to the think globally–act locally axiom. However, they may be difficult to invest in and effectively operate if the company has a long history of mass-producing standard products. Another method of making the transition to global operations is through the formation of a strategic alliance or a network to reduce the high cost of R&D or to enter a new market, for example. Most firms find that forming these alliances is much easier than running them, though. These and all other organizational responses to globalization require built-in flexibility and effective management of change and transition.

For a successful transition to global operations, it is also important that managers in different countries share a common view of the strategy and are all committed to it. If poorly implemented, the move to globalization can pit headquarters managers against country or field managers. If global strategy is perceived as a move toward the centralization of responsibility, a local manager's role may become less strategic. Autonomous units in a firm often try to protect their own turf, and subsidiary managers who joined a company because of its commitment to preserving local autonomy and adapting products to local environments may become disenchanted or even leave the organization. So effective global managers need the skills to manage the transition from independence or dependence to interdependence, from control to coordination and cooperation, and from symmetry to differentiation.

Learning, too, can be done at an organizational level. In fact, the best global companies distinguish themselves by systematizing learning systems and opportunities for the company as a whole to develop and leverage knowledge and experience. Operating managers are encouraged to look for opportunities in one country that can be transferred elsewhere. These opportunities or experiments usually are the responsibility of national managers, while their transfer is the responsibility of corporate management. The use of cross-national task forces for problems of corporate concern, such as significant expense reduction, is another way global companies try to learn and to take advantage of their global experience.

The ability of people and organizations to learn, to adapt, and to manage change will only increase in importance as markets continue to globalize. In this book, the skills addressed will help the reader develop adaptive expertise both for him- or herself, and for the organization. The cases present situations that require adaptability and flexibility, and provide opportunities to explore and practice this important skill building.

Cross-Cultural Expertise

Global managers must recognize that culture influences themselves as well as others, and they must be able not only to overcome the barriers raised by those differences but to leverage them for higher performance. That means having strong knowledge about their own and other cultures, and also using this knowledge constructively when interacting with others, designing organizational systems, and making and implementing strategic decisions.

Some famous examples of a lack of cross-cultural understanding and adaptation in marketing and product development demonstrate the obvious need for a basic level of cross-cultural expertise. For example, Procter & Gamble's (P&G's) liquid detergent failed in Europe when it was introduced in the early 1980s because European washing machines were not equipped for liquid detergent. Modifications to the detergent were made, and sales subsequently improved. Moreover, additional features that were introduced specifically for the European market, such as low sudsing action, were incorporated into the global product and launched successfully elsewhere. In another product area, P&G introduced Pampers in Japan and was delighted with the initial success. But the P&G marketing managers did not know that Japanese do laundry daily and were using Pampers only at night. Mooney, a Japanese company, introduced a disposable diaper with reusable parts, which had great appeal to the savings-conscious Japanese. P&G's market share for disposable diapers dropped from 90 percent to 10 percent almost overnight. P&G regained share by retaliating with a smaller, thinner diaper. Then, as it did with the liquid detergent, using a global-learning approach P&G brought that diaper to other markets.

More recently, Scudder Kemper, the large American mutual fund company gave up on trying to crack the Canadian market by itself after four years and took a Canadian partner.[9] The president of Scudder Canada observed that there are differences between American and Canadian investors. Americans are more comfortable as do-it-yourself, no-load fund investors, while Canadians prefer to invest through financial advisors.

Even Wal-Mart is not immune from these problems. It had difficulty in Asia when it tried to transfer its winning business formula from home. *The Economist* noted:[10]

> Basketball sets and garden games are not much use to people living in tower blocks in the most densely populated spot on earth. Nor do Hong Kongers have the space to store the bulk purchases that Wal-Mart's American customers find so alluring. Wal-Mart thought it could "just bring over something from the States and set it down", admit[ted] one of its managers.

In the food industry, as mentioned earlier, McDonald's has adapted and has different menus in different countries. Similarly, Dunkin' Donuts sells cake and yeast donuts in the United States but only yeast donuts in Brazil.

The recognition of cultural differences in global management does not necessarily come easily to North American managers, who often have less exposure to multicultural realities in their workplace than, for instance, their European or Asian counterparts. For example, Nestlé has a long history of having many nationalities among its top 100 executives (one count had it over 40). Although this type of anecdotal report may be misleading, the limited language ability of many North American managers makes the same point in another way. Language training, cross-cultural and expatriate experiences early in careers, membership on international task forces, and global content in all management training programs are among a few ways to counter the ethnocentricity of domestic managers, regardless of their country of origin.

There are signs, however, that this situation may be changing in some of the top companies in the United States. For example, Ford has a large group of internationally experienced executives and they are finding their way to the top of the organization. Four of the six group vice presidents grew up outside the United States as did its CEO and president, Jaques Nasser who was raised in Lebanon and Australia and who speaks five languages.[11]

Learning to manage global cultural diversity effectively can start with the recognition of cultural diversity at home. As a result of global movement of people through both voluntary (e.g., immigration) and involuntary (e.g., refugees) modes, most countries now have a vastly more diverse domestic labor market than they did only a decade ago. Toronto, Canada, for example, is the most ethnically diverse city in the world.[12] Over 80 languages are spoken in Toronto and one-third of Toronto residents speak a language other than English at home.[13] By the year 2001, almost 54 percent of Toronto's population will be visible minorities.[14]

Many large offices in Toronto employ people from dozens of countries. A typical team we worked with at a Toronto bank had 16 members who had been born in 14 countries across Asia, Africa, Latin America, and Europe. Only two members had been born in Canada. Other large cities around the world may not reflect this extreme multiculturalism, but they are still experiencing a shift in demographics to incorporate more cultural diversity. So the opportunities to gain insight and experience in managing cultural diversity are local as well as global.

As we discussed earlier, the cultural perspective is key to understanding global management, and cross-cultural expertise must be incorporated into the other three types of global management expertise. The text, readings, and cases in this book provide knowledge and opportunities for practice this critical skill.

Interpersonal Expertise

Because global management has become, more than ever, an exercise in cooperative decision making and action as well as the facilitation of others' ideas and actions, interpersonal expertise continues to increase in importance. The two main types of interpersonal expertise we will discuss here are communication and teamwork, but they incorporate other interpersonal skills such as negotiation, conflict resolution, and leadership.

Communicating effectively means getting your message across the way you want to, and understanding others the way they want you to. Even in domestic organizations, communication is a critical skill, and most interpersonal problems can be attributed at least in part to miscommunication. In a global organization, effective communication is both more important and more difficult. It is more important, because the cost of miscommunication is extremely high. In a now infamous example, Chevrolet tried to introduce its Nova model in Latin America without realizing that "no va" in Spanish means "it does not go." A little research and communication effectiveness would have prevented unnecessary market development costs in this case.

Even successful companies have to be continually alert to avoid problems related to communication effectiveness, and advertising examples make this point very clearly. The marketers of Coca-Cola, one of the world's most recognized brands, attribute their success to the ability of their people to simultaneously hold and understand the perspectives of the culture of their company, the culture of their brand, and the culture of the people to whom they market the brand.[15] However, during the World Cup in 1994, Coca-Cola printed the flag of Saudi Arabia on its cans. The flag contains sacred words in Arabic that Muslims believe should be treated with respect and definitely should not appear on throwaway packaging.

McDonald's carryout bags also had the flag printed on it – bags that get "crumpled up and thrown in the trash." Chanel, the fashion house in France, committed a similar faux pas when it printed Koranic verses on women's low-cut tops.[16] Pepsi outraged an ultra-orthodox Jewish organization in Israel by depicting an ape moving along the path of evolution towards a can of Pepsi. The Rabbinical Court of Jerusalem does not accept evolution as the origin of human beings and threatened to withdraw its certification that Pepsi was prepared to meet kosher regulations.[17] Three of Wal-Mart's stores in Quebec broke the law by distributing flyers in English rather than in French and wasted money in communities where many people could not read English.[18] In Europe, a Nike commercial depicting Satan and his team of demons playing soccer against a team of Nike endorsers was judged too scary and offensive by some European stations to be shown in prime time.[19] All of these cross-cultural communication errors cost their companies a great deal of money, time, and embarrassment. And all could have been prevented with more effective research into what it takes to communicate effectively in a global marketplace.

In addition to the skills necessary for effective interpersonal communication and advertising, managers need to take advantage of the increasingly global communications technology and systems. New modes of communicating through technology reduce the need for travel, but create their own challenges. Communications through technological media are much less rich than a face-to-face interaction, and miscommunication is much easier.

People from different cultures prefer different media, and prefer using them in different ways. A multi-site global R&D team we worked with finally met in person for the first time after working for more than a year and a half together. One of the first items on their agenda was agreeing on a protocol for the use of email. The different usages associated with the different cultures had resulted in a large number of miscommunications over the previous year, many associated with negative outcomes. But they felt they had to build personal relationships before talking about how to communicate electronically.

Besides the direct positive effects of good communication skills among colleagues and with customers, this latter example highlights another advantage of effective communication. Sensitive communication builds trust and strong relationships over time and these relationships help reinforce commitment in the company's direction and decisions. Moreover, strong relations reduce many of the negative effects of cultural mistakes. A mistake made with a friend is more easily forgiven and overcome than one with a stranger. In the R&D team referred to above, the time spent talking together in person made electronic communication easier, but also generally facilitated decision making as team members began to trust each others' motives.

In addition to good communication skills, global managers also require effective team skills. Even before the advent of global companies, effective teamwork was becoming essential for managerial success. As the specialization of people and differentiation in organizations increased (often driven by technological improvements, fragmentation of markets, explosions in product variations, and so on), there was a concomitant increased need for integration: for putting the specialized units back together in the service of the organization's objectives. Teams, committees, and task forces were among the devices used to accomplish the desired integration.

With the increased complexity of global operations, the ability to function in work teams – especially in culturally diverse groups – is even more important. A Conference Board Report on the experiences of 30 major MNCs in building teams to further their global interests showed the following: teams used solely for communication or providing advice and counsel still exist, but more and more firms are also using teams in different and more participative and powerful ways. Global teamwork can do more than provide improved market and technological intelligence. It can yield more flexible business planning, stronger commitment to achieving worldwide goals, and closer collaboration in carrying out strategic change.[20] Teams that span internal organizational boundaries or the company's external boundary (joint venture partners, suppliers, customers) are often required.

Interestingly, the need for transnational teamwork shows up in different ways in different functions. Consider, for example, the different assumptions about the nature and purpose of accounting and auditing in various parts of the world. In one country, financial statements are meant to reflect fundamental economic reality and the audit function is to ensure that this is so. In another country, the audit is to check the accuracy of the financial statements vis-à-vis the economic records. In still another country, it is to make sure legal requirements have been met.[21] Imagine, then, the need for cross-cultural understanding and sensitivity in auditing an international subsidiary or the teamwork needed to develop international audit standards.[22]

Other functions pick up the teamwork theme differently. In production, teams need to develop system-sensitive outlooks and processes and personal relationships across subsidiaries. Human resources managers must develop capabilities for leading multi-national teams in flexible and responsible ways. Global marketing managers need the ability to take advantage of a local execution strategy, where "not invented here" becomes "now improved here." Using this strategy, a core international team gathers ideas and passes them to local levels where the final marketing decisions are made and implemented.

In research and development, culturally diverse teams have been a reality for a long time. For example, in one American subsidiary of the French-based manufacturer of electrical distribution systems, Groupe Schneider, a research team is composed of two Americans, two Mexicans, a Pole, Russian, Frenchman, Chinese, Iranian, and Indian; another consists of two Americans, a Belgian, Thai, Filipino, Chinese, and Mexican. The first team is headed by the Belgian and the second by the Polish scientist. The manager to whom they report is an American who is working closely with the team leaders to understand the cultural complexity in their daily lives.

The advent of better and cheaper global communications technology means global teams can operate even when the members are not physically in one place. At the beginning of 1995, Ford reorganized its product development into five "vehicle platform centers" charged with designing cars for both North America and Europe. Using computer technology and satellite communications, a designer in Köln can alter a fender shape formulated by a colleague in Dearborn and get an immediate response to his revision by an audio and video hook-up.[23]

The ability to communicate effectively and work with other people in teams is so critical to the successful implementation of a global strategy that participation in global teams should occur early in the careers of managers to transform these people into potential global leaders.[24] In fact, we believe interpersonal skills represent such a cornerstone for the rest of the global manager's skills that we begin Part I by focusing on these skills, and build on this foundation throughout the rest of the book.

Summary

This review might lead the reader to conclude that an effective global manager is superhuman. But the prospect of acquiring strategic, adaptive, cross-cultural and interpersonal skills can be seen as an exciting challenge rather than an impossible task. Developing these skills is a lifelong task, and it is unlikely that a single executive will master all of them. Effective teams and organizational elements will support both skill development and also global management itself.

About This Book

This book is designed to help develop the knowledge, perspective, and skills that global managers need to function effectively in different cultural environments and to work effectively with people from other cultures. Our intention is to develop, to the extent possible using this medium, an appreciation of what it is like to work with people from other cultures and to work in other countries. In short, we intend to help the reader develop adaptive, cross-cultural, and interpersonal expertise within the context of global strategy.

In this description of the book, we begin with a discussion of our orientation to the teaching of international management behavior and how it is reflected in this book. We then outline the book and provide some specific notes on cases and using them as a learning tool.

Orientations to Teaching International Management Behavior

These orientations describe perspectives that have been developed, refined, and tested in our teaching a course of this type for over 25 years to undergraduates, graduate students, and practicing managers around the world. We have found that a combination of conceptual knowledge and contextually-based skill-building opportunities provides an effective learning package. In addition to drawing on the research of others we have conducted our own research on the issues and skills relevant to international management, and also on how best to train global managers. The result is a set of statements that reflect our approach to teaching international management behavior, as reflected in this book.

Management orientation. This book presents a problem-solving approach to international business. The implications of cultural differences and similarities for management can be examined, not isolated from business realities, but embedded in actual management situations where an appreciation of cultural influences on behavior can make a difference in outcome and performance. It is only in this context that future global managers can learn to generalize and apply the skills more broadly.

Behavioral orientation. The human element in managing effectively across cultures is just as important and, sometimes, more important than the technical or business elements. However, interpersonal skills are likely to be less developed in managers than are technical or business skills. People chosen to work in the international side of business generally have already developed a basic set of business or technical skills as a prerequisite for the assignment. These people need to complement the basic skills with people skills; if they don't, they may never get the opportunity to use the business or technical skills. The material here acknowledges clearly that business and technical skills are necessary for effectiveness, but their development is not emphasized. This book focuses on the interpersonal behavioral skills.

Process orientation. Related to the behavioral orientation is a process orientation – behaving, interacting, learning, and moving forward to meet objectives. We think this perspective is an important contributor to success in a global market. It is the "currency" of implementation, or actually putting policy decisions into practice.

Richard Pascale contrasted the Japanese "proceeding" with the American "deciding" mentality. "The process of 'proceeding' in turn generates further information; you move toward your goal through a sequence of tentative steps rather than bold-stroke actions. The distinction is between having enough data to decide and having enough data to proceed."[25] Conducting business in other countries and cultures is an activity that is filled with ambiguity and uncertainty. In this type of situation, "proceeding" may be the appropriate mode of operation. Too often the focus is on quick decisions and end results rather than on the activities necessary to achieve the end results. This achievement focus very often obscures the fact that one needs to proceed, to get better information, and to make progress – rather than come to a quick resolution of the issue – to achieve desired results. Information must be collected to put pieces of the puzzle together. An orientation that moves one closer to one's objectives is needed, accomplished through "process," or a series of interactions with other people.

The term "process" conjures up words that are active and interactive: words like exporting, managing, trading, negotiating, licensing, and joint-venturing or partnering; selecting, training, entering, leaving, and relating also come to mind. The interactions and relationships with other people in other organizations in other countries are necessary in order to be a successful exporter, manager, trader, or negotiator. The cases in this book focus on process. Often, the reader will not be able to "find a solution" or "come to a decision," but will have to suggest and outline a process. This reflects the reality of international management.

Intercultural orientation. The material in this text focuses primarily on the interaction between people of different cultures in work settings. This intercultural orientation is distinct from a comparative approach, in which management practices of individual countries or cultures are examined and compared. The intercultural perspective has been chosen because it is in the interaction of cultures that managers experience difficulties. Although the study of practices within a single culture may be helpful, it is the interaction of people with different beliefs and management practices that has an impact on managers.

Culture-general orientation. This book is intended for general managers (meaning management generalists rather than the specific position) and international staff who must function effectively in a realm of cultural diversity. This book is also useful to people who aspire to such positions in global management and staff of multinational or transnational corporations. A culture-general perspective provides a framework within which country-specific learning can take place more rapidly as necessary. It helps the reader know what questions to ask and how to interpret the answers received when conducting business globally or helping others to do the same. It makes the learner become more effective at learning and adapting to other cultures. As such, the book does not focus on culture-specific learning: the reader will not become an expert in any one culture or be able to operate in a given culture flawlessly. This is not to say that culture-specific learning will not take place. The cases and readings will convey information and knowledge specific to given cultures. However, in-depth culture-specific training is more appropriate when someone is assigned to a specific country, and may also be appropriate for staff specialists concentrating on a particular country or a limited regional area. But any kind of culture-specific training is strongly enhanced by this culture-general orientation.

Outline of the Book

The book has three main parts after this introduction: Interpersonal Effectiveness in Global Management; Implementing Strategy, Structure and Systems; and Corporate Social Behavior in a Global Economy. The first two parts build the basics of global management expertise, while the third part raises some critical issues about making competitive choices that are rarely addressed with adequate depth in international management courses.

Each section is comprised of text, a set of readings, and a set of cases. The text is a summary of the main knowledge required by global managers. It is drawn from our own research and experience and that of many others. The readings were selected carefully to complement our perspectives and add more depth that is informative and insightful. Together, the text and readings provide the conceptual background needed to address the situations in the cases and in the readers' real life experiences.

The cases put the reader in the position of a manager interacting with people from other cultures. Of course, studying a few cases in a book is not a substitute for experience. However, cases provide initial practice. In taking a manager's role, a reader psychologically puts him- or herself into another person's place and situation, sorts out the issues involved in that situation, and plans action. In this way, a reader can simulate experience. A combination of the knowledge and the experience gained from immersion in the case situations improves the judgment and skills of managers. The cases in this book are specifically intended to increase sensitivity to important cultural differences and assumptions underlying management behavior, and to issues managers are likely to encounter.

We have been involved in writing most of the cases for this book. We have lived in, or traveled to, many of the locations in the cases while working as teachers, consultants, managers, or specifically for case writing. We have worked with the managers described in the cases and have tried to bring the flavor, feeling, and tempo of these people and the countries in which they live into the classroom and to the readers of this book.

The situations described in this book may seem like unusual dilemmas to a reader with no international business experience. But before one jumps too quickly to say "I'll never go to those countries" or "I will never find myself in these situations," some individual experiences should be recounted. One person was completing a management training program and, as part of that program, a speaker came from the firm's operation in Germany to address the class. As the speaker discussed all of the problems and hassles associated with the operation, the listener was thinking, "I'm glad I'll never be sent there." He was quite surprised when, soon afterwards, he was sent to Germany as a manager. He wished he had listened more carefully to the speaker. Another manager, who appears in a case later in this book, dismissed as irrelevant a cross-cultural case taught at an executive development session. But on his first day back at the office he faced a very similar situation. He, too, wished he had paid more attention to the class discussion. In an effort to increase others' international management skills, he and the subordinate involved participated in developing a powerful case series about the situation. These cases, David Shorter and Bob Chen, are included in this book.

Disguised Cases

Ideally, we would prefer to use the real names of companies, countries, and places portrayed in the cases. However, there are many reasons why this cannot always be done. Often, the issues involved are sensitive or are perceived to be sensitive by the people in the company who have cooperated in writing the case. Also, some of the comments made about other people or other countries are not always flattering. Many of the companies depicted have ongoing business relationships with these same people and countries, and do not wish to cause offense. In allowing others to write and use these cases, some companies insist on disguising the names of people, places, and countries. Because the companies and people involved in these cases have cooperated with the case authors in order that students may benefit from their experience, their requests are honored.

Sometimes, the management of a company is sensitive only to seeing the real names of people and the company in print. In such cases, a light disguise can be used in which all the remaining information is real. Companies may also be sensitive to financial data in a case and want these as well. In these situations, the data have been slightly altered, but the important relationships are maintained. Occasionally, sensitivity to all the issues contained in a case is very high, and therefore in these instances mythical countries have been created so that no one is offended. There is nothing mythical about the situation described in such a case, only the name of the country. The number of such mythical countries has been kept to a minimum.

Though it might be preferable that the cases not be disguised, the disguise is not a critical issue with a culture-general orientation. The emphasis should be on identifying the important issues and analyzing the problems. Many of the situations described are classic and may be found in South America, Africa, or Europe. For example, one disguised case that we wrote was used in a company training program, and five experienced and knowledgeable people who read the case identified it as a project they had intimate knowledge of. Yet all five projects that these people were working on were different projects in different countries, and none was the one in the disguised case!

We have indicated on cases whether it has been disguised. The important point is that, despite the disguise, the essential elements of the problems are intact, and the cases faithfully describe the reality experienced by managers in the actual situations.

Terminology: Gender

The gender of the people in the cases is the same as the actual people in the real situations. We recognize that in some societies men are given preferential treatment in organizational life and that in other societies there are attempts to provide equal opportunity to men and women managers. The cases represent the current reality in international business, not what is necessarily desirable. The text portions of the book have been written in gender neutral or inclusive language reflecting the orientations of the United States and Canada.

Terminology: Geography and Nationality in North America

The United States and Canada have an intertwined historical, social, and economic relationship. The same is true for the United States and Mexico. Canada and Mexico, by comparison, are relatively new acquaintances and have had much less contact with each other. Due to the United States' physical location, it is natural that such bilateral relationships would develop. However, the North American Free Trade Agreement (NAFTA) created a trilateral economic relationship. One outcome is that, in the United States and Canada, people are more aware of Mexico as a business partner and not just as a resort destination.

Globalization is making its impact felt even in the area of writing textbooks. We need a way to refer to the three countries and cultures that reflects their citizens' concerns about what they are called. Citizens of the United States refer to themselves as Americans, and the rest of the world does too. However, it is equally true that people from the Americas, North and South, are "Americans." Mexicans have a word for citizens of the United States that avoids any confusion or controversy – los/las estadounidenses, or literally the United Statesers, which is too awkward in English for use here. To complicate the matter further, Canadians tend to use the designation "North American" to refer to Canadians and Americans, but not Mexicans. However, Mexico is located on the continent of North America, and therefore its citizens are also North Americans. We also could technically refer to Mexico using an abbreviated name, "the United States," since the official name of the country is the United Mexican States. Some believe that people in the United States of America have unfairly appropriated the terms American and the abbreviated name, "the United States," exclusively for their own use ignoring everyone else on the two continents.

What to do? We recognize these semantic irregularities, understand that they offend some people, and respect people's rights to their opinions regarding them. The commonly understood terms – Canadians, Mexicans, and Americans, and the United States to refer to the United States of America – will be used in this book. We will also use the Canadian terminology, North American, to refer to Americans and Canadians. In reading the book *The Labyrinth of Solitude and Other Writings* by the Mexican writer Octavio Paz, who won the 1990 Nobel Prize for Literature, we discovered that he used these terms in similar ways. We felt we were in good company.

A Final Note

This book is based on the philosophy that learning is a lifelong, continuous process. Rather than provide an illusion of mastery, we hope it stimulates and facilitates even more learning about other cultures and how to work effectively with others. For some readers, the material in this book may represent a first encounter with different cultures. Other readers may have been exposed to different cultures through previous courses or personal experience. For those with prior exposure to other people and places, the journey continues with a new level of insight. For those without prior experiences, welcome to an interesting journey!

Notes

1. Lena Zander, "The License to Lead," Ph.D. Dissertation, International Institute of Business, Stockholm School of Economics, Stockholm (1997): 175.
2. G. M. McEvoy and W. F. Cascio, "The United States and Taiwan: Two Different Cultures Look at Performance Appraisal," *Research in Personnel and Human Resources Management*, Supplement 2 (1990): 201–19.
3. *Percy Barnevik and ABB*, INSEAD case #4308: 10.
4. Bernard Daniel, Secretary-General, Nestlé, Vevey, Switzerland. Personal communication.
5. Patricia A. Galagan, "Executive Development in a Changing World," *Training and Development Journal* 44(6) (1990): 23–41.
6. The following section was based heavily on research conducted by Brenda McMillan, Joseph J. DiStefano and James C. Rush, published in "Requisite skills for global managers," Working Paper, National Centre for Management Research and Development, Ivey Business School, University of Western Ontario, London, Canada.
7. Jiping Zhang, "The building and operation of a North American business school" (Chinese) (Beijing: Tsinghua University Press, 1990). (Early English version published in 1987 by the Ivey Business School, University of Western Ontario, London, Canada.)
8. "Don't Be an Ugly-American Manager," *Fortune*, October 16, 1995: 225.
9. "Why Scudder couldn't win Canadian hearts," *Globe & Mail*, April 23, 1999.
10. "The lesson the locals learnt a little too quickly," *The Economist*, September 28, 1996: 71.
11. Stephanie Strom and Keith Bradsher, "Wedding or Wipe-Out?," *The New York Times*, May 23, 1999: Section 3, p. 13.
12. "Minorities set to be majority," *Toronto Star*, June 7, 1998: 1.
13. "Profile of Toronto and the Greater Toronto Area, 1998/99: Toronto business and market guide," Toronto Board of Trade.
14. "Minorities set to be majority," *Toronto Star*, June 7, 1998: 1.
15. Harold F. Clarke, Jr., "Consumer and corporate values: Yet another view on global marketing," *International Journal of Advertising*, 6 (1987): 29–42.
16. "Chanel apologizes for offence to Muslims," *Toronto Star*, January 23, 1994: A3.
17. Doug Struck, "Israeli court verdict on Pepsi ad: 'Uh uh!'," *Baltimore Sun*, May 16, 1992: B3.
18. "Wal-Mart flyers breach Quebec's language law," *Globe & Mail*, April 9, 1994.
19. "Nike ads stumble overseas," *Globe & Mail*, May 5, 1994.
20. Ruth G. Shaeffer, "Building global teamwork for growth and survival," *The Conference Board Research Bulletin*, 228 (1996).
21. Leslie G. Campbell, *International Auditing* (New York: St. Martin's Press, 1985): 141.
22. William S. Albrecht, Hugh L. Marsh, Jr., and Frederick H. Bentzel, Jr., "Auditing an International Subsidiary," *Internal Auditor*, 45 (5) (1988): 22–6; Joseph Soeters and Hein Schreuder, "The Interaction Between National and Organizational Cultures in Accounting Firms," *Accounting, Organizations and Society* 13 (1) (1988): 75–85; and Nicholas M. Zacchea, "The Multinational Auditor: Overcoming Cultural Differences to Apply Audit Standards," *Internal Auditor*, 45 (5) (1988): 16–21.
23. *The Globe & Mail*, January 10, 1995: B9.
24. Martha Maznevski and Joseph DiStephano, "Global leaders are team players: Developing global leaders through membership on global terms," *Human Resource Management*, forthcoming.
25. Richard Tanner Pascale, "Zen and the art of management," *Harvard Business Review*, 56(2) (1978).

PART 1

○○

Intercultural Effectiveness in Global Management

Reforms, when the ground has not been prepared for them, especially if they are institutions copied from abroad, do nothing but mischief.

Dostoyevsky, *The Brothers Karamazov*, in which the Devil speaks to
Ivan in his nightmare about changes in Hell.

Intercultural Communication and Effectiveness

A fundamental part of any global manager's reality is the intercultural nature of his or her interactions. Most managers recognize that interactions within one's own culture are difficult enough to manage effectively, as is evidenced by the attention that companies and most business schools give to training in interpersonal skills. Interactions with people from different cultures present an even greater potential for distortion or misunderstanding. The greatest challenge in global management is avoiding the "mischief," but being able to handle it well when it is unavoidable. On paper, a new product line, a new distribution strategy, a new alliance may move the company way ahead of its competition. But unless the ground has been prepared properly, managers can expect nothing close to the anticipated benefits.

This first part of the book addresses the most immediate task that international managers face when executing strategy: effective interpersonal interaction. We focus on approaches and skills to prevent unwanted misunderstandings and problems so that you can implement ideas and reforms effectively. We are not necessarily suggesting the reduction or elimination of differences because there is creative potential inherent in those differences. What might be interpreted as "mischief" or "not doing it our way" by the home country organization may, in fact, be a creative response to a situation. Multinational organizations have access to a wealth of unique perspectives that can provide enormous benefit. Rather than diminish or negate these differences, the best companies take advantage of them. They recognize that some "mischief" may be constructive and a source of competitive advantage.

We begin by describing the dynamics of typical cross-cultural situations. How do people usually respond when faced with the inconsistencies of different cultural perspectives? What tends to happen in groups with members from different cultural backgrounds? Although the most frequent responses in individuals and groups are negative or at best neutral, some people and teams grow and improve with these interactions. We spend most of this part of the text, therefore, on the knowledge and skills needed to learn from and be highly effective in cross-cultural interaction. The readings then provide more in-depth discussions on these issues, and the cases present opportunities to see the concepts in context and practice the skills.

The Dynamics of Differing World Views

To understand the typical outcomes of cross-cultural encounters, one needs to understand first the role of *assumptions* and *perceptions* in influencing our feelings and actions.

An assumption is an unquestioned, taken for granted belief about the world and how it works. Assumptions allow us to function and perform effectively every day, without thinking about how we are doing what we're doing. Assumptions help create our worldview, or the cognitive environment in which we operate. Assumptions come in many different varieties. Some are so deeply ingrained and unquestioned that it is difficult ever to surface them, and even when surfaced they are not testable. For example, assumptions about the basic nature of humans are normally surfaced and questioned only by philosophers, and even they cannot test them in an unambiguous way. Culture incorporates many of these deep assumptions, and we will elaborate on more of them presently.

Other assumptions are learned at various stages of our lives, and, once learned, are taken for granted. A child comes into the world with no knowledge of it, yet in the first few years learns to take so much for granted: day and night follow each other; manipulating switches makes things work or turns them off; things that move are either alive or powered by something; living things need nourishment; and, today, whenever you need to know something you can find out on the Internet. As we develop through life, we learn more and more, and each lesson becomes a basic building block for adding new skills and competencies. A financial analyst valuing companies takes for granted certain assumptions about efficient markets and develops analyses that eventually may affect the companies' ability to obtain resources. An advertising account manager takes for granted certain assumptions about human motivations, and produces advertising campaigns that play to those motivations and invoke them.

Assumptions influence the process of perception, or what we notice and how we interpret events and behaviors. The financial analyst is likely to focus on things such as financial ratios, earnings growth, or dividends but may not notice evidence of or value, for example, a set of programs with a long lead-time that may enhance the company's reputation for social responsibility. If she did notice this information, she would likely interpret it as something admirable but nothing that should influence stock price or ability to borrow. The advertising account manager, on the other hand, may take note only of product features that fit into his framework of assumptions about motivation for the target audience, and miss others that do not or miss other implications of those features. For example, the first marketing campaigns for cellular phones focused exclusively on the business audience, but recent campaigns have realized that the same features that attracted the first business customers are equally important for families involved in multiple activities. If marketers' asumptions had not focused exclusively on business, they may have tapped this broader consumer market much earlier.

If people did not make innumerable assumptions about the world, they would be paralyzed by their need to constantly inquire about the meaning of events and the motives of others. The key to assumptions is their accuracy and commonality. The more that others share one's assumptions, the more likely it is that effective exchange will occur. Within a culture most assumptions also are accurate enough for communication and effective interpersonal relations to occur. So, it is not surprising that a person's assumptions are most effective when he or she operates within his or her own culture and may be less effective elsewhere. We need to remember that assumptions are summary descriptions and interpretations of the world, and can never describe the world entirely accurately. There is plenty of scope for people to have different assumptions about the same phenomena. In fact, culture plays a large role in developing our assumptions, and different cultures provide different assumptions about the same things.

Assumptions influence our perceptions, which are our interpretations of events and behaviors or the meaning that the events and behaviors have for us. The expression "we see what we want to see and hear what we want to hear" is a reflection of how one's assumptions affect one's perceptions. In fact, Karl Weick, a well-known and highly respected social psychologist, has suggested that people are more likely "to see something when they believe it" rather than "to believe something when they see it".[1] Interpretations tend to be made from one's own cultural perspective and are prone to ethnocentric error. Ethnocentrism is "the evaluation of differences between groups (as in 'us better – them worse') . . . There exists a strong tendency to use one's own group's standards as the standard when viewing other groups, to place one's group at the top of a hierarchy, and to rank all others as lower."[2]

People seem to have an unfortunate tendency to move too quickly from description to interpretation and then to evaluation or labeling as good or bad. In cross-cultural situations this increases the probability of making mistakes. Resisting the quick leap to interpretation and evaluation for as long as possible will help improve cultural effectiveness.

A simple way to remember this process of social perception is captured by the acronym *DIE*, which stands for *Describe, Interpret,* and *Evaluate.* We observe something and take note of its characteristics, or describe it. In describing something we stay with the objective facts. What we are inclined to notice is influenced in part by our assumptions of what is important. For example, as professors we might notice a chair beside a desk, and notice that it has wheels on the bottom, a padded seat and back, and adjustable back and armrests. Next, we attribute meaning to what we've noticed. This interpretation process is even more influenced by our background assumptions. The wheels are for moving the chair quickly from one place to another, the padding is for comfort, and the adjustability is to customize it to a particular user. Finally, we evaluate what we've noticed. The chair is a good desk chair, and would be suitable for writing over long hours. Action is based on the evaluation part of the perceptual process: we request the chair for our offices. However, the purchasing officers of our institutions might notice and interpret things differently – the padding and adjustments add to the cost, and represent an unnecessary luxury – and turn down the purchase request. Students visiting our office might attribute some status to the chair, especially if the "visitors'" chairs in the office were more spartan, and they might react either favorably or unfavorably towards that perceived status differential.

The point is that we act based on the world we perceive, the world we see through the *Describe, Interpret, Evaluate* sequence. Since the sequence builds so heavily on our assumptions of the world and how it works, those assumptions end up influencing our own actions and what we think of others' actions.

A final important aspect of the perceptual process relates to our behavior and feelings when our assumptions are not confirmed. When assumptions are consistent with perceptions, the associated feeling is one of comfort or harmony, or, minimally, of neutral feelings. We are able to function, to get our work done, to produce. But what happens when we encounter evidence that contradicts our assumptions? These types of encounters set up a condition described by psychologists as "cognitive dissonance." It is an uncomfortable feeling of imbalance, and we are motivated to react by reducing the imbalance to achieve consistency again. There are two ways to regain consistency: changing our perceptions of the evidence to match the assumptions; and changing our assumptions to match the evidence. We are much more inclined to invoke the first method than the second, because it requires a great deal less energy and is less confusing. We usually do this by distorting what we've perceived to make it consistent with our assumptions. Why is this done? The simple answer is that people seek pleasure and avoid pain. If there is a clash between what is seen and what is assumed, people manage to reduce the negative feelings associated with the clash by distorting what they see (see figure 1).

Although the usual mode of reducing the gap between assumptions and perceptions is to distort perceptions, there is another option: altering one's assumptions. Unfortunately, this is usually an unexamined alternative. Furthermore, the closer the relationship between the assumptions in question and one's concept of self, the less likely one is to consider changing assumptions.

This tendency to make perceptions congruent with assumptions is often a source of misunderstanding between people in the same cultural milieu. It is an even bigger problem when it's moved into an intercultural context where there is a lack of shared assumptions. The definitions of how one ought to behave and, therefore, the explanations

FIGURE 1 Cognitive and Emotional States

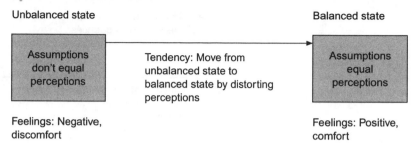

Unbalanced state

Balanced state

| Assumptions don't equal perceptions | Tendency: Move from unbalanced state to balanced state by distorting perceptions | Assumptions equal perceptions |

Feelings: Negative, discomfort

Feelings: Positive, comfort

of why a person is behaving in a particular way, often differ from one culture to another. In this situation, people get into difficulty by making inaccurate assumptions about a person or situation in a different culture.

If assumptions can be identified and understood, the capacity to verify their accuracy increases. Differences in assumptions might be anticipated, and errors in perception might be avoided. This process is similar to Samuel Coleridge's requirement for readers of poetry, namely, "the willing suspension of disbelief." In the case of poetry, the poet's power of insight often enables him or her to juxtapose two images or ideas that most people do not normally associate with each other. The reader of poetry should not let his or her assumptions overwhelm the poet's creativity in linking the elements (to disbelieve the unusual association). The challenge is to be open intellectually to the poet's assumptions about what is normal. The reward is a new vision. However, the more unusual the poet's perception of what belongs together, the more the readers' assumptions are challenged and the less likely that the poet will be appreciated or understood. Unfortunately, the more abstract the poet, the less likely the reader is to even try to understand his or her perception. Even more regrettable is the likelihood that the reader will justify his or her assumptions by dismissing the poet as "impenetrable," "impossible," "weird," or some other favorite pejorative. In intercultural situations, a similar process is often employed. People from the other culture say things and behave in ways that are not at all familiar to one's self, and the other culture is stereotyped as "primitive," "lazy," or some other negative stereotype. In this case, as with the poetry example, the common element is ethnocentric behavior, which is a major stumbling block in intercultural interaction. People tend to become aware of how their assumptions shape perceptions, values, and behavior only as they confront a different set of assumptions guiding the views and practices of other people. If people are exposed to new experiences, part of their response will include an examination of their own guiding values as well as the more common reaction of rejecting the other's values as "strange."

Figure 2 shows the influence pattern of culture on assumptions, perceptions, and management behavior, and demonstrates why culture and assumptions play such a large role in cross-cultural encounters. The cultural assumptions and the factors that contribute to their development represent the hidden bedrock upon which the guiding imperatives of activities rest. As one moves through levels from the abstract and general elements of culture to their concrete and specific manifestations (e.g., in institutions), the influence of the cultural assumptions pervades one's ways of thinking and behaving.

FIGURE 2   Influence Pattern of Culture on Assumptions, Perceptions, and Management Behavior

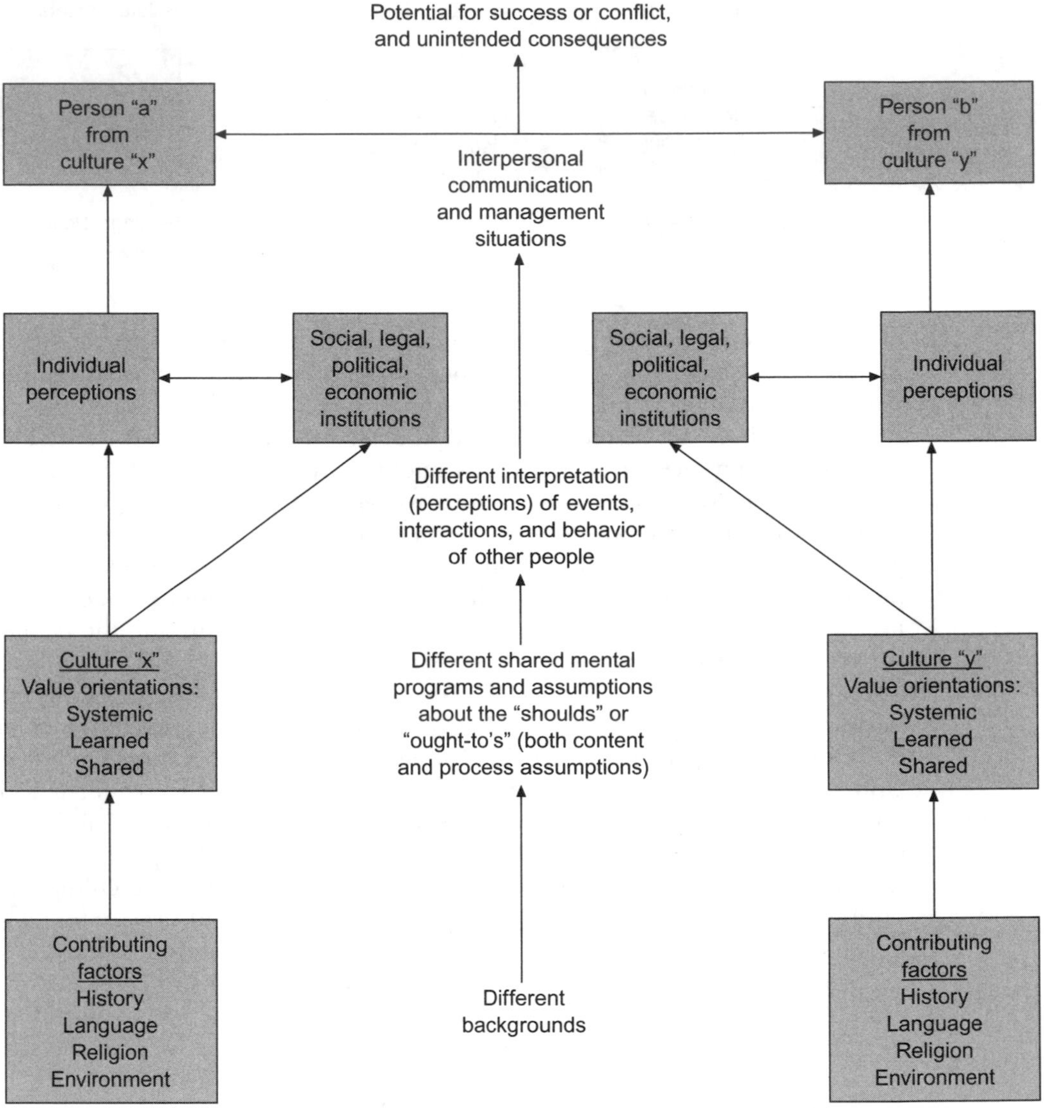

Potential for success or conflict,
and unintended consequences

Person "a" from culture "x"		Interpersonal communication and management situations		Person "b" from culture "y"

| Individual perceptions | Social, legal, political, economic institutions | | Social, legal, political, economic institutions | Individual perceptions |

Different interpretation (perceptions) of events, interactions, and behavior of other people

Culture "x" Value orientations: Systemic Learned Shared	Different shared mental programs and assumptions about the "shoulds" or "ought-to's" (both content and process assumptions)	Culture "y" Value orientations: Systemic Learned Shared

Contributing factors History Language Religion Environment	Different backgrounds	Contributing factors History Language Religion Environment

For example, people may not be conscious enough about their basic belief about human nature to articulate it. However, if you asked someone what a person would probably do if he or she found a large amount of money in an unidentified package on the street, your respondent would probably be able to reply easily. It is even more likely that they would reply with greater clarity and certainty if asked a more specific question about the kind of management control system that should be in place to prevent dishonest employees from stealing money. In general, people are more consciously aware of how they ought to behave in situations that are specific and concrete; but people are not usually aware of where those "ought's" originate from. Figure 2 connects the hidden, abstract values to conscious beliefs and behaviors associated with management. Understanding this linkage provides a way of analyzing a situation and behaving more effectively when the management practices embedded in two different cultural contexts cause problems. The cultural problems, at least intellectually, can be separated from strictly business problems.

What about when it comes to groups? How does this assumptions–perceptions process tend to play out in multicultural group settings? Not surprisingly, usually quite badly. A study reported by Nancy Adler showed that, compared to culturally homogeneous groups, multicultural groups either performed worse or better, and that more performed worse than better.[3] Every manager with whom we have worked has confirmed this result. Looking at a wide variety of diversity characteristics including gender, age, organizational tenure, and profession, research has found that the more diverse a group is, the less satisfied members are with their membership, the lower the cohesion, and the higher the absenteeism and/or turnover.[4] The experiences that lead to negative evaluations and actions tend to multiply with the number of people and intensity of the task, resulting in a disaster in terms of group relations.

For a while, the standard recommendation to managers was to avoid putting together diverse groups whenever possible. However, given the trends in demographics and global business in general outlined in the Introduction of this text, most managers have realized this recommendation is unrealistic. Global organizations inevitably have multicultural teams even within single "domestic" units, and they need multicultural teams across units.

On the positive side, some studies have shown that multicultural groups provided some advantages. Compared with culturally homogeneous groups, multicultural ones have been shown to be more creative, to develop more and better alternatives for resolving a problem, and more and better criteria for evaluating the alternatives.[5] However, even in these studies multicultural teams, on average, never performed better than the more similar teams.

Of course, there are some high-performing diverse teams. They are the ones that manage to capture the different perspectives offered by their broad membership and weave them into a synergy of innovative, effective responses to management challenges. Their path to success is described in the next section.

Map, Bridge, Integrate: The MBI Model of Managing Cultural Diversity for Personal and Team Effectiveness

The discussion that follows is based on our research on individual and team interactions in organizations. It is centered around three basic skills of Mapping to understand cultural differences among members, Bridging to communicate effectively among members, and Integrating to bring perspectives together and build on them. We have found that when these three skills are executed well, multicultural interactions between individuals or among team members result in high performance.[6] The basic model is shown in figure 3. We have used it in a wide variety of countries, situations, organizational

FIGURE 3   The MBI Model

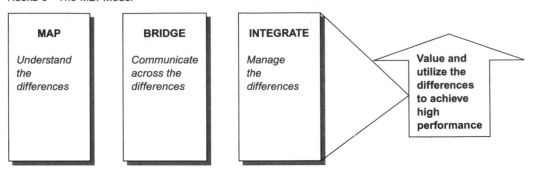

levels, and functions, and those using it have found that it helps them achieve high effectiveness with cultural diversity.

Mapping

We are all familiar with maps and their use. A good geographic map accurately provides all the information the user needs to conduct the task at hand – whether it is navigating a vacation or drilling for oil. But they contain no extraneous detail. For example, a road map does not show underlying geological formations, and a geological map does not show the location of rest stops. The skill of using a map is to know how to find oneself on the map, and then to use it in relation to the terrain to help decide where to go next.

A cultural map, rather than showing streets and highways, provides information about a group's characteristics and behavior in terms of observable patterns as discovered by experience and by research. A good cultural map for international managers provides accurate information about the ways in which cultures differ that are important to international business. Good cultural maps also simplify those differences to avoid an overabundance of detail but still permit comparisons between cultures. In our terminology, cultural mapping involves being able to describe oneself and others in terms of the map and predicting and explaining characteristics and behaviors in terms of the map. Unfortunately, cultural maps are not as ubiquitous as road maps. An international manager may also have a role as a cartographer and through his or her experience help create a map of the important features of a culture. People who live for a long time in a culture different from the one they grew up in eventually develop their own map, often unconsciously. But having a formal framework to help organize what you observe and are told helps accelerate the learning enormously. However, there has been some research that has started to chart the cultural landscape that can assist you.

Just as a good geographer uses different types or scales of maps for different purposes, a good international manager has access to several cultural maps. We will focus on one map developed by Kluckhohn and Strodtbeck that we have found to be useful across a wide variety of settings and applications. However, a number of other important cultural maps exist. Edward T. Hall, a famous anthropologist, has written several books and articles describing elements of culture that are relevant to business. In his classic article, "The Silent Language in Overseas Business," he describes cultural differences relating to the dimensions below and their impact on interpersonal behavior:[7]

- Time,
- Space,
- Things,
- Friendships, and
- Agreements.

One of his articles is included in this book as Reading 1, "Key Concepts; Underlying Structures of Culture."

Geert Hofstede has developed probably the most extensively researched framework or cultural map.[8] He identified four basic value patterns of cultures around the world:

- Individualism,
- Power Distance,
- Uncertainty Avoidance, and
- Masculinity.

He also linked these dimensions to management theories and practice. Later, with colleague Michael Bond, he identified a fifth value of *Confucian Dynamism* or Long-Term Orientation. Hofstede's framework is presented in more detail in Reading 2, "Cultural Constraints in Management Theories" and in Reading 3.

Following Hofstede, but incorporating more dimensions developed in sociology and anthropology, Trompenaars developed another map of seven dimensions.[9] The dimensions are:

- Universalism versus Particularism,
- Collectivism versus Individualism,
- Affective versus Neutral Relationships,
- Specificity versus Diffuseness,
- Achievement versus Ascription,
- Orientation Toward Time, and
- Internal versus External Control.

Trompenaars' framework has become quite popular among managers. Unfortunately space limitations prevent us from including it in detail in this book. However, we encourage interested readers to pursue it in more depth through the books he has authored or co-authored.

A fourth framework, developed by anthropologists Kluckhohn and Strodtbeck, identifies six value orientations (or dimensions) and their respective variations in different cultures.[10] Since this is the framework we use to illustrate the mapping component of the MBI model, we will discuss it in much more detail.

To paraphrase Kluckhohn and Strodtbeck, culture consists of a shared, commonly held body of general beliefs and values that define the "should's" and the "ought's" of life. These beliefs and values are taught to people so early and so unobtrusively that they are usually unaware of their influence. In a similar way, Hofstede defines culture as "the collective programming of the mind which distinguishes one group or category of people from another."[11]

The basic premise underlying Kluckhohn and Strodtbeck's Cultural Orientations Framework (COF) is that there are common themes in the issues or problems that different societies have faced throughout time, and that these universal issues provide a way of viewing culture more objectively.[12] They produced their framework by analyzing hundreds of ethnographic descriptions of worldwide cultures conducted by researchers from many different backgrounds. Kluckhohn and Strodtbeck identified six problems or issues that all societies throughout recorded history faced, but different societies developed different ways of coping with these issues. The six issues are referred to as cultural orientations, and the different responses to each issue are called variations. The six issues are:

1. Relation to nature
2. Relationships among people
3. Mode of human activity
4. Belief about basic human nature
5. Orientation to time
6. Use of space.

Some Important Caveats about Mapping

Before the Cultural Orientations Framework is presented in detail, some clarifications and caveats must be noted. The COF is a useful tool that can promote deeper cultural awareness. But like any map, it must be used thoughtfully. In this case, thoughtful use requires understanding some characteristics of the concept of culture and some assumptions underlying the framework itself. Hofstede points out that, "The culture of a country – or other category of people – is not a combination of the properties of the 'average citizen,' nor a 'modal personality.' It is, among other things, a set of likely reactions of citizens with a common mental programming."[13]

Our first caveat is to remember that variations exist in all cultures. Culture is not monolithic or uniformly manifested in a country. Not all people will react the same way, but rather patterns of reactions will be found more often in one society than in others. Because of the existence of subcultures, cultural homogeneity within any country cannot be assumed. Within larger cultures, there are always pockets of smaller cultures that can be identified as holding different dominant values. In fact, we have not been in any country where local jokes did not exist about the different cultural characteristics of various regions. For example, in Brazil, the story goes that the Paulistas (Sao Paulo) earn the money (mode of Activity-doing) so that the Cariocas (Rio) can spend it (mode of Activity-being). Both Americans and Canadians are familiar with "Down Easterners" and "Maritimers," who hold values distinctly different from those of the broader cultures in which they exist. Subcultures exist even in a small country such as Switzerland. These subcultures may be further divided by the different language groupings that make up the country, professions, religions, and so on.

An important assumption of the COF is that all variations of a particular cultural orientation exist in a given culture. That is, no culture is assumed to be so simple that all members of the culture believe that only one way of dealing with a given issue is appropriate in all situations. Rather, some of the variations are held to be more appropriate than others are. Each culture has an ordered preference of variations for solving a particular problem. Thus, one can imagine a dominant variation as reflecting the values of a majority of the people in the culture in most situations. This dominant variation may reflect the most influential preference within a culture. Other variations may also be important, but less so. In our discussions, even though a culture may be described only in terms of its most dominant variation, the reader should not confuse this simplified description of a culture with the reality of a culture's complexity or richness.

A second caveat is not to confuse personality and culture. The concept of culture is, by definition, a group-based concept (commonly held, widely shared set of values). Personality is an individual-based concept. Each person is a complex combination of personality, cultural influences, and experiences. It is often very difficult to distinguish the influence of personality from that of culture in a person's behavior. With time and experience in a culture, it becomes easier to differentiate the two influences.

Confusing the individual level with the group or societal level is such a common error that it has been identified and named in the social sciences as the ecological fallacy. It manifests itself in two ways. One manifestation is to project cultural values known to be held by a group onto an individual who is a member of the group. For example, it does not automatically follow that if the Chinese people in general hold harmony and hierarchy as dominant values, these are dominant for a particular Chinese person. The reverse is the second manifestation of the ecological fallacy: projecting from individuals to groups. If one knows a German, one should be careful not to assume that her values and beliefs reflect those of all Germans. Both types of fallacies are aspects of stereotyping and should be consciously avoided. Our second caveat also could be expressed as: "Beware of the ecological fallacy." Remember to apply concepts only at the level of analysis from which they have been derived.

Related to the interaction of personality and culture, people may make one of two potentially misleading assumptions. The first is that every individual is unique and, therefore, culture is irrelevant. The second is that culture is deterministic and all members of a culture will believe and react similarly. As discussed above, these extremes are not the case at all. Research has shown that, between these extremes, patterns exist. Within these patterns individual personality still manifests itself.

The third caveat has to do with cultural change. Cultures are dynamic. Although a culture's basic values change very slowly, they do change over time. It is important to note the time period associated with any information one uses to analyze a culture. For any particular aspect of a culture being examined, the rate of change for that element should be considered, especially if important decisions are to be based on the analysis. Of course, errors may be the result of superficial judgments, too. On the one hand, if the adoption of Western business suits were seen as a sign of the cultural change

Evidence for the empirical basis for stereotyping and for the ecological fallacy can be seen in figure 4, which shows the actual distribution of scores on a mastery scale among samples of businesspeople from the US and from Taiwan. The US cluster shows itself to be, *on average*, higher in its orientation to mastery over nature; the Taiwanese cluster, *on average*, is lower. The operative words are "on average," for we can see that there are real differences in the profiles of the two groups. Yet, it is equally clear that some members of the Taiwanese group score higher than the average of the US group, and vice versa. There are two realities visible in the diagram: there are discernible differences between the two groups from different countries, and there are also variations across individuals within both groups.

It would be a mistake to assume that one knew a person's orientation to mastery by knowing whether she or he were Taiwanese or American. Yet, we still know that there are real differences between the groups. If you had to prepare yourself for a new experience based on your best guess, you should prepare yourself to enter a culture of lower mastery in Taiwan than in the US, and vice versa, but also to find individuals who differ from the cultural mean. The point is that our knowledge cannot be used in the absence of other information to identify an individual's value orientation. We can only know something about the probability of their orientation by knowing about the group's profile.

These data were collected using the Cultural Perspectives Questionnaire, developed by Martha Maznevski and Joe DiStefano. They collected the US data, and the Taiwanese data were collected by Pei Chuan Wu. This research is reported in more detail in M. L. Maznevski, J. J. DiStefano, C. Gomez, N. Noorderhaven, and P. Wu, 1997, The Cultural Orientations Framework and International Management Research, presented at the Academy of International Business Annual Meeting in Monterrey, MX. More information on the questionnaire and its use can be obtained through Martha Maznevski's website at http://gates.comm.virginia.edu/mm4t/, or through any of the authors of this text.

FIGURE 4   Distribution of Mastery

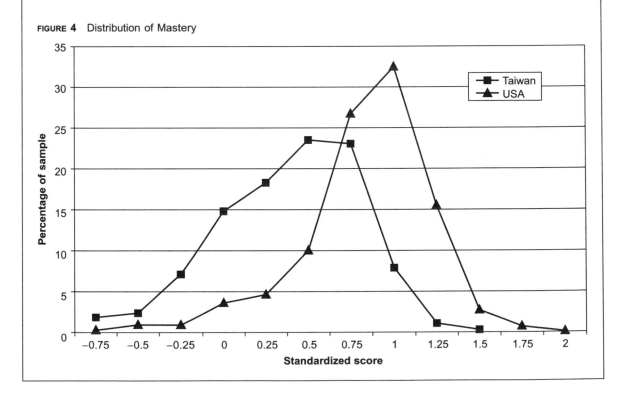

of Japanese managers, then many cultural and business mistakes would surely follow. On the other hand, intergenerational studies of Japanese families have demonstrated discernible changes in the patterns of dominant values from grandparents to grand-children. However, even though change is taking place and societies may become more modern, it does not mean that these societies are becoming more Westernized.

The fourth caveat is that culture does not necessarily mean national culture or country. It is important to note that the previous definitions of culture do not refer to a specific country. Often, however, country labels are used as shorthand notation for groups of people who hold "shared, common beliefs and values." This makes sense in international management: many of the carriers and transmitters of culture are national institutions like schools, government programs, and the media. But one could discuss age groups (seniors, baby boomers, or Generation "X"), gender, or religions as cultures, in keeping with the earlier definitions. One also could understand deaf people as a culture. For example, an article in *The New York Times Magazine* explains that "deaf activists live, proudly, in a different culture, but not a lesser one."[14] In that article M. J. Bienvenu states: "People mislabel me as disabled. In fact I am a member of American Deaf culture." This culture also has its own language: American Sign Language.

A fifth caveat is to remember that a person may be a member of many cultures simultaneously – nation, religion, school, gender, and so on. The various cultures may be similar in some ways, complementary in others, and contradictory in still others. Which cultural values most influence behavior at a given time depends on the situation.

Although we believe that the COF is helpful in promoting cultural awareness and understanding, another caveat is to recognize that a framework itself reflects a distinct orientation that will be discussed in a later section: mastery over the environment. Organizing behavioral data and expressions of preferences in an orderly and comparative fashion using a framework to better comprehend a culture can be seen as an expression of a mastery orientation.

A final caveat concerns the gap between understanding and behavior, which presents a barrier to using any framework for effectively adapting to other cultures. It is quite possible to understand exactly how another person's culture is different from your own and to see the managerial implications of these differences clearly. You may even try to avoid a problem by changing your own behavior to accommodate another person. Yet it may be impossible to do so, or doing so may be so difficult that it renders you ineffective. For a simple illustration, try standing closer to another person than you usually do during a normal conversation. A common reaction of this is to return quite quickly to a normal distance (if the other person does not readjust the distance first). If you maintain the closer distance, you may begin perspiring or using awkward pauses, gestures, or speech patterns. Some form of interference with your usual effectiveness is likely to emerge as you force yourself to behave against cultural norms. If this test seems difficult to carry out, imagine how much more frustrating the situation would be if you did not understand the cultural forces operating.

These caveats apply to the Cultural Orientations Framework, which is presented in the following section. They do not, of course, contradict the main message which is that a systematic analysis of culture's influence on management is both possible and helpful, and, once differences are understood, there are steps one can take to communicate and integrate the differences to increase the probability of exceptional performance. As an overall caution, note that the conceptual scheme should be employed as an aid to understanding, not as a simplistic answer. It would be easy to end up using the cultural categories to reinforce the stereotyping of countries and ethnic groups. Such misuse of the framework would be lamentable,[15] for its ultimate usefulness depends on the learning done subsequent to the initial analysis of a situation: using the framework as a guide to further understanding. No sterile, mechanical application of the conceptual scheme will produce useful insights. Only a dynamic, organic approach, assisted by the analytic rigor of the scheme, will lead to continued growth of understanding about a culture.

The Cultural Orientations Framework

In this discussion of the COF, we have simplified and modified slightly the terminology from Kluckhohn and Strodtbeck's original book, and made more explicit the links between the abstract concepts underlying each issue and the practical influence of the orientations and the variations on management.[16] Also, we employ the shorthand of country designations, but, as noted above, the reader should not be seduced by the labels into mistaking culture for an entire country or vice versa. For each of the six issues, we will explain the nature of the underlying assumptions and describe the variations that occur. We will also give examples of how the orientation might influence general managerial activities. These examples will illustrate how specific variations of the value orientation can yield different ways of dealing with managerial activities. In terms of the MBI model (figure 3), the COF provides the map of culture, which serves as the base for effective bridging and integration of differences.

Relation to Environment

The issue of people's relationship to the environment reflects how people in a society ought to orient themselves to the world around them, and to the supernatural. Three main variations seem to exist in the human experience.

One is *subjugation* to the environment: people see themselves as dominated by physical forces and/or subject to the will of a Supreme Being. Life in this context is viewed as predetermined or preordained, or an exercise in chance. It is felt that one should not try to alter the inevitable by acts of will, for such actions will be futile at best and blasphemous at worst. The parenthetical addition of "God willing" to a stated intention to meet with a friend in the future is an example of how this variation finds its way into language, if not into literal meaning. To a devout Muslim, the expression "Inshallah," which has the same meaning as "God willing," has a much more serious impact. The Muslim expression reflects a dominant world-view that is taken much more literally than the casual use of the similar expression by most Christians.

People who do not come from societies with an appreciation for *subjugation* often view it as a variant of fatalism: why bother working hard, for example, if everything is preordained anyway? However, this quotation from a Muslim friend of one of the authors helps explain *subjugation* as a non-fatalist orientation:

Through meditation and prayer, I am to understand what it is that Allah has planned for me – what role I am to play in His plan. Then it is my own responsibility to fulfill that role as well as I can. If I understand my role well and work hard to be effective in it, then if something happens to prevent me from doing it well I know that act was meant to happen and is part of Allah's larger plan. If I do not understand my role – which may be because I have not communicated well with Allah – and something happens to prevent me from doing it well, that act might be predetermined to help me understand my role better. If I do understand my role but I am lazy and don't work well towards it, and something happens to prevent me from fulfilling my role, that act may be my own responsibility. So it's a lot more complicated than "God determines everything," meaning every detail.

The second orientation is *harmony* with the environment: the imperative to behave in concert with the physical environment and other systems in the world around us. To a Native American in the Southwest, this may mean designing a road to skirt a clump of trees on a lovely hill. *Harmony* with the environment is not equivalent to the current meaning of strong environmentalism. Native Americans, for example, are traditionally hunters as well as gatherers. But their traditions also incorporate strong norms of studying the ecosystem to ensure that no more game is hunted than the system can tolerate without becoming unbalanced, and utilizing every single part of the animal to provide for their own needs, with no waste whatsoever. Their social traditions encourage and, in fact, regulate harmony within the tribe.

In contrast, an Anglo-Saxon civil engineer designing a road might alter the terrain by leveling the trees and the hill. In doing so, the engineer would exhibit the third variation and dominant North American value: *mastery* over the environment. A good example of the mastery orientation in this century is the goal of landing a person on the moon when the technology did not exist for accomplishing the task. The audacity of announcing that this mission was to be achieved by the end of the 1960s reflected not only a politically astute move to recapture America's confidence after the Russians launched the Sputnik satellite, but also a profound belief that if enough time, money, and brains are applied to a goal, nearly anything is achievable. This is the meaning of the mastery notion.

Much of the basis of culture is manifested in religious writings and literary works. International managers would be well advised to read the literature of the countries in which they operate for clues to understanding the cultural roots of the managerial practices that they may experience in the workplace. For example, the influence of this cultural dimension on perceptions of events is often shown in the language used to describe them. When Sir Edmund Hillary reached the summit of Mount Everest, headlines throughout the English-speaking world screamed "MAN CONQUERS EVEREST." Chinese colleagues have said that the same event reported in Mandarin would have been translated as "man befriends the mountain." Religious writings also reflect culture's influence. The mastery notion seems to pervade Genesis 26, which states: "Let them have dominion over all the Earth." In contrast, the Tao Te Ching states: "Those who would take over the Earth and shape it to their will, never, I notice, succeed."

The environment orientation influences managerial activity in many ways, two of which we will illustrate here: goal setting and budgeting. In a culture with a *subjugation* variation as the dominant influence, goals set in a managerial context will be more qualified and vague than in another cultural setting, and their achievement will not be perceived to depend solely on what people to do achieve them. In a harmony-dominated culture, goals are more likely to be moderated by the culture's need to fit with the environment. The appropriate contingencies that recognize external parameters are likely to be stated. For example, environmentalists who reflect a harmony orientation would say: "If we must consume goods, we should minimize the packaging, recycle the waste, and use biodegradable ingredients." The manager in a mastery-oriented culture, however, is likely to confidently state specific, unambiguous, and ambitious goals. The distinction between individual personality and the impact of culture is worth noting here. Which goals are set depends partially on individual differences in personality, such as the need to achieve. Cultural orientation influences the level and types of goals, and defines the way an individual should set goals.

A second managerial activity affected by orientation to the environment is budgeting. One study reported the differences between French and US subsidiaries of a large multinational corporation (MNC) with a supposedly uniform budget system.[17] This budgeting system had volumes of procedures, rules, forms, schedules, and deadlines to be followed worldwide. The French subsidiaries, which showed a very weak preference for the mastery orientation over the harmony orientation, considered the budget system an elegant exercise. They treated only the actual accounting results as real. The US subsidiaries, which showed a strong preference for the mastery orientation over the harmony orientation, treated the budget as real, relevant, and useful. They were confident of their ability to partially control events by using this managerial tool.

A budget system forced on a subsidiary operating in a cultural context where the subjugation orientation is dominant might be a futile exercise. The outcomes of the system, intended to assist managers to shape events, would be seen as predetermined by local employees in such a setting. Local managers would likely resist the process and complete the forms involved with reluctant predictions. This is distinct from what could occur if managers made specific choices as part of their activities. Some North American managers have reported such experiences with Indonesian managers.

An example of the impact of these variations in orientation to nature on management occurred when a civil engineer in a large North American construction company was given responsibility to select a site, design, and construct a fish-processing plant in a West African country. The engineer classified potential sites according to the availability of reliable power, closeness to transportation, nearness to the river for access by fishing boats from the Atlantic Ocean, location near the main markets, and availability of housing and people for employment. After evaluating these criteria and ranking the few sites in the final list, the engineer chose the optimum location. Just prior to requesting bids from local contractors for some of the site preparation, the engineer discovered, in talking to local authorities, that the site was located on ground considered sacred by the local people. These people believed this site was the place where their gods resided. None of the local people on whom the engineer was depending to staff the plant would ever consider working there! The engineer quickly revised the priorities and relocated the plant. In this case, it was lucky that the ignorance of a significant cultural barrier was discovered prior to construction. Too often these errors are realized only after a project has been completed. This true story points out the hidden workings of culture and also demonstrates that having a prior framework can assist in avoiding the problems of culturally-bounded criteria for decision making.

FIGURE 5 Variations in Relation to the Environment Orientation and Examples of Managerial Impact

Issue	Variations		
Relation to nature	Subjugation to nature	Harmony with nature	Mastery over nature

Managerial Impact			
General	Specific by Variation		
Goal setting	Qualified, hesitant, vague	Contingent, moderated	Specific, confident, unambiguous, high level
Budget systems	Futile, outcomes predetermined	Exercise, "actuals" are real	Real, relevant, useful

It is important to note that in our own research measuring these orientations we have yet to encounter any cultural group – ethnic, national, professional, etc. – that has had subjugation as its dominant orientation to the environment. Some groups definitely showed a stronger belief in subjugation than others did, and these differences may have an impact on management systems, but in no group yet have we seen subjugation higher than either mastery or harmony. So the relevant cultural differences on this variation seem to be the degree to which subjugation is assumed, in a relative way, rather than whether it is preferred to the other variations in an absolute way.

The Associated Press reported an extreme, but dramatic, example of the harmony variation in 1986. A factory in India had been closed for over two months because a cobra occupied the owner's office. The Press Trust of India (PTI) explained that since snakes are worshipped by many Hindus, the manager and the workers went to a temple for advice. They were told not to disturb the "cobra god." PTI went on to say that despite prayers, offerings, and creditor complaints, the factory remained closed for over two months. If the factory was part of a joint venture with a North American company, one can see the potential for conflict and hard feelings with North American executives who have a different orientation.

The Relation to the Environment orientation is summarized in figure 5. Under each of the variations are examples of how the cultural values manifest themselves in managerial spheres of activity. The examples in this and later figures are based on research or case studies and have been further reinforced by our own experience and that of our associates.

Relationships Among People

The concept of relationships among people is concerned with the responsibility one has to and for others. What responsibility does one have for the welfare of others? One response is that one should take care of oneself: "individualism." This attitude is dominant in North America, Australia and New Zealand, and parts of Europe. The nuclear family tends to be the outer limit of formal responsibility, and even that changes after children reach the age of majority. Independence is valued, and "Stand on your own two feet!" is the injunction. Except in unusual circumstances, such as a poor economy, parents with offspring in their twenties still living with them were viewed as having failed in their obligations to instill the "rugged individualism that made this country great!" Perhaps it is only in an individualistic society, such as the United States, that a book entitled *Looking Out for #1* could have appeared on the best-seller list. Yet quite different attitudes towards responsibility exist.

One alternative to individualism is the "group" orientation dominant in many Mediterranean, South American, and Asian cultures. In this type of society, one's allegiance and loyalty are to the extended family or group of which one is a part. In such a culture, cousins are treated with as much concern and love as siblings are in an individualistic culture. In fact, in many languages the same word is used for the English pairs grandfather/uncle, grandmother/aunt, sister/cousin, and brother/cousin; no distinction is made between the two relationships, either. The group tends to be clearly defined, and the group's members have an ultimate obligation to help and care for each other.

An important corollary exists in collective cultures that if a person is *not* part of one's own group, one has no obligation to help or care for the other person. It is assumed that his or her own group will look after the other person. On the other hand, if someone treats a stranger with the concern normally reserved for a member of one's group, then the person so treated for all intents and purposes becomes a member of the group, with all the rights and responsibilities associated with such membership. This complexity of collective can give rise to many misunderstandings. They are exemplified by the apocryphal story of an American who assisted a pedestrian brushed by a passing car in a busy street in an Asian city. Appalled by the lack of attention to the injured stranger, the American yelled at a nearby police officer, provided first aid, and insisted on hailing and paying for a taxi to take the person to a hospital. Afterward, the American muttered about the inhumanity of the local population and concluded that the incident confirmed his personal theory, "How cheap human life is in the overpopulated Asian cities." Meanwhile, the police officer's family listened, appalled, as the officer told them about the American who was so dumb as to treat a stranger like a family member. Then he was so indifferent as to send the person off in a taxi, rather than accompany the injured to the hospital personally and to attend to the victim properly afterwards.

A further variation on the relationship dimension is hierarchical, although the concept is more complex than is implied by this single word. In this variation, relationships of power and responsibility are arranged such that those lower in the hierarchy are obligated to submit to the will of those higher in the hierarchy. In return, they have the right to expect that those higher in the hierarchy will look after, protect, and provide for them. The hierarchy tends to be stable over time, such that most people remain in the same general level of the hierarchy throughout their lives. Many hierarchical societies also develop a strong collective orientation within hierarchical levels. This is characteristic of aristocratic society and caste systems. One looks after one's own kind, but knows where one's kind stands on the status ladder.

Managing a business requires managing relationships among people; therefore, the relationship variable has a pervasive influence on managerial practice and policy. Organizational structures, communication and influence patterns, reward systems, teamwork, and other managerial processes are all influenced by the relationship orientation.

In cultures where individualistic values are dominant, individuals are given much attention in the organizational structure. The focus is on the leader in the pyramidal structures. However, no matter how the organization is structured, the arrangement of relationships is treated informally. Behavior within the structures is flexible. Two-boss relationships are possible, as with a matrix organization.

In a group-dominated culture, more attention is given to horizontal differentiation. Differences between groups are the preoccupation, and the structures of work organizations reflect this concern. Hierarchical cultures emphasize vertical differentiation. Of all three possible variations, the most rigidly obeyed structures are likely to be found in the hierarchical situation. Perret found, for example, that French managers could not conceive of working in a matrix structure and faithfully reported any budget anomalies exclusively to their immediate superior, even if there were serious implications for lateral departments.[18] In contrast, American managers operated much more independently of the structure. They reported findings to anyone who had an interest in the data, regardless of his or her position in the structure. Laurent experienced the same phenomenon in teaching and research he conducted at INSEAD in France. The thought of reporting to two bosses was alien to French managers and the consideration of such an organizing principle was an impossible exercise.[19]

An interesting reversal, based on the same cultural differences, was found with respect to the importance of interpersonal relations at work. The French spontaneously raised the topic of interpersonal relations several times in unstructured interviews; the Americans mentioned interpersonal relations much less frequently and only in an instrumental context regarding work. The French valued the relations as ends in themselves. This difference between French and American managers in relating at work also shows up in communication and influence patterns. Hierarchical cultures use authority-based communications. Group-oriented cultures stress within-group patterns. Individualistic cultures maintain multiple, open arrangements to be used on an as-needed basis.

Similarly, the relationship variations have an impact on reward systems. Individually-based, group-based, and status-based systems are characteristic of each of the three types of relationship patterns. Teamwork and cooperation are also affected by the dominant pattern. In hierarchical cultures, teamwork is regulated and formal. On the one hand, in the French controller's departments studied by Perret, the hierarchical orientation was reflected in the regular work group meetings held by the managers, who rigidly controlled the agenda, data, and meeting processes. On the other hand, the American managers scheduled no routine group meetings. Instead, they dealt with others on a voluntary, informal basis whenever (but only when) the circumstances required such activity.

The skill of the Japanese in group management deserves mention. Careful examination of Japanese culture shows a more complex pattern than the popular literature leads one to believe.[20] The group orientation is combined with a strong sense of hierarchy, which coexists with an educational and social system that depends on merit (doing orientation) rather than class consciousness. The managerial implications of this include the commonly described group decision-making. They also include the less frequently mentioned respect given to a superior, who is invariably an older, experienced manager with greater practice and skill in managing groups. Another implication is that Japanese managers are encouraged to move laterally and diagonally through the organization during their careers. This is partly due to their skills in managing groups of functional

FIGURE 6   Variations in Relationships Among People and Examples of Managerial Impact

Issue	Variations		
Relationships	Hierarchical	Group	Individualistic

Managerial Impact			
General	Specific by Variation		
Organizational structure	Attention on vertical differentiation	Attention on horizontal differentiation	Informal, flexible behavior vis-à-vis structures
Communication and influence patterns	Authority-based	Within-group emphasis	Multiple, as-needed, open
Reward system	Status-based	Group-based	Individually-based
Teamwork	Regulated, formal	Normative, routine	Voluntary, informal

experts and partly because companies can depend on investment in such experience paying off in the future (because of the tradition – now eroding – of lifetime employment). In contrast, the individualistic orientation in North America stresses individual expertise that gives rise to increased specialization and career paths, primarily within a particular function.

In the survey data we have gathered to date, all the cultures and subcultures have preferred either individualism or collectivism the most, with the other of this pair second. Hierarchy has always been preferred least. Our data collection has focused on industrialized settings, so it is possible that this reflects a cultural convergence or commonality for industrialized cultures. Research has consistently shown that the more hierarchical an organization is, the more difficulty it has adapting to change. In today's dynamic environment, perhaps it is impossible to have an organization with a dominant preference for hierarchy over the long term. However, even though hierarchy was always the least preferred arrangement of responsibility, there are strong differences between countries and between subcultures within the same country.

For example, we have found some organizations to be lower than the general business population in the United States on the hierarchy orientation, and this difference was reflected in human resource management practices. One such company had a very difficult time with its subsidiary in India, which had a relatively high preference for hierarchy (although still lower than individualism or collectivism). The American managers were frustrated that their Indian subordinates would not embrace empowerment and make decisions. The Indian subordinates were frustrated that their American bosses were being so inefficient and taking so much time to discuss simple decisions with everyone, when just telling everyone what to do and then letting them go about their business would be much faster. On the other hand, we found a sample of US loan officers to be higher on the hierarchy orientation than the general US business population, with potential implications for how they process loan applications. The Relationships Among People orientation is summarized in figure 6.

Focus of Human Activity

The activity orientation does not refer to a state of activity or passivity, but rather the desirable focus of activity. The "being" orientation is characterized by spontaneity. One acts out feelings as they are experienced. This is the Dionysian mode (the Greek god of wine and good times). The "doing" orientation is the Promethean mode. Prometheus stole fire from Olympus and gave it to humans to use. As punishment, he was chained to a rock and tormented by vultures. Throughout eternity, he strained to break free of his chains, but new chains constantly reappeared when he was successful. The relentless striving to achieve and compulsive attempts to accomplish are the core of the "doing" orientation. In addition to the being and doing approaches is the thinking orientation. This is the Apollonian mode, in which the senses are moderated by thought and mind and body are balanced.

The activity dimension affects how people approach work and leisure, how preoccupied they are with work, and the extent to which work-related concerns pervade their lives. In a strongly doing-oriented culture, people are more likely to view work and work-related activities as a central focus to their existence. Decisions tend to be made with pragmatic criteria, reward systems are results-based, and there is a compulsive concern for achieving tangible performance measures. In a being-dominated culture, it is more likely that decision criteria are emotional, rewards are feelings-based, the definition of performance is much more broad, and the degree of concern for output and performance is variable, a function of individual spontaneity. In cultures with a dominant thinking orientation, decisions are more likely to be based on rational criteria, rewards are distributed logically, and output is measured against balanced objectives (such as long- and short-term profitability, quality as well as quantity of production, and so on).

In her study of French and US subsidiaries, Perret found effects of the activity orientation on the information and measurement systems of companies.[21] In the comptroller departments of the companies, the more doing-oriented US managers acted on the uniform budget system in a highly selective way. They stressed simple, operational indices and were concerned with making the system serve operational objectives. The more thinking-oriented French managers treated the system as a complex exercise and were concerned with the qualitative and broad implications of the system itself, as distinct from what the data implied for action. The French were preoccupied with absolute accuracy of all parts of the system and its calculations. The Americans were satisfied with approximations, as long as these provided data that could be used to make a difference in manufacturing departments. Although no comparative data was gathered for the being orientation, that kind of dominant variation would likely yield more of an intuitive system that would be less preoccupied with quantitative indicators. The activity orientation is summarized in figure 7.

In our own research to date, we have only twice encountered cultures that were highest on being: two R&D groups at different country sites within a large multinational corporation. In all of the other groups we have surveyed, either thinking or doing was highest, and the other of this pair was most often second highest. We think it would be very difficult for a company, especially a larger one, dominated by a being orientation to engage in business over the long term. The R&D groups with the high being orientation

FIGURE 7   Variations in Activity Orientation and Examples of Managerial Impact

Issue	Variations		
Activity	Being	Thinking	Doing

Managerial Impact			
General	Specific by Variation		
Decision criteria	Emotional	Rational	Pragmatic
Rewards system	Feelings-based	Logic-based	Results-based
Concern for output	Spontaneous	Balanced objectives	Compulsive
Information and measurement systems	Vague, feeling-based, intuitive	Complex, qualitative, broad	Simple, operational, few indices

were some of the hardest working in the company – they happened to love their work passionately. Their strength was in producing high quality innovations, but not coordinating with the rest of the company. We have found different country, organization, and subculture groups to prefer different levels of being-oriented activity, with some quite high, even though doing or thinking was higher.

Basic Nature of Human Beings

The belief about basic human nature does not reflect how one thinks about individuals, but rather one's belief about the inherent character of the human species. Does one believe that the fundamental nature of people is changeable or unchangeable? And, apart from the malleability of basic human nature, does one believe people are primarily evil, good, neutral (neither good nor evil), or mixed (a combination of good and evil)? In addressing these questions, we can see the influence of religious traditions in reflecting and shaping culture. In Christian faiths, the story of Adam and Eve in the Garden of Eden is pertinent. Adam's eating of forbidden fruit symbolizes the "fall of man," as Adam gave in to the devil. Note, however, that men and women are perfectible if they follow and worship God. In the language of the Cultural Orientations Framework these beliefs parallel the evil/changeable orientation.[22] Fundamentalists may hold such a dominant view of human beings as evil. Christians with stronger secular perspectives tend to hold a more neutral or mixed orientation. Our own understanding of Muslim and Shinto faiths and personal communications from Arab and Japanese proponents suggest that orientations emerging from these traditions may be closer to the "good" end of the spectrum. The Baha'i view "begins with the notion that human beings are essentially good, and that evil is a corruption of our true human nature."[23] This same orientation is reported by a Taiwanese manager to be the main theme of a very popular Chinese children's story.

The most obvious impact on business of the human nature value may be on control systems. A dominant evil orientation is likely to contribute a tight control system based on an underlying suspicion of people. An article in the *Wall Street Journal* stated that American workers were "among the world's most watched."[24] The primary reasons employers gave for electronic monitoring were checking on productivity and investigating theft and industrial espionage. Among the most monitored industries were retail sales, banking and finance, and telecommunications.

Cultural orientations dominated by a neutral or mixed value are likely to produce moderately tight controls, with modifications based on managers' experience with the people involved. People operating with an assumption that the basic nature of humanity is evil are less likely to modify a control system if there are no violations, because they will attribute the "good behavior" of people to the existence of the control system, not to people's innate goodness. Thus, there is a tendency to explain events in a way that is consistent with cultural values, even when other possible explanations are available. Similarly, managers who operate with the assumption that goodness is the basic human trait are likely to favor control systems based primarily on the need for management information, rather than for surveillance, checking, and control. One can imagine the opportunities for misunderstanding and mistrust in a Japanese–North American joint venture, for example, when cultural reasons produce such basic differences in why information is collected and how it is used.

There is a cultural basis in sanctions against violation of codes of conduct. An executive who was negotiating a large contract in Saudi Arabia was shopping in an open-air market. Stepping up to a currency exchange booth, the executive was very surprised to see about one-quarter of a million dollars clipped to a board in the stall. The currency dealer wandered away from the board to get some coffee after completing a transaction. The executive was stunned that such a large amount of money should be left unattended, but remembered the Islamic code's punishment for stealing – cutting off the right hand at the wrist. The severity of the punishment explained the apparently cavalier behavior of the money dealer. The executive also assumed, erroneously, that Saudis viewed basic human nature the same way as North Americans. This assumption led the executive to believe the punishment and the punishers were inhumane. However, consider an alternative explanation. If the Saudis hold human nature to be basically good, then it may follow that anyone who behaves evilly is less than human. If one is not behaving according to the expectations of what is human, then one may deserve to be identified as such by having a hand cut off.

Note that this value orientation may explain the executive's feelings towards crime and the punishment system. To most North Americans and Europeans, people's basic nature is, at best, mixed. Therefore, one should not be surprised if money were to be stolen from a neglected stall in an open-air market. A North American or European would feel that a violator should be punished, but not severely. (They tend to slap the wrist, not cut it off!) In fact, in these places, the currency dealer would probably be examined for mental stability for leaving money unattended. Simply put, control and punishment systems are created based on expectations about behavior, and the expectations are based on cultural values.[25]

An ironic end to this story occurred when the employees who were to go to Saudi Arabia after the executive had signed the contract were sent to a cross-cultural training session for one week. The first program was held at a hotel. Soon after the executive made the speech about the unattended money, the hotel, as part of a chain-wide campaign

FIGURE 8 Variations in Basic Human-Nature Orientation and Examples of Managerial Impact

Issue	Variations		
Basic human nature	Evil	Neutral or mixed	Good

Managerial Impact			
General	Specific by Variation		
Control system	Tight, suspicion-based	Moderate, experienced-based	Loose, information-based
Management style	Close supervision, top-down	Moderate supervision, consultative	*Laissez-faire*, participative
Organization climate	Adversarial, contractual		Collaborative, informal

to reduce customer theft, had put a sign on the bathroom counters in each room. The sign read: "Love is leaving the towels here when you leave!" Thus, all employees about to embark on their first trip into a markedly different culture had their own culture's view of human nature reinforced just before they left home.

The value orientation regarding basic human nature affects other areas of management beyond control and punishment systems and also likely influences management style. A culture with a dominant evil orientation is likely to be populated by managers with autocratic tendencies who practice very close supervision (Theory X). Neutral or mixed dominant orientations are likely to encourage moderate supervision and consultative managers. At the good end of the spectrum, managers are likely to prefer a *laissez-faire* style or to practice participative management (Theory Y).

Organizational climate may be consistent with the orientation on the human-nature dimension. At one extreme is an adversarial climate and a stress on contractual relations. At the other extreme, collaborative and informal relations may exist. Organizational climates probably are consistent with control systems and management styles. The consistency of managerial systems is at least partially explained by their common roots in a particular cultural orientation. Organizations develop management systems to achieve a congruence, or fit, with their environments and between the people and the tasks they perform. The systems also are probably developed to fit with cultural values, which act as hidden enforcers for their consistency. Figure 8 summarizes this human-nature orientation and its variations and potential influence on managerial practices.

Orientation to Time

There are two ways to think about time. The first involves one's general orientation toward time, rather than how one thinks about or uses specific units of time.[26] This can be illustrated by how people respond to new events. If people respond to a new challenge by looking to tradition and wondering: "How have others dealt with this kind of problem before?" then the dominant value may be past-oriented. If people primarily consider the immediate effects of an action, then the dominant orientation is more likely to be present-oriented. If the chief concern is "What are the long-term consequences of this choice?" then the dominant orientation can be described as future-oriented.

One author of this text remembers vividly his Sicilian grandfather's pattern of response to questions. The grandfather would invariably frame his answers in the form of vignettes and start with: "Well, I remember that my father would always tell me . . . ." In contrast, the author's father, who had been born in the United States, almost always answered: "What is it that you want to accomplish?" Then he would give his advice, usually in the form of alternatives rather than answers. This example also illustrates that variations in time orientation may be intergenerational as well as intercultural.

The planning horizon is this cultural variable's most obvious point of impact for managers. Past-oriented cultures are more likely to re-create past behavior when planning, while present-oriented managers will have shorter-term concerns, and future-oriented managers are more likely to consider long-term effects. The influence of precedence, current realities, or effects desired in the future may also influence decision-making. Reward systems, too, may fall under the hidden effects of time orientation. Rewards in past-oriented cultures are more likely to be based on historically determined systems. An emphasis on currently contracted arrangements that can be revised to reflect new realities is more likely to be found in cultures where the present-time orientation is dominant. Bonus systems and other incentive schemes tend to reflect a short-term future orientation, and systems that reward training and skills tend to reflect a longer-term future orientation. However, since rewards are also mediated by other variables, there are exceptions, and there is not a simple one-to-one relationship between a value orientation and a management system.

Perception of one's own time orientation may be a source of distortion. Most North American managers would like to think of themselves as future-oriented people, for whom planning is an important part of the managerial function. However, North American managers probably are much more present-oriented than they think. This contradiction is seen in the heavy emphasis given to long-term planning in traditional management textbooks and the relative absence of long-term planning in actual behavior. Other indicators of the focus of North American managers on the present are the decline in numbers of corporate planners and corporate planning departments, and financial analysts' focus on quarterly results in their assessments of company value. Although it may make more sense for line managers to do strategic planning, Henry Mintzberg demonstrated long ago how short the cycle time of activities is even for senior executives and how little planning is done as a percentage of time available.[27] With the increasing speed of global dynamics, this is even truer today.

In addition, the meaning and implications of North America's propensity to send planeloads of politicians, government bureaucrats, and business executives on trade missions to foreign countries should be pondered. One such mission targeted several Brazilian cities with a blitz of government officials and businesspeople. Upon their return, two weeks after departure, one of the managers remarked that the travel had been a waste of time since no orders had been secured during the whole trip. Even if orders were received, it reflects a predominant time orientation of now and fast – and probably downplays the amount of work done prior to the mission to facilitate the signing of deals.

FIGURE **9** Variations in Time Orientation and Examples of Managerial Impact

Issue	Variations		
Time orientation	Past	Present	Future

Managerial Impact			
General	Specific by Variation		
Planning	Extension of past behavior	Short-term	Long-term
Emphasis in decision criteria	Precedence	Current impact	Desired effects
Reward systems	Historically determined	Currently contracted	Contingent on performance

At the other extreme is the example of Konosuke Matsushita, founder of the large Japanese manufacturer, who on the fourteenth anniversary of the company announced a 250-year corporate plan divided into ten 25-year sections.[28] That is future-oriented planning! Perhaps a more practical example is that of a Japanese manager who was sent to Rio de Janeiro by a company who gave the manager a simple mission: "Get to know the people and learn Portuguese during your first year there. Then worry about starting the business." Of course, the measurement system of the Japanese company did not require their expatriates to recoup the foreign investment in the first year, either. Part of the reason is the traditional structure of the Japanese economy and the close links between companies, government, banks, and investors. But the confluence of factors facilitating the longer-term planning of Japanese companies, as compared to their North American counterparts, is not entirely an accident. Even with the recent banking crisis in Japan, Japanese companies have been trying to find ways to maintain their long-range approach. Neither is it an accident that North American managers are constrained in their planning horizons by concern for quarterly earnings per share and even by daily shifts in stock prices. A good example of the influence of North Americans' present-time orientation on management behavior was the decision of Levi Strauss to privatize the company. Their motivation was significantly related to shareholders' pressure to maximize profitability in the short term. The executives believed that this pressure constrained future-oriented strategic decision-making that would be more beneficial to the company in the longer run.

Some effects of these preoccupations are useful; some are detrimental. The important points are to understand that some of the forces that shape such behavior are cultural, that these forces operate in several spheres that tend to reinforce each other, and that these forces are not easily altered. Figure 9 summarizes the time orientation and points of potential managerial impact.

There is another aspect of time orientation that strongly influences behavior and appears to be related to the COF dimension of Activity. This aspect is the specific unit of time that is used, which is addressed by Hall in Reading 1. To North Americans, time is a valuable commodity. For example, they save, spend, and waste time. This leads North

Americans to live their lives by sacrosanct schedules. For others, such as some Arab and Latin cultures, time schedules are less critical.

There are contrasting units of time. For most North Americans, punctuality is defined as being within five to ten minutes of a previously set time. For others, it might be 45 minutes to an hour before an apology or explanation for being late is expected. North Americans, with their present/future orientation, divide the hour into quarters, but some subcultures treat five-minute intervals as the appropriate guide to behavior.

It is quite possible, therefore, that those differences in definitions of timeliness can have significant effects on business dealings. If one is driven to meet schedules and deadlines, one is likely to be viewed as lacking patience, tact, or perseverance. This is even more complicated if those who use more lengthy time units see the usefulness of the less hurried pace as a way to build relationships. One's need to "get down to business" and preserve one's schedule will then clash with the other's view of the right pace and the right way to conduct business, such as contract negotiations.

We are not suggesting that it is wrong to establish schedules or deadlines when they are reasonable. However, "reasonable" is a cultural variable. Since much of the world has more elastic and relaxed attitudes toward time, others have to learn what is reasonable in those countries and adapt to their definitions, especially when these countries act as hosts. Otherwise, at best one will rush from one country, city, or meeting to another without ever taking sufficient time to build relationships before attempting to close deals. At worst, one offends others with insensitivity and risks erecting permanent barriers to doing business.

Use of Space

People's orientation to space was not completely conceptualized by Kluckhohn and Strodtbeck, nor investigated as part of their work. It is important enough to discuss, however. We chose the words private, mixed, and public to apply to the variations of this orientation. The variable in space orientation has to do with how one is oriented towards surrounding space.[29] How does one view its use, especially the sense of "ownership" of space relative to others? The private perspective holds that space is for the exclusive use of an occupant. The private orientation holds that space is for an occupant's benefit, and it defines a large area surrounding the occupant as part of that person's territory. Protective action is taken if this larger area is "invaded" by others. In contrast, the public orientation sees space as available for anyone's use. The sense of territory is small, and defensive action to guard against invasion is taken only in the immediate area around the occupant. The mixed orientation is a blend of the private and public perspectives – an intermediate position.

The spatial dimension can have an impact on communication, influence, and interaction patterns in physical realities such as office and building layout. On one hand, managers operating in a culture dominated by a private orientation are more likely to find themselves communicating on a one-to-one basis in a secretive, serial pattern. Physically, these managers are most comfortable having a fair amount of distance between them when talking directly to each other. On the other hand, managers interacting in a culture dominated by a public orientation are more likely to engage in a wide variety of interactions using an open style. Their conversations may involve several people simultaneously, and physically close relations will not be uncommon. Cultures with a mixed orientation influence managers to be more selective in their communications, with moderately separated space between people and somewhat more organized, semiprivate arrangements.

The layout of the space within which interactions occur shows parallel effects of the dominant orientation to space. Barriers characterize private orientations. Office doors are closed; private offices are favored; large desks and formal spaces are usual. In public-oriented cultures, offices are more likely to be arranged in an open manner. Where private offices do exist, doors are more likely to be left open and fewer barriers, such as office furniture, will appear in them. The mixed orientation features a blend of these characteristics – for example, an office containing specialized spaces. Part of the layout may be formal, with an official desk providing a barrier between the occupant and visitors. An adjoining space in the same office may be furnished with more comfortable, informal furniture.

The perils of ignoring the cultural factors of space can be extremely costly. One Ontario government ministry, caught in the grips of architectural fads, decided it would modernize its office space and save money at the same time. The ministry planned to consolidate several departments in a new building and use an open office layout. Not wishing to traumatize the managers, they decided that movable partitions would provide the appropriate degree of privacy in the new situation. The move involved a total of 1,300 people. Arrangements were made to purchase sufficient dividers for all, even though the merger was to be accomplished in several steps. The first move involved 300 people, but partitions allotted for 800 people were requisitioned from storage. Puzzled, the planners went to inspect and found that most people had insisted on their own dividers. Duplicate partitions had been placed back-to-back to satisfy the managers' need for privacy and ownership!

In another situation, the CEO of a large insurance company was frustrated by the inability of divisions in the company to better integrate their efforts. Yet, the CEO was surprised when a consultant who had been in the company a total of only 14 hours had to introduce several of the 120 headquarters executives to each other. Closer scrutiny of the office layouts revealed a highly private orientation that explained both situations. Long corridors in the company formed a maze that separated people from each other. The suites of offices off the corridors all closed the doors accessing the reception areas. Inside, each of the offices that formed the group of suites also closed all their doors. The company had operated in a French-speaking milieu for over a century. However, the company was staunchly British in its culture, and the private orientation to space overwhelmed the CEO's wish for stronger integration among the departments. Even the language used in the company acknowledged the dominance of privacy; the executives openly referred to the high degree of isolation between business units as "functional solitudes." The senior management of the company, including those who used this highly descriptive language in reference to their own situation, seemed genuinely puzzled about their failure to achieve the desired degree of integration. They were, in short, oblivious to the ways their own company culture, firmly embedded in their own broader cultural values, affected the management processes. In a highly regulated environment in which the company operated, its processes, shaped by the privacy values, were

FIGURE 10 Variations in Spatial Orientation and Examples of Managerial Impact

Issue	Variations		
Space	Private	Mixed	Public

Managerial Impact			
General	Specific by Variation		
Communication and influence patterns	One-to-one, secret	Selective, semiprivate	Wide, open
Office layout	Emphasis on barriers (closed doors, large desks, etc.)	Specialized spaces (informal furniture next to formal desk)	Open concept
Interaction patterns	Physically distant, one-to-one, serial	Moderately spaced, moderated numbers, organized	Physically close, frequent touching, multiple relations (sometimes spontaneously)

adequate. As deregulation changed the industry, greater integration, flexibility, and speed were required and the old cultural values impeded adaptation to the new realities.

In addition to this spatial sense, the space-orientation value may also apply to physical goods, property, or information. People with a dominantly private orientation are likely to have a strong sense of ownership of things as well as of space. This manifests itself in the degree to which physical items are shared or viewed as community property. Links between these orientations and forms of economic activity, such as capitalism and socialism, are also possible. Figure 10 summarizes spatial orientation.

Summary

The discussion of each of the variables in the Cultural Orientation Framework has demonstrated the variety of ways in which the effects of values seep into one's assumptions and perceptions and influence behavior in one's managerial life. Figure 11 shows the full matrix with examples of each of the variations within the cells. It is worth repeating that the dominant values on one dimension are independent of dominant values on another.

When inspecting the overall matrix in figure 11, it is tempting to impose a correlation of dominant values that seem to cluster together naturally. This tendency to associate values across the dimensions as fitting with each other is most likely a result of our own cultural conditioning. Thus, North Americans probably feel that mastery, present/future, mixed/neutral, doing, individualistic, and mixed space values belong together, while Chinese readers may feel that harmony, future, good, thinking, group, and

FIGURE **11**　Completed and Summarized Cultural Orientations Framework

Issue	Variations		
Relation to environment (natural world and to life and work, in general)	**Subjugation** Predetermined Inevitable Accepting External control Dependent Fate	**Harmony** Interdependent Co-exist Live together with	**Mastery** Control events/situation Make happen Independent Internal control
Relationship among people (Whose welfare is primary?)	**Hierarchical** Vertical differentiation (and horizontal) Authority Status (age, family, seniority, etc.)	**Group** Horizontal differentiation	**Individual** Informal Variable Status (personal achievement) Egalitarianism
Activity orientation	**Being** Spontaneous Act on feelings	**Thinking** Think and feel Work and self Seeking, becoming Control self	**Doing** Achieving/striving Compulsive Performance Work is central focus
Basic human nature orientation Changeable? Unchangeable?	**Bad** Suspicion Close supervision Theory X	**Mixed/neutral** Product of social environment Consultation	**Good** Information Participation Collaborative Theory Y
Time: Orientation Daily activities	**Past** Respect tradition and proven ways Precedence Maintain continuity	**Present** Current realities Near term Respond to change	**Future** Longer term Anticipate change
	Plentiful Relaxed Elastic Less critical		**Scarce** Tight schedules Punctual Hectic
Space: Personal Ownership	**Private** Closed Secretive Distant	**Mixed**	**Public** Open Physically close

public space belong together. However, the associations are empirical, not inevitably brought about by natural law.

Earlier, we discussed the idea of a framework itself being culture-bound. The very act of conceptualizing culture in a matrix reflects a mastery orientation. An emphasis on using these conceptualizations reflects a doing value. Suggestions as to how these conceptualizations may be employed reflect neutral and individualistic orientations. Culture reaches into the very mental programs that people use to structure and process their ideas and experience. There is a danger when one applies only a dominant variation to a society. It should not be forgotten that all variations of each of the value orientations occur in most societies. Our frequent tendency to abbreviate (to save time and achieve efficiency) masks the complexity of culture and can be deceptive when trying to sort out aspects of another system of living.

The Skill of Mapping

Being able to map involves more than the knowledge of the framework. It requires *using* the framework to explain and predict others' attitudes and behavior. Mapping creates awareness and appreciation of differences and their implications in a structured and consistent way. It begins a conversation about similarities and differences using a common language and framework, and allows the conversation to move quickly and constructively to individual and situational differences. Just like any other skill, managers can practice mapping and improve their ability to map. With practice, they begin to see patterns in the values and actions of other people, and to understand those patterns from the other people's own perspectives. It is this level of mapping skill that provides a foundation for effective *bridging*.

Bridging Differences Through Communication

Understanding the lens through which others see the world is an enormous aid to intercultural effectiveness. But this understanding provides little benefit as long as it remains latent. It must be put into use to help the flow of ideas among people in a conversation, a team, or an organization. The goal of these interpersonal flows is effective communication, or the transfer of meaning from one person to another as it was intended by the first person. Most managers recognize that effective communication within one's own culture is difficult enough. Interactions with people from different cultures are even more difficult. The challenge is to interpret correctly what a person from a different culture means by his or her words and actions. Even if interaction is aided by slowing speech, speaking more distinctly, listening more carefully, or asking more questions, there still remains the problem of interpreting the message. Resolving miscommunication depends, in large part, on a manager's willingness to explain the problem rather than to blame the other person. And the quality of the explanation depends, in large part, on the manager's ability to map the other person's culture with respect to his or her own.

Although language is an important part of communication, communication is not simply a matter of understanding and speaking a language. Communication is broader than language alone. Someone who is able to speak three different languages still may not be able to understand the issues from the viewpoint of those from another culture. Or, put more eloquently by an Eastern European manager in an executive program, "I can speak to you in your language, but I can't always tell you what I am thinking in my own language."

There are three skills important to effective communication in a cross-cultural setting: preparing; decentering; and recentering.[30] While it is true that these three skills help improve all communication, in interactions within a single culture the parties can generally assume the same set of background assumptions, so the steps can be conducted

FIGURE 12   The MBI model

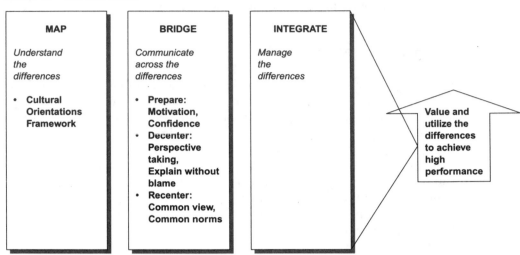

implicitly. The more culturally diverse the setting, though, the more difficult it is to accomplish these steps, and the more explicit they should be. But they also result in bigger payoffs. This component of the MBI model is summarized in figure 12.

Prepare

Preparing is about setting the ground for communication. The most important place to set the ground is in one's own mind. Two attitudes are especially predictive of effective communication: motivation and confidence. Motivation is having the will to communicate across a cultural boundary both to be understood and to understand others. We are usually very good at the former, but not as good at the latter. The confidence part of preparing is to believe that it is possible to overcome any barriers and communicate effectively. Ironically, people with little cross-cultural experience and those who have never tried to understand others from their own perspective tend to have high confidence, and confidence is decreased with the first increments of experience and insight. However, with practice and success – as aided, for example, by the tools described here – confidence increases rapidly, and this later confidence has a much more realistic foundation.

These attitudes may sound simple to control, but their manifestation is complicated by some psychological tendencies we all have. They are inherent to our nature and normally serve us well, but tend to slip us up in cross-cultural interaction. More specifically, we tend to assume:[31]

1.   The other person sees the situation the same way as we do.
2.   The other person is making the same assumptions we are.
3.   The other person is (or should be) experiencing the same feelings as we are.

4. The communication situation has no relationship to past events.
5. The other person's understanding is (or should be) based on our own logic, not their feelings.
6. If a problem occurs, it is the other person who is the one who has the "problem" or does not understand the logic of the situation.
7. Other cultures are changing and becoming, or want to become, more like our culture and, therefore, the other person is becoming more like us.

While reading a book it may seem easy to keep these in mind, but in the rush and pressure of making decisions we often forget to withhold judgment. However, there are some simple things to do that can facilitate the process, aside from just trying to remember to be motivated and confident. For example, expatriates who spend most of their time in the company of other expatriates often have little motivation to bridge the cultural communication gaps. They manifest their motivation by the company they keep. When they do run into difficulties at work, they have little practice at resolving them in more relaxed settings. A more positive sign of motivation to communicate cross-culturally is learning the language of those with whom one is working. Nothing is more likely to signal your motivation for cross-cultural communication than such an effort. Of course, having confidence that you can learn the language and that, in doing so, you will be more effective, is in itself a boost to the motivation to learn. These two elements create a positive, reinforcing circle, since having the motivation to learn will probably also boost confidence in the possibility of improving cross-cultural communication.

Even without language training, there are ways of developing motivation and confidence in cross-cultural skills. Reading and studying about the host country's culture, meeting locals and asking them to help immerse oneself in the country, and learning to apply other parts of this model are examples of how to increase confidence in one's cross-cultural communication ability and how to demonstrate the motivation to do so. Mastering a cultural framework or "map," such as the one described earlier, is another way. This gives you the motivation and confidence to ask questions that will be especially helpful in preparing yourself for future understanding. Our research shows that it is possible to learn enough about the MBI model in a two-day training program to improve performance. Therefore, there is ample reason for managers to feel both motivated and confident that preparation for bridging cultures can make a difference.

Decenter

Decentering is actively pushing yourself away from your own "center" and moving into the mind of the other person to send messages in a way the other will understand, and to listen in a way that allows you to understand them from their own point of view. Thus, one has a bicultural tongue and bicultural ears. The fundamental idea of decentering is empathy: feeling and understanding as another person does. But in the context of the communication model, decentering requires *using* one's empathy in hearing and speaking. We all know people who understand exactly how we feel, but nevertheless go ahead and say or do something hurtful anyway. This is practicing empathy without decentering.

There are two main elements to decentering. The first is perspective taking, which is the skill of being able to see things from the other person's point of view to the extent that you can speak and listen that way. The second is explaining without blame. When problems in communication do occur, it is critical that no one blames the other in a personal way, but that all parties seek an explanation in the situation – the differences in initial starting assumptions. This last point cannot be emphasized enough. In our research this emerged as the single best predictor of effective cross-cultural interaction. Teams that withhold blame and search for situation-based explanations of miscommunication almost inevitably have more effective interaction. Does this mean that all you have to do is explain without blame? No, but look at the sequence of events initiated when blame is suspended. This simple act leads a group into a positive cycle of decentering, exploring alternatives to build a shared reality, developing trust and common rules, and building confidence in the group's ability to use different perspectives productively. This conversation not only resolves the present miscommunication, but also prevents some further ones and provides ideas for creative synergy.

Good decentering is largely dependent on good mapping. The map warns you that surprises and problems may have different explanations, and also provides you with some alternatives to explore. The describe–interpret–evaluate framework identified earlier is very helpful here. When differences are encountered, the people involved should try to come to a point where they can agree on a description: what are the tangible, concrete facts we are talking about? Next they should explore their different interpretations – what do those facts mean to each person, and why? This is where the map provides a common language for sharing the analysis of interpretations. Finally, they should try to understand the different evaluations of the facts – why do some people see something as an opportunity and others as a threat? In cross-cultural situations, the greater the tendency to judge events, the greater the probability of making errors. Resisting the interpretive and evaluative modes while maintaining a descriptive posture for as long as possible is the best protection against cultural gaffes. While this may be difficult to do, it is still to be encouraged.

Recenter

The final step to effective communication is recentering, or establishing a common reality and agreeing on common rules. Like the other elements, establishing a common reality is easier said than done. But it is much easier to see the need to do so, if one is aware of the types of differences between your own values and those of others. For example, the implicit definition and purpose of "a meeting" varies from one culture to the next, with some cultures using meetings to discuss perspectives and come to a joint decision, and other cultures using meetings to publicly formalize decisions that were discussed informally among smaller subgroups of a team. A multicultural team that has not addressed even this basic definition is bound to find at least some members very frustrated with the first meeting. Again, good mapping helps to find a common definition and give the team a point of leverage. For example, members of a multi-site global R&D team differed enormously on Relationships and Environment orientations, but virtually all preferred thinking strongly over any other mode of Activity. They were able to use their common ground of the need to plan and be rational to discuss their differences and work together. A team managing a strategic alliance in a manufacturing technology firm consisted of members from all over Europe, North America, and Asia. Like the R&D scientists they had strong differences on many cultural orientations. Coincidentally, though, all were engineers for at least some part of their career, and they shared the same mastery orientation to the environment. Their common reality was based on what had to be done (changed and controlled), and they used this point to launch discussions about how to divide the work and what task processes to use.

Common norms for interacting must also be established. However, what is critical here is not necessarily agreeing on the same norms for everyone, but rather agreeing what the acceptable norms are to be. It is futile to expect someone to behave in a way that is uncomfortable to them, yet still expect them to participate to their full potential. Think back to the personal space exercise introduced earlier, where you were encouraged to stand closer to someone than you normally do when conversing. Asking some one with a predominantly thinking orientation to constantly jump in and "do" because that is the dominant mode and "you'll just have to adapt" is tantamount to asking that person not to bother contributing his or her best ideas to the group. The most effective groups find ways of allowing different members to work with the group differently. Finding these norms is a creative process. It takes time, and relies on strong relationships and trust within the group. But, like good preparing and decentering, the effort is well worth it.

An Illustration

We captured a classic example of cross-cultural communication when we videotaped a group of executives discussing the possibility of their company acquiring another firm. The group consisted of senior managers from the United States, United Kingdom, Belgium, Japan, and Uruguay. After studying various aspects of the potential deal, they came together to make a recommendation. After 20 minutes of discussion, the British manager stood up in the room and went to the flip chart and wrote: "Do Nothing!" He punctuated his writing by saying, "I don't usually entertain this option, which is always raised as a 'straw man' by business school profs, but I really think in this situation it is our best choice. The deal is far from being ready to make for a whole host of reasons." There was a moment of silence, followed by the Japanese manager clearing his throat and quietly murmuring, "Wait." The others thought that he was asking for a chance to discuss the "Do Nothing" option, but only a silence ensued. After a barely discernible pause, the British manager crossed out "Do Nothing" and wrote next to it, "Wait," and then he proceeded with his next point.

Yet the Japanese manager's "Wait" was not the same as the British executive's "Do Nothing." There was no common reality established. The British executive literally meant "don't do anything more; proceed to look for other deals until the other party indicates a change in the conditions." In contrast, the Japanese executive's "Wait" was filled with subtle actions including continuing to get to know the other parties, extending attempts to get more information about their business, and so on. If either of the speakers (or any of the other managers on the team) had been aware that, in terms of the activity dimension of the value orientation, the British executive was operating out of a dominant-doing orientation, while the Japanese manager was expressing a thinking mode, then a chance for establishing a common reality might have occurred.

The business consequences would likely have been quite different if they (a) had a map of cultural differences, (b) saw that their orientations were different and defined different realities for the acquisition situation, and (c) acted to explore their differences until they could agree on a common definition of situation. Had they done so, a different course of action (or in the British manager's sense, inaction) might have followed. In addition, both would have added to their understanding of the other's culture and its manifestation in business activity. As it was, only a review of the videotape revealed this missed opportunity. Although the Japanese manager did know that he had been misunderstood when the original incident had occurred, he had not called it to the others' attention.

In the same discussion, in the 20 minutes before the British manager wrote his recommendation to do nothing, there were three failed attempts by the manager from Uruguay to introduce the issue of who would constitute the top executive team should the deal be struck. Would the buying company or the acquired organization supply the key executives for the merged entity? He thought that this question was pertinent to the decision of whether or not to buy the organization. But each time he tried to raise the issue, his comments were brushed aside by the two American and the British managers, who were citing the lack of compatible strategies and financial problems in the negotiations. Soon their dominance in the discussion extinguished the South American's view of what was important. This, too, exemplifies the lack of a common reality. To the Latin manager, relationships were highly relevant to the deal; to the Anglo-American managers, quantitative and strategic issues were what mattered. Again, having a cultural map might have helped. The difference in relative emphasis on relationships versus mastery and doing led to a missed opportunity to reach common ground. Note also that, in both cases, it was the view of the majority of the managers present that was acted on without the other perspective even being noticed, much less engaged. In these two real examples from a single meeting, it becomes evident that having a framework to understand one's own culture and to map the differences of others can provide a way of testing whether there is a common reality or not and of building one if it is needed.

Similarly, the map helps in establishing common rules for communicating and interacting. The two examples noted above illustrate this component of the model as well as the common reality dimension. In the first situation, the Japanese manager did not call the British manager's attention to his misinterpretation of "wait." In Japan, such a comment would have meant a loss of face for the British manager. So the rule of communication is silence. But if the British manager knew he had been misunderstood, it is much more likely that he would have at least clarified what he had meant, and might have added that he had been misinterpreted. His rule for interaction is direct communication. The roots of these different rules are in varying preferences for individualism, doing, and mastery on one side versus group, thinking, and harmony modes on the other.

The example of the Uruguayan's attempt to introduce people into the acquisition equation provides another illustration of the common rules theme. Two aspects of uncommon rules were visible in that series of exchanges. First, each time he wanted to speak, the manager from Uruguay waited until there was a brief pause in the conversation; in contrast, the American and British managers often interrupted each other. Another contrast was in how the issues were raised by the two sides; the Uruguayan posed his idea tentatively, twice putting it in the form of a question ("Don't you think we should explore from which company the top officers will be drawn?"). The Anglo-Americans were much more definite and assertive in their phrasing ("That's irrelevant until we get the financials and strategy agreed to!"). Again, no common rules of interaction were established for the two parties. Until some common modes of interaction are understood and acknowledged by both parties, cross-cultural communication will be problematic.

So, if the Americans in this team knew that the Uruguayan was likely to value relationships more, they would have been more likely to hear the suggestion to consider the issue of the top executive team the first time it was made. And they would be less likely to feel and show the irritation that was evident when the videotape captured their tone of condescension the third time the Uruguayan tried to pose his idea.

Integrating to Manage and Build on the Differences

Figure 13 introduces the final component of the MBI model, integrating the differences. It is not sufficient to have a way of understanding cultural differences and bridging the gaps by effective communication. One also needs to manage the differences effectively if they are to result in higher performance of the people who are working together. There are three main integration skills: building participation; resolving conflicts; and building on ideas.

Building Participation

To realize the benefits of different perspectives and ideas (the latent possibilities among the multicultural membership of a group), it is necessary to express the ideas. Not all cultures are equally predisposed to offer their ideas openly. People from cultures with a strong hierarchical orientation, for example, are not likely to put forth their ideas in a group containing a direct superior or a higher-status person. In contrast, people from

FIGURE 13   The MBI Model

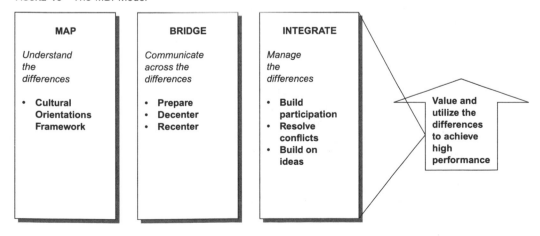

FIGURE **14**   Participation by Individuals in Two Group Discussions

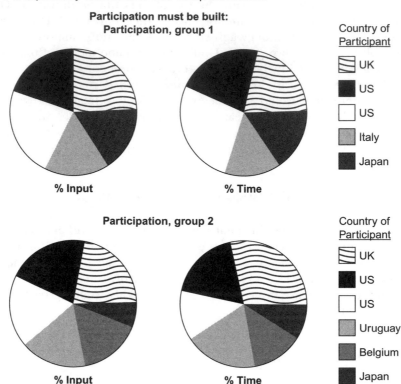

individualistic cultures are more likely to assert their ideas. The first challenge for a multicultural group, then, is to ensure that all the ideas are heard.

It is especially helpful if someone on the team monitors participation to notice whether there are systematic differences in participation rates. Figure 14 shows the pattern of participation in the meeting described above (group 2) and a parallel meeting with different individuals, first in proportion of contributions by number, then in percentage of time. If there were no differences in the rates, each shaded area would be equal in size. Aggregating the UK and US data shows a clear dominance of executives from these countries in both groups for both percentages of inputs and time. This pattern is especially clear in the second group.

There are ways of engaging all group members and facilitating their participation. In the example given earlier, the Japanese manager hardly spoke in the first half hour; his "wait" was his lone contribution during the first 20 minutes. Yet, later when the Texan in the group noticed his silence, he invited participation by saying, "If I recall, Sugano-san, a couple of years ago you had some experience in a merger similar to the one we are discussing. What do you think about this situation?" What followed was a highly relevant and cogent discourse, fluidly expressed, which had a big impact on the shape of the group's recommendation. When his involvement was sought, this otherwise infrequent participant made an important contribution.

To avoid relying solely on the observational power of a group member to notice the absence of participation, the group can set up routines to facilitate everyone's participation. For example, the group can decide that, on all important issues, a process of going around the table will be used to produce as many ideas as possible before discussion starts. Or one person can be charged with ensuring that all members have been included before an important decision is made. Another way of facilitating participation is to vary the modes of input. It might be easier, for example, for an otherwise reticent member to provide written input than to appear to be dominating or advancing his or her own interest by speaking in the group. Or it might be easier to provide ideas outside the context of formal meetings: in a private, face-to-face setting instead of a group meeting where the status issues (including the ambiguity of roles) may inhibit easy communication. Once they accept the possibility of having different norms for group members, most groups find creative ways to get everyone's input.

Resolving Disagreements

As more ideas from various viewpoints are expressed, there is an increasing likelihood that there will be disagreements. The way these conflicts are handled, then, becomes the next cross-cultural challenge. Even the way conflict gets expressed, quite apart from how it gets resolved, varies in different cultural traditions. In many cultures it is deemed inappropriate to express conflict openly. So for a manager from a culture where open expression of disagreement is valued, the first problem becomes detecting the existence of the conflict. In high-context cultures, a disagreement may be expressed very subtly or indirectly through a third party. In low-context cultures, conflict is more likely to be stated bluntly, in words of little ambiguity. When these norms (rules of communication from the earlier component of the model) are not understood, frustration or anger is likely to be the result. If I express conflict more directly, I may be frustrated by behavior that I read as sending "mixed signals" or conclude the other person is confused or cannot make up his or her mind. If I expect indirect expression of conflict, I might feel insulted by what I experience as impolite or crass comments from the other person who feels she or he is "just putting the issue on the table."

One way to deal with these issues is to use the map and communication components of the model noted in the previous section. The mapping framework provides a way to anticipate when the conflict gaps may occur; the communication techniques give tools for reaching a common understanding, and a common set of rules or norms for resolving the conflicts and avoiding them in the future. Effective communication is more than half of effective conflict resolution. The map of cultural differences may provide clues as to the other person's preferred ways of dealing with conflict. By decentering, you can adapt to the other's perspective without falling into the ethnocentric trap of blaming the other person or misinterpreting the meaning of actions by referencing your own cultural codes.

Building on Ideas

Even if the mapping framework is well understood, the communication skills are well developed, and participation and conflict issues are managed effectively, there is still a

FIGURE **15** The MBI Model

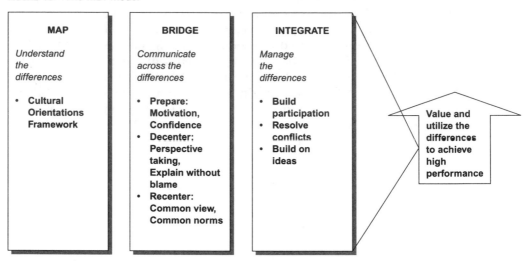

key component to realizing the potential of a multicultural group, namely, moving forward and building on the ideas. There are cultural barriers in this phase of activity, too. As mentioned earlier, some cultural preferences would lead a person to push one's ideas (individualism), while another orientation (hierarchical) is more likely to lead to deference to authority. If you are in a group with several cultures, there might be an agreement (common rules of interaction) to surface ideas without attributing them to individuals or using an individual's ideas as a starting point for discussion. The main idea is to encourage the exploration of ideas with the conscious attempt to invent new ideas, to build on the ideas initially surfaced. A real stimulus to innovation is to try to do more than combine ideas and to avoid compromises. Finally, striving to find solutions to issues or problems that are acceptable to all (another rule for interaction or norm for behavior) is another way to increase the probability of getting synergy from the diversity in the group. Trying to invent new ideas from those available and reaching for solutions to which everyone can agree are ideals that are difficult to accomplish. But even setting them as objectives will help a multicultural team achieve its potential for high performance.

Figure 15 shows the completed MBI model for interpersonal and team effectiveness.

Applying the MBI Model

There are several approaches to the application of this model. You could try to anticipate the problems that might be encountered in an intercultural situation. Or you could wait until actual problems are experienced and then use the model to help deal with them. Another approach is to differentiate the level of managerial issues involved in a situation. A problem may occur between people, or it may involve organizational-level issues, such as structures or systems. If the personal and organizational aspects are combined, a systematic way of using the model can be developed (see figure 16).

FIGURE 16   Four Approaches to Applying the Framework

Purpose of Application

	Avoiding	Resolving
Level of Issue		
Personal	Managerial preparation	Social analysis and action
Organizational	Structural and systems planning	Organizational analysis and action

To anticipate and avoid cross-cultural problems (column 1 of figure 16) at the personal or organizational level, appropriate preparation is needed. For example, if a manager is going to another country, that manager should be oriented to the culture in which he or she will operate. They can organize the information, observations, and advice provided in such an orientation by using the cultural variations of the map described as the first component of the model. The manager can then evaluate their own dominant value orientations, analyze those of the destination culture, and then decide where the main differences exist. For each value dimension where there are differences, he or she can deduce the likely areas of managerial problems by examining the examples from the figures, combined with careful thought.

A similar approach can be taken if a manager in a multinational corporation (MNC) is attempting to introduce organizational structures or systems from headquarters into a foreign subsidiary. (Part 2 of this book provides a more detailed treatment of these issues.) The difference here is that the issues involved include organizational design elements rather than people. In either case, the usefulness of the map depends upon:

1. Being explicit about one's own culture
2. Organizing what is known about another culture
3. Providing for a systematic comparison of dominant values
4. Noting value differences and using them to predict the areas in which managerial problems are likely to arise.

This four-step process may be approached by making a copy of figure 11, drawing a line connecting the cells in the matrix that designate one's own dominant cultural values, then drawing a line with a different color that designates the dominant variations of another culture. It is then easier to see the areas where managerial problems may exist, either with oneself, with others, or with respect to organizational issues.

Even though areas of potential managerial and personal problems may be predicted, the international executive still has to make a basic choice. For each kind of problem, he or she can make plans to avoid it using a dominant approach (deciding which culturally defined management practice should be followed) or a mixed strategy (blending the practices of different origins). Executives can also develop a synergistic approach to management and organization that "transcends the distinct cultures of [its] members" using the tools of communication and integration described in the overall model.[32]

It is probably unwise to select a single strategy for all kinds of problems. Some situations may require different approaches. For example, the Canadian National Railway found it necessary to insist that Inuit employees, who run their trains on a single-line track, always call in by radio if they stopped to rest.[33] (An Inuit harmony and being value is: "When tired, sleep.") In this situation, safety demanded that a dominant strategy be adopted. But when oil companies in the Arctic found that native people failed to show up for work in order to go hunting when geese were migrating (again, a harmony-influenced behavior) or when they felt like visiting relatives (a being- and group-oriented behavior), the companies hired more workers than needed and paid them only when they worked. Rather than complain about "unreliable" employees, they adopted a synergistic solution.

In addition to choosing among dominant, mixed, and synergistic strategies, there is the additional issue of deciding which party needs to adapt. A number of factors influence the decision of who should adapt and how the adaptation should be made. As a general rule, the onus for adaptation rests with the party who is seen as the foreigner. This probably is influenced by the sheer force of numbers. But this rule of the majority also misses significant opportunities for learning and inventing, as we saw in the example of the culturally mixed team of managers discussing the acquisition.

Location is another strong factor. Everything else being equal (which is rarely the case), the guest is expected to adapt to the host. Technological dependence may alter this equation. A German joint venture in Beijing may choose to emphasize German cultural values and management practice in spite of the location and overwhelming majority of Chinese population, simply as a recognition of the need to acquire information. In fact, the power of resources in general has a strong influence on who is expected to adapt. The buyer almost always expects the seller to adapt, unless the seller has something extremely rare for which there are many willing buyers.

Individual preference may also enter the equation. An expatriate dealing with Chinese in Beijing may attempt to adapt to Chinese traditions, even though there is no necessity to do so. The motives for adaptation in this situation may range from showing courtesy to a desire to learn and to increase one's own repertoire of behavior. Furthermore, no matter where a company is operating, an attempt to adapt to others' customs will be appreciated and will have a positive influence on relations.

In the variety of examples we have discussed, the range of behavior serves as a reminder that several different values can influence people simultaneously. This makes the use of a framework even more valuable, in that it provides a checklist against which to analyze a situation for cultural causes. Fixating on single explanations for events can lead to missing the complexity of the causes involved. This can lead to errors in framing the solutions to problems. Although everyone attempts to avoid problems, international managers often find themselves immersed in problems that they failed to anticipate and now must resolve (column 2 of figure 16). In such cases, the manager must avoid the tendency to blame the other party, as we noted earlier in the discussion of blame-free explanations. You should seek many alternative explanations for a problem, and be especially wary of interpreting events from only one perspective when people from more than one culture are involved. If it appears that there is a cross-cultural component to a problem, then the choice of strategy remains as described earlier. The key factor, however, is the careful analysis of the causes of a problem and the isolation of those elements that are cultural in nature. If there are no culturally-linked causes, then conventional approaches can be followed to resolve the problems.

A Final Caution: Knowledge Does Not Equal Skill

This chapter discusses the impact of culture on management and intercultural effectiveness in an analytic and almost impersonal way. It is important to know how culture works – how it affects behavior and what some of its dimensions are. It is equally important to know the components of bridging and integrating skills. Knowledge and understanding should be the bases from which one takes action. There is a danger, however, in assuming that because one has learned something, one can take such action automatically.

Intellectual understanding may not translate directly into a high degree of skill. Skills take practice. Imagine hearing someone explain, using physics and mathematical equations, how to ride a bicycle. Undoubtedly, the explanation would be correct and would display a thorough understanding of the facts and laws that would have to be observed for a person to ride a bicycle successfully. But no one would stand a chance of riding a bicycle for the first time after such a scientific lecture. Parents, teaching their son or daughter to ride a bicycle, talk about balance, turning the handlebars (and therefore the front wheel) gently, pedaling fast enough to keep the bicycle upright, and so on. Keeping these principles in mind and practicing these principles usually leads to success.

Putting knowledge into action is a skill. It is this skill that brings success. Just as the notion of "lecture and ride" is naive, so is "read and go." The child riding the bicycle has reality (hills, bumps, sand on sidewalks, other bicycles) to deal with, and so do managers working in other cultures. Managers who will conduct business in another culture cannot be told about all the hills and bumps they will face. An open mind and a willingness to learn from experiences will help the international manager get over many problems and adapt to new cultures. However, in the process of adapting, one can expect to fall off one's bicycle occasionally. We hope that the ideas presented here will decrease the number of falls and cushion their impact.

Notes

1. Karl Weick, *The social psychology of organizing* (Reading, MA: Addison-Wesley Publishing Co., 1979).
2. John Berry et al., *Cross cultural psychology: Research and applications* (Cambridge, UK: Cambridge University Press, 1992): 8.
3. Nancy Adler, International Dimensions of Organizational Behavior, 3rd edn (Cincinnati: South-Western, 1997).
4. Susan E. Jackson, "Team composition in organizational settings: Issues in managing an increasingly diverse workforce," in S. Worchel, W. Wood, & J. A. Simpson (eds), *Group process and productivity* (Newbury Park, CA: Sage 1991, pp. 138–73); and F. J. Milliken and L. Martins, "Searching for common threads: Understanding the multiple effects of diversity in organizational groups," *Academy of Management Journal,* Vol. 21, No. 2 (1996): 402–33.

5. S. C. Ling, *The effects of group cultural composition and cultural attitudes on performance* (unpublished doctoral dissertation, London, Canada: The University of Western Ontario, 1990); P. L. McLeod and S. A. Lobel, "The effects of ethnic diversity on idea generation in small groups," *Academy of Management Annual Meeting Best Papers Proceeding* (1992): 227–31; W. E. Watson, K. Kumar and L. K. Michaelson, "Cultural diversity's impact on interaction process and performance: Comparing homogeneous and diverse task groups," *Academy of Management Journal*, Vol. 36, No. 3 (1993): 590–602.

6. Martha Maznevski, *Synergy and performance in multicultural teams* (unpublished doctoral dissertation, London, Canada: University of Western Ontario, 1994); Martha Maznevski, "Understanding our differences: Performance in decision-making groups with diverse members," *Human Relations*, Vol. 47, No. 5 (1994): 531–52; Joseph DiStefano and Martha Maznevski, "Creating value with diverse teams in global management," *Organizational Dynamics*, forthcoming.

7. Edward T. Hall, "The silent language in overseas business," *Harvard Business Review* 38, no. 3 (1960): 87–96.

8. Geert Hofstede, *Culture's consequences: International differences in work related values* (La Jolla, CA: Sage Publications, 1980). "Motivation, leadership and organization: Do American theories apply abroad?", *Organizational Dynamics*, 9, no. 1 (1980): 42–63.

9. Charles Hampden-Turner and Fons Trompenaars, *The seven cultures of capitalism* (New York: Currency Doubleday, 1993). Also Fons Trompenaars and Charles Hampden-Turner, *Riding the waves of culture: Understanding cultural diversity in global business*, 2nd edn (New York: Irwin Professional Publications, 1998).

10. F. R. Kluckhohn and F. L. Strodtbeck, *Variations in value orientations* (New York: Row, Peterson & Company, 1961).

11. Geert Hofstede, *Cultures and organizations: Software of the mind* (Maidenhead, Berkshire, England: McGraw-Hill Book Company Europe, 1991).

12. This premise itself is a manifestation of the culture from which the two anthropologists were operating. The assumption that such common themes can be found, or even ought to be sought, reflects "doing" orientation and a sense that it is possible, even desirable, to "master" one's environment. The meaning of these labels and the cultural roots of the scheme will become apparent as the reader proceeds through the framework.

13. Geert Hofstede, *Cultures and organizations*, 112.

14. Andrew Solomon, "Defiantly deaf," *The New York Times Magazine*, August 28, 1994. Also Felicity Barringer, "Pride in a soundless world: Deaf oppose a hearing aid," *The New York Times*, May 16, 1993, p. 1.

15. There is evidence that effective international managers use stereotypes – or generalized descriptions – as devices to approximate reality as they enter another culture. However, after some time in a country, when they encounter the richness and variety of behavior, they drop the simplification of the stereotype and describe the mosaic of what they have experienced. Less effective managers hold on to their initial stereotypes; they exempt those who do not fit the stereotypes as exceptions that prove the rule. See Indrei Ratui, "Thinking internationally: A comparison of how international executives learn," *International Studies of Management and Organization* 12 (1983): 139–50.

16. In simplifying the terminology, we recognize that we may distort the original meaning of the authors and/or blur the distinctions made by the more precise use of the specialized language of social science. However, we have consciously elected to run this risk in the hope that, by making the ideas more accessible to managers, greater benefits will accrue than would be otherwise possible.

17. M. S. Perret, "The Impact of Cultural Differences on Budgeting" (PhD Dissertation, The University of Western Ontario, 1982).

18. Perret, *Impact of cultural differences.*

19. André Laurent, "The Cultural Diversity of Western Conceptions of Management", *International Studies of Management and Organization*, Vol. XIII, No. 1–2 (1983): 75–96.

20. Although the specific examples are becoming dated, one of the most readable and thorough studies remains Edwin O. Reischauer's *The Japanese* (Cambridge, MA: Harvard University Press, 1977).

21. Perret, *Impact of cultural differences*. Subsequent to her dissertation research, Perret replicated the original study in a consulting/accounting organization across four countries (France, United States, England, and Holland). With quality of service being the focus, she found many of the same patterns of cultural effects (M. S. Perret, personal communication, Naval Postgraduate School, Monterey CA, 1984).

22. Note that if one believes that by following the religious tenets only the *behavior* of people changes but not the fundamental *nature* (which remains marked by original sin), then the orientation would be evil/unchangeable.

23. "Introduction," *To the peoples of the world – A statement on peace* (Thornhill, Ontario: The Baha'i Council of Canada, 1990).

24. Asra Q. Nomani, "Labor letter: A special news report on people and their jobs in offices, fields and factories," *Wall Street Journal*, August 2, 1994: A1.

25. Another example of this kind of reasoning is available in Huston Smith, *The world's religions* (New York: Harper Collins, 1991). According to traditional Hindu tenets, punishment varied by the caste of the offender. For the same offense, a Follower (unskilled laborer) would receive x punishment, a Producer (craftsman, farmer, artisan) would receive $2x$, an Administrator (organizer, doer, man of affairs) would receive $4x$, and a Brahmin (intellectual and spiritual leader) would receive $8x$ to $16x$.

26. For a more complete treatment of the time variable, see Edward T. Hall, *The silent language* (New York: Doubleday and Co., 1959).

27. Henry Mintzberg, *The nature of managerial work* (Englewood Cliffs, NJ: Prentice-Hall, 1980).

28. Robert W. Lightfoot and Christopher A. Barlett, "Phillips and Matsushita: A portrait of two evolving companies," in *Transnational management: Text, cases and readings in cross-border management*, eds Christopher A. Bartlett and Sumantra Ghoshal (Homewood, IL: Richard D. Irwin, 1992): 82.

29. Hall, "The Silent Language." In Edward T. Hall, *The hidden dimension* (Garden City, NY: Doubleday, 1966), the subject of space is even more fully developed.

30. This scheme was adapted from the ground-breaking work of Rolv M. Blakar. See Blakar, "Towards a theory of communication in terms of preconditions: A conceptual framework and some empirical explorations," in *Recent advances in language, communication, and social Psychology*, eds. H. Giles and R. N. St. Clair (London: Lawrence Erlbaum Associates, Ltd., Publishers, 1985): 10–40.

31. The first five of these are drawn from Richard E. Porter and Larry A. Samovar, "Approaching intercultural communication," in *Intercultural communications: A reader*, 5th edn, eds. Larry A. Samovar and Richard E. Porter (Belmont, CA: Wadsworth Publishing Company, 1988): 15–30. The last two are corollaries of the first five, that, according to our observations, are particularly critical to cross-cultural communication.

32. Nancy J. Adler, *International dimensions of organizational behavior*, 3rd edn (Cincinnati: South Western College Publishing, 1997): 107. For a more full description of cultural synergy, see Adler's text, which devotes a full chapter to this topic. For another extensive treatment, see Robert T. Moran and Philip R. Harris, *Managing cultural differences*, 4th edn (Houston: Gulf Publishing, 1996).

33. See "The Great Slave Lake Railway," Case 9-71-C011, Case and Publications, Richard Ivey School of Business, The University of Western Ontario, London, Canada.

○ ○

Key Concepts: Underlying Structures of Culture

Edward T. Hall and Mildred Reed Hall

Culture is Communication

In physics today, so far as we know, the galaxies that one studies are all controlled by the same laws. This is not entirely true of the worlds created by humans. Each cultural world operates according to its own internal dynamic, its own principles, and its own laws – written and unwritten. Even time and space are unique to each culture. There are, however, some common threads that run through all cultures.

It is possible to say that the world of communication can be divided into three parts: *words*; *material things*; and *behavior*. Words are the medium of business, politics, and diplomacy. Material things are usually indicators of status and power. Behavior provides feedback on how other people feel and includes techniques for avoiding confrontation.

By studying these three parts of the communication process in our own and other cultures, we can come to recognize and understand a vast unexplored region of human behavior that exists outside the range of people's conscious awareness, a "silent language" that is usually conveyed unconsciously (see Edward T. Hall's *The Silent Language*). This silent language includes a broad range of evolutionary concepts, practices, and solutions to problems which have their roots not in the lofty ideas of philosophers but in the shared experiences of ordinary people. In the words of the director of a project on cross-cultural relations, understanding the silent language "provides insights into *the underlying principles that shape our lives.*" These underlying principles are not only inherently interesting but eminently practical. The readers of this book, whether they be German, French, American, or from other countries, should find these principles useful at home and abroad.

Culture can be likened to a giant, extraordinarily complex, subtle computer. Its programs guide the actions and responses of human beings in every walk of life. This process requires attention to everything people do to survive, advance in the world, and gain satisfaction from life. Furthermore, cultural programs will not work if crucial steps are omitted, which happens when people unconsciously apply their own rules to another system.

During the three years we worked on this book, we had to learn two different programs for our office computer. The first was quite simple, but mastery did require paying close attention to every detail and several weeks of practice. The second was a much more complex program that required weeks of intensive practice, hours of tutoring, and days of depression and frustration when "the darn thing didn't work." Learning a new cultural program is infinitely more complicated and requires years of practice, yet there are many similarities in the learning process.

Cultural communications are deeper and more complex than spoken or written messages. *The essence of effective cross-cultural communication has more to do with releasing the right responses than with sending the "right" messages.* We offer here some conceptual tools to help our readers decipher the complex, unspoken rules of each culture.

Fast and Slow Messages: Finding the Appropriate Speed

The speed with which a particular message can be decoded and acted on is an important characteristic of human communication. There are fast and slow messages. A headline or cartoon, for example, is fast; the meaning that one extracts from books or art is slow. A fast message sent to people who are geared to a slow format will usually miss the target. While the content of the wrong-speed message may be understandable, it will not be received by someone accustomed to or expecting a different speed. The problem is that few people are aware that information can be sent at different speeds.

Examples of Fast and Slow Messages

Fast Messages	Slow Messages
Prose	Poetry
Headlines	Books
A communique	An ambassador
Propaganda	Art
Cartoons	Etchings
TV commercials	TV documentary
Television	Print
Easy familiarity	Deep relationships
Manners	Culture

Almost everything in life can be placed somewhere along the fast/slow message-speed spectrum. Such things as diplomacy, research, writing books, and creating art are accomplished in the slow mode. Buddha, Confucius, Shakespeare, Goethe, and Rembrandt all produced messages that human beings are still deciphering hundreds of years after the fact. Language is a very slow message; after 4,000 years, human beings are just beginning to discover what language is all about. The same can be said of culture, which incorporates multiple styles of "languages" that only release messages to those who are willing to spend the time to understand them.

In essence a person is a slow message; it takes time to get to know someone well. The message is, of course, slower in some cultures than in others. In the United States it is not too difficult to get to know people quickly in a relatively superficial way, which is all that most Americans want. Foreigners have often commented on how "unbelievably friendly" the Americans are. However, when Edward T. Hall studied the subject for the U.S. State Department, he discovered a worldwide complaint about Americans: they seem capable of forming only one kind of friendship – the informal, superficial kind that does not involve an exchange of deep confidences.

Conversely, in Europe personal relationships and friendships are highly valued and tend to take a long time to solidify. This is largely a function of the long-lasting, well-established networks of friends and relationships – particularly among the French – that one finds in Europe. Although there are exceptions, as a rule it will take Americans longer than they expect to really get to know Europeans. It is difficult, and at times may even be impossible, for a foreigner to break into these networks. Nevertheless, many businesspeople have found it expedient to take the time and make the effort to develop genuine friends among their business associates.

High and Low Context: How Much Information Is Enough?

Context is the information that surrounds an event; it is inextricably bound up with the meaning of that event. The elements that combine to produce a given meaning – events and context – are in different proportions depending on the culture. The cultures of the world can be compared on a scale from high to low context.

> A high context (HC) communication or message is one in which *most* of the information is already in the person, while very little is in the coded, explicit, transmitted part of the message. A low context (LC) communication is just the opposite; that is, the mass of the information is vested in the explicit code. Twins who have grown up together can and do communicate more economically (HC) than two lawyers in a courtroom during a trial (LC), a mathematician programming a computer, two politicians drafting legislation, two administrators writing a regulation. (Edward T. Hall 1976)

Japanese, Arab, and Mediterranean peoples, who have extensive information networks among family, friends, colleagues, and clients and who are involved in close personal relationships, are high-context. As a result, for most normal transactions in daily life they do not require, nor do they expect, much in-depth, background information. This is because they keep themselves informed about everything having to do with the people who are important in their lives. Low-context people include Americans, Germans, Swiss, Scandinavians, and other northern Europeans; they compartmentalize their personal relationships, their work, and many aspects of day-to-day life. Consequently, each time they interact with others they need detailed background information. The French are much higher on the context scale than either the Germans or the Americans. This difference can affect virtually every situation and every relationship in which the members of these two opposite traditions find themselves.

Within each culture, of course, there are specific individual differences in the need for contexting – the process of filling in background data. But it is helpful to know whether the culture of a particular country falls on the high or low side of the scale since every person is influenced by the level of context.

Contexting performs multiple functions. For example, any shift in the level of context is a communication. The shift can be up the scale, indicating a warming of the relationship, or down the scale (lowering the context), communicating coolness or displeasure – signaling something has gone wrong with a relationship. In the United States, the boss might communicate annoyance to an assistant when he shifts from the high-context, familiar form of address to the low-context, formal form of address. When this happens the boss is telling the subordinate in no uncertain terms that she or he has stepped out of line and incurred disfavor. In Japan moving the direction of the context is a source of daily feedback as to how things are going. The day starts with the use of honorifics, formal forms of address attached to each name. If things are going well the honorifics are dropped as the day progresses. First-naming in the United States is an artificial attempt at high-contexting; it tends to offend Europeans, who view the use of first names as acceptable only between close friends and family. With Europeans, one is always safe using a formal form of address, waiting for the other person to indicate when familiarity is acceptable.

Like their near relations the Germans, many Anglo-Americans (mostly those of northern European heritage) are not only low-context but they also lack extensive, well-developed information networks. American networks are limited in scope and development compared to those of the French, the Spanish, the Italians, and the Japanese. What follows from this is that Americans, unless they are very unsophisticated, will feel the need for contexting, for detailed background information, any time they are asked to make a decision or to do something. The American approach to life is quite segmented and focused on discrete, compartmentalized information; Americans need to know what is going to be in what compartment before they commit themselves. We experienced this in Japan when we were asked on short notice to provide names of well-placed Japanese and Americans to be participants in a small conference. Like most prudent Americans, we were reluctant to provide names until we knew what the conference was about and what the individuals recommended would be expected to do. This seemed logical and reasonable enough to us. Nevertheless, our reluctance was read as obstructionist by our Japanese colleagues and friends responsible for the conference. In Japan the mere presence of certain individuals endows the group and its activities with authority and status, which is far more important than the topic of the conference. It is characteristic of high-context, high-information societies that attendance at functions is as much a matter of the prestige associated with the function as anything else. This in turn means that, quite frequently, invitations to high-level meetings and conferences will be issued on short notice. It is taken for granted that those invited will eschew all previous commitments if the meeting is important enough. As a general rule Americans place greater importance on how long ago a commitment was made, on the agenda, and on the relevance of the expertise of different individuals to the agenda.

Another example of the contrast between how high- and low-context systems work is this: consider a top American executive working in an office and receiving a normal quota of visitors, usually one at a time. Most of the information that is relevant to the job originates from the few people the executive sees in the course of the day, as well as from what she or he reads. This is why the advisors and support personnel who surround the presidents of American enterprises (as well as the president of the United States) are so important. They and they alone control the content and the flow of organizational information to the chief executive.

Contrast this with the office of virtually any business executive in a high-context country such as France or Japan, where information flows freely and from all sides. Not only are people constantly coming and going, both seeking and giving information, but the entire form and function of the organization is centered on gathering, processing, and disseminating information. Everyone stays informed about every aspect of the business and knows who is best informed on what subjects.

In Germany almost everything is low-context and compartmentalized. The executive office is both a refuge and a screen – a refuge for the boss from the distractions of day-to-day office interactions and a screen for the employees from continual supervision. Information communicated in the office is not shared except with a select few – the exact antithesis of the high-information cultures.

High-context people are apt to become impatient and irritated when low-context people insist on giving them information they do not need. Conversely, low-context people are at a loss when high-context people do not provide *enough* information. One of the great communications challenges in life is to find the appropriate level of contexting needed in each situation. Too much information leads people to feel they are being talked down to; too little information can mystify them or make them feel left out. Ordinarily, people make these adjustments automatically in their own country, but in other countries their messages frequently miss the target.

The other side of the coin when considering context level is the apparent paradox that high-context people, such as the French, want to see *everything* when evaluating a *new* enterprise to which they have not been contexted. Annual reports or tax returns are not enough. Furthermore, they will keep asking until they get the information they want. Being high-context, the French are driven to make their own synthesis of the meanings of the figures. Unlike Americans, they feel uncomfortable with someone else's synthesis, someone else's "bottom line."

Space

Every living thing has a visible physical boundary – its skin – separating it from its external environment. This visible boundary is surrounded by a series of invisible boundaries that are more difficult to define but are just as real. These other boundaries begin with the individual's personal space and terminate with her or his "territory."

Territoriality

Territoriality, an innate characteristic whose roots lie hundreds of millions of years in the past, is the act of laying claim to and defending a territory and is a vital link in the chain of events necessary for survival. In humans, territoriality is highly developed and strongly influenced by culture. It is particularly well developed in the Germans and the Americans. Americans tend to establish places that they label "mine" – a cook's feeling about a kitchen or a child's view of her or his bedroom. In Germany this same feeling of territoriality is commonly extended to all possessions, including the automobile. If a German's car is touched, it is as though the individual himself has been touched.

Space also communicates power. A corner office suite in the United States is conventionally occupied by "the brass," and a private office in any location has more status than a desk in the open without walls. In both German and American business, the top floors are reserved for high-ranking officials and executives. In contrast, important French officials occupy a position in the *middle*, surrounded by subordinates; the emphasis there is on occupying the central position in an information network, where one can stay informed and can control what is happening.

Personal Space

Personal space is another form of territory. Each person has around him or her an invisible bubble of space which expands and contracts depending on a number of things: the relationship to the people nearby; the person's emotional state; cultural background; and the activity being performed. Few people are allowed to penetrate this bit of mobile territory and then only for short periods of time. Changes in the bubble brought about by cramped quarters or crowding cause people to feel uncomfortable or aggressive. In northern Europe, the bubbles are quite large and people keep their distance. In southern France, Italy, Greece, and Spain, the bubbles get smaller and smaller so that the distance that is perceived as intimate in the north overlaps normal conversational distance in the south, all of which means that Mediterranean Europeans "get too close" to the Germans, the Scandinavians, the English, and those Americans of northern European ancestry. In northern Europe one does not touch others. Even the brushing of the overcoat sleeve used to elicit an apology.

The Multisensory Spatial Experience

Few people realize that space is perceived by *all* the senses, not by vision alone. Auditory space is perceived by the ears, thermal space by the skin, kinesthetic space by the muscles, and olfactory space by the nose. As one might imagine, there are great cultural differences in the programming of the senses. Americans to some extent and Germans to a greater extent rely heavily on auditory screening, particularly when they want to concentrate. High-context people reject auditory screening and thrive on being open to interruptions and in tune with what goes on around them. Hence, in French and Italian cities one is periodically and intrusively bombarded by noise.

Unconscious Reactions to Spatial Differences

Spatial changes give tone to communication, accent it, and at times even override the spoken word. As people interact, the flow and shift of distance between them is integral to the communication process. For example, if a stranger does not maintain "normal" conversational distance and gets too close, our reaction is automatic – we feel uncomfortable, sometimes even offended or threatened and we back up.

Human beings in the course of a lifetime incorporate literally hundreds of spatial cues. They imbibe the significance of these cues like mother's milk, in the context of their own culture. Just as a fragrance will trigger a memory, these cues and their associated behaviors release unconscious responses, regulating the tone, tempo, and mood of human transactions.

Since most people don't think about personal distance as something that is culturally patterned, foreign spatial cues are almost inevitably misinterpreted. This can lead to bad feelings which are then projected onto the people from the other culture in a most personal way. When a foreigner appears aggressive and pushy, or remote and cold, it may mean only that her or his personal distance is different from yours.

Americans have strong feelings about proximity and the attendant rights, responsibilities, and obligations associated with being a neighbor. Neighbors should be friendly and agreeable, cut their lawns, keep their places up, and do their bit for the neighborhood. By contrast, in France and Germany, simply sharing adjacent houses does not necessarily mean that people will interact with each other, particularly if they have not met socially. Proximity requires different behavior in other cultures.

Time

Life on earth evolved in response to the cycles of day and night and the ebb and flow of the tides. As humans evolved, a multiplicity of internal biological clocks also developed. These biological clocks now regulate most of the physiological functions of our bodies. It is not surprising, therefore, that human concepts of time grew out of the natural rhythms associated with daily, monthly, and annual cycles. From the beginning humans have been tied to growing seasons and were dependent on the forces and rhythms of nature.

Out of this background two time systems evolved – one as an expression of our biological clocks, the other of the solar, lunar, and annual cycles. These systems will be described under the headings "Time as Structure" and "Time as Communication." In the sections that follow, we restrict ourselves to those manifestations of time that have proved to be stumbling blocks at the cultural interface.

Monochronic and Polychronic Time

There are many kinds of time systems in the world, but two are most important to international business. We call them monochronic and polychronic time. Monochronic time means paying attention to and doing only one thing at a time. Polychronic time means being involved with many things at once. Like oil and water, the two systems do not mix.

In monochronic cultures, time is experienced and used in a linear way – comparable to a road extending from the past into the future. Monochronic time is divided quite naturally into segments; it is scheduled and compartmentalized, making it possible for a person to concentrate on one thing at a time. In a monochronic system, the schedule may take priority above all else and be treated as sacred and unalterable.

Monochronic time is perceived as being almost *tangible*: people talk about it as though it were money, as something that can be "spent," "saved," "wasted," and "lost." It is also used as a classification system for ordering life and setting priorities: "I don't have time to see him." Because monochronic time concentrates on one thing at a time, people who are governed by it don't like to be interrupted. Monochronic time seals people off from one another and, as a result, intensifies some relationships while shortchanging others. Time becomes a room which some people are allowed to enter, while others are excluded.

Monochronic time dominates most business in the United States. While Americans perceive it as almost in the air they breathe, it is nevertheless a learned product of northern European culture and is therefore arbitrary and imposed. Monochronic time is an artifact of the industrial revolution in England; factory life required the labor force to be on hand and in place at an appointed hour. In spite of the fact that it is *learned*, monochronic time now appears to be natural and logical because the great majority of Americans grew up in monochronic time systems with whistles and bells counting off the hours.

Other Western cultures – Switzerland, Germany, and Scandinavia in particular – are dominated by the iron hand of monochronic time as well. German and Swiss cultures represent classic examples of monochronic time. Still, monochronic time is not natural time; in fact, it seems to violate many of humanity's innate rhythms.

In almost every respect, polychronic systems are the antithesis of monochronic systems. Polychronic time is characterized by the simultaneous occurrence of many things and by a *great involvement with people*. There is more emphasis on completing human transactions than on holding to schedules. For example, two polychronic Latins conversing on a street corner would likely opt to be late for their next appointment rather than abruptly terminate the conversation before its natural conclusion. Polychronic time is experienced as much less tangible than monochronic time and can better be compared to a single point than to a road.

Proper understanding of the differences between the monochronic and polychronic time systems will be helpful in dealing with the time-flexible Mediterranean peoples. While the generalizations listed below do not apply equally to all cultures, they will help convey a pattern:

Monochronic People	**Polychronic People**
Do one thing at a time	Do many things at once
Concentrate on the job	Are highly distractible and subject to interruptions
Take time commitments (deadlines, schedules) seriously	Consider time commitments an objective to be achieved, if possible
Are low-context and need information	Are high-context and already have information
Are committed to the job	Are committed to people and human relationships
Adhere religiously to plans	Change plans often and easily
Are concerned about not disturbing others; follow rules of privacy and consideration	Are more concerned with those who are closely related (family, friends, close business associates) than with privacy
Show great respect for private property; seldom borrow or lend	Borrow and lend things often and easily
Emphasize promptness	Base promptness on the relationship
Are accustomed to short-term relationships	Have strong tendency to build lifetime relationships

The Relation between Time and Space

In monochronic time cultures, the emphasis is on the compartmentalization of functions and people. Private offices are sound-proof if possible. In polychronic Mediterranean cultures, business offices often have large reception areas where people can wait. Company or government officials may even transact their business by moving about in the reception area, stopping to confer with this group and that one until everyone has been attended to.

Polychronic people feel that private space disrupts the flow of information by shutting people off from one another. In polychronic systems, appointments mean very little and may be shifted around even at the last minute to accommodate someone more important in an individual's hierarchy of family, friends, or associates. Some polychronic people (such as Latin Americans and Arabs) give precedence to their large circle of family members over any business obligation. Polychronic people also have many close friends and good clients with whom they spend a great deal of time. The close links to clients or customers create a reciprocal feeling of obligation and a mutual desire to be helpful.

Polychronic Time and Information

Polychronic people live in a sea of information. They feel they must be up-to-the-minute about everything and everybody, be it business or personal, and they seldom subordinate personal relationships to the exigencies of schedules or budgets.

It is impossible to know how many millions of dollars have been lost in international business because monochronic and polychronic people do not understand each other or even realize that two such different time systems exist. The following example illustrates how difficult it is for these two types to relate:

> A French salesman working for a French company that had recently been bought by Americans found himself with a new American manager who expected instant results and higher profits immediately. Because of the emphasis on personal relationships, it frequently takes years to develop customers in polychronic France, and, in family-owned firms, relationships with customers may span generations. The American manager, not understanding this, ordered the salesman to develop new customers within three months. The salesman knew this was impossible and had to resign, asserting his legal right to take with him all the loyal customers he had developed over the years. Neither side understood what had happened.

These two opposing views of time and personal relationships often show up during business meetings. In French meetings, the information flow is high, and one is expected to read other people's thoughts, intuit the state of their business, and even garner indirectly what government regulations are in the offing. For the French and other polychronic/high-context people, a tight, fixed agenda can be an encumbrance, even an insult to one's intelligence. Most, if not all, of those present have a pretty good idea of what will be discussed beforehand. The purpose of the meeting is to create consensus. A rigid agenda and consensus represent opposite goals and do not mix. *The importance of this basic dichotomy cannot be overemphasized.*

Past- and Future-Oriented Countries

It is always important to know which segments of the time frame are emphasized. Cultures in countries such as Iran, India, and those of the Far East are past-oriented. Others, such as that of the urban United States, are oriented to the present and short-term future; still others, such as those of Latin America, are both past- and present-oriented. In Germany, where historical background is very important, every talk, book, or article begins with background information giving a historical perspective. This irritates many foreigners who keep wondering, "Why don't they get on with it? After all, I am educated. Don't the Germans know that?" The Japanese and the French are also steeped in history, but because they are high-context cultures, historical facts are alluded to obliquely. At present, there is no satisfactory explanation for why and how differences of this sort came about.

Time as Communication

As surely as each culture has its spoken language, each has its own *language of time*; to function effectively in France, Germany, and the United States, it is essential to acquaint oneself with the local language of time. When we take our own time system for granted and project it onto other cultures, we fail to read the hidden messages in the foreign time system and thereby deny ourselves vital feedback.

For Americans, the use of appointment-schedule time reveals how people feel about each other, how significant their business is, and where they rank in the status system. Treatment of time can also convey a powerful form of insult. Furthermore, because the rules are informal, they operate largely out of awareness and, as a consequence, are less subject to conscious manipulation than language.

It is important, therefore, to know how to read the messages associated with time in other cultures. In France almost everything is polychronic whereas in Germany monochronic promptness is even more important than it is in the United States.

Tempo, Rhythm, and Synchrony

Rhythm is an intangible but important aspect of time. Because nature's cycles are rhythmic, it is understandable that rhythm and tempo are distinguishing features of any culture. Rhythm ties the people of a culture together and can also alienate them from members of other cultures. In some cultures people move very slowly; in others, they move rapidly. When people from two such different cultures meet, they are apt to have difficulty relating because they are not "in sync." This is important because synchrony – the subtle ability to move together – is vital to all collaborative efforts, be they conferring, administering, working together on machines, or buying and selling.

People who move at a fast tempo are often perceived as "tailgating" those who move more slowly, and tailgating doesn't contribute to harmonious interaction – nor does forcing fast-paced people to move too slowly. Americans complain that the Germans take forever to reach decisions. Their time is out of phase with American time and vice versa. One must always be contexted to the local time system. There will be times when everything seems to be at a standstill, but actually a great deal is going on behind the scenes. Then there will be other times when everything moves at lightning speed and it is necessary to stand aside, to get out of the way.

Scheduling and Lead Time

To conduct business in an orderly manner in other countries, it is essential to know how much or how little lead time is required for each activity: how far ahead to request an appointment or schedule meetings and vacations, and how much time to allow for the preparation of a major report. In both the United States and Germany, schedules are sacred; in France scheduling frequently cannot be initiated until meetings are held with concerned members of the organization to permit essential discussions. This system works well in France, but there are complications whenever overseas partners or participants are involved since they have often scheduled their own activities up to two years in advance.

Lead time varies from culture to culture and is itself a communication as well as an element in organization. For instance, in France, if the relationship is important, desks will be cleared when that person arrives, whether there has been any advance notice or not. Time will be made to work together, up to 24 hours a day if necessary. In the United States and to some extent in Germany, on the other hand, the amount of lead time can be read as an index of the relative importance of the business to be conducted, as well as of the status of the individuals concerned. Short lead time means that the business is of little importance; the longer the lead time, the greater the value of the proceedings. In these countries, two weeks is the minimum advance time for requesting appointments. In Arab countries, two weeks may be too long – a date set so far in advance "slides off their minds;" three or four days may be preferable. In Japan, lead time is usually much shorter than in the United States, and it is difficult to say how many conferences on important subjects, attended by all the most competent and prestigious Japanese leaders in their fields, fail to attract suitable counterparts from the United States because of the short lead time. Although misunderstandings are blameless artifacts of the way two very different systems work, accidents of culture are seldom understood for what they are.

Another instance of time as communication is the practice of setting a date to end something. For example, Americans often schedule how long they will stay in a foreign country for a series of meetings, thus creating the psychological pressure of having to arrive at a decision by a certain date. *This is a mistake.* The Japanese and, to a lesser degree, the French are very aware of the American pressure of being "under the gun" and will use it to their advantage during negotiations.

The Importance of Proper Timing

Choosing the correct timing of an important event is crucial. Politicians stake their careers on it. In government and business alike, announcements of major changes or new programs must be carefully timed. The significance of different time segments of the day also must be considered. Certain times of the day, month, or year are reserved for certain activities (vacations, meal times, and so on) and are not ordinarily interchangeable. In general, in northern European cultures and in the United States, anything that occurs outside of business hours, very early in the morning or late at night, suggests an emergency. In France, there are times when nothing is expected to happen, such as national holidays and during the month of August, when everything shuts down for *vacances*. Culturally patterned systems are sufficiently complex so that it is wise to seek the advice of local experts.

In the United States, the short business lunch is common and the business dinner rarer; this is not so in France, where the function of the business lunch and dinner is to create the proper atmosphere and get acquainted. Relaxing with business clients during lunch and after work is crucial to building the close rapport that is absolutely necessary if one is to do business.

Appointments

The way in which time is treated by Americans and Germans signals attitude, evaluation of priorities, mood, and status. Since time is highly valued in both Germany and the United States, the messages of time carry more weight than they do in polychronic countries. Waiting time, for example, carries strong messages which work on that part of the brain that mobilizes the emotions (the limbic system). In the United States, only those people with very high status can keep others waiting and get away with it. In general, those individuals are the very ones who know enough of human relations to avoid "insults of time" whenever possible. It is the petty bureaucrat who likes to throw his weight around, the bully who takes pleasure in putting people down, or the insecure executive with an inflated ego who keeps visitors waiting. The waiting-room message is a double-edged sword. Not only does it communicate an attitude towards the visitor, but it reveals a lot about the individual who has kept a visitor waiting. In monochronic cultures, such as those in the United States and Germany, keeping others waiting can be a deliberate putdown or a signal that the individual is very disorganized and can't keep to a schedule. In polychronic cultures, such as those of France or Hispanic countries, no such message is intended. In other words, one's reading of the message should be tempered by the context, the realities of the situation, and not with an automatic projection of one's own culture.

Clearly, interactions between monochronic and polychronic people can be stressful unless both parties know and can decode the meanings behind each other's language of time. The language of time is much more stable and resistant to change than other cultural systems. We were once involved in a research project in New Mexico, conducting interviews with Hispanics. Our subjects were sixth- and seventh-generation descendants of the original Spanish families who settled in North America in the early seventeenth century. Despite constant contact with Anglo-Saxon Americans for well over a hundred years, most of these Hispanics have remained polychronic. In three summers of interviewing, we never once achieved our scheduled goal of five interviews each week for each interviewer. We were lucky to have two or three. Interviews in Hispanic homes or offices were constantly interrupted when families came to visit or a friend dropped by. The Hispanics seemed to be juggling half a dozen activities simultaneously, even while the interviews were in progress.

Since we are monochronic Anglo-Saxons, this caused us no little concern and considerable distress. It is hard not to respond emotionally when the rules of your own time system are violated. Nor was an intellectual understanding of the problem much help at first. We did recognize, however, that what we were experiencing was a consequence of cultural differences and was, therefore, a part of our data. This led us to a better understanding of the importance as well as the subtleties of information flow and information networks in a polychronic society.

Information Flow: Is it Fast or Slow and Where Does it Go?

The rate of information flow is measured by how long it takes a message intended to produce an action to travel from one part of an organization to another and for that message to release the desired response. Cultural differences in information flow are often the greatest stumbling blocks to international understanding. Every executive doing business in a foreign land should know how information is handled – where it goes and whether it flows easily through the society and the business organization, or whether it is restricted to narrow channels because of compartmentalization.

In low-context countries, such as the United States, Germany, and Switzerland, information is highly focused, compartmentalized, and controlled, and, therefore, not apt to flow freely. In high-context cultures, such as the French, the Japanese, and the Spanish, information spreads rapidly and moves almost as if it had a life of its own. Those who use information as an instrument of "command and control" and who build their planning on controlling information are in for a rude shock in societies where people live in a sea of information.

In high-context cultures, interpersonal contact takes precedence over everything else; wherever people are spatially involved with each other, information flows freely. In business, executives do not seal themselves off behind secretaries and closed doors; in fact in Japan senior executives may even share offices so that each person knows as much about the entire base of operations as possible, and in France an executive will have ties to a centrally located bureau chief to keep a finger on the pulse of information flow. In these cultures most people are already highly contexted and therefore do not need to be briefed in much detail for each transaction; the emphasis is on stored rather than on transmitted information. Furthermore, channels are seldom overloaded because people stay in constant contact; therefore, the organizational malady of "information overload" is rare. Schedules and screening (as in the use of private offices) are minimized because they interfere with this vital contact. For high-context people, there are two primary expectations: to context everybody in order to open up the information channels and determine whether the group can work together and to appraise the chances of coming to an agreement in the future. The drive to stay in touch and to keep up to date in high-context cultures is very strong. Because these cultures are also characteristically high-information flow cultures, being out of touch means to cease to exist as a viable human being.

Organizations where information flows slowly are familiar to both Americans and northern Europeans because low-flow information is associated with both low-context and monochronic time resulting from the compartmentalization associated with low-context institutions and of taking up one thing at a time. In the United States, information flows slowly because each executive has a private office and a secretary to serve as a guard so that the executive is not distracted by excessive information. Since executive territory is jealously guarded, American executives often do not share information with their staff or with other department heads. We were once hired as consultants to a large government bureaucracy in which there were problems. Our study revealed multiple causes, the most important of which was a bottleneck created by a high-ranking bureaucrat who managed to block practically all the information going from the top down and from the bottom up. Once the problem had been identified, an agency staff director remarked, "I see we have a blockage in information." In a high-context situation everyone would have already known that this was the case. In a low-context system, however, it was necessary to call in outside consultants to make explicit what some people had suspected but were unable or unwilling to identify.

Action Chains: The Importance of Completion

An action chain is an established sequence of events in which one or more people participate – and contribute – to achieve a goal. It's like the old-fashioned ritual of courtship with its time-honored developmental stages. If either party rushes things too much, omits an important procedure, or delays too long between steps, the courtship grinds to a halt.

Business is replete with action chains: greeting people; hiring and training personnel; developing an advertising campaign; floating a stock offering; initiating a lawsuit; merging with or taking over other companies; even sinking a golf putt. Many bureaucratic procedures are based unconsciously on the action-chain model. Because of the diversity of functions, it may be difficult for some people to link all these activities in their minds, but the common thread of underlying, ordered sequence ties each case to the others.

Because the steps in the chain are either technical (as in floating a stock offering or completing a merger) or else so widely shared and taken for granted that little conscious attention is paid to the details, the need to re-examine the entire pattern has largely gone unrecognized in the overseas setting.

There are important rules governing the structure, though not the content, of action chains. If an important step is left out, the action must begin all over again. Too many meetings and reports, for example, can break the action chains of individual projects, making it difficult for people to complete their work. In fact, the breaking of an action chain is one of the most troublesome events with which human beings have to contend in our speeded-up technological twentieth century.

All planning must take into account the elaborate hierarchy of action chains. Monochronic, low-context cultures, with their compartmentalized approach and dependence on scheduled activities, are particularly sensitive to interruptions and so are more vulnerable to the breaking of action chains than high-context cultures. Most Americans are brought up with strong drives to complete action chains. High-context people, because of their intense involvement with each other and their extensive, cohesive networks, are more elastic; there is more "give" in their system. Some polychronic peoples will break an action chain simply because they don't like the way things are going or because they think they can "get a better deal." For instance, we once knew a monochronic architect in New York who was designing a building for a polychronic client. The client continually changed the specifications for the building. With each change, the building design had to be revised, even down to alterations in the building's foundations. The architect found this process particularly devastating because designing and constructing a building is an incredibly complex and elaborate collection of action chains. Changing one thing is likely to throw everything else out of gear.

The relationship between action chains and disputes is important. All cultures have built-in safeguards – even though they may not always work – to prevent a dispute from escalating to an out-and-out battle. Keep in mind, however, that these safeguards apply only within the context of one's own culture. In any foreign situation where a dispute appears imminent, it is essential to do two things immediately: proceed slowly, taking every action possible to maintain course and stay on an even keel; and seek the advice of a skillful, tactful interpreter of the culture.

Interfacing: Creating the Proper Fit

The concept of interfacing can be illustrated by a simple example: it is impossible to interface an American appliance with a European outlet without an adaptor and a transformer. Not only are the voltages different, but the contacts on one are round; on the other, thin and flat. The purpose of this [article] is to serve as an adaptor for business executives operating at the interfaces between American, French, and German cultures.

The problems to be solved when interfacing vary from company to company, but some generalizations are possible.

First, it is more difficult to succeed in a foreign country than at home.

Second, the top management of a foreign subsidiary is crucial to the success of interfacing. Therefore, it is important to send the very best people available, take their advice, and leave them alone. Expect that your foreign manager or representative will start explaining things in terms of the local mentality which may sound alien and strange.

Cultural interfacing follows five basic principles:

1. The higher the context of either the culture or the industry, the more difficult the interface;
2. The greater the complexity of the elements, the more difficult the interface;
3. The greater the cultural distance, the more difficult the interface;
4. The greater the number of levels in the system, the more difficult the interface;
5. Very simple, low-context, highly evolved, mechanical systems tend to produce fewer interface problems than multiple-level systems of great complexity that depend on human talent for their success.

An example of an easy-to-interface business would be the manufacture of small components for microscopes by two divisions, one in Germany, the other in Switzerland.

The cultural distance in this case is not great since both cultures are low-context as well as monochronic, and the business operation itself does not involve different levels of complexity.

A difficult-to-interface enterprise would be a newspaper or magazine in two countries that are vastly different, such as France and the United States. Publishing is a high-context enterprise which must be neatly meshed at literally dozens of points, including writing, advertising, and editorial policy. The success of newspapers and magazines depends on writers and editors who understand their audience's culture and know how to reach their readers.

Releasing the Right Responses

The Importance of Context and Following the Rules

The key to being an effective communicator is in knowing the degree of information (contexting) that must be supplied. If you're communicating with a German, remember she or he is low-context and will need lots of information and all the details, in depth. If you're communicating with someone from France, she or he is high-context and won't require as much information. Here are two examples from our interviews:

> One German manager working for a French firm was fired after his first year because he didn't perform as expected. The German manager was stunned. His response was, "But nobody told me what they wanted me to do."

> The opposite problem was encountered by a Frenchman who resigned from a German firm because he was constantly being told what he already knew by his German superior. Both his intelligence and his pride were threatened.

In both situations, the executives were inept at releasing the right response from their subordinates.

One of the factors that determines whether one releases the right response includes observing the rules of the other culture, including the time system. In Germany a salesman can have a very fine presentation, but if he arrives late by even a few minutes, no one will be impressed, no matter how good it is. Indeed, in all probability, the Germans will not even wait around to hear it. In France form is preeminent; without it, no message can release the right response. Americans must take great care not to alienate the French by being casual and informal in their manners; if Americans are not meticulously polite and formal, their message will not get through to the French, and they and their product will suffer.

The Importance of the Right Interpreter

Releasing the right response will also depend on choosing the right interpreter. An interpreter's accent or use of the local dialect can cause a negative reaction. The importance of this facet of communication cannot be overstressed, yet it is one of the most frequent violations of the unwritten laws of communication abroad. For example, if you are trying to communicate with a Japanese executive using an interpreter who is not well educated nor extremely polite and proper, the desired response from the Japanese will not be forthcoming. A well-educated and well-mannered interpreter whose use of the language reflects a good background is also highly desirable in France and Germany.

Summary

Speed of messages, context, space, time, information flow, action chains, and inter-facing are all involved in the creation of both national and corporate character. In organ-izations everything management does communicates; when viewed in the cultural context, all acts, all events, all material things have meaning. Some organizations send strong, consistent messages that are readily grasped by employees and customers alike. Other organizations are less easy to interpret; they do not communicate clearly, or their mess-ages are incongruent. Sometimes one part of the organization communicates one thing and another part communicates something else. The cues around which these corporate and cultural messages are organized are as different as the languages with which they are associated. Most important, their meaning is deeply imbedded and, therefore, harder for management to change when making the transition from one country to another.

Many messages are implied or have a cultural meaning, and there is a tacit agreement as to the nature of that meaning which is deeply rooted in the context of the commun-ication. There is much that is taken for granted in culture that few people can explain but which every member of the culture accepts as given. Remember that messages come in many forms (most of them not in words) which are imbedded in the context and in the choice of channels.

Within all cultures there are important unstated differences as to what constitutes a proper *releaser*. Our research over the years in choosing the correct releaser has indic-ated that people cluster around preferences for "words," "numbers," and "pictures." Using the wrong format (sending numbers when words are wanted, words when the recipient only feels comfortable with numbers, or words and/or numbers to the visually-oriented person) can only release a negative, frustrated response. The fascinating thing is that the message can be the same in every case. Furthermore, it is quite evident that each culture has its own preferences in this regard.

A television ad that is effective in the United States will have to be translated into a print media message to reach Germans. Germans are print-oriented, which explains in part why there is so little advertising on German TV. Also, Germans are always looking for what is "true" and to them numbers are a way of signaling that a product is exactly as it has been represented. Germans demand facts, facts, and more facts.

It is not uncommon for Americans to experience difficulty getting the French – even those whom they know and have done business with – to reply to inquiries, even urgent ones. This can be exasperating. The reasons are many but most have to do with the importance of immediate human contacts to the French. A solution that succeeds when other methods fail is to use a surrogate to relay messages rather than relying on a letter or a phone call. Why? Because letters and telephone calls aren't personal enough. If you send a properly placed emissary, one whom the individual you are trying to reach likes and trusts and considers important, you add the necessary personal touch to your message and will thereby release the right response.

The French also stress the importance of observing the many rituals of form. If you don't use the right form, the message conveyed is that you are ignorant or ill-mannered or do not care. In any event, the response that is released is almost certain to be negative. Remember that the French deplore casualness and informality. Paying attention to the details and being correct in everything you do is the only tactic that releases the right response in France.

It is not necessary to solve every problem at once, only to show a genuine desire to do so and to take one step at a time, even if it seems to take a lifetime. The rewards are not only material but psychological and mental as well. New frontiers are not only to be found in outer space or in the microworld of science; they are also at the interfaces between cultures.

READING **2**

Cultural Constraints in
Management Theories

Geert Hofstede

Lewis Carroll's *Alice in Wonderland* contains the famous story of Alice's croquet game with the Queen of Hearts.

> Alice thought she had never seen such a curious croquet-ground in all her life; it was all ridges and furrows; the balls were live hedgehogs, the mallets live flamingoes, and the soldiers had to double themselves up and to stand on their hands and feet, to make the arches.

You probably know how the story goes: Alice's flamingo mallet turns its head whenever she wants to strike with it; her hedgehog ball runs away; and the doubled-up soldier arches walk around all the time. The only rule seems to be that the Queen of Hearts always wins.

Alice's croquet-playing problems are good analogies to attempts to build culture-free theories of management. Concepts available for this purpose are themselves alive with culture, having been developed within a particular cultural context. They have a tendency to guide our thinking toward our desired conclusion.

As the same reasoning may also be applied to the arguments in this article, I better tell you my conclusion before I continue – so that the rules of my game are understood. In this article we take a trip around the world to demonstrate that there are no such things as universal management theories.

Diversity in management *practices* as we go around the world has been recognized in US management literature for more than 30 years. The term "comparative management" has been used since the 1960s. However, it has taken much longer for the US academic community to accept that not only practices but also the validity of *theories* may stop at national borders, and I wonder whether even today everybody would agree with this statement.

An article I published in *Organizational Dynamics* in 1980 entitled "Do American Theories Apply Abroad?" created more controversy than I expected. The article argued, with empirical support, that generally accepted US theories like those of Maslow, Herzberg,

McClelland, Vroom, McGregor, Likert, Blake, and Mouton may not or only very partly apply outside the borders of their country of origin – assuming they do apply within those borders. Among the requests for reprints, a larger number were from Canada than from the United States.

Management Theorists are Human

Employees and managers are human. Employees as humans were "discovered" in the 1930s, with the human relations school. Managers as humans were introduced in the late 1940s by Herbert Simon's "bounded rationality" and elaborated in Richard Cyert and James March's *Behavioral Theory of the Firm* (1963, and recently republished in a second edition). My argument is that management scientists, theorists, and writers are human too: they grew up in a particular society in a particular period, and their ideas cannot help but reflect the constraints of their environment.

The idea that the validity of a theory is constrained by national borders is more obvious in Europe, with all its borders, than in a huge borderless country like the United States. Already in the sixteenth century, Michel de Montaigne, a Frenchman, wrote a statement which was made famous by Blaise Pascal about a century later: "*Vérité en-deca des Pyrénées, erreur au-delà.*" There are truths on this side of the Pyrénées which are falsehoods on the other.

From Don Armado's Love to Taylor's Science

According to the comprehensive ten-volume *Oxford English Dictionary* (1971), the words "manage," "management," and "manager" appeared in the English language in the sixteenth century. The oldest recorded use of the word "manager" is in Shakespeare's *Love's Labour's Lost*, dating from 1588, in which Don Adriano de Armado, "a fantastical Spaniard," exclaims (Act I, scene ii, 188): "Adieu, valour! rust, rapier! be still, drum! for your manager is in love; yea, he loveth."

The linguistic origin of the word is from Latin *manus*, hand, via the Italian *maneggiare*, which is the training of horses in the *manege*; subsequently its meaning was extended to skillful handling in general, like of arms and musical instruments, as Don Armado illustrates. However, the word also became associated with the French *menage*, household, as an equivalent of "husbandry" in its sense of the art of running a household. The theater of present-day management contains elements of both *manege* and different managers and cultures may use different accents.

The founder of the science of economics, the Scot Adam Smith, in his 1776 book *The Wealth of Nations*, used "manage," "management" (even "bad management"), and "manager" when dealing with the process and the persons involved in operating joint stock companies. British economist John Stuart Mill (1806–73) followed Smith in this use and clearly expressed his distrust of such hired people who were not driven by ownership. Since the 1880s, the word "management" appeared occasionally in writings by American engineers, until it was canonized as a modern science by Frederick W. Taylor in *Shop Management* in 1903 and in *The Principles of Scientific Management* in 1911.

While Smith and Mill used "management" to describe a process and "managers" for the persons involved, "management" in the American sense – which has since been taken back by the British – refers not only to the process but also to the managers as a class of people. This class (1) does not own a business but sells its skills to act on behalf of the owners, and (2) does not produce personally but is indispensable for making others produce, through motivation. Members of this class carry a high status, and many American boys and girls aspire to the role. In the United States, the manager is a cultural hero.

Let us now turn to other parts of the world. We will look at management in its context in other successful modern economies: Germany, Japan, France, Holland, and among the overseas Chinese. Then we will examine management in the much larger part of the world that is still poor, especially Southeast Asia and Africa, and in the new political configurations of Eastern Europe, and Russia in particular. We will then return to the United States via mainland China.

Germany

The manager is not a cultural hero in Germany. If anybody, it is the engineer who fills the hero role. Frederick Taylor's *Scientific Management* was conceived in a society of immigrants – where large numbers of workers with diverse backgrounds and skills had to work together. In Germany, this heterogeneity never existed.

Elements of the medieval guild system have survived in historical continuity in Germany until the present day. In particular, a very effective apprenticeship system exists both on the shop floor and in the office, which alternates practical work and classroom courses. At the end of the apprenticeship the worker receives a certificate, the *Facharbeiterbrief*, which is recognized throughout the country. About two-thirds of the German-worker population holds such a certificate and a corresponding occupational pride. In fact, quite a few German company presidents have worked their way up from the ranks through an apprenticeship. In comparison, two-thirds of the worker population in Britain have no occupational qualification at all.

The highly skilled and responsible German workers do not necessarily need a manager, American-style, to "motivate" them. They expect their boss or *Meister* to assign their tasks and to be the expert in resolving technical problems. Comparisons of similar German, British, and French organizations show the Germans as having the highest rate of personnel in productive roles and the lowest both in leadership and staff roles.

Business schools are virtually unknown in Germany. Native German management theories concentrate on formal systems. The inapplicability of American concepts of management was quite apparent in 1973 when the US consulting firm of Booz, Allen, and Hamilton, commissioned by the German Ministry of Economic Affairs, wrote a study of German management from an American viewpoint. The report is highly critical and writes among other things that "Germans simply do not have a very strong concept of management." Since 1973, from my personal experience, the situation has not changed much. However, during this period the German economy has performed in a superior fashion to the United States in virtually all respects, so a strong concept of management might have been a liability rather than an asset.

Japan

The American type of manager is also missing in Japan. In the United States, the core of the enterprise is the managerial class. The core of the Japanese enterprise is the permanent worker group; workers who for all practical purposes are tenured and who aspire to life-long employment. They are distinct from the non-permanent employees – most women and subcontracted teams led by gang bosses, to be laid off in slack periods. University graduates in Japan first join the permanent worker group and subsequently fill various positions, moving from line to staff as the need occurs while paid according to seniority rather than position. They take part in Japanese-style group consultation sessions for important decisions, which extend the decision-making period but guarantee fast implementation afterwards. Japanese are to a large extent controlled by their peer group rather than by their manager.

Three researchers from the East-West Center of the University of Hawaii, Joseph Tobin, David Wu, and Dana Danielson, did an observational study of typical preschools in three countries: China, Japan, and the United States. Their results have been published both as a book and as a video. In the Japanese preschool, one teacher handled 28 four-year olds. The video shows one particularly obnoxious boy, Hiroki, who fights with other children and throws teaching materials down from the balcony. When a little girl tries to alarm the teacher, the latter answers: "What are you calling me for? Do something about it!" In the US preschool, there is one adult for every nine children. This class has its problem child too, Glen, who refuses to clear away his toys. One of the teachers has a long talk with him and isolates him in a corner, until he changes his mind. It doesn't take much imagination to realize that managing Hiroki 30 years later will be a different process from managing Glen.

American theories of leadership are ill-suited for the Japanese group-controlled situation. During the past two decades, the Japanese have developed their own "PM" theory of leadership, in which P stands for performance and M for maintenance. The latter is less a concern for individual employees than for maintaining social stability. In view of the amazing success of the Japanese economy in the past 30 years, many Americans have sought the secrets of Japanese management hoping to copy them.

France

The manager, US-style, does not exist in France either. In a very enlightening book, unfortunately not yet translated into English, the French researcher Philippe d'Iribarne describes the results of in-depth observation and interview studies of management methods in three subsidiary plants of the same French multinational: in France; the United States; and Holland. He relates what he finds to information about the three societies in general. Where necessary, he goes back in history to trace the roots of the strikingly different behaviors in the completion of the same tasks. He identifies three kinds of basic principles (*logiques*) of management. In the United States, the principle is the *fair contract* between employer and employee, which gives the manager considerable prerogatives, but within its limits. This is really a *labor market* in which the worker sells his or her labor for a price. In France, the principle is the *honor* of each class in a society which has always been and remains extremely stratified, in which superiors behave as superior beings and subordinates accept and expect this, conscious of their own lower level in the national hierarchy but also of the honor of their own class. The French do not think in terms of managers versus non-managers but in terms of *cadres* versus *noncadres*; one becomes cadre by attending the proper schools and one remains it forever; regardless of their actual task, cadres have the privileges of a higher social class, and it is very rare for a non-cadre to cross the ranks.

The conflict between French and American theories of management became apparent at the beginning of the twentieth century, in a criticism by the great French management pioneer Henri Fayol (1841–1925) on his US colleague and contemporary Frederick W. Taylor (1856–1915). The difference in career paths of the two men is striking. Fayol was a French engineer whose career as a *cadre supérieur* culminated in the position of Président-Directeur-Général of a mining company. After his retirement he formulated his experiences in a pathbreaking text on organization: *Administration industrielle et générale*, in which he focused on the sources of authority. Taylor was an American engineer who started his career in industry as a worker and attained his academic qualifications through evening studies. From chief engineer in a steel company, he became one of the first management consultants. Taylor was not really concerned with the issue of authority at all; his focus was on efficiency. He proposed to split the task of the first-line boss into eight specialisms, each exercised by a different person; an idea which eventually led to the idea of a matrix organization.

Taylor's work appeared in a French translation in 1913, and Fayol read it and showed himself generally impressed but shocked by Taylor's "denial of the principle of the Unity of Command" in the case of the eight-boss system.

Seventy years later André Laurent, another of Fayol's compatriots, found that French managers in a survey reacted very strongly against a suggestion that one employee could report to two different bosses, while US managers in the same survey showed fewer misgivings. Matrix organization has never become as popular in France as it has in the United States.

Holland

In my own country, Holland, or as it is officially called, the Netherlands, the study by Philippe d'Iribarne found the management principle to be a need for *consensus* among all parties, neither predetermined by a contractual relationship nor by class distinctions, but based on an open-ended exchange of views and a balancing of interests. In terms of the different origins of the word "manager," the organization in Holland is more *menage* (household), while in the United States it is more *manege* (horse drill).

At my university, the University of Limburg at Maastricht, every semester we receive a class of American business students who take a program in European studies. We asked both the Americans and a matched group of Dutch students to describe their ideal job after graduation, using a list of 22 job characteristics. The Americans attached significantly more importance than the Dutch to earnings, advancement, benefits, a good working relationship with their boss, and security of employment. The Dutch attached more importance to freedom to adopt their own approach to the job, being consulted by their boss in his or her decisions, training opportunities, contributing to the success of their organization, fully using their skills and abilities, and helping others. This list confirms d'Iribarne's findings of a contractual employment relationship in the United States, based on earnings and career opportunities, against a consensual relationship in Holland. The latter has centuries-old roots; the Netherlands were the first republic in Western Europe (1609–1810), and a model for the American republic. The country has been and still is governed by a careful balancing of interests in a multiparty system.

In terms of management theories, both motivation and leadership in Holland are different from what they are in the United States. Leadership in Holland presupposes modesty, as opposed to assertiveness in the United States. No US leadership theory has room for that. Working in Holland is not a constant feast, however. There is a built-in premium on mediocrity and jealousy, as well as time-consuming ritual consultations to maintain the appearance of consensus and the pretense of modesty. There is unfortunately another side to every coin.

The Overseas Chinese

Among the champions of economic development in the past 30 years, we find three countries mainly populated by Chinese living outside the Chinese mainland: Taiwan, Hong Kong, and Singapore. Moreover, overseas Chinese play a very important role in the economics of Indonesia, Malaysia, the Philippines, and Thailand, where they form an ethnic minority. If anything, the little dragons – Taiwan, Hong Kong, and Singapore – have been more economically successful than Japan, moving from rags to riches and now counted among the world's wealthy industrial countries. Yet very little attention has been paid to the way in which their enterprises have been managed. *The Spirit of Chinese Capitalism* by Gordon Redding (1990), the British dean of the Hong Kong Business School, is an excellent book about Chinese business. He bases his insights on personal acquaintance and in-depth discussions with a large number of overseas Chinese businesspeople.

Overseas Chinese-American enterprises lack almost all characteristics of modern management. They tend to be small, cooperating for essential functions with other small organizations through networks based on personal relations. They are family-owned, without the separation between ownership and management typical in the West, or even in Japan and Korea. They normally focus on one product or market, with growth by opportunistic diversification; in this, they are extremely flexible. Decision making is centralized in the hands of one dominant family member, but other family members may be given new ventures to try their skills on. They are low-profile and extremely cost-conscious, applying Confucian virtues of thrift and persistence. Their size is kept small by the assumed lack of loyalty of non-family employees, who, if they are any good, will just wait and save until they can start their own family business.

Overseas Chinese prefer economic activities in which great gains can be made with little manpower, like commodity trading and real estate. They employ few professional managers, except their sons and sometimes daughters who have been sent to prestigious business schools abroad, but who upon return continue to run the family business the Chinese way.

The origin of this system, or – in the Western view – this lack of system, is found in the history of Chinese society, in which there were no formal laws, only formal networks of powerful people guided by general principles of Confucian virtue. The favors of the authorities could change daily, so nobody could be trusted except one's kinfolk – of whom, fortunately, there used to be many, in an extended family structure. The overseas Chinese way of doing business is also very well adapted to their position in the countries in which they form ethnic minorities, often envied and threatened by ethnic violence.

Overseas Chinese businesses following this unprofessional approach command a collective gross national product of some 200 to 300 billion US dollars, exceeding the GNP of Australia. There is no denying that it works.

Management Transfer to Poor Countries

Four-fifths of the world population live in countries that are not rich but poor. After World War II and decolonization, the stated purpose of the United Nations and the World Bank has been to promote the development of all the world's countries in a war on poverty. After 40 years, it looks very much like we are losing this war. If one thing has become clear, it is that the export of Western – mostly American – management practices and theories to poor countries has contributed little or nothing to their development. There has been no lack of effort and money spent for this purpose: students from poor countries have been trained in this country, and teachers and Peace Corps workers have been sent to the poor countries. If nothing else, the general lack of success in economic development of other countries should be sufficient argument to doubt the validity of Western management theories in non-Western environments.

If we examine different parts of the world, the development picture is not equally bleak, and history is often a better predictor than economic factors for what happens today. There is a broad regional pecking order with East Asia leading. The little dragons have passed into the camp of the wealthy; then follow Southeast Asia (with its overseas Chinese minorities), Latin America (in spite of the debt crisis), South Asia, and Africa always trails behind. Several African countries have only become poorer since decolonization.

Regions of the world with a history of large-scale political integration and civilization generally have done better than regions in which no large-scale political and cultural infrastructure existed, even if the old civilizations had decayed or been suppressed by colonizers. It has become painfully clear that development cannot be pressure-cooked; it presumes a cultural infrastructure that takes time to grow. Local management is part of this infrastructure; it cannot be imported in package form. Assuming that with so-called modern management techniques and theories outsiders can develop a country has proven a deplorable arrogance. At best, one can hope for a dialogue between equals with the locals, in which the Western partner acts as the expert in Western technology and the local partner as the expert in local culture, habits, and feelings.

Russia and China

The crumbling of the former Eastern bloc has left us with a scattering of states and would-be states of which the political and economic future is extremely uncertain. The best predictions are those based on a knowledge of history, because historical trends have taken revenge on the arrogance of the Soviet rulers who believed they could turn them around by brute power. One obvious fact is that the former bloc is extremely heterogeneous, including countries traditionally closely linked with the West by trade and travel, like the Czech Republic, Hungary, Slovenia, and the Baltic states, as well as others with a Byzantine or Turkish past; some having been prosperous, others always extremely poor.

Let me limit myself to the Russian republic, a huge territory with some 140 million inhabitants, mainly Russians. We know quite a bit about the Russians as their country was a world power for several hundred years before communism, and in the nineteenth century it has produced some of the greatest writers in world literature. If I want to understand the Russians – including how they could so long support the Soviet regime – I tend to reread Lev Nikolayevich Tolstoy. In his most famous novel *Anna Karenina* (1876), one of the main characters is a landowner, Levin, whom Tolstoy uses to express his own views and convictions about his people. Russian peasants used to be serfs; serfdom had been abolished in 1861, but the peasants, now tenants, remained as passive as before. Levin wanted to break this passivity by dividing the land among his peasants in exchange for a share of the crops; but the peasants only let the land deteriorate further. Here follows a quote:

> (Levin) read political economy and socialistic works . . . but, as he had expected, found nothing in them related to his undertaking. In the political economy books – in [John Stuart] Mill, for instance, whom he studied first and with great ardour, hoping every minute to find an answer to the questions that were engrossing him – he found only certain laws deduced from the state of agriculture in Europe; but he could not for the life of him see why these laws, which did not apply to Russia, should be considered universal. . . . Political economy told him that the laws by which Europe had developed and was developing her wealth were universal and absolute. Socialist teaching told him that development along those lines leads to ruin. And neither of them offered the smallest enlightenment as to what he, Levin, and all the Russian peasants and landowners were to do with their millions of hands and millions of acres, to make them as productive as possible for the common good.

In the summer of 1991, the Russian lands yielded a record harvest, but a large share of it rotted in the fields because no people were to be found for harvesting. The passivity is still there, and not only among the peasants. And the heirs of John Stuart Mill (whom we met before as one of the early analysts of "management") again present their universal recipes which simply do not apply.

Citing Tolstoy, I implicitly suggest that management theorists cannot neglect the great literature of the countries they want their ideas to apply to. The greatest novel in the Chinese literature is considered Cao Xueqin's *The Story of the Stone*, also known as *The Dream of the Red Chamber*, which appeared around 1760. It describes the rise and fall of two branches of an aristocratic family in Beijing, who live in adjacent plots in the capital. Their plots are joined by a magnificent garden with several pavilions in it, and the young, mostly female members of both families are allowed to live in them. One day the management of the garden is taken over by a young woman, Tan-Chun, who states:

> I think we ought to pick out a few experienced trustworthy old women from among the ones who work in the Garden – women who know something about gardening already – and put the upkeep of the Garden into their hands. We needn't ask them to pay us rent; all we need ask them for is an annual share of the produce. There would be four advantages in this arrangement. In the first place, if we have people whose sole occupation is to look after trees and flowers and so on, the condition of the Garden will improve gradually year after year and there will be no more of those long periods of neglect followed by bursts of feverish activity when things have been allowed to get out of hand. Secondly, there won't be the spoiling and wastage we get at present. Thirdly, the women themselves will gain a little extra to add to their incomes which will compensate them for the hard work they put in throughout the year. And fourthly, there's no reason why we shouldn't use the money we should otherwise have spent on nurserymen, rockery specialists, horticultural cleaners, and so on for other purposes.

As the story goes on, the capitalist privatization – because that is what it is – of the Garden is carried through, and it works. When in the 1980s, Deng Xiaoping allowed privatization in the Chinese villages, it also worked. It worked so well that its effects started to be felt in politics and threatened the existing political order; hence the crackdown at Tienanmen Square of June 1989. But it seems that the forces of privatization are getting the upper hand again in China. If we remember what Chinese entrepreneurs are able to do once they have become overseas Chinese, we should not be too surprised. But what works in China – and worked two centuries ago – does not have to work in Russia, not in Tolstoy's days and not today. I am not offering a solution; I only protest against a naive universalism that knows only one recipe for development, the one supposed to have worked in the United States.

A Theory of Culture in Management

Our trip around the world is over and we are back in the United States. What have we learned? There is something in all countries called "management," but its meaning differs to a larger or smaller extent from one country to the other, and it takes considerable historical and cultural insight into local conditions to understand its processes, philosophies, and problems. If already the word may mean so many different things, how can we expect one country's theories of management to apply abroad? One should be extremely careful in making this assumption, and test it before considering it proven. Management is not a phenomenon that can be isolated from other processes taking place in a society. During our trip around the world, we saw that it interacts with what happens in the family, at school, in politics, and government. It is obviously also related to religion and to beliefs about science. Theories of management always had to be interdisciplinary, but if we cross national borders they should become more interdisciplinary than ever.

Cultural differences between nations can be, to some extent, described using first four, and now five, bipolar *dimensions*. The position of a country on these dimensions allows us to make some predictions of the way their society operates, including their management processes and the kind of theories applicable to their management.

As the word culture plays such an important role in my theory, let me give you my definition, which differs from some other very respectable definitions. Culture to me is *the collective programming of the mind which distinguishes one group or category of people from another.* In the part of my work I am referring to now, the category of people is the nation.

Culture is a *construct*, that means it is "not directly accessible to observation but inferable from verbal statements and other behaviors and useful in predicting still other observable and measurable verbal and non-verbal behavior." It should not be reified; it is an auxiliary concept that should be used as long as it proves useful but bypassed where we can predict behaviors without it.

The same applies to the *dimensions* I introduced. They are constructs too that should not be reified. They do not "exist;" they are tools for analysis which may or may not clarify a situation. In my statistical analysis of empirical data the first four dimensions together explain 49 percent of the variance in the data. The other 51 percent remain specific to individual countries.

The first four dimensions were initially detected through a comparison of the values of similar people (employees and managers) in 64 national subsidiaries of the IBM Corporation. People working for the same multinational, but in different countries, represent very well-matched samples from the populations of their countries, similar in all respects except nationality.

The first dimension is labelled *power distance*, and it can be defined as the degree of inequality among people which the population of a country considers as normal: from relatively equal (that is, small power distance) to extremely unequal (large power distance). All societies are unequal, but some are more unequal than others.

The second dimension is labelled *individualism*, and it is the degree to which people in a country prefer to act as individuals rather than as members of groups. The opposite of individualism can be called *collectivism*, so collectivism is low individualism. The way I use the word, it has no political connotations. In collectivist societies, a child learns to respect the group to which it belongs, usually the family, and to differentiate between in-group members and out-group members (that is, all other people). When children grow up they remain members of their group, and they expect the group to protect them when they are in trouble. In return, they have to remain loyal to their group throughout life. In individualist societies, a child learns very early to think of itself as "I" instead of as part of "we." It expects one day to have to stand on its own feet and not to get protection from its group any more; and therefore it also does not feel a need for strong loyalty.

The third dimension is called *masculinity* and its opposite pole *femininity*. It is the degree to which tough values like assertiveness, performance, success, and competition, which in nearly all societies are associated with the role of men, prevail over tender values like the quality of life, maintaining warm personal relationships, service, care for the weak, and solidarity, which in nearly all societies are more associated with women's roles. Women's roles differ from men's roles in all countries; but in tough societies, the differences are larger than in tender ones.

The fourth dimension is labelled *uncertainty avoidance*, and it can be defined as the degree to which people in a country prefer structured over unstructured situations. Structured situations are those in which there are clear rules as to how one should

TABLE 1 Culture dimension scores for ten countries

	PD	ID	MA	UA	LT
United States	40 L	91 H	62 H	46 L	29 L
Germany	35 L	67 H	66 H	65 M	31 M
Japan	54 M	46 M	95 H	92 H	80 H
France	68 H	71 H	43 M	86 H	30* L
Netherlands	38 L	80 H	14 L	53 M	44 M
Hong Kong	68 H	25 L	57 H	29 L	96 H
Indonesia	78 H	14 L	46 M	48 L	25 L
West Africa	77 H	20 L	46 M	54 M	16 L
Russia	95* H	50* M	40* L	90* H	10* L
China	80* H	20* L	50* M	60* M	118 H

* estimated

Note: PD = power distance; ID = individualism; MA = masculinity; UA = uncertainty avoidance; LT = long-term orientation; H = top third, M = medium third, L = bottom third (among 53 countries and regions for the first four dimensions; among 23 countries for the fifth).

behave. These rules can be written down, but they can also be unwritten and imposed by tradition. In countries which score high on uncertainty avoidance, people tend to show more nervous energy, while in countries which score low, people are more easy-going. A (national) society with strong uncertainty avoidance can be called rigid; one with weak uncertainty avoidance, flexible. In countries where uncertainty avoidance is strong a feeling prevails of "what is different is dangerous." In weak uncertainty avoidance societies, the feeling would rather be "what is different is curious."

The fifth dimension was added on the basis of a study of the values of students in 23 countries carried out by Michael Harris Bond, a Canadian working in Hong Kong. He and I had cooperated in another study of students' values which had yielded the same four dimensions as the IBM data. However, we wondered to what extent our common findings in two studies could be the effect of a Western bias introduced by the common Western background of the researchers: remember Alice's croquet game. Michael Bond resolved this dilemma by deliberately introducing an Eastern bias. He used a questionnaire prepared at his request by his Chinese colleagues, the *Chinese Value Survey* (CVS), which was translated from Chinese into different languages and answered by 50 male and 50 female students in each of 23 countries in all five continents. Analysis of the CVS data produced three dimensions significantly correlated with the three IBM dimensions of power distance, individualism, and masculinity. There was also a fourth dimension, but it did not resemble uncertainty avoidance. It was composed, both on the positive and on the negative side, from items that had not been included in the IBM studies but were present in the Chinese Value Survey because they were rooted in the teachings of Confucius. I labelled this dimension: *Long-term* versus *short-term orientation*. On the long-term side, one finds values oriented towards the future, like thrift (saving) and persistence. On the short-term side, one finds values rather oriented towards the past and present, like respect for tradition and fulfilling social obligations.

Table 1 lists the scores on all five dimensions for the United States and for the other countries we just discussed. The table shows that each country has its own configuration on the four dimensions. Some of the values in the table have been estimated based on imperfect replications or personal impressions. The different dimension scores do not "explain" all the differences in management I described earlier. To understand management in a country, one should have both knowledge of and empathy with the entire local scene. However, the scores should make us aware that people in other countries may think, feel, and act very differently from us when confronted with basic problems of society.

Idiosyncracies of American Management Theories

In comparison to other countries, the US culture profile presents itself as below average on power distance and uncertainty avoidance, highly individualistic, fairly masculine, and short-term oriented. The Germans show a stronger uncertainty avoidance and less extreme individualism; the Japanese are different on all dimensions, least on power distance; the French show larger power distance and uncertainty avoidance, but are less individualistic and somewhat feminine; the Dutch resemble the Americans on the first three dimensions, but score extremely feminine and relatively long-term oriented; Hong Kong Chinese combine large power distance with weak uncertainty avoidance, collectivism, and are very long-term oriented; and so on.

The American culture profile is reflected in American management theories. I will just mention three elements not necessarily present in other countries: the stress on market processes; the stress on the individual; and the focus on managers rather than on workers.

The Stress on Market Processes

During the 1970s and 80s it has become fashionable in the United States to look at organizations from a "transaction costs" viewpoint. Economist Oliver Williamson has opposed "hierarchies" to "markets." The reasoning is that human social life consists of economic transactions between individuals. We found the same in d'Iribarne's description of the US principle of the contract between employer and employee, the labor market in which the worker sells his or her labor for a price. These individuals will form hierarchical organizations when the cost of the economic transactions (such as getting information, finding out whom to trust, and so on) is lower in a hierarchy than when all transactions would take place in a free market.

From a cultural perspective the important point is that the *"market" is the point of departure or base model*, and the organization is explained from market failure. A culture that produces such a theory is likely to prefer organizations that internally resemble markets to organizations that internally resemble more structured models, like those in Germany or France. The ideal principle of control in organizations in the market philosophy is *competition* between individuals. This philosophy fits a society that combines a not-too-large power distance with a not-too-strong uncertainty avoidance and individualism; besides the United States, it will fit all other Anglo countries.

The Stress on the Individual

I find this constantly in the design of research projects and hypotheses; also in the fact that in the US psychology is clearly a more respectable discipline in management circles than sociology. Culture however is a collective phenomenon. Although we may get our information about culture from individuals, we have to interpret it at the level of collectivities. There are snags here known as the "ecological fallacy" and the "reverse ecological fallacy." None of the US college textbooks on methodology I know deals sufficiently with the problem of multilevel analysis.

A striking example is found in the otherwise excellent book *Organizational Culture and Leadership* by Edgar H. Schein (1985). On the basis of his consulting experience, he compares two large companies, nicknamed "Action" and "Multi." He explains the differences in culture between these companies by the group dynamics in their respective boardrooms. Nowhere in the book are any conclusions drawn from the fact that the first company is an American-based computer firm, and the second a Swiss-based pharmaceutics firm. This information is not even mentioned. A stress on interactions among individuals obviously fits a culture identified as the most individualistic in the world, but it will not be so well understood by the four-fifths of the world population for whom the group prevails over the individual.

One of the conclusions of my own multilevel research has been that culture at the national level and culture at the organizational level – corporate culture – are two very different phenomena and that the use of a common term for both is confusing. If we do use the common term, we should also pay attention to the occupational and the gender level of culture. National cultures differ primarily in the fundamental, invisible values held by a majority of their members, acquired in early childhood, whereas organizational cultures are a much more superficial phenomenon residing mainly in the visible practices of the organization, acquired by socialization of the new members who join as young adults. National cultures change only very slowly if at all; organizational cultures may be consciously changed, although this is not necessarily easy. This difference between the two types of culture is the secret of the existence of multinational corporations that employ, as I showed in the IBM case, employees with extremely different national cultural values. What keeps them together is a corporate culture based on common practices.

The Stress on Managers Rather than Workers

The core element of a work organization around the world is the people who do the work. All the rest is superstructure, and I hope to have demonstrated to you that it may take many different shapes. In the US literature on work organization, however, the core element, if not explicitly then implicitly, is considered the manager. This may well be the result of the combination of extreme individualism with fairly strong masculinity, which has turned the manager into a culture hero of almost mythical proportions. For example, he – not really she – is supposed to make decisions all the time. Those of you who are or have been managers must know that this is a fable. Very few management decisions are just "made" as the myth suggests it. Managers are much more involved in maintaining networks; if anything, it is the rank-and-file worker who can really make decisions on his or her own, albeit on a relatively simple level.

An amusing effect of the US focus on managers is that in at least ten American books and articles on management I have been misquoted as having studied IBM *managers* in my research, whereas the book clearly describes that the answers were from IBM *employees*. My observation may be biased, but I get the impression that compared to 20 or 30 years ago less research in this country is done among employees and more on managers. But managers derive their *raison d'être* from the people managed: culturally, they are the followers of the people they lead, and their effectiveness depends on the latter. In other parts of the world, this exclusive focus on the manager is less strong, with Japan as the supreme example.

Conclusion

This article started with *Alice in Wonderland.* In fact, the management theorist who ventures outside his or her own country into other parts of the world is like Alice in Wonderland. He or she will meet strange beings, customs, ways of organizing or dis-organizing, and theories that are clearly stupid, old-fashioned, or even immoral – yet they may work, or at least they may not fail more frequently than corresponding theories do at home. Then, after the first culture shock, the traveller to Wonderland will feel en-lightened, and may be able to take his or her experiences home and use them advant-ageously. All great ideas in science, politics, and management have travelled from one country to another, and been enriched by foreign influences. The roots of American management theories are mainly in Europe: with Adam Smith, John Stuart Mill, Lev Tolstoy, Max Weber, Henri Fayol, Sigmund Freud, Kurt Lewin, and many others. These theories were replanted here, and they developed and bore fruit. The same may happen again. The last thing we need is a Monroe doctrine for management ideas.

Table, Figures 5, 6 and 7, and Exhibit 2

Geert Hofstede

	The 40 countries (showing abbreviations used in Figures 5, 6 and 7)				
ARG	Argentina	HOK	Hong Kong	PHI	Philippines
AUL	Australia	IND	India	POR	Portugal
AUT	Austria	IRA	Iran	SAF	South Africa
BEL	Belgium	IRE	Ireland	SIN	Singapore
BRA	Brazil	ISR	Israel	SPA	Spain
CAN	Canada	ITA	Italy	SWE	Sweden
CHL	Chile	JAP	Japan	SWI	Switzerland
COL	Colombia	MEX	Mexico	TAI	Taiwan
DEN	Denmark	NET	Netherlands	THA	Thailand
FIN	Finland	NOR	Norway	TUR	Turkey
FRA	France	NZL	New Zealand	USA	United States
GBR	Great Britain	PAK	Pakistan	VEN	Venezuela
GER	Germany (West)	PER	Peru	YUG	Yugoslavia
GRE	Greece				

From "Motivation, Leadership and Organization: Do American Theories Apply Abroad?" by Geert Hofstede, *Organizational Dynamics*, Summer 1980, pp. 42–63.

FIGURE 5 The Position of the 40 Countries on the Power Distance and Uncertainty Avoidance Scales
Power Distance Index

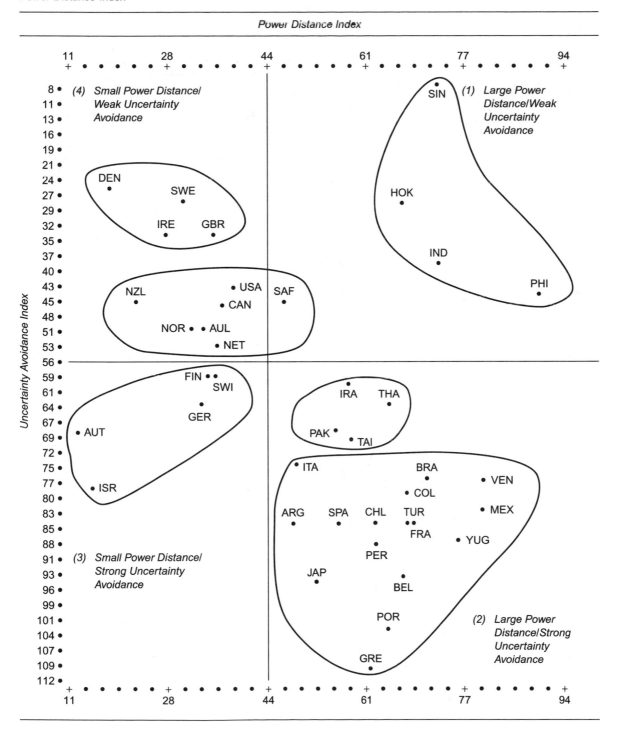

FIGURE 6 The Position of the 40 Countries on the Power Distance and Individualism Scales
Power Distance Index

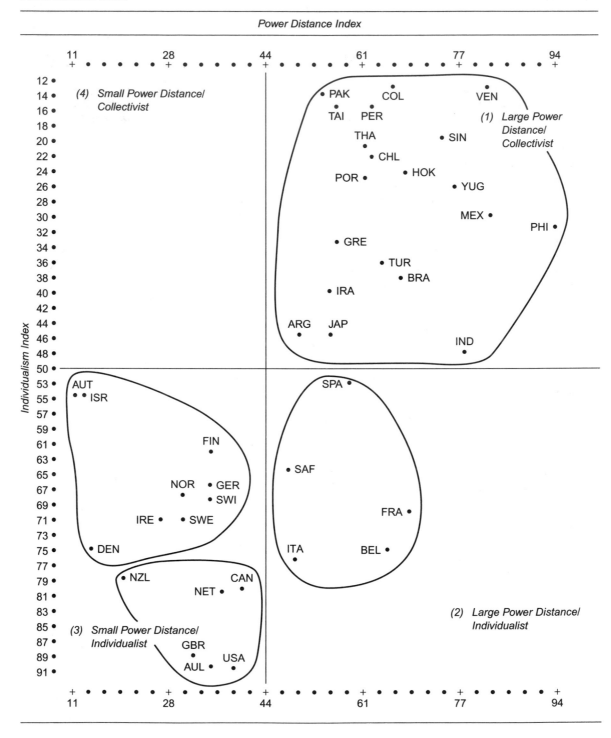

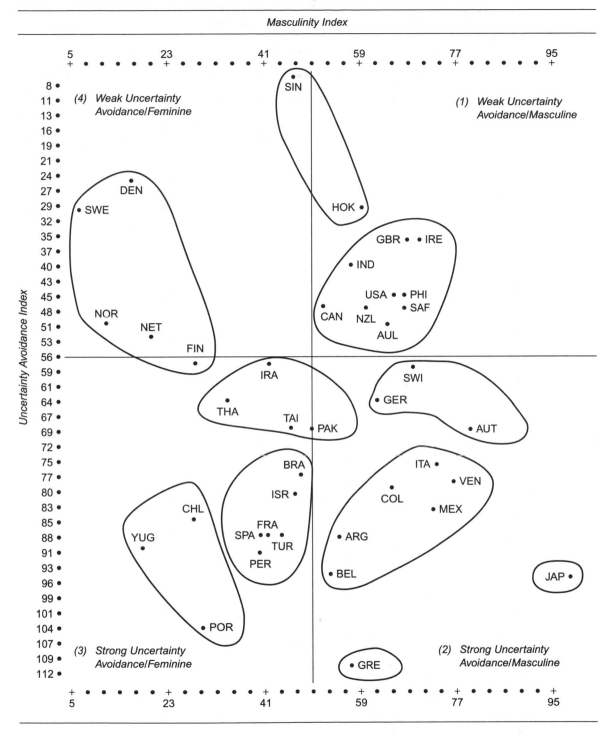

FIGURE 7 The Position of the 40 Countries on the Uncertainty Avoidance and Masculinity Scales

EXHIBIT 2 Scores on Five Dimensions for Fifty Countries and Three Regions in IBM's International Employee Attitude Survey

Country	Power Distance		Individualism		Masculinity		Uncertainty Avoidance		Confucian Dynamism	
	Index	Rank	Index	Rank	Index	Rank	Index	Rank	Index	Rank
Argentina	49	35–36	46	22–23	56	20–21	86	10–15		
Australia	36	41	90	2	61	16	51	37	31	11–12
Austria	11	53	55	18	79	2	70	24–25		
Belgium	65	20	75	8	54	22	94	5–6		
Brazil	69	14	38	26–27	49	27	76	21–22	65	5
Canada	39	39	80	4–5	52	24	48	41–42	23	17
Chile	63	24–25	23	38	28	46	86	10–15		
Colombia	67	17	13	49	64	11–12	80	20		
Costa Rica	35	42–44	15	46	21	48–49	86	10–15		
Denmark	18	51	74	9	16	50	23	51		
Equador	78	8–9	8	52	63	13–14	67	28		
Finland	33	46	63	17	26	47	59	31–32		
France	68	15–16	71	10–11	43	35–36	86	10–15		
Germany (F.R.)	35	42–44	67	15	66	9–10	65	29	31	11–12
Great Britain	35	42–44	89	3	66	9–10	35	47–48	25	15–16
Greece	60	27–28	35	30	57	18–19	112	1		
Guatemala	95	2–3	6	53	37	43	101	3		
Hong Kong	68	15–16	25	37	57	18–19	29	49–50	96	1
Indonesia	78	8–9	14	47–48	46	30–31	48	41–42		
India	77	10–11	48	21	56	20–21	40	45	61	6
Iran	58	19–20	41	24	43	35–36	59	31–32		
Ireland	28	49	70	12	68	7–8	35	47–48		
Israel	13	52	54	19	47	29	81	19		
Italy	50	34	76	7	70	4–5	75	23		
Jamaica	45	37	39	25	68	7–8	13	52		
Japan	54	33	46	22–23	95	1	92	7	80	3
Korea (S)	60	27–28	18	43	39	41	85	16–17	75	4
Malaysia	104	1	26	36	50	25–26	36	46		
Mexico	81	5–6	30	32	69	6	82	18		
Netherlands	38	40	80	4–5	14	51	53	35	44	9
Norway	31	47–48	69	13	8	52	50	38		
New Zealand	22	50	79	6	58	17	49	39–40	30	13
Pakistan	55	32	14	47–48	50	25–26	70	24–25	0	20
Panama	95	2–3	11	51	44	34	86	10–15		
Peru	64	21–23	16	45	42	37–38	87	9		
Philippines	94	4	32	31	64	11–12	44	44	19	18
Portugal	63	24–25	27	33–35	31	45	104	2		
South Africa	49	36–37	65	16	63	13–14	49	39–40		
Salvador	66	18–19	19	42	40	40	94	5–6		
Singapore	74	13	20	39–41	48	28	8	53	48	8
Spain	57	31	51	20	42	37–38	86	10–15		
Sweden	31	47–48	71	10–11	5	52	29	49–50	33	10
Switzerland	34	45	68	14	70	4–5	58	33		
Taiwan	58	29–30	17	44	45	32–33	69	26	87	2
Thailand	64	21–23	20	39–41	34	44	64	30	56	7
Turkey	66	18–19	37	28	45	31–33	85	16–17		
Uruguay	61	26	36	29	38	42	100	4		

EXHIBIT 2 *(cont'd)*

Country	Power Distance		Individualism		Masculinity		Uncertainty Avoidance		Confucian Dynamism	
	Index	*Rank*	*Index*	*Rank*	*Index*	*Rank*	*Index*	*Rank*	*Index*	*Rank*
United States	40	38	91	1	62	15	46	43	29	14
Venezuela	81	5–6	12	50	73	3	76	21–22		
Yugoslavia	76	12	27	33–35	21	48–49	88	8		
Regions:										
East Africa	64	21–23	27	33–35	41	39	52	36	25	15–16
West Africa	77	10–11	20	39–41	46	30–31	54	34	15	19
Arab Ctrs.	80	7	38	26–27	53	23	68	27		

Rank Numbers: 1 = Highest; 53 = Lowest (For Confucian Dynamism: 20 = Lowest)
From "The Confucius Connection: From Cultural Roots to Economic Growth", G. Hofstede and M. H. Bond, *Organizational Dynamics*, Vol. 16, No. 4, pp. 4–21.

READING **4**

Developing Leaders for the Global Frontier

Hal B. Gregersen, Allen J. Morrison, and J. Stewart Black

Imagine the experiences of explorers such as Magellan or Cook as they scanned the horizon of the great Pacific Ocean for days; they had no reliable charts, an unfamiliar hemisphere of stars, shark-infested waters, a crew losing confidence with each passing day, storm clouds gathering in the distance, waves crashing over the ship's bow, and wind howling. In many ways, the new business world is just as dangerous, filled with brutal storms of competitors, endless seas of change, seemingly strange cultures, confusing marketing channels, and unknown frontiers of technology.

The great difference, however, is that only a few great and courageous explorers were needed in the days of Magellan. Once the seas and their islands were charted, the coordinates didn't change. In contrast, the islands, mountains, rivers, and valleys of today's global business world are not static; they change. Markets, suppliers, competitors, technology, and customers are constantly shifting. Consequently, global business now requires all leaders to be explorers, guided by only the faintest glimmer of unfamiliar stars and excited by the opportunity and uncertainty of untapped markets.

At current growth rates, trade *between* nations will exceed total commerce *within* nations by 2015.[1] In industries such as semiconductors, automobiles, commercial aircraft, telecommunications, computers, and consumer electronics, it is impossible to survive and not scan the world for competitors, customers, human resources, suppliers, and technology.

These forces of change help explain why leadership models of the past will not work in a global future. Provincial Japanese models of leadership have worked in Japan because Japanese leaders largely interacted with other Japanese. The same has been true for American, German, or French leadership models. In the future, a new breed of leader will be needed. Recently, Jack Welch, CEO of General Electric, commented:

Reprinted from "Developing Leaders for the Global Frontier," by Hal B. Gregersen, Allen J. Morrison, and J. Stewart Black, *Sloan Management Review*, Fall 1998, pp. 21–32, by permission of publisher. Copyright 1999 by the Sloan Management Review Association. All rights reserved.

Description of Research

We conducted our research from 1994 through 1997 in two separate efforts:

First, we interviewed 130 executives in fifty firms across Europe (fifteen firms), North America (twenty-five firms), and Asia (ten firms). Of these interviews, ninety were with senior executives. We asked the executives to identify someone in their company who is "an exemplar of future global leadership – whom senior management saw as clearly being given global leadership responsibilities and who would serve as a role model of global leadership to others in the future." We conducted interviews with forty such leaders. In all 130 interviews, we asked two questions: (1) What are the key characteristics of effective global leaders? (2) What are the key means of developing these characteristics?

Second, we sent a survey to human resource managers responsible for executive development in US *Fortune* 500 firms in 1997. We received usable surveys from 108 firms. The survey asked about (1) the importance of global leadership compared to other resources (e.g., financial), (2) the quantity and quality of their global leaders, (3) the importance of global leadership characteristics (identified in the interviews described above), and (4) their current and future development efforts.

"The Jack Welch of the future cannot be like me. I spent my entire career in the United States. The next head of General Electric will be somebody who spent time in Bombay, in Hong Kong, in Buenos Aires. We have to send our best and brightest overseas and make sure they have the training that will allow them to be the global leaders who will make GE flourish in the future."[2]

Most companies lack an adequate number of globally competent executives. Based on the results of a three-year study, we found that almost all companies claim that they need more global leaders, and most want future global leaders of higher caliber and quality (*see the sidebar for details on the study*).

Of the US *Fortune* 500 firms we surveyed. 85 percent do not think they have an adequate number of global leaders (*see figure 1*); 67 percent of the firms think that their existing leaders need additional skills and knowledge before they meet or exceed needed capabilities. Jack Riechert, recently retired CEO of Brunswick Corporation, reflects the sentiments of many senior executives we interviewed: "Financial resources are not the problem. We have the money, products, and position to be a dominant global player. What we lack are the human resources. We just don't have enough people with the needed global leadership capabilities."

Another aspect of our survey is the high rating of global leadership compared to other factors in a company's global business success (*see* table 1).

Characteristics of Global Leaders

As multinational firms compete in the unpredictable business frontier, they must confront two persistent, perplexing questions:

1. What are the characteristics of leaders who can guide organizations that span diverse countries, cultures, and customers?
2. How can companies effectively develop these leaders?

FIGURE 1   Quantity and Quality of Global Leaders*

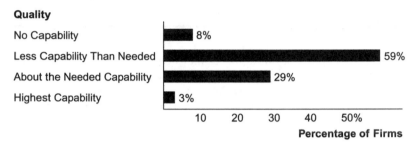

How many global leaders do firms have?

Quantity

Nowhere Near Enough	29%
Fewer Than We Need	56%
About the Number We Need	13%
More Than Enough	2%

Percentage of Firms

How capable are global leaders?

Quality

No Capability	8%
Less Capability Than Needed	59%
About the Needed Capability	29%
Highest Capability	3%

Percentage of Firms

* Based on survey of US *Fortune* 500 firms in 1997.

TABLE 1   Importance of global leadership compared to other needs*

Dimension	Average Rating
Competent Global Leaders	6.1
Adequate Financial Resources	5.9
Improved International Communication Technology	5.1
Higher Quality Local National Workforce	5.0
Greater Political Stability in Developing Countries	4.7
Greater National Government Support of Trade	4.5
Lower Tariff/Trade Restrictions in Other Countries	4.4

1 = Not at all important; 7 = Extremely important
* Based on survey of US *Fortune* 500 firms in 1997.

Our research revealed that every global leader needs a set of context-specific abilities and must have a core of certain characteristics. Roughly one-third of global business leaders' success depends on the knowledge and skills for specific contexts. For example, corporate cultures, industry dynamics, and "country of origin" management practices can permeate a company's worldwide operations and require unique knowledge and skills for successful leadership. About two-thirds of the characteristics apply generically to leaders, regardless of their managerial position, corporate culture, industry norms, or country-of-origin management practices. These general global leadership characteristics include exhibiting character, embracing duality, and demonstrating savvy. Most important, the leaders in our study saw inquisitiveness as the force underlying these characteristics.

Unbridled Inquisitiveness

While all leaders have substantial intelligence, all are not necessarily inquisitive. Constantly crossing cultural, language, political, social, and economic borders makes global business complex and uncertain. As a consequence, constant learning is required for success. Global business is physically taxing on managers. Travel, jet lag, and working in different languages and across different cultures can be tiring. For unsuccessful leaders, these aspects are just too overwhelming. Successful leaders are invigorated by the differences around them. They are driven by a sense of adventure and a desire to see and experience new things.

When studying individuals on international assignments, researchers have found this same characteristic to be important in cross-cultural adjustment and job performance.[3] They have called it adventuresomeness, curiosity, or open-mindedness. While international assignment responsibilities are not the same as global leadership, it does seem that whether a manager is crossing one country border or many, inquisitiveness is key to success (*see the sidebar on Mikell Rigg McGuire*).

Global leaders stated repeatedly that inquisitiveness is the fuel for increasing their global savvy, enhancing their ability to understand people and maintain integrity, and augmenting their capacity for dealing with uncertainty and managing tensions. Inquisitiveness enables global leaders to not only develop the characteristics of character, duality, and savvy, but also build a complex understanding of how all three work together.

Inquisitiveness: Mikell Rigg McGuire

In one of the fastest growing divisions of Franklin-Covey (the result of a merger of Franklin Quest and the Covey Leadership Center), Mikell Rigg McGuire, age thirty-five, vice president of international, deals with operations in more than sixty countries. Although she is constantly traveling with her team, rather than being stressed by the travel, she is invigorated. Before going overseas, McGuire watches international news networks and reads international magazines; she collects books and articles on the specific place she is to visit. She talks to friends who might know people in the country and calls them up to ask if they can help her understand the country. They might send her a book on art, for example, which "reflects what is important to them about the country," she commented. She continues to learn as she travels to "get that feel for the place."

On a recent assignment, her team committed to spending at least one evening out on each leg of the trip to explore the culture. They wanted to "take in a piece or flavor of that country to experience it." Sometimes they stayed in traditional local hotels, instead of generic American ones. McGuire's approach to building inquisitiveness into Franklin-Covey rests on this assumption:

> "It is pretty tough to create open-mindedness. It almost starts from infancy and increases from all your experiences. Instead, I prefer building a team of people who show a nugget of inquisitiveness and open-mindedness. Then, you mentor them. It is an ongoing process to build these capabilities, not something that happens overnight."

Personal Character

From our interviews, we determined that personal character involves two components: emotionally connecting with people from various backgrounds and exhibiting uncompromising integrity.

Emotional Connection

A genuine emotional connection with people throughout the company's worldwide operations is a function of a three-step process: (1) a sincere interest in and concern for others; (2) an effort to really listen to people; and (3) an understanding of different viewpoints. Leaders in the survey pointed out that understanding different viewpoints is *not* the same as embracing them but does lead to respecting them.[4] This process is particularly challenging when cultural and language differences confound communication. Ample opportunity exists for misunderstanding and taking and giving offense. Without the ability to connect with individuals, cultural diversity becomes a huge obstacle to effective leadership.

In the literature on expatriates, we have found similar concepts. For example, willingness to communicate with host country nationals has been found to facilitate the cross-cultural adjustment of expatriates.[5] Ethnocentricity and sociability also relate to making connections across cultures and have been discussed extensively in the literature.[6]

Fundamentally, emotional connection is important because it leads to goodwill. In turn, employees give leaders the benefit of the doubt on difficult matters, put forth their best efforts, and make sacrifices. In global organizations with webs of interrelated units that must cooperate and coordinate to meet customer needs, goodwill – rather than clear lines of command and control – is what leaders need to achieve global initiatives (*see the sidebar on Jon Huntsman*).

Integrity

Executives described integrity in terms of ethical behavior and loyalty to the company's agreed-on values and strategy. Both personal and company standards are substantially more prone to compromise overseas.[7] When far removed from corporate oversight, managers are often tempted to change themselves and their organizations to appeal to local values and demands. Yet despite the opportunities for short-term advantage, the global leaders we studied were most effective when they consistently maintained the highest ethical standards in personal and company matters. Successful global leaders indicated that integrity significantly increased the overall levels of trust throughout the organization. They pointed out that when crossing cultural, national, functional, and business unit lines, trust is an essential, irreplaceable ingredient for effective execution. They were quick to add that quite often the difference between winners and losers in global competition is great execution, not great strategy, and added that for great execution, you need employees' trust and commitment.

Connection: Jon Huntsman, Jr.

Jon Huntsman, Jr., thirty-nine, is vice chairman of Huntsman Corporation, a firm started by his father in 1970. Huntsman is the largest privately held chemical manufacturing company in the United States, with annual worldwide sales approaching $6 billion and 7,000 employees in twenty-one countries.

Despite huge responsibilities, Huntsman works hard to stay connected to his employees. In his interview, he pointed out that his company was built on acquisitions that resulted from the failures of such giants as Shell, Texaco, Monsanto, Eastman Chemical, and Hoechst Celanese. According to Huntsman, these failures occurred in part because their leaders failed to connect with employees and inspire commitment. To stay connected to employees, Huntsman and a team of senior executives visit each of the company's facilities every December and meet every employee in its plants worldwide. Huntsman commented:

"In December, we are gone every single day before Christmas. We visit every Huntsman factory, every facility around the world. We shake everyone's hand. We talk to every spouse and child and learn about what they are doing. Where are you going to school? What do you like doing? Is your family happy? What can we do for you? We also give them each a holiday gift. Maybe it's a television, or a stereo, or a cruise. We want them to know how much we appreciate them. We want to make our employees feel they are the most important people in the universe. We honestly believe this.

"Making these visits is never easy. We are gone the entire month. But I love the visits. We all derive incredible energy from them. We love the people."

Huntsman's ability to connect emotionally with employees stems from his sincere interest in them. His curiosity about their culture and their personal circumstances allows him to truly understand their capabilities, motivation, and values. This connection brings huge rewards to the company and creates goodwill where insights and ideas percolate up from the factory floor. He remarked:

"Making these visits lets us connect with our people personally. We believe that the best ideas come from the factory floor. When people have met me, shaken my hand, and talked to me, they feel they know me. I challenge them by saying, 'Here is my number. If you have a good idea, a way to work more efficiently, call me.' And they do!"

They felt that their high level of inquisitiveness actually facilitated their ability to maintain ethical integrity. All acknowledged that definitions of allowable ethical behavior varied from country to country. However, their inquisitiveness led them to probe below the surface, deep into people's ethical values. For example, one manager made the following observation: "It's true that practices differ from one country to another. 'Gifts' might be more or less accepted from one country to another. However, around the world, employees and customers alike trust managers who conduct business above board and on the basis of business merit" (*see the sidebar on Lane Cook*).

Duality

Global leaders embrace duality by managing uncertainty, essentially knowing when to act and when to gather more information, and balancing tensions, understanding what needs to change and what needs to stay the same from country to country and region to region.

Integrity: Lane Cook

In 1994, DSL, a $200 million California-based international shipping company, hired Lane Cook to work in its new Mexico City office. DSL has facilities throughout the United States as well as Hong Kong, Taiwan, Korea, China, and Singapore. It focuses on consolidated shipments for the retail industry and considers major retailers like Wal-Mart, Sears, Target, and J. C. Penney its main customers.

DSL de Mexico had been through tough times, including the dramatic devaluation of the peso against the US dollar and the loss of a major US customer that decided to build its own distribution and warehouse facility in Mexico, only 1.5 miles from DSL's building. With so much unused capacity and costs already cut to the bone, Cook was under enormous pressure to raise revenues. He believed that the key to growth was developing local business.

In 1996, Cook had nearly completed negotiations on an agreement with a medium-sized, Mexico City-based general merchandise retailer, SuperMart (a disguised name). SuperMart was to take possession of the goods in Asia and contract with DSL to ship them to Mexico via the United States. Normally, DSL would have selected the transportation company to bring the freight from the US border to Mexico City, but, in this case, the negotiator for SuperMart, Jose Hernandez (a disguised name) would sign the agreement only if he could select the Mexican transportation company. According to Cook:

> "I thought this was a little peculiar. I was even more concerned when I later heard a rumor that Hernandez had a bank account here in Mexico City as well as a bank account in Laredo, Texas, and that the trucking company he selected had promised to make a payment to his US bank account whenever a shipment was made. The Laredo bank would then wire the money to Hernandez's Mexico City account.
>
> "I had a choice. On the one hand, I could just ignore the rumors and sign the deal. We needed the business, but if the rumors were true, we weren't paying these kickbacks. Or I could investigate and ask Hernandez about the whole thing.
>
> "As I checked into it, it seemed okay, but I approached Hernandez anyway. When I did, he denied the rumor categorically. Yes, he had a bank account in Laredo, but so did many wealthier Mexicans who worried about the stability of the peso. Quite frankly, I think he was a little offended that I raised the issue, but we were able to work it out."

Cook was guided in his decision making by his commitment to three principles: first, that he was morally obligated to ensure that customers were not being cheated; second, that he not engage in any activities that reflected negatively on his company, either in Mexico or elsewhere; and third, that his peers and superiors would approve his actions. DSL de Mexico is now highly favored by sophisticated local and international retailers wanting a shipper that provides high-quality, ethical service worldwide.

Capacity for Managing Uncertainty

At the heart of any multinational, uncertainty reigns supreme, and successful leaders have a capacity for managing in changing conditions. In the global business arena, they confront a dearth of quality data and a staggering number of questions; for example: What is a country's real market potential? Is this country a good platform for global operations? How secure is the local currency? How long will it take to train local managers? While purely domestic executives face some of these same questions, the degree of uncertainty that global managers face is exponentially higher. The recent Asian financial and currency crisis underscores this point.

Once again in the literature on expatriates, we find an interesting parallel in terms of this characteristic for managing uncertainty. Researchers discuss the characteristic less

---

Managing Uncertainty: Gary Griffiths

Marriott Corporation assigned Gary Griffiths to the position of director of finance when it opened its first hotel in Poland – the Warsaw Marriott. From the outset, Griffiths faced an endless stream of significant challenges everyday. One was setting up a bank account in Poland. After calling the local bank that planned to open a branch in the hotel complex, Griffith discussed the account with the bank's vice president, who answered, "I understand what you need, but we do not have room in our system for your accounts until we open our new branch in six months. I'm sorry, but we can't help you." Then the bank vice president continued, "I can't open a business account for your company, but let me open a personal account for you." Griffiths called the treasurer of Marriott in the United States to announce that he was ready for the first transfer of cash to the hotel, $200,000. The treasurer answered, "Terrific! Give me the name on the account." Griffiths hesitantly responded, "Gary Griffiths." There was a long pause on the other end of the line.

The funds were ultimately transferred to Griffiths' personal bank account, but they were declared "missing" in the bank's system for fifty-six days, and the Warsaw Marriott still had no operating cash. Griffiths drove to Austria and picked up US $25,000 cash at the Vienna Marriott and brought it back to Poland. Re-entering Poland alone with the money, Griffiths was extremely nervous, because he had to declare to a border guard with a machine gun that he was transporting $25,000, more than fifty years of wages for the guard. Griffiths made it through safely, returned to the hotel, and deposited the money, directly into his personal account.

After living through this and other experiences filled with endless uncertainty, Griffiths concluded:

"Things are not the same when you get out there in the world. You have to be willing to understand new environments and figure out how to deal with them. You have to learn to improvise. You must be ready to change how you do business. You must relish the uncertainty of it all."

---

in terms of management and more in terms of tolerance. In fact, most studies referred to tolerance for ambiguity. Research on expatriates has found that crossing from one's home culture into a foreign one creates significant uncertainty and that those who have a reasonably high tolerance for ambiguity tend to cope and adjust better.[8]

In the global arena where uncertainty can come from not just one country but a dozen or more at a time, many managers may be tempted to do more research, which they believe will reduce the risk of poor decisions.[9] Yet, in many parts of the world and for many products, collecting accurate data sometimes takes so long that the data are useless by the time they are available. Furthermore, in today's hypercompetitive business environment, waiting for clarity works only if everyone else also waits. While global leaders allow time for research, they do not allow the search for clarity to jeopardize first-mover advantages. They quickly separate the "figure from background" and do not wait for the entire picture to come into focus before moving ahead. They know that speed and a capacity for uncertainty are tightly intertwined (*see the sidebar on Gary Griffiths*).

Unique Ability to Balance Tensions

In addition to uncertainty, managers must balance various tensions as they confront the pressures for both global integration and local responsiveness. Successful leaders indicated that it is generally a mistake to either globalize or localize *all* activities.[10] Rather, some activities like R&D may be most appropriately carried out worldwide, while other activities such as advertising and promotion may be best carried out locally or regionally. These leaders stressed that the perspective should not be one of just tolerating tensions but of embracing their inherent duality. A global executive with an engineering background commented:

> "If you design a bridge to be completely rigid, it will collapse. If you let it swing freely, no one will be able to use it. Oscillation within a range is good and necessary for the bridge to function. The same is true for global organizations and leaders. That is why effective global leaders embrace duality and tensions."

These tensions include product standardization versus local adaptation, headquarters' management style versus the subsidiary's approach, corporate labor relations policies versus host country norms, and global brand image versus local consumer preferences. Embracing duality requires leaders to view tensions as necessary *and* good (*see the sidebar on Stephen Burke*).

Savvy

Because globalization increases both the opportunities for business and the challenges in getting things done, leaders need to be more savvy, much like a high-hurdle runner needs the ability to jump higher than a low-hurdle runner. In our research, we found two dimensions: business savvy and organizational savvy.

Business Savvy

Global business savvy enables managers to recognize worldwide market opportunities. They either locate new markets for the company's goods and services or gain more efficient access to the company's existing markets. To recognize new market opportunities, to arbitrage opportunities involving cost and quality differences across company affiliates, and to maximize efficiencies by reducing redundancies, global leaders must understand competitive conditions.[11] Leaders know the sources and location of comparative advantage, country-specific conditions, countries' political and financial stability, and so on. They also understand international disciplines, such as finance, accounting, marketing, operations, human resource management, and strategy. They comprehend issues that domestic-oriented leaders just don't have to face – such as how real movements in exchange rates can create opportunities to (1) lower prices and increase market share while keeping profit margins stable, or (2) keep prices and market share constant and reap additional profits (*see the sidebar on Steve Holliday*).[12]

Organizational Savvy

Global leaders have intimate knowledge of their firms' capabilities *and* their ability to mobilize resources to capture market opportunities. They know the strengths and

Balancing Tensions: Stephen Burke

Stephen Burke, age thirty-nine, was president of broadcasting for ABC, part of Disney's recent ABC/Capital Cities acquisition. In 1992, Michael Eisner, CEO of the Walt Disney Company, asked Burke to take the position of vice president in charge of park operations and marketing at EuroDisneyland.

EuroDisneyland, a (quasi) joint venture between Disney and the French government, opened in April 1992 amid a storm of bad publicity. From the beginning, the project was beset with problems:

- Attendance was off 10 percent from projections.
- Per-person spending in the park was less than half that in Japan.
- Hotel occupancy rates were 37 percent versus 92 percent in Disney's US properties.
- Labor costs were significantly higher than those in the United States because of the inability to dramatically increase and decrease staff during peak and off seasons.
- Negative publicity and headlines abounded, like "Disney Is Cultural Chernobyl."
- Protests from French farmers continued because of the French government's appropriation of farm land for the Disney theme park.
- Some workers resisted the Disney management style and dress code.
- Construction cost overruns were nearly $2 billion.
- Operating losses were approaching $1 billion.

Burke and the local management team faced the task of devising and implementing strategic changes that would ensure growth and financial health. The first significant change was renaming the park. "Euro" seemed more like a chemical mix of unnatural ingredients than a place. Yet the name "Disneyland" was magical. Burke remarked: "With Disneyland, you get a magical place, and everybody loves Paris. By including 'Paris' in the name, the French would be more receptive. Also, by definition, we can tie the park to the city in our marketing and advertising campaigns."

After changing the park's name to Disneyland Paris, Burke continued to struggle with a central challenge: How to make the park profitable and strike a balance between Disney tradition and local culture? In the end, to retain the Disney image, Burke:

- Improved hiring to focus on outgoing, friendly Disney cast members.
- Increased training to emphasize and teach friendly service and cleanliness.
- Introduced seasonal pricing for entry to the park.
- Used traditional Disney characters throughout the park.

To adapt Disney to French culture, Burke:

- Removed the ban on alcohol in the theme parks.
- Lowered customary Disney premium prices by 20 percent to 30 percent on admission, merchandise, hotels, and food.
- Relaxed Disney's normal hierarchical managerial style and encouraged more individual initiative.
- Cut managerial staff by almost 1,000.

These and other changes had a positive impact on the park's financial results. Attendance figures rose about 17 percent. Hotel occupancy rates went up, and the hotels were fully booked during peak times. People spent more money in the park. In the third quarter of the 1995 fiscal year, the park posted its first operating profits. By the time Burke left in 1997, the press had mostly positive things to say about the park.

Burke balanced various tensions between global corporate imperatives and local market conditions. He not only managed well in the high uncertainty between headquarters in Burbank and executives in Paris, but between Disney management and local employees and among banks, creditors, the parent company, and the park's own interests. According to Burke, "Balancing tensions is both the art and fun of global leadership."

Business Savvy: Steve Holliday

Steve Holliday, age forty, is managing director of British-Borneo Oil & Gas Ltd., a medium-sized British oil and gas exploration and production company with international operations that range from Southeast Asia to the Gulf of Mexico. Holliday knows that recognizing global market opportunities is far more than "playing global chess" with competitors. Simply watching where competitors move and then defending against those moves is not enough. He commented:

"In the early 1990s, Hong Kong-based China Light & Power (CL&P) was supplying about two-thirds of Hong Kong's electric power. We saw an almost insatiable, unmet demand for electricity in southern China. So we formed a joint venture with CL&P to build a \$3.5 billion coal-powered plant at Black Point in Hong Kong's New Territories. We agreed to provide 60 percent of the capital; the rest was to come from CL&P. CL&P's expertise was in coal-fired plants, and the intention was for them to serve as plant operator.

"As the negotiations proceeded, ARCO China came into the picture. It had just discovered a major gas field in the South China Sea and wanted to find a market for its gas. In the end, Exxon had a huge power plant that would rely on a competitor's gas. Some would argue that the deal just didn't make sense. But since the plant began operations in early 1996, it has proven to be a great, highly profitable investment for Exxon."

It is this ability to think beyond the borders in a borderless world and to recognize business opportunities through the fog of time zones, cultures, and past experiences that separates global leaders from the rest.

---

weaknesses of the organization, are familiar with the company's subsidiaries and competitive positions, and know key overseas managers.[13] Due to changes in cultures, languages, government regulations, increased physical distances, and shifting time zones, as well as unclear lines of authority, the depth and breadth of organizational savvy required to execute effectively is far greater for global leaders (*see the sidebar on Ta-Tung Wang*).

Developing Global Leaders

Organizations seeking to globalize need look no further than their own leaders to determine if their efforts will succeed or fail. Does the organization have enough global leaders? If not, it must ask if its leaders are born or made. Based on our interviews, the consensus was that global leaders are born and *then* made.

Assessing Talent

Global leaders, like great musicians or athletes, need superior talent, abundant opportunity, and excellent education and training to succeed. Not everyone has the ability to become one, so companies should not give opportunity and education to just anyone. Companies need to assess whether they are hiring enough young managers with the required baseline level of leadership talent to ensure that, even with normal turnover, they will have future global leaders.

Colgate-Palmolive, a company with decades of international business experience, often hires entry-level marketing candidates who have already demonstrated such characteristics and capabilities. It intentionally hires newly minted undergraduates or MBAs who have

Organizational Savvy: Ta-Tung Wang

Ta-Tung Wang was born in the Peoples' Republic of China in 1944. After completing an undergraduate degree in Taiwan, Wang moved to the United States for graduate work. After graduation, he worked for Kentucky Fried Chicken. In 1986, he was made vice president of KFC Southeast Asia with headquarters in Singapore.

Wang saw that KFC had a competitive edge over any other major US fast-food chain in developing the Chinese market; the Chinese preferred chicken to beef. Initially, Wang found a required local partner with access to a consistent supply of KFC-approved chickens by tapping into resources at KFC's parent company (R.J. Reynolds, at the time), resulting in contacts at the Ministry of Light Industry in Beijing. These contacts led Wang to the Beijing Corporation Animal Production (BCAP), a secure supplier of KFC's most important ingredient, chicken.

After countless visits to Beijing to find a site for the restaurant, Wang learned that a three-story building across the street from Tiananmen Square was available. As lease negotiations proceeded, the city agency that controlled the lease asked Wang for ten years rent up front, a total of US $1 million in cash. Wang remarked:

> "I asked the local negotiators how they came up with the $1 million figure. They said they needed that much to finish the building. My local Chinese partners said, 'That's crazy! Don't sign.' Of course I didn't have signing authority for $1 million from KFC, but I said to the negotiators on the spot, 'Let's do it.'"

Wang knew who to call at KFC and what to say. The money arrived in Beijing a few days later. The results of this risk? According to Wang, "It was a fantastic success. KFC got all its money back in less than a year."

How did KFC achieve such returns when it could not exchange China profits into hard currency and was stuck with soft local currency RMB? Wang tapped the parent company's world-class countertrade financial skills. By this time, KFC had been sold to PepsiCo, which also owned Taco Bell and Pizza Hut. Between KFC and these other chains, there was a huge, on-going need for employee uniforms. Wang met this need by funneling most of KFC's soft currency RMB profits in China into buying uniforms for export to the United States and other countries, thus exporting the profits from China to the United States.

Without Wang's organizational savvy, KFC would never have moved so quickly and so profitably into China or found such capable partners.

FIGURE 2　Systems for Developing Global Leaders*

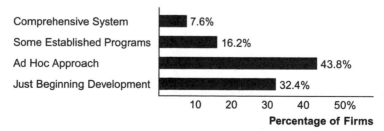

* Based on survey of US *Fortune* 500 firms in 1997.

lived or worked abroad, speak more than one language, or can demonstrate their pre-existing aptitude for global business. Still, even individuals with potential need outstanding developmental opportunities. In our research, firms with comprehensive development systems performed better financially than firms without such systems. However, most firms do not have comprehensive systems for developing global leaders (*see* figure 2).

The Development Process

How are global leaders made? The basic mental process for development is to understand the whole world, not just one country. For most of us, that requires both some rearranging and stretching of our mind-sets. However, it usually takes a pretty hard blow to the head and some real tugging before we rearrange and stretch our minds enough to encompass the whole earth.[14] Direct confrontations with new terrain can create a sharp contrast between what we know and what lies before us.

We might consider the example of one American's seemingly simple trip to a traditional Japanese restaurant. As this very tall businessman walked in, he hit his head on the wooden beam over the entry with such force that it shook and rattled the doors and windows and caused the other patrons to fear an impending earthquake. The American did the same thing the very next day. Finally, on his third trip to the restaurant, he remembered to duck when entering.

Most of us are like this person. It takes getting hit in the head – hard and probably more than once – before we are ready to change our mind-sets. And we need to expand our minds to recognize global opportunities and to marshal worldwide organizational resources. We need to emotionally connect with people who are different from ourselves and engender their good will. We need to understand people of different ethics and demonstrate integrity in a way that inspires trust. We need to embrace the constant dualities and tensions of global and local business demands. One reason that inquisitiveness differentiates between successful global leaders and those who struggle with worldwide responsibilities is that it ignites and fuels the motivation to go through this mind-altering process.

Strategies for Developing Global Leaders

In our research across Europe, North America, and Asia, we found four strategies that, when properly used, are effective at developing global leaders: travel; teams; training; and transfers.

Travel

Foreign travel, the first strategy, must put potential global leaders in the middle of the country, its culture, economy, political system, market, and so on, uninsulated by the common corporate cocoon of a western luxury hotel, car and driver, dutiful staffers, and choreographed itinerary. When Procter & Gamble CEO John Pepper travels, he visits several families' homes in each country to see firsthand how they use products, before he goes to his hotel or office. His approach helped him see that the French prefer front-load washers and would not easily change to top-load washers. This, in turn, helped Pepper better manage the introduction of a new cold-water detergent brand globally and, at the same time, find a way to meet the local need for distributing the detergent evenly throughout the clothes in front-load washers. This led to the invention of an innovative plastic ball into which a customer pours the detergent; it evenly distributes the detergent through little holes.

The successful global leaders in our survey consistently described two ways to enhance the developmental potential of international travel: first, take detours. Often the greatest contrasts and opportunities for stretching and rearranging minds are found off the beaten path. Second, get wet. Dive into the shops, markets, schools, homes, and so forth to find out what local life is really like.

Teams

The second strategy is to establish teams in which individuals with diverse backgrounds and perspectives work together closely.[15] Contrasting views and values can force members to think globally. Managed well, a culturally diverse team can also produce better business decisions.

Recently, Black & Decker implemented a 360-degree performance appraisal and feedback system, using a team from the United States and several Asian countries, including Singapore and Malaysia. Tracy Billbrough, president of Black & Decker Eastern Hemisphere, felt that the global team experience helped him better understand how to connect emotionally with people from different cultural backgrounds and appreciate why those connections aided in successful implementation.

Multicultural teams can be quite problematic, however, if not managed well. To help make teams more effective in developing global leaders:

- People should become team members before becoming team leaders.
- In general, people should be members or leaders of single-function, multicultural teams before becoming members or leaders of multiple-function, multicultural teams.
- Companies should give team members adequate training in topics such as cross-cultural communication, conflict resolution, and multicultural team dynamics.

Training

The third strategy, training, can supply all the contrast and confrontation of teams with a structured learning environment. For example, Sunkyong, one of the five largest industrial organizations in Korea, has a global leader program that involves both classroom and action learning projects for participants from the company's worldwide businesses. One project examined liquid natural gas opportunities in China. Its outcome helped Sunkyong avoid some costly mistakes; the training program teams discovered partners who were much more capable and competent than those the Chinese government had been promoting. Y. C. Kim, director of human resources, felt that exposure to various people through the company-provided training program enhanced his organizational savvy, and he met people who could help him in the future.

To enhance global leadership development, effective training programs should have these characteristics:

- Participants should come from the company's worldwide operations.
- Programs should include topics on international strategy and vision, worldwide organizational structure and design, change management, cross-cultural communication, international business ethics, multicultural team leadership, new market entry, dynamics of developing countries and markets, and managing in uncertainty.
- To ensure that the training encourages people to rearrange and stretch their minds, programs should include action learning components such as a field-based business project.

Transfers

The fourth, most powerful strategy is to provide overseas assignments.[16] We asked leaders: "What has been the most powerful experience in your life for developing global leadership capabilities?" Eighty percent identified living and working in a foreign country as the single most influential experience in their lives. Given the respondents' diverse nationalities, functional experiences, company affiliations, and so on, this finding is significant. More than any of the other three strategies, working in a foreign locale every day makes it possible to have mind-altering, head-cracking experiences.

Not everyone is open to the potential of an international assignment. People usually have one of four basic responses:

Broken heads. People with no global leadership potential have such thick heads they do not even realize when they have hit them and hence learn nothing from the assignment.
Bruised heads. Those with little potential realize that they have hit their heads, but they go back to being just as they were before the mishap and learn almost nothing.
Bright heads. People with a moderate amount of potential learn to duck after they first hit their heads; that is, they learn country-specific lessons.
Brilliant heads. When unexpectedly hit in the head, people with significant talent do not ignore it, do not try to simply reconstruct their original mind-sets, and do not create unique mental maps for each new situation and country. Instead, they continually monitor little bumps and major cracks and then update contingent, general mental maps that transcend country boundaries.

For example, NORTEL (Northern Telecom) maximizes the learning impact of international transfers by carefully managing each phase. NORTEL establishes candidate pools for international assignments, encourages informed self-selection, provides pre-departure training, establishes support mechanisms, plans for repatriation, debriefs employees and families on return, and uses repatriates' international skills and knowledge throughout the organization. NORTEL's strategic and systematic approach to international transfers produces increased market reach, quick innovation transfers, sound strategic alliances, and better global leaders.

How can firms enhance the power and effectiveness of international assignments?

Select the person carefully. Begin by thinking about how the person and the company will use the international experience in the future.

Consider the person's family. Ensure that family members are well suited for the assignment. Their difficulties could cause the global leader to lose the development potential of the assignment.

Provide training. Training helps people adjust quickly, be resilient, and better capture the potential of an assignment.

Facilitate repatriation. Companies need to retain people to leverage their international development. Unfortunately, approximately 25 percent of US expatriates who successfully complete an international assignment leave their company within a year. Companies such as Monsanto, however, employ certain strategies to retain and better utilize potential global leaders after international assignments: they provide a sponsor to help with placement and re-entry and plan for repatriation three to six months in advance. They help employees locate a suitable position before their return. They allow some "down time" for employees to put things in place at home. They provide repatriation training and facilitate the family's readjustment. They provide the opportunity to use international experience and allow for reasonable autonomy in the first job following repatriation.

Conclusion

Like explorers of old, today's global leaders face uncharted seas. While the characteristics these leaders must possess could clearly benefit domestic leaders, the difference is that global leaders cannot succeed without them. Our research suggests that most companies clearly lack the quantity or quality of global leaders they need – today or in the future. In the near term, this may create a valuable "free agent market" for those with proven capabilities until more leaders can be developed.

References

This research was funded in part by the David M. Kennedy Center for International Studies and the Center for International Business Education and Research at Brigham Young University. The authors' book, *Global Explorers: The Next Generation of Leaders*, was published by Routledge in 1999.

1. R. Daft, *Management* (New York: Dryden, 1997).
2. J. Welch, speech at General Electric, Spring 1997.
3. For a complete review of characteristics related to international assignment success, see:
   J. S. Black, H. B. Gregersen, M. E. Mendenhall, and L. Stroh, *Globalizing People through International Assignments* (Reading, Massachusetts: Addison-Wesley, 1998); and
   J. S. Black and H. B. Gregersen, *So You're Going Overseas: A Handbook for Personal and Professional Success* (San Diego, California: Global Business Publishers, 1998).
4. For a discussion of the relationship between global effectiveness and understanding culture, see:
   S. Weiss, "Negotiating with 'Romans' – Part 1," *Sloan Management Review*, volume 35, Winter 1994, pp. 51–61; and
   L. Hoecklin, *Managing Cultural Differences: Strategies for Competitive Advantage* (Wokingham, England: The Economist Intelligence Unit and Addison-Wesley, 1995).

5. For the first major review of this concept, see:
M. E. Mendenhall and G. Oddou, "The Dimensions of Expatriate Acculturation: A Review," *Academy of Management Review*, volume 10, number 1, 1985, pp. 39–47.

6. For example, see:
J. S. Black, "Personal Dimensions and Work Role Transitions: A Study of Japanese Expatriate Managers in America," *Management International Review*, volume 30, number 2, 1990, pp. 119–134.

7. M. Nyaw and I. Ng, "A Comparative Analysis of Ethical Beliefs: A Four Country Study," *Journal of Business Ethics*, volume 13, number 7, 1994, pp. 543–555; and
M. Philips, "Bribery," *Ethics*, July 1984, pp. 621–636.

8. For a review, see:
Black et al. (1998), chapter three.

9. The trade-offs between gathering too much data and too little are discussed in:
G. Stalk, "Time – The Next Source of Competitive Advantage," *Harvard Business Review*, volume 66, July–August 1988, pp. 41–51.

10. For an academic perspective, see:
A. Morrison and K. Roth, "A Taxonomy of Business-Level Strategies in Global Industries," *Strategic Management Journal*, volume 13, number 6, 1992, pp. 399–417;
M. Porter, "Changing Patterns of International Competition," *California Management Review*, volume 28, Winter 1986, pp. 9–40; and
S. Ghoshal, "Global Strategy: An Organizing Framework," *Strategic Management Journal*, volume 8, number 6, 1987, pp. 425–440.

11. For a more complete discussion of arbitrage advantages that come through globalization, see:
G. Ragazzi, "Theories of the Determinants of Direct Foreign Investment," *IMF Staff Papers*, July 1973, pp. 471–498.
For a discussion of the advantages of global integration, see:
C. K. Prahalad and Y. Doz, *The Multinational Mission* (New York: Free Press, 1987).

12. For a discussion of the impact of exchange rates on global competition, see:
R. Aliber, "The MNE in a Multiple-Currency World," in J. Dunning, ed., *The Multinational Enterprise* (London: Allen & Unwin, 1971); and
D. Lessard, "Transfer Prices, Taxes, and Financial Markets: Implications of International Financial Transfers within the Multinational Corporation," D. Lessard, ed., *International Financial Management: Theory and Application*, second edition (New York: Wiley, 1985).

13. H. Crookell and A. Morrison, "Subsidiary Strategy in a Free Trade Environment," *Business Quarterly*, volume 55, Autumn 1990, pp. 33–39; and
K. Roth and A. Morrison, "Implementing Global Strategy: Global Subsidiary Mandates," *Journal of International Business Studies*, volume 23, number 4, 1992, pp. 715–735.

14. For an excellent discussion of the challenges of learning in a global context, see:
D. Leonard-Barton, *Wellsprings of Knowledge: Building and Sustaining the Sources of Innovation* (Boston: Harvard Business School Press, 1995); and
Y. Doz, K. Asakawa, J. Santos, and P. Williamson, "The Metanational Corporation" (Banff, Canada: Academy of International Business Annual Meeting, paper, 26–29 September 1997).

15. R. Belbin, *Management Teams: Why They Succeed or Fail* (London: Heinemann, 1991);
P. Evans, E. Lank, and A. Farquar, "Managing Human Resources in the International Firm: Lessons from Practice," in P. Evans, Y. Doz, and A. Laurent, eds., *Human Resource Management in International Firms: Change, Globalization, Innovation* (London: Macmillan, 1989).

16. Black et al. (1992);
"The Fast Track Leads Overseas," *Business Week*, 1 November 1993, pp. 64–68; and
L. loannou, "Cultivating the New Expatriate Executive," *International Business*, July 1994, pp. 40–50.

CASE **1**

○ ○

Grupo Financiero Inverlat

Kathleen Slaughter, Henry W. Lane and Daniel D. Campbell

By October 1996, it had been four months since management at the Bank of Nova Scotia (BNS) increased its stake in the Mexican bank, Grupo Financiero Inverlat (Inverlat), from 8.1 percent, to an equity and convertible debt package that represented 54 percent ownership of the bank. A team of Canadian managers had been sent to Mexico to assume management of the ailing financial institution immediately after the deal was struck. Jim O'Donnell, now Director General Adjunto (DGA)[1] of the retail bank at Inverlat, had been there from the beginning.

Jim was a member of the original group that performed the due diligence to analyze Inverlat's finances before negotiations could begin. Later, he and his wife Anne-Marie (also an executive with the bank) were the first Canadians to arrive in Mexico in May 1996. Since then, 14 additional Canadian managers had arrived, and restructured the four most senior levels within Inverlat. The pace of change had been overwhelming. Jim now wondered how successful his early efforts had been and what could be done to facilitate the remaining restructuring.

A Brief Inverlat History

In 1982, in his last days as leader of the Mexican Republic, President Lopez Portillo announced the nationalization of Mexico's banks. They would remain government institutions for the next eight to ten years. Managers characterized the years under govern-

ment control as a period of stagnation in which the structure of the Mexican financial institutions remained constant despite substantial innovations in technology and practice in the banking industry internationally.

Many Inverlat managers claimed that their bank had generally deteriorated more than the rest of the banking sector in Mexico. Managers believed that there was no overall strategy or leadership. Lacking a strong central management structure, each of the bank's geographic regions began to function independently, resulting in a system of control one manager described as "feudal". The eight regions developed such a level of autonomy that managers commonly referred to Inverlat not as a bank, but as eight small banks. The fragmented structure made new product development almost impossible. When the central corporate offices developed a new product, they had no guarantee that it would be implemented in the regions and ultimately, the branches. The power struggle within the regions demanded such loyalty that employees often had to say: "I cannot support you (in some initiative) because my boss told me not to."

In 1990, an amendment to the Mexican constitution allowed majority private sector ownership of Mexican commercial banks. Between 1990 and 1992, 18 banks were privatized by the Mexican government including Inverlat. BNS, looking to expand its interests in Latin America, purchased 8 percent of the company in 1992 for C$154 million.

Under the structure of the newly privatized bank, there were three corporate cultures: that of the original bank; that of the Casa de Bolsa, the bank's brokerage house; and that of the new chair of the bank, an executive from Banamex, Mexico's largest financial institution. Many senior Banamex executives were invited to join Inverlat, some even came out of retirement to do so. The Banamex culture soon dominated the organization, as senior management tried to create a "Little Banamex." Inverlat managers without a history in Banamex said that the strategy could never function because Inverlat did not have the clients, technology, or financial resources of Banamex.

Inverlat's leaders did recognize, however, that the years of stagnation under nationalization had created a bank that had failed to create a new generation of bankers to reflect the changing times. They realized that the bank required a rejuvenation, but the managers did not have the knowledge or the capacity to effect the change.

Nowhere was the lack of development more prominent, and ultimately more devastating, than in the credit assessment function. The banks pursued a growth strategy dependent on increased lending but, unfamiliar with the challenges of lending to the private sector, failed to collateralize their loans properly or to ensure that covenants were being maintained. In early 1995, following a severe devaluation of the Mexican peso, Mexico's credit environment collapsed; so did the bank. The Mexican government assumed responsibility for the bank, and BNS was forced to write down its original investment by almost 95 percent to C$10 million.

Negotiations with BNS

Management at BNS chose to view the loss in value of their investment as a further buying opportunity and, in early 1996, they began negotiations with the Mexican government. BNS contributed C$50 Million for 16 percent of new stock in the bank and

C$125 million in bonds convertible on March 31, 2000 for an additional 39 percent of equity. If, in 2000, BNS decided not to assume ownership of the bank, they could walk away without converting the debt and retain a much smaller portion of ownership.

As the majority shareholder until 2000, the Mexican government contracted BNS to manage the bank. A maximum of 20 BNS managers would be paid by the Mexican government to manage Inverlat on the government's behalf. If BNS wanted more Canadian managers to work in the bank, BNS would have to pay for them. It was intended that the Canadian managers would remain at Inverlat only until the Mexican managers developed the skills to manage the bank effectively on their own.

With the exception of a handful of the most senior officers in the bank, employees at Inverlat had no direct means of receiving information about the progression of the negotiations with BNS. Instead, they were forced to rely on often inaccurate reports from the Mexican media. As the negotiation progressed, support among Inverlat employees for a deal with BNS was very strong. Inverlat employees did not want to become government bureaucrats and viewed BNS as a savior that would bring money, technology, and expertise.

Employee Expectations

Soon after the deal was completed with BNS, however, the general euphoria was gradually replaced by the fear of actions the Canadians were likely to take as they assumed their management role. Senior managers were worried that they would be replaced by someone younger, who spoke English and had an MBA. Rumors, supported by inaccurate reports in local newspapers, ran rampant. One newspaper reported that as many as 180 senior-level managers would be imported to Inverlat from BNS in Canada.

Anxiety mounted as speculation increased about the magnitude of downsizing that BNS would implement as it restructured the bank in its turnaround. Although BNS had purchased banks in other Latin American countries, few Inverlat employees, including the most senior management, had any knowledge about the strategies that BNS management had used. Inverlat managers felt that their employees viewed BNS as a "gringo" corporation, and expected them to take the same actions other US companies had taken as they restructured companies they had purchased in Mexico. Most believed that if any foreign bank purchased Inverlat, most of the senior management team would be displaced and up to half of the bank staff would be let go. Similarly, very few managers knew the details of the contract that limited the number of managers that could come to the bank from Canada.

Very few of the Mexican employees had had any significant contact with Canadian managers, but the majority expected behavior similar to that of US managers. Only a handful of senior-level managers had been in contact during the due diligence and the Canadians realized that they required greater insight into the Mexican culture if they were to manage effectively. As a result, the members of the senior team that were going to manage the Mexican bank arrived in Mexico one month in advance to study Spanish. The Canadian managers studied in an intensive program in Cuernavaca, a small city 80 km southwest of Mexico City. During the three-week course, lectures were available on the Mexican culture. Mexican managers were extremely impressed by this attempt by the Canadians to gain a better understanding of the situation they were entering and thought the consideration was very respectful. One manager commented that:

> At the first meeting, the Canadians apologized because it would be in English, but promised that the next would be in Spanish. The fact is, some are still in English, but the approach and the attempt were very important.

Four months later, the Canadian team was still undergoing intense tutorial sessions in Spanish on a daily basis with varying levels of success.

Canadian managers said they were trying to guard against putting people into positions simply because they were bilingual. A Canadian manager, expressing his commitment to function in Spanish, commented that:

> There are 16 Canadians down here and 10,000 Mexicans. Surely to God, the 16 Canadians can learn Spanish rather than trying to teach the 10,000 Mexicans English or having people feel that they are being left out of promotions or opportunities just because they don't speak English. This is a Spanish-speaking country and the customers speak Spanish.

Inverlat and BNS Cultures

In Canada, BNS was considered the bank with the most stringent financial control systems of the country's largest banks. Stringent, not only in deciding not to spend money in non-essential areas, but also in maintaining a tough system of policies and controls that ensured that managers held to their budgets.

Inverlat executives, on the other hand, were accustomed to almost complete autonomy with little or no control imposed on their spending. Very little analysis was done to allocate resources to a project, and adherence to budget was not monitored. Mexican managers believed that greater controls such as the ones used by BNS should be implemented in Inverlat, but they also felt that conflicts would arise.

An early example experienced in the bank was a new policy implemented by BNS management to control gifts received by managers from clients. BNS managers imposed a limit of 500 pesos[2] for the maximum value of a gift that could be received by an executive. Gifts of larger value could be accepted, but were then raffled off to all employees of the bank at Christmas. Some Mexican managers took offense at the imposition of an arbitrary limit. They felt that it was an indication that BNS did not trust their judgement. Managers thought that it would be better if the bank communicated the need for the use of good judgement when accepting gifts and then trusted their managers to act appropriately.

Mandate of BNS

Two months after the arrival of the Canadian executive team, the new bank chairman, Bill Sutton gave an address to 175 senior executives within Inverlat. The purpose of the address was threefold: to outline management's main objectives in the short term; to unveil the new organizational structure of senior-level managers; and to reassure employees that no staff reductions would be undertaken for the first year.

The primary objectives, later printed in a special companywide bulletin were the following:

1. Identify all non-performing loans of the bank.
2. Develop an organization focused on the client.
3. Improve the productivity and efficiency of all operations and activities.
4. Improve the profitability of the 315 branches.
5. Develop a liability strategy.
6. Improve the integrity of the financial information.

These objectives were generally well received by the Mexican managers. Some criticized them as being too intangible and difficult to measure. Most, however, believed that the general nature of the objectives was more practical, given the type of changes that were being made in the first year. They did agree that the goals would need to be adjusted as planning became more focused during the 1997 budget planning process.

The new management structure differed sharply from the existing structure of the bank. The original eight geographic regions were reduced to four. Managers were pleased to see that the head of each of these divisions was Mexican and it was generally viewed as a promotion for the managers.

The second change was the nature in which the Canadians were added to the management structure. The senior Canadian managers became "Directores Generales Adjuntos (DGAs)" or senior vice presidents of several key areas, displacing Mexican managers. The Mexican DGAs not directly replaced by Canadians would now report to one or more of the Canadian DGAs, but this was not reflected in the organization chart (see Exhibit 1). Mexican DGAs retained their titles and formally remained at the same level as their Canadian counterparts.

Mexican managers later reported mixed feelings by employees about whether or not they worked under a Canadian or Mexican DGA. Many felt that a Mexican DGA and his (there were no female DGAs working within the bank) employees were more "vulnerable" than a Canadian; however, senior managers also felt that they had an opportunity to ascend to the DGA position when it was being held by a Mexican. Many felt that Canadian managers would always hold the key positions in the bank and that certain authority would never be relinquished to a Mexican. This was not the message that BNS management wanted to convey. One of Jim O'Donnell's first comments to his employees was that he would only be in Mexico until one of them felt confident that they could fill his shoes.

The last message was the new management's commitment not to reduce staff levels. A policy of "no hires, no fires" was put in place. Employees were able to breathe a sigh of relief. Many had expected the Canadian management team to reduce staff by 3,000 to 5,000 employees during the first several months after their arrival.

EXHIBIT 1 Grupo Financiero Inverlat Organizational Chart (Post-Reorganization)

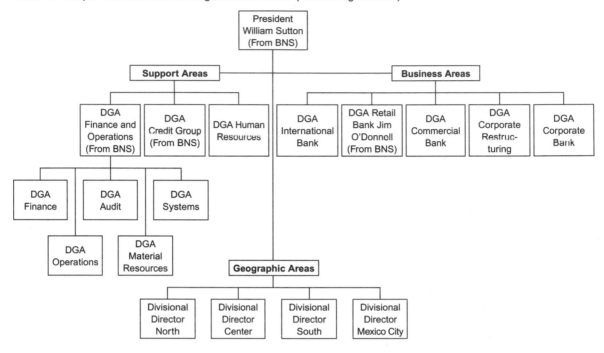

The Communication Challenge

Canadian and Mexican managers already experienced many of the difficulties that the two different languages could present. Many of the most senior Mexican managers spoke English, but the remaining managers required translators when speaking with the Canadians. Even when managers reporting directly to them spoke English, Canadians felt frustration at not being able to speak directly to the next level below. One manager commented that "sometimes, I feel like a bloody dictator" referring to the need to communicate decisions to his department via his most senior officers.

Meetings

Even when all managers at a meeting spoke English, the risk of miscommunication was high. A Mexican manager recalled one of the early meetings in English attended by several Mexicans. Each of the Mexican managers left the meeting with little doubt about what had been decided during the meeting. It was only later, when the Mexicans spoke of the proceedings in Spanish, that they realized they each had a different interpretation about what had transpired. What they found even more alarming was that each manager had heard what he had wanted to hear, clearly demonstrating to themselves the effect of their biases on their perception of events.

This problem might have been exacerbated by the way some of the Canadians chose to conduct meetings. Mexican managers were accustomed to a flexible atmosphere in which they were free to leave the room or carry on side conversations as they saw fit. Canadian managers became frustrated and changed the meeting style to a more structured, controlled atmosphere similar to what they used in Canada. The Mexican managers were told that breaks would be scheduled every two hours and that only then should they get up from the table or leave the room.

Canadian managers believed that the original conduct of the Mexican managers during meetings was due to a lack of discipline and that the new conduct would lead to higher productivity. The Canadians did not recognize the negative impact that could result from the elimination of the informal interactions that had occurred in the original style.

Beyond Language

Despite the cross-cultural training received in Cuernavaca, some Canadians still felt they had a lot to learn about the cultural nuances that could create major pitfalls. Jim O'Donnell recalled a meeting at which he and several Mexican managers were having difficulty with some material developed by another Mexican not present at the meeting. Jim requested that this manager join them to provide further explanation. Several minutes later, as this person entered the room, Jim said jokingly, "OK, here's the guy that screwed it all up." The manager was noticeably upset. It was not until later, after some explaining, that Jim's comment was understood to be a joke. Jim said it brought home the fact that, in the Mexican culture, it was unacceptable, even in jest, to be critical of someone in front of other people.

This was easier said than done. Often, what the Canadians considered a minor difference of opinion could appear as criticism that Mexican managers would prefer be made behind closed doors when coming from a more senior manager. One Mexican manager commented on the risks of disagreeing with an employee when others were present:

> When someone's boss is not in agreement, or critical of actions taken by an employee and says something during a meeting with other employees present, other managers will use it as an opportunity to also say bad things about the manager. Instead, when a disagreement arises in an open meeting, the senior manager should say "see me later, and we will discuss it".

To the contrary, the Canadian managers were trying to encourage an environment in which all managers participated in meetings and positive criticism was offered and accepted.

Mexican Communication Style

On verbal communication, one of the original Inverlat managers commented:

> In Mexico, interactions between individuals are extremely polite. Because Mexicans will make every effort not to offend the person they are dealing with, they are careful to "sugar-coat"

almost everything they say. Requests are always accompanied by "por favor", no matter how insignificant the request.

Mexicans often speak the diminutive form. For example: *Esperame* means *Wait for me.* *Esperame un rato* means *Wait for me a moment.* A Mexican would more often say *Esperame un ratito.* "Ratito" is the diminutive form meaning "a very short moment". It is not as direct.

This politeness is extended into other interactions. Every time a Mexican meets a coworker or subordinate, a greeting such as "Hello, how are you?" is appropriate, even if it is the fourth or fifth time that day that they have met. If you don't do this, the other person will think you are angry with him or her or that you are poorly educated.

One Canadian manager explained that some of the Mexican managers he dealt with went to great lengths to avoid confrontation. He was frustrated when the Mexicans would "tell him what he wanted to hear." Often these managers would consent to something that they could or would not do, simply to avoid a confrontation at the time.

Other Messages: Intended or Otherwise

Due to the high level of anxiety, Mexican managers were very sensitive to messages they read into the actions taken by the Canadians. This process began before the Canadians made any significant changes.

As the Canadians began to plan the new organizational structure, they conducted a series of interviews with the senior Mexican managers. The Canadians decided who they would talk to based on areas where they believed they required more information. Unfortunately, many managers believed that if they were not spoken to, then they were not considered of importance to the Canadians and should fear for their positions. Even after the organizational structure was revealed and many Mexican managers found themselves in good positions, they still retained hard feelings, believing that they had not been considered important enough to provide input into the new structure.

Similarly, at lower levels in the bank, because of the lack of activity in the economy as a whole, many employees were left with time on their hands. Because many employees feared staff reductions at some point, they believed that those with the most work or those being offered new work were the ones that would retain their jobs.

Communications as an On-going Process

When Jim held his first meeting with the nine senior managers reporting to him, he began by saying that none of them would have their jobs in two months. Realizing the level of anxiety at that point, he quickly added that he meant they would all be shuffled around to other areas of the retail bank. Jim explained that this would give them an opportunity to learn about other areas of the bank and the interdependencies that needed to be considered when making decisions.

Jim stuck to his word, and within two months, all but one of the managers had been moved. Some, however, had experienced anxiety about the method by which they were moved. Typically, Jim would meet with an employee and tell him that in two or three days he would report to a new area (generally, Mexican managers gave at least a month's notice). When that day arrived, Jim would talk to them for 30 to 45 minutes about their new responsibilities and goals, and then he would send them on their way.

For many of the Mexicans, this means of communication was too abrupt. Many wondered if they had been moved from their past jobs because of poor performance. More senior Mexican managers explained that often these managers would come to them and ask why Jim had decided to move them. Most of the Mexicans felt that more communication was required about why things were happening the way they were.

Accountability

Early on, the Canadian managers identified an almost complete lack of accountability within the bank. Senior managers had rarely made decisions outside the anonymity of a committee and when resources were committed to a project, it was equally rare for someone to check back to see what results were attained. As a result, very little analysis was done before a new project was approved and undertaken.

The first initiative taken by the Canadians to improve the level of analysis, and later implementation, was the use of what they called the "business case." The case represented a cost–benefit analysis that would be approved and reviewed by senior managers. Initially, it was difficult to explain to the Mexican managers how to provide the elements of analysis that the Canadians required. The Mexicans were given a framework, but they initially returned cases that adhered too rigidly to the outline. Similarly, managers would submit business cases of 140 pages for a $35,000 project.

Cases required multiple revisions to a point of frustration on both sides, but it was only when an analysis could be prepared that satisfied the Canadians and was understood by both parties, that it could be certain that they all had the same perception of what they were talking about.

Some of the Mexican managers found the business case method overly cumbersome and felt that many good ideas would be missed because of the disincentive created by the business case. One manager commented that "It is a bit discouraging. Some people around here feel like you need to do a business case to go to the bathroom."

Most agreed that a positive element of the business case was the need it created to talk with other areas of the bank. To do a complete analysis, it was often necessary to contact other branches of the bank for information because their business would be affected. This was the first time that efforts across functional areas of the bank would be coordinated. To reinforce this notion, often Canadian managers required that senior managers from several areas of the bank grant their approval before a project in a business case could move forward.

Matrix Responsibility

Changes in the organizational structure further complicated the implementation of a system of accountability. Senior management had recognized a duplication of services across the different functional areas of the bank. For example, each product group had its own marketing and systems departments. These functions were stripped away and consolidated into central groups that would service all areas of the organization.

Similarly, product groups had been responsible for the development and delivery of their products. Performance was evaluated based on the sales levels each product group could attain. Under the initial restructuring, the product groups would no longer be responsible for the sale of their products, only for their design. Instead, the branches would become a delivery network that would be responsible for almost all contact with the client. As a result, managers in product groups, who were still responsible for ensuring the sales levels, felt that they were now being measured against criteria over which they had no direct control. The Canadian management team was finding it very difficult to explain to the Mexicans that they now had to "influence" instead of "control." Product managers were being given the role of "coaches" who would help the branch delivery network to offer their product most effectively.

As adjustments were made to the structure, the Mexican manager's perception of his status also had to be considered. In the management hierarchy, the Mexican manager's relationships were with the people in the various positions that they dealt with, not with the positions themselves. When a person was moved, subordinates felt loyalty to that individual. As a result, Mexican managers moving within an organization (or even to another organization) often did so with a small entourage of employees who accompanied them.

Staff Reductions

As services within the bank were consolidated, it was obvious that staff reductions would be required. Inverlat staff were comforted by the bank's commitment to retain all staff for the first year, particularly when considering the poor state of the economy and the banking sector; but, even at lower levels of the organization, the need for reductions was apparent. Some managers complained that the restructuring process was being slowed considerably by the need to find places for personnel who were clearly no longer required.

Motivations for retaining staffing levels were twofold. First, BNS did not want to tarnish the image of its foreign investment in Mexico with massive reductions at the outset. When the Spanish bank, Banco Bilbao Viscaya (BBV), purchased Banca Cremi the previous year, they began the restructuring process with a staff reduction of over 2,000 employees. BNS executives thought that this action had not been well received by the Mexican government or marketplace.

The second reason BNS management felt compelled to wait for staff reductions was that they wanted adequate time to identify which employees were productive and fitted into the new organizational culture, and which employees would not add significant value. The problem was, quality employees were not sure if they would have a job in a year, and many managers thought that employees would begin to look for secure positions in other organizations. One Canadian manager commented that even some employees who were performing well in their current positions would ultimately lose their jobs. Many thought action needed to be taken sooner rather than later. A senior Mexican manager explained the situation:

Take the worst case scenario, blind guessing. At least then, you will be correct 50% of the time and retain some good people. If you wait, people within the organization will begin to look for other jobs and the market will choose who it wants. But as the market hires away your people, it will be correct at 90% of the time and you will be left with the rest.

Until that point, not many managers had been hired away from the bank. Many felt that this was due to the poor condition of the banking sector. As the economy improved, however, many believed that the talented managers would begin to leave the bank if job security could not be improved.

Jim felt that something was needed to communicate a sense of security to the talented managers they could already identify, but he was not certain how to proceed.

Conclusion

Jim felt that the Canadian team had been relatively successful in the early months. Many managers referred to the period as the "Honeymoon Stage." It was generally felt that the situation would intensify as managers looked for results from the restructured organization and as staff reductions became a reality. Jim then wondered how he could best prepare for the months ahead. Much of the communication with employees to date had been on an ad hoc basis. Jim did not feel they could take the risk of starting reductions without laying out a plan. The negative rumors would cause the bank to lose many of its most valued Mexican managers.

Notes

1. Director General Adjunto is the Mexican equivalent of an Executive Vice President.
2. In late 1996, one Mexican peso was valued at approximately US$0.0128.

○ ○

David Shorter

J. J. DiStefano and Neil Abramson

David Shorter sat back in his chair and thought about what he should say to Bob Chen when they met in a few minutes. Three weeks ago when David had left for holiday, he had regarded Bob as an up-and-coming member of the James-Williams team. David had seen Bob as a solid performer who wanted a career at James-Williams and who could be developed over time into a manager and perhaps eventually into a partner. David had even thought that Bob could help attract to James-Williams some of the new entrepreneurial Hong Kong companies that were coming to Toronto. Now David heard from Bob's managing partner, Jane Klinck, that Bob was threatening to resign.

David's First Day Back

David thought about the steady stream of people who had been in to see him this first morning back in the office. Jane Klinck was worried and upset. She felt that Bob was acting "crazy" and that there might be some sort of personality conflict between Bob and Mike McLeod. She hoped that David would be able to sort out the problem and find a solution that would keep Bob in the company. Mike McLeod had been in to see David, too. Mike was a fairly new partner who attracted a lot of business to James-Williams. He felt that he had not only been through the proper channels to have Bob assigned to the Softdisk Computer audit, but that he had been extremely patient with Bob. Mike said the other partners were shaking their heads about his behaviour,

Neil Abramson prepared this case under the supervision of Professor J. J. DiStefano solely to provide material for class discussion. The authors do not intend to illustrate either effective or ineffective handling of a managerial situation. The authors may have disguised certain names and other identifying information to protect confidentiality.

wondering why he was being so patient when it was standard procedure for partners to make such an assignment. Joe Silverman had been in as well. Joe was the tax partner Bob would report to starting in September, just five weeks from now. Joe hotly protested Bob's behaviour: "We can't have staff refusing assignments! Bob is way out of line! The customers must come first and this behaviour sheds a poor light on Bob. If he doesn't take the Softdisk job, he should be fired!"

The New Enterprise Group at James-Williams

David Shorter was the Practice Director of the New Enterprise Group at James-Williams. James-Williams was one of the six largest public accounting firms in Canada with 400 partners practising in 30 Canadian cities. James-Williams was the sole Canadian member of James-Williams International which provided audit, tax, consulting and other services to individuals, private businesses and governments in the Americas, Europe, the Middle East, Africa, Asia and the Pacific.

The New Enterprise Group had been set up seven years ago to provide service to smaller growth companies managed by entrepreneurs. David had been the Practice Director for the past four years. James-Williams believed that companies with gross annual revenues of between $5 and $100 million were often neglected as potential customers by Canadian public accounting firms because of their small size. Yet these companies had need of a variety of services that could be provided by James-Williams and these companies would pay high fees for their relative size. When these companies had grown beyond gross revenues of $100 million, their business could be transferred from the New Enterprise Group to the main auditing and consulting services of James-Williams and a solid relationship would exist. This was an important consideration in a mature industry where public accounting firms competed on service, reputation and price. Often, it was a long-term relationship that kept a client with a public accounting firm. These relationships enabled partners of the public accounting firms to have such an intimate knowledge of their clients' activities that they could anticipate problems and become indispensable to their clients' planning process.

The New Enterprise Group provided a range of consulting services geared to the needs of growing entrepreneurial companies. In addition to accounting and auditing services, the partners acted as principal business advisors. Client companies were particularly interested in the subjects of corporate finance and tax consulting, as well as the problems of acquisition and divestiture. Consulting was also available on strategic planning, development of business plans, marketing, human resource management, and information systems.

The New Enterprise Group was organized as a collegial system of partners who managed their own clients and activities within the performance objectives established by James-Williams, and under the general supervision of the Practice Director, who was also a partner (see Exhibit 1). Staff members below the partner level were organized on the staff system. A staff usually consisted of one or two senior staff accountants and several intermediate or junior staff accountants under a manager. A partner would have one, two or three managers and several staff reporting to him/her.

Most of the staff were either chartered accountants or in the process of becoming chartered accountants. Usually, staff would be hired out of business school as junior

EXHIBIT 1 James-Williams: The New Enterprise Group Organizational Chart (reporting relationships prior to Bob Chen's reassignment to tax)

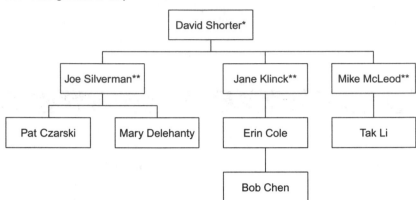

* Practice Director   ** Other Partners

staff accountants and would work on staff over a two-year period while they studied for their chartered accountant examinations. At the beginning of their second year, they were promoted to intermediate staff accountants at which level they remained until they passed the chartered accountant exams. At the beginning of their third year they wrote their exams, and, if they passed, they were promoted to senior staff accountants. If they did not pass, which was fairly common, they would have another year to prepare for a final chance at the exams.

The normal promotion process at James-Williams was for staff to remain as senior staff accountants for two years while they developed a consulting specialty of their choice. Then they might be promoted to manager and supervise six to nine staff. Most partners were selected from the ranks of the managers after they had been with the firm for ten to eleven years.

Bob Chen's Background with New Enterprise Group

Bob Chen was born in Hong Kong and came to Toronto as a high school student for Grade 13. He graduated with a Bachelor of Commerce from Queen's University in Kingston. At Queen's he achieved an overall grade point average of 75 percent[1] and was the treasurer of the Chinese Students' Society. He was recruited for James-Williams in the spring of his final year at Queen's, and began as a junior staff accountant at the New Enterprise Group in the following September.

Bob was seen as quiet and soft-spoken. One of his managers described him as "shy and accommodating. He does what he is asked to do and a bit more. Casual requests get immediate results." He was also a very private person whose politeness often meant not saying exactly what he wanted out of a situation or from another person. His civility may have masked from his colleagues his strongly felt desire for success and strongly held views about his possible contribution to the firm.

Bob was well liked by the people around him, most of whom viewed him as Westernized. Some partners and staff thought that Bob "was fairly outgoing for an Oriental" and had much better oral communications skills than previous staff from Hong Kong hired by the firm. His colleagues believed that Bob had good potential with James-Williams and hoped he would stay with the firm.

Previous Contacts between David and Bob

Two years after joining the firm, Bob wrote his chartered accountant examinations and in the following December learned the good news that he had passed. He was transferred as an audit senior to Jane Klinck, because the partner Bob had previously reported to was leaving the company. Bob was to report to Erin Cole who was the manager working under Jane.

Early in the new year, David Shorter followed his usual custom of having one-on-one meetings with staff who had passed their examinations and been promoted to senior staff accountant positions. The purpose of the meetings was not only to congratulate them on their success, but also to begin to identify their interests in professional specialization so that David could plan appropriate assignments for them within the New Enterprise Group. New assignments were usually announced after the annual performance appraisal in May, and were effective by September.

When he met with Bob in January, David was pleased with Bob's success because he had thought that Bob was a solid, but average performer and might not pass his examination the first time he wrote it. Now David decided that Bob might have higher potential within the New Enterprise Group and suggested that Bob might like to work to build a practice around attracting entrepreneurial Hong Kong-based companies to use the New Enterprise Group's services. David explained, "One of our goals is to build up our business with Hong Kong companies. Up to now, we haven't had much success because most Hong Kong money has been invested in real estate. Now, however, Hong Kong money is being invested in businesses which are in the New Enterprise Group's target market."

To be able to attract a Hong Kong practice, Bob would have to build up his auditing skills for another year, because audit was the initial function which brought companies to the New Enterprise Group and stimulated their interest in other consulting services. David remembered that he had two goals in suggesting further auditing experience for Bob. First, the New Enterprise Group had a shortage of senior auditors for this year. Second, he felt that Bob was a "keeper" who could have a long and mutually valuable future with the firm. Bob's auditing skills needed strengthening since he had done very little auditing in his first two years. David had seen previous staff with similar limitations fail as both managers and partners, because without auditing experience they could not understand the practical nature of most business problems. David noted, "Without more seasoning, he would not be as valuable to us. He would get weeded out as a technician."

But Bob had other ideas; he indicated to David that now that he had his CA designation, he wanted to develop a specialization in tax. He was open to the idea of developing a Hong Kong practice, but in the meantime he wanted an assignment that would teach him tax. David told Bob that he didn't believe Bob was ready for a tax assignment, because tax was a practical discipline that needed the ability to find creative tax solutions to business problems. Without a firm grounding in audit, staff had a tendency to quote tax regulations, rather than use the tax regulations to the advantage of their clients. "I didn't think he was ready and believed that his chargeable activity time would fall. I was under pressure to keep up the chargeable activity time of all staff." David thought that by the end of the interview he had convinced Bob of the soundness of his argument and that Bob had agreed to defer his request for a tax position.

In May, Jane conducted Bob's annual performance appraisal during which time Bob repeated his request for an assignment in tax. Her reply was similar to David's earlier commentary. Jane told Bob that she thought he needed another year of auditing work. "He had one year of decent audit work with me, but his junior year had not been enlightening in the area of audit. I thought he agreed that his junior year had not been productive in the area of audit." Jane asked David to review the performance appraisal because Bob had only been transferred to her in December. When David met with Bob in June, Bob again asked for an assignment in tax. David said no, reiterating his earlier argument that Bob needed more auditing experience. He added that Jane supported this recommendation. It was both David's and Jane's opinion that Bob was only now doing his first and second comprehensive audits. Bob seemed to accept this judgement, though he did not appear to be satisfied by it.

Over the next month, Bob requested and received two more interviews with David to request a tax assignment. David was pleased to talk with Bob because he felt that Bob's concern showed he was highly interested in his career and also highly committed to James-Williams. At the first meeting, David offered the compromise that if Bob would continue as an auditor for a year, then David would send Bob on a comprehensive three-year tax training program that was a much prized opportunity among tax consultants. "I offered to send him on this expensive course fully funded by the firm if he would agree to wait another year for a tax assignment." Bob seemed initially to agree but then asked for another meeting. At the second meeting, David finally agreed to assign Bob to a tax partner, Joe Silverman, to work in tax starting in September. "I told him that even though he could make the move into tax in September, he'd have to do some audits during his first year in tax. The firm needed to take advantage of his auditing skills as a senior. It would also keep his activities time up." Bob agreed to the conditions and David left for holiday shortly after.

Events Occurring during David Shorter's Absence

David Shorter left the New Enterprise Group to attend a Partner Development Program and for holidays at the beginning of July. During this time, Mike McLeod realized his upcoming need for a senior auditor for an important account, the Softdisk Computer Company. Softdisk's year-end required that the audit had to be done in September and October. The audit would fully occupy the time of the senior auditor during those two months. In order to make preparations for the job, the senior auditor had to be assigned to the audit by the end of July at the latest. It was more desirable for the senior auditor to be in place by July 13 in order to attend the client's physical inventory being conducted on that date. This would also provide an opportunity for the client and senior auditor to meet each other and work together prior to the actual audit.

Mike found that Bob Chen was the only senior auditor in the New Enterprise Group who might be available in September and October. Policy in the New Enterprise Group was to use internal staff as senior auditors whenever possible because the cost for hours of internal staff was less than if an auditor had to be "rented" from another division of James-Williams. Also, it would be easier for Mike to manage someone from inside the New Enterprise Group.

Since the actual audit work was to be conducted in the fall, Bob would be "officially" working for Joe Silverman in tax. Mike approached Joe Silverman and his manager, Pat Czarski, to see whether he could use Bob Chen for the audit. Joe and Pat told him that Bob was to be assigned to Joe's other manager, Mary Delehanty, who was away on holiday. But Joe and Pat thought it was a very good idea to assign Bob to the audit. The arrangements for Bob to be transferred to Joe had only been made in June and there was no tax work available for him. Further, with Mary on holiday, it was unlikely that she could find tax work for Bob to do in September and the Softdisk audit would keep Bob's billable hours at an acceptable level until they could use his services effectively.

With this approval, Mike approached Bob on July 10. He asked Bob to take the Softdisk audit and provided Bob with information on the company. In particular, Mike wanted Bob to know that the Softdisk audit would fit in with Bob's career path in tax. The audit would include international multi-jurisdictional tax issues, tax problems concerning research and development being done in Quebec, and a high-technology emphasis much valued by staff who worked in the New Enterprise Group. The tax issues were so complex and interesting that the audit had been supervised last year by a tax partner who was now in New York. Mike reassured Bob that this partner would be available for consultation if Bob had problems. Further, once Bob had done the audit, he would have first call on any further, special tax work which might be required by Softdisk. Mike suggested that Bob should contact Dominick Sousa, a manager in the New Enterprise Group who had acted as senior auditor for Softdisk last year, to confirm these details.

Mike also noted that because the prior year's work with Softdisk had been a first audit by James-Williams, extra efforts had been taken. Therefore Bob would benefit from a better planning package being in place and a high client commitment for the second year. In addition, two James-Williams staff members from last year's audit would be carried over to Bob's team, further strengthening the continuity. Finally, Mike assured Bob that Mike and Tak Li would also be available to assist as needed. Altogether, he sought to assure Bob that taking on this audit would be consistent with his professed career objectives.

It was Mike's impression that Bob had agreed to do the Softdisk audit once he had confirmed the information Mike had given him with "due diligence." "He didn't refuse. Basically, he did not say yes, but he said 'Yes, I'll consider it and will talk to the people'. I was led to believe that he would seriously consider it and I got the impression he would do it. I thought we had a reasonable exchange and that we were both being open with each other." Bob agreed to attend the physical inventory conducted on July 13. The key contact at Softdisk was also of Chinese origin, liked Bob and was pleased to have him for the audit.

Then Mike heard from Pat Czarski and from his own manager, Tak Li, that Bob had told them privately that he did not intend to do the audit. Given that Mike had thought the matter settled, he was shocked by this turn of events. He was especially surprised because Bob's attendance at the physical inventory sent a clear signal to Mike of Bob's acceptance of the assignment. Over the next week when Mike saw Bob in the office corridor or in the washroom, he checked if Bob was planning to do the audit and got the impression that Bob was still agreeable to the arrangements made earlier. But then he would hear more secondhand reports from Pat and Tak that Bob was not planning to do the audit. So Mike decided to be more direct. "I guess that I precipitated a crisis from Bob's perspective. I said, 'Don't BS me. Tell me up front. What are you going to do instead?' We had frequent contact in the hallways. I would ask him if he had a chance to talk to Dominick Sousa. But Bob wouldn't say anything about it." At this point, Mike decided that Bob was not being straight with him. He asked Pat and Tak to act as agents to see how Bob was reacting to the Softdisk project. "They would report one day that he was committed. Then the next day he had thought about it and wasn't committed any more."

This situation frustrated Mike immensely. His parents had lived in Hong Kong while Mike was growing up. His sister still lived there. "I have a better than average knowledge of cultural differences between Canadians and people from Hong Kong. I thought I was being effective." Mike decided an open discussion was necessary and wondered if Bob had not understood what a developmental opportunity the Softdisk audit was for furthering his professed career interest in tax consulting. Mike needed a fast and firm resolution to the problem because an auditor had to be in place by the end of July. If Bob would not do the job, then Mike would have to borrow a senior auditor from another James-Williams office, and the time pressure to brief such a replacement adequately would be extreme.

Mike decided to call a meeting with Bob, Pat, and Tak for July 20. "I didn't want a fight but I wasn't going to take any BS. Tak and Pat weren't getting the same story that I was. Bob was telling them 'no' and me 'maybe'. I wanted to get all four of us in a room and finally get some straight answers. I was going to tell Bob, 'You want to be a tax consultant. Well, here is the opportunity'."

On July 19, Bob met with Jane and asked for her help. Jane had supported Bob at partners' meetings and he felt she was an ally. Bob told Jane that he wanted to refuse the Softdisk job. He said he was concerned that the amount of planning time required for the Softdisk audit would interfere with a complex audit he was currently doing with a film company. He was afraid he might have to take leave from the film company audit. Jane asked if scheduling was his only concern. "Bob told me there was a bigger problem than scheduling. He didn't want to do the audit. He said he couldn't work for Mike but he wouldn't say why." Jane told Bob that he was crazy and not to do anything rash.

On July 20, Mike, Pat, Tak and Bob met for three hours. Most of the discussion centred around Mike's re-emphasizing how the Softdisk job fit with Bob's career goals in tax consulting. "I kept dragging Bob back to the career goals he said he had and showing him that if he was serious about tax then this was an opportunity. I answered all of his objections. Pat, Tak and I left the meeting once again thinking that Bob had agreed to do the job."

Meanwhile, Joe Silverman had heard about the situation and started to have doubts about the desirability of Bob joining his tax group in the fall. Since he had never worked with Bob, he approached Jane and asked for more information. Joe said the grapevine was giving him a poor impression of Bob. In Joe's view, not only was it out of line for staff to refuse assignments from partners, but also the clients' interests were the number one concern of the firm. Yet Bob did not seem to be acknowledging either of these values. If Bob would not do the Softdisk audit, then Joe thought Bob should be forced out.

Jane agreed with Joe. She was shocked by Bob's behaviour and felt, as Bob's key backer in partners' meetings, very unhappy to be caught in the middle. She called Bob into her office and told him that both Mike and Joe were furious. She told Bob that his behaviour had put him in a bad position with Joe, who was to be Bob's new managing partner. Joe was very client-oriented and was unlikely to give Bob the benefit of the doubt, because he had never seen Bob's hard work first-hand. "I told him that it didn't seem to be the right time for taking a stand. He said he believed it was a serious enough problem to resist. He was willing to leave the firm rather than work with Mike on the audit. I was shocked. I thought he enjoyed working for the firm and that he saw himself as having a good long-term career here. I don't know if he had a personal problem about working with Mike. I've talked to Mike and he doesn't know either."

On Sunday night, July 22, Bob phoned Pat to say that he would not do the Softdisk audit. Pat informed Mike who washed his hands of the matter and obtained another senior auditor from the Richmond Hill office of James-Williams.

On the morning of July 23, Bob came to see Jane. He said he would have to resign because he could not work for Mike. He also said he realized he had ruined his relationships with the partners and could not expect good performance appraisals even if he did do the audit. Jane told him he was crazy to throw away his career at James-Williams. Jane thought that maybe he was right about getting a poor performance appraisal because Joe "was fit to be tied," but she suggested that Bob wait and talk to David who was returning from holiday the next day. Perhaps David could transfer Bob since David had a high opinion of Bob's worth to the company.

David's Decision

David Shorter returned from vacation on July 23. His first day back he met with Jane Klinck and Mike McLeod who briefed him about the trouble with Bob. He also met with Joe Silverman who came to express his outrage about Bob's behaviour.

On July 24, David sat at his desk thinking. Bob would be here in a few minutes. David had some decisions to make. He knew that Bob was threatening to resign rather than do the Softdisk audit. He knew that both Mike and Joe were furious, but if Bob worked hard in the future, he did not think that Joe would give Bob poor performance appraisals. He knew that Jane had a high opinion of Bob and could not understand what was causing Bob to act this way.

David knew he had to make a decision that balanced the needs of all the people involved. On the one hand, Bob had offended some fairly important partners with whom David had to work and maintain good relationships. David was under no illusion that he could tell these partners what to do or think. They were all partners together, and they decided together. Besides, David agreed with them that it was inappropriate to let an employee with the capacity and the time to do a job refuse it. The Softdisk job also looked like a good opportunity for someone who wanted to specialize in tax. David did not know why Bob had turned it down.

On the other hand, Bob was a valuable employee given his skills and his potential for helping the New Enterprise Group attract business from Hong Kong investors. In addition to his knowledge, as reflected by his passing the uniform CA exam on his first attempt, he spoke and wrote Chinese fluently, skills relevant to James-Williams's stated goal of attracting Hong Kong business. That objective was one reason why the James-Williams office had been opened in Hong Kong. Yet the office had not done well and was now closed, so David was uncertain of the importance of Bob to the Canadian strategy.

There was the possibility of a transfer. The "Tower" (James-Williams's main group in Toronto) had been requesting that seniors interested in specializing in tax be transferred to them because they anticipated a future demand for tax specialists. Maybe that was what Bob was hoping for. David suspected that some of Bob's friends had been transferred to the Tower without any audit responsibilities and that Bob had been comparing notes with them.

David was sure of one thing. He did not want to offend the other partners in the New Enterprise Group. Perhaps he could persuade Bob to stay, and do the job, and then start tax work. Bob was an emotional kind of guy. Maybe David could get him to see reason.

Note

1. In Canada the grade point system follows the British model. At Queen's a 75 average is a B+ and is considered evidence of high achievement.

CASE 3

○ ○

Bob Chen

J. J. DiStefano and Neil Abramson

Bob Chen prepared himself for his meeting with David Shorter, Practice Director of the New Enterprise Group at James-Williams. In a few minutes, Bob might feel it necessary to resign from James-Williams. Bob had no other job to go to, and with a recession looming, it might be hard to find other employment. Nevertheless, Bob felt that his career was at stake if he was not firm.

The New Enterprise Group at James-Williams

The New Enterprise Group was a division of James-Williams located in Toronto. James-Williams was one of the six largest public accounting firms in Canada with 400 partners practising in 30 Canadian cities. James-Williams was the sole Canadian member of James-Williams International which provided audit, tax, consulting and other services to individuals, private businesses, and governments in the Americas, Europe, the Middle East, Africa, Asia, and the Pacific.

The New Enterprise Group had been set up seven years ago to provide service to smaller growth companies managed by entrepreneurs. David Shorter had been the Practice Director for the past four years. James-Williams believed that companies with gross annual revenues of between $5 and $100 million were often neglected as potential customers by Canadian public accounting firms because of their small size. Yet these companies had need of a variety of services that could be provided by James-Williams

Neil Abramson prepared this case under the supervision of Professor J. J. DiStefano solely to provide material for class discussion. The authors do not intend to illustrate either effective or ineffective handling of a managerial situation. The authors may have disguised certain names and other identifying information to protect confidentiality.

EXHIBIT 1   James-Williams: The New Enterprise Group Organizational Chart (Reporting relationships prior to Bob Chen's reassignment to tax)

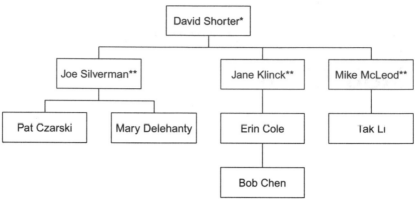

* Practice Director   ** Other Partners

and these companies would pay high fees for their relative size. When these companies had grown beyond gross revenues of $100 million, their business could be transferred from the New Enterprise Group to the main auditing and consulting services of James-Williams and a solid relationship would exist. This was an important consideration in a mature industry where public accounting firms competed on service, reputation, and price. Often, it was a long-term relationship that kept a client with a public accounting firm. These relationships enabled partners of the public accounting firms to have such an intimate knowledge of their clients' activities that they could anticipate problems and become indispensable to their clients' planning process.

The New Enterprise Group provided a range of consulting services geared to the needs of growing entrepreneurial companies. In addition to accounting and auditing services, the partners acted as principal business advisors. Client companies were particularly interested in corporate finance, tax consulting, and the problems of acquisition and divestiture. Consulting was also available on strategic planning, developing business plans, marketing, human resource management, and information systems.

The New Enterprise Group was organized as a collegial system of partners who managed their own clients and activities within the performance objectives established by James-Williams, and under the general supervision of the Practice Director who was also a partner (see Exhibit 1). Staff members below the partner level were organized on the staff system. A staff usually consisted of one or two senior staff accountants and several intermediate or junior staff accountants under a manager. A partner would have one, two or three managers and several staff reporting to him/her.

Most of the staff were either chartered accountants or in the process of becoming chartered accountants. Usually, staff would be hired out of business school as junior staff accountants and would work on staff over a two-year period while they studied for their chartered accountant examinations. At the beginning of their second year, they were promoted to intermediate staff accountants at which level they remained until they passed the chartered accountant exams. At the beginning of their third year, they wrote their exams, and, if they passed, they were promoted to senior staff accountants. If they did not pass, which was fairly common, they would have another year to prepare for a final chance at the exams.

The normal promotion process at James-Williams was for staff to remain as senior staff accountants for two years while they developed a consulting specialty of their choice. Then they might be promoted to manager and supervise six to nine staff. Most partners were selected from the ranks of the managers after they had been with the firm for ten to eleven years.

Bob Chen's Background at James-Williams

Bob Chen was born in Hong Kong and came to Toronto as a high school student for Grade 13. He graduated with a Bachelor of Commerce from Queen's University in Kingston. At Queen's he achieved an overall grade point average of 75 percent[1] and was the treasurer of the Chinese Students' Society. He was recruited for James-Williams in the spring of his final year at Queen's, and began as a junior staff accountant at the New Enterprise Group in the following September.

Early in his final year at Queen's, Bob's father, living in Hong Kong, suggested he find a job in Canada because Hong Kong would revert to the People's Republic of China in 1997. His father believed Bob's future would be better in Canada. Bob applied to a number of major Canadian public accounting firms and was told to re-apply if he was able to obtain landed immigrant status. These companies did not seem to realize that it was very hard to obtain landed immigrant status unless one had a job offer.

One firm, James-Williams, offered Bob a job. He accepted. Afterwards Bob felt very loyal to the company because their offer had made it possible for him to remain in Canada.

In September after graduation, Bob started with James-Williams in the New Enterprise Group as a junior staff accountant, doing accounting work and studying for his chartered accountant exams which were scheduled for two years hence. In the following fall he was promoted to intermediate staff accountant as was standard for all second-year staff at James-Williams. During his first two years with the New Enterprise Group, Bob worked under the supervision of several managers including Tak Li and a partner named Lara Witmer. Due to turnover of staff in the New Enterprise Group during those years, Bob was attached for various jobs to a number of managers and partners. About the time that Bob was scheduled to write his CA exams, he learned that Lara Witmer had been asked to leave the firm. Bob would be assigned to work for Jane Klinck under the project supervision of Erin Cole.

In the New Enterprise Group Bob was seen as quiet and soft-spoken. One of his managers described him as "shy and accommodating. He does what he is asked to do and a bit more. Casual requests get immediate results." He was also a very private person whose politeness often meant not saying exactly what he wanted out of a situation or from another person. His civility may have masked from his colleagues his strongly felt desire for success and strongly held views about his possible contribution to the firm.

Bob was well liked by the people around him. Some partners and staff thought that Bob was fairly outgoing and had much better oral communications skills than previous staff from Hong Kong hired by the company. His colleagues believed that Bob had good potential with James-Williams and hoped he would stay with the company.

The Beginnings of a Problem

Early in his employment at James-Williams, Bob decided he would like to specialize as a tax consultant. He knew that the normal procedure at James-Williams was for intermediate staff to wait until they had passed their chartered accountant exams before approaching the Practice Director with indications of their specialization interests. However, tax was a very popular choice and some intermediate staff in the New Enterprise Group went to David Shorter before they had passed their exams so that David would have enough time to find them assignments in their preferred areas.

Nine months after joining the New Enterprise Group, Bob met formally with David Shorter when David reviewed Bob's annual performance appraisal. At that meeting, Bob told David about his interest in becoming a tax specialist. Bob's impression of the meeting was that David had agreed to see what he could do to further Bob's interests. Bob expected that he would receive some tax assignments over the next year while he was studying for his chartered accountant exams, but no such assignments materialized.

In September, Bob wrote his exams and, in December, he received the good news that he had passed on his first attempt. The following January David Shorter called Bob in for an interview during which he congratulated Bob on passing his CA exam and asked what Bob would like to specialize in. Bob again asked for an assignment to tax, but David told him that he wasn't ready for tax because his auditing skills were not strong enough. David asked Bob to work as a senior auditor for a year in order to provide a stronger base for his tax specialization. David also asked Bob to consider the idea of specializing in Hong Kong-based entrepreneurial companies. Bob said he would think about it.

Bob was aware that the New Enterprise Group had a shortage of senior auditors. He felt that he was being asked not to pursue his career interests because of this shortage and not because of any weakness he had as an auditor. When Bob had originally mentioned his interest in tax during his first interview with David, David said he would see what he could do and had not indicated that Bob was weak in auditing. This also suggested to Bob that the main problem was the shortage. "I wanted to choose tax but I had the feeling that the partners didn't want me to because of the need for continuity in audit. I was maybe the only CA under Jane Klinck. Partners want qualified CAs on their jobs. Maybe Jane didn't want me to go to tax."

Bob was also aware that he had a reputation for doing what he was told. He tried to anticipate the needs of his supervisors and his clients, and he worked extra hard to accommodate their wishes. Partly this was his natural tendency, but he also felt a strong loyalty to the firm for hiring him and thereby providing a way for him to stay in Canada. Now he wondered if David thought he would not make a fuss if he held back in auditing for another year. "I did not usually express myself. I wondered if he thought I was too easygoing and would do whatever he wanted."

When David reviewed his annual performance appraisal in June after Bob had passed his CA exams, Bob again asked David for an assignment to tax. And again David refused, indicating that Bob needed more experience in audit. Bob did not accept this judgement and felt that he had once again been too easygoing and had failed to express himself forcefully enough.

Therefore, in late June, Bob approached David once more and after extensive discussion got David to compromise that if Bob would agree to stay in audit for the year, David would arrange to send Bob on a three-year tax training program. Bob initially agreed, but when he talked to friends in tax, they told him that the course would not teach him tax. Becoming a tax consultant required hands-on experience and the opportunity to deal with the tax problems of real companies in real situations. "I initially agreed, but decided later that it wasn't a good compromise because I wouldn't learn tax technique."

Once again Bob approached David with his concerns and David finally agreed to assign Bob to Joe Silverman, a tax consultant, in September as long as Bob agreed to finish his current audit work and was willing to accept one major audit assignment in January and February. Bob agreed and David made the arrangements for transferring Bob to Joe's tax group starting in September.

The Softdisk Audit

On July 10, soon after this series of conversations with David Shorter, Bob was approached by Mike McLeod, another partner in the New Enterprise Group, to be the senior on an audit of the Softdisk Computer Company. The audit would require Bob's full-time attention in September and October. Bob was extremely wary. He believed if he accepted the Softdisk audit, he would have very little opportunity to specialize in tax for the entire year. The problem, as Bob saw it, was that it now looked as if he might be required to do audit for six of the next eight months. He was currently doing an audit of a film company for his present managing partner, Jane Klinck. This audit had been scheduled for completion in early July, but the company's books were a mess and Bob thought he might have to continue on that job through August. In August, he would have to begin an interim audit of Softdisk. The Softdisk audit would occupy September and October. Then in January and February, he was required to do another major audit for Jane Klinck as part of his agreement with David. This left November and December for tax work, but December was a slow month due to Christmas. It didn't seem fair to Bob. He had friends who had also passed their CA exams and had been transferred directly into the Tax Department at James-Williams's main group in Toronto without having to agree to any further auditing responsibilities.

Consequently, Bob decided not to do the Softdisk audit. He told Mike McLeod that he would help out because there were no other senior auditors currently available in the New Enterprise Group. He went to the physical inventory at Softdisk in mid-July because no one else seemed to be available. At the time, he told Jane's staff manager, Erin Cole, that he would not do the Softdisk audit even though he went to observe the physical inventory.

Mike had tried to entice Bob into the audit by indicating the possibilities of learning about tax because of the intricate tax situation at the company. Bob talked about these possible advantages with others and decided that Softdisk was not as good an opportunity as Mike was describing. For one thing, Softdisk's tax complexities had been sorted out the year before by a senior tax manager, and Bob would simply be following the procedures developed at that time. Yet the situation wasn't risk free. Bob did not have adequate expertise in tax yet, and he was concerned that if he did encounter a difficult problem and made a serious mistake, he would be blamed and it would damage his career.

Bob tried to break the news gently that he would not be doing the Softdisk audit. He approached Tak Li, who now worked for Mike McLeod as a manager, and told Tak that he did not want to do the job. He also told Pat Czarski, a manager reporting to his new managing partner, Joe Silverman. Somehow the message did not seem to get through to Mike McLeod and over the next week Mike would stop Bob in the halls or in the men's room and ask if Bob had made a decision, or if Bob had any reservations that Mike could help him resolve. Mike seemed to be convinced that Bob would eventually take the job. Bob began to feel trapped. Since David Shorter had gone on vacation, he could not help sort out the situation. "I knew that Mike was quite influential in the New Enterprises Group because he had many bigger clients. He was persuasive and forceful. I wondered, 'Why is this happening to me? Why is he so determined to make me give in and take this job? Why is he going around to other partners and managers trying to get them to persuade me? He wants me to bow on this issue and I don't want to.'"

The final straw for Bob was a meeting called by Mike, including himself, Pat, Tak and Bob on July 20. Bob felt that the sole purpose of the meeting was to coerce him into taking on the Softdisk audit. After hours of pressure, Bob said he would do the job, just to end the meeting. However, he felt that he had been unfairly treated in the meeting and that he did not have to honour his agreement. "I felt isolated, like it was three against one."

Other Factors

After his meeting with Mike, Pat and Tak, Bob reviewed his situation and prospects. He knew that he had offended Mike McLeod. He had heard from Jane Klinck that he had also offended Joe Silverman who was scheduled to be his new managing partner in tax. Bob did not feel that he had a career potential with the New Enterprise Group any more.

In addition, the New Enterprise Group did not seem committed to supporting his desire to become a tax consultant. They appeared more concerned with their shortage of senior auditors. Bob felt less inclined to be loyal to a company which was not loyal to him.

Bob felt that he had the security to find another job. He had his chartered accountant designation. He was a Canadian citizen. He had money saved and his family would support him if he got into financial difficulties. He also had contacts from a management recruiting company that had tried to hire him for another company after he passed his chartered accountant exams. He decided to resign and told Jane of his intention. She discouraged him from acting rashly and convinced him to at least talk with David Shorter again when he returned from vacation on July 24. "Jane seemed to be shocked when I said I was thinking of resigning. She said, 'But you're usually so easy going!' I thought maybe they were picking on me because I'm easy going and never complain."

A Final Meeting with David Shorter

Bob expected no miracles from David before his upcoming meeting of July 24. He expected David to tell him that he was doing good work and to ask him to stay. He also expected David to ask him to do the Softdisk audit and to "tough out" the situation. Although Bob was prepared to listen, he thought he might have to resign unless David was willing to work out an acceptable alternative for him. Bob hoped David could come up with something. In the final analysis, Bob did not really want to leave. He just wanted to do tax.

Note

1. In Canada the grade point system follows the British model. At Queen's a 75 average is a B+ and is considered evidence of high achievement.

○ ○

Maria Mancini – Expatriate Compensation (A)

Joseph DiStefano and Tom Gleave

On June 16, 1996, Maria Mancini was struggling with a decision which could have important implications for her developing career. Maria had been working for almost one year in Hong Kong for Avanti International (Avanti), one of Italy's premiere luxury fashion goods retailers. During this period she became both exhilarated and overwhelmed by the pace of work and life in the city, as well as by events in the office which had unexpectedly created increased responsibilities for a new employee. At the same time, she was concerned that her present compensation package was inadequate, despite the fact that Avanti had substantially increased her salary only five days previously. Maria needed to decide if she should accept Avanti's latest raise as sufficient for the upcoming year or, instead, push for a more generous compensation package.

Maria's Background

Maria Mancini was born in 1971 to dual citizen American-Canadian parents in Toronto, Ontario. She grew up in a family where a high value was placed on acquiring a broad-based education. Her parents both held doctoral degrees from top-tier US institutions; her mother was a scholar in American history and her father taught human resource management. During her formative years, Maria was exposed to many countries and cultures, primarily in Europe and the US. At the age of 10 she lived in France where her father was a visiting professor for one year. The combination of personal travel and

Tom Gleave prepared this case under the supervision of Professor Joseph DiStefano solely to provide material for class discussion. The authors do not intend to illustrate either effective or ineffective handling of a managerial situation. The authors may have disguised certain names and other identifying information to protect confidentiality.

frequent visits by international guests to her home allowed her to experience diverse cultures throughout her life, up to and including her university days.

After finishing high school in 1990, Maria commenced studies at the University of Toronto. Four years later she received an honors BA majoring in art history with minors in comparative religion and music. During this period, she developed a greater sense of independence, while still tending to make personal sacrifices to avoid conflict and attempting to smooth over unavoidable confrontations. Prior to graduating, Maria realized that her degree offered limited potential for employment. Influenced by a number of cross-cultural experts she met through her father, she applied for fall 1994 admission to an Asian management program at Humber College in Toronto.

The Asian business program was designed for university graduates who were seeking to broaden their scope of employment possibilities in the Asia-Pacific region. The program was 20 months in duration, including an eight-month formal course component, followed by a compulsory one-year internship in an Asian-based business. The program typically attracted undergraduate and professional degree holders from a variety of disciplines, aged 28 to 32, who had four to six years of work experience. The school was initially hesitant to offer Maria a position in the program for fear that she would have difficulty securing a one-year internship in Asia, particularly since she would be competing against older, more experienced classmates. However, after several conversations with the admissions officer and program director, including interviews in Toronto, the college accepted Maria predicated on one condition: she had to secure a suitable one-year work internship in Asia *prior* to beginning her first year studies.

By August 1994, Maria had secured three separate work placement offers which were to begin the following summer in Asia. The opportunities were from a Manila-based cable television company; a Hong Kong-based distributor of roller bearings in China; and Avanti International. The interview for Avanti took place at the corporate headquarters in Milan and was conducted by Giovanni Provenzano, the firm's managing director for Europe and Asia. Two weeks after the interview, Maria received her offer of employment from Provenzano. The offer stated that she would work in Avanti's Hong Kong regional office as an assistant marketing manager commencing September 1, 1995. The contract, which was renewable upon the agreement of both parties, would remain in effect for one year and offered a starting salary of HK $14,000 per month.[1] Benefits included a basic employee insurance policy (including medical coverage), all local public holidays off and a paid annual leave of 15 working days. Working hours were stipulated as 9.00am to 6.00pm, Monday to Friday, with a one hour lunch break. Necessary overtime, "within reasonable limits," would not be paid. Maria accepted the terms of the contract.

Maria commenced the Asian management program in September 1994 and finished the course component in early May 1995. During this period she studied a variety of international business courses, Asian cultures and histories, and the Mandarin language. At one point during the year, she faxed Avanti an offer to undertake a free market research project on the company's behalf as part of a course requirement. However, Avanti did not reply. Having made the dean's list for her academic performance, Maria was especially pleased with her "A" in international finance, because she had not taken any math-related courses since junior high school. These successes helped her to develop significantly greater self-confidence and assertiveness. After completing her course work, she left for Suzhou, China (located about 75 kilometres northwest of Shanghai) for five weeks of intensive Mandarin lessons. This program was intended to help consolidate the learning she received during the academic year. On the day that she arrived in Suzhou, she received a fax from Avanti's Hong Kong office urgently requesting her to meet with the general manager and marketing manager in Hong Kong the next weekend. She replied that she would meet them in Hong Kong on Saturday, June 12, 1995.

Avanti International SPA

Avanti International (Avanti) was a Milan-based "house of fashion" which retailed luxury brand goods, such as ready-to-wear knitwear, belts, and small leather accessories. The company's product positioning was meant to appeal to sophisticated consumers seeking elegance and refinement in their fashion statements. The primary competitors for Avanti, particularly within the Asia-Pacific region, were Zegna and Prada.

The senior people at Avanti's head office with whom Maria had contact included:

Giovanni Provenzano (46) was the managing director of Avanti's European and Asian divisions. He was acknowledged as being the second most senior individual in the family-run company, next to his brother, Vincenzo, who was chairman and CEO. After she was hired, Maria met Giovanni twice for about one half hour each, once in Milan and the other while he was visiting the Hong Kong office.

Luigi Ditullio (52) was an engineer who had worked for Andersen Consulting prior to joining Avanti as director of Asian operations. It was widely recognized in the company that Luigi was Giovanni's most valued and trusted assistant. He also had the most direct contact with the Hong Kong office of any senior individual working at Avanti's head office. He visited Asia at least twice a year in order to review business development in the region, both with the Hong Kong staff and with Avanti's franchisees. Maria had met Luigi once each in Milan and Hong Kong, although she had spent less time with him than with Provenzano.

Guiseppe Parise (58) was the recently appointed director of human resources after previously serving as the director of MIS. Maria suspected that he was appointed to this new role because "HR had no power." Although Maria was never personally introduced to Guiseppe, she did contact him by phone to discuss the company's travel policy.

Avanti's Hong Kong Operation

Avanti's regional office in Hong Kong (Avanti-HK) provided sales, promotion, and operations support to numerous markets throughout East and Southeast Asia. The company distributed its products through exclusive retail franchise agreements by country (or territory). This arrangement existed for Taiwan, China, Japan, Korea, the Philippines, and Hong Kong, where a total of 80 retail outlets were serviced by Avanti-HK. Additionally, products were distributed through duty free stores inside the boarding areas of airports in the region locations which provided a strategic fit for Avanti's popularity with the Japanese tourist market.

As was the case with most luxury goods manufacturers, business growth in Asia far outpaced that in Europe and North America. In the Asia region Avanti-HK's sales volumes varied widely within the different countries and territories it serviced. For example, sales for every six-month period in Hong Kong were eight times the typical six-month sales volume in Taiwan. The explanation for the relatively poor performance in Taiwan was that Avanti selected an exclusive franchise partner who was undercapitalized. This caused the Taiwanese partner to devote considerably more time and effort managing its other struggling businesses at the expense of the Avanti franchise.

The general manager in charge of the Hong Kong office when Maria first began working was Georgio Gascalione, a Canadian of Italian lineage. Previously, Georgio had attended Stanford University where he obtained an undergraduate degree in economics before pursuing an MBA at IMD in Switzerland. Maria believed that "he was perfect for the job. He was fluent in Italian, well-educated, business savvy and had six years of industry experience working in Japan prior to coming to in Hong Kong in 1992." The marketing manager was Rosaria Verde. Rosaria was born into a family that had a "passion for fashion." Her father owned and operated a knitwear business, her mother acted as a fashion consultant, her brother was a fashion photographer and her sister was a fashion designer for Calvin Klein in New York. Prior to working for Avanti, Rosaria had worked at an Italian advertising agency, as well as at a Milan-based silk manufacturing company where she worked in the marketing department. The remaining staff in the Hong Kong office consisted of two accounting clerks and one shipping clerk.

Developments at Avanti-HK

On June 12, 1995, Maria took the train from Suzhou to Shanghai and then flew to Hong Kong to meet with Georgio Gascalione and "a very pregnant" Rosaria Verdi. The message that they greeted her with was: "We need you now. We need to train you before Rosaria goes on maternity leave in early September." Given the situation, Maria agreed to cut short her Mandarin studies in Suzhou and to start working for Avanti-HK on July 1, 1995, two months prior to the original starting date of September 1.

After agreeing to an early start date, Maria spent another two weeks in Suzhou and then cut short her immersion training to return to Canada to take care of her personal affairs. Four days later she flew back to Hong Kong in preparation for her new career. Her first week was spent with Rosaria who provided an overview of Maria's responsibilities. This training was short-lived, however, as Rosaria left for Italy one week later. She spent the duration of the summer working in Italy and, in September 1995, began her four-month maternity leave. This meant that Maria not only had to learn her own job responsibilities, she also had to assume, by default, many of Rosaria's responsibilities. (See Exhibit 1 – Job Description for Assistant Marketing Manager; Exhibit 2 – Maria's List of Assumed Responsibilities.)

While the learning curve remained steep over the next several months, Maria was satisfied with her job performance, particularly in light of the limited training and supervision she had received. However, as she interacted more frequently with Georgio, she detected that he had become increasingly frustrated in his job. This was because he felt he lacked any legitimate decision-making authority. In October 1995, after being

EXHIBIT **1**   Job Description – Assistant Marketing Manager (June 1995)

Avanti International

Assistant Marketing Manager

Responsible to: Marketing Manager

Nature and scope:
The assistant marketing manager is based in the Hong Kong office, where five people are employed. The Hong Kong office is responsible for coordinating the company's network of exclusive distributors throughout East and Southeast Asia (Hong Kong, China, Australia, New Zealand, Taiwan, Thailand, Singapore, the Philippines, Malaysia, Indonesia and Vietnam).

The assistant marketing manager works directly with the marketing manager to support the distributors in terms of: planning of advertising campaigns and public relations activities; opening of new points of sale; training of sales staff; and merchandising at the point of sale. The objective is to provide the distributors with all the necessary information and know-how to operate the Avanti boutiques in a manner consistent with the company's worldwide corporate image, and ensure that the distributors apply this information correctly.

Principal accountabilities:
1. Participates in the implementation of advertising campaigns, and ensures that each country's advertising campaign is carried out in accordance with the approved budget and media plan.
2. Assists the marketing manager in selecting public relations materials received from head office in Italy, modifying them if necessary for specific requirements of each national market, disseminating the materials to each distributor, and ensuring that the materials are used actively to obtain PR coverage.
3. Works with the marketing manager in coordinating the point-of-sale activities including architectural fit-out renovations, display programs and promotions, staff uniforms and packaging.
4. Maintains the database of Avanti International shops. Maintains the database of the competitors' point-of-sale. Coordinates the collection and analysis of market survey information from distributors.

---

repeatedly sought by various head-hunters for several senior positions with Avanti's competitors and other high-end fashion retailers, he tendered his resignation. Only through repeated entreaties to defer his departure was Avanti able to keep him as long as it did. He subsequently left Avanti in January 1996, after Rosaria returned from her maternity leave.

Upon her return, Rosaria took on much of the work that Georgio was doing on market development. She was also permitted to have one half day off per week in order to spend time with her baby. At the same time, Maria took on some of the company's budgeting duties, as well as some of the work that Rosaria had been doing in areas related to architecture and window display coordination, buying analysis, and customer support. Maria also became more involved in public relations, as well as in the management and reconciliation of advertising invoices. By May 1996, Maria had carefully considered the problems she was experiencing due to her low salary. After almost one year of working for Avanti-HK, she had no savings and was concerned about her ability to meet her upcoming income tax obligations. Furthermore, she was living in less than ideal conditions. She described the two-bedroom, 54-square-metre (600-square-foot) apartment that she shared with one other roommate as being:

EXHIBIT 2 Maria's List of Assumed Responsibilities (July 1995 to July 1996)

Public Relations
- Liaised between Avanti International and franchisees for queries and problems
- Received, sorted, prepared and distributed press releases
- Collected press clippings and sent to Avanti International

Advertising
- Attended media planning meetings – Hong Kong
- Worked with HKG franchise on Beijing loose insert project
- Thoroughly checked all invoices and media and ensured that all problems were resolved before sending to Italy for payment
- Worked on 1997 advertising budget based on client buy and projected buy
- Updated and distributed international address lines each season

Architecture
- Monitored parts of the architecture process
- Managed all prop orders for new shop openings/renovations
- Ensured that all historic photos were ordered and delivered for new shops/renovations
- Managed all furniture and fittings orders necessary from Italy
- Worked on updating order forms and creating a more efficient process
- Developed basic point-of-sale (POS) database
- Kept POS books and photographic records updated

Display windows
- Helped to implement the first seasonal window display
- Collected relevant window measurements of all shops in region including information on possible problem locations
- Compiled files of information for future projects
- Worked on coordinating window program with merchandise delivery
- Sent feedback to Italy regarding problems and worked on solutions to defective panels

Christmas
- Managed orders of Christmas cards for clients
- Managed Christmas catalogue orders for clients
- Worked as above on Christmas display windows

Open To Buy Orders (OTB)
- Put together a general form for collecting OTB information from clients
- Collected and analyzed information from clients – sought clarification when needed

February 1996 – spent three and a half weeks in Milan for basic corporate orientation.

Dingy and claustrophobic. All the windows were frosted and had bars on them. There was no hint of sunlight in the apartment whatsoever. I could barely squeeze out of my bed in the morning because the space was so limited. Cockroaches partied every night in the kitchen, which itself was nothing more than a closet with twin propane burners for a stove.

Given that her one-year contract with Avanti was due for renewal, Maria began to calculate what she thought was a "fair and equitable compensation package." According to Maria, "a common measure for determining a subsistence standard of living in Hong

Kong is 'rent times three'." Since her rental obligations were HK $9,000 per month, Maria believed she required a minimum of HK $27,000 per month "to stay above the water." In retrospect, Maria commented:

> I originally took Avanti's offer of HK $14,000 per month because I didn't know any better and because I realized I had no experience and had a lot to learn. However, after listening to some of my colleagues in the Humber program, I realized that this amount was going to be insufficient. Therefore, in April 1995, before I started my job, I approached Giovanni about my concerns and he quickly responded by offering me a starting salary of HK $19,000.

On June 11, 1996, just as she was trying to decide how to broach the issue of a raise with Avanti's head office, Maria received a "call out of the blue" from Luigi Ditullio. She was taken aback when he told her that she was receiving an unsolicited raise to HK $23,333 per month, retroactive to March 1, 1996.

> I was very surprised to receive the raise. Unfortunately, Luigi is the type of person who doesn't let you get a word in edgewise, so I did not even have a chance to respond. It happened so fast I did not know what to say or think. There I was, one moment getting a raise and the next listening to a dial tone.

Deciding What to Do

In assessing her current situation, Maria tried to be as objective as possible. On the one hand, she realized that Avanti had been forthcoming in raising her salary in the past. First, she received an immediate increase to her request in April 1995, prior to beginning work in Hong Kong. Second, she received the unsolicited increase the previous week. On both occasions she was quite appreciative of Avanti's efforts, while also remaining pleased by the good relationships she had established with people in the company. On the other hand, Maria felt that, in light of her initial salary, the high cost of living in Hong Kong and her assumption of responsibilities she believed were well in excess of those outlined in her original job description, a strong case could be made for a requesting a more generous compensation package. This course of action was not without risk, however, as she was quite uncertain as to how Avanti would react to any overture she made for more money. Thus, Maria faced a dilemma. While she did not wish to jeopardize the growing rapport she had established with Avanti, she also felt that the economic realities of Hong Kong, coupled with greater assumed responsibilities, warranted a further increase in pay.

Note

1. The Hong Kong dollar was pegged to the US dollar at about HK$7.74 = US$1.00.

Japanese-American Seating Inc. (A)

Joyce Miller and J. Michael Geringer

In mid-January 1991, Jim Needham was facing one of the first challenges of his new position as general manager at Japanese-American Seating Inc. (JASI). Located in southwestern Ontario, JASI was a joint venture between a Japanese seat manufacturer and a Michigan-based seat assembler. When Needham arrived at the beginning of the year, the JASI plant had been through 20 months of commercial production under his predecessor, Bill Stanton. After several hours of discussion in a recent meeting about how to strengthen project management, Needham's Japanese managers had finally gotten his agreement to hire a project coordinator who would report to the materials manager and schedule and control engineering projects. But the more he considered the situation, the more uneasy Needham felt about enlarging the role of the materials department. Could he renege on his earlier decision, or should he just let this one go?

The North American Automotive Industry

The automotive industry accounted for a large part of manufacturing activity in both Canada and the United States, and contributed significantly to the expansion and recession of these economies. In the past decade, the "Big Three" U.S. automakers had experienced an unprecedented decline in market share and profitability, and they continued

 Joyce Miller and Professor J. Michael Geringer prepared this case solely to provide material for class discussion. The authors do not intend to illustrate either effective or ineffective handling of a managerial situation. The authors may have discussed certain names and other identifying information to protect confidentiality.

EXHIBIT 1   The Big Three Automakers and the North American Automotive Industry

	1973	1978	1987	1988	1989
General Motors Corporation					
Quality (defects per 100 cars)	–	–	176	165	158
Productivity (cars per person per year)	11.4	12.1	11.3	12.9	12.6
Inventory turns	5.4	6.7	18.0	18.8	20.0
Profit per unit ($)	490	684	435	692	645
Return on sales (%)	6.7	5.5	3.5	4.4	3.8
Market share (%)	51.5	47.3	34.7	34.9	35.0
Ford Motor Company					
Quality (defects per 100 cars)	–	–	156	169	143
Productivity (cars per person per year)	13.7	13.8	18.7	19.9	20.9
Inventory turns	5.3	6.5	15.6	17.3	18.0
Profit per unit ($)	260	360	1023	1014	663
Return on sales (%)	3.9	3.7	6.4	5.7	3.9
Market share (%)	29.8	26.5	23.1	23.7	24.6
Chrysler Corporation					
Quality (defects per 100 cars)	–	–	178	202	169
Productivity (cars per person per year)	13.0	13.1	16.2	18.0	19.5
Inventory turns	5.6	6.3	16.8	21.6	26.3
Profit per unit ($)	127	(129)	853	649	649
Return on sales (%)	2.1	(1.5)	4.5	3.0	1.0
Market share (%)	15.6	11.2	12.3	13.9	13.7

Source: Annual reports and industry sources

to battle against foreign car companies (Exhibit 1). A recent study noted that sales of vehicles made by North American manufacturers had dropped dramatically as the popularity of overseas models increased, particularly those from Japan, Taiwan, and South Korea. In the 1984–89 period, annual North American vehicle production was relatively flat at about 13 million units, roughly 30% of global production. Captive imports represented a growing phenomenon, and accounted for nearly 5% of North American motor vehicle sales in 1990. Pure imports accounted for an additional 24% of 1990 sales. Captive imports were vehicles imported by American companies. For instance, Chevrolet marketed the Isuzu I-Mark as the Spectrum, General Motors' LeMans and Optima were manufactured in Korea by Daewoo, and Chrysler imported several products made in Thailand by Mitsubishi.

Overall, foreign nameplates had captured about a third of the North American automobile market, despite trade barriers designed to keep them at bay. Honda now claimed 10% of the North American passenger vehicle market, and Toyota had a 7.5% share. These companies beat the quotas by agreeing to voluntary restraints, and building plants in North America, sometimes in conjunction with domestic producers. These operations were called "transplants." The total transplant production in Canada for 1991–92 was forecast at 460,000 units or 16% of Canadian capacity, an explosive increase since 1988, when transplants represented only 3% and 9.5%, respectively, of total Canadian and U.S. production capacity. Under the Auto Pact, vehicles manufactured in

Canada and having at least 50% Canadian or U.S. content could be exported duty-free to the U.S. This also applied to vehicles built by transplant operations.

In response to the challenge posed by foreign manufacturers, the Big Three had invested over US$8 billion in the past five years to upgrade capacity and launch quality programs aimed at matching the Japanese. As well, they were streamlining the manufacturing process by using just-in-time (JIT) principles and contracting out subassemblies. Outsourcing was part of an industry-wide effort to reduce costs. Where car makers used to retool and redesign components almost annually, they were now pushing the burden of design and engineering down to parts suppliers.

These developments had a dramatic impact on organizations supplying seats to the automotive manufacturers. Until the early 1980s, the seat industry was highly fragmented, and could be described as a series of hand-offs, from engineering through to marketing. Each supplier concentrated on one or two areas, such as headrests or suspension systems. The automakers handled most of the "cut-and-sew" activities in-house. By 1991, however, 40% of seat production was being outsourced to suppliers who designed and manufactured complete seating systems. A complete system included the frame, foam pads, cover, seat tracks, lumbar support, recliner, headrest, and trim. At this time, to cut overheads and increase quality control, the automakers were reducing the number of suppliers, and the seat industry was becoming more competitive.

Japanese-American Seating Inc. (JASI)

In 1987, Kasai Kogyo Ltd., a seat manufacturer based in Tokyo, and Banting Seat Corporation, a seat assembler headquartered in a Detroit suburb, formed a 65–35 joint venture to exclusively supply seats on a JIT basis to Orion Manufacturing Corporation. JASI was one of several companies established in southwestern Ontario as dedicated suppliers to Orion. Located 15 km away, Orion was a recently negotiated Japanese-American joint venture which expected to begin producing four cylinder subcompact cars in early 1989. The Orion plant would have the capacity to produce 200,000 vehicles annually, most of which would be shipped to the U.S. Actual production volumes would depend on the market's acceptance of these vehicles as well as cyclical movements of the industry.

Banting and Kasai were leaders in automotive seating in their respective countries. Banting employed about 5,000 people in their North American operations and another 2,000 abroad. They were an established supplier to the Big Three with over $1 billion in annual revenues. After several years of reorganization, Banting had shed all of their non-automotive businesses, and were focused exclusively on seating (approximately 70% of revenues) and other automotive interior parts. Banting's objective was to attain a position of leadership in the automobile seating industry. During the late 1980s, they had invested heavily in R&D and manufacturing facilities in the U.S., as well as acquiring several smaller European producers of automotive seating and interior components.

Kasai employed about 4,200 people and had $1.5 billion in annual sales. Nearly 80% of Kasai's revenues were from the automotive industry, with the remainder coming from office and communications equipment, chemical products, building materials, and miscellaneous machinery. Overall, while heavily involved in their traditional business of automobile parts, Kasai's objective was to achieve greater growth and stability through product diversification and overseas market expansion.

While Banting relied on a myriad of raw materials suppliers to assemble their seating systems, Kasai had a more vertically integrated operation. Kasai owned 12 plants and 26 affiliated companies in Japan, most of them involved in auto-related activities. By applying just-in-time principles to seat production, Kasai had gained a strong reputation within the Japanese auto parts industry. In the 1980s, in an effort to follow their customers and to increase penetration of international markets, Kasai had aggressively expanded their sales network throughout the world, with regional sales headquarters in the U.S., Canada, Spain, Brazil, Taiwan, and Thailand. Although Kasai had also pursued international manufacturing through 11 joint ventures worldwide, the JASI operation marked the company's entry into North American production. The JASI venture was initiated, in part, to help Kasai maintain its supplier relationship with the Japanese firm which was the majority partner in Orion.

The venture was to be run as a profit center. Banting held the minority participation, and JASI would supply Orion on an exclusive basis for a five-year period. The contract called for 3–5% annual price cuts. Construction on the 120,000 square foot facility began in mid-1988, and was completed in early 1989. An investment of $20 million was required and breakeven was expected within four years. The plant had the capacity to produce 245,000 seats annually and would eventually employ 220 people on two shifts.

JASI's Start-up

Under the terms of the joint venture agreement, Banting would design the plant, contribute a general manager, and negotiate the purchase of major raw materials and components. Kasai would contribute their expertise in production and process technology and provide a president to head the venture. Orion placed great value on having an important representative from Japan on-site.

The start-up team was composed of Sumio Imai, president, Bill Stanton, general manager, Akira Hoshino, finance, Tadashi Abe, Orion design engineer, Katsuhiko Ito, engineering, and Yuji Yamanaka, manufacturing/quality director (Exhibits 2 and 3 have organization charts for mid-1989 and January 1991). This was the first time any of the Japanese managers had worked in North America. The Japanese who went abroad were typically on a five-year rotation. Rotating people to gain a cross-section of experience within a company was a widely accepted practice and was, in fact, the foundation of management training and development in Japan. Lifetime employment was still the common practice in Kasai.

Except for Imai, all the Japanese managers brought their families to Canada. Imai, who chose to return to Tokyo three or four times a year for three-week periods, commented:

> My children have finished university and are working; it made sense to do it this way. I go back regularly to spend time with my family and to maintain business connections. The biggest challenge of going on rotation is actually returning. I mean this in a couple of ways.

EXHIBIT 2 Organization Chart, May 1989

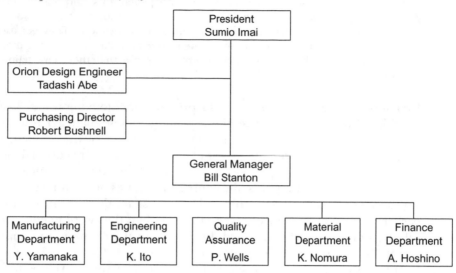

EXHIBIT 3 Organization Chart, January 1991

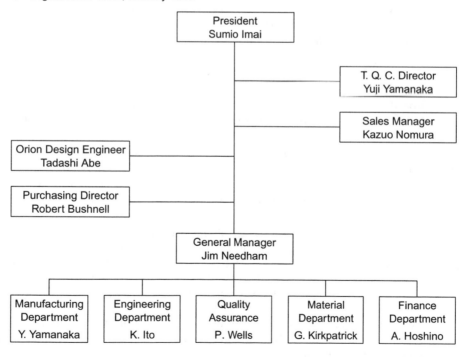

First, companies are dynamic, always changing, and it is important to know the organization. This takes time. It is not uncommon for people to spend many evenings after work socializing with colleagues, building up networks. Second, those who relocate their families to another country often find returning quite an adjustment. They get used to the lower cost of living and the bigger houses. Some people have difficulty getting their children back on track for the best universities. There is a sense that they have gained "bad habits" abroad.

JASI adopted the principles of the JIT production system known as "kanban," which was considered to be Toyota's invention. As one Japanese manager remarked, "Toyota has been doing it for 30 years and is seen as the master of the kanban system. In Japan, everybody likes and lives under kanban." Where the conventional production system was built on an earlier process continuously forwarding products to a later process regardless of its requirements, the kanban system was built on reversing this conception. To supply parts used in assembly under this system, the later process traced back to an earlier process, and withdrew materials only when they were needed. In this way, wasteful inventory could be eliminated. Imai was an early champion in applying the kanban system to the production of seats at Kasai.

In JASI's case, the kanban referred to a triangular vinyl envelope which accompanied parts and products as they moved through the plant. The kanban provided information about picking up or receiving an order so that only what was needed would be produced. The kanban controlled the flow of goods by serving as a withdrawal order, a work order, and an order for conveyance. Associates picked and replaced parts in small batches according to the kanban.

Work cells contained several machines designed for quick, easy changes and short set-up times so that a single operator could do a series of tasks. At any one time, there was no more than 4–8 hours of inventory in the plant, from parts through to the seats waiting on the rack for shipping. Seat storage and shipping were geared to the "live broadcast" of cars coming out of Orion's paint section which fixed the order through final trim and assembly. To meet JIT requirements, units were shipped sequentially based on material and other options according to Orion's production schedule. JASI typically had a 3.5–4 hour window to deliver a particular seat set to Orion. There was a substantial financial penalty for late or incorrect delivery. Incoming seats were transferred directly to the final assembly line in the correct position without having to sort through an entire truckload to locate a specific unit. An industry analyst observed:

> Kanban systems require a lot of training: training workers to monitor inventory levels and training suppliers to operate under JIT principles. Suppliers have to understand the concept of delivering 50 pieces at 10 a.m.; not before, not after, and not 49. It's about supplying the right quantities of the right product at the right time. It's changing the philosophy away from protecting business behind the delivery door; it's about partnerships.

JASI had approximately 100 suppliers of small stampings, nuts and bolts, cloth, foam, frame, recliners, and other raw materials. At some point, certain activities like manufacturing foam might be brought in-house in a separate facility.

In September 1988, Kazuo Nomura joined the company as materials manager. Following the Japanese model, Nomura had both purchasing and sales responsibilities, and oversaw all aspects of cost, material, and production control. In addition to being a liaison with Orion, handling suppliers, and scheduling incoming materials, he controlled engineering projects. However, expediting materials was taking up an extraordinary amount of his time. Nomura explained:

> North American suppliers don't give us the kind of support we're used to in Japan. I'd end up having regular quarrels with suppliers just trying to explain the kanban process. It was taking longer than I expected to get them to buy in, to deliver small quantity shipments on a JIT basis, and I was getting frustrated. It was hard to handle everything. Our reputation with Orion was key, and I was dedicated to building this relationship. In January 1990, I became sales manager, and JASI hired a Canadian, George Kirkpatrick, to take over materials. By this time, many of my responsibilities had been parcelled out to other departments. Kirkpatrick would schedule parts in and products out, keep suppliers onstream, ensure manufacturing had the materials to keep the plant going, and interact with Orion regarding product sequencing and shipping.

During start-up, the management team generally worked well together despite some differences in management style. Stanton had designed the plant, knowing nothing about Japanese management and production principles that would be used to operate it. Over a six-month period beginning in November 1988, three groups of two or three salaried managers and technicians went to Japan to learn about Kasai's production system, and see the same seats they would be making being built at the Tokyo facility. Throughout this time, JASI was producing pilot seats, programming and debugging the numerically controlled metal benders and robot welders, and training people how to properly fit seat covers.

Overall, there were few technical problems or difficulties with the non-unionized workforce. The area had an abundant labor pool, particularly with the recent influx of East European and Southeast Asian immigrants. Stanton's policy was to recruit young people without industry experience; and have them work in teams and cross-train. With a monthly absenteeism rate of 3%, where the industry average was 5%, JASI was considered a highly successful venture, especially on the interpersonal side.

JASI began commercial production in April 1989, coinciding with Orion's start-up. Over the next 20 months, the company made steady progress in training their workforce and suppliers, containing costs, and meeting the price cuts scheduled into the contract with Orion. From the start, JASI had adopted the Japanese concept of "kaizen." Literally translated, this meant continuous improvement. This philosophy encouraged associates to submit ideas for new methods, rationalized set-ups, more efficient ways of operating machinery, and so on.

The Japanese managers considered that JASI operated relatively autonomously from both parent companies, particularly Kasai. Their communications with Kasai were principally about issues of product quality; major problems with customers, especially regarding product quality issues; engineering changes, and the development and testing of prototypes; and proposed investments. For example, in response to model changes at Orion, they would send samples of parts prototypes for testing in Kasai's labs, since JASI lacked the required capabilities. Interactions with Banting often involved operational details, such as purchasing materials, changing suppliers, and introducing new products. They also communicated with Banting regarding cultural issues which the Japanese managers were unfamiliar with, such as donations to a local charity, or staging a company party for employees and their families.

On a monthly basis, both parent companies received a statement outlining the venture's general financial status. While Kasai had never requested additional detailed financial data, Banting had occasionally asked for figures on overtime, production costs, and output, particularly during the venture's start-up. JASI's managers were strictly required to consult with both parents, including detailed documentation, whenever funding was required for new investments. One Japanese manager noted that requests for investment funds had never been rejected, and parent inquiries associated with these requests had diminished substantially as the venture became more established. However, he noted that where Kasai would allow the venture to have a negative cash flow for five years, Banting had a significantly shorter horizon and seemed to require stricter budgetary control.

As a sole supplier of a major component, quality or delivery problems on JASI's part could shut down Orion's plant. Of all of Orion's suppliers, JASI believed it faced the greatest potential for problems; the fabric, foam, and weave of the knit all affected the final product. Most returns were because of variances within tolerances. Nomura was the key liaison between the two companies, and he met daily with Imai to report current issues. He travelled frequently to the Orion site, and was in daily contact with the purchasing, engineering, and quality departments to feed information back into the JASI plant. Nomura explained:

> For minor problems, Orion's quality department talks directly with our quality area. If problems are deeper, I get involved. I'll set up a meeting with people from both sides to analyze the current system and get at the root cause, then I report back to Orion about how we're implementing improvements. Everyone has their mind on corrective action and there's a lot of informal communication. We're still small enough to respond fast. When significant new investment is required, I'll get the president and general manager involved. Otherwise, it's up to me.

Showing a high degree of responsiveness and taking quick action to correct returns had enabled JASI to build an excellent reputation to the extent that the company had recently been taken off Orion's regular quality audit list, which meant that performance reviews would only be conducted every six months. By this time, a strongly knit culture had developed, both in management and on the plant floor.

When Orion geared up production in September 1990, JASI brought on a second shift which added 100 people to the payroll. Work groups had to be split up to train the new associates. Defects increased and productivity deteriorated significantly during this period. At this time, the Canadian Auto Workers (CAW) made a successful bid to unionize the workforce. In October, the CAW was certified as the official bargaining unit and began negotiations with JASI management.

Jim Needham's Arrival

In Fall 1990, Banting finalized a deal to acquire a German seat assembler, giving the firm entry into the country which represented about one-third of the automotive manufacturing

market in Europe. European seat makers had traditionally sold foam and metal components, but there was increasing pressure from the car makers to deliver complete
seating systems on a JIT basis. Stanton was asked to take over the management of the
plant in Germany, and Jim Needham was offered the general manager position at JASI,
a promotion from his current position managing a seat assembly plant in Michigan.
Needham, age 41, expected to spend at least three years at JASI. He reflected:

> Bill took the job in Germany because he felt he couldn't do much more here; he was ready
> to take on a new challenge. I accepted the job in mid-November and started commuting
> back and forth several times a week. A lot of my time was taken up with paperwork and
> immigration matters. I had to buy a house, move my family here at the beginning of the
> year, and get my two kids settled into new schools. My wife and 12-year-old son seemed to
> make the transition okay. But my 16-year-old daughter wasn't exactly thrilled about moving
> to a small rural town in another country. At first, it seemed like there was just one brick on
> my back after another.

Needham had worked for Banting for the past six years, coming up through the ranks
from manufacturing manager. He continued:

> I'm an old factory nut, and I was really impressed with the JASI plant: how well it was laid
> out, the robotics and metal bending capabilities, the high-tech product testing. JASI was
> making all their own frames whereas the plants I'd worked in before were building seats
> with purchased parts. I'd been through some consensus training but I had limited experi-
> ence working with the Japanese. In Michigan, we were doing JIT, we had cards on the seats
> and were scheduling the replacement of batches. We thought we were doing a lot, but I've
> never seen kanban worked as thoroughly through the production process as here. It's hard
> to learn how to make kanban work, and making it work right is a real trick.
>
> Right now, I'm concerned about the union negotiations. I'd worked with the United
> Auto Workers in the past but the CAW has the reputation of being a more militant organ-
> ization. I hope that we won't get into the typical adversarial relationship. JASI's wage
> structure is good and the benefits package is solid. We have a progressive-thinking union
> rep who seems open to a different approach. I'm not anticipating a lot of restrictions; the
> union knows our relationship with Orion, that the company will be growing.
>
> I think Bill took the decision to unionize quite personally. Bill put everything he had into
> this plant, and he had a strong feeling of personal ownership here. He was into all the
> details. Once he was convinced of something, he went all out to make it happen. He has
> quite a forceful personality with a decisive, direct style, even authoritarian at times.

Needham did not have a lot of preparation before taking on his new position. He
remarked:

> I only had 3–4 days with Bill, and I spent that time trying to get down the mechanics of the
> organization. I knew that I was coming into a tightly knit group. And I was coming into
> a situation where I couldn't even speak directly with my own boss and some of my key
> managers. Nomura and Hoshino had a working knowledge of English, but I'm not sure
> how much the other Japanese comprehend. They spend a lot of time together interpreting
> for each other. I suspect that Imai understands more than what he can express in English.
> Whenever Imai has a meeting with an Anglo, he'll always have someone else there, usually

Nomura, to interpret. Still, I have to be careful. What gets said may be just the best way someone knew how to say it and not necessarily their intent.

It's hard to figure out the dynamics of the management group. Imai is gregarious and outgoing while Yamanaka gravitates towards the role of the "keeper;" he keeps situations in control, he's more grounded. Nomura seems to be the linking pin in the whole operation. Bill tried not to tell me too much; he didn't want to predispose me to certain individuals. One thing Bill emphasized was the need to maintain operational control, especially in order to achieve better cost/benefit ratios. He gave the example that the Japanese continually look for improvements and might request that eight people be assigned to the task of rearranging a work cell. They'll justify it as being for the good of the company, but the benefit might not come until four or five years later. Bill noted that this could generate problems at Banting, since Mr. Begar, an Executive Vice President at Banting and their senior representative on JASI's board, as well as other executives at headquarters would expect me to regularly report key production data as Bill had done, and they would not be pleased if the figures varied substantially from budget.

I'm mostly learning as I go along. I realize that I can't do things the same way I did before. I didn't think people could tolerate an American coming in swinging. The last thing I want anyone to think is that I'm a dictator; I've worked for those types before, and it never works. I want to take the long view; changes will come over time. At the beginning, the important thing is to not make too many quick judgments or life-threatening decisions, to just get involved where you really need to.

I'm starting to have some interaction with Hoshino on the budget, and it's possible that he could be a window into the Japanese group, someone who I can put the sticky questions to and find out about personalities and political ramifications in Japan. At the moment, I'm very much the new guy. I have a sense that people might be looking for changes in the way things get done. I bring a new set of ears, and ideas that didn't get through before will be resubmitted. People are redefining relationships, and this isn't necessarily a bad thing. There are good reasons for making changes at this level: there's the saying that you can't change the players but you can sometimes change the coach. Maybe I'll have a chance to make the improvements my predecessor couldn't crack.

Shortly after Needham's arrival, the media reported that early January 1991 sales of North American vehicles had plunged as worries about the faltering economy and the Persian Gulf crisis continued to erode consumer confidence.

Managing in a Cross-Cultural Environment

Needham knew that his job at JASI would be more difficult, at least initially, than those he had gone into previously. He recounted:

I'm used to reading a situation quicker. I come from a system where a good boss listens to his manager, then makes a decision; his people understand it and follow it. The Japanese look for consensus, and this is hard to get to. Management meetings are long. Recently, we spent an hour only to find that we had two versions of the same vacation policy, one for the Japanese and one for the North Americans. We spent another two hours trying to hammer out a single policy. There's always a risk that everyone will nod their heads, and then the Japanese will go off and run the business their way and the North Americans will go off and do things differently. People forget that they're supposed to be learning from each other;

there's always some tension, and sometimes it's hard to get over the humps. The North Americans aren't familiar with the kanban system and sometimes they don't go far enough; they had something that worked before. Put that against the Japanese guys who know and believe in their system.

I see my role as bringing up issues for discussion. If I walked in with the solution to a problem, there would be immediate resistance. We need the extra step here, and I'm patient enough to go through it.

Through a series of conversations, Needham discovered that the Japanese were used to relying heavily on their technicians. In Japan, once these people were told the rules, there was apparently little need to follow up. However, he noticed that JASI's floor technicians were not consistently enforcing such simple things as wearing safety glasses. Shop rules and discipline seemed to be foreign ideas to his Japanese managers. Needham elaborated:

The Japanese don't seem to recognize that the workforce might slip; they aren't trained to look for such problems. Even if they become aware of something, they appear to overlook it. I don't know if it's just a cultural difference, a case of not feeling comfortable dealing with the situation. For instance, it recently happened that someone was stealing and my Japanese guys didn't seem to realize that a person who behaved this way would have to be fired.

Another difference between the Japanese and North American systems was the role of the materials department. In Japan, this department was a large, central hub which ran new engineering and information programs, and scheduled and controlled all aspects of projects. In North America, these activities were typically handled by engineering or manufacturing. As a whole, JASI's Japanese management group felt strongly that the company needed to get better at project management to achieve continuing quality improvements and cost reductions.

The January Meeting

On January 11, 1991, Jim Needham convened a two-hour meeting with virtually the entire management team, including Imai, to discuss the project management situation. Project management was intimately linked with costs. The decisions made in this meeting would affect everyone. The Japanese managers felt strongly that the materials department should enlarge its role and regain its original status. As the venture had moved toward commercial production, many of the responsibilities Nomura originally had as materials manager had been dispersed across departments as he dedicated more of his time to building JASI's relationship with Orion. The Japanese felt that the key to better project management was to centralize this function back in materials. They argued adamantly that a project coordinator needed to be hired in.

Reporting to the materials manager, the project coordinator would launch projects and follow them through to completion. For example, if an engineering study proposed joining three pieces to bolt onto a seat, the project coordinator would find parts suppliers and obtain quotes to facilitate a make or buy decision. This person would also interact with engineering, quality, and manufacturing to ensure each department carried out its responsibilities on the project. The Japanese contended that creating such a position would mean that everyone was informed of the status of ongoing projects. Starting up new projects would be smoother, less costly, and better quality. Needham responded:

> I kept telling people I wasn't convinced that we needed to add an extra person. This hadn't been slotted in and I didn't want to bastardize the budget within the first month. I thought that the job could be handled by someone else already in the organization. I had recently talked to the quality manager, Paul Wells, and he was willing to schedule and follow up projects. This wouldn't make for as big a role for the materials department as the Japanese wanted: the real responsibility would still be with the pieces, but I didn't feel comfortable giving up some of my own authority when I still didn't completely understand the operation. My Japanese managers persisted. One even remarked that when I went to Japan in April, I'd learn why project management should be done in materials. After several hours of discussion, I finally relented.
>
> I suspected that Imai and the others were pleased with the outcome. They were comfortable that I went after consensus, and I had a feeling they would like JASI to operate even more like a Japanese organization.

A few days after agreeing to hire a project coordinator, Needham was having serious second thoughts. Besides concerns that the company was still too small to warrant this additional person and the accompanying costs, he did not feel that the materials department was ready to take on this level of responsibility, and ultimately, he was not comfortable defining the department as largely as it was in Japanese operations. Delegating this additional authority to lower-level managers before he was comfortable in his new position might also limit his own decision-making authority in the future. But what could he do now?

Needham was to meet with Imai at 8 a.m. tomorrow for their weekly meeting, and the agenda which Imai had sent to him was quite full. In addition to addressing several important strategic and operational issues, such as improving integration of local suppliers within JASI's kanban system, production planning and quality control issues, and finalizing a strategy for upcoming negotiations with union representatives, Needham and Imai had been asked by the materials manager to formally approve the proposal to hire a project coordinator, including funding to retain a personnel recruiting firm and placement of position advertisements. In fact, this latter issue was the first item on their agenda, along with review of the quality control report for the prior two weeks, which showed a continuing decline in production defects. Could he change his mind? And how would he even go about doing it?

CASE **6**

○ ○

Footwear International

R. William Blake

John Carlson frowned as he studied the translation of the front-page story from the afternoon's edition of the *Meillat*, a fundamentalist newspaper with close ties to an opposition political party. The story, titled "Footwear's Unpardonable Audacity," suggested that the company was knowingly insulting Islam by including the name of Allah in a design used on the insoles of sandals it was manufacturing. To compound the problem, the paper had run a photograph of one of the offending sandals on the front page. As a result, student groups were calling for public demonstrations against Footwear the next day. As Managing Director of Footwear Bangladesh, Carlson knew he would have to act quickly to defuse a potentially explosive situation.

Footwear International

Footwear International is a multinational manufacturer and marketer of footwear. Operations span the globe and include more than 83 companies in 70 countries. These include shoe factories, tanneries, engineering plants producing shoe machinery and moulds, product development studios, hosiery factories, quality control laboratories, and approximately 6,300 retail stores and 50,000 independent retailers.

Footwear employs more than 67,000 people and produces and sells in excess of 270,000,000 pairs of shoes every year. Head office acts as a service center and is staffed with specialists drawn from all over the world. These specialists, in areas such as marketing, retailing, product development, communications, store design, electronic data processing, and business administration, travel for much of the year to share their

Reproduced by permission of the author. © R. William Blake, Faculty of Business Administration, Memorial University of Newfoundland, St. John's, Canada A1B 3X5.

expertise with the various companies. Training and technical education, offered through company-run colleges and the training facility at headquarters, provide the latest skills to employees from around the world.

Although Footwear requires standardization in technology and the design of facilities, it also encourages a high degree of decentralization and autonomy in its operations. The companies are virtually self-governing, which means their allegiance belongs to the countries in which they operate. Each is answerable to a board of directors which includes representatives from the local business community. The concept of "partnership" at the local level has made the company welcome internationally and has allowed it to operate successfully in countries where other multinationals have been unable to survive.

Bangladesh

With a population approaching 110,000,000 in an area of 143,998 square kilometers (see Figure 1), Bangladesh is the most densely populated country in the world. It is also among the most impoverished, with a 1987 per capita gross national product of U.S.$160 and a high reliance on foreign aid. More than 40% of the gross domestic product is generated by agriculture and more than 60% of its economically active population works in the agriculture sector. Although the land in Bangladesh is fertile, the country has a tropical monsoon climate and suffers from the ravages of periodic cyclones. In 1988, the country experienced the worst floods in recorded history.

The population of Bangladesh is 85% Moslem, and Islam was made the official state religion in 1988. Approximately 95% of the population speaks Bengali with most of the remainder speaking tribal dialects.

Bangladesh has had a turbulent history in the twentieth century. Most of the country was part of the British-ruled East Bengal until 1947. In that year it joined with Assam to become East Pakistan, a province of the newly created country of Pakistan. East Pakistan was separated from the four provinces of West Pakistan by 1,600 kilometers of Indian territory and, although the East was more populous, the national capital was established in West Pakistan. Over the following years widespread discontent built in the East, whose people felt that they received a disproportionately small amount of development funding and were underrepresented in government.

Following a period of unrest starting in 1969, the Awami League, the leading political party in East Pakistan, won an overwhelming victory in local elections held in 1970. The victory promised to give the league, which was pro-independence, control in the National Assembly. To prevent that happening the national government suspended the convening of the Assembly indefinitely. On March 26, 1971, the Awami League proclaimed the independence of the People's Republic of Bangladesh and civil war quickly followed. In the ensuing conflict hundreds of thousands of refugees fled to safety across the border in India. In December India, which supported the independence of Bangladesh, declared war and twelve days later Pakistan surrendered. Bangladesh had won its independence, and the capital of the new country was established at Dhaka. In the years immediately following independence industrial output declined in major

FIGURE 1 Bangladesh

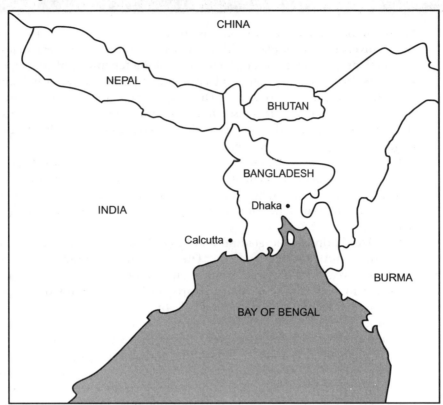

industries as the result of the departure of many of the largely non-Bengali financier and managerial class.

Throughout the subsequent years, political stability proved elusive for Bangladesh. Although elections were held, stability was threatened by the terrorist tactics resorted to by opposition groups from both political extremes. Coups and counter coups, assassinations, and suspension of civil liberties became regular occurrences.

Since 1983, Bangladesh had been ruled by the self-proclaimed President General H. M. Ershad. Despite demonstrations in 1987, which led to a state of emergency being declared, Ershad managed to retain power in elections held the following year. The country remains politically volatile, however. Dozens of political parties continually maneuver for position and alliances and coalitions are the order of the day. The principal opposition party is the Awami League, an alliance of eight political parties. Many of the parties are closely linked with so-called opposition newspapers, which promote their political positions. Strikes and demonstrations are frequent and often result from cooperation among opposition political parties, student groups, and unions.

Footwear Bangladesh

Footwear became active in what was then East Bengal in the 1930s. In 1962 the first major investment took place with the construction of a footwear manufacturing facility at Tongi, an industrial town located thirty kilometers north of Dhaka. During the following years the company expanded its presence in both conventional and unconventional ways. In 1971, the then Managing Director became a freedom fighter, while continuing to oversee operations. He subsequently became the only foreigner to be decorated by the government with the "Bir Protik" in recognition of both his and the company's contribution to the independence of Bangladesh.

In 1985, Footwear Bangladesh went public and two years later spearheaded the largest private-sector foreign investment in the country, a tannery and footwear factory at Dhamrai. The new tannery produced leather for local Footwear needs and the export market, and the factory produced a variety of footwear for the local market.

By 1988, Footwear Bangladesh employed 1,800 employees and sold through eighty-one stores and fifty-four agencies. The company introduced approximately 300 new products a year to the market using their in-house design and development capability. Footwear managers were particularly proud of the capability of the personnel in these departments, all of whom were Bangladeshi.

Annual sales in excess of 10,000,000 pairs of footwear gave the company 15% of the national market in 1988. Revenues exceeded U.S.$30 million and after tax profit was approximately U.S.$1 million. Financially, the company was considered a medium contributor within the Footwear organization. With a population approaching 110,000,000, and per capita consumption of one pair of shoes every two years, Bangladesh was perceived as offering Footwear enormous potential for growth both through consumer education and competitive pressure.

The managing director of Footwear Bangladesh was John Carlson, one of only four foreigners working for the company. The others were the managers of production, marketing, and sales. All had extensive and varied experience within the Footwear organization.

The Incident

On Thursday, June 22, 1989, John Carlson was shown a copy of that day's *Meillat,* a well-known opposition newspaper with pro-Libyan leanings. Under the headline "Footwear's Unpardonable Audacity," the writer suggested that the design on the insole of one model of sandal produced by the company included the Arabic spelling of the word "Allah" (see Figure 2). The story went on to suggest that Footwear was under Jewish ownership and to link the alleged offense with the gunning down of many people in Palestine by Jews. The story highlighted the fact that the design was on the insole of the sandal and therefore, next to the bottom of the foot, a sign of great disrespect to Moslems.

FIGURE 2   Translation of the *Meillat* Story*

Unpardonable Audacity of Footwear

In Bangladesh a Sandal with Allah as Footwear trade mark in Arabic designed in calligraphy has been marketed although last year Islam was made the State Religion in Bangladesh. The Sandal in black and white contains Allah in black. Prima facie it appears it has been designed and the Alif "the first letter in Arabic" has been jointly written. Excluding Alif it reads LILLAH. In Bangladesh after the Satan Rushdies Satanic Verses† which has brought unprecedented demonstration and innumerable strikes (Hartels). This International shoe manufacturing organization under Jewish ownership with the design of Allah has made religious offence. Where for sanctity of Islam one million people of Afghanistan have sacrificed their lives and wherein occupied Palestine many people have been gunned down by Jews for sanctity of Islam in this country the word Allah under this guise has been put under feet.

Last night a group of students from Dhaka university came to Meillat office with a couple of pairs of Sandal. The management staff of Footwear was not available over telephone. This sandal has got two straps made of foam.

* The translation is identical to that with which Carlson was given to work.
† Salman Rushdie was the author of the controversial book *The Satanic Verses*. The author had been sentenced to death, in absentia, by Ayatollah Khomenei, the leader of Iran, for crimes against Islam.

Carlson immediately contacted the supervisor of the design department and asked for any information he could provide on the design on the sandals. He already knew that they were from a medium-priced line of women's footwear that had the design on the insole changed often as a marketing feature. Following his investigation the supervisor reported that the design had been based on a set of Chinese temple bells that the designer had purchased in the local market. Pleased by the appearance of the bells, she had used them as the basis for a stylized design, which she submitted to her supervisor for consideration and approval (see Figure 3).

All the employees in the development and marketing department were Moslems. The supervisor reported that the woman who had produced the offending design was a devout Bengali Moslem who spoke and read no Arabic. The same was true of almost all the employees in the department. The supervisor confirmed to Carlson that numerous people in the department had seen the new design prior to its approval and no one had seen any problem or raised any objection to it. Following the conversation Carlson compared the design to the word Allah, which he had arranged to have written in Arabic (see Figure 4).

Carlson was perplexed by the article and its timing. The sandals in question were not new to the market and had not been subject to prior complaints. As he reread the translation of the *Meillat* article, he wondered why the Jewish reference had been made when the family that owned Footwear International was Christian. He also wondered if the fact that students from the university had taken the sandals to the paper was significant.

As the day progressed the situation got worse. Carlson was shown a translation of a proclamation that had been circulated by two youth groups calling for demonstrations against Footwear to be held the next day (see Figure 5). The proclamation linked

FIGURE 3 The Temple Bells and the Design Used on the Sandal

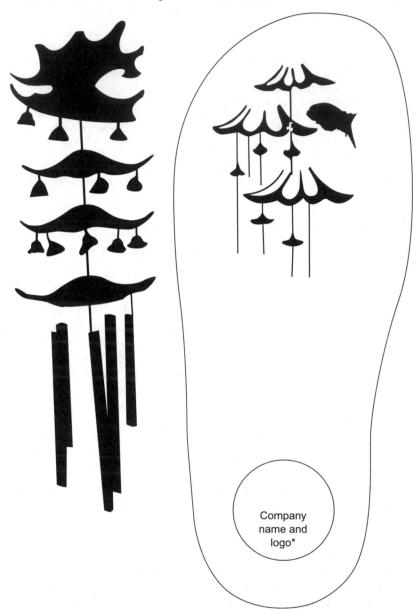

* The company's name and logo appeared prominently on the insole of the sandal. Both of the images in the exhibit were redrawn from copies of facsimiles sent to headquarters by John Carlson.

FIGURE **4** The Arabic Spelling of *Allah* (This was redrawn from a facsimile sent to headquarters by John Carlson.)

FIGURE **5** Translation of the Student Group's Proclamation*

The audacity through the use of the name "Allah" in a sandal.
Let Rushdies Jewish Footwear Company be prohibited in Bangladesh.
Dear people who believe in one God It is announced in the holy Quran Allahs name is above everything but shoe manufacturing Jewish Footwear Shoe Company has used the name Allah and shown disrespect of unprecedented nature and also unpardonable audacity. After the failure of Rushdies efforts to destroy the beliefs of Moslems in the Quran, Islam and the prophet (SM) who is the writer of Satanic verses the Jewish People have started offending the Moslems. This time it is a fight against Allah. In fact Daud Haider, Salman Rushdie Viking Penguin and Footwear Shoe Company all are supported and financed by Jewish community. Therefore no compromise with them. Even at the cost of our lives we have to protest against this conspiracy.
For this procession and demonstration will be held on 23rd. June Friday after Jumma prayer from Baitul Mukarram Mosque south gate. Please join this procession and announce we will not pardon Footwear Shoe Companys audacity Footwear Shoe Company has to be prohibited, don't buy Jewish products and Footwear shoes. Be aware Rushdies partner.
Issued by Bangladesh Islamic Jubashibir (Youth Student Forum) and Bangladesh Islamic Satrashbir (Student Forum).

---

* The translation is identical to that with which Carlson was given to work.

Footwear, Salman Rushdie, and the Jewish community and ominously stated that "even at the cost of our lives we have to protest against this conspiracy."

More bad news followed. Calls had been made for charges to be laid against Carlson and four others under a section of the criminal code that forbade "deliberate and malicious acts intended to outrage feelings of any class by insulting its religion or religious believers" (see Figure 6). A short time later Carlson received a copy of a

FIGURE **6**   Section 295 of the Criminal Code

[295-A. *Deliberate and malicious acts intended to outrage religious feelings of any class by insulting its religion or religious believers*. Whoever, with deliberate and malicious intention of outraging the religious feelings of any class of [the citizens of Bangladesh], by words, either spoken or written, or by visible representations insults or attempts to insult the religion or religious beliefs of that class, shall be punished with imprisonment.

. . . In order to bring a matter under section 295-A it is not the mere matter of discourse or the written expression but also the manner of it which has to be looked to. In other words the expressions should be such as are bound to be regarded by any reasonable man as grossly offensive and provocative and maliciously and deliberately intended to outrage the feelings of any class of citizens. . . . If the injurious act was done voluntarily without a lawful excuse, malice may be presumed.

FIGURE **7**   The Statement of the Plaintiff

The plaintiff most respectfully states that:

(1)   The plaintiff is a lawyer, and a Bangladeshi Citizen and his religion is Islam. He is basically a devout Moslem. According to Islamic tradition he regularly performs his daily work.
(2)   The first accused of this . . . is the Managing Director of Footwear Shoe Company, the second accused is the Production Manager of the said company, the third accused is the Marketing Manager, the fourth accused is the Calligrapher of the said company and last accused is the Sales Manager of the said company. The said company is an international organization having shoe business in different countries.
(3)   The accused persons deliberately wanted to outrage the religion of Muslims by engraving the calligraphy of "Allah" in Arabic on a sandal thereby to offend the Religion of majority this Muslim Country. By marketing this sandal with the calligraphy of "Allah" they have offended the religious feelings of millions of Muslims. It is the solemn religious duty and responsibility of every devout Muslim to protect the sanctity of "Allah." The plaintiff first saw the sandal with this calligraphy on 22nd June 1989 at Elephant road shop.

The accused persons collectively and deliberately wanted this calligraphy under the feet thereby to offend the religion of mine and many other Muslims and have committed a crime under provisions of section 295A of the Penal Code. At the time of hearing the evidence will be provided.

Therefore under the provisions of section 295A of the Penal Code the accused persons be issued with warrant of arrest and be brought to court for justice.

The names of the Witnesses
(1)
(2)
(3)

statement that had been filed by a local lawyer, although no warrants were immediately forthcoming (see Figure 7).

While he was reviewing the situation Carlson was interrupted by his secretary. In an excited voice she informed him that the Prime Minister was being quoted as calling the sandal incident an "unforgivable crime." The seriousness of the incident seemed to be escalating rapidly and Carlson wondered what he should do to try to minimize the damage.

CASE **7**

○ ○

Hazelton International

Henry W. Lane and Lorna L. Wright

Dan Simpson, the in-coming project manager of the Maralinga-Ladawan Highway Project, was both anxious and excited as he drove with John Anderson in their jeep up the rutted road to the river where they would wait for the ferry. John was the current manager and was taking Dan, his replacement, on a three-day site check of the project. During this trip John was also going to brief Dan on the history of the project and the problems he would encounter. Dan was anxious about the project because he had heard there were a number of messy problems, but was excited about the challenge of managing it.

Hazelton, a consulting engineering firm, was an advisor on the project and so far had little success in getting the client to heed its advice. After two years of operation, only 17 kilometers of the 245 kilometer highway were under construction.

Background

Since 1965 Hazelton had successfully completed assignments in forty-six countries across Africa, Asia, Europe, South and Central America, and the Caribbean region. A large proportion of the projects had been in Africa but the company was now turning is attention to developing its Asian operations. Since its beginning, Hazelton had done only ten projects in Asia – less than 10% of all its projects.

Henry W. Lane and Lorna L. Wright prepared this case solely to provide material for class discussion. The authors do not intend to illustrate either effective or ineffective handling of a managerial situation. The authors may have disguised certain names and other identifying information to protect confidentiality.

Hazelton provided consulting services in transportation, housing and urban development, structural engineering, and municipal and environmental engineering, to both government and corporate clients around the world. Specific services included technical and economic feasibility studies, financing, planning, architecture, preliminary and final engineering design, maintenance programming, construction supervision, project management, and equipment procurement.

Projects ranged from extremely large (building an international airport) to very small, requiring the skills of only a single expert (advising on a housing project in Malaysia). The majority of these projects were funded by international lending agencies (ILAs) such as the World Bank, African Development Bank and aid agencies like the U.S. Agency for International Development (USAID) and the Canadian International Development Agency (CIDA). The previous year Hazelton's worldwide annual fee volume exceeded U.S. $40 million.

Hazelton staffed its overseas projects with senior members of its permanent staff. In addition, experts with international experience and capabilities in the applicable language were used whenever possible. Both these principles had been adhered to in the Maralinga-Ladawan project.

Maralinga-Ladawan Highway Project

Soronga was a nation of islands in the Pacific Ocean. This project required design and construction supervision services for a 245 kilometer highway along the western coast of the island of Tola from Maralinga in the north to Ladawan in the south (see Figure 1). Sections of the highway past Ladawan were being reconstructed by other firms funded by aid agencies from Japan and Australia.

In addition to supervising the project, Hazelton was responsible for a major training program for Sorongan engineers, mechanics, operators, and administrative staff.

This was the fifth largest project ($1.6 million in fees) that Hazelton had ever undertaken (see Figure 2). It was a joint venture with two other firms, Beauval Ltd. and McPherson Brothers International (MBI), whom Hazelton involved to strengthen its proposal. Hazelton acted as the lead firm on behalf of the consortium and assumed overall responsibility for the work. Over the life of the project, the three firms would send twenty-two expatriates, including highway designers, engineers, mechanics, and operators.

MBI was involved because it was a contractor and Hazelton felt it might need those types of skills when dealing with a "force account" project. Usually, Hazelton supervised the project and left the actual construction to experienced contractors. This project was different. Force account meant that the construction workers would be government employees who would not be experienced in construction work.

Beauval had been working in Asia for seventeen years and had established a base of operations in Kildona. It had done several projects on the island of Hako but this would be the first on the island of Tola. This local experience helped the proposal gain acceptance both in the eyes of the financing agency, and the client, the Sorongan Highway Department (SHD).

The financing agency provided a combination loan and grant for the project and played a significant role in the selection of the winning proposal. The grant portion

FIGURE 1 Map of Soronga (not to scale)

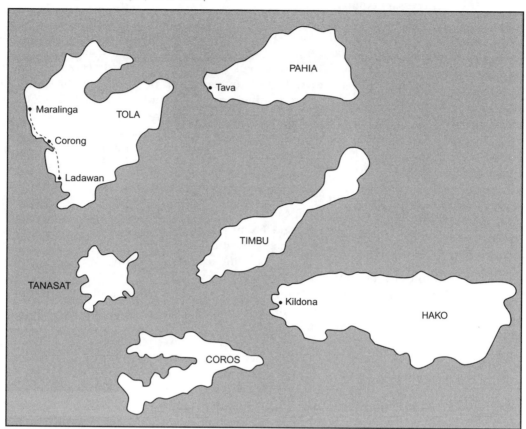

FIGURE 2 Hazelton's Six Largest Projects

Project	Location	Fee
1. International airport	Africa	$4 million
2. Highway supervision	South America	$3.4 million
3. Highway feasibility	South America	$2.25 million
4. Highway design	South America	$2.25 million
5. Highway betterment	Soronga	$1.63 million
6. Secondary roads: graveling	Africa	$1.32 million

paid for the salaries of the expatriates working on the project while the loan funds were for necessary equipment.

Under the contract's terms of reference, Hazelton personnel were sent as advisors on the techniques of road construction and equipment maintenance. The training component was to be the major part of the project with the actual construction being the training vehicle. The project was to last five years with Hazelton phasing out its experts in about four years. The Sorongans would be trained by that point to take over the project themselves. The training program would use formal classroom instruction and a system of counterparts. Each expatriate engineer or manager would have a counterpart Sorongan engineer or manager who worked closely with him in order for the expertise to be passed on. At the mechanic and operator levels, training programs would be set up involving both in-class instruction and on-the-job training.

SHD's responsibilities included providing counterpart staff, ensuring that there was housing built for the expatriates, and providing fuel and spare parts for the equipment that would be coming from Canada.

It was thought that a force account project – with government staff doing the work – would be the best way to marry the financial agency's objective of training with the Sorongan government's aim of building a road. It was one of the first times that SHD had found itself in the role of contractor.

Hazelton was in the position of supervising one arm of the organization on behalf of another arm. It was working for the client as a supervising engineer, but the client also ran the construction. Hazelton was in the middle.

In Soronga's development plans this project was part of the emphasis on developing the transportation and communication sector. It was classed as a *betterment* project, meaning that Soronga did not want undue resources going toward a "perfect" road in engineering terms; merely one that was better than the present one and that would last. An important objective also was to provide employment in Tola and permit easier access to the rest of Soronga, because the province was a politically sensitive area and isolated from the rest of the country.

Tola

Tola was the most westerly island of the Sorongan archipelago. It was isolated from the rest of the country because of rough terrain and poor roads. It was a socially conservative province and fundamentalist in religion. The majority of Tolanese were very strict Moslems. The ulamas (Moslem religious leaders) played an important role in Tolanese society, perhaps more so than in any other part of Soronga.

Economically, the province lagged behind Hako, the main island. The economy was still dominated by labor-intensive agriculture. Large-scale industry was a very recent development with timbering providing the biggest share of exports. A liquefied natural gas plant and a cement factory were two new industries begun within the past two years.

From its earliest history, Tola had enjoyed a high degree of autonomy. In 1821 it signed a treaty with a European country guaranteeing its autonomy in commerce. This was revoked in 1871 when that European country signed a treaty with another European colonial power, recognizing the latter's sovereignty over the whole of Soronga. The

Tolanese understood the implications of this treaty and tried to negotiate with their new master to retain Tola's autonomous standing. Neither side was willing to compromise, however, and in 1873 the European country declared war on Tola. This war continued for fifty years, and the fierce resistance of the Tolanese against colonization became a model for Soronga's own fight for independence later. Even after the Tolanese officially surrendered this did not mean peace. Guerrilla warfare continued, led by the ulamas. With the advent of World War II and the arrival of the Japanese, resistance to the Europeans intensified. At the end of the war, the Japanese were expelled and the European colonizers returned to Soronga, but not to Tola.

With the independence of Soronga, Tola theoretically formed part of the new nation, but in practice it retained its regional social, economic, and political control. In 1961, however, the central government in Kildona dissolved the province of Tola and incorporated its territory into the region of West Pahia under a governor in Tava. Dissatisfaction with this move was so intense that the Tolanese proclaimed an independent Islamic Republic in 1963. This rebellion lasted until 1971, when the central government sought a political solution by giving Tola provincial status again. In 1977 Kildona granted special status to the province in the areas of religion, culture, and education.

Tola's long periods of turmoil had left their mark on the province and on its relations with the rest of the country. It was deeply suspicious of outsiders (particularly those from Hako, since that was the seat of the central government), strongly independent, and fiercely proud of its heritage and ethnic identity. Although all Tolanese could speak Sorongan because that was *the* only language used in the schools, they preferred to use their native language, Tolanese, amongst themselves. The central government in Kildona had recently become concerned about giving the province priority in development projects to strengthen the ties between the province and the rest of the country.

Progress of the Project

The First Year

Negotiations on the project took longer than expected, and the project actually began almost a year after it was originally scheduled to start. Hazelton selected its personnel carefully. The project manager, Frank Kennedy, had been successful in a similar position in Central America. He had also successfully cleaned up a problem situation in Lesotho. In September Frank and an administrator arrived in Soronga, followed a month later by the major design team, bringing the total expatriate contingent to ten families. They spent a month learning the Sorongan language but had to stay in Kildona until December because there was no housing in Maralinga. The houses had not been finished; before they could be, an earthquake destroyed the complex. Eventually, housing was rented from Australian expatriates working for another company who were moving to a complex of their own.

Hazelton was anxious to begin work, but no Sorongan project manager had been specified, and the vehicles did not arrive until late December. When the vehicles did arrive, the fuel tanks were empty and there was no fuel available. Neither was there provision in SHD's budget to buy fuel nor lubricants that year. The project would have to wait until the new fiscal year began on April 1 to have money allotted to it. Meanwhile, it would be a fight for funds.

The Second Year

By the beginning of the year the equipment was on site, but the Sorongan counterpart staff still were not. Hazelton had no control over SHD staff, since it had no line responsibility. When the SHD project manager finally arrived, he was reluctant to confront the staff. Senior SHD people on the project were Hakonese, whereas most of the people at the operator level were local Tolanese. There was not only the Hakonese–Tolanese strain but an unwillingness on the part of the senior staff to do anything that would stir up this politically volatile area.

Frank was having a difficult time. He was a construction man. There were 245 kilometers of road to build and nothing was being done. It galled him to have to report no progress month after month. If the construction could start, the training would quickly follow. On top of the project problems, Frank's wife was pregnant and had to stay in Singapore, where the medical facilities were better. His frustration increased, and he began confronting the Sorongan project manager, demanding action. His behavior became counter-productive and he had to be replaced. The person chosen as his replacement was John Anderson.

John Anderson

John Anderson was a civil engineer who had worked for Hazelton for fifteen years. He had a wealth of international experience in countries as diverse as Thailand, Nigeria, Tanzania, and Kenya. He liked the overseas environment for a variety of reasons, not the least of which was the sense of adventure that went with working abroad. "You meet people who stand out from the average. You get interesting points of view."

Professionally, it was also an adventure. "You run across many different types of engineering and different ways of approaching it." This lent an air of excitement and interest to jobs that was lacking in domestic work. The challenge was greater also since one didn't have access to the same skills and tools as at home: As John said, "You have to make do."

Even though he enjoyed overseas work, John had returned to headquarters as Office Manager for Hazelton. His family was a major factor in this decision. As his two children reached high school age, it became increasingly important for them to be settled and to receive schooling that would allow them to enter university. John had no intention of going overseas in the near future; however, when it became evident that a new project manager was needed for Soronga, loyalty prompted him to respond without hesitation when the company called.

John had been the manager of a similar project in Nigeria where he had done a superlative job. He had a placid, easy-going temperament and a preference for operating by subtle suggestions rather than direct demands. Hazelton's top management felt that if anyone could make a success of this project, John could.

John's Perceptions of the Project

From the description of Maralinga in the original project document, John knew he would face problems from the beginning. However, when he arrived on site, it wasn't as bad as he'd expected. People were friendly, the housing was adequate, and there was access to an international school run by the Australians.

The work situation was different. The equipment that had come from Canada could not be used. Bridges to the construction sites had not been built and the existing ones could not support the weight of the machines. The bridgework would have been done before the road project started. Roads had to be widened to take the construction equipment, but no provisions had been made to expropriate the land needed. Instructions were that the road must remain within the existing right-of-way. Technically, SHD could lay claim to fifteen meters, but they had to pay compensation for any crops lost, even though those crops were planted on state land. Because of these problems, the biggest pieces of machinery, such as the crusher plant, had to be taken apart and moved piece by piece. Stripping a machine down for transportation took time, money, and labor – all in short supply.

The budgeting process presented another problem. It was done on an annual basis rather than for the entire project period. It was also done in meticulous detail. Every liter of fuel and every nut and bolt had to be included. The budget was extremely inflexible, too. Money allocated for fuel could not be used for spare parts if the need arose.

When the project was initially planned, there was plenty of money, but with the collapse of oil prices, the Sorongan economy was hit hard and restrictions on all projects were quickly instituted. Budgets were cut in half. The money originally planned was no longer available for the project. Further problems arose because the project was a force account. The government bureaucracy could not react quickly, and in construction fast reactions were important. Revisions needed to be approved quickly, but by the time the government approved a change, it was often too late.

The training component of the project had more than its share of problems. Counterpart training was difficult because Sorongan managers would arbitrarily reassign people to other jobs. Other counterparts would leave for more lucrative jobs elsewhere. Among the mechanics, poor supervision compounded the problems. Those who showed initiative were not encouraged and the spark soon died.

John's Arrival on Site

John arrived in Soronga in March. SHD budgets were due soon after. This required a tremendous amount of negotiating. Expenses had to be identified specifically and in minute detail. By September the process was completed, and the project finally, after more than a year, had funds to support it.

Shortly after John's arrival, the project was transferred from the maintenance section of SHD to the construction section. The Sorongan project manager changed and the parameters of the job began to change also.

SHD would not allow realignment of the road. To change the alignment would have meant getting property rights, which was an expensive, time-consuming process and inconsistent with a project that SHD saw as road improvement rather than road construction. This meant that half the design team had no work to do. Their roles had to be quickly changed. For example, the chief design engineer became costing, programming, and budgeting engineer.

The new SHD project manager was inexperienced in his post and concerned about saving money and staying within budget. Because of this, he was loath to hire more workers to run the machinery because the rainy season was coming and construction would slow down. The workers would have to be paid but little work would be done. By October, with the rainy season in full swing, it was evident that the money allocated to the project was not going to be spent, and the project manager frantically began trying to increase activity. If this year's budget was not spent, it would be very difficult to get adequate funds for the next year. However, it was difficult to spend money in the last months because no preparatory work had been done. It took time to let tenders and hire trained staff.

The new SHD project manager was Hakonese, as was his predecessor. Neither understood the local Tolanese situation. Getting access to gravel and sand sites necessitated dealing with the local population, and this was not handled well, with the result that it took a long time to acquire land rights. The supervisors were also mainly Hakonese and could exercise little control over the work force. Discipline was lax. Operators wouldn't begin doing any constructive work until 9:30. They would quit at 11:30 for a two-hour lunch and then finish for the day at 5:00. Drivers hauled material for private use during working hours. Fuel disappeared at an alarming rate. One morning when a water truck was inspected before being put into service, the Hazelton advisor discovered the water tank was full of fuel. No explanation as to how the fuel got there was forthcoming, and it soon vanished again.

Bridges were a problem. It had been almost two and a half years since the original plans had been submitted, and SHD was now demanding changes. Substructure were not yet in place and the tenders had just been let. When they were finally received by mid-year, SHD decided that Canadian steel was too expensive and they could do better elsewhere. The tendering process would have to be repeated, and SHD had not yet let the new tenders.

Although there was no real construction going on, training had begun. A training manager was on site, and the plan was to train the mechanics and equipment operators first. The entire program would consist of four phases. The first phase would involve thirty people for basic operator training. The second would take the best people from the first phase and train them further as mechanics. In the third phase, the best mechanics would train others. The fourth phase would upgrade skills previously learned. SHD canceled the second phase of training because they considered it to be too costly and a waste of time. They wanted people to be physically working, not spending time in the classroom. Hazelton felt that both types of training were needed and the cancellation raised difficulties with the financing agency, who considered the training needs paramount.

SHD, as a government agency, was not competitive with private companies in wages. It was not only losing its best engineering people to better-paying jobs elsewhere, but it could not attract qualified people at the lower levels. Its people, therefore, were inexperienced and had to be taught the basics of operating mechanical equipment. Ironically, equipment on the project was some of the most sophisticated available.

SHD was directing the construction, but there didn't seem to be any plan of attack. The SHD manager was rarely on site and the crews suffered badly from a lack of direction. Time, materials, and people were being wasted because of this. Bits and pieces of work were being started at different points with no consideration given to identifying the critical areas.

In June there was a push to get construction underway. There was a need to give the design people something to do and a desire to get the operators and mechanics moving, as well as the equipment, which had been sitting idle for several months. Finally, there was the natural desire to show the client some concrete results. Hazelton was losing the respect of the people around them. Most people were not aware that Hazelton was acting merely in an advisory capacity. The feeling was that they should be directing the operations. Since Hazelton was not taking charge, the company's competence was being questioned.

The rainy season was due to begin in September and would last until the end of December. This was always a period of slow progress because construction was impossible when it rained. Work had to be stopped every time it rained and frequently work that had been done before the rain had to be redone.

Besides the problem of no progress on construction, some of the expatriate staff were not doing the job they had been sent out to do. Because there was little design work, the design engineer was transformed into a costing and budgeting administrator. No bridges were being built, so the bridge engineer was idle. No training was being done, so the training manager was declared redundant and was sent home.

It was difficult for Hazelton to fulfill even its advisory role because SHD personnel were not telling them what they were doing next. A communication gap was rapidly opening between SHD and Hazelton. Communication between SHD in Tola and SHD in Kildona was poor also. It appeared that the Kildona headquarters was allowing the Tola one to sink or swim on its own. Little direction was forthcoming. It didn't seem as if SHD Kildona was allocating its best people to the project, either.

The one bright spot of the year was that the project was now under the construction section of SHD rather than the maintenance section, and thus they could understand the situation from a construction point of view. The feeling was that things would improve because now the people in headquarters at least understood what the field team was up against and what it was trying to accomplish.

The Third Year

At the beginning of the year, there was little to be seen for the previous year's work.

The Hazelton staff and their Sorongan counterparts worked out of a small two-story building in the SHD office compound in Maralinga. The Sorongans occupied the top floor and Hazelton, the bottom. A field camp and trailer site had been set up in Corong, the halfway point between Maralinga and Ladawan. The plan was to move construction out from this area in both directions.

John, his mechanic supervisor, and the bridge engineer made the five-hour trip out to the site at the beginning of each week, returning to Maralinga and their families at the end of the week. The second mechanic and his wife lived on-site, whereas the erstwhile design engineer, now in charge of budgeting and administration, stayed primarily in the Maralinga office.

SHD was beginning to rethink its position on using force account labor. There were signs that in the next fiscal year it might hire a contractor to do the actual work because the force account was obviously not satisfactory. SHD also underwent another change in project manager. The third person to fill that position was due on-site in April but arrived at the end of May. The new manager began making plans to move the Sorongan base of operations to Corong. The Hazelton expatriates, for family reasons, would remain based in Maralinga.

The project now also underwent its third status change. It was now being given back to the maintenance section of SHD again. The budget process had to be started again. Hazelton, in its advisory role, tried to impress on the SHD staff the advantages of planning ahead and working out the details of the next year's work so that there would be funds in the budget to support it.

Construction had at last started, even though in a desultory fashion. However, Ramadan, the month of fasting for Moslems, was looming on the horizon and this would slow progress. This meant no eating, no drinking, and no smoking for Moslems between sun-up and sundown, which had obvious consequences for a worker's energy level. Productivity dropped during this period. This had not been a major problem the previous year because not much work was being done. Following Ramadan, there would be only two months to work at normal speed before construction would have to slow again for the rainy season.

John's briefing of Dan having been completed, they continued the site check. John wanted Dan to inspect the existing bridges as they arrived at them.

CASE **8**

○ ○

An International Project Manager's Day

Lorna Wright and Henry W. Lane

Situation

The Maralinga-Ladawan Highway Project consists of 14 expatriate families and the Sorongan counterpart personnel. Half of the expatriates are engineers from Hazelton. The other expatriates are mechanics, engineers, and other technical personnel from Beauval and MBI, the other two firms in the consortium. All expatriate personnel are under Hazelton's authority. This is the fifth largest project Hazelton has ever undertaken, with a fee of $1.63 million.

You arrived in Maralinga late on March 28 with your spouse. There was no chance for a briefing before you left. Head office had said *John Anderson*, the outgoing project manager, would fill you in on all you needed to know.[1] They had also arranged for you to meet people connected with the project in Kildona.

On March 29 you visited the project office briefly and met the accountant/administrative assistant, *Tawi*, the secretary, *Julip*, and the office messenger/driver, *Satun*. You then left immediately on a three-day site check of the 245 kilometer highway with John. Meanwhile, your spouse has started settling-in and investigating job prospects in Maralinga.

On your trip you stopped at the field office in Corong. *Chris Williams*, Second Mechanic and his wife, Beth, were living there. Chris was out at the timber company site

Lorna Wright, Research Assistant, prepared this case under the supervision of Associate Professor Henry W. Lane solely to provide material for class discussion. The authors do not intend to illustrate either effective or ineffective handling of a managerial situation. The authors may have disguised certain names and other identifying information to protect confidentiality.

to get help in recovering a grader that had toppled over the side of a ravine the night before, so you weren't able to see him. However, you met his Sorongan counterpart and he advised you that everything was going well, although they could use more manpower.

You noted that Corong did not have any telephone facilities. The only communication link, a single side-band radio, had been unserviceable for the past few weeks. If you needed to contact Chris, it would involve a five-hour jeep ride to Corong to deliver the message.

You were able to see the haphazard way the work on the road was proceeding and witnessed the difficulty in finding appropriate gravel sites. Inspecting some of the bridges you had crossed made you shiver too. Doing something about those would have to be a priority, before there was a fatality.

You returned to Maralinga on April 1 and met some of the staff and their families. Their comments made it clear that living conditions were less than ideal, the banking system made it difficult to get money transferred and converted into local currency (their salaries, paid in dollars, were deposited to their accounts at home), and the only school it was possible to send their children to was not appropriate for children who would have to return to the North American educational system.

That evening John left for another project on another continent. It is now Tuesday morning, April 2. This morning, while preparing breakfast with your spouse, the propane gas for your stove ran out. You have tried, unsuccessfully, on your way to work to get the gas cylinder filled, and have only now arrived at the office. It is 10:00 a.m. You have planned to have lunch with your spouse at noon and you are leaving for the airport at 2:00 p.m. for a week in Kildona to visit the Beauval office, the SHD (Sorongan Highway Department) people, and the IAA (International Aid Agency) representative for discussions concerning the history and future of this project (it takes about one-half hour to drive to the airport). This trip has been planned as part of your orientation to the job. Since the IAA representative and the senior man in the Beauval office were both leaving for other postings at the end of the month, this may be the only opportunity you will have to spend time with them.

On your arrival at the office, Julip tells you that *Jim*, one of the surveyors, and his wife *Joyce*, are arriving at 10:30 to discuss Joyce's medical problems with you. This is the first opportunity you have had to get into your office and do some work. You have about 30 minutes to go through the contents of your in-basket and take whatever action you feel is appropriate.

Instructions

For the purpose of this exercise, you are to assume the position of Dan Simpson, the new project manager for the Maralinga-Ladawan Highway Project.

Please *write out* the action you choose on the Action Forms provided. Your action may include writing letters, memos, telexes, or making phone calls. You may want to have meetings with certain individuals or receive reports from the office staff.

For example, if you decide to make a phone call, write out the purpose and content of the call on the Action Form. If you decide to have a meeting with one of the office staff or another individual, make a note of the basic agenda of things to be discussed and the date and time of the meeting. You also need to think about establishing priorities for the various issues.

To help you think of the time dimension, a calendar follows. Also, Maralinga is 12 hours ahead of Eastern Standard Time.

Note

1. See Case 7.

SUNDAY	MONDAY	TUESDAY	WEDNESDAY	THURSDAY	FRIDAY	SATURDAY
March 24	25	26	27	28 Arrival in Maralinga	29 Site check with John	30
31 Return	April 1	2 TODAY —	3 Visit to Kildona —	4	5	6
7	8	9 Return to Maralinga	10	11	12	13
14	15	16	17	18	19	20
21	22	23	24	25	26	27
28	29	30	May 1	2	3	4

Note: You are in a Muslim area. People do not work Friday afternoons. Saturday morning usually is a workday.

Organization Chart

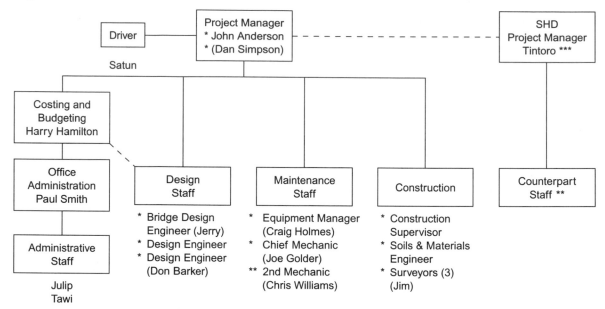

NOTES

* These people travel to Corong and other locations frequently.

** Stationed in Corong.

*** Located on the floor above Dan Simpson in the same building.

Note: The 2 expatriates responsible for the training component had been sent home. The remaining 6 expatriates called for under the contract had not yet arrived in Soronga and the 2 construction supervisors recently requested by SHD would be in addition to these 6 people.

Transportation Availability: (1) PROJECT OWNED – a) 1 Land Rover for administrative use by HQ Staff, b) 1 car shared by all the families, c) most trucks are in Corong, however there usually are some around Maralinga (2) PUBLIC – a) peddle-cabs are available for short distances (like getting to work), b) local "taxis" are mini-van type vehicles which are usually very overcrowded and which expatriates usually avoid, c) there are a few flights to Kildona each week.

PART 2

○ ○

Implementing Strategy, Structure, and Systems

Introduction

Today's global organizations need well-prepared managers. As we explained earlier, understanding other cultures and developing good intercultural skills should help you to work effectively in other cultures and with other people in multicultural teams.

This chapter was revised for this edition by Profesor Nicholas Athanassiou, College of Business Administration, Northeastern University.

Today, these are important managerial competencies. However, as a manager in the global economy you will need more than these interpersonal and team skills. You will have to understand the potential cultural bias that might exist in your company's strategy, structures, administrative systems, and normal mode of operations.

The cultural bias exists because most multinational companies (MNCs) have evolved systems and practices within a particular organizational heritage that has been influenced by the national culture of their home countries. For example, Lincoln Electric's corporate culture of rugged individualism – with its origins in the mid-western United States – shaped its early strategy for international development. When Lincoln transferred, unchanged, its US manufacturing labor selection, compensation and incentive systems abroad, it experienced limited success in markets that were culturally "close," or similar, to the USA – UK, Australia – and failure in others that were culturally were "distant," or less similar – Indonesia and France. Only with the emergence of a new generation of internationally experienced top managers who understood the extent to which Lincoln Electric was dependent on its American context were the company's strategy, organization structure and systems modified to allow for cultural differences. Then, Lincoln's international business began to recover.[1]

If executives are not aware of the cultural assumptions underlying their firm's systems and practices, then their use in another country may lead to unforeseen negative consequences. Thus, in addition to awareness of the firm's own cultural assumptions, a company's top managers need to understand how these assumptions will interact with other national cultures in their various markets. As we explained in Part 1, culture is the collectively held body of general beliefs and values that define the "shoulds" and the "oughts" of life that people usually cannot articulate. They are acquired through the process of *socialization* in which shared experiences create shared mental models and accepted ways of operating. Since all knowledge and practices in companies are not necessarily systematized and documented, or made *explicit*, it means that there is a great deal of implicit or *tacit* knowledge required to manage a company effectively.[2] To learn and to understand the "unwritten" knowledge of their companies and markets, managers have to have direct experience in these markets and in their foreign operations.

As an MNC spreads more of its activities beyond its home market and begins to create a global network, top managers need to develop their cultural "filters" through the acquisition of this personal, experiential knowledge. Specifically, this knowledge should include important overseas country market environments, company activities embedded in these country markets, and the linkages among this worldwide network of activities and be shared by executives to create a top management group perspective. The experiences, the understood but unwritten information, as well as the explicit policies and practices, create the operating and cultural filters necessary for top managers to decode, interpret, and understand context dependent information flowing from the company's various markets. With this properly interpreted information, they can make informed strategic decisions and influence the design and implementation of culturally sensitive organization structures and systems to achieve organizational goals.[3]

This is the topic of Part 2 of this book: executing strategy and designing the appropriate structures and systems for use in another culture. This introduction to Part 2 has five sections. In the first section, the overview, we elaborate on key concepts of strategy and how culture affects them. In the second section we discuss the key strategy formulation issues that concern companies that do business internationally. This discussion leads to an elaboration on multinational corporations' structures in section three and systems in section four. Finally, we address some critical issues associated with expatriate and inpatriate managers who are a fundamental means for worldwide strategy implementation.

Overview

The formulation and implementation of a strategy is an expression of the organization's purpose or mission in relation to its environment. This requires understanding market demands and external constraints, such as culture and government policies. Managers must interpret information from the external environment, combine this interpretation with a thorough understanding of the organization's internal strengths and weaknesses, and translate the implications into appropriate organizational action that will lead to desired goals. Examples of appropriate organizational action include choosing structures, work systems, and administrative mechanisms to motivate people toward the desired goals.

Organizations have long been understood as sociotechnical systems, that is to say, they have both social and technical elements. The "technical" part is the numerous technical and/or functional tasks of the business. These include acquiring inputs such as capital and raw materials, as well as using specific technology and work processes to create finished products or services. Each of the major functional areas of an organization – such as production, marketing, or finance – are systems within the larger organizational system. Each has a set of tasks and operations necessary to the functioning of the entire organization. The "social" component is the human element, the people – the individuals and groups, with their skills, needs, expectations, experience, and beliefs, who carry out the tasks and operations. Top managers have to link the social and technical elements of a company, as well as to solve problems that arise within and between the two in order to achieve the organization's strategic goals.

Managers use certain "tools" to organize their people, to focus them on their tasks, and to link them with other groups and departments. These relational tools provide the form and feel of the organization and channel the activities of employees at all levels. For example, structure creates reporting relationships between people at various levels of responsibility and facilitates the completion and coordination of critical tasks. It sends messages to organization members about what behavior is expected of them, on what tasks to work, towards what goals to work, with whom to work, whom to obey, and whom to direct. Structure includes such things as the division of labor, as well as the recombination of specialized functions though the use of internal formal and informal networks of managers, special integrating roles for individuals and various types of teams and task forces.

Managers also use rules, procedures, and a variety of other administrative mechanisms to align people and jobs. An example would be budgets and performance appraisals that direct behavior toward specific tasks and goals. The range of administrative devices includes selection criteria and hiring processes, training and development programs, allocation of rewards, information and control systems, and performance evaluation methods. Organizational theorists would suggest that there needs to be an alignment – or "fit" – internally between strategy, structure, work tasks, and people and externally between the organization and its environment in order to be effective and successful. Organizational systems should help to promote this alignment. However, if they are not designed carefully, they may actually hinder it. Simply stated, this means having the right people who have the right skills and attitudes, organized and motivated in the right way, producing the products and services customers want. Easy to say, but not always easy to do.

Structures and systems should be tools to help organizations and their employees succeed. They should be adaptable to changing conditions and workforces and not be ends in themselves. Judgment is required in assessing the likely impact of systems on people in jobs and in adjusting them to support job achievement and organizational results.

The discussion up to this point addresses what any top manager has to consider in arriving at an appropriate strategy and designing structures and administrative mechanisms to achieve the organization's goals. An additional element of judgment is required of MNC managers who must work across national boundaries. They need to be able to judge the impact of home country and host country cultures on management systems and practices. What distinguishes global business from domestic business are home-host country cultural differences and differences in policies and operations among national governments. Managers don't necessarily give much thought to national culture in their domestic context, but they must learn to do so when crossing national borders. For example, in the conduct of domestic business North American companies tend to decide about strategy, structure, and systems with the use of rational, economic, and cost–benefit analyses. In the domestic context, it is not important for managers of these companies to understand that their analyses are based on their own country's particular set of cultural assumptions that may not be shared completely by managers in other countries. Nor is it necessary for the North American managers to arrive at strategic decisions through conscious reference to their implicit set of domestic cultural assumptions; all managers of all domestic companies are assumed to share similar domestic cultural assumptions (though they don't necessarily). Yet these assumptions of commonality must be abandoned when a manager operates in multiple national markets. Further, domestic government policies pertain to all organizations equally and pose similar demands on all domestic market decision makers. Doing business across borders requires paying conscious attention to multiple cultures and to multiple government policies.

Geert Hofstede has commented that "theories reflect the cultural environment in which they were written."[4] Management concepts and practices are explained by theories regarding organization, motivation, and leadership. Therefore, theories of management systems and practices may be culture-bound if they are based on a set of inputs that reflect one culture's practices. These practices may work well in the culture that developed them because they are based on local cultural assumptions and paradigms about the right way to manage. Hofstede also asked the question: "To what extent do theories developed in one country and reflecting the cultural boundaries of that country apply to other countries?"[5] Can structures, systems, and practices developed in one country be transferred to another where cultural assumptions and paradigms about the right way to manage may be different? If so, can they be transferred as is, or do they need to be modified?

Consider, for example, the introduction of a piece-rate incentive system in a small sewing operation in Botswana by a well-meaning expatriate manager.[6] Instead of producing more garments in order to receive more pay, the workers, who had previously enjoyed a close relationship with the manager, went on strike – an unusual action in the rural community where the workers lived. Their actions puzzled her, especially since the workers were highly dependent on their jobs to support their families. Furthermore, the walkout was led by the most productive workers, those people who should have benefited from the new scheme. In this case, the manager's confusion about the reasons for the walkout could easily have led to charging the workers with laziness, and a rapid deterioration of working relationships could have resulted. Fortunately, she asked the workers and other experienced people in the village for advice. This culturally-based conflict was resolved when the manager adopted a group-based incentive that was more consistent with the values of the workers. This incentive, however, violated the expatriate manager's own sense of equity when less productive workers received the same financial rewards as the best producers. However, it was effective in the local context.

The values underlying managerial systems, in this case a reward system, may not be obvious. It might be easier to conclude that workers were the problem than it might be to examine the assumptions underlying an incentive scheme. And, if the scheme is one's own design, it is even less likely that one would consider it a source of a problem.[7] Similarly, what are the cultural assumptions underlying practices such as empowerment, self-directed work teams, and 360-degree feedback? Numerous other examples of the impact of values on systems and management styles are provided in Part 1 in the elaboration of the *Map* component of the MBI model for improving interpersonal and team effectiveness, and you may want to go back and review that discussion.

Management also creates the culture and climate of the organization. A set of values and philosophy will develop in every organization, whether it is created explicitly with careful forethought, or whether it happens implicitly without specific guidance and is perhaps less effective. Management's values and style can create an atmosphere of trust, problem solving, and adaptation to another country or one of mistrust, obedience, and domination.

A framework to help guide the exploration of implementing strategy in another culture is shown in Figure 1.[8] We encourage you to use this framework as an analytic tool but not to think of it and organizations in a static way. Organizations are dynamic. Analysis is only the beginning. It simply provides an initial outline for action. As we pointed out earlier, the implementation process is critical. Successful implementation means finding the right combination of strategy, structure, and systems that motivates people to strive for high performance. It involves listening to, understanding, and working with people from different cultures in the organization.

FIGURE 1   Organizational Systems Framework

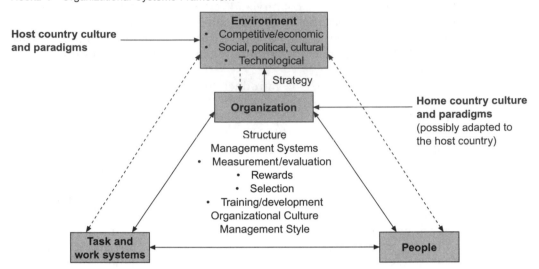

Strategy in Global Organizations

A Global Balancing Act: Global Integration and Local Responsiveness

Two fundamental forces influence companies operating in multiple, national markets: those pushing towards *global integration* and those pulling towards *local responsiveness*.[9] Forces for *global integration* push MNCs to minimize duplication of efforts and to increase efficiencies by placing specific value chain activities in suitable locations around the world. This allows them to capitalize on the interaction between the company's competitive advantage in the particular activity and the country's locational comparative advantage for such an activity.[10] For example, the USA's Silicon Valley is considered by technology companies around the world to be a prime location for R&D operations because of the high concentration of professionals, institutions, and companies with leading-edge technology expertise who nurture each other's learning. Similarly, countries in Southeast Asia have become locations of choice for manufacturing of technologically intensive components because of the quality–cost–availability profile of their local labor forces. This ability to concentrate each value chain activity in one best location from which to service corporate global activities increases when organizations can move goods and ideas around the world without being constrained by national borders. At the extreme, each activity is located in the part of the world from which the firm can best serve the rest of its global activities. This creates complex interdependencies among the MNC's different geographic locations. Such interdependencies usually are among activities that are more likely situated in culturally different locations and, thus, create unique cross-cultural managerial challenges. This is true in the most "pure" form of MNCs that have adopted a global strategy, generally referred to as global companies. Crookell identified three forces enabling organizations to move towards globalization – global integration: declining tariffs and easier world trade; global communications, which have led to similar tastes in some products and international standards for these products; and easier international coordination, again due to modern communication systems.[11]

The second of the two main forces that has an impact on strategy is pressures for *local responsiveness*. These pressures determine the extent to which an MNC has to tailor its strategy, systems, and products to serve the particular needs of a specific national market. Because of different cultural preferences for certain products and services, structural relations and systems, it is rarely possible, in the long term, to run a business in another country in exactly the same way as it is run at home. To achieve local responsiveness, the value chain activities of the company are tailored to a particular country's needs and become unique to this market. At the extreme, all the value chain activities must be tailored to meet each of its markets needs. A fully, locally responsive MNC would be following what is generally described as a *multidomestic strategy*. Four elements tend to promote localization of strategy: non-tariff barriers, such as requirements to have a local partner or local standards for products; foreign exchange shortages; cultural differences that influence consumer tastes and preferences even as some products become global; and flexible production technology that reduces the cost advantage of large-scale production while permitting greater local customization.[12] Moreover, cultural preferences that influence how people work and how they relate to each other, as well as government policies regarding human-resource practices, favor localization of structures and systems. A successful company will adapt at least some elements of its operations to the local culture.

In addition to balancing globalization and localization, a successful global organization engages in *global learning*, that is, the transfer and sharing of new ideas and knowledge among units.[13] A new production technology, marketing strategy, or product feature designed for one market can often be transferred to other markets. The keys are learning to see links among units that may look different on the surface and effectively transferring elements that can be adapted. Organizational structures and systems, as well as individuals play an important role in facilitating global learning.

All companies that operate internationally are subject to environmental pressures of global integration and local responsiveness. The degree to which a company must and can balance these two forces more to one, the other, or both dimensions to operate optimally depends on the characteristics of the industry in which it competes and on the company's own structural idiosyncrasies. Top managers must recognize the optimal balance between global integration and local responsiveness suitable for the particular MNC to compete successfully. This recognition leads to the choice of the MNC's worldwide strategy.

One accepted classification of MNC strategies that is based on the integration–responsiveness framework recognizes four strategies: the *global*; the *multidomestic*; the *international*; and the *transnational*.[14] First, an MNC that follows a strategy that is highly dependent on global integration for many of its value chain activities and that is dependent on local responsiveness for few of its value chain activities is following a *global strategy*. Such a company is characterized by a high degree of complex interdependencies among its subsidiaries around the world and has a governance structure that is tightly and centrally controlled. Its managers have to be culturally aware and its senior management around the world is likely to be dominated by a cadre of seasoned career foreign assignment managers who share similar corporate values. Companies like Ericsson (telecommunications) and Matsushita (consumer electronics) have been recognized as companies with global strategies.

Second, one that follows a strategy minimally dependent on global integration of few of its value chain activities and highly dependent on local responsiveness with many of its value chain activities idiosyncratically designed for each or most of its overseas markets is following a *multidomestic strategy*. These organizations may operate differently in each country; in an extreme case, each country or region would have its own manufacturing, marketing, and research and development. These firms can be thought of as a confederation of loosely coupled organizations with strong local and weak central control. The managers of its subsidiaries are independent "feudal lords" who may or may not be expatriate managers depending on the company's administrative heritage. Nestlé, Unilever, Procter & Gamble, McDonalds, and KFC, while not representing the extreme end of the spectrum, tend to have multidomestic strategies. A multidomestic strategy enables a firm to tailor its strategy to specific markets but does not optimize global efficiency.

Third, an MNC that follows a strategy that depends minimally on global integration pressures and minimally on local responsiveness pressures follows an *international strategy*. Essentially, it simply replicates its home market systems in each of its foreign subsidiaries. These companies are very centralized and their subsidiaries are simply outlets for headquarters decisions. The product categories most suitable to such a strategy would include commodities. For example, grain businesses (AMD, Cargill) are large organizations that deal with commodity products that are traded around the world on the basis of price. Also, the ball bearing industry to a certain extent can be seen as an industry suitable to an international strategy. For this industry there are many consumers (any manufacturer of machinery that has moving parts) and a rather undifferentiated product that depends on technical specifications that can be applicable anywhere in the world.

Finally, an MNC that is simultaneously highly globally integrated and highly locally responsive is following a *transnational strategy*. This strategy distributes the global responsibility for specific activities to the managers who manage the subsidiary to which the activity has been assigned. Each country manager can report to different persons with different worldwide activity responsibilities. The local responsiveness is achieved by managing each distributed value chain activity with enough flexibility so that the local manager can make the essential compromises necessary to achieve as high a local market fit as possible. The transnational strategy is extremely costly to implement and requires managers who are cross-culturally and interpersonally skilled and flexible. Few, truly transnational corporations exist.

When implementing strategy, the ideal balance of global integration and local responsiveness and how best to implement global learning depends on the home country, host country, industry, company size and experience, and many other factors. Rather than present a single ideal solution (since none exists), in Part 2 we try to help you become knowledgeable about how to assess the costs and benefits related to implementation of various strategies, structures, and systems. In this way, informed decisions can be made about entering and managing in other countries.

New Market Entry Mode Decisions

Executives must make an additional decision when developing global strategy. They must decide what is the appropriate business form, or entry mode, with which to operate in each overseas market.[15] Entry modes establish the legal form in a foreign market; the extent to which the MNC owns the organization; the degree to which it maintains operating control; and the extent to which this new organization is part of a set of business relationships that extend beyond one country market.

Companies can choose from a large range of entry and ownership forms. These options vary in terms of the amount of capital and other investment required in the host country. One set of foreign market entry options include modes that limit the MNC's activities to *exporting* products and *licensing* technology to other companies in the foreign market, which can require relatively little investment of resources. There are market entry modes that require capital and human resources investment but permit full control of the *wholly-owned businesses or subsidiaries* which can be purchased intact or developed as new, "greenfield" sites. A third set of market entry alternatives includes hybrid modes, such as a variety of *equity joint venture* and *strategic alliance* forms. An international equity joint venture involves creating a new entity owned jointly by two or more "parent" organizations to enter a market where at least one of the parent organizations is non-resident. Management responsibilities are contractually controlled. The percent of equity held by each parent generally defines who has formal strategic control. A strategic alliance, on the one hand, may involve a contractual agreement to cross-sell complementary products or to engage in other activities on a cooperative basis. Passenger airline carriers have formed global strategic alliances to share reservation systems, complementary routes, aircraft purchasing and technical specifications, maintenance facilities and crews, ground services staff, and even pilots and cabin crews.

Costs and benefits are associated with each of these operating modes and ownership structures. The costs to be considered usually include capital, management time and commitment, impact on strategy, and the cost of enforcing agreements. Some benefits include repatriation of profits, political security, contribution to parent-company knowledge, and local distribution capability.

Culture's Influence on Strategy and Implementation

The existence of potential costs and benefits suggests that rational managers will weigh them in coming to their decision and choose the "right" one. However, what appears to be a rational, straightforward process in a manager's home market environment may not work in practice in a foreign environment. What a home manager considers "rational" may not be so in another country whose local managers give higher value to different priorities. Further, in some circumstances, managers may not have a choice, as suggested by theory, and the decision may, in effect, be made for them. For example, governments of many developing countries want to increase investment and employment and simply exporting products to them may not be a long-term option for an

MNC. Other governments may require joint ventures with local partners so that there will also be local ownership of the industrial capacity of the country and a transfer of technology. However, the majority of developing countries are market economies and, although they may require some amount of local ownership, firms can choose a local partner for a joint venture or find other ways of providing for local ownership.

Once the decision has been made for a firm to initiate international operations, to expand its international activities, to use a certain entry mode, or to change its mode of operations, the issues become those of execution. Someone has to travel to another country to negotiate a contract, arrange a distributorship, or work with people from another culture to make a project or joint venture a reality. Once this person leaves the office to negotiate the contract in Europe or to start up the plant in Southeast Asia, what really takes place? There are a lot of questions to ask and issues to be faced before the business becomes a reality. Very often costs are underestimated at the start of the project and do not become apparent until later, when they outweigh the expected benefits. We believe that North Americans, in particular, have an initial tendency to overestimate the time necessary for new market entry effort benefits to materialize and underestimate the extent of the initial and ongoing costs of doing business internationally. When the true costs become apparent, a firm begins to learn whether or not it has the commitment and staying power to carry on.

In addition to start-up and operating considerations, culture influences how managers think about strategic options. As we demonstrated in Part 1, different cultural patterns are associated with different approaches to decision making, and these differences find their way into company strategy. Reading 6, "From Battlefields to Corporate Boardrooms: Lessons from Sun Tzu's *Art of War*" describes how some people in the Asia-Pacific region may think about strategy differently than Westerners do. As the author points out, Sun Tzu's *Art of War* may provide a useful start to "understanding the philosophy and thinking to the oriental mindset." This does not imply that, when in China, for example, one must always use a Chinese strategy. However, to be successful, a company must understand its competitors' ways of thinking. It is equally critical to understand that a company's own local managers might interpret the company's strategy differently from how it was originally intended and act on those interpretations in a way unpredictable to home country managers!

The role of relationships in international strategy is worthy of special note. Often in North America, relationships are viewed as instrumental, as a means to ends, if they are thought of at all in a business context. In contrast, much of the world outside the United States and Canada values relationships in and of themselves. They form a basis of trust and linkage upon which a business activity may be built. Relationships are a major determinant of strategy, if not part of the strategy themselves. Given such striking differences in outlook on relationships, it is not surprising that partnership problems are one of the most frequently cited reasons for joint venture failure.[16]

The Right Strategy: Some Questions

What strategy will give the right balance between the forces of globalization and localization for a particular company? What strategy maximizes global learning? When developing an international strategy, the costs and benefits of different approaches must be weighed. Some critical questions are:

1. Which parts of the strategy are so important that they absolutely cannot be changed? (These should be designed and managed globally to gain advantages of economies of scale or to assure protection from appropriation by competitors.)
2. Which parts of the strategy depend on local people – as customers, employees, or allies – to be implemented effectively? (These should be localized to gain advantages of local capabilities.)
3. What legal constraints are there? How much choice does the firm have? On what issues?
4. What kinds of experiences does the firm already have? How can previous learning be leveraged? Has the firm developed the human resources necessary to pursue a particular strategy? How can the company gain experience and knowledge needed for future moves?
5. How would the strategy be interpreted in the local culture? Is that acceptable (even if not how it was originally intended)? And, often most importantly,
6. Does the company have the commitment and patience to follow through with its global strategy?

Business Risk

Besides dealing with issues of strategy and implementation under relatively "normal" conditions, executives also may find themselves in difficult situations. These situations usually reflect historical or economic events and cultural factors of a given country or region, and could pose a threat to corporate assets, or to employees. Some of these difficult situations include expropriation, currency collapse and, at an extreme, civil war.

In the late 1980s and early 1990s it appeared that the world was becoming an easier place in which to live and do business. China had opened up to the rest of the world; Mikhail Gorbachev introduced *perestroika* and *glasnost*; the Cold War ended, and countries in Eastern Europe were permitted to decide their own destiny; Germany was reunited; South Africa abandoned apartheid; and Iran and Iraq ended a long, bloody war. However, places like Tiananmen Square, Kuwait, Bosnia, Chechnya, and Chiapas took over the headlines. Even Canada narrowly escaped being split up when, in October 1995, the citizens of Quebec voted to remain in Canada by a very narrow margin. The issue of Quebec's sovereignty was not resolved by this referendum, and it still remains to be resolved.

Different challenges and opportunities had taken over by the end of the 1990s. The suddenness and depth of the Asian economic crisis in 1997 shook confidence in the economies of South Korea, Thailand, Malaysia, and Indonesia which sank into deep recessions. Brazil's economy threatened to follow suit as capital markets' attitudes towards emerging economies chilled. The Indonesian government collapsed and rioters reappeared on the streets. This situation presents the managerial challenge in Case 20, "Building Products International: A Crisis Management Strategy," in Part 3 of this text.

The wars in Bosnia and Kosovo reminded Europe that, even with the European Union and the Euro, it had not yet entirely escaped from the legacies of the late nineteenth and early twentieth centuries. Finally, China's openness, which never quite reappeared after the Tiananmen Square events, changed in hue as the reversion of Hong Kong and economic growth increased this country's desire for an active global political role. On the positive side, the twenty-first century is being greeted with a mostly favorable economic outlook. Even so, executives could be tempted to say: "Well, as part of our strategy let's concentrate on places like the United States and Western Europe."

It is interesting to recall that countries and regions such as China, the Soviet Union, Eastern Europe, and Mexico at one time or another became "darlings" for investment by foreign companies. Then, when the political climates changed or the countries experienced economic problems, companies started to rethink their involvement, and some left.

We believe that global business is a long-term proposition. Companies cannot succeed by jumping in and out of countries when the going gets a little tough. Not only is it expensive, but customers and suppliers often remember when they were "deserted." One executive known to us attributes part of his company's success in Mexico to the fact that it did not pull out in 1982 like many companies did when the country defaulted on its debts. It was still operating in Mexico in 1989 when the economy started to open up and it has been very successful there.

Nestlé had some of its operations in South America nationalized and later returned. It then went through a second full cycle of nationalization and return. Although the company contested and fought the actions as best it could, the attitude of senior executives was one of patience, knowing that these things happen and that, eventually, the regime would change and the assets would be returned. This company has had a real commitment to its global business and a long-term perspective, both of which have contributed to their unusual success.

In 1994, China added another dimension to business risk when it ordered McDonald's to vacate its restaurant near Tiananmen Square in a seeming breach of a 20-year lease.[17] Multinationals long have had to factor into their strategies political, social, and economic instability. But the apparent ease with which Chinese authorities revoked the contract gave companies reason to "consider the unsettling notion that contracts, often reached through grueling and tiresome negotiations with Chinese business partners, may be as readily disposed of as a wrapper of a Big Mac."[18] However, the concept of a contract may mean a very different thing to the Chinese than to Americans or Canadians.

Many countries could be considered difficult places in which to do business – bad risks. It is important to have a realistic attitude toward these situations and to learn to live and work in a world of uncertainty and risk. The more you learn about other countries, the better you understand the risks involved. This enables better decisions to be made about entering a certain country and the steps necessary to manage the risks in the country.

The following story illustrates this well. One of us was having dinner with the president of a British bank's Canadian subsidiary and was describing some of his activities in East Africa to the bank president. The bank president commented about how risky it was to operate in Africa. This comment surprised the author, who understood the difficulties involved but had thought it possible to manage them. The bank president then described all the countries in South America in which the bank was operating and making money. To the author, South America had to be one of the riskiest places to operate at that time, and he said so. The bank president replied, "Not really; the bank had been there for a long time, and we understand the situation." Therein lies the moral: familiarity with and understanding of a country provide the necessary perspective for accurately assessing risks, determining acceptable levels of risk, and managing those risks.

Companies need to have strategic and tactical plans for managing risks. Large companies can develop specialists in assessing risks to contribute to informed decision making, and smaller ones can access specialist firms or consultants for information relevant to specific decisions. All companies are advised to listen to expatriates and locals working in the field when they provide systematic assessments of their environments required periodically as part of the normal business plan by the home office. Individual managers can add to the quality of their own decision making by reading broadly, by understanding the history of regions in which they operate, and by seeking (and paying attention to) information from international field personnel. As globalization increases, more international representation in the senior ranks of corporate headquarters personnel will also increase the ability to assess risks in specific countries. A global viewpoint, an understanding of the culture, political and social situations, and a long-term commitment to global operations are essential.

Operating globally is different from operating at home, and those differences must be understood. The costs of entering the game can be high. But the experience can be rewarding financially for the corporation, as well as personally and professionally for the manager.

Structures: Organizing for Effectiveness

Once the decision has been made to establish operations in another country, executives must decide how to structure the organization. Typical structures include *international, geographical* (regional), *product or project, matrix,* and *networked* or *transnational.* Each of these structures had its strengths and weaknesses and would be appropriate for different situations. The two main factors that influence strategic choice are the pressures to be responsive to the local country and culture and the forces pushing toward global integration. The two additional criteria to be considered in the choice of the appropriate structure with which to implement the strategy are the extent to which a company's sales and profits are derived from foreign operations and complexity of the company's product line.[19]

In the international division structure, all business conducted outside the firm's home country is organized through one division. This form is often a starting point for firms that are beginning to internationalize and that probably have relatively little international business as a percentage of total revenues. As the overseas involvement of a firm increases, the international division structure may evolve into a geographical division structure in which all products for a particular region are grouped together in separate geographic regions around the world. This structure is typically more suitable with a multidomestic or an international strategy. In the product or project division structure, responsibility for all markets around the world is given to specific product line or project divisions. This form tends to be adopted by MNCs that are involved in multiple product lines or businesses overseas. The matrix structure form combines regional and product emphases. Finally, a new form of organization, referred to as a network organization (and sometimes what is implied by the term "transnational"),[20] is beginning to emerge in some multinational corporations. A network organization combines many or all types of organizational units in relationships of varying degrees of ownership and relationship intensity with the home country's headquarters. The latter two organization forms are mostly adopted by large diversified MNCs and tend to be costly to implement and maintain. The divisional, and more so, the matrix and network forms of organization are seen to be more suitable for companies that adopt a global or a transnational strategy.

This book does not attempt to pursue in detail an exposition of the advantages and disadvantages of each structure. There are many books and readings on the topic of international organization and organizational architecture that comprehensively cover these issues.[21] Beyond considering the strategic advantages or disadvantages of the various structural forms a company can use, one needs to recognize the cultural values and assumptions upon which these structures may be based.

Culture's Influence on Structure

Organizational structures are not free from the influence of culture. Each structure carries with it identifiable assumptions about the legitimacy of certain practices and relationships and defines the locus of authority, responsibility, and bases of power differently. Each legitimizes a different pattern of communication and interaction. In addition to fitting certain competitive situations or product characteristics, some structures may be more acceptable than others in a given culture, as some may require, or, conversely, discourage behavior and interactions that are inappropriate in that culture. In Part 1, both the text and Reading 2, "Cultural Constraints on Management Theories" provide insights into the impact of cultural differences on management theories and organizational structures.

Laurent also has investigated the relationship between culture and organizational structure.[22] He believes that attempts to communicate alternative management processes and structures to managers will fail unless the "implicit management gospels" that they carry in their heads are addressed. He became convinced of this when he was trying to explain matrix organizations to French managers to whom the idea of reporting to two bosses was "so alien that mere consideration of such organizing principles was an impossible, useless exercise."[23]

The proposition that guided Laurent's research was that the national origin of managers significantly affected their views of what they considered proper management. His research uncovered differences in the basic conception of organization and found that these differences clustered by nationality. He demonstrated differences on four dimensions of organization: organizations as political systems; authority systems; role formalization systems; and hierarchical relationship systems. In another study comparing French and American managers, the results indicated that the two groups held very different views regarding structure. The US managers held an instrumental conception

TABLE 1 Two views of organization

Instrumental	Social
Positions are defined in terms of task	Positions are defined in terms of social status and authority
Relationships between positions are defined as being ordered in any way instrumental to achieving organizational objectives	Relationships are defined as being ordered by a hierarchy
Authority is impersonal, rational, and comes from role or function; it can be challenged for rational reasons	Authority comes from status; it can extend beyond the function and cannot be challenged on rational grounds
Superior–subordinate relationships are defined as impersonal and implying equality of persons involved; subordination is the acceptance of the impersonal, rational, and legal order of the organization	Superior–subordinate relationships are personal implying superiority of one person over the other; subordination is loyalty and deference to the superior
Goal attainment has primacy over power acquisitions	Achievement of objectives is secondary to the acquisition of power

Source: Giorgio Inzerelli and André Laurent, "Management Views of Organization Structure in France and the USA," *International Studies of Management and Organization*, 13, nos. 1–2 (1983): 97–188.

of structure, while the French held a social conception.[24] A comparison of these two views is presented in Table 1.

Organizational Structures: Some Observations

Given pressures to globalize, localize, and learn, how should an organization structure itself internationally? As alluded to above, many forward-looking multinationals, such as ABB, are implementing network organizations. The network allows a multinational to have a very high degree of structural flexibility. It provides all the advantages of balancing strategies in a matrix organization and adds the flexibility inherent in alliances with other organizations. For example, a network organization might include global research and development in some product areas and local R&D in others, global marketing for some product lines and local marketing for others, and so on. It also might have several different types of alliances for projects having different roles in the firm's overall strategy or for product lines at varying stages of development. However, as might be predicted, a network structure is exceptionally difficult to manage effectively. Some of these challenges can be seen in Case 11, "ABB Poland."

The emerging forms of network organizations will also put high demands on managerial sensitivity and skills and on organizational responsiveness. One example of such a network between a supplier and buyer is now being built between two multinational giants, Xerox and Schneider Electric, one of Xerox's suppliers of components for its equipment and for the manufacturing technologies to make it.[25] Both companies have provided us with access to the development of their relationship, which promises extraordinary benefits to both parties as well as enormous challenges. On the vendor side of the network, the Schneider Electric global account manager responsible for relations with the buyer has to have:

- clear vision and mission statements;
- empowerment, broad acceptability and cooperation for local implementation;
- an effective communication network with identified regional managers at several levels and a formalized matrix structure;
- "solution-selling" competence;
- cultural adaptability.[26]

The two organizations have had numerous sets of senior executive meetings and formalized an agreement for the vendor to be the preferred supplier for its entire product line, worldwide. This arrangement has the potential for increasing Schneider Electric's worldwide sales to Xerox dramatically; Xerox has the potential for significant cost savings. If they can successfully implement their innovative ideas, competitors will be looking to duplicate the advances, but from a position of considerable disadvantage.

Schneider Electric has now developed responses for all of the following key questions:

- Who are the potential customers for the new global linkages?
- What multinational processes should be established?
- How can effective global account managers be developed?
- How to plan and budget for customer-specific efforts?
- How to measure performance and reward results?

The organizations have provided each other with significant proprietary information in order to build the knowledge necessary to answer these questions. Even R&D streams from Xerox have been disclosed to Schneider Electric, whose response has included realigning its product development efforts to fit the future needs of its global customer. Responsibilities at both a global and local level have been matched off against local and centralized operational bases, and weaknesses have been identified and are being corrected. With the initial planning complete, and one relationship now launched, Paris-based Schneider Electric has identified 25 global account managers, including those from its Square D North American subsidiary, and started their training and development in early 1995.

This example of a network structure reflects virtually all of the elements of global managers described earlier. Its implementation will require daily use of all components of the MBI model of interpersonal and team effectiveness. Finally, it will stretch the capacity of organizational designers and of more conventional managers who will now have to share power and be much more flexible than in the past. Although this form of network is only starting to emerge among global companies, the trends identified by these two companies suggest that they are at the leading edge of a major development.[27] Implementing structures such as these is not always easy as can be seen in Case 10, "Global Multi-Products Chile."

We now turn our attention to a more familiar organizational arrangement – the joint venture. The management of joint ventures is a particularly important and particularly troublesome element of network organizations. Cooperative alliances, such as joint ventures, are used for many reasons. Companies, for example, may need to share financial risk, respond to government requirements, secure access to natural resources, acquire particular technical skills, gain local management knowledge and experience, or obtain access to markets and distribution systems. From the multinational's perspective, two important reasons for using joint ventures are the need to understand and have access to local markets and to have local general management knowledge, skills, and experience in the joint venture company.

Alliances are not an automatic solution to a lack of understanding of another culture, as executives sometimes think. An additional cultural interface, besides the one with the external marketplace, is created with the partner in the venture. The choice of a partner is a critical decision. As Geringer explains:

> Selecting partners with compatible skills is not necessarily synonymous with selecting compatible partners. . . . Although selecting a compatible partner may not always result in a successful JV, the selection of an incompatible partner virtually guarantees that venture performance will be unsatisfactory.[28]

How does one choose a partner? Where does one look? What characteristics should a partner have? What are one's expectations? What are the potential partner's expectations? There are a number of criteria that should be considered: "complementarity of technical skills and resources, mutual need, financial capability, relative size, complementarity of strategies and operating policies, communication barriers, compatible management teams, and trust and commitment between partners."[29] More detail on some of the issues that develop at the internal interface of culture between partners is highlighted in Reading 7, "Cross-Cultural Cooperative Behavior in Joint Ventures in LDCs."

In establishing joint ventures, managers often make some common mistakes. There can be a tendency to concentrate on the end result and desired outcome and not to think as carefully as is necessary about the process of getting there. Executives contemplating a joint venture need to think about the relationships that must be built in the process of creating a joint venture and the commitment of time and effort necessary to make the venture successful. They need to think more accurately, not about the joint venture, but about joint venturing – a process orientation.

Another common mistake is that the emphasis is likely to be placed on the "visible" inputs to the decision and the "tangible" aspects of the business. These visible inputs include the legal structure of the venture, the financial considerations of ownership and *pro forma* operating statements, and the market analyses – all the things managers (and specialists like lawyers and accountants) learned in school and deal with daily. These are important considerations and need to be given careful thought, but they are not the only considerations. There are many operational issues to be considered in establishing a joint venture that go beyond the legal and economic ones. These may not be given enough careful thought in advance and may be left to be resolved as problems arise.[30] The "invisible," "intangible," or "non-quantifiable" components of the venture are often ignored or disregarded. Issues like trust, commitment, and partners' expectations are overlooked, possibly because these are not usually part of the managers' prior training.

The situation is analogous to an iceberg in that approximately one-seventh of it is visible above the water's surface and six-sevenths is below the surface. The result of not knowing what is hidden can be disastrous for ships, and for companies.

In summary, the successful management of a complex international organization, whatever its form, depends in great part on the systems used to manage people, to which we now turn.

Systems: Managing the Global Organization

Companies employ a large number of systems to manage their people and operations. These include job design, recruiting and selection, evaluation, training and development, and compensation and benefits systems. Negotiating, decision making, and management styles are also important components of the management process; cultural assumptions are incorporated into these as well. Although there is some contention as to whether cultures around the world are converging or diverging and in what areas, there is no doubt that, in the realm of systems and practices preferred in a given country, culture plays an influential role. Each set of cultural values gives rise to a different system, preferred behavioral style, or management systems that are acceptable or even desirable. Those of one country (such as hiring of friends and relatives in many Latin countries) are often unacceptable or even ridiculed in another (such as the United States and Canada). In Part 1, the text and readings provided numerous examples of how culture influenced management systems and processes and details will not be repeated here.

A Perspective on Human Resource Management Systems

It is important to recognize that even the idea of what human resource systems are and how they should be designed (or whether they can be designed) may be culturally influenced. For example, Brewster has observed that the concept of human resource management, as developed originally in the United States, reflects a degree of organizational autonomy from external constraints, such as government and unions that does not exist in many other countries.[31] As this model of HRM is extended into the international arena, the autonomous orientation continues to be reflected. The starting point for decisions is the firm's strategy and the goal of HRM is to fit people, practices, and systems to it in order to increase global competitiveness. Although these frameworks recognize differing host country sociopolitical and legal situations, they usually are considered simply exogenous factors that must be recognized and accommodated.

Managers in Europe, for example, have much less autonomy over human resources decisions since workers and governments have greater influence on private organizations' human resources and, thus, create significant constraints and restrict organizational decision-making autonomy. This different orientation may be more than a matter of semantics according to Brewster, and "there is a need, therefore, for a model of HRM which goes beyond seeing these features as external constraints, and integrates them into the concept of HRM."[32]

Much of the international HRM literature in North America focuses on expatriate issues such as selection and training. However, when a firm operates in a foreign environment, it is not just expatriate policies that comprise the human resource management issues. There are local laws governing the hiring and firing of employees that may be unfamiliar to the firm. There could be substantial financial ramifications for firing a person. Consistent with the culture-general orientation adopted in this book, the specifics of various laws will not be covered here. Whether it will cost two years' salary if a person is fired or six months' salary is not the issue. The specifics of laws of all countries are subject to continual change. What is important is that executives recognize that such laws exist and that these laws are significant constraints on management discretion. A manager in a foreign country has to know the laws governing personnel practices.

In some countries, hiring quotas – laws requiring the hiring of people of specified ethnic or racial backgrounds – may be in force. These laws are similar in concept to the affirmative action laws in North America. Usually, these quotas have high political sensitivity and significant impact on foreign corporations that are guests in the host country. What does the manager do when the best person for the job is from a particular group, but he or she cannot hire any more people from that group? How does one manage in this situation? Does the manager try to avoid the issue, ignore it, procrastinate, actively recruit – and at what cost? How does the manager maintain cooperation and discipline in an organization when employees come from distinct subgroups that historically have been adversaries?

Where quotas exist, corporations usually are under pressure to employ local people not just at low levels, but in the higher managerial ranks as well. In a number of countries, serious localization pressures are experienced. What is the firm's plan for building local management capacity? How is the firm going to carry out this plan? What price is the firm prepared to pay? The firm's answers to these questions, and its localization policy, can significantly contribute to success or failure in a foreign environment.

The use of local managers has increased. In many developing countries, larger pools of better-educated management talent are appearing. In developed countries, where sufficient management talent exists, there are employment and immigration laws with which a firm must comply. In all cases, in order to attract competent local management, a firm has to offer competitive wages, benefits, working conditions, development, and advancement opportunities.

Finally, interpersonal differences and the potential for conflict exist, not just between expatriates and locals, but also between local groups – based on ethnic, tribal, linguistic, or religious differences. The citizenry of many countries is not homogeneous in terms of culture, language, and religion. However, an outsider naively may believe that the inhabitants of a country think and behave similarly. Such conflict between local people is apparent in countries of Europe, South and Southeast Asia, Africa, the Middle East, and parts of the Americas.

Organizational Systems: Transfer, Adapt, or Create?

An important decision facing management in international operations is whether existing practices, systems, and styles can be transferred from one culture to another or whether they must be changed and adapted in some way when they appear to be in conflict with the norms of another culture. On the one hand, the answer is not always to change a system, even if it is different than in the host country. Sometimes people in another culture simply need to be trained to use a system (remembering, of course, that the best training format may be influenced by the culture). On the other hand, neither is the answer always to assume that training is all that is required. Each response has a proper time and place.

The decision regarding transferring, adapting, or possibly even creating a new hybrid should be the result of careful, informed judgment based on understanding the cultural biases of the systems and the cultural norms of the country in which the operations are located. Are there rules? Not really, but careful analysis can help sort out the issues and help managers solve the problem. Questions such as "How important is it that we do it identically to the way it's done at home?" can guide one's decisions. It may not be important that the procedures are exactly the same; rather, results may be more important. Just because it is the way headquarters does it, or wants it done, does not mean that it is right for a different cultural environment. What are important are the *business imperatives*, tasks that must be done well for the firm to make money.[33] Differing business imperatives and cultural accommodation requirements can be compared in the situations presented in "Grupo Financiero Inverlat" (Case 1) and "Japanese-American Seating Inc." (Case 5).

Systems and structures are tools to help managers do their job. They are culturally determined tools in their assumptions about human motivation and behavior. If they become ends in themselves, they often become barriers to effective performance. This is true in one's own culture and even more so when they are in conflict with the values and beliefs of other cultures. The difficulty is learning to recognize one's own cultural assumptions built into the tools that may impede one from seeing that they can be changed or adapted. We remind you that the *Map* scheme described in the "Cultural Orientations Framework" discussion in Part 1 provides a powerful analytic tool for testing the cultural assumptions underlying organizational systems and structures. A global organization may even find practices abroad that could be effective at home, leading to management innovation throughout the company.

Expatriates and Inpatriates: A Key Means for Coordination and Integration

In an era of globalized business, coordination and integration are essential key contributors to successful strategy implementation by a global network of geographically dispersed activities embedded in differing cultural environments. Formal systems are employed extensively by MNCs to achieve their objectives. Further, in an era of ever-increasing electronic communication and data processing system options, they are creating sophisticated enterprise information systems to coordinate their dispersed activities, the activities of their suppliers and the activities of their customers. However, those culturally influenced dimensions of information flow that provide the deepest comprehension of market-specific knowledge may not be transferable electronically. It is impossible to understand deep-rooted, tacit knowledge that explains the most important nuances of operations in a particular cultural context because this knowledge is acquired experientially and must be shared through face-to-face interactions.[34] Yet, it is the successful acquisition and sharing of experiences and lessons learned across the internationally dispersed corporate activities that gives a firm sustainable competitive advantage. One solution to this challenge is the use of a cadre of expatriate and inpatriate managers whose key role is this acquisition and sharing of knowledge. These managers create stocks of social capital – relationships internal and external to the MNC around the globe – and intellectual capital – individual managers' stocks of explicit and implicit knowledge and experience – that become essential to the meaningful and value creating integration of global operations.[35]

In addition to expatriate and inpatriate managers, greater numbers of other managers and their staff are going to be interacting in more ways with people from other cultures within and beyond the MNC's boundaries. Expatriates employed in a foreign subsidiary will be working with host country nationals from many levels in the organization and, most likely, from government, Headquarters personnel will interact with inpatriate managers transfered to headquarters from regional operations. Also, managers located anywhere within the organization can be interacting with local country managers and staff members from other cultures as headquarters and local operations become more interconnected electronically and through *ad hoc* personal meetings.

Corporations must consider their human resource management policies, including expatriation, in light of globalization. It should be evident by now that the new global manager must develop a way of thinking and acting that is qualitatively different from the way in which managers have thought or acted either domestically or internationally (operating in just two or a few countries). Cross-cultural understanding and experience are essential in today's business environment, and foreign assignments can be a critical part of every manager's development.

American companies went through a period of reducing the number of expatriates they sent overseas for numerous reasons.[36] One major reason was the expense associated with relocating them and their families. Their salaries were usually higher than those of local managers, and they usually received benefits to make an overseas move attractive. Benefits often included items like housing or a housing allowance, moving expenses, tax equalization, and schooling for children. Many of these benefits were not usually provided to local employees. In addition to lowering costs, having fewer expatriates has reduced conflict between employees and groups in the local environment and increased the development of host country managerial and technical capabilities.

Although this trend can be seen as a positive step in the globalization process, there is a question about whether another explanation for the reduction may be an inability to function abroad successfully.[37] Estimates of expatriate failure rate run at 20–50 percent, and the average cost per failure to the parent company ranges from $55,000 to $150,000.[38] There also are studies claiming the failures are 30–70 percent. The accurate identification of the actual rate of failure is less important than the disturbing fact that this range represents a large number of managers who cannot, or at least did not, function successfully in other cultures. The reduction in expatriate personnel has ramifications for strategic management and control, such as less identification with, and knowledge about, the global operations and organization and less control by headquarters over local subsidiaries. One scholar concludes:

there is increasing value to expatriate assignment as firms become global competitors. . . . A means must be found to provide this experience to as many managers as possible. That would probably involve shorter-term expatriate assignments whose purpose is avowedly developmental – for both the individual and the organization.[39]

MNCs must think about "inpatriation" (from the home country and headquarters perspective) as well as expatriation as a strategic tool. It can be a tool that is used to develop managers with a global orientation, but that is also used to manage key organizational and country relationships.[40] Recently, we have dealt with some companies that were either increasing the number of inpatriates to headquarters or actually increasing the flow of expatriates, while avoiding some of the previous financial disadvantages. These inpatriate assignments were usually short term, two to three months, at headquarters for a special project. This had a double advantage of exposing the inpatriate to headquarters processes, concerns, and perspective, while allowing headquarters personnel to become acquainted with cultural orientations and views of headquarters from around the world. At the same time, some of these firms were establishing formal policies that required international experience as a prerequisite for consideration for promotion to senior ranks – and eliminating many of the perks that were formerly needed as incentives for executives to accept an international assignment. The emphasis in the use of inpatriates or expatriates should be:

> on long-term commitment to learning about international markets. If high potential individuals are carefully selected and trained for overseas positions, they will not only facilitate the maintenance of an international network of operations in the short-term but should be allowed to continue providing informational support upon their return.[41]

It might sound straightforward, but the process of developing globally-minded managers with the requisite skills is more difficult than it appears. The quotation above contains the conditions that most often are not met – if high potential individuals are carefully selected and trained – and which are crucial to the successful use of expatriation for development and strategic purposes. Careful selection and preparation of expatriates for their foreign assignments should be high priority issues for multinationals. Managing their performance and careers while away, and upon return, should also receive attention. Unfortunately, this is not always the case.

Experience in a job in another country does not automatically ensure a manager's increased sensitivity to cultural issues or an ability to transfer whatever has been learned to other managers. Cross-cultural training, even for experienced people, can add significantly to their understanding of their past experiences and to their skill in future assignments. Reading 9, "Serving Two Masters: Managing the Dual Allegiance of Expatriate Employees," outlines recommendations for managing expatriates to maximize globalization, localization, and global learning.

Selection

In 1973, published research showed that people were selected for international assignments based on their proven performance in a similar job, usually domestically.[42] The ability to work with foreign employees was at, or near, the bottom of the list of important qualifications. Unfortunately, over 25 years later the situation has not changed dramatically for the better.[43] Very often technical expertise and knowledge are used as the most important selection criteria. Although these are important considerations, they should not be given undue weighting relative to a person's ability to adapt to and function in another culture. It does no good to send the most technically qualified engineer or finance manager to a foreign location, if they cannot function there and have to be brought home prematurely. As we noted earlier, the cost of bad selection decisions is high to the corporation as well as to the individual and to his or her family.

Kealey developed a useful model for thinking about overseas effectiveness that focuses on adaptation, expertise, and interaction.[44] He states that for a person to be effective he or she "must adapt – both personally and with his/her family – to the overseas environment, have the expertise to carry out the assignment, and interact with the new culture and its people."[45] An increasingly important decision to be considered, particularly by American and Canadian companies, is the international assignments of female managers. This has become an issue as more women have graduated from business schools and decided that they want international careers. It is also a relevant concern both under employment equity guidelines and legislation, which encourage or require companies to promote women into positions of higher responsibility in organizations, and in the interest of simply ensuring that talented resources are used effectively throughout the organization. Reading 8, "Competitive Frontiers: Women Managing Across Borders" focuses on this subject and calls into serious question some of the myths about barriers to women working internationally. Case 15, "Ellen Moore: Living and Working in Korea" describes the experience and challenges of a woman managing a consulting contract in Korea.

Training

The training that a person undergoes before expatriation should be a function of the degree of cultural exposure to which they will be subjected.[46] Two dimensions of cultural exposure are the degree of integration and the duration of stay. The integration dimension represents the intensity of the exposure. On the one hand, a person could be sent to a foreign country on a short-term, technical, trouble-shooting matter and experience little significant contact with the local culture. On the other hand, a person could be in Japan only for a brief visit to negotiate a contract, but the cultural interaction could be very intense and might require a great deal of cultural fluency to be successful. Similarly, an expatriate assigned abroad for a period of years is likely to experience a high degree of interaction with the local culture from simply living there.

This model, shown in Figure 2, suggests that, for short stays and a low level of integration, an "information-giving approach" will suffice.[47] This includes, for example, area and cultural briefings and survival-level language training. For longer stays and a moderate level of integration, language training, role plays, critical incidents, case studies, and stress reduction training are suggested. For people who will be living abroad for one to three years and/or will have to experience a high level of integration into the culture, extensive language training, sensitivity training, field experiences, and simulations are the recommended training techniques. Effective preparation would also stress the

FIGURE 2 Relationship between Degree of Integration into the Host Culture and Rigor of Cross-Cultural Training and between Length of Overseas Stay and Length of Training and Training Approach

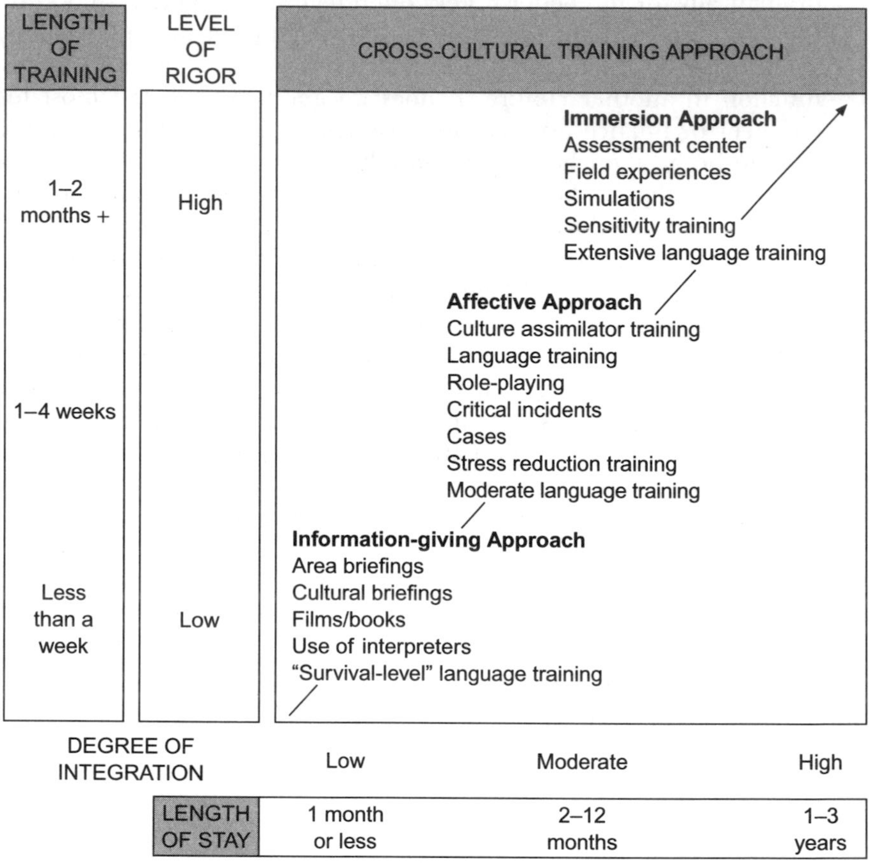

LENGTH OF TRAINING	LEVEL OF RIGOR	CROSS-CULTURAL TRAINING APPROACH
1–2 months +	High	**Immersion Approach** Assessment center Field experiences Simulations Sensitivity training Extensive language training
1–4 weeks		**Affective Approach** Culture assimilator training Language training Role-playing Critical incidents Cases Stress reduction training Moderate language training
Less than a week	Low	**Information-giving Approach** Area briefings Cultural briefings Films/books Use of interpreters "Survival-level" language training

DEGREE OF INTEGRATION	Low	Moderate	High
LENGTH OF STAY	1 month or less	2–12 months	1–3 years

Reprinted with permission of John Wiley and Sons Inc., "Expatriate Selection, Training, and Career Pathing: A Review and Critique," M. E. Mendenhall, E. Dunbar, and G. R. Oddou: *Human Resource Management*, 2b, no. 3 (1987): 340. Copyright © 1993.

realities and difficulties of working in another culture and the importance of establishing good working relationships with the local people.

The Canadian International Development Agency (CIDA) has recently developed an approach to training for situations in the top right-hand corner of the figure. After extensive pre-departure training, expatriates are sent abroad. Shortly after they begin in their new posting, CIDA provides more training for the expatriates with their new co-workers, thus facilitating a productive integration. During the expatriates' stay abroad, periodic "refreshers" or debriefing sessions are held. Finally, the expatriates are actively involved in repatriation training both prior to and after their return home. The expatriates' spouses and families are also provided with similar training and resources. Although CIDA has not yet formally evaluated the new program, it appears to provide an exemplary model for expatriate training.[48]

The Reality of Culture Shock

Notwithstanding a strong desire to understand and to adapt in order to be effective as a manager, nearly everyone experiences disorientation when entering another culture. This phenomenon, called culture shock,[49] or more appropriately acculturative stress, is rooted in our psychological processes.[50] The normal assumptions that the manager uses in his or her home culture to interpret perceptions and to communicate intentions no longer work. When this happens, whether in normal attempts to socialize or in a business context, confusion and frustration result. Frustration occurs because the manager is used to being competent in such situations and now finds that he or she is unable to operate effectively.

An inability to interpret surroundings and behave competently can lead to anxiety, frustration, and sometimes, to more severe depression. Most experts agree that some form of culture shock is unavoidable, even by experienced internationalists.[51] People who repeatedly move to new cultures likely dampen the emotional swings they experience and probably shorten the period of adjustment, but they do not escape it entirely. In fact, research on intercultural effectiveness has found that those who are eventually the most effective tend to report experiencing greater difficulty in their initial adjustment. This is because those who are most sensitive to different patterns of human interaction are likely to be both disrupted by changes in these patterns and likely to become adept at new patterns.[52]

One can think of four modes of responding to a new environment.[53]

- Going Native (assimilation): "acceptance of the new culture while rejecting one's own culture,"
- Being a Participator (integration): "adaptation to the new culture while retaining one's own culture,"
- Being a Tourist (separation): "maintenance of one's own culture by avoiding contact with the new culture," and
- Being an Outcast (marginalization): "the inability to either adapt to the new culture or remain comfortable with one's own culture."

The pattern usually experienced by people who move into a new culture comes in three phases: first, the elation of anticipating a new environment and the early period of moving into it; second, the distress of dealing with one's own ineffectiveness and, as the novelty erodes and reality sets in, the realization that one has to function in a strange situation; and third, the adjustment and effective coping with the new environment.

The critical aspect of these phases is that during the first and second periods, performance is usually below one's normal level. The period of adjustment to normal or above-average performance takes from three to nine months, depending on previous experience, the degree of cultural difference being experienced, and the individual personality. It should be noted that culture shock is not a shock experienced as, for example, a result of conditions of poverty. Culture shock is more the stress and behavioral patterns associated with a loss of control and a loss of sense of mastery in a situation.

During a person's adaptation to a new environment, frequently observed symptoms are similar to most defensive reactions. People reject their new environment and the people that live there, often with angry or negative evaluations of "strangeness." Other symptoms include: fatigue; tension; anxiety; excessive concern about hygiene; hostility; an obsession about being cheated; withdrawal into work, family, or the expatriate community; or, in extreme cases, excessive use of drugs and alcohol.

The vast majority of people eventually begin to accept their new environment and adjust. Most emerge from the adjustment period performing adequately and some people perform more effectively than before. A smaller percentage either "go native," which is usually not an effective strategy, or experience very severe symptoms of inability to adjust (alcoholism, nervous breakdown, and so on).

These types of reactions seem to occur independently of the type of cultural change or the direction of a move. North Americans going to the former Soviet Union exhibit patterns similar to ex-Soviets coming to North America. However, one does not have to leave one's own country to experience culture shock, as the following demonstrates. A volunteer on a project in Ghana experienced the symptoms of culture shock, even after participating in an orientation program organized by the sponsoring agency. More severe symptoms of culture shock were reported on returning to an urban-base MBA program. However, the ultimate culture shock came upon graduating and starting work for a manufacturer located in a small, rural community in one of Canada's Maritime Provinces. In all three experiences, the patterns were the same, and the sharpest disorientation occurred within this person's native country, perhaps because it was least expected. It is important to note that this individual experienced a "reverse culture shock" on the return home. "Return shock," or "re-entry shock," also is an adjustment phenomenon that people experience and for which they need to be prepared.[54]

Different people have different ways of coping with culture shock. Normal stress management techniques, regular exercise, rest, and balanced diet are helpful. As noted earlier, some use work as a bridge until they adjust. Usually, the work environment does have some similarities to that of one's home culture. But for the spouse who does not work and who is often left to cope with the new environment on his or her own, the effects can be more severe. Language training is one very effective way of coping and provides an entry into the host culture. Education about the local history, geography, and traditions of the new culture and then exploration of the new environment also help adjustment. Whatever methods are employed, it is wise to remember that everyone experiences culture shock. One can only moderate its effects through diligent preparation.

Support systems are especially important during the adjustment period. One obvious source of support is the family. Doing more things together as a family, more often, is a way to cope with the pressures. Another is to realize that it is acceptable to withdraw from the new culture, temporarily, for a respite. Reading newspapers from home or enjoying familiar food is a good cultural insulator – if not carried too far. After eight months in Switzerland, an eight-year-old asked her grandfather to bring her cheddar cheese and a Hershey bar on a visit, even though she had grown to enjoy Swiss fondue and Swiss chocolate! It is important that the use of such temporary interruptions to one's reality be restricted to bridges to the new culture, not as permanent anchors to an old environment.

In company situations, it must be understood that the international manager in a new culture goes through these stresses. Local colleagues should not be surprised at less than perfect performance or strange behavior and can provide crucial sources of support for the managers and their families.

When one goes overseas or sends someone overseas, there are two jobs to accomplish. There is the functional or technical job – for example, the engineering, finance, marketing, or plant management responsibilities. This is obvious. However, too often it is only this job that people identify, focus on, and prepare for. The other job is cultural adaptation. If one cannot adapt successfully, one may be requested to go (or may be sent) home early – often in a matter of months. One may never get a chance to use one's technical or functional skills.

The financial and psychological costs of not adapting are heavy. A high failure rate may be a significant problem for North American companies. One study found that of the US companies sampled, only 24 percent had an early return rate of 10 percent or less, compared with 97 percent for the European companies and 86 percent for Japanese companies.[55] The single most pervasive reason why expatriates fail is because their spouses fail to adjust. It is not only important for expatriate managers to prepare for their new jobs, but also to see that their spouses (male or female) are prepared as well.[56] Many of the expatriate adaptation issues are seen in Case 16, "Marconi Telecommunications Mexico."

Repatriation

Selecting the right people, training them properly, and sending them and their families to their foreign posting is not the end of the exercise. Reintegrating these people into the company after the foreign assignment so that the company can continue to benefit from their experience and expertise has been proven to be a problem. Research suggests that the average repatriation failure rate – those people who return from an overseas assignment and then leave their companies within one year – is about 25 percent.[57] If companies want to retain their internationally experienced managers, they will have to do a better job managing the repatriation process. There are indications that some companies, such as Monsanto, Coherent Inc., ABB, and Intel, are recognizing this situation and have developed programs to address it.[58]

The international assignment may be an important vehicle for developing global managers, achieving strategic management control, coordinating and integrating the global organization, and learning about international markets and competitors, as well as foreign social, political, and economic situations. However, this idealized goal of becoming a global, learning organization will only happen if the right people are selected for foreign assignments, trained properly, repatriated with care, valued for their experience, and then used in a way that takes advantage of their unique background.

Conclusion

Organizing to do business globally reguires balancing a need for achievement of efficiencies through global integration and a parallel, sometimes countervailing, need for local responsiveness, all the while ensuring that learning is taking place globally in the organization. Strategy, structure, and systems are tools for relating to global markets and for organizing a global business. The effective application of these tools is, however, influenced by culture as well as by industry and other factors. The text and readings in this part should guide you in developing a framework of both the choices that must be made in developing a global organization and the factors that influence those choices. The cases that follow provide opportunities to see the elements in action and to apply the understanding gained.

Notes

1. Hastings, Donald F., "Lincoln Electric's harsh lessons from international expansion," *Harvard Business Review* 77, no. 3, February–March (1999): 162–178.
2. Nonaka, Ikujiro and Hirotaka Takeuchi, *The Knowledge Creating Company* (New York: Oxford University Press, 1995).
3. Athanassiou, Nicholas, "The impact of internationalization on top management team characteristics: A tacit knowledge perspective," (1995), Unpublished Doctoral Dissertation, The University of South Carolina; and Athanassiou, Nicholas and Douglas Nigh, The impact of company internationalization on top management team advice networks: A tacit knowledge perspective, *Strategic Management Journal* 19, no. 1 (1999): 83–92.
4. Geert Hofstede, "Motivation, Leadership, and Organization: Do American Theories Apply Abroad?" *Organizational Dynamics* 8, no. 2, Summer (1980): 50.
5. Ibid.
6. See "The Botswana Uniform Agency [Pty] Ltd." (A) and (B), Cases 9-79-C020 and 9-79-C021, Case and Publications Department, Ivey Business School, The University of Western Ontario, London, Canada.
7. The tendency to attribute success to one's own skill and to blame others for failure is not a cultural universal, however. An Oriental perspective might well reverse the direction of explanation for success and failure and credit others for positive outcomes while assuming the blame for problems. The writers take a North American perspective in discussing examples in the text unless otherwise noted.
8. This organizational design framework and analytic model has been adapted from a number of writers on the contingency theory of organizations: James D. Thompson, *Organizations in Action* (New York: McGraw-Hill, 1967); Paul R. Lawrence and J. W. Lorsch, *Organization and Environment* (Homewood, IL: Richard D. Irwin, 1969); Jay R. Galbraith, *Designing Complex Organizations* (Reading, MA: Addison-Wesley, 1973); Jay W. Lorsch and John J. Morse, *Organizations and Their Members: A Contingency Approach* (New York: Harper & Row, 1974); Jay R. Galbraith, *Organization Design* (Reading, MA: Addison-Wesley, 1977); Jay W. Lorsch, "Organization Design: A Situational Perspective," *Organizational Dynamics*, 5 (1977) American Management Association, 1977; Jay R. Galbraith and Daniel A. Nathanson, *Strategy Implementation: The Role of Structure and Process* (St. Paul, MN: West, 1978); John P. Kotter, Leonard A. Schlesinger, and Vijay Sathe, "Organization Design Tools," *Organization: Text, Cases and Readings on the Management of Organizational Design and Change* (Homewood, IL: Richard D. Irwin, 1979). See also H. W. Lane, "Systems, Values and Action: An Analytic Framework for Intercultural Management Research," *Management International Review*, 20, no. 3 (1980): 61–70.
9. C. A. Bartlett and S. Ghoshal, *Managing Across Borders: The Transnational Solution*, 2nd edn (Boston: Harvard Business School Press, 1998); and C. K. Prahalad and Y. L. Doz, *The Multinational Mission: Balancing Local Demands and Global Vision* (New York: The Free Press, 1987).

10. B. Kogut, "Designing Global Strategies: Comparative and Competitive Value-Added Chains," *Sloan Management Review* 26, no. 4, Summer (1985): 15–28.

11. Harold Crookell, "Organization Structure for Global Operations," in *International Management: Text and Cases*, eds Paul W. Beamish, J. Peter Killing, Donald J. Lecraw, and Harold Crookell (Homewood, IL: Richard D. Irwin, 1991).

12. Ibid.

13. Bartlett and Ghoshal, op. cit., 1998.

14. Bartlett and Ghoshal, op. cit., 1998.

15. P. W. Beamish, J. P. Killing, D. J. Lecraw, and A. J. Morrison, *International Management: Text and Cases*, 2nd edn (Burr Ridge, IL: Richard D. Irwin, 1994).

16. Beamish, et al., op. cit.

17. *The Wall Street Journal*, November 22, 1994: A16.

18. *The Economist*, November 26, 1994: 36.

19. Bartlett and Ghoshal op. cit., 1998; and Stopford, John M., and Louis T. Wells Jr., *Managing the Multinational Enterprise: Organization of the firm and ownership of the subsidiaries* (New York: Basic Books, 1972).

20. C. A. Bartlett and S. Ghoshal, "Managing across Borders." See also C. K. Prahalad and Y. L. Doz, *The Multinational Mission: Balancing Local Demands and Global Vision* (New York: The Free Press, 1987).

21. See, for example, C. A. Bartlett and S. Ghoshal, *Managing Across Borders: The Transnational Solution*, 2nd edn (Boston: Harvard Business School Press, 1998); and C. K. Prahalad and Y. L. Doz, *The Multinational Mission: Balancing Local Demands and Global Vision* (New York: The Free Press, 1987).

22. André Laurent, "The Cultural Diversity of Western Conceptualizations of Management," *International Studies of Management and Organization* 13, nos 1–2 (1983): 75–96.

23. Ibid., 75.

24. Giorgio Inzerilli and André Laurent, "Managerial Views of Organization Structure in France and the USA," *International Studies of Management and Organization* 13, nos 1–2 (1983): 97–188.

25. An indication of the importance of this phenomenon is Arthur D. Little's establishment of an international award for the "Best of the Best Supply Chain Management Practitioners" (PR Newswire, press release, December 7, 1994). Both Xerox and Schneider Electric were winners in 1994.

26. This list is a partial set of requirements as described by the first global account manager for the vendor (personal communication, September 1994).

27. The authors are grateful for the opportunity to attend the second major planning meeting between these companies in October 1994 and for the permission to provide this glimpse into their groundbreaking efforts.

28. J. Michael Geringer, "Partner Selection Criteria for Developed Country Joint Ventures," *Business Quarterly* 53, no. 1 (1988): 55.

29. Ibid.

30. P. W. Beamish, *Multinational Joint Ventures in Developing Countries* (London: Routledge, 1988).

31. Chris Brewster, "Developing a European Model of Human Resource Management," *Journal of International Business Studies* 26, no. 1 (1995).

32. Ibid. For a comparison of these two orientations, besides the Brewster article, see Randall S. Schuler, Peter J. Dowling, and Helen De Cieri, "An Intergrative Framework of Strategic International Human Resource Management," *Journal of Management* 19, no. 2 (1993): 419–459.

33. This statement is a good example of the North American instrumental orientation.

34. N. Athanassiou, 1995.

35. Nahapiet, Janine and Sumantra Ghoshal, "Social capital, intellectual capital, and the organizational advantage," *Academy of Management Review* 23, no. 2 (1998): 267–284. Nonaka, Ikujiro, "A dynamic theory of organizational knowledge creation," *Organization Science* 5, no. 1 (1994): 14–37.

36. Stephen J. Kobrin, "Expatriate Reduction and Strategic Control in American Multinational Corporations," *Human Resource Management* 27, no. 1 (1988): 63–75. Roth Kendall, David Schweiger, and Allen Morrison, "Global strategy implementation at the business unit level: Operational capabilities and administrative mechanisms," *Journal of International Business Studies*, 22, no. 3 (1991): 369–402.

37. Ibid.

38. Mark E. Mendenhall, Edward Dunbar, and Gary R. Oddou, "Expatriate Selection, Training, and Career Pathing: A Review and Critique," *Human Resource Management* 26, no. 3 (1987): 331–345.

39. Kobrin, "Expatriate Reduction."

40. Nakiye A. Boyacigiller, "The International Assignment Reconsidered," in *International Human Resource Management*, eds Mark Mendenhall and Gary Oddou (Cincinnati, OH: South-Western College Publishing, 1995).

41. Ibid., 154.

42. E. L. Miller, "The International Selection Decision: A Study of Some Dimensions of Managerial Behavior in the Selection Decision Process," *Academy of Management Journal* 16, no. 2 (1973): 239–252.

43. Mendenhall, Dunbar, and Oddou, "Expatriate Selection."

44. Daniel J. Kealey, *Cross-Cultural Effectiveness: A Study of Canadian Technical Advisors Overseas* (Ottawa: Canadian International Development Agency, 1990). This study was based on a sample of over 1,300 people including technical advisors, their spouses, and host-country counterparts.

45. Ibid., 8.

46. Mendenhall, Dunbar, and Oddou, "Expatriate Selection."

47. Ibid.

48. M. Matteau, *Towards Meaningful and Effective Intercultural Encounters* (Hull, Canada: Intercultural Training and Briefing Centre, Canadian International Development Agency, 1993).

49. Some suggested readings on the topic of culture shock include: Ingemar Torbiorn, *Living Abroad: Personal Adjustment and Personnel Policy in the Overseas Setting* (Sussex, England: John Wiley, 1982); Nancy Adler, *International Dimensions of Organizational Behavior*, 3rd edn, Chapters 8, 9 (Cincinnati, OH: South-Western College Publishing, 1997); Kalvero Oberg, "Culture Shock: Adjustment to New Cultural Environments," *Practical Anthropology* 7 (1960): 177–182; C. L. Grove and I. Torbiorn, "A New Conceptualization of Intercultural Adjustment and the Goals of Training," *International Journal of Intercultural Relations* 9, no. 2 (1979).

50. Research on stress and adapting to stressful situations also suggests that there are physiological contributions as well. One reference that links physiology and culture shock is Gary Wederspahn, "Culture Shock: It's All in Your Head . . . and Body," *The Bridge* (1981): 10.

51. For these generalizations we are drawing on Torbiorn, *Living Abroad*; the research literature described by Adler, *International Dimensions*; an excellent, but unpublished paper by Clyde B. Sargent, "Psychological Aspects of Environmental Adjustment," Kalvero Oberg, "Culture Shock," *Practical Anthropologist*, 7 (1960): 177–182; and our own experience with numerous executives and students around the world.

52. Kealey, "Cross-Cultural Effectiveness."

53. Ibid., 39. This framework was developed by J. W. Berry, "Acculturation as Varieties of Adaptation," in *Acculturation: Theory, Model, and Some New Findings*, ed. A. Padilla (Washington, D.C.: AAAS, 1980).

54. See Adler, *International Dimensions*, Ch. 8.

55. See Rosalie L. Tung, "Selection and Training Procedures of U.S., European, and Japanese Multinational," *California Management Review* 25, no. 1 (1982): 57–71.

56. J. Stewart Black and Gregory K. Stephens, "The Influence of the Spouse on American Expatriate Adjustment and Intent to Stay in Pacific Rim Overseas Assignments," *Journal of Management* 15, no. 4 (1989): 529–544.

57. J. Stewart Black and Hal R. Gregersen, "When Yankee Comes Home: Factors Related to Expatriate and Spouse Repatriation Adjustment," *Journal of International Business Studies* 22, no. 4 (1991): 671–694; J. Stewart Black, Hal R. Gregersen, and Mark E. Mendenhall, "Toward a Theoretical Framework of Repatriation Adjustment," *Journal of International Business Studies* 23, no. 4 (1992): 737–760.

58. Charlene Marmer Solomon, "Repatriation: Up, Down, or Out?," *Personnel Journal* 74 (1995): 28–37.

○ ○

Global Execution: Have you Forgotten what 95% of Management is all About?

Piero Morosini

Mergers and acquisitions (M&As), joint ventures (JVs) and other forms of strategic alliance have continued to grow at a record pace as we enter the twenty-first century. However, numerous studies across an enormous range of performance parameters, industries and countries show that more than 50 percent of all M&As, JVs and alliances fail. More disturbingly, these studies clearly suggest that the failure rate has not decreased over the past three decades. Quite on the contrary, evidence of similarly complex business initiatives such as global re-engineering or major organizational change programs also show a failure rate of over 50 percent.

Does this mean that the strategic role of M&As and other large-scale business moves have been exaggerated in the emerging global economy? Are the expectations from these initiatives too high? Or have managers and researchers simply been overlooking key factors? Indeed, in the case of global M&As, a survey conducted amongst CEOs with extensive acquisition experience showed that, before a M&A deal was implemented, strategic and financial issues took priority over "cultural," organizational and personnel aspects. However, these factors took clear priority over strategic and financial issues *following* the conclusion of an M&A deal.

So, Are National Cultural Differences to Blame?

Most conventional management theories view national cultural distance as a "barrier" or "risk factor" detrimental to the performance of global business. For example, a number of researchers have argued that cross-border M&As, global technology transfers or

All the studies, research findings and company cases quoted in this article are described in detail in: *Managing Cultural Differences. Effective Strategy and Execution Across Cultures in Global Corporate Alliances*, Piero Morosini, 1998, Pergamon Press, Oxford, U.K.

similar initiatives are more difficult to implement between culturally distant countries such as the US and Japan, than with relatively closer nations, say Britain and the US. Nevertheless, some pundits have forcefully denied the existence of such cultural "barriers." Quite surprisingly, however, both camps offer little or no evidence to back their views.

In the first formal study linking national cultural distance and the performance of cross-border acquisitions, we surveyed over 400 transactions in a broad range of industries, companies, and countries. The national cultural distance between the acquirer and the target was measured employing proven quantitative scales.

Contrary to previous theories, it was found that national cultural distance was not necessarily detrimental to the performance of cross-border acquisitions. Rather, *when handled effectively*, national cultural differences actually enhanced performance. Indeed, it became clear that execution factors were much more dominant for performance than strategic variables. Specifically, companies with strong global execution capabilities were found to primarily excel at:

1. Articulating and communicating common business values across national cultures
2. Developing and aligning key people able to work effectively across borders

It is ironic that "execution" is only now emerging as a field of management research in its own right. Arguably, it should have been the first. In fact, a problem common to conventional approaches to global business has been the separation between the thinker and the doer. In a global context, culture and organizational realities are just too changeable, complex, and unpredictable. Any attempt to isolate cultural or organizational knowledge from the intuition of the managers "in the field" can easily become an over-simplistic approach. Indeed, obstacles to making such knowledge explicit confirm our findings that companies strong in cross-cultural execution possess unique competitive advantages. ABB, the Swedish/Swiss electrical engineering giant, provides a case in point to illustrate this.

How Does a Company Build Global Execution Capabilities?

During the 1988–1996 period, ABB more than doubled its revenues to about $34 billion, with dramatic increases in profitability, productivity, and international coverage. In the culturally unfamiliar former communist countries of Central and Eastern Europe, ABB built up a multibillion dollar business from scratch in less than five years, acquiring companies at a rate exceeding one per month immediately after the fall of the Berlin Wall in 1989. This ABB did without increasing its headquarters staff above 200 people. In the event, most pundits praised the "multi-domestic" organization ABB put in place during those years, and focused on describing the key characteristics of the "global managers" responsible for coordinating the company's critical resources internationally. However, most firms that tried to actually implement multi-domestic principles in their organizations – some of them prior to ABB – failed to obtain similar performance results, even when counting on global managers of high caliber and international exposure.

FIGURE 1 Why did it work in ABB? – Building common *business values* across national cultures

Global Execution, Piero Morosini, Copyright 1998©

So, how did ABB manage it? The company excelled at five key execution areas (see Figure 1):

- Setting in place the "building blocks" for global coordination
- International assignments and personnel policies
- Communication mechanisms
- Coordination mechanisms
- Leadership.

By working effectively across *all* these five areas, ABB's ten-person Executive Committee plus its 500 multicultural global manager group, were able in less than one decade to radically transform a 210,000 strong company, operating with 5,000 profit centers in 140 countries. Let us now look at each of these execution areas in more detail.

Building Blocks

In the case of ABB, these were:

A. A common company language (English)
B. A company constitution (explicit in ABB's "book of values")
C. A unified reporting and control system (ABACUS)
D. Clear career policies for global managers
E. Clear company performance rules and measurements.

Beyond the mere existence of these building blocks, what set ABB apart from other cases was the direct involvement of top management to "walk the talk" and ensure that these key blocks functioned in a consistent way. For example, one important principle in ABB's book of values: that its 500 global managers are "givers" rather than "receivers" (meaning that they continuously make available staff needed elsewhere, instead of hanging on to them), is firmly embedded in their promotion and incentive policies. Every year, the company's CEO and Executive Committee personally revise and decide upon every global manager's compensation and career advancement.

International Assignment Policies

ABB did much more than resorting to the familiar long-term expatriate assignments or short-term rotation and trainee programs common to several multinationals. Rather it made extensive use of innovative mechanisms that allowed it to *pre-position* key resources long in advance and gather *tacit* knowledge inside culturally distant countries. Two such mechanisms were:

Cloning

Although in 1995 many companies were still holding back from entering the former communist countries of Eastern Europe and Russia, ABB was by then employing over 10,000 people and generating close to $1.5 billion in the area, mostly through acquisitions. Several years before the 1989 fall of the Berlin Wall, the company began to hire "locals" with high managerial potential in the area, and placed them in established ABB subsidiaries, usually in Germany, Sweden or the US. Here, they became familiar with ABB's ways and methods. Once acquisitions were made in their home countries after 1989, the "cloned" managers were sent back to turn the acquired companies around. The unique experiential knowledge of both ABB and the local cultural and business environment gave the "cloned" management enormous capacity for speed of execution, with turnaround times averaging 18 months in the newly acquired firms. Similarly, companies as diverse as Nestlé, Mckinsey & Co. and Tetra Laval have used cloning as a key mechanism to quickly turn around acquisitions or to start up operations in culturally distant countries.

Adopting

This is a complement to cloning. During the first years of major change, new acquisitions in Eastern European and other transitional economies were formally adopted by an established ABB subsidiary in a nearby country. The adoptive parent provided functional, technological, and human support, with a significant part of its incentive compensation tied to their "adopted" company's performance. Parent companies were carefully selected for cultural affinity in the same way that global managers are. Through "adopting," an ABB subsidiary develops unique cross-cultural managerial experience that can be continuously leveraged in other expansion programs. Similarly, once they became well established, the adopted Eastern European acquisitions became parents of other target companies further East, which had in turn been staffed by "cloned" locals. And so on, rolling out over the new markets with increasing speed and momentum (see Figure 2).

FIGURE 2   ABB's approach to execution in Eastern Europe: 1988–1996

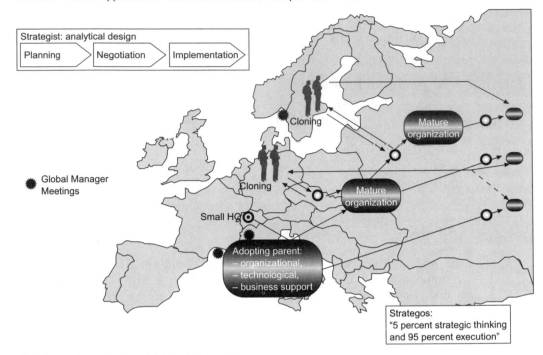

Global Execution, Piero Morosini, Copyright 1998©

Communication Mechanisms

During ABB's 1988–1996 transformation, former CEO Percy Barnevik was himself passionately involved in preparing, delivering, and following-up on a highly structured communications program. These communications took a variety of forms and reached numerous ABB constituencies, from day-to-day routine communications to regular Group Executive Committee meetings and continuous visits to ABB's local subsidiaries.

Communications reached a climax during the annual *Global Manager Meetings*. Their purpose was to foster and consolidate common company values, business practices and key achievements across ABB's multicultural group of 500 global managers, while at the same time building an *esprit de corps* under the CEO's leadership. During the company's Eastern European expansion, these meetings were turned into a critical educational tool, extensively promoting and rewarding initiatives such as "cloning" and "adoption" (see Figure 2). Similar kinds of intensive communication mechanisms, continuously involving the CEO and top management, can be observed at the heart of General Electric's aggressive growth programs overseas.

Co-ordination Mechanisms

Also during this period, ABB pioneered and implanted a number of coordination mechanisms to continuously share best practices, establish internal benchmarks and align key managers in the complex transformation programs, breaking initial resistance to change at an early stage.

One example of such mechanisms is the *International Centers of Excellence*. These are manufacturing sites or assembly plants that have achieved high performance and "best practice" standards relative to other ABB centers. When a major change initiative was required somewhere, ABB invited key "local" managers to visit a center of excellence to see how best practices, working methods, and productivity standards were achieved and maintained. Often, these centers of excellence were carefully selected to ensure cultural affinity with the visiting companies.

Leadership

Beyond the media "hype" that surrounded ABB's global transformation during 1988–1996, the company's top leadership truly was distinct in their strict adherence to a few managerial principles and simple business values. Thus Barnevik, who defined management as "5 percent strategic thinking and 95 percent execution," combined a clear vision with spending over 200 days "on the road" every year, visiting ABB subsidiaries all over the world and building direct communication with several managerial levels and key customers. Such a mixture of a "thinker" and a "doer" – of tacit and explicit knowledge – found within the same individual, constitute a key characteristic of leaders in companies such as ABB, General Electric and Daewoo. They bring to mind the ancient Greek military figure of the *Strategos*, or the war fleet commander. Instead, our modern managerial term: "Strategist" (although etymologically rooted in that Greek notion) has often come to signify an analytically focused leadership, rather detached from the market battlefields.

The Art is Not in the Concept

The key point of effective execution is not the success of any particular mechanism utilized by a "successful" firm, but a company's ability to continuously learn and adapt a series of execution mechanisms that suit particular "local" contexts. At the same time, to develop managers capable of coordinating resources across national cultures in concert with the firm's values and objectives.

For example, after the Berlin Wall fell, South Korea's Daewoo was in no position to *clone* and *adopt* local talent in the way ABB had. Instead, the company sent young, bright South Korean staff on *International Missions* of several years into situations where they would have no option but to mix with the local culture. As a result, the company developed a group of "insiders" in countries from Poland and Romania to Ukraine and Uzbekistan, who not only spoke the local languages but also had developed critical social and political networks. Daewoo had to do this through its Western European subsidiaries, since South Korea did not even have diplomatic relations with most former communist regimes until well after 1989. However by 1995, driven by their Korean insiders turned "global managers", Daewoo had already invested several billion US dollars in these countries and was able to quickly turn around major acquisitions in sectors ranging from automotive to shipbuilding and banking.

During the early 1990s, both ABB and Daewoo shared the strategic objectives of expanding into Eastern Europe. What set them apart from many other companies, which pursued similar strategies and failed, was their ability to work across the five key execution areas (Figure 1). The specific methods open to them to achieve that depended on their own initial resources and the particular circumstances they each faced. Nevertheless, both companies realized early on that, with the right managers and building blocks in place, national cultural differences need not be a problem.

Among the main barriers to building global execution capabilities are large headquarters and an abundance of centralized procedures. Combined with career promotion and incentive schemes favoring centralized roles over more international ones, these factors often compromise a company's ability to rotate key executives, inexorably attracting talented managers to headquarters after a short time period overseas. Lack of top management involvement, clear performance measures and international assignment policies, a common company language and standardized control systems are among other typical impediments to global execution.

To conclude, there is no fixed "recipe" how a company should approach its journey towards developing global execution capabilities. The five key execution areas described earlier are not unlike the artist's palette: they provide the basic colors, and perhaps a bit of initial inspiration, but they are no substitute for the subjective experience and unique context behind any major work of art. Similarly, determined companies that move quickly to build execution capabilities can turn cultural diversity into concrete advantages, and reap the enormous rewards of global coordination in ways that are unique and difficult to replicate.

○ ○

From Battlefields to Corporate Boardrooms: Lessons from Sun Tzu's *Art of War*

Chow Hou Wee

Introduction

Sun Tzu's *Art of War*, written around 400 to 320 BC, is the oldest military classic known in Chinese literature. It is also probably the most revered and well-known military text outside China. The significance and importance of Sun Tzu's work in influencing military thought has seldom been questioned. For example, this book is known to influence Japanese military thinking as Sun Tzu's writings were introduced to Japan around 716 to 735 AD (Griffith 1982). Even in the 1990/91 Gulf War, Sun Tzu was cited repeatedly by reporters and analysts. The wide acceptance of Sun Tzu's thinking can be noted by the fact that his works have been translated into many languages, and the book can be found among the "must read" list in major military schools around the world.

What is perhaps less known is the applicability of Sun Tzu's *Art of War* to business practices. Yet it is interesting to note that the idea of an analogy between the world of business and that of the battlefield is not a novel one. The metaphor is accepted, consciously or not, in such familiar phrases as the US–Japan trade war and a militaristic turn of phrase in the boardroom now borders on being a cliche. It was in July 1985 that the *New York Times Magazine* carried Theodore White's argument that while America may have won the military war, Japan was busy winning the economic war. Several years later, *International Business Week* (April 9, 1990) and *Asia Magazine* (May 8–10, 1992) both carried the headline "Car Wars" on their covers. Both issues featured prominently the continuous US–Japan–Europe rivalries in their conquest for market shares in the world automobile industry. In an earlier issue of *International Business Week* (January 22, 1990), Carla Hills was also featured prominently on its cover and in its cover story as the US "Trade Warrior." In her role as the new US trade negotiator, it was reported that she would have to battle with the Japanese and European policy makers, while keeping the US protectionists at bay. In another cover page of the Asian edition of *Fortune Magazine* (June 23, 1997), the headline was entitled "Killer Strategies." In that lead featured article, the author argued that companies that were prepared to break the rules were the ones that made shareholders rich (Hamel 1997).

Military jargon, cliches, and analogies have also found their way into the writings of renowned journalists, executives, and scholars. For example, Enricho and Kornbluth (1987) described how Pepsi won the "Cola Wars" against Coke. Saporito (1992) documented that price wars would never end for companies in the airline, automobile, computer, food, retailing, and steel industries because of over-investment in the past. This had forced many companies in these industries to chase market share at all costs. Labich (1992a, b) used the term "Sky Wars" to describe the battle for market share among the three leading aircraft manufacturers, Airbus, Boeing, and McDonnell-Douglas. This was followed by Zellner (1992), who reported how the American airlines are killing each other through price wars, and Labich (1992b), who documented how deregulation in the airline industry had led many of Europe's airlines to war. Schlender (1993b) commented on how the American manufacturers of personal computers had begun to attack the Japanese market with new spiffy machines, innovative software, and sharply lower prices.

Indeed, the term "war" and related military jargon have never ceased to be used as titles for articles written for business readers. Examples include "Information Wars: What You Don't Know Will Hurt You" (Stewart 1995); "Picking the Winners in the New Communications War" (Kupfer 1995); "My Life as a Corporate Mole for the FBI" (Henkoff 1995); "Northwest and KLM: the Alliance from Hell" (Tully 1996); "The Holy War Over Capital Gains" (Birnbaum 1997); "The Next Big War in Telecom" (Kupfer 1998); "The Spying Game moves into the U.S. Workplace" (Casimiro 1998); "Spy vs Spy" (Behar 1999); "China's Spies Target Corporate America" (Robinson 1998); "Steeling for a Trade War" (Costa 1999); "The Battle to Control Telecom" (Kupfer 1999); "War Breaks Out in TV Land" (Gunther 1999); and the list goes on.

Various studies relating the application of military strategies to business practices have been undertaken (for example, Kotler and Singh, 1981; Stripp, 1985). In a publication by Ries and Trout (1986), they chose to rely on the works of German general Karl von Clausewitz to illustrate the parallels between military concepts and marketing practices. In addition, Kotler et al. (1985), Lazer et al. (1985), Ohmae (1982) and many others have often described the Japanese economic conquest of the world in the 1980s as very much like a well-orchestrated military campaign. In an article, Sullivan (1992) cited the works of Abegglen and Stalk (1985) in describing Theory F (for fear) as one of the factors for the success of Japan. According to Theory F, large Japanese corporations were obsessed with analyzing their competitors so as to exploit competitive advantages. In addition, they had a growth bias in their strategic orientation.

Few writers, however, have given recognition and acknowledgement to the oldest known military treatise in the world, Sun Tzu's *Art of War*. Yet this manual, written in China centuries before the birth of Christ, can be said to contain the foundations on which all modern military strategies are based. It is proposed that the achievement of Sun Tzu's *Art of War* transcends the military context and offers the basis for an insight into the nature of modern business practices. In particular, and this is an underlying thesis, a study and understanding of Sun Tzu provides a valuable platform for exploring the exact nature of the analogy between business and war, and in doing so it offers a pregnant framework for interpreting one of the most startling economic trends in the late twentieth century: the relative rise of the Japanese economy. Besides Japan, the Korean *chaebols* have been known to mirror the corporate strategies of the Japanese *keiretsus*. While the Asian financial crisis, which began in July 1997, dealt a very severe blow to the growth of many Asian economies (Chowdhury and Paul 1997; Krugman 1997; Rohwer 1998), there are already positive signs that a number of them, including Japan and Korea, are on the track of recovery.

There are other reasons for focusing on Sun Tzu's works. With the opening up of China, there is an increased desire to know their thoughts, especially in the area of strategic management and practices. This is necessary if one wishes to do business with them. Here, it is significant to note that while the Chinese have turned to the Western world for much help in the area of training and consulting, they have also begun actively to research their own classics to relate their applications to management. Sun Tzu's *Art of War* has emerged as a favorite, and today, there are many publications in China that attempt to relate this classic to strategic thinking and practice (for example, Li et al. 1984; National Economic Commission, 1985). In fact, in a recent publication on the negotiating strategies of the Chinese, the author devoted a fair number of pages to Sun Tzu's *Art of War* (Fang 1999, pp. 155–163). Fang (1999) and Wee and Lan (1998) also cited other well-known military strategies and tactics that are commonly used by the Chinese strategist. These are in addition to many similar publications that exist today in Hong Kong, Taiwan, Japan, and South Korea. In fact, Sun Tzu is a highly regarded guru in these countries.

If one subscribes to the belief that the twenty-first century may belong to the Asia-Pacific region, it is important to note that its key players – Japan, Taiwan, South Korea, Hong Kong, and Singapore – have many cultural similarities that could be traced to their roots in China. Together with China, they can form a significant economic force that few countries can ignore. Without doubt, there is a need for practitioners and researchers in the Western world to begin understanding the philosophy and thinking of the oriental mind-set. Sun Tzu's *Art of War* may provide a useful start in this learning process.

A detailed exposition on how Sun Tzu's works can be applied to business practices can be found in Wee et al. (1996). Selected application of Sun Tzu's principles can also be found in Wee (1989, 1990, 1993, 1994, 1995, 1997; and Lee, Chng and Wee 1994). The purpose of this reading is to highlight some of the salient concepts that are embedded in the works of Sun Tzu, which could be applied to strategic thinking and business practices. Without doubt, there are many other concepts in the works of Sun Tzu that could be used for business practices. What will be highlighted here represents only the "tip of the iceberg" on the application possibilities of Sun Tzu's *Art of War* to modern business operations and management.

Strategy, Structure, and Behavior

One of the most important aspects in the conduct of war is the relationship between strategy, structure, and behavior. In the words of Sun Tzu:

> To control a large force in combat is similar to that of a small force. It is a matter of formations and signals.

FIGURE 1   Strategy, Structure and Behavior

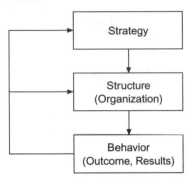

He went on to say:

> Order and disorder depend on organization.

Implicit in these sayings is that structure actually breeds behavior, regardless of the size of the army. As such, the way a general organizes an army would affect the behavior of the troops in battle. Similarly, the way a company is organized and structured will also determine the behavior of the employees. For example, if a company wants to become international, it must be structured in such a way so as to reward those employees with international experience. Otherwise, no one would want to work abroad.

What, then, determines structure? In war, it is always *strategy*. In other words, the strategy must be the genesis of any organizational design and structure. Undeniably, with proper feedback, one's strategy could be modified. However, the starting point for any planning exercise in war has to be strategy. For example, in the 1991 war against Iraq, the US-led forces decided on the strategy before embarking on how to organize for combat. In fact, General Norman Schwarzkopf was himself a product of the strategy.

There is a definitive requirement as to why structure and organization must follow the crystallization of the strategy in war. First, there is a need for *flexibility*. This is because battle conditions are quite fluid, and the general on the ground must be given the maximum flexibility to organize and structure his troops and formations depending on the battle situations. Second, as battle conditions change, the general must change his strategy accordingly. In other words, he has to constantly reorganize according to his strategy. Although he begins with a battle plan, that plan can never be cast in stone. He must constantly reorganize his troops for battles as he changes his plan (strategy) to meet the dynamic conditions of war. In sum, he has to be very proactive and seize on any available opportunity to win. This was true of ancient wars, and is still applicable today. Figure 1 shows the relationships between strategy, structure, and behavior.

Interestingly, there is no lack of support in the business literature for the relationship between strategy and structure. For example, Chandler (1962) concluded that once a corporate strategy is in place, its structure will follow. Bartlett and Ghoshal (1989, p. 20) argued that organizational structure should fit the strategic requirement of the business

TABLE 1 Strategy, structure, and behavior

Strategy → Structure	Structure → Strategy
(1) Believes in flexibility (fluidity)	(1) Creates rigidity ("Cast in stone")
(2) Able to cope in an uncertain and dynamic environment	(2) Prefers to operate in a static or stable environment
(3) Change is a necessity	(3) Change is to be avoided
(4) Adopts a proactive approach	(4) Develops a reactive posture
(5) Tends to promote creativity	(5) Tends to build bureaucracy
(6) Stimulate learning in the organization	(6) Retards progress in the organization
(7) Able to tackle risks head-on	(7) Avoids risks if possible

and the firm's dominant strategic capability. Similar views were expressed by Lorange and Vancil (1976), Henderson (1979), Lorange (1980, 1982), and Ohmae (1989). Unfortunately, there are other scholars who counter-argue that it is often the other way around – that is, it is often the structure that drives the strategy (for example, Pascale 1990, p. 100). This lack of consensus on how strategy affects structure or vice versa has influenced, to some extent, the way many companies manage themselves for competition.

It is important to point out that there are fundamental differences in the likely outcome/behavior between a strategy-led versus a structure-led approach. These differences are shown in Table 1. In the current highly competitive and technology-driven environment, it would be more logical to subscribe to a strategy-led approach as it would result in behavior/outcome as illustrated in the left column of Table 1. In fact, even Japanese companies are discovering that their bureaucratic structures are now affecting their competitiveness (Schlender 1993a; Taylor 1996b; Desmond 1998; Bremner, Thornton and Kunii 1999; and Keenan and Landers 1999). Companies should not be confined by fixed organizational charts. Instead, they should organize their companies around their strategies and the changing environment (Dumaine 1991; Katzenbach and Smith 1993; Kirkpatrick 1993; Guyon 1997; and Hamel 1997). In fact, a fair number of articles in Hesselbein, Goldsmith and Beckhard (1997) have been devoted to discussing issues pertaining to the organization of the future.

The Need to be Combat-ready All the Time

It is very important to emphasize that in the realm of the military, the army must always maintain a highly vigilant state of combat readiness. Thus, even though there may be no war, troops are trained to the highest level of combat fitness in *peacetime*. In fact, it is during peacetime that the army can seize on the opportunity to build up its resources so as to act as a deterrent to any hostile move by the enemy. This principle is well illustrated by Sun Tzu:

> In the conduct of war, one must not rely on the enemy's failure to come but on one's readiness to engage him; one must not rely on the enemy's failure to attack but on one's ability to build an invincible defence.

The need to adopt a "war mentality" or to be in a constant state of combat readiness even in peacetime is well understood by any military general. This concept of "combat readiness" can also be meaningfully applied to business. Such a business philosophy or orientation will constantly motivate the company to want to scale greater heights, and to seize on every opportunity to improve itself. It would always have the mentality to want to grow. In fact, the obstacle to growth would be its own resource availability and capability rather than the constraints imposed by its competitors and the environment. Unfortunately, many companies tend to become victims of their own successes. This is because when they become successful, they forget about what brought them there. They no longer become "hungry" for growth, especially when profits are good. Instead, they are contented with only maintaining their status quo, and would only *react* when threatened by the competitors. In other words, they cease to build invincible defenses around their successful businesses, and instead wait for the arrival of the competitors, or worse, they hope that their competitors will not come after them!

It is important that the correct competitive posture be adopted for any company to excel. Let me illustrate with an example. When a company is not in the number-one position in any market, business, or product, in terms of either sales or profitability, it would be its greatest goal to strive for the number-one position. However, what should its goal be if it has already attained the number-one position? Here, it would not be surprising to find answers like "protect the number-one position," "defend the number-one position," "maintain the number-one position," and "stay in the number-one position." There is a fundamental flaw in such responses in that they all reflect a reactive mind-set, not a proactive posture. If you are already number one, you are the leader, and you should lead! Thus, the more appropriate answer should be to *distance oneself* as far as possible from the rest of the competitors. It must be pointed out that any time you are within the sights of your nearest competitor, you become vulnerable. This is because you are providing the most logical reason and target for the competitors to catch up, or even overtake you. However, if the gap is very large, it becomes almost impossible to catch up. In fact, the gap itself would demoralize any competitor!

The attitude of not having a combat-ready mind-set did, in fact, cause many American and European companies to adopt a complacent posture during the 1970s and 1980s despite the fact that Japanese companies were fast gaining market shares on them. These Western corporate giants actually began from a position of strength after the Second World War, and they were leaders in many world markets and products. Unfortunately, their great success caused them to be complacent, and many failed to take a proactive stance, and made little effort to build strong defenses. For example, instead of investing more into reseach and development, and expanding their market shares, many of them became lethargic and were more interested in short-term profits and dividends. By slowing down their innovation process, and by not paying attention to building up their market shares, they were literally throwing open invitations to their lesser-known Japanese competitors. By adopting such a reactive posture, these Western giants made themselves vulnerable, and, as history has shown, many of them have become victims of their own successes. It was not until the 1990s that Western companies like those in the automobile industry became more aggressive and combat-fit to take on the Japanese (Taylor 1992; Rapoport 1993a). In addition, there were also strong calls for US industry to be more aggressive in research and development investments

(Faltermayer 1993). Interestingly, of late, many European and American companies appear to have swung to the other extreme. Mega mergers and the quest for size to gain competitive advantages have become a new business fad, so much so that 1999 was labelled as the year of merger by *Fortune* magazine (Colvin 1999). Indeed, the year was characterized by mega mergers among many industrial giants like Exxon and Mobil, Travelers Group and Citicorp, NationsBank and Bank America, Bell Atlantic and GTE, Daimler-Benz and Chrysler, British Petroleum and Amoco, and so on.

Among many well-known multinational corporations, IBM is an example of how an industry giant has failed to be protective and combat-fit at all times. Clearly, IBM overwhelmingly dominated the computer industry, especially the mainframe market, for almost four decades. In fact, its mainframe computers were its cash cow. Unfortunately, IBM failed to capitalize on its dominance to further distance itself from the rest of its competitors. Instead, it became complacent and lost its zeal for innovation. Worst of all, it failed to realize that the industry was moving towards personal computers. As a result, it was forced into a very defensive position (Dobrzynski 1993) for many years. Fortunately, it managed to make a comeback through the Internet business (Kirkpatrick 1996) and had also made credible inroads into the notebook market by the late 1990s. In fact, IBM has shifted radically to focus more on e-business and services as the core of its business for the future (Kirkpatrick 1999).

Achieving Relative Superiority at the Point of Contact

In military combat, one of the most important factors to ensure success is to understand the principle of *relative superiority at the point of contact*. In war, it does not matter how large a force you have at home or how rigorously the troops have been trained (although better training would improve their combat readiness and effectiveness). Rather, what matters most is what happens at the point of contact – that is, the side who can gain relative superiority at the point of contact will win. In fact, Sun Tzu underlined this concept when he said:

> The strength of an army does not depend on large forces. Do not advance basing on sheer numbers. Rather, one must concentrate the forces and anticipate correctly the enemy's movements in order to capture him.

The above statement reflects what we commonly call "niching" in business. Sun Tzu went on to elaborate what he meant by achieving relative superiority, and how a small force can take on a larger one if it can exploit the principle underlying point of contact:

> The enemy must not know where I intend to attack. For if he does not know where I intend to attack, he must defend in many places. The more places he defends, the more scattered are his forces, and the weaker is his force at any one point.

He went on to say:

> If he [the enemy] prepares to the front, his rear will be weak; if he defends the rear, his front will be fragile. If he strengthens his left, he will weaken his right; if he strengthens his right, he will weaken his left. If he tries to prepare for everywhere, he will be weak everywhere.

Thus, no one can be invincible whether it is an army or an organization. There are bound to be weak spots among the mightiest of armies and the strongest of business organizations. Even the mighty Japanese companies can become vulnerable, as demonstrated when the Japanese economy began to slow down in the early 1990s, and as Japanese companies faced increased competition from the rest of the world (Schlender 1992, 1993a, 1995; Taylor 1996a; Desmond 1998; Bremner, Thornton and Kunii 1999). The challenge for the smaller force (company) is to concentrate its entire force against a fraction of the larger force at those weak spots where superiority can be attained. As such, even small companies can find their places in any competitive environment, so long as they can develop their unique expertise and cater to specific market niches. In fact, it is tautologous to state that almost all large companies, including the multinational corporations (MNCs), began by being small. Almost all of them began with some kind of niching strategy before pursuing growth and expansion relentlessly. Indeed, in the modern world of high-technology, many companies like Yahoo, American Online, eBay, Amazon.com, Priceline.com, @Home, and Dell Computers have emerged from small companies to become industry giants with high market capitalization within a very short period of time. They succeeded by finding niches in the marketplace.

Relative superiority at the point of contact can also be achieved if one learns to choose battlegrounds carefully. In the words of Sun Tzu:

> Therefore, those who are skilled in warfare will always bring the enemy to where they want to fight, and are not brought there by the enemy.

> To be certain to succeed in what you attack is to attack a place where the enemy does not defend or where its defence is weak. To be certain of holding what you defend is to defend a place the enemy does not attack or where the defence is invulnerable to attacks.

Note that Sun Tzu's principles on the choice of battlegrounds have been applied to business as well. For example, the Japanese are renowned for their clever choice of battlegrounds in their economic conquest of the world (for example, Ohmae 1982, pp. 240–241). In the earlier years, they deliberately avoided head-on confrontation with the Western corporate giants. In exporting, they deliberately selected markets that the Americans were not interested in or had ignored completely like Southeast Asia. Even when they gained strength, and were ready to penetrate the Western markets, they spared no effort in understanding the characteristics of their battlegrounds. In fact, Kotler et al. (1985, p. 49) documented how Toyota skilfully exploited the beachheads (frontiers) they captured on four key West Coast cities in the USA – Los Angeles, San Francisco, Portland, and Seattle – in their penetration of the American automobile market.

Despite the fact that many Japanese companies are now very strong and capable of head-on competition, they are still known to enter markets that are ignored by their competitors. In addition, they have continued to invest heavily in understanding the characteristics of their markets. For example, it is widely known that Japanese firms are very active in new economies like Vietnam and Myanmar, and even in Eastern Europe.

In products, the Japanese have also deliberately sought out neglected and unfilled market segments. For example, in automobiles and consumer durables, the small-size segments were ignored completely by American and European manufacturers. Japanese manufacturers concentrated their entire initial efforts in making small cars, small television sets, mini hi-fi components, desktop photocopiers, etc. Today, they have built up so much expertise and many skills in these areas that are unrivalled by the Western corporations.

Even in the design and styling of products, the Japanese manufacturers would enter areas where the Western corporate giants were reluctant to do so. For example, while American automobile manufacturers hesitated to make cars with right-hand drive for other overseas markets, the Japanese companies have been doing so for more than 40 years! In fact, in making the changes, the Japanese manufacturers would even go into the minute details of adjusting and shifting all the necessary gadgets within the car to accommodate different driving positions, something that even the leading German and European car makers like Mercedes, BMW, Saab, Volvo, Citroen, and Renault have failed to do. It was not till the 1990s that these European car makers realized the seriousness of the Japanese threat. With concerted efforts, some of these European car makers like Mercedes and BMW have begun to seize the initiative from the Japanese (Taylor 1996a).

In choosing areas ignored by the competitors in their economic assault on the world market from the 1960s to the 1980s, the Japanese gained themselves several distinctive advantages. First, as these were areas ignored by the rest, the Japanese manufacturers had all the opportunities and time to improve themselves without being threatened by their stronger Western counterparts. Second, as there was no competition, they were given, by default, unlimited access to exploit the market(s) available. Even in instances where there was competition, it tended to be weak and scattered, and this allowed the Japanese companies to concentrate their entire force against a fraction of those of their competitors. Finally, as a result of having been given an unrestricted scope for building up their market shares in specific product areas, they have developed enough expertise and strengths to challenge the leaders. A good example is that of the automobile industry. Toyota, Nissan, and Honda are now capable of challenging their Western competitors in the luxury car markets with models like the Lexus, Cima, and Legend.

It must be pointed out that Japanese companies began from a position of weakness, not strength. In fact, the whole nation was almost destroyed after the Second World War, and the efforts to rebuild the country and its industries were almost insurmountable. When Japanese products first appeared in the international arena they were known to be of inferior quality, cheap and imitated items. Today, Japanese products have become synonymous with high quality and reliability. Among many reasons for its success, the ability to choose the battleground carefully, and the application of the principle of relative superiority at the point of contact are definitely two of the contributing factors.

Of course, Japanese companies are not the only ones who exploited the principle of relative superiority. In the publishing industry, World Scientific Publishing Co. Pte Ltd (WSP), a company based in Singapore, started off by publishing conference proceedings – an area ignored by larger publishers because of the small market. In doing so, WSP was put into contact with scientific authors who provided strong editorial support for their publications. Subsequently, WSP decided to focus on publishing high-level textbooks – largely graduate-level text – that depend on editorial strengths that it has built up over the years. This was an area ignored by the larger publishers, who tended to concentrate on the large undergraduate textbook market. WSP deliberately avoided head-on competition with the larger publishers as it lacked marketing strengths. Its *forte* was in editorial work, not marketing. Thus, by concentrating on technical and scientific publications, WSP has today built up a very strong niche in an area which the larger publishers find difficult to exploit.

Similarly, for many years, the courier giants like UPS, Federal Express, and TNT were too contented with focusing their businesses in the United States and Europe. They ignored Asia completely. In contrast, DHL, which was a very small player in the American and European markets, decided to build its presence in Asia. Today, DHL is a very dominant leader in Asia with over 40 percent of the market share. The other three larger players can only manage around 15 percent each, and they are now trying very hard to seize market share from DHL.

Role of Intelligence

Without doubt, intelligence plays a pivotal role in the conduct of war. Generals develop their combat strategies based on intelligence gathered on the enemy, weather, and terrain. According to Sun Tzu:

> The reason why the enlightened ruler and the wise general are able to conquer the enemy whenever they lead the army and can achieve victories that surpass those of others is because of foreknowledge.

What is interesting is his view on where the foreknowledge or intelligence should come from:

> This foreknowledge cannot be elicited from spirits nor from the gods; nor by inductive thinking; nor by deductive calculations. It can only be obtained from men who have knowledge of the enemy's situation.

Thus, there is a need to rely on *human intelligence* to actively collect, store, analyze, and utilize information for the development of effective strategies. There is no scope for superstitious practices or hunches when it comes to planning for war. The importance of using human intelligence can be supported by the fact that Sun Tzu expounded on the use of five different types of secret agents for gathering information on the enemies (see Wee et al. 1996, pp. 237–44).

Business espionage should be condemned and frowned upon (Beltramini 1986; Pooley 1982; Waller 1992; Labich 1992c). However, to pretend that business espionage does not exist would be an exercise in futility and naivety. If anything, industrial espionage is rife and commonly practiced in the business world (Nelan 1993; Henkoff 1995; Robinson 1998; Casimiro 1998).

Besides espionage, it is important to point out that there are many "above-board" methods of gathering market and competitive information that could be used for the development of business strategies – for example, surveys, industrial studies, market studies, and trade missions (Eells and Nehemkis 1984; Savidge 1992). In today's business environment where competition is rife, consumer tastes are fast changing and information technology becoming more widespread, the need to rely on intelligence for effective decision making has become more eminent (Brock, 1984; Gordon, 1982; Attanasio, 1988; Bergeron and Raymond, 1992). Many scholars have even argued for systematic ways of collecting and analyzing information on their competitors and the markets (Sammon et al. 1984; Fuld 1985; Gilad and Gilad 1988; Gilad 1989).

In the Asia-Pacific region, it is worth noting that many companies still lack organized intelligence in developing their corporate strategies. Instead they still rely on hunches and guesses in their decision making. Some of the more superstitious chief executive officers (CEOs) and bosses even call in geomancers and temple mediums/priests for consultation in strategic decisions! At the same time, they also rely heavily on personal contacts and family ties to conduct their business. There is nothing wrong in trying to evoke the spiritual dimension and to count on personal networking for business decisions. However, over reliance on such practices at the expense of good and available market information and data would be sheer commercial stupidity. In fact, part of the blame for the Asian economic and financial crisis that began in July 1997 and persisted till mid-1999 can be attributed to the stubborn overlooking of market information, development and trends by the government and companies in many Asian economies (Dumaine 1997).

It is also worth noting that many Japanese companies are known to pursue market intelligence relentlessly. For example, the Japanese general trading companies (GTC), the Ministry of International Trade and Industry (MITI), and the Japanese External Trade Organization (JETRO) have each established worldwide networks of intelligence systems. Together with Japanese companies, they form a formidable market intelligence force unrivalled by any other country in the world. Even the smaller companies are known to depend on the mainstream companies and government-related agencies for information.

According to de Mente (1992), author of more than 20 books on Japan, including *Japanese Etiquette and Ethics in Business* (1960) and *How to Do Business with the Japanese* (1962), knowledge flows unfettered in Japan. Japanese tend to treat the search for and utilization of information as an ongoing activity. This is very different from Westerners, who tend to seek and utilize just enough information to get by or to accomplish immediate short-term goals. Interestingly, the Japanese treatment of information in business is very similar to that for the conduct of war, where information and intelligence are extremely important for decision making.

As a further observation, Japanese executives are known to be highly religious but not superstitious. For example, their corporate ceremonies are filled with spiritual rituals and are accompanied by rich customs and traditions. However, when it comes to decision making, they rely heavily on market intelligence. They are never clouded by superstitions and hearsay. In contrast, many Chinese businessmen in Southeast Asia (including Hong Kong) are highly superstitious, but not religious. In other words, they tend to believe in the spiritual realm more often without substantiation – and rely less on using market information and data. Yet in their daily lives and corporate rituals, religion does not appear to play a major role.

At this point, it may be worthwhile to point out that the Japanese superiority in corporate intelligence may lose its edge in the future world of high-technology and computerization. Based on the predictions made by Kirkpatrick (1997) and Schwartz (1999), the new technology world is going to be highly wired through the Internet and other related technologies (Schlender 1999). The rush and race to wire Europe and Asia have begun in the most earnest manner (Prochnick 1997; Baker, Ewing and Capell 1999; Chowdhury 1999; Kraar 1999). In other words, with the Internet, data can now be retrieved and obtained electronically much faster than by conventional means. In addition, content development is increasing at a geometic function as well. All these mean that it will not only be easier to obtain more data in the future, but that the data can be obtained in analyzed format and form that can be used readily for business decision making. In fact, Davis and Meyer (1998), in their latest book entitled *Blur*, argue how the speed of change in the connected economy would radically affect future business practices and lifestyle. Unfortunately for the Japanese, all these developments are based and done through the *English language* – a severe handicap faced by the Japanese. Thus, the weak command of the English language may become a big obstacle to Japanese companies by the turn of the century. It takes years for anyone to develop a strong command of any language!

Shaping and Flexibility

Sun Tzu used a very simple and common medium, water, to illustrate the need to be flexible in combat:

> The guiding principle in military tactics may be likened to water. Just as flowing water avoids the heights and hastens to the lowlands, an army should avoid strengths and strike weaknesses. Just as water shapes itself according to the ground, an army should manage its victory in accordance with the situation of the enemy. Just as water has no constant shape, so in warfare there are no fixed rules and regulations.

Thus, the wise general is someone who is able to apply the principle of flexibility to take advantage of the changing circumstances in war. Note that one of the most remarkable statements is that there are no fixed rules and regulations when it comes to execution of plans. In other words, the general has the ultimate authority to decide what he deems most appropriate, given the situation that confronts him.

The principle of flexibility in business can best be illustrated by Japanese companies. For example, Japanese production systems are known to be very flexible. To begin with, they rely heavily on subcontracting systems which are geared towards flexibility in many ways. First, it cushions the impact of falling demand and orders, as the burden (such as problems of retrenchment of workers) is passed to the subcontractors. Second, it allows the buyer to source from multiple suppliers, and hence the possibility of obtaining supplies at lower prices. Third, it creates competition among the subcontractors, which inevitably raises quality and service standards. Finally, competition among the various suppliers also tends to increase the overall efficiency and productivity of the production system.

Going beyond purchasing, the Japanese shopfloor is organized in a very flexible manner to capitalize on changes in product designs, order sizes, and so on. To complement such a system, Japanese workers are trained to perform more than one function and their job rotation system ensures that their level of competency is not affected. At the final product stage, Japanese products are known to be shaped according to the demands of the markets that they are selling to, even though the market size may be small. For example, while the United States ignored the markets in Southeast Asia in the 1960s and 1970s, the Japanese courted this part of the world enthusiastically with products that were designed specifically for them. Despite their huge successes today, the Japanese have continued to be flexible in their product offerings to newer markets in the Asia-Pacific region. For example, when China needed cars after that country had opened up aggressively in the 1980s, the Japanese were prepared to do "reverse engineering" in order to sell the Chinese cheap, large, and efficient cars. In contrast, the Western companies were reluctant to do so. The results of such flexible policies are very telling by the size of Japanese market shares in these countries. In the words of Kotler et al. (1985, p. 254):

> Flexibility has been the visible trademark of the Japanese. They have not engraved their strategies in stone. They have not become so committed to a specific strategy that they have been blinded by it. Rather, they remained committed to broad strategic thrusts, and they have demonstrated tremendous flexibility in pursuing these thrusts . . . They have continually adapted to the market and competitive environment and their evolving position within it.

In recent years, top US and European companies have begun to close the quality gap against Japanese products. In response, Japanese manufacturers have shifted to flexible manufacturing systems and strategies as their new competitive weapon. They do this by focusing on more and better product features, flexible factories that can accommodate varying production orders and designs, expanded customer service, innovation, and technological superiority (Stewart 1992b; Taylor 1996b; Desmond 1998). However, it is significant to note that in the car industry, several European car makers like Mercedes and BMW have stolen the glamor back from the Japanese car makers. In the high-technology businesses like telecommunications and computers, the American and European companies are now miles ahead of the Japanese. This is because in the realm of high-technology where individual creativity and entrepreneurship are critical, the Americans and Europeans have decisive edges over the Japanese.

Business situations are always very dynamic as they are affected by various factors – the consumers, the competitors, the government, the general public, the state of technology, the state of the economy, and so on. To compete successfully, the company must be adaptive to changes in its environment, and must not be bound by past practices or traditions. In fact, in their book, Bartlett and Ghoshal (1989) argued that the future transnational corporations, among other things, must able to maintain organizational flexibility in order to compete effectively. Their views were supported by Stewart (1992a). For example, there are no fixed rules on how a company should go about developing its overseas markets (Bartlett and Ghoshal 1989). If one company cannot do it alone, there is nothing to stop it joining forces with other companies with similar interests, even if they are direct competitors.

Indeed, strategic alliances and mergers are becoming an important development in the conduct of business today as they can also provide for flexibility (Sherman 1992). Toshiba, the oldest and third-largest Japanese electronics giant, has made strategic alliances a cornerstone of its corporate strategy (Schlender 1993c). As of 1999, it had no less than 25 strategic partners in the USA, Europe, Canada, and even South Korea. In taking such a flexible approach, Toshiba has been able to enhance its global position in both technology and marketing. Besides Toshiba, many other Japanese companies have created strong partnerships by investing in sagging European rival companies (Rapoport 1993c). In doing so, they have created additional leverages for themselves to compete in the future. Besides the Japanese, the South Koreans are pursuing similar flexible strategies in their quest for world market share (Kraar 1992, 1993).

Perhaps one of the most startling calls made for flexibility in recent years must be from Gary Hamel, a management guru. In a cover story of *Fortune* magazine, he argued that the companies that did best for their shareholders thrive by taking risks, that is, by breaking the rules (Hamel 1997). To excel, Hamel further advocated that companies must adopt a "gung-ho" approach and be prepared to change the rules of the competition by reinventing new rules! In his study, he even documented how it was important to turn a company's business upside down in order to forge ahead. While these may sound like radical and futuristic ideas, they are none the less not too far from the philosophy of Sun Tzu! However, some authors like Sennett (1998) and Carr (1999) have also begun to sound words of caution. To them, too much flexibility may corrode a person's character and lead to the loss of important virtues like commitment, loyalty, and integrity – essential attributes of a corporate executive.

Innovation and Use of Initiative

Innovativeness is another interesting concept advocated by Sun Tzu. This can be illustrated as follows:

> Therefore, do not repeat the tactics that won you a victory, but vary them according to the circumstances. He [the general] must be able to change his methods and schemes so that no one can know his intentions. He must be able to alter his camp-sites and marching routes so that no one can predict his movements.

This non-repetitiveness of tactics implies a constant search for new ways of meeting the challenges offered by the ever-changing circumstances. In addition, the use of new approaches will also prevent the enemy (competitor) from anticipating one's plans, as one becomes unpredictable through continual innovation. In essence, the strategy to be adopted should be novel and situation dependent, rather than relying on seemingly proven strategies.

It is important to note that while shaping and flexibility are more reactive in that they flow according to the situation, innovativeness is more proactive in that it attempts to dominate or control the situation: "Thus, those skilled in manipulating the enemy do so by creating a situation to which he must conform."

Innovation is very much desired in business. This is especially so in the present environment where technology is becoming increasingly important as a competitive edge. There must be a constant search for different ways of doing things. In the process, the solutions may not conform to past practices and traditions. For example, despite the setbacks faced by many Japanese companies in the early 1990s, especially in the computer and automobile industries (Schlender 1993a, b; Taylor 1993), they are looking for new ways to overcome their problems In fact, some enlightened Western writers even cautioned the Western world not to rejoice over the economic woes of the Japanese companies in the early 1990s. If anything, based on how they had overcome the oil crisis in the 1970s and the rising yen in the late 1980s, Japanese companies are likely to emerge even stronger after they have resolved their difficulties in the 1990s (Stewart 1992b; Taylor 1993). Already, companies like Honda are beginning to take corrective actions (Taylor 1996b) and the Japanese economy had shown signs of an economic recovery as of the first quarter of 1999 when its GDP registered a healthy 1.9 percent growth.

While innovation is a proactive, deliberate, and systematic approach to problem solving, the use of *initiative* requires both the proactive and reactive dimensions. In other words, it requires the individual to be very responsive to changes in situations, as well as able to take pre-emptive actions. Thus, resourcefulness at the point of decision making is essential. In addition, the exercise of initiative is often instantaneous and an intuitive act of the individual who is faced with the decision. In the words of Sun Tzu: "There are situations when the orders of the ruler need not be obeyed." In fact, he illustrated this as follows:

> If the situation is one of victory, the general must fight even though the ruler may have issued orders not to engage. If the situation is one of defeat, the general must not fight even though the ruler may have issued orders to do so.

Thus, the use of initiative requires the general to make decisions at the point of battle as there is little time for him to consult the ruler (who is often not at the battlefield). The general must decide on the spot what his next move is to be. If the situation dictates that he should attack, he must do so, even if he had prior orders not to engage. This is because there are so many variations and changes at each step of the battle. If the general cannot exercise initiative under such circumstances and must await the orders of the ruler for each move, it is like telling your superior that you would like to have his permission to put out a fire. By the time the order to do so is approved, the ashes would be cold!

It must be pointed out that in exercising initiative, the general must advance without seeking personal fame and glory and must retreat without fear of being punished. At all times, he must have the welfare of the people and the interests of the ruler at heart. Thus, in exercising his initiative under such circumstances, he has not betrayed the trust given to him, nor should his loyalty be questioned.

> Therefore, the general who advances without seeking personal fame and glory, who retreats without fear of being punished, but whose main concern is for the welfare of the people and the interests of the sovereign, is the precious gem of the state.

The use of initiative requires the general to capitalize on the situations facing him, and to be able to exploit the resources available to him:

> Therefore, the adept in warfare seeks victory from the situation, and does not rely on the efforts of individuals. Thus, he is able to select suitable men to exploit the situation.

Initiative also extends beyond pragmatism. This is because pragmatism, to a large extent, is reactive in nature. Initiative, however, encompasses both the reactive and proactive dimensions. Other than reacting very expediently and effectively to changes in the environment, it also involves constantly looking for better ways to win:

> If the enemy provides an opportunity, quickly capitalize on it. Effective strategies must constantly change according to the situation of the enemy.

In the same way, a company must encourage the flow of innovative ideas and the exercise of initiative on all fronts from the conception of product/service ideas to the actual implementation of marketing strategies. Pascale (1990) even argued for innovative ways of managing conflicts in order to stay ahead of competition, while Naisbitt and Aburdene (1985) advocated innovative human resource management and organization as the future corporate challenge. Hamel (1997) even advocated the breaking of rules! No matter what it is, it is important that at any time when opportunities arise as a result of the changing environment or other factors, the company must be capable of capitalizing on them. It must not shy away, even though the execution process may have to be modified. At times, it may also entail changes to plans that are already made.

Briefly, innovativeness and initiative are very much related to creativity. In recent years, creativity has been actively pursued by organizations and their corporate executives. This has resulted in no shortage of literature on the subject. For example, de Bono (1971) propounded lateral thinking for management. Ackoff (1978) wrote his famous book on the art of problem solving. Miller (1986) and Adams (1986) argued for the need to foster innovation and ideas at the place of work. Goman (1989) attempted to provide pointers to creative thinking in business. Yu (1990) proposed an integrated theory of habitual domains as the basis for forming winning strategies. Yet despite all this available literature, the books remain only academic if corporate executives are unable to translate them into actionable plans and projects for the company.

Need to be on the Offensive in Combat

While Sun Tzu acknowledged the need for strong defense, he also advocated the need for offense. If possible, one should attack plans at inception, and avoid open conflicts. However, if open combat is inevitable, the best way to win is through attacking:

> Invincibility in defense depends on one's own efforts, while the opportunity of victory depends on the enemy. It follows that those who are skilled in warfare can make themselves invincible, but cannot cause the enemies to be vulnerable.

It is important to understand the rationale behind the need for attacking in open combat. An invincible defense can ensure that one does not lose, but cannot guarantee a victory. At best, it can only result in a draw. At worst, it can even lead to "self-choking" and isolation. Victory can only be achieved by capturing the enemy's territory (or destroying his forces). It cannot be won by defending one's territory or troops. Indeed, the focus on attack has led to the development of niching strategies for those with smaller forces and weaker equipment. To achieve success with niching, one must constantly keep in mind that in direct confrontation, it is the relative superiority of forces at the point of contact that matters most. Thus, absolute superiority alone in numbers and resources are not sufficient in winning. What is more important is to develop and use strategies that allow the achievement of relative superiority.

The logic on attack applies to business as well. For example, strong defense of a company's market share can reduce the probability that its competitors will not steal its customers. However, its market share is unlikely to increase unless it seeks new and potential customers and those of its competitors. There is hardly any other viable option in the case of open competition. In fact, even if a company chooses not to attack, there is no guarantee that its competitors will not pursue its customers! In businesses where economies of scale prevail, the need to pursue market share (as a means to reduce costs and hence increase profits) is even more urgent and important. Perhaps this is one of the reasons behind the increasing number of mega mergers that occurred in the late 1990s (Colvin 1999).

This principle of attack in open combat is well illustrated by Samsung, one of the largest South Korean companies. Moving away from making imitated products, it invested over US$2.5 billion a year into training, research, and production facilities. It also began a deliberate policy to pursue market share in the long run by forgoing short-term profits (Kraar 1993). Samsung was not an exception. Many other South Korean companies were pursuing similar aggressive strategies to expand their stakes in the world market in the 1980s and early 1990s (Kraar 1992). Their ambitious plans were finally halted with the onslaught of the Asian financial and economic crisis that began in July 1997. Interestingly, many American and European high-technology companies are pursuing the same strategy today. For example, Amazon.com invested the bulk of its earnings regularly into research and development with the intention of dominating the market and reaping the profits only in the future (Kraar 1999).

Moving to a more macro level, the analogy of attack can be extended to international trade among nations. Over the last two decades, the successes of countries like Japan and the newly industrialized economies (NIEs) – namely Hong Kong, Singapore, South Korea, and Taiwan – have been largely due to their attacking strategies in international trade (for example, Kraar 1992). They opted for an export-oriented strategy as the engine for economic growth rather than relying on domestic factors like developing import substitution industries. The results are well known. In addition, countries like Singapore even capitalized on the 1997 Asian economic and financial crisis to widen its gap against other competitive economies. Instead of retreating and cutting back expenditure, Singapore used the crisis as a catalyst to force economic change and the development of new and more competitive industries like software, banking, and other services (Clifford, Shari and Einhorn 1999).

Ironically, when threatened with the export offensive strategy of Japan and the NIEs, many Western European countries, the USA and Canada tended to embark on defensive strategies (Smith 1992; Rapoport 1992, 1993b). They used various measures to protect their domestic markets, and devoted relatively less attention to making their industries more competitive and export-oriented (Smith 1992). Without doubt, their protective measures only ensured that they would not lose further foreign exchange. However, with equal certainty, they could not earn the needed foreign exchange! Fortunately, many Western companies began to go on the offensive in the early 1990s (Taylor 1992; Faltermayer 1993; Kirkpatrick 1993; Rapoport 1993a). With the 1997 Asian economic and financial crisis, many American and European companies had even moved aggressively into Asia to pick up corporate bargains at basement prices.

Focus More on the Heart in Execution

Without doubt, in developing his strategies and plans, the general cannot afford to allow them to be affected by his personal feelings and emotions (that is, matters of the heart). Instead, planning and strategizing have to be done cold-bloodedly and with the coolest of minds. He has to use the best men to do the most life-threatening assignments; he must not be biased or influenced by his feelings for the men. However, when it comes to the execution of the plan and in motivating the morale of the troops, the general has to switch from a pure mind-driven mentality to a heart-oriented posture. This is because in war, the general cannot rely on material benefits to motivate his troops. Instead, he has to appeal to their sense of national pride and loyalty. He appeals to their emotions and feelings, and uses the moral cause as justification for aggression. For this reason, the general even joins his troops and, if needed, drinks from the same coffee mug and eats from the same mess tin. In doing so, he wins their hearts, which is very important for building up comradeship and team spirit ingredients so essential for winning wars. Indeed, no shrewd general would think of motivating his soldiers in combat with extra pay or bonus!

While it is very easy for anyone to comprehend the need to focus on the heart in the motivation of an army for war, it is harder to translate that into applications to business. If anything, many Western companies tend to develop policies that appeal to the mind rather than the heart. There are fundamental differences between these two approaches, as shown in Table 2. Appealing to the heart is more an art rather than a science. For example, to appeal to the heart, there is a need to take a long-term perspective and the

TABLE 2 The heart and mind approach in the management of people

The heart (feelings and emotions)	*The mind (logic and reason)*
(1) Social orientation	(1) Task orientation
(2) Personal and people-centered	(2) Impersonal and systems-driven
(3) Takes a long-term perspective	(3) Breeds short-term mentality
(4) Builds loyalty and group values	(4) Develops self-interest and individualism
(5) Contributions assessed over one's lifetime	(5) Contributions assessed on economic value
(6) Reliance on psychic rewards	(6) Focus on tangible benefits
(7) Expertise not vulnerable to external exploitation	(7) Expertise can be bought and sold
(8) Management more an art	(8) Management more a science

employee's contributions have to be viewed over a lifetime. There is a need for strong social interactions, and the CEO has to adopt a much more personal and people-centered approach. When the heart can be won over, the employees are likely to be highly loyal and less likely to be lured away by higher perks offered by the competitors. In other words, they will find satisfaction in working for the organization as they tend to rely more on psychic rewards. The heart approach facilitates the cultivation of group values, which in turn, favors the development of team building and team work.

In general, Japanese and many Asian companies tend to focus more on appealing to the hearts in the management of their employees. In contrast, Western companies, largely due to their cultural influences, tend to focus more on appealing to the minds in their personnel management. They do this largely by offering higher salaries and perks. If special expertise is needed, they will not hesitate to "head-hunt" for it, and this includes hiring the CEO. For example, IBM hired a new CEO in 1993 as it was felt that there was no senior executive within the existing organization capable of doing the job. Interestingly, despite the seemingly elaborate "head-hunting" exercise, the computer industry did not appear to give IBM's new CEO much respect (Dobrzynski 1993). In short, the Western approach tends to treat management as more of a science, and adopts a much more "clinical" approach in the way the organization is handled.

In business practice, the heart and mind are not mutually exclusive. Neither am I saying that one approach is superior to the other. Rather, my arguments are that the Japanese and Asian companies tend to pay more attention to the heart factors in the management of employees, while the Western companies tend to be more mind-driven. There is nothing wrong with being more mind-driven so long as a healthy balance can be maintained. For example, if teamwork is necessary to achieve success, then there is a need to inject more heart into the organization. This is where I find much of the literature on team building and teamwork lacking. While many of these works tend to expound on the importance and contributions of teamwork and team building, they tend to treat the subject in a rather "clinical" manner (for example, Dyer 1987; Johansen et al. 1991; Katzenbach and Smith 1993). Little attention is given to building up social bonds within the team – that is, focusing on building up the heart. Ironically, when one traces back into history, it was Mayo's (1933) classic Hawthorne experiment that clearly demonstrated the emergence of the team idea in an organized work setting – one that operated with the heart. In that well-documented Hawthorne experiment, the group maintained high productivity over a five-year period largely because of mental rewards resulting from a strong team spirit. The leader of that group managed by appealing to the heart, not the mind! In fact, Mayo's works were very much supported by McGregor (1960) when he wrote *The Human Side of Enterprise*, and Likert (1961) who authored *New Patterns of Management*. Perhaps it is timely for Western executives to revisit some of these classic works to rediscover the need for the heart in management.

Conclusion

The analogy between war and business is a fruitful exercise, but it is too often taken for granted. For example, in the conduct of war, *leadership is crucial*. In fact, a general is carefully trained over many years and only attains his rank based on his military accomplishments. He is never "parachuted" into the army as his stars must be earned through the rank-and-file. In addition, it is a military practice to rotate generals, depending on the war mission at hand. It is no wonder that Sun Tzu's writings are largely focused on the general and his strategies.

Ironically, in the world of business, little attention is paid to the training of leaders. If anything, it is quite typical for a company to be plagued with succession problems. Worse still, even when a corporate general is doing well on the job, he is often allowed to carry on as if in perpetuity until the company gets into serious trouble. In fact, this is the typical case of many American companies, as illustrated by the removal of Robert C. Stempel as Chairmen of General Motors in late 1992.

Of course, there are limits to the analogy between war and business in that the former is an extreme situation, demanding exceptional responses and a suspension of normal life. War, after all, involves killing and being killed, and often allows for various forms of behavior, espionage, and control of the media, for instance. These activities are unlikely to be tolerated in peacetime. Even allowing for the notion of a "just war" one may feel that a war mentality is not necessary or desirable for a successful business life. Yet it is equally difficult to deny that many military concepts can be applied meaningfully in business. In particular, they help to develop a mentality among corporate executives to win business wars. Thus, Sun Tzu's *Art of War*, a treatise highly regarded by many Asian corporate strategists, may provide some inspiration in this direction.

References

Abegglen, J. C. and Stalk, Jr., G. (1985), *Kaisha: The Japanese Corporation*, New York, Basic Books.

Ackoff, R. L. (1978), *The Art of Problem Solving*, New York, John Wiley.

Adams, J. L. (1986), *Conceptual Blockbusting: A Guide to Better Ideas*, Reading, MA, Addison-Wesley.

Attanasio, D. B. (1988), "The multiple benefits of competitor intelligence," *The Journal of Business Strategy*, May/June, 16–19.

Baker, S., Ewing, J. and Capell, K. (1999), "The race to wire Europe," *Business Week*, 7 June, 30–34.

Bartlett, C. A. and Ghoshal, S. (1989), *Managing Across Borders: The Transnational Solution*, Boston, MA, Harvard Business School Press.

Behar, R. (1999), "Spy vs Spy," *Fortune*, 139, No. 2, 1 February, 64–67.

Beltramini, R. F. (1986), "Ethics and the use of competitive information acquisition strategies," *Journal of Business Ethics*, 5, 307–11.

Bergeron, F. and Raymond, L. (1992), "Planning of information systems to gain a competitive edge," *Journal of Small Business Management*, January, 21–6.

Birnbaum, J. F. (1997), "The Holy War over capital gains," *Fortune*, 135, No. 3, 17 February, 14.

Bremner, B., Thornton, E. and Kunii, I. M. (1999), "Fall of a Keiretsu," *Business Week*, 15 March, 34–40.

Brock, J. J. (1984), "Competitor analysis: some practical approaches," *Industrial Marketing Management*, 13, 225–31.

Carr, N. G. (1999), "Being virtual: Character and the new economy," *Harvard Business Review*, 77, No. 3, May/June, 181–186.

Casimiro, S. (1998), "The spying game moves into the U.S. workplace," *Fortune*, 137, No. 6, 30 March, 68.

Chandler, A. D. Jr. (1962), *Strategy As Structure*, Cambridge, MA, MIT Press.

Chowdhury, N. and Paul, A. (1997), "Where Asia goes from here," *Fortune*, 136, No. 10, 24 November, 28–29.

Chowdhury, N. (1999), "Yahoo! Hello, Asia," *Fortune*, 139, No. 12, 21 June, 45.

Clifford, M. L., Shari, M. and Einhorn, B. (1999), "Remaking Singapore Inc.," *Business Week*, 5 April, 19–22.

Colvin, G. (1999), "The year of the megamerger," *Fortune*, 139, No. 1, 11 January, 32–34.

Costa, L. A. (1999), "Steeling for a trade war," *Fortune*, 139, No. 1, 11 January, 24.

Davis, S. and Meyer, C. (1998), *Blur: The Speed of Change in the Connected Economy*, Reading, MA, USA, Addison-Wesley.

de Bono, E. (1971), *Lateral Thinking for Management*, London, McGraw-Hill.

de Mente, B. L. (1992), "In Japan, knowledge flows unfettered," *Singapore Straits Times*, 30 March.

Desmond, E. W. (1998), "Can Canon keep clicking?" *Fortune*, 137, No. 2, 2 February, 42–45.

Dobrzynski, J. H. (1993), "Rethinking IBM," *Business Week*, 4 October, 44–55.

Dumaine, B. (1991), "The bureaucracy busters," *Fortune International*, 123, No. 13, 17 June, 26–34.

Dumaine, B. (1997), "Asia's wealth creators confront a new reality," *Fortune*, 136, No. 11, 8 December, 42–52.

Dyer, W. G. (1987), *Team Building: Issues and Alternatives*, Reading, MA, Addison-Wesley.

Eells, R. and Nehemkis, P. (1984), *Corporate Intelligence and Espionage*, New York, Macmillan.

Enricho, R. and Kornbluth, J. (1987), "The other guy blinked: how Pepsi won the cola wars," *World Executive Digest*, April, 44–48.

Falternayer, E. (1993), "Invest or die," *Fortune International*, 127, No. 4, 22 February, 16–22.

Fang, Tony (1999), *Chinese Business Negotiating Style*, London, U.K., SAGE Publications, Inc.

Fuld, L. M. (1985), *Corporate Intelligence: How to Get It, How to Use It*, New York, John Wiley.

Gilad, B. (1989), "The role of organized competitive intelligence in corporate strategy," *Columbia Journal of World Business*, Winter, 29–35.

Gilad, B. and Gilad, T. (1988), *The Business Intelligence System*, New York, American Management Association.

Goman C. K. (1989), *Creative Thinking in Business*, Guildford, U.K., Biddles Limited.

Gordon, I. H. (1982), "Competitive intelligence – a key to marketplace survival," *Industrial Marketing*, 67, No. 11, November, 69–75.

Griffith, S. B. (1982), *Sun Tzu: The Art of War*, Oxford, Oxford University Press.

Gunther, M. (1999), "War breaks out in TV land," *Fortune*, 139, No. 12, 21 June, 19–20.

Guyon, J. (1997), "Why is the world's most profitable company turning itself inside out?" *Fortune*, 136, No. 3, 4 August, 62–67.

Hamel, G. (1997), "Killer strategies that make shareholders rich," *Fortune*, 135, No. 12, 23 June, 30–44.

Henderson, B. (1979), *Henderson on Corporate Strategy*, Cambridge, MA, Abt Books.

Henkoff, R. (1995), "My life as a corporate mole for the FBI," *Fortune*, 132, No. 5, 4 September, 38–47.

Hesselbein, F., Goldsmith, M. and Beckhard, R. (1997), *The Organization of the Future*, San Francisco, USA, Jossey-Bass Publishers.

Johansen, R., Martin, A., Mittman, R., Saffo, P., Sibbet, D. and Benson, S. (1991), *Leading Business Teams*, Reading, MA, Addison-Wesley.

Katzenbach, J. R. and Smith, D. K. (1993), *The Wisdom of Teams: Creating the High-Performance Organization*, Boston, MA, Harvard Business School Press.

Keenan, F. and Landers, P. (1999), "Staggering giants," *Far Eastern Economic Review*, 162, No. 13, 1 April, 10–14.

Kirkpatrick, D. (1993), "Could AT & T rule the world?" *Fortune International*, 127, No. 10, 17 May, 18–27.

Kirkpatrick, D. (1996), "IBM and Lotus: Not so dumb after all," *Fortune*, 134, No. 1, 8 July, 36–40.

Kirkpatrick, D. (1997), "Ten tech trends to bet on," *Fortune*, 136, No. 9, 10 November, 72–79.

Kirkpatrick, D. (1999), "Big blue dinosaur to e-business animal," *Fortune*, 139, No. 8, 26 April, 66–71.

Kotler, P. and Singh, R. (1981), "Marketing warfare in the 1980s," *Journal of Business Strategy*, Winter, 30–41.

Kotler, P., Fahey, L. and Jatusripitak, S. (1985), *The New Competition*, Englewood Cliffs, NJ, Prentice-Hall.

Kraar, L. (1992), "Korea's tigers keep roaring." *Fortune International*, 125, No. 9, 4 May, 24–28.

Kraar, L. (1993), "How Samsung grows so fast," *Fortune International*, 127, No. 9, 3 May, 16–21.

Kraar, L. (1997), "Korea's chaebol sail into an era of radical change," *Fortune*, 136, No. 11, 8 December, 56–60.

Kraar, L. (1999), "The art of the c-deal," *Fortune*, 139, No. 12, 21 June, 40–42.

Krugman, P. (1997), "What ever happened to the Asian miracle?" *Fortune*, 136, No. 4, 18 August, 12–14.

Kupfer, A. (1995), "Picking the winners in the new communications war," *Fortune*, 132, No. 2, 24 July, 122–124.

Kupfer, A. (1998), "The next big war in telecom," *Fortune*, 138, No. 10, 23 November, 133–32.

Kupfer, A. (1999), "The battle to control telecom," *Fortune*, 139, No. 3, 15 February, 94.

Labich, K. (1992a), "Airbus takes off," *Fortune International*, 125, No. 11, 1 June, 22–28.

Labich, K. (1992b), "Europe's sky wars," *Fortune International*, 126, No. 10, 2 November, 20–31.

Labich, K. (1992c), "The new crisis in business ethics," *Fortune International*, 125, No. 8, 20 April, 83–86.

Lazer, W., Murata, S. and Kosaka, H. (1985), "Japanese marketing: towards a better understanding," *Journal of Marketing*, 49, No. 2, 69–81.

Lee, K. S., Chng, P. L. and Wee, C. H. (1994), "The art and the science of strategic marketing: Synergizing Sun Tzu's *Art of War* with game theory," *Journal of Strategic Marketing*, 2, No. 2, June, 112–139.

Li S. J., Yang, X. J. and Tang, J. R. (1984), *Sun Tzu's Art of War and Business Management*, China, Kwangsi People's Press (translated)

Likert, R. (1961), *New Patterns of Management*, New York, McGraw-Hill.

Lorange, P. (1980), *Corporate Planning: An Executive Viewpoint*, Englewood Cliffs, NJ, Prentice-Hall.

Lorange, P. (1982), *Implementation of Strategic Planning*, Englewood Cliffs, NJ, Prentice-Hall.

Lorange, P. and Vancil, R. F. (1976), "How to design a strategic planning system," *Harvard Business Review*, 54, No. 5, September/October, 75–81.

Mayo, E. (1933), *The Human Problems of an Industrial Civilization*, Division of Research, Graduate School of Business Administration, Harvard University, Boston, MA.

McGregor, D. (1960), *The Human Side of Enterprise*, New York, McGraw-Hill.

Miller, W. C. (1986), *The Creative Edge: Fostering Innovation Where You Work*, Reading, MA, Addison-Wesley.

Naisbitt, J. and Aburdene, P. (1985), *Re-inventing The Corporation*, New York, Warner Books.

National Economic Commission (1985), *Classical Chinese Thoughts and Modern Management*, Economic Management Research Institute, China, Yunnan People's Publishing (translated).

Nelan, B. W. (1993), "A new world for spies," *Time*, 5 July, 28–31.

Ohmae, K. (1982), *The Mind of the Strategist: The Art of Japanese Business*, New York, McGraw-Hill.

Ohmae, K. (1989), "Planting for a global harvest," *Harvard Business Review*, 67, No. 4, July–August, 136–145.

Pascale, R. T. (1990), *Managing On The Edge: How the Smartest Companies Use Conflict to Stay Ahead*, New York, Simon and Schuster.

Pooley, J. (1982), *Trade Secrets: How To Protect Your Ideas and Assets*, Berkeley, CA, Osborne, McGraw-Hill.

Prochniak, A. L. (1997), "Asia's infotech," *Fortune*, 136, No. 4, 18 August, 44–45.

Rapoport, C. (1992), "Getting tough with the Japanese," *Fortune International*, 125, No. 9, 4 May, 30–35.

Rapoport, C. (1993a), "Europe takes on the Japanese," *Fortune International*, 127, No. 1, 11 January, 14–18.

Rapoport, C. (1993b), "Europe's slump," *Fortune International*, 127, No. 9, 3 May, 22–27.

Rapoport, C. (1993c), "Japan to the rescue," *Fortune International*, 128, No. 9, 18 October, 30–34.

Ries, A. and Trout, J. (1986), *Marketing Warfare*, New York, McGraw-Hill.

Robinson, E. A. (1998), "China's spies target corporate America," *Fortune*, 137, No. 6, 30 March, 52–55.

Rohwer, J. (1998), "Asia's meltdown: The risks are rising," *Fortune*, 137, No. 3, 16 February, 32–33.

Sammon, W. L., Kurland, M. A. and Spitalnic, R. (1984), *Business Competitor Intelligence*, New York, John Wiley.

Saporito, W. (1992), "Why the price wars never end," *Fortune International*, 125, No. 6, 23 March, 20–25.

Savidge, J. (1992), *Marketing Intelligence*, USA, Book Press Inc.

Schlender, B. R. (1992), "How deep a slump, and which way out?" *Fortune International*, 126, No. 14, 14–18.

Schlender, B. R. (1993a), "Japan: hard times for high tech," *Fortune International*, 127, No. 6, 22 March, 18–23.

Schlender, B. R. (1993b), "PC wars in Japan," *Fortune International*, 127, No. 14, 12 July, 14–18.

Schlender, B. R. (1993c), "How Toshiba makes alliances work," *Fortune International*, 128, No. 8, 4 October, 42–7.

Schlender, B. R. (1995), "Sony on the brink," *Fortune*, 131, No. 11, 12 June, 32–48.

Schlender, B. R. (1999), "E-business according to Gates," *Fortune*, 139, No. 7, 12 April, 48–51.

Schwartz, N. D. (1999), "The tech boom will keep on rocking," *Fortune*, 139, No. 3, 15 February, 28–38.

Sennett, R. (1998), *The Corrosion of Character: The Personal Consequences of Work in the New Capitalism*, New York, W. W. Norton & Company.

Sherman, S. (1992), "Are strategic alliances working?," *Fortune International*, 126, No. 6, 21 September, 33–34.

Sherman, S. (1993), "The new computer revolution," *Fortune International*, 127, No. 12, June 14, 20–40.

Smith, L. (1992), "A dangerous fix for trade deficits," *Fortune International*, 125, No. 9, 4 May, 96–97.

Stewart, T. A. (1992a), "The search for the organization of tomorrow," *Fortune International*, 125, No. 10, 18 May, 53–58.

Stewart, T. A. (1992b), "Brace for Japan's hot new strategy," *Fortune International*, 126, No. 6, 21 September, 24–32.

Stewart, T. A. (1995), "Information wars: What you don't know will hurt you," *Fortune*, 131, No. 11, 12 June, 87–89.

Stripp, W. C. (1985), "Sun Tzu, Musashi and Mahan: The integration of Chinese, Japanese and American strategic thought in international business," *Proceedings of the Inaugural Meeting of the Southeast Asian Region Academy of International Business*, Hong Kong, The Chinese University of Hong Kong, pp. 109–118.

Sullivan, J. J. (1992), "Japanese management philosophies: From the vacuous to the brilliant," *California Management Review*, 34, No. 2, Winter, 66–87.

Taylor III, A. (1992), "U.S. cars come back," *Fortune International*, 126, No. 11, 16 November, 24–53.

Taylor III, A. (1993), "How Toyota copes with hard times," *Fortune International*, 127, No. 2, 25 January, 18–22.

Taylor III, A. (1996a), "Speed! Power! Status!" *Fortune*, 133, No. 11, 10 June, 39–46.

Taylor III, A. (1996b), "The man who put Honda back on track," *Fortune*, 134, No. 5, 9 September, 30–38.

Tully, S. (1996), "Northwest and KLM: The alliance from hell," *Fortune*, 133, No. 12, 24 June, 48–59.

Waller, D. (1992), "The open barn door: U.S. firms face a wave of foreign espionage," *Newsweek*, 4 May.

Wee, C. H. (1989), "Planning for war and business: lessons from Sun Tzu," *Pointer*, Singapore, January–March, 3–20.

Wee, C. H. (1990), "Battlegrounds and business situation: lessons from Sun Tzu," *Singapore Business Review*, 1, No. 1, 21–43.

Wee, C. H. (1993), "Application of military strategies to business: Why they are more relevant to Japanese than American companies," *The International Executive*, 35, No. 2, 95–124.

Wee, C. H. (1994), "Managing change: Perspectives from Sun Tzu's *Art of War*," *Journal of Strategic Change*, 3, July/August, 189–199.

Wee, C. H. (1995), "From battleground to marketplace," *Asian Business*, April, 42–44.

Wee, C. H. (1997), "Fighting talk," *People Management*, Personnel Publications, United Kingdom, 3, No. 21, October, 40–44.

Wee, C. H., Lee, K. S. and Hidajat, B. W. (1996), *Sun Tzu: War and Management*, Reading, MA, Addison-Wesley.

Wee, C. H. and Lan, L. L. (1998), *The 36 Strategies of the Chinese: Adapting Ancient Chinese Wisdom to the Business World*, Singapore, Addison-Wesley Longman.

Yu, P. L. (1990), *Forming Winning Strategies: An Integrated Theory of Habitual Domains*, Berlin, Springer-Verlag.

Zellner, W. (1992), "The airlines are killing each other again," *International Business Week*, 8 June, 30.

○ ○

Cross-Cultural Cooperative Behavior in Joint Ventures in LDCs

Henry W. Lane and Paul W. Beamish

Joint ventures (majority and minority), alliances and global strategic partnerships are emerging as the organizational forms of the future in global businesses (Perlmutter and Heenan, 1986). Minority joint ventures are particularly common in less-developed countries (LDCs) (Franko, 1989). Of the approximately 25,000 foreign affiliates worldwide of US-based companies, "minority equity affiliates outnumber majority and fully owned affiliates put together" (Contractor and Lorange, 1987).

Cooperative ventures may be a way to improve global prospects but they frequently do not meet performance expectations (Radway, 1986). For example, executives both from foreign parent companies and from local companies we have surveyed were dissatisfied with the performance of more than one-half of their international joint ventures. None were totally satisfied with all their joint ventures.

Many Western corporations seek cooperative ventures as a "quick fix" to global competitiveness without understanding the relationships being established and the behavioral and cultural issues involved. Strategic alliances are challenging the old distinction of competitors and collaborators (Hax, 1989). Companies now may be both – simultaneously. Minority affiliations are requiring new sets of attitudes and behaviors. Domination based on financial ownership and tight control is giving way to partnership based on mutual interests, trust, and the management of ongoing relationships. Control is exercised through influence as much as through budgets and reporting systems. Alliances and joint ventures may force a shift in executive behavior towards improved skills in working collaboratively, communicating and gaining consensus (Palmer, 1987).

The potential benefits of cooperative ventures are real, but not guaranteed. The anticipated benefits may never be achieved. The principal observation from our research (Beamish, 1984, 1988; Lane and DiStefano, 1988; Beamish and Wang, 1989) is

© 1990, Gabler Verlag. Reprinted with permission by *Management International Review*, vol. 30, Special issue, pp. 87–102.

that the problems and failures are related primarily to a deterioration of relationships and unresolved conflicts between partners resulting from defects in the process of initiation and implementation and to the lack of management attention after the venture has started operating. The defects often stem from the unobtrusive influence of culture on behavior and on management systems (Hofstede, 1980), which may create unresolved conflict. In fact to some, compatibility between partners is the most important factor in the endurance of a global alliance; and differences between national cultures, if not understood, can lead to poor communication, mutual distrust, and the end of the venture (Perlmutter and Heenan, 1986).

We believe that the behavioral and cultural differences contributing to successful or unsuccessful cooperative ventures have not yet been fully explored or understood, particularly in North America. In this article we describe some North American behavioral patterns and cultural influences that may be unnoticed barriers to cooperation and to increased global effectiveness. Specifically, we examine these influences on the process of establishing and managing joint ventures in LDCs. There is no simple formula for achieving success, but there are ways to improve the prospect for success. We have encountered numerous instances of culturally conditioned assumptions and behavior preventing North American executives and their companies from being successful in cooperative ventures. We also believe that the proper preparation of these executives to function in multicultural cooperative ventures has been an almost neglected human resource issue in the literature (Shenkar and Zeira, 1987) and by companies in practice (Beamish, 1984, 1988; Lane and DiStefano, 1988).

Methodology

The data on which this article is based come from a variety of sources, countries, and methodologies. We have studied the impact of culture on management and the creation and management of joint ventures in Latin America, Africa, Southeast Asia, and the Caribbean region.

One author has conducted structured interviews in five countries with forty-six executives involved with sixty-six joint ventures in twenty-seven LDCs, and completed detailed case studies of twelve companies in the Caribbean region. In most cases, the international vice president of the foreign parent was interviewed, but in some cases it was the CEO. In addition, senior executives of the local parent in twelve joint ventures were also interviewed. Although some of the companies were headquartered in the United Kingdom, the majority were American and Canadian. The focus of this work was on the creation and management of LDC-based joint ventures. More recently, this author's work has shifted to joint ventures in LDCs where there is a planned economy.

The other author, using primarily a case-research methodology, developed fifteen cases of nine Canadian and American companies working in South America, East and North Africa, and Indonesia. The data for these cases came from interviews with parent company executives of fourteen companies; parent and headquarter executives of three companies and the local partner of two joint ventures; company records, secondary sources, and, sometimes, participant observation as a consultant helping to establish the joint venture. The focus of these cases was on the impact of culture on management systems/procedures, decision making and behavior. Four of the companies studied were involved in joint ventures in South America, East Africa, and Indonesia. Discussions also were held with parent company executives from three other companies with joint ventures in West Africa and Southeast Asia.

We believe the data from this mixture of methodologies and from the two different perspectives of the authors (organizational behavior and business strategy) provide a realistic picture of issues managers face in joint ventures in developing countries. Questionnaires and structured interviews completed in numerous companies provide a necessary breadth of understanding the types of problems managers experience in their joint ventures. Clinical research provides an important depth of understanding of individuals, their motivations, problems, decisions, and their operating environments.

In addition, both authors have taught, worked, and consulted in numerous countries and bring this experience to bear in their observations and analyses as well.

International Human Resource Management and International Business

There is a clearly emerging field of international human resource management. For the most part the focus is the expatriate managers – recruiting them, selecting them, compensating them, and training them. The concerns, in corporations and in the literature, are managing the international transition and the expatriates' ability to adapt and to function effectively in another culture (Harari and Zeira, 1978; Tung, 1981; Mendenhall and Oddou, 1985, 1986; Adler, 1986; Lane and DiStefano, 1988).

Much is known about attitudes and skills that favor adaptation and intercultural effectiveness, in general. Very often what is missing, however, are the business issues – the context within which adaptation and intercultural communication skills must take place. We believe there is a need to improve the training of executives who are involved internationally by linking cross-cultural effectiveness training more closely to the context and issues they will face. Not all executives will be expatriates, but they are more likely in the future to be functioning as part of multicultural teams, particularly as the use of cooperative ventures increases. There is evidence that this is being recognized (Adler, 1986). However, the business context will have to be addressed in training as well.

The international business literature, generally, has not addressed the issue of implementing joint ventures and alliances well either, although there is evidence that some researchers are taking an interest in the joint venture implementation process (Geringer, 1988). While strategy formulation is a cognitive and analytic process, effective implementation requires different skills. Executives must travel to another country and/or work closely with people from other cultures to start operations and manage the ongoing business. The interaction between people with different cultural backgrounds can be intense. Successful implementation requires both an understanding of the business and the partners' cultures. Too much emphasis on the task of getting the job done and ignoring the relationships with the people can lead to failure (Moran, 1980). The HRM focus has concentrated on the selection of executives and their adaptive behavior independently of the business context, and the international business literature has concentrated on strategy and structure issues independently of the implementation/ behavioral processes involved.

We believe there is a need to link the two foci. It is going to be increasingly important to train executives in specific cross-cultural business issues related to cooperative ventures, but before that can be done it will be necessary to understand, through research, what these issues are. There has been a distinct lack of attention paid to this issue by academics. In their review of the literature on personnel problems in international joint ventures, Shenkar and Zeira (1987) found only one study (and twenty years old at that) that addressed the "lack of training for functioning in an international joint venture structure." In this article we have tried to merge the international business policy and behavioral orientations to highlight issues for improving training and cross-cultural skill development as it relates specifically to joint ventures, and particularly to joint ventures that North American companies establish in LDCs.

Focus on the Venture Process Not the Anticipated Result

Problems that eventually may debilitate a joint venture can develop at any point in the process. We have seen recurring behavioral patterns that lead to performance difficulties in the decision to form the venture and the assessment of the company as a joint venturer; the partner selection criteria and process; the design of the organization; and the management of the ongoing relationship between the partners.

The Decision to Form the Venture

It is important to understand clearly why the company wants a joint venture. Many ventures are poorly conceived and probably should not be formed (Hendryx, 1986). Strategic and economic benefits are obvious first considerations for entering a cooperative venture, but they are not the only considerations.

Even if there are sound strategic and economic reasons for the venture, a Western company may lack the necessary skills and qualities to be a good joint venturer. The firm's capability and commitment to function in a cooperative mode must be realistically assessed. This assessment should provide insight into how the company will respond in the difficult situations that undoubtedly will be encountered. The first indication of whether or not the company is likely to be a successful international joint venturer is its commitment to international business and to working in difficult conditions. Rational strategies have a way of deteriorating as Western executives encounter the practical difficulties common in LDCs and become frustrated (Lane and DiStefano, 1988).

In some cases, the internal evaluation and reward systems of a corporation may encourage, unduly, the formation of joint ventures. Two examples we have seen of the pressure on executives to conclude deals expeditiously were a manager's drive to achieve objectives set in the MBO process and a corporation's push to repatriate funds before fiscal year-end from the conversion of a wholly owned subsidiary to a minority joint venture. The obvious lesson is to ensure that evaluation and reward systems do not "force" executives to make hasty decisions in support of poorly conceived objectives or without adequate implementation plans.

Although performance appraisal, reward systems, and financial reporting and control systems may encourage short-sighted and short-term behavior, they also can be used to reinforce behavior more likely to lead to success. If the venture is worth doing, it is worth doing properly. Even if it is small, someone in the company should be assigned responsibility for it, and it should be important to them. The importance of the venture should be reflected in the corporation's HRM systems, and the individual's personal performance targets. Used properly, in any context, the performance systems should encourage the establishment of a limited number of realistic targets. The unilateral setting of business goals and executives' performance targets at headquarters by the parent company without input from the local partner can lead not only to unmet objectives, but to potential conflict and to deterioration of the relationship if the partner disagrees with them or if pressure is put on the local partner to meet these objectives (Lane and DiStefano, 1988). One dimension on which many North Americans, in particular, establish unrealistic expectations is time (Porter and Samovar, 1976; Lane and DiStefano, 1988), expecting business activities to be completed more quickly than is often possible.

Before seeking and entering into a joint venture in a developing country, a company must recognize that developing business in the Third World is a long-term proposition and investment. Overseas travel is expensive and negotiations are slow. In most of the world establishing a personal relationship is the prerequisite to doing business (Lane and DiStefano, 1988). It is necessary to spend the time (and, therefore, money) that this will require. Expectations of early or easy returns are early indications of future problems.

There are also personal pressures to act quickly, and the potential for mistakes in the name of efficiency is enormous. North Americans have a tendency to over-schedule their time. Corporate executives sandwich brief trips to the LDC between more important activities or assign already over-extended staff one more project to investigate. Time is money and, therefore, not to be wasted. How will someone on a tight schedule cope with unreliable or unavailable data and the inability to arrange appointments with government officials and local businessmen who are busy or are out of the country? The quickest, easiest, and least expensive option is to rely on secondhand information prevailing in the diplomatic and expatriate communities, and on the conventional wisdom that is paraded as informed analysis. The results can be disastrous.

North Americans often find they do not like conditions in the developing world. They want to leave quickly, so they push to complete a project or resolve a partnership more quickly than they should. The executives assigned to conduct market studies or to search for partners, in addition to their technical business preparations, should be psychologically prepared for the frustrations of lost baggage, immigration difficulties, climate extremes, lots of travel, little sleep, different standards of hygiene, and intestinal difficulties.

An unwillingness to spend the requisite amount of time in a country also may be indicative of an unrealistic superiority complex. One hears the following attitude expressed in various ways: "We're a good company with good products. They should be happy to work with us. We'll wine and dine them. They'll be impressed." Often, the people you want to meet have never heard of you or your company. And, another dinner in a nice restaurant does not impress them. Tight schedules and an over-inflated corporate ego can translate into poor search and implementation practices. These attitudes are barriers to business success.

Developing an awareness of the impact of culture and management systems on business behavior and decisions (Hofstede, 1980b), requires training and constant attention. North American executives need to develop both a self-awareness of how their culture influences them, as well as an awareness of how their partners' cultures influence their partners' behavior. Business or technical skills are only part of the required package of skills for executives involved in cooperative ventures. Without cultural sensitivity, adaptability, interpersonal, and communication skills, the executives from the foreign parent may not survive long enough in the LDC to utilize the business or technical skills that they were sent to use; or if they do survive, poor relationships with the local executives often reduce these expatriates' effectiveness. Training and skill development must address the need for technical and cross-cultural skills and be tied as closely as possible to the specific situations to be encountered.

Partner Selection: Criteria and Process

Identifying and selecting a partner is possibly the most important consideration in establishing a cooperative venture. It also may be the most difficult and time-consuming. Even though partner selection could be the determining factor in success or failure, it usually is not given the time and attention that it deserves. The most common problems cited with joint ventures in LDCs involve the local partner (Beamish, 1988). However, it is too easy to automatically blame one's partner when conflict arises and not to question one's own contribution to the problem.

A number of firms we encountered were impatient to find a partner in order to enter an attractive market. As a result, they were careless in their selection process and mistakenly traded poor partner quality for quick action. Partners are often selected only for short-term and political reasons. When the situation changes and the partner has nothing more to offer, the relationship often ends.

One large North American MNE which had for years operated a wholly owned subsidiary in a developing country found itself constrained by local government regulations on foreign ownership which limited the repatriation of dividends. To expand the business and to remit dividends a significant level of local equity participation was required. A joint venture was the obvious solution and a minority joint venture would permit the maximum local investment base and repatriation of the maximum allowable dividends. This was a significant change for the company, which had operated primarily through wholly owned subsidiaries or joint ventures which it controlled.

The company searched for a local corporation or individual who would not be actively involved in the business. The legal requirements regarding ownership would be met and the North American parent could control and run the joint venture. An apparently satisfactory partner was found, and more than a year was spent completing the financial and legal arrangements. Within six months of starting the joint venture, however, there was substantial conflict between the partners over differences of opinion about strategy and operating procedures. The relationship deteriorated during the next three years over a variety of issues and ended in the local courts. The issue brought to the court was the inappropriate procedures used by the local partner in distributing stock to the local employees as part of the "nationalization" process. The general consensus at the North American parent was that the short-term financial gain probably did not offset the significant costs incurred in management time, direct expenses, stress on employees, and possible damage to the firm's reputation in that part of the world. In our opinion, the company was not committed to the use of the minority joint venture form and did not have a long-term need for its partner. It essentially wanted to buy his nationality. The marriage of convenience did not work.

To be successful, a partnership must operate on the principle of fair exchange. There must be value in the relationship for both parties. Major differences in the performance of joint ventures in developing countries relate to whether there exists a long-term need and commitment between the partners. When there is, the ventures are more likely to be stable and successful. "Need" refers to the requirement for skills or resources in the venture, such as access to raw materials, distribution channels, labor, political connections, and local knowledge. Unfortunately, there is a tendency to think of these needs primarily from the perspective of the foreign parent.

In our opinion, the best joint venturers – meaning those who work toward ensuring the long-term viability of the business – are the companies that recognize their specific long-term needs and recruit partners to fill these needs. They also recognize the needs of their local partner and how they will fill those needs. Specifically, foreign parent companies look to their local partner for general knowledge of the local economy, politics, and culture, and for the supply of general managers (Beamish, 1988).

Our research and experience indicate that good local partners are more likely to have access to competent local managers than do foreign firms. In most developing countries the demand for qualified managers by foreign firms and by local firms and parastatals is high. In some countries this pressure is increased by laws requiring the "localization" of human resources in foreign companies and joint ventures. However, even in those countries where an adequate supply of trained managers exists, these good local managers often are not accessible to foreign firms.

For example, in one East African country, we heard for years from foreign executives about the problem of attracting good local managers. It seemed that they did not exist, according to these foreign executives. Yet, our experience in our training programs and with our contacts with local firms indicated otherwise. Discussions with numerous local managers showed that they avoided foreign firms in favor of working for parastatals, local firms, or starting their own businesses. Most of them had been denied promotions that went to expatriates from the foreign company or foreign parent. They believed that it was almost impossible to advance to senior executive positions in foreign firms or foreign controlled joint ventures. The foreign parent, therefore, needs to consider carefully how it will assign expatriates to the venture so that it can develop its executives without interfering with the development and progression of the local managers. Once this potential conflict has been identified the partners together can work out a plan to satisfy the needs of both.

Local partners also have needs to which the foreign parent can contribute. Technology can be an important contribution – if the foreign parent is undertaking regular technological improvements. Many joint ventures in LDCs have collapsed after the simple technology provided by the foreign parent had been assimilated by the local partner and there was no upgrading of it. The local partner may feel there is no longer a major advantage to having a foreign partner, and strike out alone. For its part, the foreign parent may feel betrayed since it provided the technology with a view towards developing a long-term relationship and no longer receives the expected stream of earnings. There may also be a need for export opportunities. Given a local partner's interest in increasing total sales and generating foreign exchange, some foreign parents have ensured that they will be needed over the long term providing, incrementally, access to their distribution network, usually on a regional basis.

Our studies in the Caribbean region have shown that the better performing companies were using the joint venture structure voluntarily and that there was a hierarchy of importance to the local partner's contributions. Foreign parent companies in higher-performing joint ventures had chosen local partners for their knowledge of the local economy, politics, and customs and to provide managers. The foreign parents viewed these needs as continuing and long term.

In our experience, Western corporations tend to think that local knowledge is a short-term need and that the company will learn quickly about an LDC. However, the local scene keeps changing. There is clear evidence that joint ventures in LDCs face very different environments than in developed countries (Beamish, 1985). New players appear, as well as new attitudes, regulations, and laws. Learning must keep pace. Expatriates living in the country often can be out of touch with the country and culture (Lane and DiStefano, 1988). They may become insulated from reality by the exclusiveness of the expatriate community and by acceptance of this community's often inaccurate perceptions of local people and conditions. The research in the Caribbean indicated that the acquisition of information about local conditions and understanding of them was the most important long-term need. Local people can fill this need best. As one international VP noted: "In many LDCs it takes about twenty years to really understand the local system – and we just can't leave our [expatriate] managers there that long."

The temptation to have a local politician or government official as a joint venture partner is often strong. However, in the developing world, governments can change rapidly and without notice. A partner should be expected to bring more to the partnership than position or contacts. A partner should be able to make a contribution to the ongoing operation. The best advice seems to be: use industrialists of some stature in the same or a similar business – if you can find them. The next best choice would be a firm that offers a complementary service such as product distribution. As you move further from your business base, the ability of your partner to contribute substantially to the venture and to provide qualified general managers declines.

Finding the right partner takes time and effort, and there is no substitute for active, rigorous exploration. As we talked with executives, we were amazed at how some partners were found. Some had been met "fortuitously" at cocktail parties in Latin America, or Trinidad, or in a hotel bar in Nigeria. Non-rigorous search for a partner may result in taking the first person who comes along, which most likely is a mistake. One company suggests that twelve to eighteen months is not an unusual amount of time spent in finding and selecting a partner.

One reason finding a partner can take so long is that quality business people in many developing countries are likely to be more relationship-oriented than North Americans (Pye, 1986; Harris and Moran, 1979). They want to establish a personal relationship first and then do business. Initially, they want to focus on the North American as a person. Do they feel comfortable with and trust him? However, North Americans usually want to discuss business right away. In North America, we generally conduct business, and out of the business a personal relationship might develop. Building relationships takes time and patience, commodities we often lack.

Potential partners should be visited in their milieu to see how they live and how they run their business. We also would suggest trying to find ways in which to work together on smaller projects to "test" the working relationship. It is easier and more satisfactory to increase investment in a small project than to write-off one's large investment.

In North America, a multinational company is a separate legal entity and is usually viewed that way. Company goals are established and executives work to achieve those goals for the company. In many market-economy LDCs, business people are inclined to view their business ventures personally. The businesses often are closely held and the owners heavily involved in decision making. The company may simply be an extension of the owner's personality. Partnerships with members of prominent families in LDCs are common (Lane and DiStefano, 1988). Very often the culture of these countries dictates putting family interests ahead of rational business development. Thus, the business is viewed less objectively or in a less detached manner. Conflicts between the foreign parents and local partners over future company goals and the distribution and use of profits are frequent.

Size differentials can create problems (Davis, 1969; Lane and DiStefano, 1988). Large foreign parents tend to be systematic and slow in their decision making. They also have a long-term investment orientation and a willingness to reap rewards in the future. In contrast, their local partners often are entrepreneurs who manage intuitively and make decisions very quickly. Such partners more likely will have immediate financial needs.

Foreign parents often have to face the issue of multiple business interests on the part of their local partners. They should not be unrealistically scared away from an excellent local partner because of the partner's seemingly unfocused diversity of interests. However, it is a legitimate concern that such interests will dilute the partner's attention to the joint venture unless a solid local management team is put into place. This is an area in which expectations must be established clearly. For its part, the foreign parent has a responsibility to provide quality expatriates who can contribute to the venture and not use it as a dumping ground for extraneous executives or merely as a training ground for inexperienced people.

The most obvious link between the partner selection process and human resource management is in the selection and preparation of the "search and selection" executives. The executives responsible for partner search and selection must know more than finance and operations. They must be sensitive to the impact of culture on behavior and have some background on the social, economic, political environment, and history of the potential host country. They need education in the specific culture of their venture partner and training in the behavioral skills necessary to build long-term relationships. The human resource management (HRM) function at headquarters should be responsible for organizing these briefings. They could also contribute to partner search and selection by ensuring that these executives are supported by specialists like interpreters, for example. In fact, given the importance of partner selection and that "partner problems" are the greatest difficulty in joint ventures, it may be wise to consider using teams with a balance of skills and perspectives in the search process.

Another area where the HRM function could contribute is in the evaluation of a potential partner's HRM systems and practices. These may give an indication of the partner's concern for his human resources and his compatibility on this dimension with the foreign parent. The future training needs of the partner's firm can also be assessed. Achieving a profitable venture may require more than an investment of money and technology by the foreign parent. The development of local human resources could contribute to the joint venture's competitive advantage and protect the foreign parent's investment, particularly in countries where there are strong localization pressures. Another area that is important to understand from the beginning is the industrial relations climate of the country and the firm. The local partner's attitude towards unions and his relationship with them could be important to the profitability of the joint venture.

Designing the Venture

Decisions must be made about the equity structure, how and by whom the venture will be staffed, and who has decision-making responsibility in specific areas. These decisions must be made jointly by the partners. Lawyers and accountants can help codify the basic operating agreement made by the principals to the joint venture, but should not determine that agreement. One executive went so far as to say that these people should not be involved until the general agreement and expectations have been made clear by the principals and their commitment to functioning as a joint venture also has been made. The most important issue is to establish a fair, equitable, and workable commercial relationship. Lawyers often take an adversarial perspective, rather than a commercial one, and complicate understandings with legal terminology. Working relationships need to be defined and established by the partners.

Decision-making control can either be shared or dominated by one of the partners. In LDCs, shared decision-making control is recommended (Beamish, 1988). The concept of shared control – especially *how* to do it – is confusing to some managers. Even if they support shared control in principle, they cannot see how to put it into practice. Shared control conjures up an image of two or more people making every decision, no matter how small. Even when decisions are shared within a joint venture, they are in fact frequently not being jointly made, but rather divided or split between the partners based on knowledge, skill, experience, and understanding of the particular issue. An element of specialization is maintained. The foreign partner may have a better understanding of the technology and the local partner a clearer grasp of the local market and political conditions. However, since there is an interaction between product and market there must be an interaction between partners. Some decisions will have to be jointly made, arrived at through consensus after discussions. Not to do so ignores the others' expertise. More of the decisions are likely to be made by one partner or the other, as agreed upon at the time of the joint venture formation, when the expectations and contributions of each should be made explicit.

Consensus decision making takes time and creates potential conflict within a single culture. The potential for misunderstanding and conflict across cultures can be enormous. However, since not every decision has to be made this way, it is not an onerous requirement. It may not be as efficient as allowing one partner to make all the decisions but, we believe, it is more effective since the partners usually have different experience bases, different knowledge and skills, and different information. However, it requires people who are sensitive to the partners' needs and culture and who are willing to understand, learn and be persuaded, as well as being persuasive. Managing successfully in a minority joint venture seems to require a shift from control through financial and legal structures to influence through creating relationships and through behavioral interaction. Ownership and other legal considerations of a venture are often complicated, tangible, structural relationships that are important. However, we have observed that these issues often divert attention and effort from the even more important, dynamic, but less tangible human relationships.

The use of a large proportion of local managers rather than expatriates is recommended to ensure the foreign parent acquires the necessary knowledge of the local economy, politics, and culture. Although the supply of competent local managers is increasing, the demand for such managers is high. The solution for many companies has been to offer equity to the general manager (and in some cases to other senior local managers). This not only improves the probability of attracting and retaining a qualified management team but also provides motivation for good performance. The use of a large number of local managers also increases the need for training executives in the foreign parent company's headquarters in cross-cultural issues.

It is recommended that foreign parents take a minority or equal amount of equity. There usually are tax advantages and preferential treatment regarding dividend repatriation for the foreign parent owning less than 50% of the equity. Many executives are skeptical about equal ownership. This is understandable if ownership is thought of as the critical element in decision making and control. The actual equity positions of each partner do not necessarily reflect their respective levels of influence. Ownership is not the same as control. Foreign parents with a minority equity position in their LDC-based joint ventures can maintain an equal voice in the operations of the business. However, it will take the time and skill of a sensitive, concerned, and knowledgeable executive from the foreign parent to do it. Also with a general manager and other senior local managers holding equity, the foreign parent can be the single largest shareholder and still be in a minority equity position. Minority equity does not have to mean that the foreign parent will have a minority voice in the joint venture's operations.

An "our way is best" orientation can unduly influence the ownership structure, selection, and staffing of a venture. Majority ownership and the use of North Americans in management positions often reflects a lack of trust in local nationals; and that this, in turn, may only reflect our lack of understanding of the local culture. Mistrust and misunderstanding are certain barriers to success. Yet where are the skills taught; or how are cultural sensitivity and understanding, as well as an ability to establish trust and build relationships factored into selection decisions for the people chosen to work in LDCs? Our experience and research indicate that these issues are not yet addressed very well. Learning to work as part of a multicultural management team is going to be recognized as an important management skill eventually. In fact, some of the more successful cross-cultural joint ventures are engaging in mixed management team, cross-cultural training (Radway, 1986).

Ongoing Management and Relationship

The real work, operating the joint venture, begins after the partner has been selected and the management structure decided upon. It requires a commitment by the corporation to persevere and to work to achieve its target and not to quit as the inevitable problems appear. Commitment is necessary for success and is required at each step in the process. Commitment is required to overcome initial uncertainties associated with a new country or partner. One executive with a highly successful international corporation has stated, "Commitment is probably the single most critical factor for successful entry into foreign markets." He referred specifically to many facets of commitment: financial commitment; commitment to customer and partner support; to product integrity; to company employees around the world; to understanding the politics, economics, and culture of trading partners; to the building of trust and sharing of information; to the building of cooperative relationships.

Without commitment, the numerous problems that come with the "territory" of cooperative ventures can become overwhelming and provide reasons for quitting: the venture is requiring more attention and resources than expected or forecast, and no longer looks as good as it did at the start. Commitment is probably the most important attribute in the ongoing management of a cooperative venture. A sense of duty to the venture and partner is the basis on which problems are addressed and solved, changes made, and help provided. One company's entry into Nigeria required nearly ten years of very difficult work to make the venture a success. As much as the foreign parent felt it needed a local partner, however, it seems doubtful that the venture would have succeeded without a long-term commitment to problem solving as well. This outcome is not surprising since this company had developed the minority joint venture as a modus operandi in the developing world. It had invested in learning how to operate profitably in this mode, and it selected executives as representatives to the ventures who understood the company's philosophy and who could work well with the local parent company and joint venture management.

Many other companies have not learned these relationship skills. Some foreign parents take an arm's-length investment approach to the joint venture. The foreign parent is reluctant to visit the joint venture when problems arise and is unwilling to supply special skills to the venture from the parent organization if they are needed. At the other extreme the foreign parent manages the joint venture as if it were a wholly owned subsidiary. The local partner is not kept informed or involved in decision making. The foreign parent does not like to hold regular meetings and is only willing to include the local partner in discussions if the management contract specifies that they are obligatory. In each of these extremes, the foreign parent has forgotten that it is a joint venture and that both partners have something to contribute.

A successful relationship requires constant attention and nourishing. As one executive explained, "good local partners have to be cherished and taken care of." He was not talking about doing anything illegal either. His company invests heavily in travel and communications to maintain its personal relationships.

Many foreign parents with joint ventures that are currently performing poorly or likely will soon experience difficulties. When problems arise, many of them will blame their local partner, the local government, the general state of the local economy – in fact, almost anyone or anything except themselves or their systems. Yet, there is evidence to suggest that they should look internally for the explanation.

Of the many joint ventures we investigated, several involved the turnaround of poor performers. In every case, among the changes made by the foreign parent was a rethinking of their attitudes towards the value of local partners. Accompanying these turnarounds was the recognition that the local partner was needed for specific contributions and that sharing the decision making might, after all, make sense. We were also able to compare two joint ventures of similar companies in similar situations that yielded very different results. One North American company's success resulted from its understanding of its partner, his culture, and from its executives' skill in building and maintaining good relationships. The other North American company's joint venture was unsuccessful because its executives could not (or chose not) to behave in a similar cooperative manner.

A successful joint venture is a stable, healthy, and profitable business relationship based on cooperation and two-way communication that meets the needs of both partners over the long term. Success should be viewed as a mutual condition, not a one-sided one. However, executives may need help in overcoming some unanticipated obstacles on the road to success: their corporate systems; their own culture; and their own behavior. Cross-culture cooperation cannot be taken for granted. It takes effort and insight. Learning to behave cooperatively will require a change in attitude, specific training, and practice. It is an area of executive development to which human resource management professionals should pay more attention.

References

Adler, Nancy (1986). *International Dimensions of Organizational Behavior*, Boston: Kent Publishing Co.

Beamish, Paul W. (1984). *Joint Venture Performance in Developing Countries*, Ph.D. dissertation, School of Business Administration, The University of Western Ontario.

—— (1985). "The Characteristics of Joint Ventures in Developed and Developing Countries," *Columbia Journal of World Business*, Winter.

—— (1988). *Multinational Joint Ventures in Developing Countries*, London: Routledge.

Beamish, Paul W. and H. Y. Wang, (1989). "Investing in China via Joint Ventures," *Management International Review*, 29, no. 1: 57–64.

Contractor, Farok J. and Peter Lorange (1987). *Cooperative Strategies in International Business*, Lexington, MA: D. C. Heath.

Davis Stanley (1969). "U.S. versus Latin America: Business and Culture," *Harvard Business Review*, November–December.

Earley, P. Christopher (1987). "Intercultural Training for Managers: A Comparison of Documentary and Interpersonal Methods," *Academy of Management Journal*, 30, no. 4: 685–698.

Franko, Lawrence, G. (1989). "Use of Minority and 50–50 Joint Ventures by United States Multinationals During the 1970s: The Interaction of Host Country Policies and Corporate Strategies," *Journal of International Business Studies*, 20, no. 1.

Geringer, J. Michael (1988). *Joint Venture Partner Selection: Strategies for Developed Countries.* Westport, CT: Quorom Books.

Gomes-Casseres, Benjamin (1989). "Joint Ventures in the Face of Global Competition," *Sloan Management Review*, Spring: 17–26.

Harari, Ehud and Yoram Zeira (1978). "Training Expatriates for Managerial Assignments in Japan," *California Management Review*, 20, no. 4: 56–62.

Harris, Phillip R. and Robert Moran (1979). *Managing Cultural Differences.* Houston: Gulf Publishing.

Hax, Arnoldo, C. (1989). "Building the Firm of the Future," *Sloan Management Review*, Spring: 75–82.

Heenan, David A. and Howard V. Perlmutter (1979). *Multinational Organizational Development.* Reading, MA: Addison-Wesley.

Hendryx, Steven R. (1986). "Making the Deal Work," *Harvard Business Review*, July–August: 75–84.

Hofstede, Geert (1980). *Culture's Consequences.* Beverly Hills, CA: Sage Publications.

—— (1980b). "Motivation, Leadership and Organization: Do American Theories Apply Abroad?," *Organizational Dynamics*, Summer.

Killing, J. Peter (1982). "How to Make a Global Joint Venture Work," *Harvard Business Review*, May–June.

—— (1983). *Strategies for Joint Venture Success.* London: Croom-Helm.

Lane, Henry W. and J. J. DiStefano (1988). *International Management Behavior: From Policy to Practice.* Scarborough, Ontario: Nelson Canada.

Ling, Sing Chee, "Managing Multi-Cultural Work Groups," Ph.D. dissertation (1990), School of Business Administration, The University of Western Ontario, London, Canada.

Mendenhall, Mark and Oddou, Gary (1986). "Acculturation Profiles of Expatriate Managers: Implications for Cross-Cultural Training Programs," *Columbia Journal of World Business*, Winter: 73–79.

Mendenhall, Mark and Oddou, Gary (1985). "The Dimensions of Expatriate Acculturation: A Review," *Academy of Management Review*, 10, no. 1: 39–47.

Moran, Robert (1980). "Cross-Cultural Dimensions of Doing Business in Latin America," in *Reference Manual on Doing Business in Latin America*, eds D. R. Shea, F. W. Swacker, R. J. Radway, and S. T. Stairs, Center for Latin America, University of Wisconsin, Milwaukee.

Palmer, Russell E. (1987). "Trends in International Management: Towards Federations of Equals," *Business Quarterly*, 52, no. 1.

Perlmutter, Howard V. and David A. Heenan (1986). "Cooperate to Compete Globally," *Harvard Business Review*, March–April: 136–152.

Porter, Richard and Samovar, Larry (1976). "Communicating Interculturally," in *Intercultural Communication: A Reader*, 2nd edn, eds Larry Samovar and Richard Porter, Wadsworth Publishing Co.

Pye, Lucien W. (1986). "Making the Deal," *Harvard Business Review*, July–August: 74–80.

Radway, Robert J. (1986). "Joint Ventures with Foreign Partners: Capital, Control and Culture Problems," *The Currency Forecasters Digest*, November–December: 24–30.

Schwind, Hermann (1985). "The State of the Art in Cross-Cultural Management Training," *International HRD Annual*, Volume 1, ed. Robert Doktor, American Society for Training and Development.

Shenkar, Oded and Yoram Zeira (1987). "Human Resource Management in International Joint Ventures: Directions for Research," *Academy of Management Review*, 12, no. 3: 546–557.

Tung, Rosalie (1981). "Selection and Training of Personnel for Overseas Assignments," *Columbia Journal of World Business*, 16, no. 1: 68–78.

Competitive Frontiers:
Women Managing Across Borders

Nancy J. Adler

It doesn't make any difference if you are blue, green, purple, or a frog, if you have the best product at the best price, they'll buy.

— **American woman manager based in Hong Kong**

About the single most uncontroversial, incontrovertible statement to make about women in international management is that there are very few of them. The evidence is both subjective and objective (17). As an executive in a global firm, would you hire a woman for an international management position? Would you send her abroad as an expatriate manager? Would she succeed? Would hiring her increase or decrease your firm's competitiveness?

Global Competition

Business today increasingly competes on a worldwide basis. Few firms have the luxury of competing primarily within their own domestic market. Whereas some firms use country-specific multidomestic strategies, and thus compete in independent domestic markets, a much greater number have embraced globally integrated strategies structured around worldwide lines of business (11). As global competition continues to intensify, firms are evolving transnational strategies. Such strategies simultaneously require the local responsiveness demanded by multidomestic strategies, the worldwide integration demanded by global strategies, along with an increased emphasis on organizational learning and innovation (14). These business dynamics lead to:

> transnational networks of firms and divisions within firms, including an increasingly complex web of strategic alliances. Transnational firms . . . are less hierarchically structured

than firms operating in the previous phases. Power is no longer centered in a single head-quarters that is . . . dominated by any one national culture. As a consequence, both structural and cultural dominance are minimized, with cross-cultural interaction no longer following any predefined "passport hierarchy" (10).

These organizational changes are affecting the numbers and roles of women managers.

Women and Transnational Corporations

Given the increasing importance of transnational corporations, it is encouraging that their impact on women in management, to date, has been primarily positive. Transnational corporations include women in ways that domestic, multidomestic, and multinational firms do not. First, the extremely competitive business environment forces transnational firms to select the very best people available. The opportunity cost of prejudice – of rejecting women and limiting selection to men – is much higher than in previous economic environments. As *Fortune* succinctly stated: "The best reason for believing that more women will be in charge before long is that in a ferociously competitive global economy, no company can afford to waste valuable brainpower simply because it's wearing a skirt" (18:56). This competitive advantage is heightened by a growing worldwide education differential favoring women.

Second, whereas domestic and multidomestic companies hire primarily local nationals and, therefore, must closely adhere to local norms on hiring – or not hiring – women managers, transnational corporations are not similarly limited. Because the corporate culture of transnational firms is not coincident with the local culture of any particular country, transnationals have greater flexibility in defining selection and promotion criteria that best fit the firm's needs rather than those that most closely mimic the historical patterns of a particular country. Said simply, transnationals can and do hire local women managers even in countries in which the local companies rarely do so.

U.S.-based transnational corporations, for example, have often hired local women managers when local firms would not. This dynamic has been particularly pronounced in Japan, where foreign corporations have had difficulty attracting top-ranked male applicants (25;35). American firms have led the way in hiring well-qualified Japanese women, while Japanese firms are still extremely reluctant to hire them (36). Interestingly, while still hiring fewer women than most American firms, Japanese multinationals operating in the United States hire more women managers in their American affiliates than they do in their home country operations (33).

By hiring women, transnationals act as role models for firms in many countries that have not seriously considered promoting significant numbers of women into managerial positions. The greater the number of expatriates involved in foreign affiliates, the less likely they are to follow local human resource practices – including being less likely to restrict the number of women managers (33). The firm's transnational character allows it organizational freedoms and imposes competitive demands not present in domestic or multidomestic environments.

Third, transnational corporations have begun to send women abroad as expatriate managers (4). Because transnationals use expatriates and local managers, they can benefit from the greater flexibility that many cultures afford foreign women. As will be described, most countries do not hold foreign women to the same professionally limiting roles that restrict local women (6;23). The outstanding success of these women expatriate managers in all geographical areas – Africa, the Americas, Asia, Europe, and the Middle East – is encouraging firms both to continue sending women abroad (6;30) and to begin to promote more local women into management (23).

Fourth, whereas domestic, multidomestic, and multinational firms have been characterized by structural hierarchies, transnationals are increasingly characterized by networks of equals. Recent research suggests that women work particularly well in such networks:

> women . . . are countering the values of the hierarchy with those of the web. . . . when describing their roles in their organizations, women usually refer . . . to themselves as being in the middle of things. . . . Inseparable from their sense of themselves as being in the middle . . . [is] women's notion of being connected to those around them (22:52,45–46).

Not surprisingly, transnational firms see women managers as bringing needed collaborative and participative skills to the workplace (31).

Fifth, leading management scholars have identified innovation as a key factor in global competitiveness (14;21;32). An inherent source of innovation is well-managed diversity, including gender diversity (8). Women bring diversity to transnational corporations that have heretofore been primarily male dominated.

Transnational corporations thus include more women than their predecessors could (or would) and benefit organizationally from their professional contributions in new ways. They benefit both from women's increased representation at all levels of the organization as well as from their unique ways of contributing to the organization that complement those of men.

Fundamental Assumptions: Different Approaches

Given the current scarcity of women in the managerial ranks, transnational firms can use two approaches to unleash the potential of women managers: they can increase the number of women managers and executives, and they can encourage their unique contribution. Unfortunately, many of their predecessors – domestic, multidomestic, and multinational firms – adopted neither approach or limited themselves by focusing on only one of the two approaches.

As shown in Table 1, firms have traditionally made one of two fundamentally different assumptions about the ideal role of women in management. Although generally implicit, the first reflects an equity approach based on assumed similarity, while the second defines a complementary contribution approach based on assumed difference.

The first focuses on increasing the representation of women managers; the second, on increasing their utilization at all levels of the organization. The first, the equity approach, based on assumed similarity, has been used most pervasively in the United States. In this approach, firms assume that women are identical, as professionals, to men, and therefore equally capable of contributing in ways similar to those of men.

TABLE 1 Two approaches to women in management

Assumptions	Equity Approach Contribution	Complementary Approach
Fundamental assumptions:	Similarity	Difference
Women's and men's contributions	Identical	Complementary
Fairness based on	Equity	Valuing difference
Strategic goal:	Equal access	Recognizing and valuing difference
Assessment	Quantitive	Qualitative
Measured by	Statistical proportion of women at each hierarchical level	Assessing women's contribution to organization's goals
Process	Counting women	Assessing women's contribution
Measurement of effectiveness:		
Women's contribution	Identical to men's	Complementary to men's
Norms	Identical for men and women	Unique to men and women
Based on	Historical "male" norms	Women's own contribution
Referent	Men	Women
Acculturation process:	Assimilation	Synergy
Expected behavior	Standardized	Differentiated
Based on	Male norms	Female norms
Essence	"Dress for success" business suit	Elegant, feminine attire
Example	United States: "the melting pot"	France: "Vive la différence!"

Source: (7).

From this equity perspective, the primary question is one of entry into and representation within management. Is the firm hiring and promoting sufficient numbers of women managers? Primary change strategies include affirmative action programs, equal rights legislation, and structural changes designed to avoid tokenism and to train women in managerial skills traditionally neglected during their formal education and informal socialization.

Given the equity approach's emphasis on equal entry into and equal representation within the male-dominated world of management, the equity approach's implicit goal for women managers is assimilation. Firms expected women to think, dress, and act like the men who had traditionally held the aspired-to management positions. Understandably, firms measured effectiveness against male norms: could she do what he had been doing as well as he had been doing it? Or, according to *Fortune* (31:58): "If you can't join 'em, beat 'em . . . the way to overcome [discrimination] is to . . . start outdoing men at their own game." The potential for women to make unique, but equally valuable, contributions to organizations remained outside the logic of the equity approach and therefore largely unrealized.

In contrast, the second approach, the complementary contribution approach, is based on the assumption of difference, not similarity. Originally used to describe Swedish managers (34), it has been pervasive throughout Europe and Japan and is evident in most other areas of the world. In the complementary contribution approach, firms assume women and men differ and therefore are capable of making different, but equally valuable, contributions to the organization (13;16;19;20;24;26;27;28). Unlike in the equity approach, the goal is not assumed to be equal statistical representation but, rather, equivalent recognition of and benefit from women's and men's differing patterns and styles of contribution at all levels of the organization.

From this second perspective, change strategies focus first on identifying the unique contributions of women and men managers; second, on creating enabling conditions to encourage and reward both types of contribution; and third, on creating synergy – on combining women's and men's contributions to form more innovative and powerful organizational solutions to business challenges. Under this second set of assumptions, firms expect women managers to think, dress, and act like women. Women managers' thinking and behavior, though similar in many ways to that of their male colleagues, is seen to differ in important respects.

Progress, as measured by the equity approach, is quantitative – a statistical accounting of the proportion of women managers in the organization by rank, salary, and status. As measured by the complementary contribution approach, progress is qualitative – an assessment of the organization's track record in encouraging and rewarding women and men for making unique contributions and for building organizationally effective combinations of those contributions; that is, for increasing innovation and organizational learning.

Interestingly, each approach has tended to be labeled as heresy when viewed through the eyes of the other. From the perspective of the equity approach, viewing women (or any other distinct group) as different was seen as tantamount to judging them as inferior (16). Recognizing differences among women and men managers was implicitly equated with prejudice (8). From this point of view, only one best way to manage exists, and equity demands that women be given equal access to that one way. By contrast, the complementary contribution approach posits that there are many equally valid, yet different, ways to manage. The best approach, based on recognizing, valuing, and combining differences, is synergistic. From this second perspective, not to see a woman manager's uniqueness is to negate her identity and, consequently, to negate the potential for her unique contribution to the organization.

To predict what women's roles in management will be in the late 1990s and the twenty-first century, we must understand the underlying assumptions that firms make in each country about the role of women in management (15). To what extent is difference viewed as heresy as opposed to a potential resource? To what extent is uniqueness seen as a constraint rather than as a valuable asset? Unlike their predecessors, transnational firms view women managers' increased representation and potentially unique contribution as complementary sources of competitive advantage rather than as either–or solutions, or, even more limiting, as societal constraints.

Unexpected Success: Women Managing Across Borders

Cross-border business is fundamental to transnational firms. Unlike their predecessors, such firms define managerial roles transnationally, with expatriate assignments forming a central component. Given the historical scarcity of local women managers in most countries, firms have questioned if women can function successfully in cross-border managerial assignments. They have believed that the relative absence of local women managers formed a basis for accurately predicting the potential for success, or lack thereof, of expatriate women.

Given the importance of these questions to future business success, a multipart study was conducted on the role of women as expatriate managers. The research revealed the story of a noun, *woman*, that appears to have gotten mixed up with an adjective, *foreign*, when predicting expatriate managers' success. It revealed a set of assumptions that managers and executives make about how foreigners would treat expatriate women, based on their beliefs about how foreign firms treat their own local women. The problem with the story is that the assumptions proved to be false. Moreover, because the assumptions fail to accurately reflect reality, they are inadvertently causing executives to make decisions that are neither effective nor equitable.

The first part of the study sought to determine the proportion of women that companies select for expatriate positions. It surveyed 686 major North American multinational firms. The firms reported sending over thirteen thousand (13,338) expatriate managers abroad, of whom 402, or 3%, were women. Thus, North American firms send thirty-two times as many male as female expatriate managers abroad (1;4). In comparison with this 3% in international management, women held 37% of domestic U.S. management positions, twelve times as many as they held abroad (38).

Although the 3% represents significantly fewer women working as expatriate managers than the proportion holding domestic management positions, this should not be viewed strictly as a poor showing but rather as the beginning of a new trend. The vast majority of women who have ever held expatriate management positions were sent so recently that they are currently still working abroad.

Given transnationals' needs for the best-qualified managers – whether women or men – the second, third, and fourth parts of the study sought to explain why so few women hold international management positions. Each part addressed one of the three most commonly held myths about women in international management:

Myth 1: Women do not want to be international managers.
Myth 2: Companies refuse to send women abroad.
Myth 3: Foreigners' prejudice against women renders them ineffective, even when they are interested in international assignments and are successful in being sent.

These beliefs were labeled myths because, although widely held by both women and men, their accuracy had never been tested.

Myth 1: Women Do Not Want to Be International Managers

Is the problem that women are less interested than men in pursuing international careers? The study tested this myth by surveying more than a thousand graduating MBAs from seven top management schools in the United States, Canada, and Europe (3;5). The results revealed an overwhelming case of no significant difference: female and male MBAs display equal interest, or lack of interest, in pursuing international careers. More than four out of five MBAs – both women and men – want an international assignment at some time during their careers. Both female and male MBAs, however, agree that firms offer fewer opportunities to women than to men, and significantly fewer opportunities to women pursuing international careers than to those pursuing domestic careers.

Although there may have been a difference in the past, women and men today are equally interested in international management, including expatriate assignments. The first myth – that women do not want to be international managers – is, in fact, truly a myth.

Myth 2: Companies Refuse to Send Women Abroad

If the problem is not women's lack of interest, is it that companies refuse to select women for international assignments? To test if the myth of corporate resistance was true, human resource vice presidents and managers from sixty of the largest North American multinationals were surveyed (2). Over half of the companies reported that they hesitate to send women abroad. Almost four times as many reported being reluctant to select women for international assignments than for domestic management positions. When asked why they hesitate, almost three-quarters reported believing that foreigners were so prejudiced against women that the women managers could not succeed even if sent. Similarly, 70% believed that dual-career issues were insurmountable. In addition, some human resource executives expressed concern about the women's physical safety, the hazards involved in traveling in underdeveloped countries, and, especially in the case of single women, the isolation and loneliness.

Many of the women who succeeded in being sent abroad as expatriate managers report having confronted some form of corporate resistance before being sent abroad. For example:

Malaysia:	Management assumed that women didn't have the physical stamina to survive in the tropics. They claimed I couldn't hack it [in Malaysia].
Thailand:	My company didn't want to send a woman to that "horrible part of the world." They think Bangkok is an excellent place to send single men, but not a woman. They said they would have trouble getting a work permit for me, which wasn't true.
Japan and Korea:	Everyone was more or less curious if it would work. My American boss tried to advise me: "Don't be upset if it's difficult in Japan and Korea." The American male manager in Tokyo was also hesitant. Finally the Chinese boss in Hong Kong said, "We have to try!" Then they sent me.

A few women experienced severe resistance from their companies to sending any women managers abroad. Their firms seemed to offer them an expatriate position only after all potential male candidates had turned it down. For example:

Thailand:	Every advance in responsibility is because the Americans had no choice. I've never been chosen over someone else.

Japan: They never would have considered me. But then the financial manager in Tokyo had a heart attack, and they had to send someone. So they sent me, on a month's notice, as a temporary until they could find a man to fill the permanent position. It worked out, and I stayed.

Although most of the women are sent in the same capacity as their male expatriate colleagues, some companies demonstrate their hesitation by offering temporary or travel assignments rather than regular expatriate positions. For instance:

Hong Kong: After offering me the job, they hesitated: "Could a woman work with the Chinese?" So my job was defined as temporary, a one-year position to train a Chinese man to replace me. I succeeded and became permanent.

These sentiments concur with those of 100 top-line managers in Fortune 500 firms, the majority of whom believe that women face overwhelming resistance when seeking managerial positions in international divisions of U.S. firms (37). Similarly, 80% of U.S. firms report believing that women would face disadvantages if sent abroad (30). Thus, the second myth is in fact true: firms are hesitant, if not outright resistant, to sending women managers abroad.

Myth 3: Foreigners' "Prejudice" Against Women Expatriate Managers

Is it true that foreigners are so prejudiced against women that women could not succeed as international managers? Would sending a woman manager abroad be neither fair to the woman nor effective for the company? Is the treatment of local women the best predictor of expatriate women's potential to succeed? The fundamental question was, and remains, the following: is the historical discrimination against local women worldwide a valid basis for predicting expatriate women's success as international managers?

To investigate the myth that foreigners' prejudice against women renders them ineffective as international managers, a survey was taken of over a hundred women managers from major North American firms who were on expatriate assignments around the world. Fifty-two were interviewed while in Asia or after having returned from Asia to North America (6;23). Since most of the women held regional responsibility, their experience represents multiple countries rather than just their country of foreign residence.

Who Are the Women Expatriate Managers?

The women were very well educated and internationally experienced. Almost all held graduate degrees, the MBA being the most common. Over three-quarters had had extensive international interests and experience prior to their present company sending them abroad. On average, the women spoke two or three languages, with some speaking as many as six fluently. In addition, they had excellent social skills. Nearly two-thirds were single and only three (6%) had children.

Firms using transnational strategies sent more women than did those using other strategies, with financial institutions leading all other industries. On average, their international assignments lasted two and one-half years, with a range from six months to six years. The women supervised from zero to twenty-five subordinates, with the average falling just below five. Their titles and levels within their firms varied. Some held very junior positions – for example, assistant account manager – others held senior positions, including one regional vice president. In no firm did a woman expatriate hold her company's number one position in the region or in any country.

The women were considerably younger than the typical male expatriate. Their ages ranged from twenty-three to forty-one years, with the average age being just under thirty. This reflects the relatively high proportion of women sent by financial institutions – an industry that sends fairly junior managers on international assignments – and the relatively low proportion sent by manufacturing firms, which select fairly senior managers for expatriate positions (such as a country or regional director).

The Decision to Go

For most firms, the women expatriates were "firsts." Only 10% followed another woman into her international position. Of the 90% who were "firsts," almost one-quarter represented the first woman manager the firm had ever sent abroad. Others were the first women sent to the region, the first sent to the particular country, or the first to fill the specific expatriate position. Clearly, neither the women nor the companies had the luxury of role models or of following previously established patterns. Except for several major financial institutions, both the women and the companies found themselves experimenting, in the hope of success.

Most women described themselves as needing to encourage their companies to consider the possibility of assigning international positions to women in general and to themselves in particular. In more than four out of five cases, the woman initially suggested the idea of an international assignment to her boss and company. For only six women did the company first suggest the assignment.

Since most firms had never considered sending a woman manager abroad, the women used a number of strategies to introduce the idea and to position their careers internationally. Many explored the possibility of an international assignment during their original job interview and eliminated companies from consideration that were totally against the idea. In other cases, the woman informally introduced the idea to her boss and continued to mention it at appropriate moments until the company ultimately decided to offer her an expatriate position. A few women formally applied for a number of international assignments prior to actually being selected and sent.

Many women attempted to be in the right place at the right time. For example, one woman who predicted that Hong Kong would be her firm's next major business center arranged to assume responsibility for the Hong Kong desk in New York, leaving the rest of Asia to a male colleague. The strategy paid off; within a year, the company elevated their Hong Kong operations to a regional center and sent her to Asia as their first woman expatriate manager.

Most women claimed that their companies had failed to recognize the possibility of selecting women for international assignments, rather than having thoroughly considered the idea and then having rejected it. For the majority of the women, the obstacle appeared to be the companies' naiveté, not malice. For many women, the most difficult hurdle in their international careers involved getting sent abroad in the first place, not – as most had anticipated – gaining the respect of foreigners and succeeding once sent.

Did it Work? The Impact of Being a Woman

Almost all of the women expatriate managers (97 percent) reported that their international assignments were successful. This success rate is considerably higher than that reported for North American male expatriates. Although the women's assessments are subjective, objective indicators support the contention that most of the assignments, in fact, had succeeded. For example, the majority of the firms (after experimenting with their first woman expatriate manager) decided to send more women abroad. In addition, most companies promoted the women on the basis of their foreign performance or offered them other international assignments following completion of the first one.

Advantages

Given the third myth, women would be expected to experience a series of difficulties caused by their being female and, perhaps, to create a corresponding set of solutions designed to overcome each difficulty. This was not the case. Almost half of the women expatriates (42%) reported that being female served as more of an advantage than a disadvantage; 16% found it to be both positive and negative; 22% saw it as being either irrelevant or neutral; and only 20% found it to be primarily negative.

The women reported numerous professional advantages to being female. Most frequently, they described the advantage of being highly visible. Foreign clients were curious about them, wanted to meet them, and remembered them after the first encounter. The women therefore found it easier than their male colleagues to gain access to foreign clients' time and attention. The women gave examples of this high visibility, accessibility, and memorability:

Japan:　　　　　　　It's the visibility as an expat, and even more as a woman. I stick in their minds. I know I've gotten more business than my two male colleagues. . . . [My clients] are extra interested in me.

Thailand:　　　　　　Being a woman is never a detriment. They remembered me better. Fantastic for a marketing position. It's better working with Asians than with the Dutch, British, or Americans.

India and Pakistan:　In India and Pakistan, being a woman helps in marketing and client contact. I got in to see customers because they had never seen a female banker before. . . . Having a female banker adds value to the client.

Again contrary to the third myth, the women managers discovered a number of advantages based on their interpersonal skills, including that the local men could talk more easily about a wider range of topics with them than with their male counterparts. For example:

> *Japan*:   Women are better at putting people at ease. It's easier for a woman to convince a man. . . . The traditional woman's role . . . inspires confidence and trust, less suspicion, not threatening.
>
> *Indonesia*: I often take advantage of being a woman. I'm more supportive than my male colleagues. . . . [Clients] relax and talk more. And 50% of my effectiveness is based on volunteered information.
>
> *Korea*:   Women are better at treating men sensitively, and they just like you. One of my Korean clients told me: "I really enjoyed . . . working with you."

Many women also described the high social status accorded local women and found that such status was not denied them as foreign women. The women often received special treatment that their male counterparts did not receive. Clearly, it was always salient that they were women, but being a woman was not antithetical to succeeding as a manager.

> *Hong Kong*: Single female expats travel easier and are treated better. Never hassled. No safety issues. Local offices take better care of you. They meet you, take you through customs. . . . It's the combination of treating you like a lady and a professional.
>
> *Japan*:   It's an advantage that attracts attention. They are interested in meeting a *gaijin*, a foreign woman. Women attract more clients. On calls to clients, they elevate me, give me more rank. If anything, the problem, for men and women, is youth, not gender.

In addition, most of the women described benefiting from a "halo effect." The majority of the women's foreign colleagues and clients had never met or previously worked with a woman expatriate manager. Similarly, the local community was highly aware of how unusual it was for North American multinationals to send women managers abroad. Hence, the local managers assumed that the women would not have been sent unless they were "the best," and therefore expected them to be "very, very good."

> *Indonesia*: It's easier being a woman here than in any place in the world, including New York City. . . . I never get the comments I got in New York, like "What is a nice woman like you doing in this job?"
>
> *Japan*:   They assumed I must be good if I was sent. They became friends.

Some women found being female to have no impact whatsoever on their professional lives. Many of these women worked primarily with the overseas Chinese:

> *Hong Kong*: There are many expat and foreign women in top positions here. If you are good at what you do, they accept you. One Chinese woman told me: "Americans are always watching you. One mistake and you are done. Chinese take a while to accept you and then stop testing you."
>
> *Asia*:   There's no difference. They respect professionalism . . . including in Japan. There is no problem in Asia.

Disadvantages

The women also experienced a number of disadvantages in being female expatriate managers. Interestingly enough, the majority of the disadvantages involved the women's relationship with their home companies, not with their foreign colleagues and clients. As noted earlier, a major problem involved the women's difficulty in obtaining an international position in the first place.

Another problem involved home companies initially limiting the duration of the women's assignments to six months or a year, rather than offering the more standard two to three years. While temporary assignments may appear to offer companies a logically cautious strategy, in reality they create an unfortunate self-fulfilling prophecy. When the home company is not convinced that a woman can succeed (and therefore offers her a temporary rather than a permanent position), it communicates the company's lack of confidence to foreign colleagues and clients as a lack of commitment. The foreigners then mirror the home company's behavior by also failing to take the woman manager seriously. Assignments become very difficult or can fail altogether when companies demonstrate a lack of initial confidence and commitment. As one expatriate woman working in Indonesia stated: "It is very important to clients that I am permanent. It increases trust, and that's critical."

A subsequent problem involved the home company limiting the woman's professional opportunities and job scope once she was abroad. More than half of the women expatriates experienced difficulties in persuading their home companies to give them latitude equivalent to that given to their male counterparts, especially initially. For example, some companies, out of supposed concern for the woman's safety, limited her travel (and thus, the regional scope of her responsibility), thereby excluding very remote, rural, and underdeveloped areas. Other companies, as mentioned previously, initially limited the duration of the woman's assignment to six months or a year, rather than the more standard two to three years. For example:

Japan:	My problem is overwhelmingly with Americans. They identify it as a male market . . . geisha girls.
Thailand (petroleum company):	The Americans wouldn't let me on the drilling rigs, because they said there were no accommodations for a woman. Everyone blames it on something else. They gave me different work. They had me on the sidelines, not planning and communicating with drilling people. It's the expat Americans, not the Thais, who'll go to someone else before they come to me.

A few companies limited the women to working only internally with company employees, rather than externally with clients. These companies often implicitly assumed that their own employees were somehow less prejudiced than were outsiders. In reality, the women often found the opposite to be true. They faced more problems from home country nationals within their own organizations than externally from local clients and colleagues. As one woman described it:

Hong Kong: It was somewhat difficult internally. They feel threatened, hesitant to do what I say, resentful. They assume I don't have the credibility a man would have. Perhaps it's harder internally than externally, because client relationships are one-on-one and internally it's more of a group; or perhaps it's harder because they have to live with it longer internally; or perhaps it's because they fear that I'm setting a precedent or because they fear criticism from their peers.

Managing foreign clients' and colleagues' initial expectations was one area that proved difficult for many women. Some found initial meetings to be "tricky," especially when a male colleague from their own company was present. Since most local managers had never previously met a North American expatriate woman who held a managerial position, there was considerable ambiguity as to who she was, her status, her level of expertise, authority, and responsibility, and therefore the appropriate form of address and demeanor toward her.

People's Republic of China: I speak Chinese, which is a plus. But they'd talk to the men, not to me. They'd assume that I, as a woman, had no authority. The Chinese want to deal with top, top, top level people, and there is always a man at a higher level.

Asia: It took extra time to establish credibility with the Japanese and Chinese. One Japanese manager said to me: "When I first met you, I thought you would not be any good because you were a woman."

Since most of the North American women whom local managers had ever met previously were expatriates' wives or secretaries, they naturally assumed that the new woman was not a manager. Hence, they often directed initial conversations to male colleagues, not to the newly arrived woman manager. Senior male colleagues, particularly those from the head office, became very important in redirecting the focus of early discussions back toward the woman. When this was done, old patterns were quickly broken and smooth ongoing work relationships were established. When the pattern was ignored or poorly managed, the challenges to credibility, authority, and responsibility became chronic and undermined the women's effectiveness.

As mentioned earlier, many women described the most difficult aspect of the international assignment as getting sent abroad in the first place. Overcoming resistance from the North American home company frequently proved more challenging than gaining local clients' and colleagues' respect and acceptance. In most cases, assumptions about foreigners' prejudice against women expatriate managers appear to have been exaggerated. The anticipated prejudice and the reality did not match. It appears that foreigners are not as prejudiced as many North American managers had assumed.

The *Gaijin* Syndrome

One pattern is particularly clear: first and foremost, foreigners are seen as foreigners. Like their male colleagues, female expatriates are seen as foreigners, not as local people. A woman who is a foreigner (a *gaijin*) is not expected to act like the local women. Therefore, the societal and cultural rules governing the behavior of local women that limit their access to managerial positions and responsibility do not apply to foreign women. Although women are considered the "culture bearers" in all societies, foreign women are not expected to assume the cultural roles that societies have traditionally reserved for their own women. As one woman expatriate in Japan stated: "The Japanese are very smart: they can tell that I am not Japanese, and they do not expect me to act as a Japanese woman. They will allow and condone behavior in foreign women that would be absolutely unacceptable in their own women." Similarly a Tokyo-based personnel vice president for a major international bank explained that: "Being a foreigner is so weird to the Japanese that the marginal impact of being a woman is nothing. If I were a Japanese woman, I couldn't be doing what I'm doing here. But they know perfectly well that I'm not" (29:1,27).

Many of the women expatriates related similar examples of their unique status as "foreign women" rather than as "women" per se:

Japan and Korea:	Japan and Korea are the hardest, but they know that I'm an American woman, and they don't expect me to be like a Japanese or Korean woman. It's possible to be effective even in Japan and Korea if you send a senior woman with at least three or four years of experience, especially if she's fluent in Japanese.
Asia:	It's the novelty, especially in Japan, Korea, and Pakistan. All of the general managers met with me. . . . It was much easier for me, especially in Osaka. They were charming. They didn't want me to feel bad. They thought I would come back if they gave me business. You see, they could separate me from the local women.
Pakistan:	Will I have problems? No! There is a double standard between expats and local women. The Pakistanis test you, but you enter as a respected person.
Japan:	I don't think the Japanese could work for a Japanese woman . . . but they just block it out for foreigners.
Hong Kong:	Hong Kong is very cosmopolitan. I'm seen as an expat, not as an Asian, even though I am an Asian American.

Conclusion

It seems that we have confused the adjective *foreign* with the noun *woman* in predicting foreigners' reactions to expatriate women. We expected the most salient characteristic of a *woman* expatriate manager to be that she is a woman and predicted her success based on the success of the local women in each country. In fact, the most salient characteristic is that expatriates are *foreign*, and the best predictor of their success is the success of other foreigners (in this case, other North Americans) in the particular country. *Local managers see women expatriates as foreigners who happen to be women, not as women who happen to be foreigners.* The difference is crucial. Given the uncertainty involved in sending women managers to all areas of the world, our assumptions about the greater salience of gender (female/male) over nationality (foreign/local) have caused us to make false predictions concerning women's potential to succeed as international executives and managers.

The third myth – that foreigners' prejudice precludes women's effectiveness as international managers – is, in fact, definitely a myth. Of the three myths, only the second myth proved to be true. The first myth proved false: women *are* interested in working internationally. The third myth proved false: women *do* succeed internationally, once sent. However, the second myth proved to be true: companies are hesitant, if not completely unwilling, to send women managers abroad. Given that the problem is caused primarily by the home companies' assumptions and decisions, the solutions are also largely within their control.

Recommendations

In considering women managers for international assignments, both the companies and the women need to approach the decision and the assignment in a number of new ways.

Recommendations to Companies

Do Not Assume That it Will Not Work

Do not assume that foreigners will treat expatriate women managers the same way they treat their own local women. Our assumptions about the salience of gender over nationality have led to totally inaccurate predictions. Therefore, do not confuse adjectives with nouns; do not use the success or failure of local women to predict that of foreign women managers.

Do Not Confuse the Role of a Spouse With That of a Manager

Although the single most common reason for male expatriates' failure and early return from international assignments is the dissatisfaction of their wives, this does not mean that women cannot cope in a foreign environment. The role of the spouse (whether male or female) is much more ambiguous and, consequently, the cross-cultural adjustment is much more demanding for the spouse than for the employee (8). Wives have had trouble adjusting, but their situation is not analogous to that of women managers and therefore is not predictive.

Do Not Assume That a Woman Will Not Want to Go Abroad

Ask her. Although both single and married women need to balance private and professional life considerations, many are very interested in taking international assignments. Moreover, the proportion of women interested in working abroad is identical to that of men and can be predicted to increase over the coming decade.

Offer Flexible Benefits Packages

Given that most expatriate benefits packages have been designed to meet the needs of traditional families (employed husband, non-employed wife, and children), companies should be prepared to modify their benefits packages to meet the needs of managers who are single (women and men) and dual-career couples. Such modifications might include increased lead time in announcing assignments, executive search services for the partner in dual-career couples, and payment for "staying connected" (including telephone and airfare expenses) for couples who choose some form of commuting rather than both simultaneously relocating abroad.

Give Women Every Opportunity to Succeed

Accord her full status at the outset – not that of a temporary or experimental expatriate – with the appropriate title to communicate the home office's commitment to her. Do not be surprised if local colleagues and clients initially direct their comments to male managers rather than to the new woman expatriate during their first meeting with her. However, do not accept such behavior; redirect discussion, where appropriate, to the woman. Such behavior from foreign colleagues should not be interpreted as prejudice but rather as a reaction to a new, ambiguous, and unexpected situation.

Recommendations to Women Expatriate Managers

The women expatriates had a number of suggestions for the women managers who will follow in their footsteps.

Assume Naiveté, Not Malice

Realize that sending women abroad is new, perceived as risky, and still fairly poorly understood. In most cases, companies and foreign managers are operating on the basis of untested assumptions, many of which are faulty, not on the basis of prejudice. The most successful approach is to be gently persistent in "educating" the company to be open to the possibility of sending a woman abroad and granting her the status and support usually accorded to male peers in similar situations.

Be Outstanding

Given that expatriating women is perceived as risky, no woman will be sent abroad if she is not seen as technically and professionally well qualified. In addition, beyond being extremely well qualified, arrange to be in the right place at the right time.

Address Private-Life Issues Directly

For single women the issue of loneliness and for married women the issue of managing a dual-career relationship must be addressed. Contact with other expatriate women has proven helpful in both situations. For dual-career couples, most women consider it critical to have discussed the possibility of an international assignment with their husbands long before it became a reality and to have developed options that would work for them as a couple. For most couples, this means creating alternatives that have never, or rarely, been tried in the particular company.

Realize that expatriate status inadvertently helps to solve some of the role overload problems experienced by women who are managers, wives, and mothers. Since most expatriate managers can afford household help while on an expatriate assignment, but not in their home countries, they are able to reduce substantially the demands on their time. As one American expatriate manager in Hong Kong stated, "It would be impossible for me to do what I'm doing here if I was still in the United States. There just wouldn't be enough time!"

Global competition is, and will continue to be, intense in the 1990s. Transnational corporations, faced with the most intense global competition, may well continue to lead in hiring and promoting women into significant international management positions. Can they risk not choosing the best person just because her gender does not fit the traditional managerial profile? Needs for competitive advantage, not an all-consuming social conscience, may answer the question, if not in fact define it. Successful companies will select both women and men to manage their international operations. The option of limiting international management to one gender has become an archaic "luxury" that no company can afford. The only remaining question is how quickly and effectively each company will increase the number and use of women in their worldwide managerial workforce.

Acknowledgments

I would like to thank the Social Sciences and Humanities Research Council of Canada for its generous support of the research reported here. I owe special thanks to Dr. Homa Mahmoudi for her creativity and professional insight in helping to conduct the Asian interviews. This article is based on Dr. Adler's recent work on transnationals (9;10) and her research on women expatriate managers (1–6;23). The equity and complementary contribution approaches were originally presented in Adler and Adler and Izraeli's first book, *Women in Management Worldwide* (12).

References

All quotes by the women expatriates are taken from Dr. Adler's research interviews. While the names of the women cannot be released, each of them was working in the country listed at the time of the interview.

1. Adler, Nancy J. (1979) "Women as Androgynous Managers: A Conceptualization of the Potential for American Women in International Management," *International Journal of Intercultural Relations*, 3, no. 4: 407–435.

2. Adler, Nancy J. (1984a) "Expecting International Success: Female Managers Overseas," *Columbia Journal of World Business*, 19, no. 3: 79–85.

3. Adler, Nancy J. (1984b) "Women Do Not Want International Careers: And Other Myths About International Management," *Organizational Dynamics*, 13, no. 3: 66–79.

4. Adler, Nancy J. (1984c) "Women in International Management: Where Are They?" *California Management Review*, 26, no. 4: 78–89.

5. Adler, Nancy J. (1986) "Do MBAs Want International Careers?" *International Journal of Intercultural Relations*, 10, no. 3: 277–300.

6. Adler, Nancy J. (1987) "Pacific Basin Managers: A Gaijin, Not a Woman," *Human Resource Management*, 26, no. 2: 169–191.

7. Adler, Nancy J. (1986–1987) "Women in Management Worldwide," *International Studies of Management and Organization*, 16, no. 3–4: 3–32.

8. Adler, Nancy J. (1991) *International Dimensions of Organizational Behavior*, 2nd edn, Boston: PWS-Kent Publishing.

9. Adler, Nancy J. (1993) "Competitive Frontiers: Women Managers in the Triad," *International Studies of Management and Organization*, 23, no. 2: 3–24.

10. Adler, Nancy J., and Bartholomew, Susan (1992) "Managing Globally Competent People," *Academy of Management Executive*, 6, no. 3: 52–65.

11. Adler, Nancy J., and Ghadar, Fariborz (1990) "Strategic Human Resource Management: A Global Perspective," in *Human Resource Management in International Comparison*, Rudiger Pieper ed., Berlin: de Gruyter: 235–260.

12. Adler, Nancy J., and Izraeli, Dafna N. (eds.) (1988) *Women in Management Worldwide*. Armonk, NY: M. E. Sharpe.

13. Aptheker, B. (1989) *Tapestries of Life: Women's Work, Women's Consciousness, and the Meaning of Daily Experience*. Amherst: University of Massachusetts Press.

14. Bartlett, Christopher A., and Ghoshal, Sumantra (1989) *Managing across Borders: The Transnational Solution*. Boston: Harvard Business School Press.

15. Berthoin Antal, Ariane, and Izraeli, Dafna N. (1993) "A Global Comparison of Women in Management: Women Managers in Their Homelands and as Expatriates," in *Women in Management: Trends, Issues and Challenges in Managerial Diversity, Women and Work*, Vol. 4, Ellen Fagenson ed., Newbury Park, CA: Sage.

16. Calvert, Linda McGee, and Ramsey, V. Jean (1992) "Bringing Women's Voice to Research on Women in Management: A Feminist Perspective," *Journal of Management Inquiry*, 1, no. 1: 79–88.

17. Caulkin, S. (1977) "Women in Management," *Management Today* (September): 58–63.

18. Fisher, Anne B. (1992) "When Will Women Get to the Top?" *Fortune*, September 21: 44–56.

19. Fossan, J. (1989) "Women in Organization," *Implementing Strategies and Achieving Change*. Seminar Research Report, Berlin: Aspen Institute.

20. Gilligan, Carol (1982) *In a Different Voice*. Cambridge, MA: Harvard University Press.

21. Hammond, Valerie, and Holton, Viki (1994) "The Scenario for Women Managers in Britain in the 1990s," in *Competitive Frontiers: Women Managers in a Global Economy*, Nancy J. Adler and Dafna N. Izraeli eds., Cambridge, MA: Blackwell Publishers: 224–242.

22. Helgesen, S. (1990) *The Female Advantage: Women's Ways of Leadership*. New York: Doubleday.

23. Jelinek, Mariann, and Adler, Nancy J. (1988) "Women: World-Class Managers for Global Competition," *Academy of Management Executive*, 2, no. 1: 11–19.

24. Korabik, Karen (1988) "Is the Ideal Manager Masculine? The Contribution of Femininity to Managerial Effectiveness." Paper presented at the annual meetings of the Academy of Management, Anaheim, CA.

25. Lansing, P., and Ready, K. (1988) "Hiring Women Managers in Japan: An Alternative for Foreign Employers," *California Management Review*, 30, no. 3: 112–127.

26. Loden, M. (1987) *Feminine Leadership or How to Succeed in Business without Being One of the Boys.* New York: Times Books.

27. Miller, Jean Baker (1976) *Toward a New Psychology of Women.* Boston: Beacon Press.

28. Miller, Jean Baker (1982) "Women and Power," Working Paper. Wellesley, MA: Wellesley College, Stone Center for Development Services and Studies.

29. Morganthaler, E. (1978) "Women of the World: More U.S. Firms Put Females in Key Posts in Foreign Countries," *Wall Street Journal*, March 16: 1, 27.

30. Moran, Stahl, and Boyer, Inc. (1988) *Status of American Female Expatriate Employees: Survey Results.* Boulder, CO: International Division.

31. Perry, Nancy J. (1992) "If You Can't Join 'em, Beat 'em," *Fortune*, September 21: 58–59.

32. Porter, Michael (1990) *The Competitive Advantage of Nations.* New York: The Free Press.

33. Rosenzweig, Philip M., and Nohria, Nitin (1992) "Human Resource Management in MNC Affiliates: Internal Consistency or Local Isomorphism," working paper, Boston: Harvard Business School.

34. Steen, Gunilla Masreliez (1987) "Male and Female Culture: A View From Sweden," working paper presented at the International Federation of Training and Development Organizations Conference.

35. Steinhoff, Patricia G., and Tanaka, Kazuko (1988) "Women Managers in Japan," in *Women in Management Worldwide*, Nancy J. Adler and Dafna N. Izraeli eds., Armonk, NY: M. E. Sharpe: 103–121.

36. Steinhoff, Patricia G., and Tanaka, Kazuko (1994) "Women Managers in Japan," in *Competitive Frontiers: Women Managers in a Global Economy*, Nancy J. Adler and Dafna N. Izraeli eds., Cambridge, MA: Blackwell Publishers: 79–100.

37. Thal, N., and Cateora, P. (1979) "Opportunities for Women in International Business," *Business Horizons*, 22, no. 6: 21–27.

38. *Yearbook of Labor Statistics* (1986) (1987) (1991) Geneva: International Labor Office. Copyright 1994. "Competitive Frontiers and Women Managers in a Global Economy," Nancy J. Adler and Dafna N. Izraeli (eds.) Reprinted with permission of Blackwell Publishers.

Serving Two Masters: Managing the Dual Allegiance of Expatriate Employees

J. Stewart Black and Hal B. Gregersen

Each year hundreds of thousands of expatriate managers all over the world find themselves torn between their allegiance to the parent firm and their allegiance to the local foreign operation. To understand this tension, consider the following situation. A Dutch expatriate manager in a multinational consumer products firm is faced on the one hand, with a parent firm that wants a set of products introduced in the host country (a large developing nation) as part of its global brand image strategy. On the other hand, the host country government wants high-technology transferred into the country, not just consumer products placed on store shelves. Market research suggests that local consumers are interested in some of the core products but not others and in products not currently part of the firm's core set. The parent firm has a philosophy encouraging participative decision making, but host national employees expect managers to make decisions without burdening them.

Faced with serving two masters, many expatriate managers end up directing their allegiance too far in one direction or the other, creating serious costs and consequences for both themselves and their organizations. For example, if individuals are too committed to the local operation relative to the parent firm, it is difficult for the home office to coordinate with them. A senior Honda executive commented to us that Honda had incurred "non-trivial" costs trying to coordinate its global strategy for the new Honda Accord because some expatriate managers were too focused on the local situation. Expatriates who are overly committed to the parent firm relative to the local operation often inappropriately implement policies or procedures from the home office. The medical equipment division of a large U.S. multinational firm recently tried to implement home office financial reporting and accounting procedures that simply did not apply to and would not work in its newly acquired French subsidiary.

Reprinted from *Sloan Management Review*, Summer 1992, pp. 61–71, by permission of publisher. © 1992 by the Sloan Management Review Association. All rights reserved.

FIGURE 1   Forms of Expatriate Allegiance

Allegiance to the Parent Firm	Low	Expatriates who see themselves as free agents	Expatriates who "go native"
	High	Expatriates who leave their hearts at home	Expatriates who see themselves as dual citizens
		Low	High
		Allegiance to the Local Operation	

Perhaps most important, the high competitive pressure, great geographical distances, and wide cultural diversity of global operations combined with ineffective management of expatriates can set off a vicious cycle that erodes or even destroys a firm's global competitive position:

1. Unbalanced allegiance can lead to a variety of failures during and after international assignments.
2. As managers hear about these failures, firms find it increasingly difficult to attract top international candidates.
3. Increasingly worse candidates are sent overseas, producing even worse organizational results and more failed careers.
4. This further limits the pool of willing and qualified candidates.
5. Over time the firm's overseas competitive position erodes.
6. This cycle spirals downward until it becomes nearly unstoppable.

Today's multinational firms need managers who are highly committed to both the parent firm and the local operation and who can integrate the demands and objectives of both organizations. As one senior executive put it, the bottom line question is: "How can we get expatriate managers who are committed to the local overseas operation during their international assignments, but who remain loyal to the parent firm?" Unfortunately, our research suggests that expatriate managers with high dual allegiance are a rare commodity.[1]

This is not surprising in light of studies of dual commitment in domestic contexts, such as commitment to a union and an organization (that is, United Auto Workers and General Motors) or commitment to a profession and an organization (that is, nursing and a specific hospital). These studies have found that certain factors have different effects on the two targets of commitment and that people hold different patterns of commitment. Some individuals are unilaterally committed to one organization over the other, some have low levels of commitment to both, and others have high levels of commitment to both.[2]

In this article we present a description of the patterns, causes, and consequences of expatriate dual allegiance. In brief, expatriate managers can be grouped into one of four allegiance patterns. They can be overly committed to the parent firm or the local operation, highly committed to both organizations, or committed to neither. These four basic patterns are presented in the Figure 1 matrix. Much more important than the patterns of dual allegiance are the factors that cause them and the related organizational and individual consequences. We describe the causes and consequences associated with each pattern and illustrate them with actual cases generated through numerous interviews and surveys (most managers asked that their names and firms be disguised). We also examine what firms are doing now and what they can do in the future to more effectively manage their expatriate managers.

Free Agents

As an undergraduate, Paul Jackson majored in Asian studies and studied for two years in Japan. At graduation, he had intermediate fluency in Chinese and near fluency in Japanese. He immediately went on to receive a master's degree from the American Graduate School of International Management in Phoenix. He was hired by a major east coast bank and two years later was sent on a three-year assignment to Hong Kong. The expatriate package Paul and his family received made life in Hong Kong enjoyable. However, Paul felt little loyalty to the parent firm back home or the Hong Kong operation. First and foremost, Paul was committed to his career. Because he was such a hard charger, the bank invested a substantial amount of time and money into him for language and technical training. He worked hard but always kept an ear out for better jobs and pay. Two years into his Hong Kong assignment, he found a better position in another firm and took it. Four years into that company and assignment, he took a job with a different U.S. bank and its Taiwan operation. Four years later, he took a job as vice-president and general manager for the Japan subsidiary of a large west coast bank.

When we interviewed Paul about his work history, he said: "I can't really relate to your question about which organization I feel allegiance to. I do my job, and I do it well. I play for whatever team needs me and wants me. I'm like a free agent in baseball or a hired gun in the old West. If the pay and job are good enough, I'm off. You might say, 'have international expertise, will travel.'"

Interestingly, Paul was actually part of a network we discovered of "hired-gun free agents" in the Pacific Rim. The network consisted of a group of about ten American managers hired as expatriates (not as local hires), who were either bi- or trilingual, and who had spent over half of their professional careers in Asia. This group of free agents passed along information to each other about various firms that were looking for experienced expatriate managers for their Asia operations.

Hired-Gun Free Agents

These expatriates have a low level of commitment to both their parent firms and their local operations. They are first and foremost committed to their own "gun-slinging" careers. When asked what long-term career implications this approach might have for them, these expatriates commonly indicated that it would be very difficult for them to ever "go back home" and move up the headquarter's hierarchy in any firm. However, most did not want to for several reasons. First, they felt the experience their children received from both an educational (schools are generally international, private, and paid for by the firm) and general life perspective was far superior to what they would receive back home. Second, the expatriates would be worse off financially if they went home and had to give up the extra benefits of their expatriate packages. Third, most were confident that they would not be given a job back home with the status, freedom, and importance of those jobs they held overseas. Consequently, most of these hired guns seemed happy with their lives and careers overseas.

Firms tend to view these expatriates with some ambivalence. On the one hand, even though these hired guns receive special benefit packages, they tend to be slightly less expensive than sending expatriates from the home country. Furthermore, these expatriates have already demonstrated their specialized skills, such as language, and their ability to succeed in international settings – qualities that are often lacking in a firm's internal managerial or executive ranks. This may be especially important to U.S. firms; on average 15–20% of their expatriate managers fail in their overseas assignments, at great cost to the firm, because they have serious problems adjusting to the foreign culture.

On the other hand, these free agent expatriates often leave the firm with little warning. Replacing them is usually costly and difficult and can have negative consequences for both the parent firm and the local operation. Sometimes these hired guns serve their own short-term career objectives at the expense of the firm's long-term interests. Also, as mentioned, few of these expatriates are willing to repatriate to the home office. This makes integrating their international experience or specific country or regional knowledge into the firm's global strategy formulation process next to impossible.

Plateaued-Career Free Agents

Our research uncovered another type of expatriate with low levels of commitment to both the parent firm and the local operation. This type of expatriate typically comes from the ranks of home country employees rather than of hired international experts. These expatriates are generally not committed to the parent firm before leaving for the overseas assignment in part because their careers have often plateaued. They take the international assignment because they do not see themselves going anywhere in the home operations, and they hope an international stint will change things. Or they are simply attracted by the sweet financial packages common to most overseas assignments. Unfortunately, many of the factors that led to low commitment before the international assignment result in low commitment to the local operation once the manager is overseas.

Several factors can contribute to development of this type of expatriate. First, if firms simply allow candidates for overseas assignments to self-select, they open the door for this type of expatriate. As one expatriate said: "I figured I was stalled in my job [back in North Carolina], so why not take a shot at an overseas assignment, especially given what I'd heard about the high standard of living even mid-level managers enjoyed overseas." Research has shown that certain personal characteristics correlate with successful adjustment to international assignments.[3] A self-selection process leaves personal characteristics of the expatriates to chance. Second, placing a low value on international operations can increase the probability that plateaued managers will apply for overseas assignments and decrease the probability that high-potential managers will volunteer for them. In such an environment, high-potential managers know that the place to get ahead is not overseas somewhere, out of sight and out of mind, but at home. Finally, lack of pre-departure cross-cultural training can also reinforce low levels of commitment to the parent firm and the local operation. U.S. firms may be particularly vulnerable to this factor; roughly 70% of all U.S. expatriates receive no pre-departure cross-cultural training.[4] Lack of firm-sponsored training can contribute to the view that "the company doesn't care about me, so why should I care about it?" Lack of training can also inhibit the expatriate from understanding the foreign culture and becoming committed to the local operation.

Unlike the hired guns, many of the plateaued-career free agents are not happy in their overseas assignments. Their low level of commitment often results in little effort to adjust to the local operation and culture. At worst, they fail the assignment. A failed overseas assignment not only inhibits the individual's career advancement, it can strike severe blow to the individual's identity and self-confidence. Of course, there are also costs to the firm. Beyond the $100,000 to $250,000 it costs to bring the employee and family home and send out a replacement, the firm incurs the costs of damaged client and supplier relationships.[5] The lack of leadership during the replacement process can contribute to damaged internal and external relations. Failed assignments can also generate rumors back home that international posts are the "kiss of death" for a career, which in turn makes it more difficult to attract good candidates in the future.

Even if lack of commitment doesn't result in a failed assignment, it can still be costly to the person and the organization. Bob Brown was a typical plateaued manager for a major U.S. aircraft manufacturer who transferred to Taiwan three years before his interview with us. Bob was not very excited about living in Taiwan and neither was his family. His wife and daughter repeatedly asked to go back home. Bob pointed out that there was really no job for him to go back to. His daughter became so distraught that she began doing extremely poorly in school. This and other pressures put a severe strain on Bob's relationship with his wife. In an interview, Bob summed it up by stating that his home life was in shambles and that work was merely a paycheck, but a fat one (his compensation and benefit package was worth about $210,000 per year).

Perhaps the parent and local firm were getting their money's worth out of Bob, but it seems unlikely. Past studies have found that of those expatriates who complete their assignments, about one-third are considered ineffective.[6] Also, it is hard to imagine that a manager whose career has plateaued back home could be paid two to three times a normal compensation package and still provide a good return on that expense. If, as we suspect, such managers cannot, then this represents a serious economic loss to firms.

To summarize, low commitment to the parent firm and the local operation seems to be found in two general types of expatriate managers – hired-gun free agents and plateaued-career free agents. Although the causes and consequences of each type are different, both types represent potentially serious costs to the individual, parent firm, and local operation, since 41% of our sample fell into this group.

Going Native

The next allegiance pattern involves having high levels of commitment to the local operation but low levels of commitment to the parent firm. These expatriates usually form a strong identification with and attachment to the country's culture, language, values, and business practices. Consequently, these expatriates are often referred to as those who "go native."

Gary Ogden had been with a large computer company for fifteen years. He was the country manager for the firm's instrument division in France and had been in Paris for about four years, his third international assignment. Of his fifteen years with the parent firm, over half had been spent overseas, including six of the last eight years. Given that this was his third international stint, it had not taken long for Gary, his wife, and their three daughters (ages six, nine, and eleven) to settle in to life in France. His girls had enrolled in regular French schools when they moved to Paris and were now fluent for their ages. Gary's French was not perfect but he was comfortable in business situations. He had spent long hours trying to understand the local business situation, and he thought that corporate was constantly requesting and demanding things that either worked against objectives for the French unit or couldn't be done effectively or sometimes at all in France. Still, Gary loved it so much in France that he had already requested an extension, even though his contract only required him to stay another six months. When asked to describe his commitment to the parent firm and the local operation, he responded, "My first commitment is to the unit here. In fact, half the time I feel as if corporate is a competitor I must fight rather than a benevolent parent I can look to for support."

Our research suggests that individuals like Gary Ogden who have spent a number of years overseas, who adjust to the local culture, and who feel at odds with corporate headquarters are the most likely to go native. As managers spend more time away from the home office, their identities seem less and less tied to the parent firm. The firm becomes both literally and psychologically distant, as compared to the local operation. Additionally, the lack of formal communication with the home office through mechanisms such as sponsors (individuals assigned to keep in touch with specific expatriates) also serves to cause or reinforce this commitment pattern. Firms that are structured in international divisions and have cadres of "career internationalists" may be particularly vulnerable to this pattern.

What are the consequences of going native in terms of expatriate allegiance? Let us consider the individual's perspective. First, Gary felt that he had effectively managed the local situation. He pointed out that his knowledge of the language, culture, and union structure had enabled him to avoid an almost certain and probably very costly strike. Unfortunately, because the strike never happened, Gary felt that corporate did not recognize his achievement. Second, because Gary knew that his career depended to some extent on the evaluations made of him back at corporate, when he had to "fight" the parent firm, he had to do it subtly: "Sometimes I would simply ignore their directives if I didn't think they were appropriate or relevant to our operations. If it's really important, eventually someone from regional or corporate will hassle me, and I'll have to respond. If it isn't important or if they think I implemented what they wanted, they just leave me alone. As long as the general results are good, it doesn't seem as if there are big costs to this approach." Gary also indicated that on occasion he had to fight corporate more overtly. Although this may have cost him back at corporate, fighting these fights and especially winning them helped him gain the trust and loyalty of the local national employees. Their greater loyalty made it easier for him to be effective in the country. Interestingly, this effectiveness often later earned him points and slack back home.

Third, when Gary was repatriated after international assignments, he disliked the lack of responsibility compared to what he enjoyed overseas and the general lack of appreciation and utilization of his international knowledge. He nearly quit the firm both times he was repatriated. His low commitment to the parent firm heightened his dissatisfaction. Gary stated that both times it was receipt of another overseas assignment that kept him from leaving the firm.

From the parent firm's point of view, one of the common problems associated with expatriates who go native is the difficulty of getting corporate policies or programs implemented at the local level. Often the intense commitment to the local foreign operation leads these expatriates to implement what they think is relevant, in a way they deem appropriate, and then to ignore or fight the rest. This can be very costly, especially when the parent firm is trying to closely coordinate activities in a wide variety of countries for the good of global corporate objectives.

Also, to the extent that low commitment to the parent firm contributes to repatriation turnover, the parent firm loses the opportunity to incorporate the knowledge and experience of these expatriates into its global strategy or to incorporate some of these individuals into their succession plans. Interestingly, our research found that most expatriates, regardless of commitment pattern, do not feel that the international knowledge and experience they gained overseas is valued by their firms (91% of U.S. expatriates, 97% of Japanese expatriates, and 89% of Finnish expatriates). In general, firms do not seem to be utilizing these valuable resources.

Despite the negative aspects of expatriates who go native, many corporate executives recognize that these expatriates are not all bad. The high level of allegiance to the local operation generally leads these expatriates to identify with and understand the host national employees, customers, and suppliers. This understanding can translate into (1) new products and services or adapted products and services that are well targeted to the local market, and (2) managerial approaches that are suited to the host national employees.

The importance of a managerial style modified to suit host national employees must not be overlooked, especially by U.S. firms. Although most U.S. firms assume that good managers in New York will do fine in Tokyo or Hong Kong and consequently select expatriates based primarily on domestic track records, evidence suggests that managerial characteristics that are related to performance in the United States are not related to performance in foreign countries.[7]

This potentially positive aspect of these expatriate managers may be particularly true in firms at a multidomestic stage of globalization.[8] In most multidomestic firms, each overseas unit competes in its national or regional market independent of the firm's other organizational units in other countries. The primary information flow is within the local operation, rather than between it and the parent firm. There is a premium on understanding the local market and the host national people and culture. Expatriates with relatively high allegiance to the local operation may be particularly beneficial in this situation.

In summary, managers who have spent a lot of time away from the parent firm, who can adjust to foreign cultures, and who lack formal communication ties to the parent firm are the most likely to go native; they constituted about 15% of our sample. There are pros and cons to this pattern for both the individual and the parent firm. Expatriates who go native often have valuable insights into the local operation, culture, and market; they can adapt procedures, products, or managerial approaches to fit the local situation. They may also be less likely to return prematurely and to invoke the serious costs associated with early returns. However, they also can frustrate global coordination efforts and may not be committed enough to the parent firm after repatriation to pass their knowledge on for country, regional, or global strategic planning.[9]

Hearts at Home

The third type of expatriate manager is highly committed to the parent firm but has little allegiance to the local foreign operation. We refer to these expatriates as those who "leave their hearts at home;" they constituted about 12% of our sample. These expatriate managers identify much more strongly with the parent firm than they do with the local operation and the local country's culture, language, and business practices.

Earl Markus was the managing director of the European headquarters of a large building-supply firm's "do-it-yourself" retail division. This was Earl's first international assignment in his twenty-two years with the firm. He was married and had two children, both of whom were in college and therefore did not move with their parents to European headquarters in Belgium. Earl had worked his way up from a store manager to southwest regional manager and eventually to vice president of finance over the previous twenty-two years.

The European operations were fairly new, and Earl saw his mission as expanding the number of retail outlets from the current nine in Belgium to fifty throughout western Europe. The president and CEO of the U.S. parent firm had assigned the CEO, Frank Johnson, to work closely with Earl during his three-year assignment.

One year into the assignment, Earl was on schedule and had opened fifteen new outlets in three countries. But he was very frustrated. He said that he had seriously considered packing up and going home more than once during the year. He claimed Europeans were lazy and slow to respond to directives. When asked about his allegiance, he said that there was no contest. He was first and foremost committed to corporate, and when the next two years were up, he was headed back home. As an example of how things had gone, Earl described the implementation of the inventory system.

About eight months into the assignment, Frank Johnson suggested that Earl implement the new computerized inventory system that had just been phased into U.S. outlets. Frank was excited about the system's ability to reduce costs and shrinkage (i.e., theft), and he had high expectations of similar benefits for its use in Europe. For proper operation, the system required daily recording of sales and weekly random physical inventory of specific items. These reports needed to be transferred within forty-eight hours to the central office, which would generate total and store-by-store reports. The forms and procedure manuals were printed, and a two-day seminar was held for all European store managers and directors of operations and relevant staff members. Two months later, Earl inquired about how the system was operating. It wasn't. He said all he got from his managers were "lame excuses" about why the system would not work, especially in Belgium.

This case illustrates some of the main causes and consequences of expatriates' allegiance being tilted strongly in favor of the parent firm. It is not surprising that our research found a significant correlation between long tenure in the parent firm and allegiance to it. These expatriates had invested time, sweat, and heartache with the parent firm, and they expected a "return" on this investment. Over time, the expatriates' identities had intertwined with the identities of the parent firm. A high level of allegiance to the parent firm was a natural consequence.

Our research found two other factors that, in combination, contributed to this allegiance pattern. The first factor was poor adjustment to the host country and culture, in part fostered by selection processes that primarily considered domestic track records. Because these expatriates could not relate to the host country's culture and people, they could not develop a strong sense of allegiance to the local operation. The second factor was having a sponsor in the home office who was formally assigned to the expatriate to maintain a formal tie. This tie focused attention and allegiance toward the parent firm and away from the local operation.

What personal and organizational consequences resulted from this allegiance pattern? Earl Markus was frustrated; he had considered leaving the overseas assignment several times. It was his fear of negative career consequences more than anything else that kept him from going. In addition to early return costs, which we discussed in the section on free agents, organizations can also incur the cost of having ineffectual managers. These managers often try to implement and enforce programs that are inappropriate for the local operation, or they implement them in ways that offend local employees, customers, or suppliers. Earl's inventory implementation effort antagonized employees and created an adversarial relationship that hampered other programs and changes he subsequently tried to initiate.

However, just as in the case of going native, not all the consequences of leaving one's heart at home are bad. Our research found that U.S. expatriates who had a high commitment to the parent firm during the international assignment were more likely to want to stay with the parent firm after their repatriation. Thus, to the extent that these expatriates gain valuable experience, knowledge, and skills during their international assignments, their parent firms have greater opportunities to gain future returns from them. Unfortunately, the low commitment to the local operation reduces the knowledge these expatriates can gain. Nevertheless, expatriates who leave their hearts at home can provide another advantage. They often make it easier for the home office to coordinate activities between headquarters and the subsidiary. In Earl's case, it was very easy for the corporate purchasing agent to utilize the buying power of headquarters' centralized purchasing activities for the European operations. This coordination gave the European operations access to substantial price savings.

The ability to coordinate easily with the home office may be particularly beneficial for firms at the export stage of globalization. The primary objective of most firms at this stage is to sell in foreign markets products developed and manufactured in the home country. Information flows primarily from the parent firm to the local operation. The home office plays a key coordinating role, and good coordination with the subsidiaries is important. Expatriates with relatively high commitment to the parent firm are less likely to resist following the home office's coordination efforts than expatriates with low levels of commitment to the parent.

Dual Citizens

The final category consists of expatriate managers who are highly committed to both the parent *and* the local operation – dual citizens. We use the word "citizen" because it seems to reflect this group's behavior, attitudes, and emotions. These managers tend to see themselves as citizens of both the foreign country and their home country and as citizens of both the local operation and the parent corporation. They feel responsible for serving both organization's interests.

Joan Beckenridge was the director of a prominent U.S. consulting firm's Japan office. This was Joan's second international assignment in her thirteen years with the firm. Her first assignment was a one-year special project stint in Singapore seven years before. Joan was one of three candidates considered for the job in Japan and had been selected based not only on her past performance but also on assessments by outside consultants. Because the job required a high degree of interaction with host nationals in a novel culture, Joan was given five months' notice before departing for Japan. During this time she received about sixty hours of cross-cultural training. In addition, her spouse received about ten hours of survival briefing. Four months after arriving in Japan, Joan received another forty hours of cross-cultural training. She also took advantage of hundreds of hours of language training, paid for by the parent firm.

Perhaps most important, Joan had a clear set of objectives for her assignment. The Japan office had been established to serve the Japanese subsidiaries of the firm's U.S. clients. At this point, the office's growth was limited by the slowed pace of expansion of U.S. client firms to Japan. Joan was charged with developing Japanese clients. This would serve two objectives. First, it would increase the office's growth potential, and second, it would make it easier to secure Japanese firms' U.S. subsidiaries as clients, which would expand U.S. operations.

Despite these preparations, Joan found herself frustrated in one area. Headquarters and the local operation had differing expectations regarding business and entertainment expenses. Headquarters did not realize how much time and money it took to cultivate effective relationships in Japan. Joan's Japanese business associates were fond of pointing out that their country had the highest business entertainment expenses as a percentage of sales in the world. Joan felt the tension between corporate "bean counters" who worried over entertainment expenses and local staff who floated contact opportunities that Joan could not develop. However, unlike many expatriates in similar situations, Joan had a mechanism for working out these differences. She had a high-level sponsor at corporate who was officially assigned to help her. Through this sponsor, Joan could educate corporate and bring corporate and local expectations in synch.

It was also clear from the beginning how this assignment fitted Joan's overall career path and how her repatriation would be handled. Although she was not guaranteed a specific position upon repatriation, Joan knew what her general opportunities would be if she met her objectives in Japan.

Perhaps the most important factor in Joan's effectiveness was that she had a great degree of autonomy in deciding how to achieve the assignment's objectives. She had the flexibility to deal with the inevitable conflicts and ambiguities that cropped up in the job.

When asked about her allegiance, Joan said, "I feel a strong sense of allegiance to both companies [the local operation and the parent firm]. Although they sometimes have different objectives, I try to satisfy both whenever I can." When the two organizations conflicted, Joan would work to bring them together rather than simply following one or the other.

The personal and organizational consequences of Joan's dual-citizenship orientation were primarily positive. Joan indicated that it was sometimes frustrating to be torn between parent and local needs but that the clarity of her objectives, the latitude she had to pursue them, and the relative infrequency and small magnitude of the conflicts made the work rewarding and satisfying. Joan did well in her five years in Japan and received a substantial promotion upon repatriation to a position in which her knowledge was utilized in domestic and international expansion plans. For the organization, Joan's dual-citizenship orientation helped her build solid relations with Japanese clients and government officials and helped the home office establish relationships with Japanese clients' U.S. subsidiaries. Joan believed her dual focus also gave her a greater ability to recruit high-quality Japanese employees, which was difficult for competitors.

Thirty-two percent of our sample of U.S. expatriate managers fit this allegiance pattern. Although it would be inaccurate to say that these expatriates never returned home early, never left the firm after repatriation, or never had adjustment or performance problems during international assignments, this group had a higher probability than the others of completing the foreign assignment, staying with the firm upon repatriation, and adjusting well to the overseas stay. These expatriate managers were much more interested than the others in understanding the needs, objectives, constraints, and opportunities of both the local operation and the parent firm. They talked of using this understanding to benefit both organizations. They could effectively implement corporate policies in the local operation and pass information from the local operation back to corporate in order to help shape strategy and policy development.

As indicated in Joan Beckenridge's case, *role conflict* played an important part in determining commitment. When the parent and local organizations had different expectations, demands, and objectives, the managers who had to negotiate these differences suffered from role conflict. The greater the role conflict, the less managers felt responsible for the outcomes and the less they felt committed to either organization. As one expatriate put it: "It's hard to feel responsible for what happens when you're being torn in opposite directions." In contrast, the greater the consistency between the two organizations, the more expatriate managers felt responsible for what happened and the more they felt committed to both organizations.

Role ambiguity produced a similar dynamic. Whereas role conflict follows from clear expectations that conflict, role ambiguity occurs when expectations from both organizations simply are not clear. Poor coordination between the parent firm and the local operation was a common source of role ambiguity. When we asked one expatriate manager how much responsibility he felt for what happened on his job, he replied: "How can I feel responsible, when I don't even know what I'm supposed to do or what's expected of me?" In contrast, the clearer the role, the more expatriates felt responsible for what happened at work and committed to both organizations.

Another factor related to dual allegiance was *clarity of repatriation programs.* Over 60% of U.S. firms have no systematic or formal repatriation program.[10] Clear, systematic repatriation programs facilitate high levels of commitment to both organizations. Such programs seem to free expatriates from worrying about going home and allow them to focus on the job at hand. This facilitates allegiance to the local operation. Such programs also seem to communicate that the parent firm cares about their expatriates and has thought about reintegration. This creates a greater sense of obligation to the parent firm.

The most powerful factor in creating dual allegiance was *role discretion.* Role discretion is the freedom to decide what needs to be done, how and when it should be done, and who should do it. The more discretion expatriate managers have, the more they feel responsible for what happens at work and committed to the local operation. Because they generally view the parent firm as responsible for the amount of freedom they enjoy, this translates into a greater sense of commitment to the parent firm as well. Part of the reason that discretion is the most powerful factor is that most expatriate managers experience some role conflict and ambiguity. Role discretion gives the manager the freedom to define expectations and resolve conflicting ones.

Although dual citizens are desirable for any firm at any globalization stage, they are most critical for firms at the coordinated multinational stage. Such firms need information to flow back and forth between the home office and foreign subsidiaries and from one foreign subsidiary to another. They need managers who identify with both the people back home and those in the local operation. They need managers who will stay in the assignment, who will try to meet the needs of both organizations, and who will stay with the firm after repatriation so that their international experience, knowledge, and skills can be utilized.

Policy Implications

Although most executives in multinational firms are aware of the issues concerning expatriate allegiance, few of the expatriates we interviewed said that their firms understood the cause and consequences of the different allegiance patterns or had systems for developing dual-citizen expatriates. However, many firms had found ways to counterbalance "lopsided" allegiance. Below we present what some of these firms are doing, and we propose steps for developing dual-citizen expatriates.

Strategy 1: Counterbalancing Going Native

Managers who have several years of international experience and who have successfully adjusted to foreign cultures in the past are most likely to go native. Although these managers tend to have a low commitment to the parent firm, they are also good candidates to send overseas because they lower the risks and associated costs of failed assignments and premature returns. What can firms do if their current policies tend to produce too many expatriate managers like Gary Ogden?

Limit Time Away from Corporate

Honda brings expatriates home to Japan for a few years before they go overseas again. This method reinforces the link between the manager and the parent firm. Honda believes that it is not logical to expect career internationalists who move from one foreign assignment to the next to be highly committed to the parent firm.

Send Managers with Strong Ties to Corporate

Firms can send managers overseas who have longer tenure in the parent firm. The longer managers have been with the firm, the more they have invested in it, the more they identify with it, and the more they are committed to it. Also, long tenures build personal connections that keep individuals involved with corporate. However, this recommendation is problematic for firms such as General Electric (GE), General Motors (GM), and Ford, which increasingly use international assignments to develop younger, high-potential managers.

Establish Corporate Sponsor Programs

GE uses sponsors to counterbalance the tendency to go native. The company assesses the expatriate's career objectives and chooses a senior manager, often in the function to which the expatriate is likely to return, who is willing to serve as sponsor. The sponsor maintains contact with the expatriate throughout the assignment, including face-to-face meetings; evaluates the expatriate's performance during the assignment; helps clarify the expatriate's career objectives and capabilities before repatriation; and provides career advice and help finding a position back at headquarters. Some divisions even commit to hiring the expatriate manager back into a specific position before the foreign assignment begins.

Executives at several firms with sponsorship programs gave us additional advice. Overall, they recommended that sponsor assignment be systematized. First, the sponsor should be senior enough relative to the expatriate to be able to provide a broad view of the organization. Second, the sponsor should receive specific guidelines about the form, content, and frequency of contacts with the expatriate. Too often the sponsor is simply assigned, and that's it. If the sponsor takes the initiative and fulfills the responsibility, things go well. Otherwise, the sponsorship is in name only. Finally, the responsibility of planning for repatriation should not rest solely with the sponsor but should be incorporated into the firm's career systems.

Provide Pre-departure and Post-arrival Cross-Cultural Training

Most U.S. firms do not provide any cross-cultural training for international assignments. While it may seem that pre-departure training would increase a tendency to identify with the host culture and thus go native, our data indicate that such training creates a sense of obligation to the parent firm stemming from the firm's demonstrated concern for the expatriate.[11] Although we only examined the impact of pre-departure training because fewer than 10% of the expatriates received post-arrival training, we suspect that a similarly positive effect could be generated by providing training after arrival if the expatriate understands that the parent firm, and not the local operation, is paying for and sponsoring the training.

Strategy 2: Counterbalancing Hearts at Home

Although many U.S. executives seem unconcerned with the tendency of expatriates to leave their hearts at home, our research suggests that the consequences of this tendency are just as serious as those for going native. The lack of organizational practices in this area forces us to rely on our research for ways that firms might counterbalance the tendency of managers like Earl Markus to leave their hearts at home.

Send Younger Managers

The managers most likely to be highly committed to the parent firm and much less committed to the local operation are those with long tenures at the parent firm and little international experience. Thus, firms such as GE, GM, and Ford, which are increasingly sending younger managers overseas for career development, are perhaps unintentionally counterbalancing the hearts-at-home tendency.

Facilitate Cross-Cultural Adjustment

Helping the expatriate manager adjust to the non-work environment is another powerful counterbalancing force. Ironically, many of the perks – such as company housing, car, and driver – that are given to senior expatriate executives actually isolate them and inhibit their adjustment to the environment. Family members, especially the spouse, are often more directly exposed to the foreign environment because they do not have the insulation provided by the corporate structure. Therefore, a firm's efforts to facilitate the family's adjustment can have a positive effect on the manager's adjustment.[12]

Provide Cross-Cultural Training for the Family

Ford is one of the few U.S. firms that tries to consistently provide training and preparation for the families and especially spouses of its expatriates. Although Ford executives did not intend this training to counteract the hearts-at-home tendency, our research suggests that this is a likely consequence.

Encourage Host National Sponsorship Programs

Interacting with host nationals outside of work can help both families and managers adjust. Host nationals, who understand their own culture, are the best sources of instruction and especially feedback in getting along on a daily basis. However, such interaction is not always easy to develop. Firms can help by asking host national employees and their families to assist specific expatriates during the first few months. Care should be taken to match the sponsoring family's characteristics (that is, number and ages of children) with those of the expatriate family. Several Japanese auto firms actually have hired Americans who speak Japanese to help their expatriate managers and families adjust to life in the United States.

The Amos Tuck School's joint MBA program with the International University of Japan has a sponsorship program. A special employee in Japan is assigned to help U.S. professors with logistical problems, such as housing and travel, during their stay. Several Tuck professors who spent a term in Japan expressed pleasant surprise at the willingness of both the special employee and other employees to go beyond logistical assistance and to help them navigate the cultural and business terrain. This assistance gave them important insights into the culture and people and helped them adjust to the new environment.

Strategy 3: Creating Dual Citizens

Although these mechanisms are useful for counterbalancing negative tendencies, the most important steps firms can take are those that create high levels of dual allegiance. Our research suggests that the primary target for fostering expatriates like Joan Beckenridge is the job.

Plan Overseas Jobs Strategically

A firm that clearly defines the expatriate's job, reduces conflicts concerning job expectations, and gives the expatriate a fair amount of freedom in carrying out assigned tasks will foster a high level of dual allegiance. The idea is simple, but execution is complex.

One of the easiest but rarely utilized techniques for increasing role clarity is allowing the incumbent and the new manager an overlap period of several days or weeks. The more complex the job and the less experienced the new entrant, the longer the overlap. Several expatriates specifically mentioned this method as a relatively low-cost means of facilitating adjustment and effectiveness. Expatriates in Japan and Korea said that this overlap was necessary for properly introducing the replacement to employees, clients, and suppliers. Of course, sometimes there is no incumbent, and this option is not available.

Role clarification in and of itself does not necessarily reduce role conflict. In fact, clarification of job expectations can reveal previously hidden role conflicts, which most often stem from the differing expectations of the parent firm and the local operation. Thus firms must try to increase role clarity and decrease role conflict simultaneously. This requires understanding and integrating the perspectives of the parent firm and the local operation.

A firm's best intentions cannot entirely eliminate role ambiguity and conflict. This is probably why role discretion emerged as the single strongest factor in promoting high dual allegiance. Having a fair amount of freedom to decide what tasks to do, how and when to do them, and who should do them gives expatriates the flexibility to cope with ambiguity and conflict. However, too much discretion without clear objectives may make expatriates unintentionally work against the best interests of the parent firm, the local operation, or both. Firms need to consider all three job elements simultaneously.

We believe that role clarity, conflict, and discretion are best approached not as targets of manipulation but as outcomes of broader policy and strategic processes. If a firm wants to make significant, long-term, and effective changes in the expatriate manager's job, it should carefully assess the following issues:

1. Why is the expatriate being sent to this particular post? (Because there are no host nationals capable of filling the position? In order to provide developmental experience for the expatriate?)
2. How will job success be measured? What do you really want this particular person to do in this position?
3. Are the objectives of the parent firm and the local unit consistent? Are they consistent between the local unit as a whole and the individual's department?
4. How much should the parent firm coordinate and control the local operation? How much freedom and autonomy should the local unit have? Is the expatriate's level of discretion consistent with these coordination needs?

Without an assessment of these strategic issues, firms may adjust expectations in ways that are dysfunctional for the firm's overall strategy. For instance, firms may provide overlap time that serves only to clarify the severe expectation conflicts between the two organizations. Or firms may give too much freedom to expatriate managers. Consequently, such ad hoc adjustments are likely to have short-term positive results at best and severe negative results at worst. In contrast, an analysis that begins with the broader context naturally leads to appropriate job adjustments and a higher probability of a high dual allegiance.

Some readers may feel that their firms have moved beyond the coordinated multinational stage. Global firms need managers who are capable not just of dual citizenship but of world citizenship. Many firms are moving in this direction, but our data suggest that most expatriate managers are still struggling to successfully reach dual allegiance. It seems to us that the first practical step toward developing global managers for global firms is to develop managers who see themselves as dual citizens. Dual-citizen expatriates are best developed through: (1) careful selection processes; (2) cross-cultural training before and after arrival; (3) well-planned career systems that lead to clear, consistent job expectations and appropriate discretion levels; and (4) repatriation programs that effectively utilize expatriates' knowledge, skills, and experience. These steps will help expatriates more successfully serve two masters and help firms more effectively manage their expatriates.

Notes

1. H. B. Gregersen and J. S. Black, "Antecedents to Dual Commitment during International Assignments," *Academy of Management Journal*, 35 (1992): 65–90. This article is based primarily on two international research projects. First, we did a questionnaire study of 321 U.S. expatriate executives and managers while they were on assignment in Europe (Belgium, England, the Netherlands, and Germany) and the Pacific Rim (Japan, Korea, Taiwan, and Hong Kong). These expatriates had worked on average more than fourteen years in their U.S. multinational firms representing a wide range of industries. We also completed in-depth interviews with more than thirty expatriates in both Pacific Rim and European countries. Second, we completed a study of expatriate commitment during repatriation for 174 Americans, 173 Japanese, and 104 Finns returning to their respective home countries after international assignments.

2. C. V. Fukami and E. W. Larson, "Commitment to the Company and Union: Parallel Models," *Journal of Applied Psychology*, 69 (1984): 367–371; M. E. Gordon and R. T. Ladd, "Dual Allegiance: Renewal, Reconsideration, and Recantation," *Personnel Psychology*, 43 (1990): 37–69; H. B. Gregersen, "Multiple Commitments at Work and Extrarole Behavior during Three Stages of Organizational Tenure," *Journal of Business Research*, 25 (1992); and N. B. Tuma and A. J. Grimes, "A Comparison of Models of Role Orientations of Professionals in a Research-Oriented University," *Administrative Science Quarterly*, 26 (1981): 187–206.

3. J. S. Black, "Personal Dimensions and Work Role Transitions," *Management International Review*, 30 (1990): 119–134; and M. E. Mendenhall and G. Oddou, "The Dimensions of Expatriate Acculturation," *Academy of Management Review*, 10 (1985): 39–47.

4. J. S. Black and M. Mendenhall, "Cross-Cultural Training Effectiveness: A Review and a Theoretical Framework for Future Research," *Academy of Management Review*, 15 (1990): 113–136.

5. J. S. Black, "Work Role Transitions: A Study of U.S. Expatriate Managers in Japan," *Journal of International Business Studies*, 19 (1988): 277–294; J. S. Black and H. B. Gregersen, "Antecedents to Cross-Cultural Adjustment for Expatriates in Pacific Rim Assignments," *Human Relations*, 44 (1990): 497–515; L. Copeland and L. Griggs, *Going International* (New York: Random House, 1985); and K. F. Misa and J. M. Fabricatore, "Return on Investment of Overseas Personnel," *Financial Executive*, 47 (1979): 42–46.

6. See R. L. Tung, *The New Expatriates* (Lexington, MA: Lexington Books, 1988) for a review.

7. J. S. Black and L. W. Porter, "Managerial Behavior and Job Performance: A Successful Manager in Los Angeles May Not Be Successful in Hong Kong," *Journal of International Business Studies*, 22 (1991): 99–114; and E. Miller, "The International Selection Decision: A Study of Managerial Behavior in the Selection Decision Process," *Academy of Management Journal*, 16 (1973): 234–252.

8. M. Porter, "Changing Patterns of International Competition," *California Management Review*, Winter (1986): 9–10.

9. H. B. Gregersen, "Commitments to a Parent Company and a Local Work Unit during Repatriation," *Personnel Psychology*, 45 (1992): 29–54.

10. M. G. Harvey, "Repatriation of Corporate Executives," *Journal of International Business Studies*, Spring (1989): 131–144.

11. Research consistently shows that good pre-departure training helps expatriate managers adjust to and perform well in their jobs overseas. See Black and Mendenhall, "Cross-Cultural Training."

12. See also J. S. Black and G. K. Stephens, "The Influence of the Spouse on U.S. Expatriate Adjustment in Overseas Assignments," *Journal of Management*, 15 (1989): 529–544.

○ ○

Andersen Consulting (Europe): Entering the Business of Business Integration

Mary Ackenhusen and Sumantra Ghoshal

A partner in Andersen Consulting defined its business as "helping clients manage complexity." As information systems technology progressed over the decades, Andersen emerged as the world's largest information systems consulting company through "analyzing and then systematizing business' current information requirements into commodity products and then quickly proceeding to the next tier of complexity." According to Terry Neill, head of services for the company's UK office: "Andersen's greatest challenge is constant commoditization of its products and services. Our success depends on our ability to stay ahead of the commoditization envelope."

In the 1940s, Andersen's expertise lay in designing the complex manual accounting processes required in corporations to meet the increased reporting demanded by the Securities and Exchange Commission (SEC) in the United States. The business had become routine by the 1950s with many companies able to do the work as efficiently and cost-effectively as Andersen, but by this time Andersen had moved on to the next emerging business system requirement which had never been done before: payroll systems. These had become commonplace by the 1960s and the firm had proceeded on to the development and integration of computerized accounting and payroll systems. Likewise, with the introduction of personal computers, networks, and fast-paced change in the capability of hardware and software, the 1970s and 1980s offered a constant stream of new opportunities as the company's clients struggled to exploit these new technologies to manage the increasing complexity of their businesses.

The emerging business integration market, described by Andersen as the clients' need for an integrated business, information, and people strategy was the company's

This case was written by Mary Ackenhusen, Research Associate, under the supervision of Sumantra Ghoshal, Associate Professor at INSEAD. It is intended to be used as a basis for class discussion rather than to illustrate either effective or ineffective handling of an administrative situation. Reprinted with the permission of INSEAD. © 1992 INSEAD, Fontainebleau, France.

target for the 1990s. Building from its unequaled strength in systems integration, Andersen sought to broaden its capabilities so as to be able to help clients formulate and implement strategic thrusts that encompassed all activities and functions on an integrated basis.

This new business vision presented an enormous challenge for the company. While there was a broad agreement among the senior partners on the need for pursuing the business-integration market, there were considerable differences of opinion on how to implement the strategy without sacrificing the strengths inherent in Andersen's traditional organizational values and management processes. There were also some significant differences in the market structures in different countries that called for a delicate balancing between the need for a coherent worldwide business integration strategy and the demand for different implementation approaches to suit the context of different national operations. Further, the thrust into the business integration market also required the development of two new skill areas – namely, strategy and change management – and the seamless integration of those skills into the existing organizations which supported Andersen's unique strengths in systems integration and information technology. To integrate the client's business, Andersen needed first to integrate its own business, which could prove to be the most difficult task the company had faced yet.

Arthur Andersen and Company

In 1913, Arthur Andersen, the son of Scandinavian immigrant parents, purchased a small audit firm in Chicago which has since grown into the major accounting and consulting firm of Arthur Andersen. Andersen's vision was to establish "a firm that will do more than routine auditing . . . a firm where we can measure our contribution more by the quality of the services rendered than by whether we are getting a good living out of it." For more than three-quarters of a century, his philosophies have continued to influence the firm's culture as well as the profession of accounting as a whole.

Andersen wanted to build a practice with intelligent, well-trained people, but he could not find them through the profession's traditional method of hiring high school and commercial school graduates. At this time he was also teaching accounting at Northwestern (a major U.S. business school) and he began recruiting his brightest students. This meant he had to pay more for his staff, but he found that the extra productivity and comprehensive understanding of business they brought with them was worth the higher cost. Andersen also started the then-unheard of practice of paying his employees during their training period. In other accounting firms, the employee paid the firm during this period of apprenticeship.

Andersen ingrained in his company the concept that the client always came first, regardless of personal sacrifice – evenings and weekends were not sacred. "The client deserves our best, regardless." To help support this philosophy, Andersen initiated the practice of paying overtime to his employees in the face of strong criticism from the major accounting firms of the day.

Extensive professional training, which became a well-known distinguishing feature of the company, had its roots in the 1920s. Training was strongly advocated by Andersen, beginning with mandatory lectures given by him and by other senior partners several times a week in the office and expanding to a rigorous course developed in the 1940s designed to teach common standards to all U.S. Andersen employees. From the beginning, these courses were taught by insiders. It was Andersen's belief that "lectures should be given by men in our own organization who have pedagogical inclinations because these men [understand] our methods and procedures."

The culture built by Andersen was one of inscrutable professional honesty even at the cost of losing a client. He always said that if the staff "thought straight and talked straight," they would earn the respect of clients. According to former CEO Duane Kullberg: "Those remain words we live by – not simply a hand-me-down slogan."

The firm outpaced market growth in the 1950s and 1960s, expanding internationally and domestically through a mixture of a few high-quality acquisitions and the establishment of new offices. This period also saw the beginnings of the consulting arm of the business which helped fuel growth in the 1970s when the market for audit began to stagnate. The consulting business continued to be the major impetus for growth through the 1980s.

Andersen Consulting

The origins of the Andersen Consulting practice lay in the industrial engineering function sponsored by the firm's founder, the purpose being to "show the strong or weak points in company position or management, and seek to correct such weak spots." This function was given second priority to the audit business through the 1940s until, in 1951, Joe Glickauf, an influential partner, built a copy of an advanced-design computer which had been developed at the University of Pennsylvania. When he presented it to the partners with his vision of what it could mean for the future of business systems, they voted to give full support to the development of the area. The implementation of an automated payroll system at GE in 1952 was Andersen's first computer-based project – it is believed to be the first commercial application of a computer.

Since the 1950s, Andersen's consulting business has grown quickly with the advancement of information technology and its capabilities. The strong culture and training infrastructure established by Arthur Andersen for the accounting practice have proven to be key strengths in this business also. Initially, clients came from the customer base in the audit business but by 1990 their share had declined to less than 20%. By 1990, Andersen Consulting had emerged as the largest player in information systems consulting and was, in fact, the largest consulting company in the world, with over 20,000 professionals, operating in more than fifty countries. Worldwide revenues of $1.9 billion represented a compounded annual growth rate of 30% between 1985 and 1990 (see Exhibit 1). The company designed and implemented large-scale information systems and provided all associated services including programming and training of client personnel. Andersen also developed and marketed its own proprietary software and was an increasingly active player in the business of facilities management (that is, managing computer operations outsourced by its clients).

Andersen, the man, always stressed homogeneity within Andersen, the firm, with his maxim, "one firm, one voice." Continuous reinforcement of this principle through standardized training and extensive formalization of work procedures positioned the

EXHIBIT 1   Andersen Consulting Financial Summary

	Worldwide			EMEAI		
Year	Net Revenues ($MM)	Partners	Professionals	Net Revenues ($MM)	Partners	Professionals
1991	2,256	755	21,668	908	191	7,751
1990	1,850	692	18,188	663	172	6,263
1989	1,433	586	15,373	465	143	4,974
1988	1,106	529	12,009	360	123	3,743
1987	828	469	9,231	236	108	2,858

Source: company document.

EXHIBIT 2   Worldwide Organization

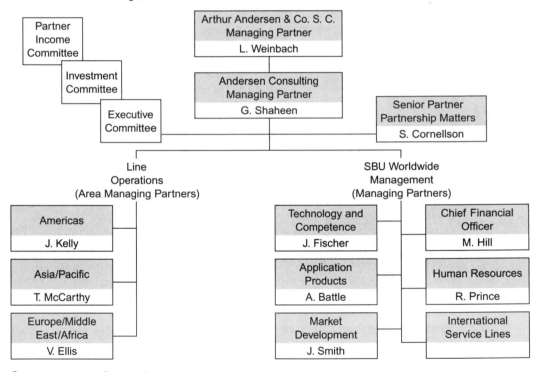

Source: company document.

firm for consistent service and methods across all offices and all countries. By the late 1980s, maintenance of the "one firm" concept became increasingly difficult as Andersen began to branch off into two distinctly different businesses – audit and tax, on the one hand, and consulting, on the other – with vastly different professional norms, market structures, business approaches, and compensation levels in the two activities. Matters came to a head with the increasing demand of consulting partners for remuneration consistent with the significantly higher profitability and growth of the consulting practice, and in 1988 the two businesses were formally separated into two divisions. The consulting arm was renamed Andersen Consulting and was given the freedom to develop its own compensation system and management structure (Exhibit 2). While a twenty-four-member board of partners retained responsibility for providing oversight of the company as a whole, both strategic business units now had significant strategic and operational autonomy so that each could respond most effectively to its own market and business needs.

Andersen Consulting (Europe, Middle East, Africa, and India)

Andersen Consulting in Europe, the Middle East, Africa, and India (EMEAI) emerged as a separate entity when the management of the tax/audit and consulting businesses was divided. In 1990, Andersen EMEAI had offices in eighteen countries staffed with 6,500 professionals who generated total 1990 billings of $695 million. This made it the largest consultancy in Europe in terms of gross revenues. The EMEAI practice had been growing at a rate of 28% per year in people terms over the preceding five years.

The Andersen organization (see Exhibit 3 for the EMEAI organizational structure) was built around a geographic base of country practices. A matrix structure, including industry functions, specialty skills, and functional skills was overlaid on top of this legally autonomous aggregation of national practices, creating an organization of considerable complexity.

Each country or country group was managed by a country managing partner who had reporting to him or her, three industry sector heads and several heads of specialty skill or functional areas. The three industry sectors were financial services, industrial and consumer products, and government and services. The number and types of specialty and functional heads depended on the size and expertise of the office and included strategy and change management. Every professional in a country reported to either an industry, specialty skills, or functional head. Additionally, larger countries often had a varying number of industry subsector heads (that is, oil and gas) and functional managers (that is, logistics). These partners had no direct reports and reported into one of the industry sectors.

Each country was responsible for effectively utilizing its professionals to meet annual, and multiannual, fee, and productivity targets. A country managing partner's most important job was the management of his or her people resource to assure they were either utilized within the country practice or loaned out to support a job outside the country practice and therefore still effectively utilized.

Vernon Ellis, the managing partner of EMEAI, was based in the United Kingdom. Each country's managing partner reported to him, as did the European heads of each of the three industry sectors and the heads of the specialty and functional skill areas. These regional sector or functional managers were responsible for practice leadership, which included setting strategy and assisting in the staffing and execution of projects in their respective areas, and were linked to their counterparts in the country offices through what were referred to as "dotted line relationships."

EXHIBIT 3 Andersen Consulting EMEAI Organization

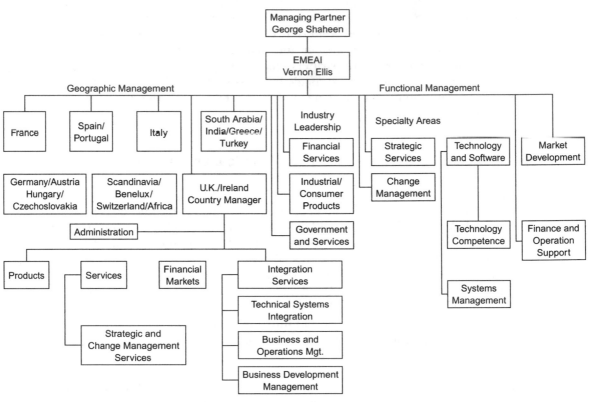

Source: company document.

The Andersen Way

While all professional service firms assert that people are their key asset, at Andersen Consulting this assertion was translated into a set of institutionalized practices that lay at the core of what was often described both within and outside the company as the "Andersen way." The company invested heavily in building the capabilities of its people and the systems which supported them. These assets were then effectively leveraged through the project team structure to provide value to the client.

Building Capabilities: Developing People

The training infrastructure was one of the key distinguishing features of Andersen. Every new employee worldwide was required to take a six-week course, Computer Application Programming School (CAPS), taught in Andersen's luxurious St. Charles (Illinois) education facility which was referred to, not inappropriately, as "the university." This rigorous course taught the fundamentals of computer applications and programming through intensive work sessions designed to simulate project work at a client site. Eighty-hour weeks and the requirement of business attire throughout the program made the simulation realistic and also emphasized that "at Andersen, training is serious business." The same methods were used to teach liberal arts majors and engineers alike in the Andersen methodology of systems design and implementation. As one senior partner described:

> CAPS is a real shock at first . . . you wonder how you'll be able to keep up, it is very intense . . . , but then you find that everyone is in this together and you begin working as a team helping each other to pull through. And since then, this group has been my main network within the company. The experience created a career-long bond with these cohorts.

Andersen Consulting educated all its professionals in a uniform approach to each aspect of a job whether it was systems design, programming, project management, or writing a proposal for new business. The tools were designed to eliminate any ambiguity in the nuts and bolts of a project. This common tool set embodied in numerous, thick reference manuals were used worldwide to assure consistency in firm performance and to enhance the ability of consultants from different countries and disciplines to work together. In combination, the uniform training program at St. Charles with the immense documentation tools provided the core of Andersen's success in management information consulting: the ability to hire new undergraduates and in six weeks turn them into productive, billable programmers.

Training continued throughout a professional's career with a standardized system that required everyone to spend nearly 1,000 hours over a five-year period in training, undertaking a prespecified set of courses at predesignated intervals (see Exhibit 4). All training still conformed to Andersen's original contention that the best teacher came from within, allowing the more senior professionals to impart their learning to the new recruits. All offices of the company around the world were allocated a fixed number of hours of training they had to staff and faculty roles were allocated within the office among partners and other experienced staff. The internal faculty was supplied with standard material for teaching their classes, but was also encouraged to embellish their sessions with examples from their most recent assignments. These new case stories were then incorporated into the teaching material that was provided to the next faculty for the same sessions. Approximately £35,000 was spent on a new employee in the first five years and an extraordinary 10% of Andersen's revenue was allocated to professional training. Internally, training was emphasized as an important benefit of working for Andersen: "Your skills aren't just good news for the client. After training with Andersen Consulting, you could work for anyone, anywhere or you could work for yourself."

The majority of Andersen's recruiting had historically been targeted at young undergraduates directly out of university. Each recruit had to undergo extensive interviewing and the objective was to seek out bright achievers who could best be "molded" into the Andersen pattern with the expectation of a long career in the firm. Recruiting was a major activity for all professionals at Andersen's including the partners.

EXHIBIT **4**   Graduate to Manager

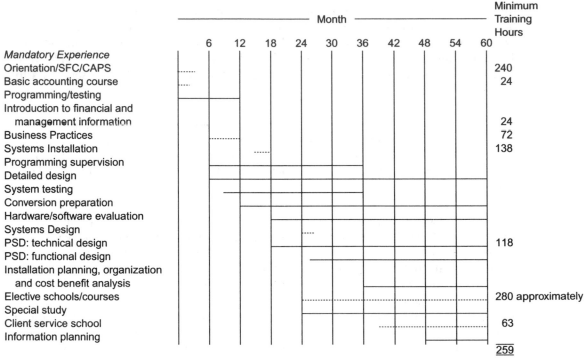

Notes: (1) Start and finish points are the earliest and latest respectively; (2) Number of days is the minimum requirement; (3) This sets out the guidelines for the *minimum* path to manager; (4) Training programmes are set in bold, others represent work experience.
Source: company document.

Likewise, the development and nurturing of new recruits was an important part of upper management's role. Andersen partners were involved in subordinate development through a formal counselling program. Each new employee was assigned a counselling partner upon arrival and met with this partner every six months to discuss performance, career interests, and other pertinent topics. Each partner counselled twenty to thirty professional personnel.

The typical career path with Andersen Consulting began with one to two years as an assistant consultant working mainly on large systems integration projects as a programmer, with regular formal and informal training in information technology and business skills. The next three to five years as a senior consultant were spent broadening technical and business skills in client engagements with more specialized training. In five to eight years, a professional could be expected to take on the role of project manager and in nine to twelve years, most recruits still with the firm would be expected to become a partner.

Like universities, Andersen followed the up or out principles of a meritocracy: each individual either performed well and moved up the ladder, or left the firm, opening up opportunities for those behind in the queue. The evaluation process was tough: only 50–60% of new professional recruits would make manager and perhaps 10% would ever become a partner.

Assistant and senior consultants were evaluated on their performance every three months by their project managers. The evaluations were taken very seriously by both sides and were a valuable tool for performance improvement. Theoretically, project managers were evaluated themselves every six months by their project partner, but these often turned into self-evaluations due to limited partner time for the process. Consultant and manager compensation was strictly based on merit, though the range between an outstanding performer and a satisfactory performer was less than in other comparable companies. There was no bonus or profit-sharing below the partner level.

To facilitate personal development and professional contacts, Andersen Consulting prided itself on its vast and varied methods of communication within the firm. Every industry, functional, and country group had at least one newsletter which helped the fast-paced professionals stay on top of new projects, successes, and issues in their areas of interest. Likewise, these groups often sponsored conferences and circulated files of interesting papers on current issues. For those consultants with a wide area of interest, oversaturation, not lack of communication, was the problem.

The ongoing training at St. Charles and the European center in Eindhoven in Holland provided professional and social stimulation. To help retain a small-firm feeling, personnel groups of 100–200 people were formed solely for the purpose of regular social gatherings. Upward communication with the partners was also facilitated through informal partner/manager dinners held on a regular basis.

The end result was a strong cultural glue which helped Andersen employees to understand each others' objectives, methods, and motivations across offices and functions. They grew up together after college with the same experiences and values. As one manager remarked: "It's hard for outsiders to work at Andersen. They just don't know our vocabulary, our systems. While those who grow up in Andersen can carry out a task based on one sentence directions, an outsider will be lost. Andersens' can think alike." Other firms in the industry expressed both their envy and their scorn for this strong internal homogeneity by the label "Andersen Androids" which was almost a source of pride within the company.

Leveraging Capabilities: Managing Project Teams

The project team was the main organizational unit of Andersen for leveraging the capabilities of its people to deliver value to the client. Each team was made up of at least one partner, one manager, and a number of junior level consultants, and utilized the worldwide network of experts to participate on the team or advise. The ratio of partner time to consultant time attributed to the project determined the economics of the project and, therefore, of the firm. At Andersen, the partner to consultant ratio was very low with, for example, only 180 partners out of 6,500 professionals in EMEAI, which resulted in high compensation for the partners leveraged off the large base of associate and senior consultants. Somewhat offsetting the favorable economics of a high consultant-to-partner ratio, target utilization rates were lower than the industry norm due to the

EXHIBIT 5   Economics for Typical Professional Service Firm

	Relative Number of Professionals by Level	Relative Net Billings per Head by Level	Relative Compensation of Professionals by Level
Consultant	100	100	100
Manager	40	156	250
Partner	20	208	633

Key Assumptions
1   Target utilization: consultant (90%), manager (75%), partner (75%)
2.   Relative net billing per head = relative billing rate/hours × utilization rate × available hours; relative billing rate/hours: associate (100), manager (187), partner (250)
3.   Relative compensation = salary + bonus
Source: "Professional Service Firm Management," D. Maister, 1985.

emphasis on training and other forms of personnel development. Target rates for partner, manager, and consultant levels were 50%, 75%, and 80%, respectively. Nevertheless, this ability to leverage the expertise of partners across a large base of consultants was why Andersen partners were among the most highly compensated in the industry. (See Exhibit 5 to review the economics of a typical professional service firm.)

A project manager was chosen by the partner managing the case, based on skills, past experience, and availability. The company had a database detailing each professional's skills and experience by industry and client, as well as his or her current assignment and availability. Partners complained, however, that it was too hard to codify all the important characteristics of a team player and the database was typically used only as a last resort. The personal networks of the partners were often more important for selecting project managers and later staffing the teams.

With the partner's guidance, the project manager built the team and provided day-to-day management in the execution of the project. To staff a project, the manager would call on the worldwide resources of Andersen to get the proper fit. For example, for a project at Jaguar, the U.K. office, which had done relatively little work in the automotive field, borrowed personnel from the Paris office, which had worked extensively with Renault and Peugeot. The manager was also responsible for meeting budget and time commitments and for the professional development of team members. People management was a very important part of this job.

Availability was the key to forming a team, and therefore the scheduling database, which detailed who was available and when, was the most utilized formal database within Andersen. Each consultant was expected to be 80% utilized on client projects, with the other 20% of his or her time being spent in training, other personal development activities, or downtime. The Andersen culture would rarely allow someone to be pulled from a case before its completion: the client's needs came before the business's. Therefore, there was a relatively limited pool of available talent to be placed on a team and there were considerable pressures to utilize anyone not currently on a team. Though Andersen professionals had some latitude in choosing projects which met their own career-development needs, most conceded that the system did not and probably could not be expected to support this objective fully.

Providing Stewardship: The Role of Partners

Partners at Andersen spent 50% of their time on case work, 25% selling new projects, and 25% on development of subordinates. The partners were seen as the entrepreneurs of the business because they traditionally developed their own portfolio of business based on their own contacts and interests.

Each partner owned a piece of the firm and participated in the management of the firm on a one-person, one-vote basis. According to one partner: "This is how we challenge sacred cows. Ownership is a great driver of arguments and strong opinions."

Partners shared costs on a worldwide basis. Partner income was determined by a distribution formula based on the number of his or her units. Unit allocations were set by a partner committee which evaluated business generated, business performed, development of personnel, teamwork, practice leadership, unique skills, and other areas. Practice management partners evaluated all partners working for them and other partners could contribute to the review process as they felt appropriate. All management partners were evaluated by a comprehensive process of upward evaluation which was set up to be non-attributable, though many partners chose to discuss their feedback with the management partners they were evaluating. All partners received a listing of the unit allocations of every other partner in the world. Though there was an appeal process, it was rarely used. In general, the partners approved of the fairness of the evaluation and compensation systems. As described by one: "It may not be perfect every year, but over a period of time, everyone seems to get what they are due."

The partners saw themselves as the stewards of the firm who should continue to strengthen the firm for those who would follow. Sacrificing immediate personal income for the long-term benefit of the firm was a cherished norm. The first international expansion of the company in 1957 provides a good example. The proposal to open new offices in Paris, London, and Mexico was brought to the partners' meeting after the profits for the year had already been disbursed to them. Client needs required immediate opening of these offices, and the partners decided to pay back 40% of their income so that the firm could expand even though many of them would not serve in the company long enough to reap the benefits. Likewise, year after year, the partners continued to approve the tremendous investment in the training of future generations of Andersens. When a partner retired he took with him only his initial capital investment in the firm, and no appreciation or goodwill accumulated over his period of partnership. One partner reflected: "The style of the organization is set by high-quality people with high values which we pass on to the next generation. It's a strong cultural influence."

The Business of Business Integration

The information technology (IT) consulting business could be divided into two broad segments. The first segment, also the larger and the more traditional of the two, was the IT professional-services market that included custom software development, consulting, education and training, and systems operations. The other, more complex, segment was the systems-integration market, which was when one company took the technical and administrative responsibility for tying together information networks potentially involving multiple hardware and software vendors and multiple corporate functions. Systems integration projects usually ranged from $1–10 million in the commercial sector, but could go as high as $100 million for large-scale government projects.

In 1989, the IT professional service market for Europe exceeded $15 billion and was growing at the rate of 20% per year. The 1994 market size was expected to approach $39 billion, of which 68% was attributed to custom software development. The systems integration market was only $1.9 billion in 1989 but was expected to grow to $6 billion by 1994 (over 30% per year), with over half of this revenue coming from associated consulting services. In comparison, the systems integration market in the United States had grown to $8.8 billion by 1990 and was expected to grow to $20.5 billion by 1995.

Both the size and growth rate made the systems-integration and professional-services markets very enticing to most key competitors in the information field. The high growth rate was attributable to the decentralization of in-house information systems departments, fast-paced technological changes with the associated new product introductions, the externalization of in-house corporate services, and the ongoing restructuring of major industrial markets.

European competition in such attractive markets was stiff and was continuing to attract new entrants. In professional services, the market was quite fragmented with the key competitors being: IBM (5.3%); Cap Gemini Sogeti, the French software multinational (4.7%); and Volmac, a Dutch software company which received 90% of its revenues from the Netherlands (2.0%). Andersen was ranked number thirteen with a 0.8% market share. The top three competitors in systems integration and their European market shares were IBM (12.5%), Cap Gemini Sogeti (11.8%), and Andersen Consulting (10.2%) (see Exhibit 6 for other competitors).

Many of these companies also competed in the related businesses of facilities management and packaged software. Facilities management was an important market because it could often be an entry into a systems-integration project; likewise, it helped systems-integration firms hone their technical skills. Packaged software was important because many clients demanded standardized solutions from a vendor before they would consider a later purchase of professional services. Andersen Consulting had become quite active in both markets.

From Systems Integration to Business Integration

The systems-integration market had been experiencing serious quality problems as projects fell short of client expectations in functionality, cost, and completion deadlines. It was increasingly believed that the potential of IT could not be realized until a firm had a clear business strategy to direct the use of IT and had made the necessary organizational changes for IT to support a new way of doing business. Overlay of new IT capabilities on existing business practices rarely yielded the potential or expected benefits: the real payoff lay in utilizing the new technology to support fundamental redirection of business strategy and management processes. This realization was the driving force behind the need for an integrated business philosophy and hence the potential of

EXHIBIT 6 IT Professional Services and Systems Integration (Europe) – Key Competitors

Company	1988 European Prof. Services Est. Revenue ($MM)	1988 European Prof. Services Market Share (%)	1988 European Systems Integr. Est. Revenue ($MM)	1988 European Systems Integr. Market Share (%)	1989 World Revenue ($MM)	1989 World Profit ($MM)	Revenue CAGR (%) 1986–1989	Profit CAGR (%) 1986–1989
IBM	660	5.3	190	12.5	62,710	3,758	6.3	–7.8
CAP Gemini	590	4.7	180	11.8	1,202	89.4	34	40
Volmac	245	2.0	*	*	283	53	12†	4.1†
Finsel	225	1.8	*	*	625	N/A	N/A	N/A
SEMA	220	1.8	80	5.3	478	18	55	44
Bull	220	1.8	35	2.3	5,890	–48	23	N/A
Olivetti	200	1.6	45	2.9	7,406	166	7.3	–29
Unisys	180	1.4	55	3.6	10,097	–639	11	–145
Digital	140	1.1	*	*	12,742	1,073	19	20
SD-Scicon	140	1.1	85	5.6	462	5	66	3
Andersen	105	.8	155	10.2	1,442	N/A	31	N/A
Logica	75	.6	65	4.3	280	20	29	42
Siemens	80	.6	65	4.3	32,398	836	8	2
Others	9,470	75	962	63	–	–	–	–
Total	12,550	100	1,520	100				

* Market share is insignificant and included in "others."
† CAGR is 1987–1989
Source: company document.

a business-integration consulting market as the next level of complexity beyond the systems-integration market.

According to Andersen's preliminary market research, only a few European clients recognized the need to better integrate their functional consulting requirements to produce an integrated business strategy through the engagement of one firm. Nevertheless, the company felt confident the market was going that way and had decided to build the competencies and infrastructure to exploit what they expected to be the new opportunity of the 1990s.

Key competitors in the emerging business-integration market were potentially the same as in the systems-integration market, with the addition of the general consulting firms. The traditional software and hardware companies such as Cap Gemini, IBM, and DEC were considered to be strong competitors with perhaps unequaled technical expertise but lacking in project-management skills. Systems integrators like SD-Scicon and SEMA, two European-based companies specializing in software services and integration, were also seen to be technically strong and farther along in the task of building the needed project-management skills. The large accounting firms were serious competitors in terms of project-management skills, with less perceived competence in technical areas. Lastly, the general consulting firms, McKinsey, PA Consulting, and others, had excellent reputations for their ability to develop and implement corporate strategies, easy access to corporate board rooms, some experience in systems design, but minimal systems-implementation experience.

Many of these companies had already begun to prepare for an expanded business-integration market by taking action to broaden their skill base or geographic scope through mergers, acquisitions, and alliances. IBM had taken minority positions in numerous companies with large European market shares, and Andersen had developed numerous strategic alliances with companies such as DEC, IBM, and Sun Microsystems. SEMA and SD-Scicon were both results of recent mergers.

Andersen's Entry into Business Integration

The need to link an IT project to the rest of the business was not a new concept to Andersen, though it was not formally recognized as Andersen's strategic thrust under the name of "business integration" until 1988. Even before formal recognition of the strategy, specialists were being groomed in two key areas where Andersen did not yet have a reputation and skill base: namely strategy and human-resource change management. In 1987, these became the separate practice areas of strategic services and change management. Shortly thereafter, the formal concept of business integration with its associated four bubble graphic (see Exhibit 7) was adopted by Andersen Consulting, who described business integration as:

> A seamless combination of skills from each of the four areas: strategy, technology, operations, and people. In developing business solutions it [is] necessary to consider all four areas and select in the appropriate balance, using different proportions in different situations. [This requires] people who are not narrowly based in a single discipline but who combine knowledge and understanding of each of these different areas.

EXHIBIT 7   The Business of Business Integration

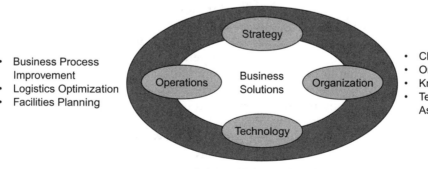

Source: company document.

In support of the four functions, four centers of excellence were formed: strategic services, change management, operations, and information technology. The strategic services group worked with clients to develop and implement successful strategies in all areas of corporate activity. The change management group worked with organizations to position their people, processes, and technology to master change with maximum benefits. The operations group helped clients develop effective day-to-day processes, including implementation of JIT systems, plant relayouts, quality assurance systems, and so on, and the Information Technology group contained very specialized hardware and software experts to assist in implementing state-of-the-art customer solutions. For most country organizations, only strategic services and change management were distinct skill sets; operations and information technology were still located within other functional or industry groups.

These specialty areas were geared to building up repeat and continuous experience in their respective areas of a world-class nature. The IT generalist background of a standard Andersen consultant was deemed unsuitable to efficiently support these speciality areas to the level needed to compete in the emerging business-integration market. As described by Vernon Ellis: "You could try to produce a complete Renaissance man but it is impossible these days. The business world is too complex. . . . We need both generalists and specialists. Some people will be in just one bubble, some in the middle of all the bubbles, and some at specific intersections."

In numbers, these specialists were few compared to the rest of Andersen. In 1989–90, there were 170 strategy specialists and 290 change specialists within EMEAI. The majority of Andersen professionals were the IT generalists (the "engine room," as described by one consultant) in the middle of the graphic bubble chart – although the vast majority of these "IT generalists" specialized in an industry or industry sector. IT generalists were the people doing the execution and had a "delivery mechanism" skill set. They were expected to have a good general business understanding of each of the specialist areas as well as a thorough knowledge of the IT area, Andersen's traditional strength. The project manager's challenge was to glue the expertise of the specialists and the business understanding of the generalists together into a successful project team.

The Experience at National Power

A business-integration case often developed through an evolutionary process. As described by Vernon Ellis: "Usually we start with one aspect of a project and hopefully it broadens into a business integration project. Our aim is not to sell more work but to make sure the end result is better implementation."

National Power in the United Kingdom was recently given the mandate to privatize and called on Andersen Consulting to assist them in this major operational, organizational, and cultural change. Tim Forrest, who was also the industry head for oil and gas energy in Europe, served as the partner on the initial engagement.

The team was composed of fifteen Andersen consultants and included specialists from each of the centers of excellence. Forrest estimated that the project fell into the four areas of business integration as follows: strategy (10–15%), information technology (40–50%), operations (25%), and change management (15%).

The first three months were spent deciding on the new mission of the company. The objectives articulated by National Power upon engaging Andersen were: (1) to become a cost-effective supplier of electricity, (2) to take advantage of market opportunities, and (3) to diversify into new businesses to optimize revenue.

Tim Forrest gave his view on what Andersen offered as strategic input to this mission:

> It was really to make the strategy work. It was partly to flesh out the ideas they had, because they were very conceptual. Within each area, there were myriad things that needed to be done in every part of the organization. The strategic services people talked to a variety of National Power managers at different levels to get some specific definitions of what the company would do differently in the future and to ascertain what it would take to do those things differently.

In evaluating the contribution of the change management personnel, Forrest commented:

> Initially they were focused on IT because the IT department had been 1,200 people two years ago. At the beginning of the year it was split three ways . . . 300 were all that was left. . . . Basically they were in a very depressed state, they didn't know what the company was trying to do. . . . They didn't understand the IT strategy or the business strategy, so initially the change management people were very much focused on talking to as many senior people as they could within the IT department to find out what their concerns were. . . . Once they got these people reasonably motivated and fired up, they then started to optimize the communication the other way [to the user community].

The technology and operations content of National Power was the type of work that Andersen had specialized in for many years. After developing strategic objectives, critical success factors, and key performance indicators for each area, elaborate IT systems and operational systems were designed in the areas of work management, inventory management, operational information, and project management systems.

In evaluating the relationship between the various centers of excellence and the generalist practice, Tim Forrest stated:

> The core of the business is still the same [the IT/operations concentration]. Change management helps us to do lots of things we've done for the last twenty years, only we now do them very much better. There's nothing particularly new about change management, . . . they're extremely good at forcing us to think more about cultural change and the impact of technology on people . . . quite honestly, the strategy input is a bit the same, or at least on many projects it is like that. Strategy is forcing the project team to think: "Well what are we really trying to do with this system?" . . . In relation to our main practice, it is the discipline that helps us do our main job better.

The Challenge of Managing Complexity

By 1990, the strategy of business integration had been well communicated and widely accepted within Andersen, though there were some different internal views on how the company was pursuing the market. Vernon Ellis recognized this lack of clarity: "There are still conferences and debates on the strategy, which reflects an emerging understanding with no clear answer yet. We may be actually facing dichotomies to a certain extent which are not capable of resolution."

Balancing Conflicting Demands

At the core of these dichotomies lay the conflicting needs for building best-in-class capabilities in each of the skill areas needed to support the business integration strategy and the demand for integrating those skills internally in a manner that would provide Andersen with some competitive advantage over the scores of other companies targeting the same opportunity. As described by Terry Neill:

> We are the best in the business-systems piece. What goes with strategy or change is that we have to be the best in each piece. In strategy, there are established leaders like McKinsey, and our challenge is to develop a reputation as good as theirs. The change management business is still fragmented, just like the IT marketplace in the 1960s and 1970s, with small "guru"-style firms and individuals. We are doing the same thing in change management that we did there.

Gerard Van Kemmel, managing partner of France agreed: "I don't believe clients will buy a business-integration project unless the supplier is the most skilled and best value in each area. Otherwise, a customer will hire the best firms and integrate themselves."

The other internal viewpoint stressed the importance of integrating the functional pieces of a customer solution.

> I don't think we want our strategic services practice to be the same as McKinsey's. We want the market to accept that we do strategic services work, but if that was all we had, we would be no better than McKinsey. I think that's why the integration bit, the fact that we can talk readily across into the other areas, and that we offer the portfolio, is a very strong message. Otherwise, we could just divide the building into four wings and put McKinsey down one wing, Andersen down another wing, someone who was good at change in another wing, and then some technology experts down the fourth wing.

And, while the two perspectives were not necessarily contradictory, their operational implications were not easy to reconcile. As described by an external industry analyst:

> If you want to be the best in each piece, you have to grow each activity separately – specialize each group with the most challenging assignments dedicated to its particular area. If you want to really integrate, you need to develop a different model of what strategy and change is all about, redefining them from the perspective of integrated delivery. Best-in-class specialization and effective integration require not just different structures and management processes, but even different definitions and visions of what each bubble represents.

Further, some differences of views still lingered on the right balance between allowing individual partners and local practices the freedom to develop their businesses entrepreneurially, identifying and exploiting local opportunities, and the need for pursuing a coherent worldwide business integration strategy. As described by Ellis:

Historically, our partners have been entrepreneurs, and that is how Andersen has been so successful. Partners built their own practices based on their skills, interests, and contacts. They managed the projects start to finish. Now we need a different approach. A worldwide strategy requires that the partner finds the best person for each job, and often that person may not be him. We need a change in the partner mindset.

Terry Neill also suggested that perhaps there was a need to consider some fundamental organizational changes to adapt to the new strategic approach,

Everyone here is a doer – that's our style – but sometimes we don't have enough people fully dedicated to thinking things through and that, sometimes, shows up. We have had occasional false starts. Perhaps we need a dedicated internal strategy and planning group – with young partners spending two or three years in the role – in much the same way as officers in the military spend short periods in staff roles as a key part of their career development.

Responding to National Differences

The corporate vision of business integration was not always mirrored at the country operating level. For example, the United Kingdom and French offices pursued the business-integration market with varied implementation strategies due to the competitive and cultural differences of the two markets and historical differences in the two practices.

EXHIBIT **8**   Andersen Consulting United Kingdom/Ireland

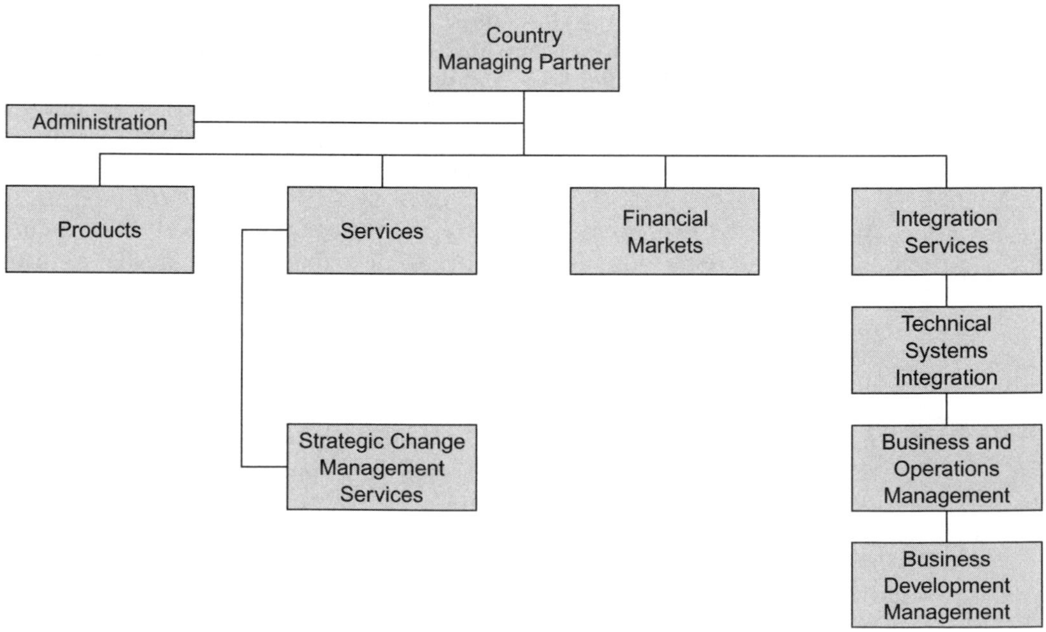

Source: company document.

EXHIBIT 9   France

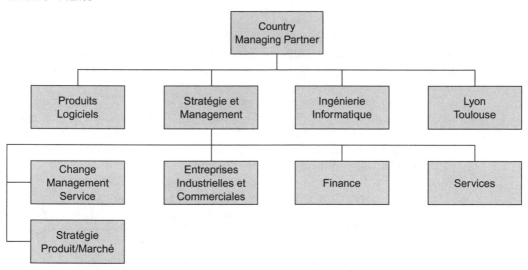

Source: company document.

The French information-technology market was the most developed in the world in terms of percentage of GNP spent on IT and was also the largest market in Europe. The market structure reflected a much clearer dichotomy between IT and business consulting. In the IT area, the market had several large, world-class competitors, such as Cap Gemini and SEMA, who were able to compete successfully with Andersen on a cost basis. From this "IT only" view of the French market, Andersen was sometimes seen as a small player. In contrast, it was historically very strong in the sector of management consulting.

By some measures, the United Kingdom was the third largest IT market in Europe and also very competitive. Andersen was very successful in the United Kingdom because the market was willing to pay a relatively high rate due to the perception of extra value being added when performed by an "integrator." This meant that Andersen could often command significantly higher rates in the United Kingdom than France for IT work. On the other hand, Andersen's U.K. competitors would often try to position Andersen as IT consultants so as to undermine the market perception of Andersen's strengths in the business-consulting area.

Culturally, in France, the corporate IT function was perceived to be of lesser stature than in the United Kingdom. In the United Kingdom, the top IT job was a key management position charged with helping the company integrate its business and information technology strategies. In France, the position of IT director was not seen to be the way to the top – top positions in corporations were reserved for the graduates of the elite *grandes écoles* system, a group to which the IT directors did not typically belong. The IT director had little or no voice in corporate strategy and top management issues. The result was that IT directors ran a relatively insular and controlled world without top management interference. When they hired consultants, they looked for firms who were cheap, had a flexible workforce, and most importantly, would allow them full control of the project. A successful consultant in France would never go around the IT director to top management.

These market differences led to very different recruiting and development systems in the two countries. To develop and maintain the French strength in management consulting, the French office had always recruited from the *grandes écoles* educational system. These individuals were trained in the fundamentals of IT through the traditional Andersen course work (CAPS and so on) but were only required to work in IT for a very limited time period (six to twelve months) after which they were assigned to the management consulting practice.

The majority of Andersen employees in the French office focused on the IT business were not recruited from the *grandes écoles*. They were on different pay scales – although these were significantly in excess of their French IT competitors. One career track within this organization did draw from the *grandes écoles* system; these were the employees who helped integrate the IT business with management consulting when needed and who were the future partners of the IT business.

In contrast, the United Kingdom had always been much stronger in the IT business and recruited to develop and maintain this skill. Recruits came from the top British schools, were trained in the Andersen methodology, and were then required to work in systems design and programming for three to five years.

Because of these competitive, cultural, and historical differences, the French and U.K. national organizations pursued some very different approaches in implementing the business-integration strategy. The U.K. implementation replicated the corporate vision as laid out by Ellis. The four centers of excellence were integrated at the country level to present a "seamless combination of skills" to the clients. The strategy and change-management areas were distinct organizations reporting into the services industry subsector. The professional-development infrastructure was the same for all professionals in terms of training requirements, salary structure, and promotion opportunities.

The French model maintained separate organizations for the information-technology business – *ingénierie informatique* – and the management-consulting business – *stratégie et management*. Within *stratégie et management*, there was a very successful stand-alone practice in change management. The *strategic services* function was not a separate area within the management-consulting arm because the French management felt their professionals were well schooled in strategy, making it unnecessary to develop this expertise in a separate group. Although the two organizations sometimes sold their services separately, more than 80% of their work was for common clients.

While recognizing that the French model was very different from the corporate blueprint, local management strongly believed that its approach was better suited at least for the French market. First, a distinct IT organization showed a commitment to Andersen's core expertise in information technology with a focus on productivity and skills. Secondly, the structure recognized the French market's IT-business dichotomy and made IT directors more comfortable because they could deal with a separate consulting group as they always had in the past. Thirdly, the structure allowed for recruitment of people with different profiles and expectations and made it possible for the company to remain as a cost-effective competitor in the traditional IT business, while protecting the high-quality image necessary for success in the management-consulting and business-integration fields. Lastly, it allowed clients to easily buy only one service from Andersen (just IT or just consulting) as a stand-alone piece of work and to do the business integration themselves.

The long-term vision of how Andersen's strategy should be developed also varied between the two country offices. The United Kingdom was organized by three main industry groups: financial markets, products, and services. A fourth division, integration services, housed specialist technology, software, and systems-management skills. The U.K. practice had three further centers of excellence – strategy and change management, housed in services, and operations/logistics, housed in products. The French vision planned for a center of excellence structure within each of the three industry groups (financial services, products, and services) as soon as each area had enough critical mass to justify the organization.

Developing New Capabilities

Of the four centers of excellence, the newly formalized areas of strategic services and change management were still establishing themselves both internally and externally.

Change management was challenged to establish a distinct skill set for itself. Its historical roots were to provide training to clients in support of large, complex systems being installed by Andersen. However, since 1988, change management's scope had expanded rapidly to reflect the cultural and organizational challenges of major transformational change in large organizations. Change management was defined in three practice areas: technology assimilation which supported the training and education needed to ensure that the expected benefits of major IT investments were fully delivered; knowledge transfer which covered training in all its aspects, including the use of training technologies; and organization change which included the strategic and tactical aspects of process and organizational change.

Much of Andersen's change management work in 1988 and 1989 was still in the training area (knowledge transfer), but the balance was rapidly changing as partners recognized the key role of the people and change dimensions in executing Andersen's business-integration strategy. Because the change management market subsector was very fragmented with few large players, cost was an important element of competition.

Strategic services marketed the following services in support of business integration: strategic management studies, competitive/industry analysis, market and sales planning, operational planning, information technology strategy, organizational strategy, and change management. In reality, most strategic services work seemed to have an operational bent. As one partner described the practice:

> Most of the strategy work, after all, is concerned with sorting out strategies to optimize a business, rather than what company should I go and acquire in the marketplace. In other words, it's what I would call internal strategic consulting, rather than external strategy consulting.

Some partners had expressed concerns about the potential overlaps between the change management and strategy skill sets as change management moved into organizational change work. Others shared Terry Neill's view:

> Executing our business-integration vision requires that we be able to mobilize project teams with a portfolio of skills in systems, strategy, process, and change management. We need

world-class skills in each dimension and the ability to bring them together for a client without the client having to concern himself about divisions which could be created by the internal structures of Andersen Consulting. We now have a dozen large, high-quality U.K. clients where we are making business integration a working reality. These companies are seeing the value of the skills portfolio and that will accelerate the removal of internal barriers. We are winning with those organizations who see the skills of strategy and execution being inextricably intertwined.

To fill the specialist needs, Andersen broke with its tradition of hiring recent graduates and 50% of the center of excellence hires were brought in as experienced "outsiders" at senior and manager levels, while the other 50% came from within the firm or were recruited at an MBA level from the outside. In general, strategic services recruited MBAs from top business schools, and change management brought in experienced individuals from the fields of organization change, industrial psychology, and education. Though Andersen prided itself on growing organically and not through acquisition, a small manufacturing consulting firm was acquired in 1988 in the United Kingdom to enhance the skill base of the operations specialty practice.

The new recruiting model and acquisition strategy required a rapid build up of expertise and internal training. Some partners felt that Andersen made a slow start in this area. Nevertheless, good progress was made in 1990 and 1991 in building training and methodologies for the emerging change management and strategy skill sets. Andersen's ability to roll out and deploy new training and approaches quickly and effectively was seen by several partners as the key to success in delivering on the business-integration vision. On-the-job training was somewhat hindered because project opportunities for inexperienced newly trained specialists could only grow at the rate at which Andersen was succeeding in taking its business integration strategy to the market.

Absorbing a large number of outsiders was a significant challenge for a firm whose strong cultural roots were passed on from one generation of recruits to the next through the institutionalized mechanisms represented in the "Andersen way." Normally, similar training, work tools, experiences, and ways of thinking made a team work smoothly. With the development of specialists within the centers of excellence, some of the common parameters were diluted. These outsiders came in at middle management levels with different ideals and methods weakening the cultural glue that had traditionally bound together a team of Andersen consultants.

The more experienced professionals hired from the "outside" did not view the traditional Andersen training program as an appropriate initiation for a senior employee. A recent MBA from a top institution recruited into strategic services was required to take the full six-week CAPS course at St. Charles and then work for several months on a systems project – the typical progression for an undergraduate recruit. His view was that the requirement added no value, and he did not think it compared favorably to the first few months of strategy work that his counterparts at the strategy boutiques experienced. Likewise, a newly hired senior manager in change management who had refused to participate in the six-week course said: "I would quit before I would take the CAPS course!"

Furthermore, there was a concern within the strategic services practice that the Andersen compensation/development philosophy was hampering their ability to recruit and retain top individuals. They felt there was a need to at least approach some of the benefits which were found at their competitor's shops. Base compensation was on par with the competition, but in the boom times for strategy consulting in the 1980s, some partners felt that Andersen's unwillingness to have bonuses might have put the firm at some disadvantage in recruiting. On the other hand, Andersen grew by nearly 40% in the United Kingdom in 1991, while most of its competitors were laying off large numbers of people. Most felt that its approach was thus vindicated – especially since so many strategy consultants from other firms applied to join Andersen, partly because of its rapidly growing reputation in the strategy area.

The generalists, in contrast, complained that the recently recruited specialists did not know how to do things in the "Andersen way" and did not want to take the time to learn. The opinion of a member of the change management group who had come through the traditional Andersen career path was: "If you change the infrastructure and make it different than the rest of Andersen, the result will be a loss of trust." Another generalist consultant agreed: "We're somewhat suspicious of the strategic services and change management types, especially if they are an external hire but even if they were moved from the IT area of the practice."

A specialist in the change management field saw the tension between the groups differently: "Although less than 50% of our consulting practice is now in the United States, our origins in the Midwest leave strong cultural values. We tend not to appreciate gurus or luminaries. Apartness, or individual aggrandizement, is neither revered, rewarded, or encouraged."

The result of these difficulties was that the turnover in strategic services and change management was higher than for the firm in general. Consequently, Andersen had begun to fine-tune the profile of a successful outside hire to more closely match the characteristics of an Andersen undergraduate recruit and the traditional Andersen culture. Additionally, the mandatory computer-based training that all Andersen recruits had been required to take in the past at St. Charles was shortened, and in some cases waived, for outside manager-level recruits. There was no formal policy in this area, but increasing flexibility seemed to be the direction in which Andersen was heading.

Integrating the Multinational Network

Andersen saw one of its competitive advantages to be its ability to serve a multinational client, or a client who would like to become multinational, through its own network of multinational offices to provide an integrated, pan-European, or even worldwide solution. This service created a need within Andersen for professionals who embodied a multinational perspective in terms of language, culture, and business knowledge. As one partner explained:

> There are very few (companies) who can pull into a project the resources from around the world. I've got over 20,000 people, and somewhere in the world we can find that somebody who really does understand a particularly difficult problem.

But as Andersen grew in size and organizational complexity, the firm was finding it increasingly difficult to take advantage of its enormous people resources to develop, identify, and effectively utilize this multinational specialist. As expressed by Terry Neill:

> A key impediment could become our ability to share knowledge quickly. In the past we have done it entirely by the personal network . . . now we're too big to do this. We need to improve our own IT network. But we also need to protect and improve our informal human network. Both are difficult, but both are challenges we must respond to urgently.

After an individual was identified as being needed on a project team, the country manager had to agree to release the individual. Because the country manager was responsible for his or her own profits, and these specialists tended to be very effective on national cases, deployment of people to regional or worldwide project teams was becoming more and more a source of conflict. There were incentives within the partnership evaluation system which measured how well each partner supported the multinational practice needs, but in reality, it was recognized that country interests came first.

Andersen was also finding it hard to hire and develop enough consultants who wanted and had the ability to participate in multinational cases. Language and cultural differences were difficult to overcome and many consultants preferred not to work outside their local area.

In 1991, a pilot program was introduced in the strategic services area to try to better develop and manage the valuable multinational specialist resource. Breaking from the traditional structure in which all professionals reported within a geographic region, a multinational specialist team was formed, which had a small centralized core in one country and a network of specialists located in various other countries, all reporting directly to the head of the team. As expressed by Bill Barnard, the partner in charge of market development for Europe who developed the program:

> In areas where we have very few specialists, we can't afford to have them only work in one country. We need to move them into different countries to work multinationally, which causes conflicts with the country managers. Some conflict is good but we need to protect these people and to help them get repeat experience and develop their skill sets. Otherwise, their experience gets lost.

Andersen also attacked this problem by trying to hire and develop people who liked multinational activity and by stressing in the education process that international relocation was part of the job. A human resource program introduced in 1990 supported a small group of individuals for development through exchange programs across Europe. Nevertheless, Bill Barnard predicted that it would take until the end of the century before Andersen worked as a truly integrated European operation.

CASE **10**

○ ○

Global Multi-Products Chile

Henry W. Lane and Dan Campbell

Introduction

As he drove to his office in Providencia, a modern commercial and residential area in Santiago, Bob Thompson, Managing Director of Multi-Products Chile, was eagerly anticipating the upcoming week. He had spent a pleasant weekend with his family that had started well on the previous Friday afternoon with what he saw as real progress at work.

He had received an e-mail from one of the sales representatives in the North branch office reporting the minutes of the first branch sales meeting ever held in the company. Among other items, the minutes stated that the team had identified six accounts on which they were going to work together under the Integrated Solutions program and that they had chosen a team leader.

Thompson was surprised but delighted. The sales reps never knew what this type of meeting could accomplish or what they could do as a group. He had not expected these teams to function so well from the beginning. Maybe making changes in the organization would not be as difficult as he first had thought.

Upon entering his office, Thompson learned that two of his Business Unit managers were anxious to see him. The first, to whom the formally designated Integrated Solutions Manager reported, commented that he was just checking about the e-mail with Thompson and politely asked, "Have you seen the e-mail from the North? What's your opinion about the comments about Integrated Solutions? Isn't this our responsibility?"

Dan Campbell prepared this case under the supervision of Professor Harry Lane solely to provide material for class discussion. The authors do not intend to illustrate either effective or ineffective handling of a managerial situation. The authors may have disguised certain names and other identifying information to protect confidentiality.

The second Business Unit manager was more concerned and was disturbed with the tone of the e-mail: "What do you think about the note? These comments go way beyond the responsibilities of the branch people."

His earlier mood of satisfaction had turned to consternation. It appeared to him that his top executives, members of his Management Operating Committee, were suggesting a stop to his changes before they got out of hand. He found himself starting to have doubts about what he was doing. Maybe this wasn't going to be so easy after all. Should he keep pushing ahead with change when his senior management team did not appear to support it? He began to reflect on events that had led to this point.

Background

Multi-Products Inc. was founded in the early 1900s to manufacture abrasives. The company's creation of the world's first waterproof sandpaper in the early 1920s, followed by numerous other new products, established the company's identity as an innovative, multi-product, manufacturing company. By 1998, the company manufactured and distributed over 50,000 products for a diverse range of applications. Some products were brands found in households and offices all over the world. Others became components of customer products such as computers, automobiles, and pharmaceuticals. Many became the standards in their industry. All these products were the result of combining the company's core technologies in ways that solved their customers' problems.

In 1996, international sales totaled U.S.$14.2 billion, an increase of 5.8 percent over the previous year, and income from continuing operations was U.S.$1.52 billion, an increase of 11.7 percent over 1995. International sales represented 53 percent of total sales. Multi-Product subsidiaries operated in over 60 countries outside of the United States and were the channels to sell products into almost 200 countries.

The Company Vision

According to Bob Thompson, the global growth drivers for the company were: 1) technology and innovation; 2) the supply chain; and 3) a customer focus. The 1996 annual report stated the company vision this way:

Our vision is to be the most innovative enterprise and the preferred supplier by:

- Developing technologies and products that create a new basis of competition.
- Earning our customers' loyalty by helping them grow their businesses.
- Expanding internationally, where we already generate more than half of our sales.
- Improving productivity and competitiveness worldwide.

Technology and Innovation

In 1996, nearly 30 percent of sales came from products introduced within the previous four years. Those new products were derived from about 30 "technology platforms" where Multi-Products believed it possessed a competitive advantage. These technologies ranged from adhesives and fluorochemistry, to even newer technologies like micro-replication with potential in abrasives, reflective sheeting, and electronic displays.

These technology platforms were considered the path to the goal of developing products that would create a new basis of competition. The Chairman of Global Multi-Products had high expectations for these programs:

> We have about 30 programs under way. These products serve high-growth industries and offer the potential to generate several billion dollars of new sales by the end of this decade.

Innovation in Customer Service

Historically, sales efforts were by product group. Often, sales representatives from one product group built strong relationships with customers that could benefit from products from other divisions as well. As a result, in the early 1980s, in an effort to take advantage of these opportunities, the company implemented a program referred to as "Related Sales." In 1988, this program was replaced by "Customer Focused Marketing" that sought to re-orient the sales and marketing effort around the needs of customers, instead of the company's product groups.

In the early 1990s, the process was carried a step further with "Integrated Solutions." Company documents explained the program:

> Customers rely on Multi-Products not only for innovative, high quality products, but also for solutions to other important needs. We help them develop, manufacture and merchandise their products; meet occupational health and safety standards; expand globally; and strengthen their businesses in other ways. We aim to be the first choice of customers. We strive for 100 percent customer satisfaction.
>
> Multi-Products has an innovative way of doing business through which the client can easily access the [company's] products. The system has been labelled "Integrated Solutions" and voices the ideal of "one voice, one face, one company", which means that a single employee can provide you access to all products and solutions.

Multi-Products in Latin America

The company had a long history in Latin America. In 1996, it celebrated 50 years of operations in Brazil, and in 1997, the same in Mexico. The 1996 annual report explained:

> In Latin America, we operate in 16 countries. We've posted annual sales growth of 15 percent during the past five years. Throughout the area, Multi-Products is fulfilling the need for better roads, telecommunications systems and other types of infrastructure improvement. In addition, demand for health care and consumer products is strong. We manufacture or convert[1] products in a dozen Latin American countries.

Managing Directors in the region reported to the vice president, Latin America, Africa, and Canada, who, in turn, reported to the Executive Vice President, International Operations.

Multi-Products Chile[2]

Multi-Products began operating in Chile in January 1976. With an initial investment of almost U.S.$2 million, operations began in a large shed that served as the warehouse, production, and administration areas. In adherence to Chile's foreign investment legislation at the time, the company was required to establish a manufacturing operation as part of its investment.

Since its beginnings, Multi-Products Chile strove to project a presence throughout the country. The first company branch was created in Concepción in the south of the country during 1977; the second in Valparaíso near Santiago, two years later; and in 1982, a third branch was established in Antofagasta north of Santiago.

In 1992, Multi-Products Chile was asked to be formally responsible for the company's expansion in Bolivia. The local office enabled Multi-Products to directly satisfy the needs of the Bolivian market.

In 1997, the company's sales totalled approximately U.S.$60 million with more than 8,000 products. Multi-Products Chile served multiple markets with multiple technologies and products, each of them with solid positions in their category. It supplied numerous manufacturing and service sectors, such as the health and first aid area (hospitals, drugstores, dentists); the industrial sector (safety products, abrasives, reflectors, packing systems, electrical and mining products, graphic communication products); the mass consumption area (cleaning, hardware, and bookstore products); office, audio-visual and automobile sectors, and the large productions areas, such as forestry and construction.

Multi-Products' reputation for innovation also was recognized in Chile. *El Mercurio* conducted a survey in 1998 of 117 directors and general managers of medium and large-sized companies headquartered in Chile. Multi-Products Chile was ranked sixth in response to the question: "Which are the top companies in Chile in innovative capacity and incorporation of technology?"

In 1998, the company had a staff of 270 that included 80 sales representatives, nine technical support staff, 45 people in manufacturing, and the remainder in management, administrative, and maintenance positions.

Chile: A Brief History[3]

In 1970 a Marxist government was elected in Chile. Soon after elections, Salvador Allende's government began a program of "economic reform." The banking, communications, textiles, insurance and copper mining industries were nationalized. Problems were soon apparent: Chile's currency reserves were gone; business groups were dissatisfied; the U.S. led a boycott against international credit for Chile; and strikes paralyzed the country. In 1973 inflation reached 300 percent.

In 1973, General Augusto Pinochet and the military took control of the country. Although General Pinochet's government was criticized for its human-rights record, it began to introduce market-oriented reforms, such as reducing government's control of the economy, privatizing industries including those considered "strategic" and lowering import duties.

Sixteen years of military rule and a peaceful transition to a democratically elected government in 1990 that followed a similar economic path, provided the base for Chile's economic success. Chile boasted one of the best economies in the Western hemisphere: greater than seven percent average growth rates, single digit inflation, a high personal savings rate (23 percent), and a fully funded pension system.

In 1998, Chile's 14.4 million inhabitants shared a per capita GDP in excess of U.S.$5,200, one of the highest in Latin America. While 60 percent of the country's population and economy was concentrated in the Santiago and Valparaíso region in the country's center, strong growth in the mining sector to the north, and the creation of a salmon fisheries industry to the south, had begun to decentralize economic activity.

Chilean Culture

Numerous Chilean managers at Multi-Products Chile shared their opinions about Chilean culture.

> Compared with the rest of Latin America, we are formal, closer to Argentina. We are the most serious people in Latin America. We often describe other Latin American cultures as less formal and see them as paying less attention to details. We are very professional at all levels and some people think Chileans are boring.
>
> We are also polite and indirect. For example, an e-mail or Lotus Notes that might be five lines from the United States, might be two pages long, on the same subject, if written by a Chilean.
>
> Many Chileans are workaholics. We work from 8 a.m. to 8 p.m. and we often take work home with us on weekends. However, we still have scheduling problems. Time is flexible. A meeting scheduled for 10:00 may not start until 10:20.

Another manager observed:

> Why are we, as a country, not as developed as the United States over the same period of time? Chileans are more isolated from one another. I have been living in the same place for three or four years, and I don't know my neighbors. Nothing, names, number of children, nothing. In Chile, we tend to care about ourselves, our families, and maybe our friends, but that's it.
>
> We haven't paid enough attention to implement programs that make people work together. We haven't paid enough attention to organization development or to developing a sense of community. We don't have a tradition of taking responsibility for a wider group.

Another commented on the "silo effect" stating that, in addition to age and educational background differences, recent political history had polarized society and had not encouraged trust. He commented:

> Things are starting to change slowly, but the wounds haven't healed in 10 years. This is the biggest barrier to working in teams. People didn't trust each other, don't trust each other.

Bob Thompson

Prior to going to Chile, Bob Thompson had been an executive with Multi-Products Canada. Multi-Products Canada was a mature company with a well-trained sales force backed by good technical support that Thompson felt was the company's classic model and was essential to long-term success.

However, in 1991–2, facing a flat economy and stagnating organization, Multi-Products Canada began a change process that sought to empower managers within the organization. Thompson commented:

> The message was that we just couldn't continue with that style of management. We needed to get the best out of people. We needed to be more creative. I think the change process was successful. People felt part of the company in a much deeper way. I, personally, felt very positive about it.

In Chile, his predecessors had always come from the United States; in fact, most had spent considerable time in the head office. Thompson, on the other hand, had spent his career outside of the head office and, in keeping with the Canadian subsidiary's model of management, was more comfortable with broadly shared authority. He believed in encouraging positive risk-taking and empowerment.

Multi-Products Chile had been successful, growing at about 17 percent per year, which was acceptable for a subsidiary in an emerging market. Multi-Products liked to grow at between two and four times the growth rate of the local gross domestic product and it maintained a strong focus on incrementally improving profitability.

Although there was no crisis in Multi-Products Chile when Thompson arrived in early 1996, profitability had declined and the message to him was that it could be improved. As Thompson sized up the organization, he believed it could achieve those profitability objectives. On the other hand, he could make more substantial changes to achieve the potential that headquarters felt existed in Chile.

Customer and Distribution Channel Changes

The group of retailers and distributors that Multi-Products Chile had traditionally served was changing quickly. Bob Thompson commented:

> The last five years have been dramatic. Big American retailers are here or are coming. That has meant that our organization needed to change.

U.S. superstores were rapidly changing the retail market in the country. One manager commented that in the past, local superstores might have represented 60 percent of retail sales, with small sole-proprietorships making up the rest. This superstore segment had been growing at 8–10 percent per year. In 1998, he believed superstores, local and foreign, represented over 90 percent of the business.

As the level of sophistication increased among retailers, expectations of their suppliers increased as well. Purchasing managers, due to the volume of products they were purchasing, were reluctant to deal with distributors, preferring instead to deal directly with suppliers. They also expected lower prices. Multi-Product managers commented:

> Customers are asking for direct service at lower prices. With the big U.S. retailers, negotiation requirements have changed. We have lost power. Our products have traditionally had solid margins and I feel they were higher in the past. Before we might have averaged 80 percent margins. Now, it is difficult to have a different price from everyone else because communication systems like the Internet let people know the world price.

One manager recounted the entry of a new office products retailer into the Chilean market:

> They have been putting a lot of pressure on margins. We are assisting them to enter the market with special programs but it is costly. We have competitors, but Multi-Products has the most complete line of products. We try to add more value to the product. For example, our competitor may sell one kind of tape, where we will sell six.

Retailers were demanding more than just price discounts. They demanded a commitment to advertising support before they would place a product on their shelves. In the case of the office supplies retailer, Multi-Products paid 5 million pesos[4] for a photograph of its office products to be included in a supplementary catalogue. The catalogue would be followed up by a telemarketing campaign that was also a new concept for Chile.

Retailers also wanted more timely delivery to reduce inventories and better communication with their suppliers around ordering, billing, and logistics. One manager commented:

> We had to learn to make the delivery and leave the invoice at the same time. As an industrial products company we were used to loading a big truck and sending it to the customer. In consumer products, we use smaller trucks and make more stops. We had to wait at the new, large retailers because the big, traditional consumer goods suppliers had more clout and were unloaded first.

Retailers wanted to reduce the number of Multi-Product sales representatives they were dealing with from four or five down to one. As a result, that sales person had to have access to information about all of the company's products being delivered to that retailer, even though they might originate from multiple product divisions.

The company also wanted to consolidate and had re-organized product responsibilities to achieve this. For example, where the Marketing Manager for Consumer Goods had been responsible for tape sales within his or her channel, responsibility for all tape sales, industrial and consumer, now resided with another manager in the Home and Office Division. This meant that the Marketing Coordinators of the Home and Office and Consumer Products Division now had to work together more closely than in the past. Cross-divisional selling had become an established fact. One manager commented:

> We have to learn to work together. They have the products and product knowledge. We have the relationship with the superstores and the skill in negotiating with them. Last year 44 percent of our division's sales were from non-consumer products to supermarkets, home centers and hardware stores.

In many instances, the company continued to use distributors, in part, because nearly 80 percent of their product sales went to industrial users. In some industries, the number of distributors had decreased after consolidation and the sophistication of the remaining distributors was increasing. Managing the relationship with distributors had become increasingly difficult as sales representatives began selling directly to end users previously serviced by a distributor.

It was not just the retail sector that had changed, but industrial products companies as well. The mining industry used to be government-controlled but large, mining multinationals were commonplace and they operated differently. One executive commented, "Everything has been challenged. We need new skills."

New Role for Sales Representatives

Changes in the company's customer base were resulting in new responsibilities and requirements for Multi-Products' sales representatives. Generally, Chile was a fairly structured society. In business, titles conferring status in the organization were very important. The selling role was not held in the same regard as other positions, and levels of education tended to be lower. Indeed, it was often difficult for sales reps to access more senior managers in the selling process. Thompson commented that "the idea of a sales executive meeting with a client's executive does not exist commonly here."

A business unit manager described a typical sales call in the past:

> When sales representatives visited a business, they would usually sit down and have a coffee with their contact. A significant portion of their conversation would revolve around non-business-related topics such as the client's family or maybe football. The relationship was very important. Eventually, the sales representative would inspect the client's inventories and make suggestions for orders of our products.

Because of increased client sophistication and more advanced products from Multi-Products, more was required from a sales representative. Another Business Unit manager commented:

> A sales rep now needs to teach as well as to sell. In the past, they were specialists. They may have only sold simple office products. Now they need to know how to sell a multi-media projector, connect it to a notebook computer and train clients on how to use it, too! People need to be more professional in their commercial relationships and make an effort to learn. We don't sell products anymore, we sell solutions.

Instead of casual sales visits, it was not uncommon now to have a team of five or six sales people, coordinated by one single client contact, making presentations that could last two or three days. Consumer products sales reps also were now focused on visiting a given number of stores in a day and handling smaller orders faster and more frequently since there were no warehouses – just the shelves in the customers' stores. Not all the sales reps were happy with this conversion from maintaining a relationship with a store owner to being, in their view, an "ant" running all over the place.

Multi-Products Chile had started placing more emphasis on recruiting high caliber people including those for sales positions. However, most university graduates showed much greater interest in positions that appeared to offer faster mobility to executive positions such as in marketing.

Integrated Solutions and Key Accounts in Multi-Products Chile

When Thompson arrived in Santiago, he learned that, although there was an awareness of the "Integrated Solutions" approach, little real progress appeared to have been made. He commented:

> This was our most important commercial activity globally, but it was not present in Chile. Our product line is so broad and deep, that customers were confused. "Why can't we see just one sales representative?" they would ask.
>
> The company had been organized for distribution-based selling, taking product lines to distributors. We needed to start understanding client and business applications of products . . . acting like a consultant. This approach proved new and challenging for the organization.

Sales representatives were responsible for sales of a specific product or line of products. Performance was measured on the ability of a representative to sell certain products, and there was no incentive to sell products from other areas of the company. As a result, customers who purchased a range of products from Multi-Products were forced to deal with several different sales representatives. If the customer was a multinational, it would often have to deal with a separate sales organization in each country in which it did business.

Structural Changes

When Bob Thompson arrived at Multi-Products Chile, he found an organization that had been very successful with traditional distribution-based selling. The deeper Multi-Products "footprint" that he was used to, especially technical support groups, was limited. He added technical support positions along with a technical council to foster its development. As well, marketing, sales, and manufacturing councils were added in time.

He also created the new position of Integrated Solutions Manager, reporting to the manufacturing products business unit manager. This person would be responsible for the implementation of Integrated Solutions in Chile and would coordinate the sales teams that would service large clients where the program was being implemented.

A short time later, a position of National Accounts Leader for Key Accounts was also created, reporting directly to Thompson. A new manufacturing manager was hired from Multi-Products Argentina where a more established manufacturing organization existed. See Exhibit 1 for a diagram of the revised organizational structure.

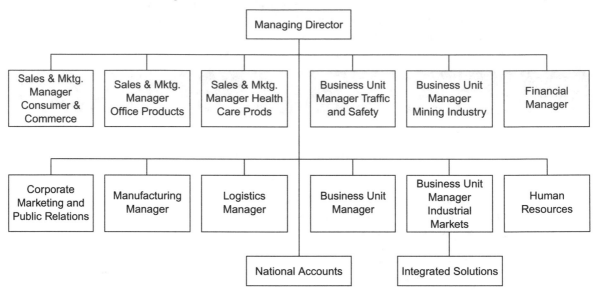

EXHIBIT 1   Multi-Products Chile Organization Chart

Accounts of special significance to Multi-Products Chile would now be viewed in one of two ways: Key Accounts and Integrated Solutions Targets.

Key Accounts

The Key Account concept was not new to Multi-Products Chile. However, in the past, a key account was identified as a customer with the potential to purchase large quantities of the company's products. Multi-Products Chile sold directly to these customers using programs different from distributors especially in pricing structure and logistics support, but the sales effort remained similar. Multiple sales representatives from each of the product areas selling to the client would service the account. Little, or no, coordination existed between the product groups.

Now, Key Accounts were those customers whose relationship with Multi-Products took on a strategic significance beyond a buyer/supplier relationship in that Multi-Products' technology could augment the customer's business and possibly change the basis of competition. Multi-Products Chile wanted to identify strategic partnerships with its customers where activities such as research and product development could be coordinated between the organizations, creating long-term competitive advantages for both organizations.

In 1998, this process had only been initiated, and partners, as well as the specific nature of the desired relationships with these partners, were in the process of being determined. However, the criteria for selecting Key Accounts were: a) a strong relationship with Multi-Products Chile, b) purchase potential, c) potential importance as an

Integrated Solutions account, and d) an important company in Chile concerned about the environment and society and having the same values as Global Multi-Products Inc.

Multi-Products Chile was one of the first of the company's Latin American subsidiaries to create this formal Key Accounts position. The National Accounts Leader felt that his challenge was going to be to convince the other Multi-Products companies to be consistent in their business model and prices with the Chilean company so that multinational customers could benefit from the relationship. He commented:

> This is a strategic program and will take a big change in mentality. We can't think short term, anymore. Free trade is helping to stabilize the country but we could still have big changes. This is the reason that business executives in Chile think short term.

Integrated Solution Targets

The real start of Integrated Solutions was in August 1997 with the collection of data about which customers would make the best targets for an initial effort. The idea was to discover those product divisions that had good relationships with clients and use the relationship to sell other products. Where the National Account Program, Key Accounts, was a strategic approach to link with a few very large accounts to create new products, Integrated Solutions was a broadly based tactical approach involving many more accounts.

Integrated Solutions represented an opportunity to sell products from multiple product groups to a client in a concerted effort. By early 1998, more than 30 customers had been identified as targets.

The next stage involved taking an "x-ray" of these companies to determine which products the company was already using. A group of specialists would map a customer's business process to find opportunities for other products that might reduce a customer's costs. This process was complicated because a single company could purchase its products directly from Multi-Products Chile, although from different product groups, as well as from a range of distributors. Once managers knew what the company was purchasing, they could measure any increase in sales to those accounts and measure that against the general market to determine if the Integrated Solutions effort was succeeding.

An individual sales representative was then selected as the leader for a specific client and would act as the single point of contact for all sales to that client, including sales outside of the sales representative's own product area. These sales representatives would then request support from other representatives as required. This leader was determined by selecting the person having the best relationship with the client, who usually was obvious.

Sales Representatives and Integrated Solutions

Managers often described the Multi-Products Chile organization as silos, with individual product groups functioning independently of one another. One manager commented:

> We used to describe the situation as feudal. There were some sales reps that supported other divisions, but there was no program to formalize the activity.
>
> Salespeople feel they have ownership over their product areas. They would ask: "Why would I use my time opening doors for another sales rep when I can use that time to visit my own customers?"

With the implementation of Integrated Solutions, it was recognized that sales staff needed to work as a team, helping one another to sell products. Everyone had not adjusted well to working with other product divisions. Some managers demanded: "Give me the products and I will sell them and earn the commission!" One manager commented:

> Not all the sales people are with the program; 15 percent are with the program, another 60 percent are with the program but are not leading it. The others are saying: "I will look after my own business and nothing else."
>
> Sales people need a change in terms of mentality. They also need to develop new sales techniques and knowledge about the products. The younger people are generally more adaptable to the change.

The increased sophistication in the buying process of some of the company's clients had also caused problems. Some sales representatives felt they had less influence in the process. They had grown accustomed to pushing new products that had been created in the US. Now marketing people were often involved in the initial process of approaching retailers with new products and negotiating the terms of sale.

Compensation also became an issue, because sales representatives usually were measured against sales targets in their product areas.

Sales Representative Compensation

When sales representatives joined Multi-Products Chile, they were given a six-month grace period during which time their compensation was 100 percent fixed. After that time, 40 percent of their compensation was fixed while the remaining 60 percent was variable or "at risk," and tied to the achievement of various targets. As a sales representative became more senior, the variable portion was reduced to 20 percent which reduced uncertainty about pay. As one manager commented, "We Latins don't like uncertainty."

The variable compensation targets were set by the sales manager, and were designed to encourage desired activity for that period. For example, 20 percent of the variable pay could be for the sale of new products. Other percentages could be used for sales calls on new clients, or sales of certain high-margin items. To accommodate Integrated Solutions, a sales manager could include sales of other product areas as a target within a sales representative's variable compensation. These targets were usually adjusted annually to meet the needs of the sales division.

Sales representatives could also receive additional pay in extra compensation for exceeding their targets. For example, sales reps with 30 percent variable compensation could earn up to 130 percent of their salary and a senior sales rep with 20 percent variable compensation could earn up to 120 percent.

The Sales Contest

Until two years earlier, the sales contest was designed and administered by the Human Resources Department when it was transferred to Corporate Marketing. The Corporate Marketing Manager invited the Sales Council,[5] of which he was the head, to design a new program.

The new program eliminated the prizes that had been given in the past such as trips and microwave ovens which, as was clearly evident, the winners usually sold. Instead, it provided monetary rewards. If sales reps made 123 percent of their target they would get, in effect, a bonus payment of x percent. If the sales team of which they were a part met its objectives, they would get an additional y percent. And, if the Business Unit met its objectives, they could receive another z percent. In total, they could earn up to an additional $2,500.

This new sales contest presented difficulties for Bob Thompson. The Manager of Human Resources and other managers were not pleased with it. They felt that: a) it was too expensive, potentially costing as much as the whole training and education budget; b) it should not have been monetarized; c) it permitted everyone to get a prize; and d) it had become part of the compensation system which was senior management's responsibility.

Thompson knew there was dissatisfaction among his managers with the new sales contest. His Human Resources Manager preferred to see changes in the plan but Thompson liked some elements of the design and since it came into effect when sales growth exceeded 23 percent it was to a degree self-funding.

Initiating the Change Process

In late 1996, soon after Thompson's arrival, a retreat was held in Iquique, a resort area north of Santiago, for senior managers from Multi-Products Chile as well as from Multi-Products Bolivia and Peru. Prior to the managers of the three countries meeting as one group, they met individually to confirm their primary mission and goals. The Chile group appeared to struggle at working together.

One of the purposes of the retreat was to establish a general mission statement for the region created by the three countries. The discussion went poorly. Managers seemed to have trouble defining a clear mission and did not touch on broader objectives for the region. As the discussion, originally scheduled for two or three hours, entered its second day, Thompson became increasingly disappointed, not only with the group's inability to reach a conclusion, but with what appeared to him to be the quality of the discussions. Frustrated, Thompson stopped the discussion and asked the group why things were going so poorly. To his surprise, one of the Chilean managers stood up and said: "We don't trust each other."

Thompson had hired a consultant to act as a professional facilitator for the retreat. As part of his services, he later provided a report outlining his conclusions about the meeting and the group. His executive summary included the following points about the executive team:

Generally, this appears to be a strong task- and results-oriented group. They are autonomous in doing what they do and are well adjusted to standard requirements. Because of this they are able to focus on task structure and output evaluation but are less aware of group process and its importance to productivity and teamwork. At times they seem isolated and defensive. There are also some unresolved personal conflicts with no methodology about resolving those conflicts.

This information gave Thompson some idea about the nature of the Multi-Products Chile organization, and pointed out some challenges to be met as he worked to make it more responsive to the customers and markets they served.

Additionally, the company conducted company-wide employee surveys every three years. They included information from various levels of the organization, about employees' opinions on various aspects of the company, such as salaries, empowerment, and safety. As a part of the data analysis, a comparison was made of the opinions of senior managers in contrast with the opinions of lower level employees on each dimension. While opinions differed on many issues, certain areas showed senior managers having a much more positive opinion than their employees (a difference of ≥ 20 percent). These included work conditions, training, job progress, pay, safety, and empowerment.

About the change process, one executive observed:

> There has been resistance and conflict generated because of the changes. Maybe it has been too aggressive or too quick. People need to understand why we are changing and we are addressing this. We are in the process of changing even though not much has really changed yet.
>
> These programs promote involvement beyond your scope of responsibility. They are long-term programs, sophisticated techniques. They won't create sales tomorrow. We are measured by our results and there is no need to change. The company is doing well. There are no rewards for thinking strategically. You can be comfortable and do well not doing these things. Thompson is doing it because he thinks it is right. It takes courage. Others do only what they are rewarded for.

Conclusion

Thompson's secretary interrupted his reflections to remind him that he had a meeting shortly with his human resources manager. Thompson thought to himself that, maybe, he had introduced enough change to Multi-Products Chile and that it was not necessary to go further. After all, business was good and things were going well.

Notes

1. "Converting" meant taking products originally received in bulk, and packaging or sealing them for consumption in the local market.
2. Much of this information was taken from company documents.
3. This section is adapted from *The Economist*, January 24, 1998; *Santiago; What's on*; Turiscom S. A., January 1998; and *Chile Handbook*; Charlie Nurse, Footprint Handbooks, 1997.
4. In January 1998, U.S.$1 purchased 450 Chilean pesos.
5. The composition of this council included the corporate marketing manager, and senior sales representatives from the business units.

CASE **11**

○ ○

ABB Poland

Ann Frost and Marc Weinstein

Introduction

In May 1996, Artur Czynczyk,[1] the recently appointed human resource director for ABB Poland, pondered his next step in promoting the much needed restructuring of the companies acquired by ABB in Poland since 1990. At a meeting of ABB Poland's top management earlier that month, at corporate headquarters in Warsaw, he had reported his findings: the restructuring of operations within individual companies was stalled and the current personnel staff appeared incapable of facilitating the needed change process. Having had only limited success over the past two and a half years in facilitating change indirectly, Czynczyk needed a plan for what to do next.

ABB Organizational Structure

ABB, a Swedish-Swiss multinational, entered the Polish market in 1990 with its acquisition of Zamech, a Polish manufacturer of turbines. ABB's entry was precipitated by the huge market potential in the former COMECON countries for infrastructure development. ABB's acquisitions in Poland stayed true to ABB's core businesses as the company acquired Polish companies in the power generation, power transmission and transportation fields (see Exhibit 1). By 1993, ABB was the third largest foreign investor in Poland after Fiat and International Paper. By 1996, ABB Poland had emerged as an important

Professors Ann Frost and Marc Weinstein prepared this case solely to provide material for class discussion. The authors do not intend to illustrate either effective or ineffective handling of a managerial situation. The authors may have disguised certain names and other identifying information to protect confidentiality.

EXHIBIT 1 ABB's Acquisitions in Poland 1990 to 1997

Year	Company Name	City	Major Product	1996 Employment
May 1990	ABB Zamech	Elblag	• Steam turbines, gas turbines • Service and retrofit of the complete turbine islands • Environmental protection systems (previously ABB Flakt Industry) • Pre-insulated district heating pipes • Gears and marine propellers • Casting steel and copper alloys • Service station turbochargers • Gas and oil equipment • Car industry robots	3,400
Oct 1990	ABB Dolmel	Wrocław	• Turbogenerators • Industrial generators • Hydrogenerators for small hydro power plants	615
Oct 1990	ABB Dolmel Drives	Wrocław	• Induction and synchronous motors • Marine generators • Generators for diesel-electric generating sets • DC winder motors for mines • Traction auxiliary machines • DC motor trams • Starters for induction slip-ring motors • Lifting magnets • Electromagnetic separators	603
April 1992	ABB Elta	Łódź	• Power transformers • Distribution transformers • High voltage (HV) switchgear • Insulation kits • Galvanizing services	932
Dec 1992	ABB Industrial Components	Warsaw	• Sale of products allocated within BA IIM, ILA and IAH as the core business • Network control & protection active in TNP BA	44
Oct 1993	ABB Instal	Wrocław	• MV switchboards • LV switchboards MNS, KNS, INS • Complex performance of electric power engineering objects	164
Jan 1994	ABB Centrum	Wrocław	• Complete solutions for power plants and heating power plant control	69
March 1994	ABB Industry	Warsaw	• Production, engineering and sales of drives, rectifiers, excitation systems and instrumentation • Industrial control systems	117

EXHIBIT 1 (*cont'd*)

Year	Company Name	City	Major Product	1996 Employment
June 1997	ABB Elbud	Kraków	• Construction, overhauling, upgrading and refurbishing of HV overhead lines, transformer substations and underground cable lines • Erection of steel-constructed masts • Assembly, testing and start-up of telemetry and remote control in HV, VHV substations	500
June 1997	ABB Elpar	Łódź	• MV switchgear • HV switchgear • Network control and protection equipment	230
Sept 1997	ABB Donako	Wrocław	• Design and manufacturing of tools and process equipment, and steel sheet punching	171
Sept 1997	ABB Huta Katowice Service	Dabrawa Gornicza	• Service	100
Oct 1997	ABB Service	Legnica	• Service	200

employer in the Polish economy, employing 7,500 people in 13 companies located throughout the country (see Exhibit 2).

ABB Poland was organized using the same matrix structure that the company utilized throughout the rest of the world (see Exhibit 3). The basic matrix consisted of geographic regions and three product segments: power, transmission and distribution (T&D); and industry and building systems. Together these three segments comprised over 50 business areas (BAs). BA leaders operated as global optimizers and strategists for specific product lines such as power transformers or high voltage switchgears. Their role was to decide which factories made which products, what export markets each factory would serve, how factories should pool their expertise, and how research and development funds ought to be allocated for the benefit of the business worldwide. The BA leader also tracked talent. When a new plant manager for a particular business area was required anywhere in the world, then that BA leader was responsible for identifying an appropriate candidate from a shortlist of people that he or she maintained from the global operation.

Within national boundaries, ABB coordinated its activities through the use of country organizations (see Exhibit 4). Significant benefits to the component companies were derived on this basis. For example, the country organization could successfully recruit top people from the universities, build an efficient distribution and service network across product lines, circulate good people among local companies and maintain productive relations with top government officials. The country president also had responsibilities similar to those of a CEO of a large domestic firm: negotiating labor agreements; maintaining banking relationships; and managing high-level contacts with customers.

EXHIBIT 2 Map of Poland

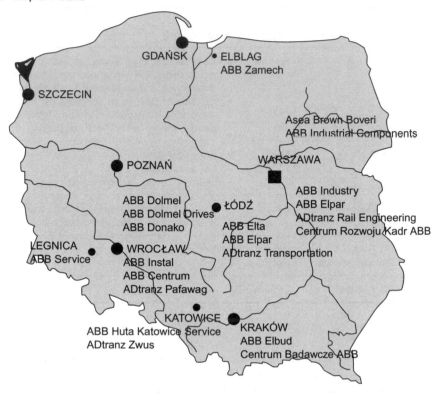

EXHIBIT 3 ABB's Matrix Structure

Region / Segment	Europe, Middle East, Africa	The Americas	Asia
	National Holding Companies (Finance, Human Resources, Legal Affairs, Communications)		
Power			
Transmission & Distribution			
Industry & Building Systems			

EXHIBIT 4 National Organization Chart

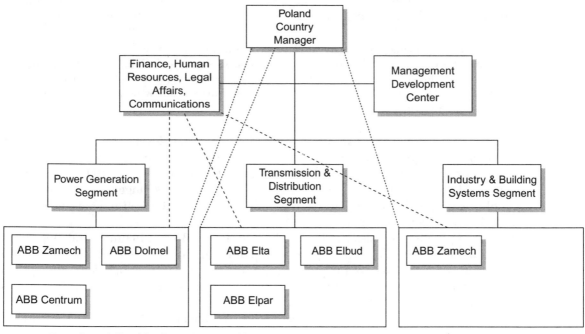

---------------- Reporting relationship of company presidents
- - - - - - - Reporting relationship of functional directors

The matrix organization produced clear benefits for ABB. ABB was a highly profitable company, leanly organized, and extremely responsive. However, to outsiders, ABB's organization structure appeared complex and difficult to manage. Percy Barnevik, the architect of ABB and its organizational structure, however, believed the organization was actually very simple for managers to operate within.

> The only way to structure a complex global organization is to make it as simple and local as possible. ABB is complicated from where I sit. But on the ground, where the real work gets done, all of our operations must function as closely as possible to stand-alone operations. Our managers need well-defined sets of responsibilities, clear accountability and maximum degrees of freedom to execute. I don't expect most of our people to have "global mindsets," to do things that hurt their business but are "good for ABB." That's not natural.[2]

Barnevik also stressed the importance of local accountability and autonomy.

> ABB is a huge enterprise. But the work of most of our people is organized in small units with P&L responsibility and meaningful autonomy. Our operations are divided into nearly 1,200 companies with an average of 200 employees. These companies are divided into 4,500 profit centres with an average of 50 employees.... We are fervent believers in decentralization.[3]

Given the autonomy accorded to company presidents and the need for local "insiders," ABB shied away from the use of expatriate managers at the company level. Commenting on the need to have nationals managing their own companies Barnevik stated:

> We can't have managers who are "un-French" managing in France because 95 per cent of them are dealing every day with French customers, French colleagues, French suppliers. That's why global managers also need humility. A global manager respects a formal German manager – Herr Doktor and all that – because that manager may be an outstanding performer in a German context.[4]

When they were used, expatriates usually filled corporate-level roles such as country presidents or segment managers.[5] In Poland, David Hunter, an American, was country manager from the founding of ABB Poland in 1990 until the end of 1996 when he was replaced by a Pole, Miroslaw Gryszka. In February 1996, Frank Duggan, a long-time ABB employee originally from Ireland, was appointed head of the Polish Transmission and Distribution (T&D) segment.

Entering the former eastern bloc for the first time, ABB (and Hunter and Duggan in turn) found conditions in the acquired companies far from the standards it was used to in western Europe. Many of the problems ABB management encountered were typified by the example of Elta, a manufacturer of transformers located in Łódź,[6] Poland. As part of the T&D segment, Elta fell under the responsibility of Frank Duggan. Arriving in Poland after spending several years with ABB in Thailand, he found what was in his words, "a bloody disaster."

ABB Elta – Historical Background

After a year of negotiation, ABB acquired 51 percent of Elta Transformers and Traction Apparatus Factory (Elta) in April 1992. As was ABB's usual practice as a multidomestic firm, Elta entered into the ABB matrix system with its internal management structure intact and its existing managers in place. Located in Łódź, a city of about 850,000 inhabitants about an hour's driving time southwest of Warsaw, Elta was founded in 1925 to manufacture transformers for the Łódź power station. Nationalized in the wake of the imposition of Soviet-style socialism after World War II, by 1969, Elta was producing high voltage switchgear, power transformers, and distribution transformers for both Poland and the then Soviet Union.

Because of its strategic importance in the Polish economy as a supplier of critical infrastructure materials, Elta was not a part of an industry association during the socialist period. Instead, company management reported directly to the Ministry of Industry. Following closely upon the Leninist principle of "dual power," all offices of the government were shadowed by parallel positions within the party. Administrative positions within the government were staffed by professional bureaucrats, who rose to power through party ranks. At the same time, the principle of "democratic centralism" required every party member to obey the orders of his superior. As a result, all power in the country flowed directly from the top. Similar structures reached down into the bureaucracy of Elta as well. Thus, Elta's factory-level party structures were well entrenched and employment, promotion, and investment decisions at Elta were even more sensitive to political considerations than was usually the case in Polish enterprises.

Because Elta was a state-owned firm operating in a command economy, the central government set production targets, allocated contracts and set prices. Top management took its orders from the state ministry and relayed them down the organizational hierarchy. If unanticipated cost overruns occurred (and with the very crude accounting methods Elta had in place, this was common), they were simply funded by additional bank loans and allowed to accumulate on the books indefinitely.

Long before the Communists came to power in Poland, the working class was seen as a key element in Polish society. As early as 1918, workers were organizing into trade unions and forming worker councils to demand a role in determining wages, working conditions, and limits on managerial authority. After the imposition of Communist rule, these worker councils were seen to be so consistent with the values of socialist organization that they were officially sanctioned by the new regime. Worker councils were empowered to negotiate wages, shape employment policies, and to participate in workplace decision making. Even after the fall of Communism in 1989, state-owned firms retained their worker councils.

Consistent with the status of workers in a socialist economy, blue-collar workers at Elta earned 105 percent of the average wage. Technical employees and engineers earned 98 percent of the average and other support services earned about 90 percent of the average. Top management's salaries were not much higher than blue-collar wages. Living in a socialist economy in which most necessities were provided or heavily subsidized by the state (housing, medical care, education, day care, vacations, recreation activities) and in which consumer goods were scarce, wage increases only led to an increase in the oversupply of money. While both engineers and blue-collar workers tended to be very skilled, both groups were highly alienated and lacked independent initiative. Over the years, they had been socialized to defer decisions to others.

ABB Elta – Production

ABB Elta was made up of six separately managed divisions: power transformers, distribution transformers, high voltage switchgear, insulation component production, galvanizing and engineering. The first three divisions produced final products, while the latter three were support divisions. The insulation component production division produced the insulation kits used in the two types of transformers. All insulation kits were produced by hand. The galvanizing division was responsible for the zinc coating of small metal parts used in the production of the transformers and switchgear to prevent rusting and corrosion. Each part was galvanized by hand-dipping in liquid zinc. Finally, the engineering center provided engineering expertise including design and troubleshooting to Elta as a whole.

The main production area within Elta, where the insulation kits, switchgear, and both types of transformers were produced, had been thoroughly modernized after ABB's acquisition of the facility. This plant was bright, clean, and the floor area relatively uncluttered. However, other parts of the Elta facility remained as they had been for 40 or more years. The paint shop, where all transformer casings were painted before final assembly, was dark, covered with decades of grime, cluttered, fume-filled and lagged considerably behind Western health and safety standards. Men painted with hand-held spray guns, often immersed up to their knees in paint, and without eye or breathing protection. Although masks were available, they were so uncomfortable and they distorted the painters' vision so badly few wore them. Despite these conditions, especially in contrast to the refurbished main production site, most people saw there being no alternative way to set up the painting facility to overcome these drawbacks.

The organization of production, even in the modernized plant at ABB Elta, was similarly underdeveloped. Power transformers are enormous pieces of equipment standing approximately 15 feet high, 12 feet long and 6 feet wide. Distribution transformers look like a scaled-down version of power transformers with dimensions of approximately 5 feet high, 6 feet long, and 3 feet wide. Each transformer was individually built. Production was highly labor intensive from the stacking of pre-cut metal pieces to produce the core, to the addition of insulation, to the welding of the housing. Work in process was managed very inefficiently with semi-finished transformers or enormous pieces of transformers having to be moved multiple times. There was no integration of design and manufacturing. Mistakes in design were often only discovered upon final testing, which then necessitated a laborious deconstruction of the transformer to correct the problem before its consequent rebuilding.

However, despite ranking near the bottom of the list of ABB's 26 power transformer plants in terms of productivity, Elta's product was price competitive at the time of its acquisition by ABB due to comparatively low wages. Where western European or North American workers in a comparable ABB facility might earn up to US$2,500 per month in wages, Elta's Polish workers earned only about US$350. But, Polish wages were rising and were expected to reach Western levels relatively soon. Productivity had to improve markedly if Elta was to survive.

ABB Elta – Human Resource Management

Historically, employees at Elta were assigned to jobs on an almost random basis with little thought as to the needs of the job or the skills and abilities of the employee. Recruitment and selection processes were simple: applicants who showed up to be hired when there was an opening were hired. Performance appraisal was little more than a yearly ritual in which managers gave their subordinates high ratings and filed the results with the personnel department. These ratings were rarely shared with subordinates and were never used as a development tool. There were also no well-thought-out plans for employee training or career development. The compensation system in place was equally unsophisticated. Blue- and white-collar employees alike were paid salaries, dispensed in cheque or cash on a weekly basis. As stated earlier, wages were highly compressed with top management earning only slightly more than the average blue-collar worker. The human resource system in place created a number of problems for Elta as it struggled to restructure.

Elta's personnel department was typical of that found throughout the Polish economy. An internal ABB study found that Elta's 104-person personnel staff (for the most part long-tenured female employees), was consumed entirely by administrative work including the tracking of absenteeism, tardiness, disciplinary problems, and pay administration. Without computerization, these were tedious and laborious tasks. The rest of the time was taken up by myriad other duties including monitoring and enforcing employment laws, reporting company statistics to government offices, organizing workers' holiday excursions, and undertaking special projects such as restructuring the employee cafeteria.

After years of significant growth in the post-war period, Elta's employment levels peaked at over 3,000 in the early 1980s, making it one of Łódź's largest and most prominent employers. During the 1980s, however, Elta experienced a number of years of low demand as a result of the deterioration of the Russian economy. As demand from the former Soviet bloc declined precipitously, many Elta employees left the company to find work elsewhere. After its acquisition by ABB in 1992, and on the heels of several years of losses as the Polish economy went through economic shock therapy after 1990, Elta needed to successfully restructure to be able to compete successfully in the deregulated economy. Elta continued to downsize, laying off people in order of reverse seniority. By 1996, employment stood at about 940.

The Need to Restructure

When Frank Duggan arrived to head up the T&D segment for Poland in early 1996, he found conditions in Elta appalling, even when compared to his most recent posting in Thailand. He immediately recognized change had to occur and to occur quickly if the Polish companies were to survive. If the management of the companies did not improve dramatically and quickly, ABB Poland would find itself holding a set of uncompetitive companies as their one source of competitive advantage – low wages – was eroded, as wage levels rose to Western levels. (See Exhibit 5 for a summary of ABB Elta's financial performance.) Although an engineer by training himself, Duggan was stunned by the attitudes of the managers and technical personnel he found within his segment's companies. Duggan recounted:

> Quite frankly, our managers think empowerment is a load of crap. A survey we did a few months ago told us that. The same survey told us that workers don't want to be empowered either. Basically, the technical people here focus on the technology, not the people. But, come on, people are the only thing we have to differentiate ourselves with. This is old technology. Anybody can buy it. What we have here is nothing different from anybody else.

EXHIBIT 5   ABB Elta Financial Performance 1992 to 1996

	1992	1993	1994	1995	1996
Revenues (thousand $)	21,997	34,023	39,416	45,266	62,887
Net Profit (Loss) (thousand $)	1,876	1,329	1,606	136	747
Employment	1,911	1,303	1,190	932	951

Elta's condition was not unusual in the companies that ABB was acquiring during the first half of the 1990s in Poland. Observing these conditions, David Hunter, the country manager for Poland, recognized the need for significant restructuring. He knew, however, that it would have to be driven from inside the companies and that it would likely entail a considerable amount of time and resources. His first course of action was to set up an external training organization to which company managers could be sent to develop a number of critical skills needed in the new environment. Not only would managers within the ABB Poland companies require knowledge related to the operation of a market economy and modern business practices, but they would also require English language skills, the language of ABB. To help in this endeavor, Hunter contracted with a consultant to locate an appropriate director for the training center he envisioned.

The consultant found Artur Czynczyk. Studying for a doctorate in sociology and lecturing at the University of Warsaw in 1989, the then 28-year-old Czynczyk found plenty of consulting opportunities to supplement his meager university salary after the fall of Communism. It was in his role of advising clients on labor-management relations and organizational restructuring, that Czynczyk came to the attention of the consultant hired by Hunter in early 1993.

The Management Development Center (MDC) opened in May 1993 with a threefold purpose: to aid in the development of ABB employees and to facilitate the restructuring of ABB companies; to integrate the various acquired companies in Poland into a country-based organization; and to integrate the ABB Poland organization into the larger ABB global network. Having understood the lack of knowledge in several critical areas – finance, marketing and sales, and human resource management, in particular – Czynczyk and his staff had set about developing and delivering training to managers of ABB Poland to help them "get up to speed" and begin to proactively change their organizations. Between 1993 and 1996, MDC trained more than 3,000 people during more than 600 program days.

After two and a half years, it became clear that the MDC-developed training was not having a significant effect upon organizational performance. Only a few managers, from any particular organization or area in an organization, came to MDC at a given time. Company presidents perceived MDC as a "corporate" organization designed to achieve "corporate" goals, such as integration, about which the individual companies cared very little. More importantly, many middle-ranking managers faced significant constraints in applying their newfound knowledge in their organizations after their training and were frustrated by their inability to utilize skills newly acquired at MDC training sessions. Eventually, Hunter concluded that additional steps were needed. In late 1995, Hunter asked Czynczyk to move to corporate headquarters as human resource director of ABB Poland. In January 1996, Czynczyk assumed this new position overseeing the human resource management of ABB Poland's 7,500 employees.

Czynczyk realized the stakes involved in restructuring ABB Poland's companies. He also had the experience of operating the MDC behind him and the knowledge of what was needed inside the individual companies. He realized he needed to have access directly into the companies if he was to create the kinds of changes that were required to successfully restructure the companies of ABB Poland. He wondered what he would do and who he would use to lead the change.

Notes

1. Pronounced "Chinchick."
2. Taylor, W. 1991. "The Logic of Global Business: An Interview with ABB's Percy Barnevik." *Harvard Business Review*, March–April, pp. 90–105.
3. Ibid.
4. Ibid.
5. In Poland, segment managers played a more important role in guiding company policy than did the BA leaders.
6. Pronounced "Woodge" (where the "oo" sounds like the "oo" in wood).

CASE 12

○ ○

Five Star Beer – Pay for Performance

Brian Golden and Tom Gleave

In June 1997, Tom McMullen (President – Alliance Brewing Group) and Zhao Hui Shen (General Manager – Five Star Brewing Co. Ltd) met to discuss the "pay for performance" systems which Zhao had been implementing at Five Star's two breweries over the past several months. McMullen needed to determine whether or not these incentive systems were properly designed to ensure that the breweries would produce higher quality beer at progressively lower costs. If not, he needed to consider how he might suggest that these and other systems be changed in order to achieve Alliance Brewing's cost and quality objectives.

Five Star's ASIMCO Connection

The majority owner of Beijing Asia Shuang He Sheng Five Star Brewing Co. Ltd (Five Star) was the Beijing-based investment group, Asian Strategic Investments Corporation (ASIMCO). The primary shareholders of ASIMCO were Trust Company West, Morgan Stanley–Dean Witter Reynolds and senior management. The senior management team consisted of the following people:

> Jack Perkowski (Chairman and CEO) – a former investment chief at Paine Webber (New York City) and graduate of both Yale University (cum laude) and the Harvard Business School (Baker Scholar).

Tom Gleave prepared this case under the supervision of Professor Brian Golden solely to provide material for class discussion. The authors do not intend to illustrate either effective or ineffective handling of a managerial situation. The authors may have disguised certain names and other identifying information to protect confidentiality.

Tim Clissold (President) – a physics graduate from Cambridge University who turned accountant with Arthur Andersen in the 1980s. Clissold had worked in England, Australia, China and Hong Kong for Andersen before entering London's School of Oriental and Asian Studies where he became fluent in both spoken and written Mandarin.

Michael Cronin (Chief Investment and Financial Officer) – also worked as an accountant for Arthur Andersen throughout the 1980s in Australia, the UK and Hong Kong. Previously, Cronin had worked for over five years at 3i, Europe's largest direct investment organization.

Ai Jian (Managing Director) – a Chinese native and graduate from Northwestern Polytechnical University in Xian, China. Ai's previous working experience included senior posts in the foreign relations department of China's Ministry of Foreign Trade and Economic Cooperation. He was a native Mandarin speaker and also fluent in English.

The motivations underlying ASIMCO's investment in the Chinese beer industry were twofold. First, the industry was experiencing high, sustainable growth rates. This high growth was spurred by the increasing levels of disposable incomes in China, to the point where it was expected that the Chinese beer market would become the world's largest (overtaking the U.S.A) within the next several years. Second, the industry was highly fragmented and was undergoing a significant restructuring. This high degree of fragmentation was a consequence of China's legacy of central planning. Given its increasing adoption of market-driven mechanisms, China's central government was encouraging (or passively allowing) the rationalization of certain industries, including the beer industry. The industry consensus was that the number of breweries was expected to be reduced from over 800 to less than 600 nationwide over the next several years, while managing to steadily increase overall beer volume. This meant that surviving firms would need to seek economies of scale, maintain high-quality production and ensure development of strong management teams as the competition intensified.

ASIMCO's investment strategy was to identify Chinese companies that had the potential to be globally competitive and to support these firms with capital, Western management skills and leading-edge technologies. The partners they sought were expected to be aggressive, profit-oriented and industry leaders. Whenever a potential opportunity was discovered, ASIMCO would marshal its skills and international resources to perform due diligence, negotiate contracts, and obtain necessary approvals. ASIMCO would subsequently provide capital, Western management expertise, and technological know-how to the joint venture and devise an exit strategy designed to realize the value created.

ASIMCO viewed itself as an agent of change in helping to transform formerly inefficient state-owned enterprises into market-driven and export-ready competitive firms. By June 1997, ASIMCO had entered into 13 automotive parts manufacturing, two automotive parts distribution and two beer manufacturing joint ventures. The sum total of these investments, all of which were majority positions, was about U.S.$360 million. All minority positions were held by various Chinese partners. The Five Star joint venture was ASIMCO's largest single investment in its portfolio with a total capital outlay of U.S.$70 million for a 63 percent stake in the company. The minority interest partner was the First Light Industry Bureau (FLIB) with a 37 percent stake. The FLIB was a division of the Beijing municipal government and had ownership interests in many diverse business activities. ASIMCO's other joint venture in brewing was a 54 percent

EXHIBIT **1**   ASIMCO's Ownership in Brewing Joint Ventures

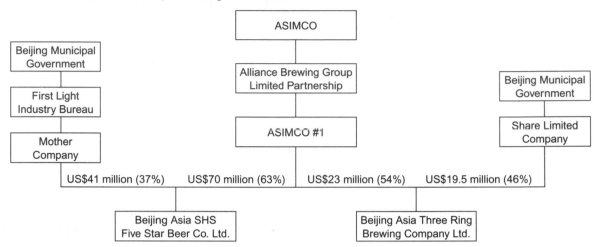

interest in the Three Ring Beer Company, an investment valued at U.S.$23 million. Both of the brewing joint ventures were formalized in January 1995 (See Exhibit 1).

Alliance Brewing Group

Alliance Brewing Group (ABG) was a management services group which was specifically established to provide support to both of ASIMCO's brewery joint ventures. This gave ABG the mandate to support three different, yet related, brewing facilities. These breweries were as follows:

Brewery	Owner	Annual Capacity
Shuang Sheng	Five Star	90,000 tons
Huadu	Five Star	180,000 tons
San Huan	Three Ring	130,000 tons

(Total production for the three breweries was currently running at about 250,000 tons per year.)

ABG was organized into separate corporate-level support functions which included marketing, brewing and quality control, operations services, financial control, and new business development. The President of ABG was Tom McMullen, an American expatriate who formerly worked in the consumer packaged goods business in the U.S. after graduating from the Wharton School of Business (See Exhibit 2).

The overall goal of ABG was to help both brewing companies realize their return on invested capital targets. With respect to Five Star, this was expected to be accomplished through the achievement of five key objectives, which included (in order of priority) the following:

EXHIBIT 2 Alliance Brewing Group – Partial Organization Chart

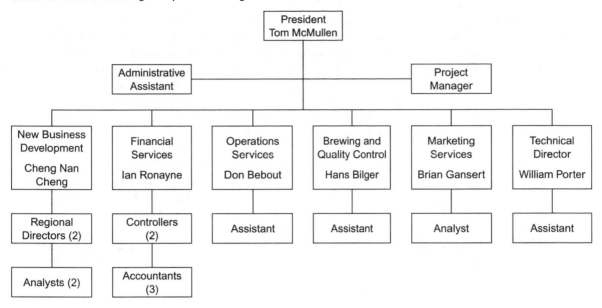

1. Improved product and packaging quality.
2. Reduced production costs in an effort to gain better margins.
3. The development of professional sales, marketing and distribution systems.
4. The development of a system which rewarded good performance and punished bad performance.
5. An increased understanding between Five Star's two breweries that separate production facilities did not mean separate companies. Rather, they were part of the same brewing company.

According to McMullen, one of the more meaningful signs of progress that ABG was able to make over the past year was the development of rational and integrated financial reporting systems. These new systems took more than one year to develop but eventually allowed both Chinese and expatriate managers to "talk from the same page." As evidence of the importance of the need for reliable and timely financial information, particularly with respect to the need for Chinese management to understand the importance of meeting budgeted targets, ABG had installed its own financial personnel at both of its beer companies.

Five Star's Recent History

Five Star was one of the oldest brewing companies in China, with its origins dating back to 1915. Like most breweries in China, Five Star originally served its local markets, the main one being Beijing and the surrounding Hebei province. This focus on local markets developed as a consequence of competing interests from local governments which, in turn, led to the industry's fragmented structure. Over the years, however, Five Star was able to gain some market share in areas beyond the immediate region. This market penetration was accomplished through the establishment of licensing agreements between Five Star and other regional brewers throughout the country.

Prior to the early 1990s, the company enjoyed a majority share of the local Beijing market. This market position had developed because Five Star had a lengthy history in the region and, as a state enterprise which was wholly owned by the Beijing municipal government, was conferred special privileges. For example, in 1957, Chinese Premier Zhou Enlai decreed that Five Star was to be the exclusive beer supplied at all State banquets, thus bringing the company name to national prominence.

By the early 1990s, Five Star's market position began to deteriorate as it found itself competing in the same territories in the Beijing area with one of its largest licensees, Three Ring Beer. In 1993, Five Star entered into a licensing agreement which allowed Three Ring to produce and market Five Star beer for sale in specific territories on the northeastern outskirts of Beijing. However, Five Star soon found that Three Ring was "stealing" sales by deliberately encroaching on Five Star's exclusive territories within the core areas of the city. Three Ring was successful in securing significant market share due to its offer of lower pricing (for virtually the same products) and the lack of wholesaler and retailer loyalty. ASIMCO acquired a majority stake in both brewing companies in January 1995. This left ABG with the challenge of ensuring that the two companies refrain from directly competing with each other.

The progressive intrusion by Three Ring was compounded by the deteriorating quality of Five Star's products. It was only after it acquired ownership control that ASIMCO discovered that Five Star was experiencing greater quality difficulties than originally thought. Perhaps most disturbing of all was the consistently poor performance and apathetic attitude of Mr. Xu, Five Star's former General Manager. According to Tom McMullen:

> Xu was completely lacking in competence in virtually all respects. He was simply a victim of the old state-enterprise culture which encouraged senior managers to have a minimum of initiative and innovation. He perceived himself to be a king in his castle, while ABG in general, and me in particular, were seen as interlopers. Unfortunately for him, he discovered the hard way that his position was less secure than he believed.

Admittedly, McMullen had much less control than he originally expected when he signed on with Five Star. Having worked in the U.S. for over 20 years, McMullen was accustomed to the idea that employees could be hired, disciplined and terminated as deemed necessary. However, in China, such activities were regulated to a much greater extent and often involved political considerations. For example, the person in charge of the human resource management and training functions at Five Star was Mr. Qi, resident member of the Communist Party of China. (See Exhibit 3 and Appendix 1).

EXHIBIT 3 Five Star Beer Organization Chart

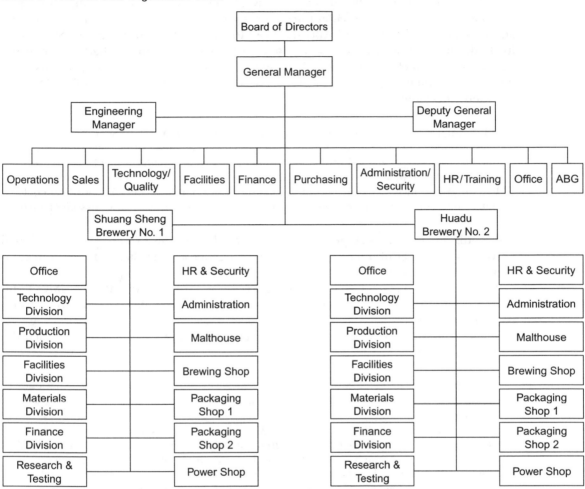

The Imperative for Quality

The high degree of industry consolidation, coupled with increasing Sino-foreign joint venture activity involving numerous world famous beer companies (such as Heineken, Beck's and Budweiser), meant that Five Star was beginning to experience greater competition from very capable rivals. This created a critical need for Five Star to provide higher quality beer and packaging. The common criteria by which product quality was evaluated included consistency in taste, clarity, carbonation, fill levels and labelling. The challenge of achieving consistency across all of these quality dimensions was great. Numerous documented incidences of foreign matter inside bottles, as well as unfilled or short-filled bottles and cans had been documented. Many packaging issues had also been identified and typically included poorly labelled or poorly sealed bottles and cans. One particularly poignant incident occurred shortly after the joint venture was formed and signalled to ASIMCO and ABG the need for drastically improving Five Star's quality. In this instance, a customer found a bottle which was half-full that had been released with a ripped label that was glued on sideways, despite having passed at least four inspection workers. Upon hearing the news of this episode, Tim Clissold (ASIMCO President) declared:

> It is beyond rational thought how our workers allowed this bottle to be sent out for public consumption. And when inquiries were made as to how this type of thing could happen, the line manager simply laughed with embarrassment. This is the result of the old central planning mentality in which there was no connection between reward and effort. These workers had no proper incentive or disincentive to ensure full product quality. The workers could not be fined or punished, nor were they entitled to extra wages for extra work completed.

The bottle in question was permanently displayed in ASIMCO and ABG's combined offices as a reminder of the need for ensuring diligence at every stage of the production and marketing process.

After realizing that quality issues facing Five Star were considerable, ASIMCO and ABG moved quickly to resolve the problems. ABG's professional staff was to focus on reducing costs, but a priority emphasis was placed on quality. Three key brewing professionals, the only non-Chinese to take an active role at any of the breweries, led the effort. They were:

> Don Bebout (VP – Operations Services), an American with over 19 years of experience working for Miller Brewing. He was particularly skilled in the areas of packaging and labelling.
>
> Hans Bilger (Master Brewer and ABG's Quality Manager) had a lifetime of brewing experience. In his native Germany, he grew up helping his father run a family-owned brewery before embarking for the U.S. where he spent nearly 30 years involved in a variety of positions, both with U.S. brewing giants and microbreweries.
>
> William Porter (Technical Director) was also an industry veteran from the U.S. where he worked for over 20 years at such breweries as Miller, Lone Star and Pabst. Although Porter's "home" brewery was with the Three Ring brewing joint venture, he was often called upon to offer technical advice to Five Star.

These three ex-pats were each provided with dedicated assistants, all of whom were fluently bilingual. This assistance was essential since none of the three ex-pats spoke Mandarin. Among the three assistants, Zhou Yue reported directly to Don Bebout and held a graduate degree in fermentology. She had previously worked for several years at China's National Institute for Food and Fermentology. Similarly, Bi Hong, assistant to Bilger, was a genetics technologist and had also worked for the National Institute for Food and Fermentalogy. She also received 13 months of brewery training while studying in France.

A major concern of ABG's operations and quality staff was the need to achieve higher quality targets while "milking" the existing equipment. When ASIMCO took its majority stake in Five Star, the company was believed to possess some of the best equipment of any brewery in China, although some of it required refurbishing due to lack of regular maintenance. Given the recent influx of well-funded foreign brewers, Five Star appeared to be at a technological disadvantage when it came to ensuring product and packaging quality.

The Need for Management Control and Motivation

Regarding the level of management control and commitment that is necessary for ensuring consistent quality, Hans Bilger (Master Brewer) offered the following remarks:

> The skills needed to produce quality beer on a consistent basis are minimal. What you need are the monitoring procedures, the discipline to adhere to those procedures and the clear reporting of information to the appropriate people. The tasks of monitoring operations, recording data and communicating results on a regular basis are not sophisticated. The problems arise when management does not take control by ensuring that procedures are followed or that information is shared. For example, line workers are expected to regularly record the temperatures in the brewing vats. This is done often enough, but the results are frequently not communicated to the people who use this information. This is a symptom of the silo mentality around here. There really is no cross-functional coordination. And in the event that any results are communicated, you end up getting what you want to hear and not the real story, even when there is a problem. This shows that our quality problems are management-related and that the senior managers at the brewery need to become committed to quality.
>
> Quality is a way of life. It is a mindset. The senior managers at the brewery have yet to fully understand these concepts. Part of the problem could be that they are rewarded on volume output, not quality output. This is because brewing in China is a low margin business and, therefore, breweries need to pump out the volume in order to make any profits. This means that some managers are reluctant to take any measures which will impede their ability to produce as much as they can.
>
> Ideally, I would like to see Five Star have an independent quality department reporting directly to the General Manager, not to the Deputy GM and Chief Engineer as is now the case – despite what the formal organization chart suggests. Both the 'Number 1' and 'Number 2' breweries would have their own divisional labs which would feed their results to Five Star's quality assurance office on a regular basis. This quality assurance department would also be given policeman-like powers. Someone has to be able to say "this is not good enough," and then have the authority to take corrective action. Unfortunately, this type of arrangement goes against the strong tradition of hierarchical reporting in China.

Hiring Mr. Zhao

In response to the need to replace Mr. Xu, and after a thorough recruiting process, ASIMCO and ABG agreed to hire Zhao Hui Shen. Mr. Zhao, formerly a factory manager at a piano manufacturing plant where he had worked for over 20 years, came highly recommended by the FLIB. Clissold was skeptical about hiring Zhao due to his obvious lack of brewing industry experience. However, Zhao won Clissold's confidence when confronted about this apparent liability by stating that, "you will not hire me to make the beer, you will hire me to manage the people who make the beer."

Zhao was expected to work impartially for the Five Star joint venture company. He was also expected to draw upon the resources of ABG in an effort to improve the overall quality and productivity of Five Star's brewing operations. Within the joint venture company, Zhao reported to the Board of Directors. The Board's membership consisted of Jack Perkowski, Ai Jian, Tom McMullen, Mr. Zhao and a representative from the FLIB.

Zhao was viewed by many others at ABG and Five Star as representing a new generation of Chinese manager. This was because he had taken a very aggressive and hands-on approach to managing the business, a style which was a distinct departure from the state-owned enterprise culture of the past. Zhao commented:

> You have to change the way of thinking from traditional enterprise methods. Nowadays we must think of management by objective. I want people to think about how they can achieve their goals, not how to waste time thinking of excuses for not achieving them and then relying on the government for money.

Zhao's Performance-Related Pay Systems

One of ABG's key objectives was to help the breweries adopt a "pay for performance" culture. ABG believed that it must try to get people to care about their work and about themselves, particularly since jobs were taking on an entirely new role in Chinese life. ABG was seeking to instill a culture which would see employees take greater control over their destinies.

When it came time (in January 1997) to begin the development of specific pay for performance systems, Zhao requested the assistance of ABG. However, ABG was unable to offer extensive support at that time due to limited resources and its other priorities. In March 1997, ABG offered to assist Zhao in developing the systems, but Zhao then declined the offer because he did not want ABG to change what he had already initiated. He did, however, offer to reveal his key objectives to ABG. This led McMullen to acknowledge that the issue of establishing a pay for performance system may have been a higher priority for Zhao than it was for himself.

In developing the compensation systems, Zhao believed that monetary punishment could be used as a strong incentive for better performance, something McMullen referred to as "using more stick than carrot." One such example of this approach involved the bottle-filling line, where one of the key measures of quality was to ensure that all bottles were filled to the proper level. To ensure that properly filled bottles were distributed from the brewery, each filling line was assigned two people to manually check for empty bottles, while four additional people were used to manually check for short-fills. When the bottles were filled they were date-stamped and coded so that the product could be traced to its original filling and labelling lines. In the event that an empty or short-filled product was found in the marketplace (whether it be by Five Star's sales people, distributors or final customers), all six people on the originating filling line would be fined a total of 500 renminbi, or about 83 Rmb each.[1] This fine would be deducted from their salaries in which each line worker received an average compensation of about 1,000 Rmb per month, an amount which was almost double that of similar positions in Chinese wholly owned breweries.

There was some debate in the plant as to whether or not this was an effective system. Hans Bilger (Master Brewer) felt that this approach was too harsh. He believed that, at a filling rate of 12,000 bottles per hour over a six-hour shift, the employees would become too tired to identify all empty bottles or short-fills. On the other hand, Yang Xiang, a bilingual technician working for the Operations Service group, felt that this type of system was "to some extent fair." He felt that somebody must take responsibility for these types of errors and that it might be more effective if the line supervisors were fined, not just the line workers.

Another example of a disincentive for poor performance involved a fine levied on the brew house for poor sanitation in the rice mill under its responsibility. The beer that Five Star brewed typically consisted of 30 percent rice grain and 70 percent malt. A rice mill was utilized on-site to provide the appropriate supplies. A common problem in the mill was the high level of dustiness, due primarily to the lack of care in cleaning, as well as an occasionally malfunctioning dust collection system. This presented a danger of insect infestation which, apart from affecting beer quality, also posed a threat of flammable explosion. In the spring of 1997, after Bilger submitted one of his periodic inspection reports which gave the mill a failing grade, seven line workers in the mill and associated brew house were deducted 100 Rmb each from their next pay cheque. As was the case in the previous example, the affected employees also earned 1,000 Rmb per month.

One of Zhao's more widely discussed systems involved the sales force. Given that Five Star was seeking to re-establish its market position within the greater Beijing area, a strong emphasis was placed on boosting sales and thus increasing market share. Although sales people began by earning a starting salary of only 600 Rmb per month, they could earn up to ten times this amount depending upon their sales performance. Unfortunately, Mr. Zhao had encountered some difficulty recruiting people who were prepared to receive compensation based largely upon their own efforts. Additionally, there were widely held suspicions among some of the ABG operations and quality staff that this particular system had invited abuse in the proper recording of sales. Although these staffers had "heard rumors" of this type of activity, they had no concrete evidence. Any inquiries about the company's latest sales performance were met with "stony silence."

The implementation of Zhao's various performance-related pay schemes had given rise to a general debate among ABG's operations staff. The nature of the debate centered around which direction or approach would best motivate employees to strive for quality. The divergent views expressed by the operations staff were highlighted by the contrasting opinions between William Porter and Hans Bilger. Porter contended that cash payouts were a more effective incentive for improving performance than the recognition for a job well done. He believed that the employees would "far sooner have more renminbi in their jeans than a pat on the back." Bilger, on the other hand, suggested that pride of workmanship and the recognition of a job well done were more powerful motivators than cash rewards. His reasoning was that China was a status-conscious society where a high value was placed on securing the favorable opinion of one's peers and superiors. Despite a significant amount of spirited discussion, no clear consensus had emerged among ABG's operations staff as to whose view was more compelling.

Decision

The next Board meeting was scheduled for mid-July 1997, at which time McMullen wished to offer the members an update on the design and implementation of the pay for performance systems at Five Star. Therefore, as McMullen contemplated how he might suggest to Zhao different ways for improving these systems, he needed to consider several important factors. First and foremost, he needed to consider the cultural, historical, social, and business contexts in which Five Star and ABG found themselves. McMullen was keenly aware that the receptivity to pay for performance systems was only beginning to be slowly accepted in China. Moreover, he needed to recognize the far greater knowledge that Zhao possessed about Chinese behavioral habits and culture. Therefore, he could not presume that what would be effective in North America would be effective in China. McMullen was also intrigued by the debates which had surfaced among his own operations staff. Did the notion of "punishments" have some merit in China? Would workers respond most to cash rewards or were they more likely to be motivated by some form of recognition? The only thing which seemed clear to McMullen was that the motivation and quality problems had no easy solutions.

Note

1. The June 1997 exchange rate was about 8.28 Rmb = U.S.$1.00.

Appendix 1
Labor Market Conditions and Human Resource Development Practices in China

China's labor market in 1997 was experiencing significant structural changes as market-oriented reforms took hold. State policy efforts to establish a new social welfare system and to implement state-owned enterprise (SOE) reform have had a profound effect on labor market conditions and human resource management practices in both domestic and foreign-funded enterprises. The first national labor law came into effect in 1995 and brought with it a lower level of government intervention in human resource management (HRM) at the enterprise level and more equal treatment for domestic and foreign enterprises. It is expected that this law will eventually allow all types of firms to acquire greater control over wage setting as well as the power to hire, discipline, and dismiss workers, areas which have traditionally been highly regulated by government. In the meantime, China's labor market remains under-developed: labor mobility is restricted, and HRM is a new concept. Therefore, both domestic and foreign enterprises are now operating in a highly uncertain environment which reflects a combination of the old planned economy practices with those of newer Western approaches to HRM.

In 1994, China's labor force totalled 615 million, or approximately 51 percent of the country's total population of 1.2 billion. This labor force is expected to grow by an average of 20.9 million persons per year between 1995 and 2006. Importantly, no national social welfare system has been established in China. Social welfare has traditionally been the responsibility of the SOEs, the dominant form of industrial organization in the Chinese economy since the "liberation" of 1949. However, as market forces take greater hold in China, the SOEs will find it increasingly difficult to maintain these responsibilities for delivering a wide range of social services including subsidized housing, education, and health care.

Until recently, HRM in China has been defined by the tenure employment structure of the planned economy. In the old SOE system, labor was regarded as a passive input in the production process rather than a productive factor. As a result, traditional human resource management included only personnel administration activities, such as registering the recruited workers, recording increases in wages and promotions (by seniority), filing job changes, and maintaining workers' files. Although training was provided, most of it involved indoctrinating workers with the Communist Party's prevailing policies. The focus was on the use of workers rather than their career development. Compensation was not directly linked to performance and served as little incentive for better performance. From an enterprise's overall performance perspective, it is clear that these practices were not aligned with a strategy to be productive and competitive in a market-oriented economy.

Source: The Conference Board of Canada, Opportunities and Risks for Canadian Business in China, 1996.

CASE **13**

○ ○

Moscow Aerostar

Henry W. Lane and Christine Shea

Background

The Moscow Aerostar Hotel opened for business on May 1, 1991. The hotel was a joint venture between Russia's national airline, Aeroflot, and an aerospace multinational, IMP Group Limited, based in Halifax, Nova Scotia. The relationship between the two companies began when an IMP company won a contract to service and refuel Aeroflot flights landing in Gander, Newfoundland. While on business in Moscow in 1988, Ken Rowe, IMP's Chairman and Chief Executive Officer, noticed an unfinished concrete building on Leningradski Prospect near the site of the 1980 Moscow Olympic Games. Aeroflot owned the building which originally had been designed to house athletes during the games, but had never been completed. Ken Rowe accepted the challenge of converting the unfinished building into a Western-style hotel.

> "It's been a challenging four years," admits Rowe. "Launching a joint venture in partnership with a former communist country isn't the same as working with any other country in the world. We had to overcome many obstacles, build a lot of bridges between the Russians and ourselves and navigate through some unknown waters. With the current political situation in Russia, we're coming up against something new every day!"[1]

Most of the materials used to remodel the building had to be imported: electrical equipment from Spain; mechanical equipment from England, Belgium, the United States and Canada; kitchen equipment from Germany; and bathroom fixtures from Italy

Christine Shea prepared this case under the supervision of Professor Henry Lane, solely to provide material for class discussion. The authors do not intend to illustrate either effective or ineffective handling of a managerial situation. The authors may have disguised certain names and other identifying information to protect confidentiality.

and Canada. Construction workers also were brought in from other countries such as Poland and Hungary. The hotel was completed only four months behind schedule – "a miracle by Russian standards."[2]

The hotel carried a four-star rating and had achieved an average occupancy rate over 80 percent. Since it opened it had developed a reputation "as an oasis of Western efficiency in the midst of the Russian economic and political hurricane."[3] It boasted a restaurant offering full buffet breakfast, lunch, and dinner (including lobster dinners three days per week); a steak and seafood restaurant; a business office for guests complete with fax machine with satellite hook-up, photocopiers, and word-processing services; a meeting room capable of accommodating 80 to 150 persons for meetings, press conferences or cocktail parties; a fitness room including sauna, rowing equipment, and universal gym; and a caviar and vodka bar, in addition to 417 well-appointed rooms. Room rates were 15 to 20 percent lower than the competition (which generally had been awarded five-star ratings) and ranged from $205 per night for single occupancy including breakfast[4] to $395 per night for a triple-occupancy suite. Restaurant prices were comparable to prices at similar hotel restaurants in the West.

Achieving this standard of quality and service had not come easily. It took a talented and dedicated group of professionals to make it a reality. However, even though it already had established a positive reputation, working to maintain it continued to challenge the Aerostar's management team. Andrew Ivanyi, a Canadian, was the General Manager of the Moscow Aerostar Hotel. According to him, the development of managerial talent was one of the biggest obstacles facing the Aerostar.

The plan had been to drastically reduce the number of expatriates running the hotel within two years of opening, but after one year the number of expatriates had grown instead. Because of the low productivity resulting from having to operate with a staff which was completely inexperienced in the hotel business, the Aerostar required twice as many employees to operate than comparable hotels in the West. It had 550 Russian employees.[5] There were 20 expatriates managing the hotel when it opened and this number was to be reduced to 10 by January 1993. Instead, by June 1992, there were 22 expatriate managers. The number of employees and expatriate managers had a major impact on the budget.

Recruiting

Recruitment of staff began with an advertisement in a Russian newspaper which had home-delivery only and was geared to young people. If the position required fluency in English for the front desk, for example, then the advertisement would be in English which acted as an initial screen. The response to recruitment advertisements had been good and the calibre of the applicants was high. Many of the people who applied were university graduates (e.g., medical doctors, psychology professors, engineers, nurses, and lawyers). Recently, however, a decline in good applicants was prompting hotel management to consider a "hire-a-friend" campaign in which employees would be encouraged to bring in people they knew to apply for work.

Initially, the Aerostar used an Aeroflot application form which had many questions that would have been considered illegal to ask in Canada. For example, applicants had to provide their age, number of children, whether their parents belonged to the Communist Party, where they had worked before, what diseases they had had, and whether they had ever done military service. Many of these questions have since been removed, but some remain. They still inquire about how many children applicants have and how old they are. Children are almost sacred in Russia and it was important to know whether there was anyone at home to look after them. According to Laurie Sagle, Director of Training and Personnel, it was not uncommon for a mother to take three weeks off from work to stay at home with a child who had a simple cold. Medical certificates of absence from doctors were readily available and, just for a cold, people might take a week or two off for rest. Laurie commented that it seemed like people always wanted to rest:

> "Last weekend was a four-day holiday with beautiful weather and we were outside in the parks and walking. Many of the local people stayed in their homes and rested. We had to emphasize during orientation that their hard currency bonus was based on performance and attendance. If they're not here, they're not performing."

Unlike other joint venture hotels in Moscow, the Aerostar did not rely on Russian managers to interview and select the Russian staff. Hotel policy specified that at least one, and usually two, expatriates be involved. The initial interview consisted of a ten-minute screening to see if the applicant appeared to be hireable for some job in the hotel. Interviewers checked for mastery of the English language and general grooming. If the applicant passed, a second interview was arranged on the spot since many of the applicants had no telephone. The second interview was longer and usually was conducted by a manager of a functional area. Laurie suggested that this had presented somewhat of a problem since the applicants were often very reluctant to specify which area interested them:

> "Generally, they have no idea. They don't know the hotel business. They're used to being told everything. They've never been given a selection or choice before. However, you do get some who really want the front desk, for example, and those who do won't change their minds. If you don't have a job for them there, they don't want to work for you."

It was very difficult to know the right questions to ask during interviews. For example, one of the questions commonly asked in the West – "Why do you want to work here?" – did not elicit the desired response in Moscow. The usual answers included: "I want to meet foreigners" and "I want to improve my English." Questions such as: "Why should we hire you?" and "What good qualities or attributes do you have for our business?" would be followed by stunned silence since Russian people considered bragging to be rude. Asking the applicant why he or she should be hired over someone else did not help since the typical answer was that the other person would probably be a better choice. According to Laurie, the most telling replies were to the question: "What did you do in your last job?" The typical answer might be: "Oh, we had meetings, we discussed issues, we solved problems." When asked to specify what they actually did or accomplished, few people were able to answer.

"Finally, I had someone who was honest and said, 'Oh, I did nothing, I just sat at my desk all day.' Most would say they discussed problems and when asked if anything was fixed, they would say they discussed it. It's a country that philosophizes. You could get almost no one to tell you what they did."

Another difficulty arose concerning reference checks. People were stunned when they received the call asking about an applicant, and nobody would give a bad reference even though a Russian made the call. The hotel gave up on all reference checks except those to other joint ventures in the city:

"We call the personnel and training managers at the other hotels and ask them about the person: 'Fired for theft' might be the reply. Let's face it, who is going to quit a job where they get paid three times the norm plus a currency bonus? Very few people quit. Most that leave are let go."

Orientation

There was a five-day orientation program during which new employees were taught the concept of profit, the organization chart, and what the departments do (e.g., house-keeping, stewarding, business centre), so that they would know if guests asked. They toured the hotel and had lunch in the cafeteria as a group. The rules and regulations were explained and they were given information on grooming, uniforms, receiving a salary paid in cash, and discipline issues.

Laurie explained that the hotel's expectations were made very clear during the first week of training:

"I tell them that class starts at nine in the morning and if they're not here on time, the door is going to be shut. That's because time is a cultural difference we've observed; people are late all the time. Maybe it's because previously there was not a lot of work to be done, so it's not a big deal. We are trying to instill values we think are important. Punctuality is a big issue. How can we open a restaurant if the staff is not there to serve the guests? We're providing service so we have to be punctual."

The second day of training consisted of the first "Customer Service" component. Recruits were taught the hotel's two customer service standards: **Smile and Help**. Role playing and evaluations were used to show them how to smile and how to help guests by answering questions or by meeting requests. They were taught five steps for meeting a guest's requests and how they were supposed to follow up. Then they were taught general fire safety rules.

The third day included listening and communicating skills in the morning. Employees were taught how to clarify and confirm requests, and why they must listen, for example. In the afternoon, those who were going to use telephones were taught "telephone courtesy" – what to say, how to put someone on hold, how to take a proper message, what to ask, and why it was important to repeat the message to make sure it had been correctly understood. Telephone courtesy courses were not offered at the hotel in Toronto where Laurie previously was the training manager, but in Russia they were needed. As Laurie said:

"They have never done any of this so it's more important that they get it right at the beginning before they have a lot of guest contact."

On the fourth day, there was a review, more role playing and a written test. So far, everyone had passed, but anyone who did not achieve at least 75 percent on the test was reviewed. In the afternoon, women received cosmetic training. They would bring their own make-up since there was no point in teaching them about make-up to which they would not have access. Laurie said:

"I tell them about some of the surveys comparing women photographed with no make-up and wearing a business suit, another with too much make-up and a business suit, and a third with the appropriate amount of make-up and a business suit. The photos were sent to a sample of CEOs who were asked to rate the women's credibility. The woman who rated highest on productivity and efficiency was the one with an appropriate amount of make-up on because she looked like she was ready for business. They find that fascinating. We tell them that if they are at the front desk with absolutely no make-up on, they may be 25 or 30 years old but look like a little girl, and it is really hard to handle a guest's problems or complaints."

In Toronto, the make-up classes were optional. But in Russia, there was nowhere to learn this information and, unfortunately, the Russian women who wore make-up wore too much. The class was held for all female employees.

Apparently, Russians were accustomed to learning by memorizing. Questions dealing with memorized facts were no problem (e.g., What does the bar offer? What's the cost of a taxi?). The problem came with questions about what to do in certain situations. Role playing had been used but had met with some difficulty since Russians were not very comfortable with that training method. Laurie said that she wanted them to practice during the training sessions because it was a safe place to do it. They were afraid of looking stupid, but she stressed that it was better to make mistakes in training than with a guest. Everyone was required to participate. At first, Laurie found it frustrating that the employees never asked questions. She encouraged them to ask questions by explaining that when they said nothing, she assumed that they were not interested and did not want to be there.

On the fifth day, the employees went to the departments in which they would be working and were shown how to do the job by the supervisor.

Laurie's degree in Hotel and Restaurant Management, her diploma in Teaching and Training Adults and her experience as Training Manager at a major hotel in Toronto had not prepared her for some of the adjustments she discovered that she had to make in Moscow. In most cases, she had to completely rewrite the examples she used for her courses in Moscow. For example, one of her exercises for teaching trainees the meaning of good service consisted of asking trainees to think of a time when they were in a hotel or restaurant and received good service. In North America, people had difficulty coming up with examples of good service – precisely the point of the exercise. So, the trainer asked them to think of examples of bad service which then led to the reverse of these examples constituting good service or hospitality. In Moscow, nobody understood the word "service." Laurie had to change the exercise to: "Raise your hand if you've ever had a guest at your house." Since Russian people loved to entertain friends and took great pride in their hospitality, everyone would raise their hand. Laurie then asked them to list some of the things they did in preparation for the evening. The answers started coming, at first tentatively and then with more assurance: "I go out and buy some Vodka!" (everyone would laugh); "I wear my good clothes!"; "I clean the house!". "And this, what you do when you entertain guests at home", explained Laurie, "is exactly what service and hospitality are all about." And then they understood.

Laurie found that she had to incorporate social skills training into her program also in order to eliminate unacceptable behavior. For example, she described a reception catered by the hotel at which the staff were drinking while they were working:

"On New Year's Eve, we held a dinner-dance for foreigners. They bought tickets, just like at home. The staff had to work and we provided taxis home when they were done. Well, they ended up drinking all night in the back rooms. They would take someone's glass away and drink what was left in it. They felt that this was New Year's Eve and this was a party. They did not seem to realize that they were here to work. Drinking is a big thing that's culturally accepted."

Supervisory Training Program

Department heads selected employees from their departments for promotion to supervisor on the basis of their work performance in the department. Once an employee was promoted, he/she would be scheduled to attend the next scheduled Supervisory Orientation Supplement (SOS) and the next Supervisor Training Program.

The SOS was a general orientation during which new supervisors were given information to help them in their new jobs. They were shown how to read profit and loss statements. Their responsibilities as supervisors were explained and they were given guidance about how to discipline employees.

The Supervisor Training Program consisted of eight sessions. Two sessions were held each month and were typically attended by groups of 22 supervisors.

Session 1: Introduction

The purpose of this two-hour session was to clarify management's expectations with respect to the supervisors' behavior during the training program. The students were expected to arrive on time for classes, do their homework, participate in class, and practice what they learned in class in their daily work. The students were asked what they expected to learn from this training program and why they thought they were there. This question puzzled most of them and some of them admitted that they were there simply because their supervisors had told them to be there. Exhibit 1 lists the educational background of a typical group of supervisors.

During the introductory session, they also completed the Hersey and Blanchard situational leadership questionnaire for use in analyzing and evaluating their management style during Session 2.

EXHIBIT **1**   Educational Background of a Typical Group of Hotel Supervisors

Current Position at The Aerostar	Educational Background
Staff English Teacher	Degree from the Pedagogical Institute of English and French
Maintenance Engineering Supervisor	Degree from the Moscow Civil Engineering Institute
Security Supervisor	Degree from the Highest School of the Militia and a 5-year Law Degree
Laundry Supervisor	High School Diploma
Interpreter/Training Department Administrator	Degree from the Pedagogical Institute of English and German
Switchboard Supervisor	Degree from the Pedagogical Institute of English and German
Restaurant Supervisor	Degree from the Pedagogical Institute of Musical Education
Bellman Supervisor	Degree from the Institute of Geological Prospecting
Engineering Supervisor	Degree from the Power Engineering Institute
Housekeeping Supervisor	High School Diploma

Session 2: Situational Leadership

During this four-hour session, the results of the situational leadership questionnaire were discussed with each participant. Laurie stressed that there was not "one best leadership style." Instead, situational leadership theory advocated the tailoring of one's leadership style to the requirements of each specific issue being addressed and each employee involved. Supervisors were taught to evaluate the competence and commitment level displayed by each of their employees on each task which they were required to perform. Supervisors were taught to rate their employees at Level 1, "Disillusioned Learner," on tasks for which they possessed low competence and low commitment; Level 2 "Enthusiastic Beginner," on tasks for which the employee possessed low competence but high commitment; Level 3, "Reluctant Contributor," on tasks for which they possessed high competence but varying levels of commitment; and Level 4, "Peak Performer," on tasks for which they possessed both high competence and high commitment. Four different leadership styles were to be used depending on the level attained by the employee on a particular task.

Session 3: Listening and Communications

This was a general session on why listening is important and how to improve one's listening skills. Laurie used various activities to get these points across. One of these, for example, was the "Broken Telephone Line Game" in which each participant whispered a predetermined message to the next person and the message became garbled by the time it reached the end of the line. Another activity was to have two people sit back-to-back and have one of them instruct the other to draw something based on verbal instructions only. What was drawn was always quite different from what the communicator had intended.

Session 4: How to Train Employees

During this session, supervisors were taught the five steps to follow for teaching job skills: tell them; show them; let them try it; observe their performance; and praise any progress. Students practiced these steps by writing job tasks which involved breaking simple jobs down into steps because, as Laurie pointed out, "you can't teach a job, you can only teach the steps."

Session 5: Giving Feedback

This session was to teach the supervisors the importance of giving specific, timely, and sincere feedback for the improved performance of their employees. Most of the session was spent practicing and observing the effect of negative feedback, no feedback, positive but not sincere feedback, and positive and sincere feedback on performance. The exercises almost always pointed to positive and sincere feedback being associated with the highest quality work.

Session 6: Coaching Theory

This was the most difficult session because it dealt with confronting employee problems. Supervisors were taught to overcome their tendency to define and solve the problem on the spot (e.g., You are late. Buy a new alarm clock and get here on time). Instead, they were to attempt to get the employee to admit that a problem existed and then, to try to engage the employee in coming up with his or her own alternative solutions to encourage more commitment to the selected solution. Supervisors were taught five steps to follow: (1) get the employee to admit that there was a problem; (2) discuss alternative behaviors; (3) decide which alternative behavior was to be selected; (4) follow up and verify that the employee was changing his/her behavior; and (5) provide recognition of any behavioral change, no matter how small.

Session 7: Coaching Practice

This session began with a ten-minute review of coaching theory. The rest of the session was devoted to practicing what had been learned by playing the roles of supervisors and employees dealing with realistic hotel situations.

Session 8: Exam

Two weeks after Session 7, the student supervisors were given a three-hour written test and a behavioral exam on what they had learned. Finally, the supervisors were rewarded for completing the course with a certificate presented by the hotel manager at a special luncheon in the hotel restaurant.

Laurie reminisced about some of the difficulties encountered with the first group of graduates:

> "When the first group completed the supervisory training course, the manager and I decided that because this was our first group and because they had done so well and were so eager, we would take them to the Aerostar restaurant for lunch. Normally, they are not allowed in there. It was a fiasco! I had an inkling that it might be so and had talked about what was appropriate to have for lunch and what they could order: one appetizer, one main course and one dessert, which would be a big lunch for us. A lot of them ordered two appetizers, like a soup and shrimp. One man ordered two main courses, some of them ordered two desserts – they would have something like chocolate mousse *and* ice cream – even after we had talked to them about it! It was almost like they thought they would never get in here again, so they had to try it all. It was a 'live for now, we've got it so we had better try it' behaviour. I took responsibility for it and my boss and I laughed about it later. But in the next session, I really went into detail about appropriate behavior at a business luncheon. No one had ever told them the importance of how one was perceived by a business associate!"

Expectations and Compensation

Management made it very clear that a job at the Aerostar meant more opportunities, better pay and better treatment than the employees would receive from a Russian organization, but it also meant more work than they had to do before in order to meet the higher expectations. The staff agreed that they worked harder than they ever had. Yet, Laurie felt that less was demanded of them than Western staff. There seemed to be no real work ethic. It was not uncommon for people to complain because they felt the work was physically too difficult and shift work interfered with time spent with their family. Added Laurie, "They're not even talking about children; they're talking about their parents!"

Russian employees in May 1992 were paid a ruble salary the equivalent of $25 per month which was about twice the state average. The typical salaries offered by state organizations for teachers and medical doctors would not exceed 1,500 rubles per month (or about $13). It was illegal to pay in hard currency, but each employee received a performance-based bonus in the form of a gift certificate for a hard currency shop. This bonus could be worth as much as $140 per month for some employees, or almost ten times what the average state employee earned! In spite of this, the employees continued to demand more. When asked their opinions about the rewards they received for their work, the typical responses included:

> "The salary is not good, but management treats me well."

> "The hotel is not doing enough for me, I expected more."

> "In general, I am pleased with what I am earning, but, with respect to the West, it's nothing."

> "The bonus is not very useful, things are quite expensive at the hard currency shops."

The lack of expression of gratitude or appreciation by the Russian employees for their high rate of pay and for other things provided by hotel management was a source of frustration to management. On the first anniversary of the opening of the hotel, a banner was displayed thanking the employees for their hard work and each one was personally handed a food basket containing a bottle of French red wine, a kilo of French cheese and a pineapple. Only one employee said thank you. In fact, one employee said that he did not like red wine and asked for a bottle of white. At Christmas, the manager had food packages delivered to directors of agencies and organizations which dealt with the Aerostar. He received no thanks. Apparently, even a recent 30-percent raise was greeted with: "Is that all? Give me more." According to Laurie:

> "There are a limited number of joint ventures and good jobs here but they still don't look at what they have compared to others. The glass is always seen as half-empty, not half-full. After a while you get frustrated with that. Then you get someone who comes up and thanks you for something and you feel really good about it all again and you think, 'OK, it's going to take a while but someone has appreciated something.'"

Developing Managers

At other joint venture hotels, Russian "deputies" were paired with managers trained in the West in the hope that they would develop the skills required to do the job eventually on their own. But even that did not result in them meeting North American standards. Sending Russians to North America for training was not seen as a viable alternative because of the cost involved and the small amount of learning and skill transfer associated with the process.

Andrew Ivanyi was frustrated with the hotel staff's lack of interest in the hotel business as a career:

> "The problem is that they don't see these jobs as their lifetime careers. They all want intellectual work, and manual labor unless it is taking place in a factory is not appealing to them."

In the West, promotion to line management was viewed as prestigious, but in Russia it just seemed to mean extra work. According to Laurie, there seemed to be little pride associated with a promotion to supervisor. In fact, Russian supervisors often questioned why everyone could not attend the special functions established for supervisors only or receive the rewards such as gift certificates and benefits set aside for supervisors. Lately, the benefits offered to supervisors have been changed to make them substantially more attractive than those offered to other employees. For example, the hard currency bonuses were now twice as much for supervisors as for other employees. In addition, supervisors were given their birthdays off with pay; were able to borrow video films from the hotel library for free; were reimbursed up to half of the tuition fees paid for courses directly relevant to their jobs in the hotel; were allowed to use their currency bonuses for travel outside Russia; and wore special name tags as a sign of their position. Still, with all of these attempts at trying to make supervisory positions more attractive to the hotel employees, Laurie was not sure that they were having the desired effect.

"How do we make them appreciate what they have here and want to be supervisors?" wondered Laurie

Notes

1. Moscow Aerostar Hotel press release, March 1992.
2. *The Globe and Mail,* February 9, 1993, p. B25.
3. Ibid.
4. Ibid.
5. Ibid.

CASE **14**

Robert Mondavi Corporation: Caliterra (A)

Brian R. Golden, Henry W. Lane and David T. A. Wesley

Alan Schnur, senior vice president of the Robert Mondavi Corporation, recalled how Michael Mondavi, president and CEO, had personally asked him to head up the company's joint venture in Chile. A Ph.D. in Psychology, he had previously been a senior management consultant with Towers Perrin, a leading global consulting firm that specialized in Organizational Strategy.

Schnur had been working with the Mondavi family for more than a year, when in early 1996, he was asked to present the family with a list of qualified candidates to manage the new joint venture in Chile. "You missed a name," Michael Mondavi replied. Schnur was sure that he hadn't. Mondavi quickly added, "Have you looked in the mirror?" Schnur was surprised by the offer. After all, his background was not in the wine industry and he had been working with the company for less than two years. Nevertheless, Mondavi believed that Schnur's Spanish-language skills and expertise in human resource management would be critical in managing the cross-cultural issues that were sure to arise.

Within months, Schnur was becoming all too aware of the challenges. Mondavi's success was built around producing the best quality wines in the industry, but distributors were complaining about the quality of Mondavi's first shipments of Chilean wine.

Then, in early March 1997, just as the situation appeared to be improving, Schnur received an alarming phone call from Chile. Wine valued at $450,000[1] had become contaminated due to poor sanitation. Furthermore, without a new winery, conditions were only going to continue to deteriorate. A few days later Schnur was at the Mondavi board meeting when Robert Mondavi looked him in the eye and said, "Fix it!"

David T. A. Wesley prepared this case under the supervision of Professors Brian R. Golden and Henry W. Lane solely to provide material for class discussion. The authors do not intend to illustrate either effective or ineffective handling of a managerial situation. The authors may have disguised certain names and other identifying information to protect confidentiality.

Company Background

The Robert Mondavi Winery was founded in 1966 when Robert Mondavi, an alumnus of Stanford University (Chemistry and Economics), and his oldest son, Michael Mondavi, purchased land in Northern California's Napa Valley. Robert Mondavi already had 30 years of winemaking experience when he founded the winery. The new facility was the first major winery constructed in the United States since the end of prohibition.

At the time, Napa Valley did not enjoy a reputation for fine wine. "Throughout the 1950s and early 1960s," recalled Robert Mondavi,

> . . . we in California had enormous potential; I knew we could become one of the great wine-producing regions of the world. But the American wine industry was still in its infancy, and no one seemed to have the knowledge, the vision, or the guts to reach for the gold, to make wines that could stand proudly next to the very best from France, Germany, and Spain.[2]

The Mondavi family was one of the first to invest in new French oak barrels for ageing their wines. Friends of the family warned that the plan was a "one-way ticket to financial disaster."[3] Michael Mondavi recalled,

> Starting a winery was big news. After all, this was the first new winery constructed since 1934. People in the valley thought we were crazy. Our winery was referred to as "Robert's Folly" or the "test-tube winery." They said, "Look at the way he's spending money on French oak barrels." It simply wasn't done.[4]

The Mondavis began construction of the winery in 1966 and, despite criticism that the undertaking would be impossible, completed the construction in time for the next harvest.

> Though a lot of people said we couldn't do it, we brought in a harvest and made wine that very same year – before we even had a roof on the winery![5]

After a difficult start, Mondavi wines began to develop a reputation for quality, and by the early 1970s were winning awards. Eventually, Robert Mondavi came to be regarded as the single most influential person in elevating the status of California, and particularly Napa Valley, wines.

A facility was purchased in Woodbridge in 1979 for the production of California varietal wines. In 1979, Robert Mondavi also began the production of Opus One, an ultra-premium[6] Bordeaux-style red wine, in a joint venture with the Baron Philippe de Rothschild of Chateau Mouton Rothschild in France. A year earlier, in 1978, the Baron had proposed the joint venture to produce Napa Valley wines under French and American supervision.

The Rothschilds began producing wines in 1853 when the Baron Nathaniel de Rothschild became the owner of the Chateau Mouton Estate in Bordeaux, France. Only two years later the Mouton-Rothschild label was classified by the French government as a Premier Cru, a designation awarded to the top five wines in the country. The company's low-priced brand, Mouton-Cadet, was introduced in 1933 and went on to become the world's most successful wine brand. The high profile attached to the Opus One joint venture had much to do with the Rothschild's stature within the wine community, and proved valuable in raising the status of Mondavi's other brands.

Negotiations for the Opus One joint venture were conducted very informally one morning at the Baron's chateau near Bordeaux, France. The agreement, which specified relatively few details, was settled in two hours, and became the model for Mondavi's future joint ventures. Until a dedicated winery could be built and vineyards planted, Robert Mondavi was to manage the production of Opus One wines using Mondavi facilities. "Ours was an accord built on shared passions and mutual trust," Mondavi recalled.

> And not once . . . did the Baron ever change one iota of our initial agreement, nor did he waver from our initial goals and spirit.[7]

The Mondavis placed great importance on aesthetics. The Opus One winery, for example, was constructed under the most detailed architectural planning, reflecting Robert Mondavi's passion for "high art." A leading interior designer from Paris ensured that the finest art and fabric adorned the interior. A leading wine journalist wrote of the winery:

> First you descend a stately spiral staircase that opens onto a dimly lit hallway. At the end of the hall is a tasting room with a dramatic curved glass wall that overlooks a sweeping semicircular vista – to your right and left, rows of barrels stretch away into obscurity. The effect is breathtaking.[8]

The total construction cost for the 30,000-barrel per year facility was an unprecedented $26.5 million.

International Focus

The company continued to expand throughout the 1980s, acquiring several smaller California wineries. The 1990s saw significant expansion into international production. In 1995, the Mondavis entered into a joint venture with the Frescobaldi family to produce and market Italian ultra premium wines at $50 per bottle. Marchesi de' Frescobaldi, established in 1308, was one of Italy's oldest wineries, and with annual production of 5.5 million bottles, one of the largest.

In December 1996, Mondavi began producing wines in the Languedoc region of France under the brand name Vichon. Languedoc had a reputation for producing the worst wines in France, but, as he had done in Napa Valley, Robert Mondavi planned to elevate the status of the region by introducing higher quality wines. In this case, however, Mondavi could not find a suitable partner in the region, and decided to go it alone.

Robert Mondavi explained the reason for expanding internationally:

> We are going offshore to produce wines because we realize that each country has its own particular style and character which is involved with the wine and cuisine of that country.

This is also true of our country. We want to be able to supply, in America, wines of these different types to go with various international cuisine. We want to take the Mondavi winemaking style to the other great winemaking regions of the world, and we want to make wine that reflects that unique character for the people in this country.[9]

A worldwide wine grape shortage in 1995 and 1996 resulted in higher costs, particularly in California. From 1995 to 1997, Mondavi's profit margin declined from 53.8 percent to 44.8 percent. However, during the same period, the company grew significantly and, in 1997 alone, increased its vineyards by 1,000 acres, or approximately 25 percent. As a result, the company achieved record revenue and income despite declining margins. Margins were expected to recover as soon as grape harvests improved and grape prices, which accounted for approximately 30 percent of costs, returned to normal.

Quality

Quality had always been of critical importance to the Mondavi family. "I am an uncompromising perfectionist," recalled Robert Mondavi. "And I became an absolute fanatic about detail."[10] This attention to detail helped Mondavi win numerous international awards. In 1997, the company began compiling a database of the awards won by Mondavi wines. For the years 1990 to 1997 alone, the database already included several hundred awards.

In each wine region where Mondavi had interests, a flagship brand represented the best the region had to offer. In California it was Opus One and in Italy it was Luce. These ultra premium wines retailed for $50 to $100 per bottle and were regularly ranked among the top 100 wines in the world by magazines such as *The Wine Spectator*. Although these brands were profitable, their main purpose was to lend recognition and prestige to the entire family of wines under them. The consumer, it was hoped, would recognize that Mondavi's less expensive table wines were produced in the same regions and under the same careful management as the flagship brands.

From the 1970s to 1996, Mondavi exports increased from 1 to 10 percent of sales, making it the largest exporter of premium California wines. The company had an initial public offering in 1993, while retaining control of 92 percent of voting shares among family members. Imported wine from Mondavi's joint ventures accounted for 3.5 percent of the approximately seven million cases sold in 1997, and 27.4 percent of the company's sales growth.

In 1998, Mondavi was one of the world's larger wine companies, with 890 employees and sales in 90 countries. Revenue from sales amounted to $325.2 million.

The Chilean Wine Industry

The production of wine in Chile began with the planting of vineyards by Jesuit missionaries in the sixteenth century. These first vineyards were established more than two centuries ahead of California's. In 1840 Chile began exporting bulk wine to neighboring countries, thereby becoming the first wine-exporting nation in the Americas.

In 1877, the European wine industry was devastated by a phylloxera plague.[11] By the end of the century two-thirds of European vineyards had been destroyed. California, Australia, South Africa and most other wine-producing regions eventually became infested. Only Chile, due to its isolation, remained untouched. Chile also benefited from near ideal growing conditions, such as dry summers, mild winters, and ideal soil conditions. Situated at 36 degrees south latitude, Chile's wine region was directly opposite California's 36 degrees north latitude. Chile and California also shared their proximity to the Pacific Ocean to the west and mountain ranges to the east.

Industry in Decline

Many of the most reputable vineyards were family-owned and cultivated over several generations. In 1970, as part of the 'agrarian revolution' introduced by the Marxist government of former president Salvador Allende, most of Chile's vineyards were expropriated. The newly formed National Wine Company took control, but its heavily laden bureaucracy and lack of professional oenologists precipitated a sharp decline in quality and productivity. Exports all but collapsed and Chile's reputation for quality eroded. Although the government of General Augusto Pinochet[12] returned the vineyards to their original owners, the wine industry continued to struggle well into the next decade. Entire wineries were sold for only a few hundred thousand dollars, including land, buildings, equipment, and cellars.[13]

Chile's largest potential market was the United States. Although it ranked well behind Europe in per capita wine consumption, the U.S. was less protective with regard to wine imports. However, while most of Chile's production was geared toward red wine such as Cabernet Sauvignon, reds only accounted for 30 percent of wine sales in the U.S. in the 1970s. Vintner Concha y Toro was among the first to realize the problem and, in the late 1970s, began efforts to produce higher quality white wines. Nevertheless, most companies did not have the resources to improve quality and continued to use antiquated equipment, such as fermentation vats made out of cement. Only a few used stainless steel, and fewer still used new oak barrels.

In the 1980s domestic consumption in Chile went into rapid decline. Bulk wine prices fell to as low as five cents per litre. "Between 1985 and 1990, nearly two-thirds of the country's vineyards were ripped out to make way for more profitable fruits like nectarines, peaches, and plums. The total number of hectares of vineyards fell from 120,000 to 45,000 in that five-year period as the Chilean people turned away from wine in favor of soft drinks, beer and liquid yogurt drinks, among other novelties."[14] The remaining producers realized that exporting was the only way to survive. By 1996, exports accounted for nearly 60 percent of sales.

The American Connection

By a stroke of luck, the decline in wine sales in Chile coincided with strong growth in sales in the United States. For the first time, in 1980, wine sales in the U.S. exceeded spirits by 100 million litres.[15] Efforts to improve quality eventually paid off. In the United States, sales of Chilean wine grew by an average of approximately 50 percent per year from 1987 to 1991 to rank Chile as the third largest wine exporter to the United States. Total volume exported to the U.S. increased from only 50,000 cases in 1978 to 1.3 million cases in 1991. In subsequent years, Chile remained the third largest exporting nation.

Despite the many similarities, California presented a much more difficult growing environment compared to Chile. Vintners waged constant war on diseases such as phylloxera. To combat these diseases, California developed the most advanced viticulture research program in the world at the University of California, Davis. In total, California producers spent an estimated $2 billion fighting disease.

In contrast, Chile had what one leading wine expert referred to as "absurdly easy" growing conditions. Starting a vineyard was almost as simple as sticking vines in the ground. Direct foreign investment and the transfer of expertise allowed Chile to greatly increase the quality of its wines. For example, while in the mid-1980s most producers used cement fermentation vats, stainless steel was becoming the norm in the 1990s. Stainless steel vats, while more expensive, were much easier to clean than cement. They also had cooling jackets on the outside of the vats which controlled temperature and prevented the wine from overheating.

Chile further benefited from a shift in consumption toward red wine that followed the release of a study done at Cornell University in 1991 that found a lower incidence of heart disease among red wine drinkers. Red wine sales surged, growing by 151 percent from 1991 to 1997 and capturing nearly 40 percent of U.S. table wine sales.

Then in 1995 and 1996, poor weather and phylloxera resulted in a decline in the California grape harvest while, at the same time, consumer demand in the U.S. was increasing. Under normal circumstances, diverse weather conditions ensured that when some regions experienced poor crops, others would be plentiful. However, the California shortage coincided with a drought in Europe that resulted in a worldwide grape shortage. Price increases from between 5 and 10 percent for California wines made Chilean wines more attractive to value-conscious consumers. In 1996, Chile more than doubled its exports to the United States, far exceeding increases from other major wine regions, and Chilean vintner Concha y Toro became the second largest import label in the U.S. (1.7 million cases).

Chile offered several advantages over the United States. At an average $2.00 per hour, Chile's labor costs were one-tenth that of California's. Although technology had made labor less important, planting and maintenance both continued to be labor-intensive. And Chile's relatively low land prices provided further incentive for foreign investment compared to other southern hemisphere producers.

Most California vintners viewed Chile as a temporary solution to the wine grape shortage. For many, their involvement in Chile was limited to sourcing contracts with Chilean producers. Under such contracts, bulk wine was shipped to California and bottled under California brand names.[16] As soon as the shortage ended, these companies planned to pull out of Chile.

From Shortage to Glut?

Many vintners responded to the continuing surge in demand for Chilean wine by planting new vineyards. Increased grape prices encouraged significant new vine planting in other major wine-producing regions of the world as well, such as Australia and South Africa. However, most of the newly planted vines were not expected to produce harvests until 2001. Meanwhile, worldwide wine consumption was in steady decline, especially among younger consumers.

Caliterra Brand

Viña Errazuriz

Viña Errazuriz [err-AH-soo-rees] was founded in 1870 by Maximiano Errazuriz Valdivieso, a Chilean of Basque origin. Don Maximiano[17] purchased land in the Aconcagua Valley, imported grapevines from France, and hired a French oenologist to apply wine-growing techniques that were considered advanced for that era. The Errazuriz name became important in Chile, and after Chile's independence from Spain, the country saw four presidents and two archbishops from the Errazuriz family.

By the 1950s the family's estate had grown to over 1,000 hectares and was considered the largest single estate winery in the world. Alfonso Chadwick Errazuriz, a direct descendant of the founder, became head of the winery in 1983, at a time when the Chilean wine industry was in rapid decline. Chadwick invested heavily in new equipment in order to improve the quality of Errazuriz wines, thereby enhancing their suitability for the demanding export market.

In 1989, Alfonso Chadwick's son, Eduardo Chadwick, formed a partnership with Franciscan Vineyards of California to produce wines specifically for the U.S. market. Since many Americans had difficulty pronouncing Errazuriz, the name Caliterra was chosen instead, but was used exclusively in North America. In essence, Caliterra and Errazuriz were the same and used the same grapes, wineries, and production facilities. Franciscan merely acted as a U.S. agent for the wine.

Within a short period, Chadwick and Augustin Huneus, president of Franciscan Vineyards, began to disagree over the future of the brand. While Chadwick planned to develop Caliterra internationally, Huneus wanted to focus on the United States. When Huneus, a Chilean by birth, purchased land in Chile and began developing his own facilities, Chadwick started to question Huneus' long-term commitment to Caliterra. Eventually, Huneus and Chadwick decided to part ways and the joint venture agreement was dissolved.

After the passing of Alfonso Chadwick Errazuriz in 1993, Eduardo Chadwick became president of Errazuriz. Aside from a brief interruption during the Allende era, when most wineries were nationalized, the company remained in the sole control of family members through five generations.

In the early 1990s, Errazuriz produced between 200,000 and 300,000 cases[18] of wine annually and employed approximately 50 full-time staff, not including seasonal labor.

Robert Mondavi

With an eye toward Chile, the Mondavi family met with several Chilean producers during a visit to Chile in 1991. Eduardo Chadwick was not seeking a partner at the time, but as a courtesy to Robert Mondavi, Augustin Huneus arranged for Chadwick to act as Mondavi's guide. Caliterra's commercial director explained:

> Augustin arranged for Chadwick to escort Mondavi. The wine industry is very competitive in the market, but very friendly in production. There is lots of exchange in information. You open your doors to everybody. It is a wide open and very friendly industry.

After careful consideration, the Mondavi family decided to partner with one of the four larger wine companies, but negotiations broke down when the Mondavis sensed that their prospective partner was not 100 percent behind the joint venture. While many California producers went to Chile to make up for a temporary grape shortage, Mondavi was committed to a long-term partnership as part of the company's internationalization strategy. Therefore, they needed a partner who also had a long-term commitment.

Eduardo Chadwick, who was then in his early thirties, approached Robert Mondavi with a sense of eagerness. Chadwick, like many in the industry, held the father of the modern California wine industry in high esteem and hoped to benefit from the reputation and expertise Mondavi would bring to Caliterra. He knew that Chile's climate and soil conditions were capable of yielding among the best wines in the world, but achieving world-class status would be difficult without a world-class partner to help improve quality and lend prestige to the brand.

For his part, Robert Mondavi was impressed by the young Chadwick. His passion for quality winemaking and his willingness to learn were reminiscent of Mondavi's own early years in the wine industry. Schnur explained:

> Robert Mondavi saw something of himself in Eduardo Chadwick. We were looking for someone who was passionate about wine, but eager to learn. It seemed to fit. Chadwick seemed like he could be part of the family.

Family-owned conglomerates, known as *Grupos Industriales*, were common throughout Latin America and most of Chile's wineries, including Errazuriz, were owned by such companies. The owners of Santa Rita, for example, also owned the country's only major glass factory. Owning a winery was an important status symbol for such families, and Chile's elite were often referred to as *Apellidos Vinosos* (wine families). In a country where personal relations were extremely important, some believed that in order to succeed in business, one had to partner with the *Apellidos Vinosos*. They "serve to give status to business operations," one journalist wrote.[19]

Chadwick's other business interests included a Coca-Cola bottling plant, a brewery, a malt factory, and mining interests. In total, Caliterra and Errazuriz only accounted for about 5 percent of Chadwick's holdings. For this reason, Mondavi's marketing manager did not view Chadwick entirely as a young Robert Mondavi:

> Yes, wine is a passion, but it's not a big part of Chadwick's business. To Mondavi it is everything!

Nevertheless, Errazuriz managers estimated that Chadwick spent 70 percent of his time on Errazuriz and Caliterra.

The general manager of Errazuriz commented:

> Errazuriz is much smaller than Polar (Coca-Cola bottling), but it's Eduardo's baby. It is the business that he loves. He is very involved in Errazuriz. . . . There is no relation between involvement and the size of the company.

The Mondavis' first reaction when Chadwick approached them with the idea of forming a joint venture was not positive. The general manager for Errazuriz explained:

> Mondavi was impressed with his passion and enthusiasm, but he had nothing to show. Errazuriz was too small. It was not part of the big group (Chile's five largest wineries).

In June 1995, Chadwick met with the Mondavi family again at VINEXPO. By this time, negotiations with Mondavi's other potential partner in Chile had failed and the family was more receptive to Chadwick's offer.

One point in Chadwick's favor was "the story." "When you sell a bottle of wine, you sell a lot more than a bottle of wine," Alan Schnur noted. Wine embodied Western culture and civilization. This was reflected in the sometimes extravagant rituals associated with wine drinking. Errazuriz, as "one of Chile's oldest and most respected wineries," conveyed an image to the consumer that was consistent with Mondavi's other products. The consumer needed a reason to choose Caliterra over the plethora of competing wines that had been introduced in recent years.

By the end of VINEXPO, Chadwick and Mondavi agreed to a 50/50 joint venture to be formalized in early 1996. The deal provided for a $12 million equity investment to develop vineyards and construct modern winery facilities by 1999. A lack of technology had been the greatest stumbling block for most Chilean wineries and, until the new winery was complete, Caliterra wines would be shipped to the U.S. in bulk and bottled at Mondavi's California facilities. Mondavi also arranged to take over as the exclusive agent for Viña Errazuriz in the U.S. In total, Caliterra would account for less than 5 percent of Mondavi's worldwide business.

In order to give the joint venture the best possible start, the Mondavis arranged to send the company's entire sales force of 122 to Chile for a one-week course on the Chilean wine industry. This involved touring the facilities of Errazuriz and competing wineries, such as Concha y Toro. The purpose was to familiarize the sales force with the Chilean geography, culture, and wine industry. However, Errazuriz did not have enough staff to provide much interaction between its Chilean employees and the American sales force.

Schnur's impression of the Chileans was very positive:

> Our partners are wonderful people, very warm and very friendly. They would fit in here in California. When we are in Chile, we stay in their homes. We need to be friends.

Transfer of Technology

Mondavi planned to transfer vineyard management experience gained under California's difficult growing environment to Chile. With growing seasons six months apart, viticulturists and oenologists from Chile would have the opportunity to spend time at Mondavi facilities in California working with Mondavi staff. Eventually the joint venture would have its own dedicated staff selected jointly by Errazuriz and Mondavi, but in the meantime, Caliterra would remain under Errazuriz management and Mondavi would pay Errazuriz for this service.

"We took everything we had and brought it to the table and they took everything they had and brought it to the table," Schnur noted. Errazuriz had much to offer in the way of local expertise in culture, human resources, accounting, and government relations, while Mondavi was more advanced in the areas of viticulture, oenology, and international marketing.

When Mondavi viticulturists visited the Chilean vineyards they were struck by the sophisticated irrigation system that channelled water from the Andes Mountains to flood the vineyards of the dry wine-growing regions of the country. Combined with hot dry summers, this system produced beautiful large grapes that could be made into very fruity but overly oxidized and flat wines (see Exhibit 1 for an explanation of wine terms).

In California, drip irrigation provided only enough water for the vines to grow and would "stress" or "starve" the vines to produce smaller, but more flavorful, grapes. Under this method, harvests were smaller and, therefore, more costly, but they were also much better suited for the production of premium wines.

Additionally, Chilean vine rows were spaced widely to allow easy irrigation and harvest. This would need to be replaced with close spacing of the rows to optimize sunlight absorption and reduce wind damage.

Caliterra's chief winemaker commented:

> With Mondavi, there had been a period of rapid change. Caliterra's quality standards went up immediately.[20]

The Quality Issue

Prior to the joint venture, sales of the Caliterra brand had been sluggish, amounting to 55,000 cases annually. The bottles were plain and the brand competed on price. Shortly after the joint venture was finalized, Mondavi's newly appointed brand manager for Caliterra wanted to reposition the wine in the premium or higher segments, along with the other brands in Mondavi's portfolio. He proposed changing the bottle design, label, and cork. Just about everything associated with the image of the wine would be redesigned. In order to make a fresh start, Mondavi's marketing team felt that recalling all unsold wine, bottled prior to the joint venture, would be in the company's best long-term interest.

While Errazuriz was supportive of changing the position of the brand, they did not feel it necessary to pull existing wine from store shelves. Errazuriz had already paid

EXHIBIT **1**   Glossary of Wine Terms

Flat:
Tasting term for a wine that is too low in acidity. A flat wine is lacking in crispness, as if something important is missing from the wine. Flat wines are difficult to drink and enjoy even if the flavor is good.

Fruity:
Term applied to a fine young wine which has the aroma and flavor of fresh fruit.

Oenology:
The science and technical study of winemaking.

Oxidized:
A fault in wine owing to excessive exposure to air. Can be detected both by nose and by palate.

Red wine:
Made by fermenting red grapes in the presence of their skins so that pigments in the skins can color the wine. Red wines are often aged in wooden barrels one to two years before bottling.

Table wine:
A wine between 10% and 14% alcohol by volume. It may be red, white, rosé and vinted off-dry.

Varietal:
The wine name taken from the grape variety used to make it. The following are some varietal names: Pinot Blanc, Chardonnay, Gewürztraminer, Riesling, Pinot Noir, Merlot, Cabernet Sauvignon.

Vintage:
Harvesting, crushing, and fermentation of grapes into wine. Applied to the crop of grapes or the wine of one season.

Vintner:
Common term for anyone in the wine business. It was originally reserved for those who grew grapes and produced wine, but common usage to date includes anyone in wine, whether in sales, marketing or production.

Viticulture:
The science, art, and study of grape growing.

Adapted from Fetzer and Sumac Ridge wine glossaries.

Franciscan Vineyards to sell the wine on incentive,[21] but most of it remained on store shelves. Withdrawing from the market, even temporarily, would be very costly in terms of lost sales and the cost of destroying existing bottles. The Mondavi people struggled to convince their Chilean counterparts that it was in the long-term best interest of the brand to absorb the cost of recalling the brand.

At the same time, the first Errazuriz wines began to arrive in the U.S. as a Mondavi import. This was the first time in the company's history that Mondavi had agreed to be an agent for another company's wine. It wasn't long before Schnur started fielding calls from distributors complaining that the bottles had scuff marks on the labels. Schnur soon learned that this was only the most evident symptom of a serious quality problem. Once they were returned to Mondavi, the bottles were discovered to have different fill levels, corks inserted at different depths, labels incorrectly placed on the bottle, and back labels with translation errors. Furthermore, many of the boxes used to ship the wines had broken.

Schnur got on the phone to Chile. How could this have happened? Why weren't the shipments checked? He listened for a response, but when it came, it was not what he expected. Schnur could not believe what he was hearing. The shipments *were* checked. They *knew* about the defects. But then why were they released? His counterpart responded, "Who's going to notice!"

With the company's reputation at stake, Schnur decided to issue a general recall of the Errazuriz brand. What concerned Schnur the most was the Chilean company's reaction. "When someone comes to Mondavi with a quality problem, we jump a mile."

While Schnur did not want to "Mondavi-ize" his Chilean partners by having them make clones of California wines, prudence dictated that someone from Mondavi should be sent to Chile. Two Mondavi managers were asked to go. Mondavi's bottling manager was sent to investigate the bottling problem and William Johnson, an accounting manager, was sent to act as a communications bridge between the two companies.

Soon after his arrival, Mondavi's bottling manager discovered that many of the bottles had dust particles in them and a disturbing number had been tainted by poor quality cork. The bottling manager remained in Chile for three weeks at the request of Errazuriz, providing advice on how to improve processes.

While most of the concerns were addressed, some problems continued to arise. For example, after he had returned to California, Mondavi's bottling manager was contacted by Errazuriz and told that new flange labels were peeling off during shipping. It was later discovered that Mondavi had similar problems when new labels were introduced some 15 years earlier. However, to Mondavi this problem was ancient history and the Mondavi people never expected they would encounter it again so many years later.

The Changing View of Quality in Chile

The Chileans viewed quality differently from Americans. Errazuriz was used to selling in the low end of the premium sector, and within Chile, Errazuriz was viewed as a quality wine.

The commercial director for Errazuriz described the company's position:

> Packaging was not as much of a concern, nor was marketing. We were concerned about value for money, selling on price. Our concerns were the varietal, price, and brand, and there was no disagreement in the past with Franciscan Vineyards.

The general manager (GM) of Errazuriz added:

> Errazuriz was in the high quality segment in 1995, but the standard reference point for quality has been going up. Packaging was not that important to the domestic market.
>
> We were doing things better than the Chilean industry, but not the same as Mondavi's standards. In Chile you don't see that love for work well done. This is something that is changing. Our intention is to learn faster and copy our partner.

Caliterra's GM in Chile echoed this view:

> Here we will try to get it right, but if we make a mistake, that is okay. We need to battle against thinking that it is okay to make mistakes.

In order to ensure that quality standards would be met in the future, Mondavi decided to introduce its procedures manual in Chile. This manual ran to several hundred pages in length and was normally used in conjunction with *The Technology of Wine Making*, an industry standard textbook.

Errazuriz managers, having been accustomed to making more intuitive and spontaneous decisions, became "extraordinarily frustrated" by the complexities of these quality controls. Schnur agreed that such controls did not allow the same flexibility Errazuriz had had in the past:

> We are slow and we plan in too much detail. We have a process written for everything, from how to change a cork to how to buy land. The most difficult need to reconcile is our need for planning versus their need to act.

One Chilean manager commented:

> It was very efficient to have one person making the decision. I would ask the general manager about changing the label, for example, and it took about five minutes to get Chadwick's approval.

Suppliers

The GM for Errazuriz believed that a major source of difficulty was with suppliers. In the United States, most suppliers had high quality standards and Mondavi did not need to inspect every shipment to ensure that it met company specifications. Chile was another matter. Suppliers who produced the company's bottles, corks, labels, and boxes had limited competition and high demand for their products.

> We are more concerned about quality than the Americans because we don't have good suppliers and we have to reject a lot. Mondavi doesn't have to worry about quality control because they can rely on their suppliers, but in Chile we have to check on everyone.

For example, Chile had only one major bottle manufacturer, Cristalerias Chile S.A., owned by the same family that owned Santa Rita wines. When Mondavi deemed that the glass color was unacceptable for Caliterra, Errazuriz went to Cristalerias to ask for changes. Cristalerias responded by saying that they would be unable to make the requested changes. To Mondavi, this was unacceptable and Errazuriz was asked to make the request again. Their response was, "We can't go back a second time." How could they tell the bottle manufacturer that the glass did not meet their standards without potentially harming Caliterra's relationship with their only supplier?

Results

Eventually, Errazuriz agreed to Mondavi's proposed recall of the Caliterra brand. "In contrast to the 55,000 cases per year that Errazuriz was selling before the recall, we sold 172,000 cases in the first nine months after repositioning," commented Mondavi's marketing manager. But he also commended Chadwick for his concern over the cost of a general recall.

> You can make the greatest wine in the world and not make a penny. They are teaching us how to focus on this (earnings).

Caliterra's commercial director recalled:

> Caliterra really changed as a company and as a brand. It had a different packaging and a different price. The idea was to launch a new wine in the premium sector.

Caliterra's own growth put a strain on the company's resources and the staff's ability to focus on quality improvements. From sales of 55,000 cases per annum prior to the joint venture, volume growth increased quickly under the joint venture as shown in the following table.

TABLE 1   Caliterra 1995 to 1998

Year	1995	1996	1997	1998*	1999*	2000*
Capacity (000 litres)	0	0	0	5,300	6,300	10,800
Hectares under cultivation	20	20	158	227	290	350
Word Sales Volume (cases)[22]	245,000	620,000	460,000	550,000	700,000	835,000

* projected

William Johnson

William Johnson worked as an accounting manager at Mondavi's Napa headquarters. After 20 years with Mondavi, he had become bored with his job and saw no opportunity for advancement within the company. Many thought it would be only a matter of time before Johnson would decide to leave the company. The decision to assign Johnson to be Caliterra's controller in late 1996 was intended as a means of resolving communication difficulties between the two companies and to provide Johnson with new and interesting challenges.

When Johnson arrived in Santiago in January 1997, he spoke no Spanish and had no prior experience working in Latin America. His main job would be to interpret Caliterra's financial statements and convert them to U.S. GAAP so that they could be read and understood by managers in California. He had no decision-making authority within Errazuriz or Caliterra.

From the time of his arrival, Johnson remained an outsider. The Caliterra managers bypassed him for decisions. Not having any friends or family in Chile, he became lonely and isolated. One Chilean manager offered this view:

> Bill Johnson was his own biggest enemy . . . He was isolated here because of his character. The company was so disorganized, but this guy was impossible. He didn't learn any Spanish. He needed to talk Spanish, otherwise it was impossible to convince people to work with him. He was viewed as a spy here, and he was not receiving help from anybody.

Another manager agreed with this view, but also felt that Johnson had been instrumental in arranging an important media event around the launch of a new brand:

> Bill was critical for communicating details about preparation for launch. Without him, communication with the Mondavi family would have been a disaster. He knew them and what they wanted and he told them that everything was being arranged the way they wanted.

The Merlot Reserve

Normally, Errazuriz would utilize its own winery in the Aconcagua Valley or rent facilities at other wineries to process Caliterra wine, but for the 1997 harvest, increased worldwide demand for Chilean wine was placing enormous strain on existing facilities. In the past the company had never experienced problems finding space either at the Errazuriz winery or through contracts with other wineries. No one foresaw potential capacity constraints until harvest was upon them.

Suddenly, Errazuriz was scrambling to find wineries with available capacity. Ultimately, it had no other choice but to negotiate a contract with a winery it had never done business with in the past. A large portion of the harvest went into cement fermentation vats at the rented facility which turned out to have insufficient running water and substandard sanitation.

Cement vats were no longer common in the United States because they were difficult to clean and could not be temperature-controlled. In Chile, most wineries had converted to stainless steel vats, but for the 1997 harvest, those wineries had already allocated existing space for their own production or that of competing wineries.

The wine, a Merlot Reserve, was a super-premium brand that was popular among U.S. consumers and commanded higher margins than some less popular varietals. It amounted to approximately 13 percent of the Chilean harvest for that year, and was expected to help make up for Mondavi's short harvest in California.

Errazuriz sent its winemaker to the facility once a week to test the wine. One week he discovered that the wine had become contaminated. To the Mondavis, wasting such a large quantity of premium wine grapes was "sacrilege." However, both Errazuriz and Mondavi had quality standards that gave them no other option but to dispose of the Merlot Reserve.

The loss could have been prevented with better planning and the use of Wine Availability Reports (see Exhibit 2) that predicted harvests and available winemaking

EXHIBIT 2 Wine availability report, projected U.S. case sales of Caliterra wines

	F1997	F1998	F1999	F2000	F2001	F2002	F2003	F2004	F2005	F2006	F2007
WHOLESALE SALES											
CABERNET RESERVE	4,479	13,800	15,000	18,000	20,000	22,000	24,000	25,000	26,000	27,000	28,000
CABERNET	40,714	57,200	90,000	104,000	111,000	118,000	124,000	132,000	140,000	148,000	160,000
MERLOT RESERVE	–	2,000	7,000	15,000	20,000	24,000	26,000	30,000	31,000	32,000	34,000
MERLOT	46,400	58,000	97,000	116,000	130,000	145,000	155,000	164,000	173,000	180,000	195,000
CHARDONNAY RESERVE	4,760	19,000	15,000	18,000	20,000	22,000	24,000	25,000	25,000	26,000	27,000
CHARDONNAY	44,500	77,500	87,000	99,000	106,000	113,000	120,000	127,000	135,000	142,000	148,000
SAUVIGNON BLANC	18,200	43,500	36,000	43,000	48,000	52,000	54,000	55,000	55,000	55,000	55,000
TOTAL WHOLESALE	159,053	271,000	347,000	413,000	455,000	496,000	527,000	558,000	585,000	610,000	647,000
RETAIL SALES											
CABERNET RESERVE	100	100	100	200	200	200	300	300	300	300	300
CABERNET	100	100	200	200	300	300	400	400	400	400	500
MERLOT RESERVE	–	100	100	200	200	200	300	300	300	300	300
MERLOT	100	100	200	200	300	300	400	400	400	400	500
CHARDONNAY RESERVE	100	100	100	200	200	200	300	300	300	300	300
CHARDONNAY	100	100	200	200	300	300	400	400	400	400	500
SAUVIGNON BLANC	100	100	200	200	300	300	400	400	400	400	500
TOTAL RETAIL	600	700	1,100	1,400	1,800	1,800	2,500	2,500	2,500	2,500	2,900
DIRECT SALES											
CABERNET RESERVE	–	100	100	200	200	200	300	300	300	300	300
CABERNET	–	100	200	200	300	300	400	400	400	400	500
MERLOT RESERVE	–	100	100	200	200	200	300	300	300	300	300
MERLOT	–	100	200	200	300	300	400	400	400	400	500
CHARDONNAY RESERVE	–	100	100	200	200	200	300	300	300	300	300
CHARDONNAY	–	100	200	200	300	300	400	400	400	400	500
SAUVIGNON BLANC	–	100	200	200	300	300	400	400	400	400	500
TOTAL DIRECT	–	700	1,100	1,400	1,800	1,800	2,500	2,500	2,500	2,500	2,900
TOTAL SALES											
CABERNET RESERVE	4,579	14,000	15,200	18,400	20,400	22,400	24,600	25,600	26,600	27,600	28,600
CABERNET	40,814	57,400	90,400	104,400	111,600	118,600	124,800	132,800	140,800	148,800	161,000
MERLOT RESERVE	–	2,200	7,200	15,400	20,400	24,400	26,600	30,600	31,600	32,600	34,600
MERLOT	46,500	58,200	97,400	116,400	130,600	145,600	155,800	164,800	173,800	180,800	196,000
CHARDONNAY RESERVE	4,860	19,200	15,200	18,400	20,400	22,400	24,600	25,600	25,600	26,600	27,600
CHARDONNAY	44,600	77,700	87,400	99,400	106,600	113,600	120,800	127,800	135,800	142,800	149,000
SAUVIGNON BLANC	18,300	43,700	36,400	43,400	48,600	52,600	54,800	55,800	55,800	55,800	56,000
TOTAL SALES	159,653	272,400	349,200	415,800	458,600	499,600	532,000	563,000	590,000	615,000	652,800

Source: Robert Mondavi.

resources. In California, Mondavi often planned the sale of vintage wine from five to ten years in advance, and made extensive use of the reports for this purpose. The reports made clear that existing facilities would not be sufficient and would have allowed time for the company to make alternative arrangements in advance. "Wine availability defines everything. They should have known!" Schnur explained.

Because the loss followed so shortly after the bottling problems, the lack of trust Mondavi managers had in the ability of the joint venture partners to manage Caliterra was only reinforced. "We simply assumed, 'of course they will have running water'," Schnur recalled. The incident became infamous at Mondavi, where the managers referred to it as "the lost Merlot."

Confidence in the ability of Errazuriz to manage the joint venture had been shaken. The marketing manager's view was typical:

> We assumed that they must be a sophisticated export company, but they are a minimalist company. They create the wine, they create the label, then they give it to the agent and say, "go sell it."

The New Winery

The contaminated Merlot Reserve highlighted an even more serious concern. While Mondavi was expecting to have several years to build a new on-site winery, capacity constraints for the next harvest were only going to get worse. If projections held true, Caliterra was facing a capacity shortfall of at least five million litres. The only alternative would be to have the new winery ready before the next harvest, less than a year away.

In 1996, a site with the potential for 600 hectares of cultivatable land had been chosen in the Colchagua Valley, an isolated area of the country three hours south of Santiago. Construction of a new winery with an estimated cost of $6 million was slated to begin in 1998. La Arboleda, as it was known, was almost entirely surrounded by mountains, and consisted of nothing more than desert scrub and grazing land. It had no access road, no electricity, and no irrigation.

Even in California, where advanced infrastructure already existed, the task of building a large-scale winery in such a short time seemed nearly impossible. The Opus One winery, the model for the planned winery in Chile, was located along the major highway that runs through Napa Valley, and had ready access to power and irrigation. Nevertheless, Opus One took nearly six years to build, after unforeseen difficulties with flooding and geothermal activity required costly and time-consuming design changes.

The Chileans, on the other hand, did not anticipate such problems at La Arboleda, even though nearly all of the winery equipment would need to be imported from overseas. They believed they could complete the winery in time for the next harvest and were urging Schnur to trust them.

Time was running out. With only 10 months until the next harvest,[23] something had to be done. Schnur thought it might be possible to have a new winery completed on time, if everything went right. Others at Mondavi were not so sure. As he began to consider what to do next, Schnur knew he had to make a decision quickly.

Notes

1. Estimated by Mondavi based on the company's price to wholesalers and distributors. All currency values given in the case are in U.S. dollars unless stated otherwise.
2. Mondavi, Robert, *Harvests of Joy*, Harcourt Brace, Orlando, 1998.
3. Ibid.
4. Company records.
5. Mondavi, Robert, *Harvest of Joy*, Harcourt Brace, Orlando, 1998.
6. In 1998, Opus One wines retailed for $90 per bottle (750 ml).
7. Mondavi, Robert, *Harvests of Joy*, Harcourt Brace, Orlando, 1998.
8. Opus One, *The Wine Spectator*, November 15, 1995.
9. Chat with Robert Mondavi, *The Wine Spectator*, October 25, 1997.
10. Mondavi, Robert, *Harvests of Joy*, Harcourt Brace, Orlando, 1998.
11. The grape phylloxera is an aphid-like insect that feeds on grape roots. Phylloxera originated in the Americas and was unintentionally imported into Europe in the mid-nineteenth century.
12. General Augusto Pinochet became president of Chile after leading a military coup that saw the overthrow of Allende's democratically elected government.
13. Miguel Torres of Spain, for example, purchased the Ahrex winery for $200,000 in 1979, including a large estate and 50 hectares of vineyards. (A hectare is equivalent to 10,000 square meters, or 2.471 acres.)
14. Chile: California Dreaming, *The San Francisco Examiner*, February 8, 1998.
15. The Maturing of American Wine, *The Economist*, September 5, 1981.
16. In order to be classified as a Chilean wine, grapes had to be produced, crushed and fermented in Chile.
17. "Don" is a title which denotes a person of rank, note, or distinction and is used before the person's given name only.
18. A case of 12 bottles (750 ml each) of Chilean wine typically sold for between US$20 and $30 F.O.B. wholesale.
19. Translated from: Las Andanzas del Chiquillo Veloz Contadas por él Mismo, *La Tercera*, June 18, 1997.
20. Translated from: Enólogos Jóvenes, *Communicaciones UVA*, 1998.
21. Selling on incentive amounted to paying merchants to reduce the price and clear out the remaining wine.
22. As an export label, nearly all of Caliterra's sales were outside Chile.
23. The next Chilean harvest would be in February 1998.

CASE **15**

Ellen Moore (A): Living and Working in Korea

Henry W. Lane, Chantell Nicholls and Gail Ellement

Ellen Moore, a Systems Consulting Group (SCG) consultant, was increasingly concerned as she heard Andrew's voice grow louder through the paper-thin walls of the office next to her. Andrew Kilpatrick, the senior consultant on a joint North American and Korean consulting project for a government agency in Seoul, South Korea, was meeting with Mr. Song, the senior Korean project director, to discuss several issues including the abilities of the Korean consultants. After four months on this Korean project, Ellen's evaluation of the assigned consultants suggested that they did not have the experience, background, or knowledge to complete the project within the allocated time. Additional resources would be required:

> I remember thinking, "I can't believe they are shouting at each other." I was trying to understand how their meeting had reached such a state. Andrew raised his voice and I could hear him saying, "I don't think you understand at all." Then, he shouted, "Ellen is not the problem!"

WSI in Korea

In 1990, Joint Venture Inc. (JVI) was formed as a joint venture between a Korean company, Korean Conglomerate Inc. (KCI), and a North American company, Western

Chantell Nicholls and Gail Ellement prepared this case under the supervision of Professor Harry Lane solely to provide material for class discussion. The authors do not intend to illustrate either effective or ineffective handling of a managerial situation. The authors may have disguised certain names and other identifying information to protect confidentiality.

EXHIBIT 1　Organizational Structure – Functional View

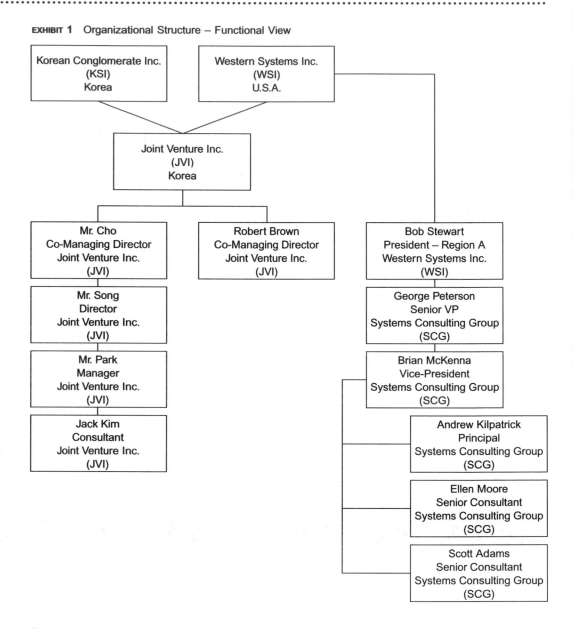

Systems Inc. (WSI) (Exhibit 1). WSI, a significant information technology company with offices worldwide employing over 50,000 employees, included the Systems Consulting Group (SCG). KCI, one of the largest Korean "chaebols" (industrial groups), consisted of over 40 companies, with sales in excess of US$3.5 billion. The joint venture, in its eighth year, was managed by two Regional Directors – Mr. Cho, a Korean from KCI, and Robert Brown, an American from WSI.

The team working on Ellen's project was led by Mr. Park and consisted of approximately 40 Korean consultants further divided into teams working on different areas of the project. The Systems Implementation (SI) team consisted of five Korean consultants, one translator, and three North American SCG consultants: Andrew Kilpatrick; Ellen Moore; and Scott Adams, (see Exhibit 2).

This consulting project was estimated to be one of the largest undertaken in South Korea to date. Implementation of the recommended systems into over 100 local offices was expected to take seven to ten years. The SCG consultants would be involved for the first seven months, to assist the Korean consultants with the system design and in creating recommendations for system implementation, an area in which the Korean consultants admitted they had limited expertise.

Andrew Kilpatrick became involved because of his experience with a similar systems implementation project in North America. Andrew had been a management consultant for nearly 13 years. He had a broad and successful background in organizational development, information technology, and productivity improvement, and he was an early and successful practitioner of business process re-engineering. Although Andrew had little international consulting experience, he was adept at change management and was viewed by both peers and clients as a flexible and effective consultant.

The degree of SCG's involvement had not been anticipated. Initially, Andrew had been asked by SCG's parent company, WSI, to assist JVI with the proposal development. Andrew and his SCG managers viewed his assistance as a favor to WSI since SCG did not have plans to develop business in Korea. Andrew's work on the proposal in North America led to a request for his involvement in Korea to gather additional information for the proposal:

> When I arrived in Korea, I requested interviews with members of the prospective client's management team to obtain more information about their business environment. The Korean team at JVI was very reluctant to set up these meetings. However, I generally meet with client management prior to preparing a proposal. I also knew it would be difficult to obtain a good understanding of their business environment from a translated document. The material provided to me had been translated into English and was difficult to understand. The Korean and English languages are so different that conveying abstract concepts is very difficult.
>
> I convinced the Koreans at JVI that these meetings would help demonstrate our expertise. The meetings did not turn out exactly as planned. We met with the same management team at three different locations where we asked the same set of questions three times and got the same answers three times. We did not obtain the information normally provided at these fact-gathering meetings. However, they were tremendously impressed by our line of questioning because it reflected a deep interest and understanding of their business. They also were very impressed with my background. As a result, we were successful in convincing the government agency that we had a deep understanding of the nature and complexity of the agency's work and strong capabilities in systems development and implementation – key cornerstones of their project. The client wanted us to handle the project and wanted me to lead it.

JVI had not expected to get the contract, because its competitor for this work was a long-time supplier to the client. As a result, winning the government contract had important competitive and strategic implications for JVI. Essentially, JVI had dislodged an incumbent supplier to the client, one who had lobbied very heavily for this prominent

EXHIBIT 2   Organizational Structure – SI Project Team

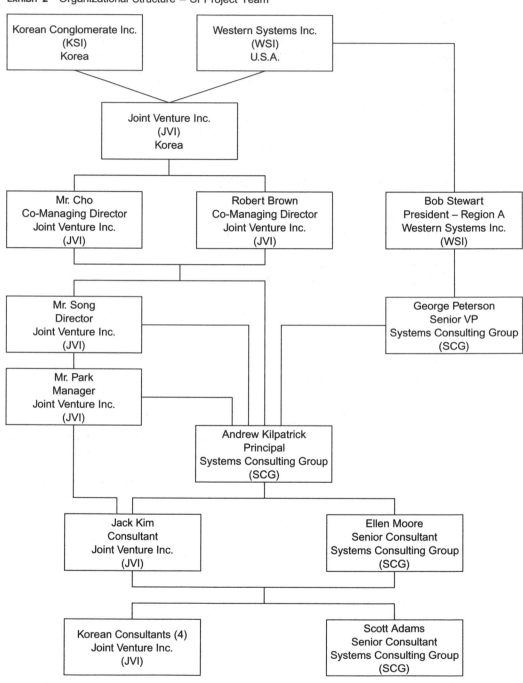

contract. By winning the bid, JVI became the largest system implementer in Korea and received tremendous coverage in the public press.

The project was to begin in June 1995. However, the Korean project team convened in early May in order to prepare the team members. Although JVI requested Andrew to join the project on a full-time basis, he already had significant commitments to projects in North America. There was a great deal of discussion back and forth between WSI in North America, and JVI and the client in Korea. Eventually it was agreed that Andrew would manage the SI work on a part-time basis from North America, and he would send a qualified project management representative on a full-time basis. That person was Ellen Moore.

At that time, Andrew received immediate feedback from the American consultants with WSI in Korea that it would be impossible to send a woman to work in Korea. Andrew insisted that the Korean consultants be asked if they would accept a woman in the position. They responded that a woman would be acceptable if she were qualified. Andrew also requested that the client be consulted on this issue. He was again told that a woman would be acceptable if she were qualified. Andrew knew that Ellen had the skills required to manage the project:

> I chose Ellen because I was very impressed with her capability, creativity, and project management skills, and I knew she had worked successfully in Bahrain, a culture where one would have to be attuned to very different cultural rules from those prevalent in North America. Ellen lacked experience with government agencies, but I felt that I could provide the required expertise in this area.

Ellen Moore

After graduating as the top female student from her high school, Ellen worked in the banking industry, achieving the position of corporate accounts officer responsible for over 20 major accounts and earning a Fellowship in the Institute of Bankers. Ellen went on to work for a former corporate client in banking and insurance, where she became the first female and youngest person to manage their financial reporting department. During this time, Ellen took university courses towards a Bachelor Degree at night. In 1983, she decided to stop working for two years, and completed her degree on a full-time basis. She graduated with a major in accounting and minors in marketing and management and decided to continue her studies for an MBA.

Two years later, armed with an MBA from a leading business school, Ellen Moore joined her husband in Manama, Bahrain, where she accepted a position as an expatriate manager for a large American financial institution.[1] Starting as a Special Projects Coordinator, within one year Ellen was promoted to Manager of Business Planning and Development, a challenging position that she was able to design herself. In this role, she managed the Quality Assurance department, coordinated a product launch, developed a senior management information system, and participated actively in all senior management decisions. Ellen's position required her to interact daily with managers and staff from a wide range of cultures, including Arab nationals.

In March 1995, Ellen joined WSI working for SCG. After the highly successful completion of two projects with SCG in North America, Ellen was approached for the Korea project:

> I had never worked in Korea or East Asia before. My only experience in Asia had been a one-week trip to Hong Kong for job interviews. I had limited knowledge of Korea and received no formal training from my company. I was provided a 20-page document on Korea. However, the information was quite basic and not entirely accurate.

After arriving in Korea, Ellen immediately began to familiarize herself with the language and proper business etiquette. She found that English was rarely spoken other than in some hotels and restaurants which catered to Western clientele. As a result, Ellen took advantage of every opportunity to teach herself the language basics:

> When Andrew and I were in the car on the way back to our hotel in the evening, we would be stuck in traffic for hours. I would use the time to learn how to read the Korean store signs. I had copied the Hangul symbols which form the Korean language onto a small piece of paper, and I kept this with me at all times. So, while sitting back in the car, exhausted at the end of each day, I would go over the symbols and read the signs.

The third SCG consultant on the project, Scott Adams, arrived as planned three months after Ellen's start date. Upon graduation, Scott had begun his consulting career working on several international engagements (including Mexico, Puerto Rico, and Venezuela), and he enjoyed the challenges of working with different cultures. He felt that with international consulting projects the technical aspects of consulting came easy. What he really enjoyed was the challenge of communicating in a different language and determining how to modify Western management techniques to fit into the local business culture. Scott first met Ellen at a systems consulting seminar, unaware at the time that their paths would cross again. A few months later, he was asked to consider the Korea assignment. Scott had never travelled or worked in Asia, but he believed that the assignment would present a challenging opportunity which would advance his career.

Scott was scheduled to start work on the project in August 1995. Prior to arriving in Seoul, Scott prepared himself by frequently discussing the work being conducted with Ellen. Ellen also provided him with information on the culture and business etiquette aspects of the work:

> It was very fortunate for me that Ellen had arrived first in Korea. Ellen tried to learn as much as she could about the Korean language, the culture, mannerisms, and the business etiquette. She was able to interpret many of the subtleties and to prepare me for both business and social situations, right down to how to exchange a business card appropriately with a Korean, how to read behavior, and what to wear.

About Korea[2]

Korea is a 600-mile-long peninsula stretching southward into the waters of the western Pacific, away from Manchuria and Siberia to the north on the Asian mainland. Facing eastward across the Sea of Japan, known to Koreans as the East Sea, Korea lies 120 miles from Japan. The Republic of Korea, or South Korea, consists of approximately 38,000 square miles, comparable in size to Virginia or Portugal. According to the 1990 census, the South Korean population is about 43 million, with almost 10 million residing in the capital city, Seoul.

Korea has an ancient heritage spanning 5,000 years. The most recent great historical era, the Yi Dynasty or Choson Dynasty, enlisted tremendous changes in which progress in science, technology, and the arts were achieved. Although Confucianism had been influential for centuries in Korea, it was during this time that Confucian principles permeated the culture as a code of morals and as a guide for ethical behavior. Confucian thought was designated as the state religion in 1392 and came to underpin education, civil administration, and daily conduct. During this time, Korean rulers began to avoid foreign contact and the monarchy was referred to as the "Hermit Kingdom" by outsiders. Lasting over 500 years and including 27 rulers, the Yi Dynasty came to a close at the end of the nineteenth century. Today, in Korea's modern era, the nation is quickly modernizing and traditional Confucian values mix with Western lifestyle habits and business methods.

Although many Korean people, particularly in Seoul, have become quite Westernized, they often follow traditional customs. Confucianism dictates strict rules of social behavior and etiquette. The basic values of the Confucian culture are: (1) complete loyalty to a hierarchical structure of authority, whether based in the family, the company, or the nation; (2) duty to parents, expressed through loyalty, love, and gratitude; and (3) strict rules of conduct, involving complete obedience and respectful behavior within superiors–subordinate relationships, such as parents–children, old–young, male–female, and teacher–student. These values affect both social and work environments substantially.

Managing in Korea

Business etiquette in Korea was extremely important. Ellen found that everyday activities, such as exchanging business cards or replenishing a colleague's drink at dinner, involved formal rituals. For example, Ellen learned it was important to provide and to receive business cards in an appropriate manner, which included carefully examining a business card when received and commenting on it. If one just accepted the card without reading it, this behavior would be considered very rude. In addition, Ellen also found it important to know how to address a Korean by name. If a Korean's name was Y. H. Kim, non-Koreans would generally address him as either Y. H. or as Mr. Kim. Koreans would likely call him by his full name or by his title and name, such as Manager Kim. A limited number of Koreans, generally those who had lived overseas, took on Western names, such as Jack Kim.

Work Teams

Teams were an integral part of the work environment in Korea. Ellen noted that the Korean consultants organized some special team-building activities to bring together the Korean and North American team members:

On one occasion, the Korean consulting team invited the Western consultants to a baseball game on a Saturday afternoon followed by a trip to the Olympic Park for a tour after the game, and dinner at a Korean restaurant that evening. An event of this nature is unusual and was very special. On another occasion, the Korean consultants gave up a day off with their families and spent it with the Western consultants. We toured a Korean palace and the palace grounds, and we were then invited to Park's home for dinner. It was very unusual that we, as Western folks, were invited to his home, and it was a very gracious event.

Ellen also found team-building activities took place on a regular basis, and that these events were normally conducted outside of the work environment. For example, lunch with the team was an important daily team event which everyone was expected to attend:

You just couldn't work at your desk every day for lunch. It was important for everyone to attend lunch together in order to share in this social activity, as one of the means for team bonding.

Additionally, the male team members would go out together for food, drink, and song after work. Scott found these drinking activities to be an important part of his inter-action with both the team and the client:

Unless you had a medical reason, you would be expected to drink with the team members, sometimes to excess. A popular drink, soju, which is similar to vodka, would be poured into a small glass. Our glasses were never empty, as someone would always ensure that an empty glass was quickly filled. For example, if my glass was empty, I learned that I should pass it to the person on my right and fill it for him as a gesture of friendship. He would quickly drink the contents of the glass, pass the glass back to me, and fill it for me to quickly drink. You simply had to do it. I recall one night when I really did not want to drink as I had a headache. We were sitting at dinner, and Mr. Song handed me his glass and filled it. I said to him "I really can't drink tonight. I have a terrible headache." He looked at me and said "Mr. Scott, I have Aspirin in my briefcase." I had about three or four small drinks that night.

Ellen found she was included in many of the team-building dinners, and soon after she arrived in Seoul, she was invited to a team dinner, which included client team members. Ellen was informed that although women were not normally invited to these social events, an exception was made since she was a senior team member.

During the dinner, there were many toasts and drinking challenges. During one such challenge, the senior client representative prepared a drink that consisted of one highball glass filled with beer and one shot glass filled to the top with whiskey. He dropped the whiskey glass into the beer glass and passed the drink to the man on his left. This team member quickly drank the cocktail in one swoop, and held the glass over his head, clicking the glasses to show both were empty. Everyone cheered and applauded. This man then mixed the same drink, and passed the glass to the man on his left, who also drank the cocktail in one swallow. It was clear this challenge was going around the table and would eventually get to me.

I don't generally drink beer and never drink whiskey. But it was clear, even without my translator present to assist my understanding, that this activity was an integral part of the team building for the project. As the man on my right mixed the drink for me, he whispered that he would help me. He poured the beer to the halfway point in the highball glass, filled the shot glass to the top with whiskey, and dropped the shotglass in the beer. Unfortunately, I could see that the beer didn't cover the top of the shot glass, which would likely move too quickly if not covered. I announced "One moment, please, we are having technical difficulties." And to the amazement of all in attendance, I asked the man on my right to pour more beer in the glass. When I drank the concoction in one swallow, everyone cheered, and the senior client representative stood up and shouted, "You are now Korean. You are now Korean."

The norms for team management were also considerably different from the North American style of management. Ellen was quite surprised to find that the concept of saving face did not mean avoiding negative feedback or sharing failures:

It is important in Korea to ensure that team members do not lose face. However, when leading a team, it appeared just as important for a manager to demonstrate leadership. If a team member provided work that did not meet the stated requirements, a leader was expected to express disappointment in the individual's efforts in front of all team members. A strong leader was considered to be someone who engaged in this type of public demonstration when required.

In North America, a team leader often compliments and rewards team members for work done well. In Korea, leaders expressed disappointment in substandard work, or said nothing for work completed in a satisfactory manner. A leader was considered weak if he or she continuously provided compliments for work completed as required.

Hierarchy

The Koreans' respect for position and status was another element of the Korean culture that both Ellen and Scott found to have a significant influence over how the project was structured and how people behaved. The emphasis placed on hierarchy had an important impact upon the relationship between consultant and client that was quite different from their experience in North America. As a result, the North Americans' understanding of the role of a consultant differed vastly from their Korean counterparts.

Specifically, the North American consultants were familiar with "managing client expectations." This activity involved informing the client of the best means to achieve their goals and included frequent communication with the client. Generally, the client's customer was also interviewed in order to understand how the client's system could better integrate with their customer's requirements. Ellen recalled, however, that the procedures were necessarily different in Korea:

The client team members did not permit our team members to go to their offices unannounced. We had to book appointments ahead of time to obtain permission to see them. In part, this situation was a result of the formalities we needed to observe due to their rank in society, but I believe it was also because they wanted to be prepared for the topics we wanted to discuss.

The Korean consultants refused to interview the customers, because they did not want to disturb them. Furthermore, the client team members frequently came into the project office and asked the Korean consultants to work on activities not scheduled for that week or which were beyond the project scope. The Korean consultants accepted the work without question. Ellen and Scott found themselves powerless to stop this activity.

Shortly after arriving, Scott had a very confrontational meeting with one of the Korean consultants concerning this issue:

> I had been in Korea for about a week, and I was still suffering from jet lag. I was alone with one of the Korean consultants, and we were talking about how organizational processes should be flow-charted. He was saying the client understands the process in a particular manner, so we should show it in that way. I responded that, from a technical standpoint, it was not correct. I explained that as a consultant, we couldn't simply do what the client requests if it is incorrect. We must provide value by showing why a different method may be taken by educating the client of the options and the reasons for selecting a specific method. There are times when you have to tell the client something different than he believes. That's what we're paid for. He said, "No, no, you don't understand. They're paying our fee." At that point I raised my voice: "You don't know what you are talking about. I have much more experience than you." Afterwards, I realized that it was wrong to shout at him. I pulled him aside and apologized. He said, "Well, I know you were tired." I replied that it was no excuse, and I should not have shouted. After that, we managed to get along just fine.

The behavior of subordinates and superiors also reflected the Korean's respect for status and position. Scott observed that it was very unusual for a subordinate to leave the office for the day unless his superior had already left:

> I remember one day, a Saturday, when one of the young Korean consultants who had been ill for some time, was still at his desk. I made a comment: "Why don't you go home, Mr. Choi?" Although he was not working for me, I knew his work on the other team was done. He said, "I can't go home because several other team members have taken the day off. I have to stay." I repeated my observation that his work was done. He replied: "If I do not stay, I will be fired. My boss is still here, I have to stay." He would stay and work until his boss left, until late in the evening if necessary.

Furthermore, Scott found that the Korean consultants tended not to ask questions. Even when Scott asked the Korean consultants if they understood his instructions or explanation, they generally responded affirmatively which made it difficult to confirm their understanding. He was advised that responding in a positive manner demonstrated respect for teachers or superiors. Asking a question would be viewed as inferring that the teacher or superior had not done a good job of explaining the material. As a result, achieving a coaching role was difficult for the North American consultants even though passing on their knowledge of SI to the Korean consultants was considered an important part of their function on this project.

Women in Korea

Historically, Confucian values have dictated a strict code of behavior between men and women and husband and wife in Korea. Traditionally, there has been a clear delineation in the respective responsibilities of men and women. The male preserve can be defined as that which is public, whereas women are expected to cater to the private, personal world of the home. These values have lingered to the present day, with Korean public life very much dominated by men.

Nevertheless, compared to the Yi dynasty era, the position of women in society has changed considerably. There is now virtual equality in access to education for men and women, and a few women have embarked on political careers. As in many other areas of the world, the business world has until recently been accessible only to men. However, this is changing as Korean women are beginning to seek equality in the workplace. Young Korean men and women now often participate together in social activities such as evenings out and hikes, something that was extremely rare even ten years ago.

Dual-income families are becoming more common in South Korea, particularly in Seoul, although women generally hold lower-paid, more menial positions. Furthermore, working women often retain their traditional household responsibilities, while men are expected to join their male colleagues for late night drinking and eating events which exclude women. When guests visit a Korean home, the men traditionally sit and eat together separately from the women, who are expected to eat together while preparing the food.

Although the younger generation are breaking from such traditions, Scott felt that the gender differences were quite apparent in the work place. He commented:

> The business population was primarily male. Generally, the only women we saw were young women who were clerks, wearing uniforms. I suspected that these women were in the workforce for only a few years, until they were married and left to have a family. We did have a few professional Korean women working with us. However, because we are a professional services firm, I believe it may have been more progressive than the typical Korean company.

The Systems Implementation Team

Upon her arrival in Korea, Ellen dove into her work confident that the Korean consultants she would be working with had the skills necessary to complete the job in the time frame allocated. The project work was divided up among several work groups, each having distinct deliverables and due dates. The deliverables for the SI team were required as a major input to the other work groups on the project (see Exhibit 3). As a result, delays with deliverables would impact the effectiveness of the entire project:

> JVI told us they had assigned experienced management consultants to work on the project. Given their stated skill level, Andrew's resource plan had him making periodic visits to Korea; I would be on the project on a full-time basis starting in May, and Scott would join the team about three to four months after the project start. We were informed that five Korean consultants were assigned. We believed that we had the resources needed to complete the project by December.

Jack Kim

J. T. Kim, whose Western name was Jack, was the lead Korean consultant reporting to Mr. Park. Jack had recently achieved a Ph.D. in computer systems from a reputable

EXHIBIT 3   Project Time Frame

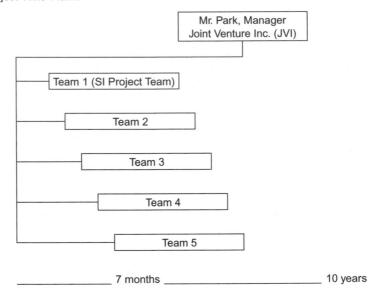

American university and he spoke English fluently. When Andrew initially discussed the organizational structure of the SI team with Mr. Park and Jack, it was agreed that Jack and Ellen would be co-managers of the SI project.

Three weeks after her arrival, Jack informed Ellen, much to her surprise, that he had never worked on a systems implementation project. Additionally, Ellen soon learned that Jack had never worked on a consulting project:

> Apparently, Jack had been made the lead consultant of SI upon completing his Ph.D. in the United States. I believe Jack was told he was going to be the sole project manager for SI on a daily basis. However, I was informed I was going to be the co-project manager with Jack. It was confusing, particularly for Jack, when I took on coaching and leading the team. We had a lot of controversy – not in the form of fights or heated discussions, but we had definite issues during the first few weeks because we were clearly stepping upon each other's territory.

Given Jack's position as the lead Korean consultant, it was quite difficult for Ellen to redirect team members' activities. The Korean team members always followed Jack's instructions. Scott recalled:

> There were frequent meetings with the team to discuss the work to be completed. Often, following these meetings the Korean consultants would meet alone with Jack, and it appeared that he would instruct them to carry out different work. On one occasion, when both Andrew and Ellen were travelling away from the office, Andrew prepared specific instructions for the team to follow outlined in a memo.
>
> Andrew sent the memo to me so I could hand the memo to Jack directly, thereby ensuring he did receive these instructions. Upon his return, Andrew found the team had

not followed his instructions. We were provided with the following line of reasoning: you told us to do A, B and C, but you did not mention D. And, we did D. They had followed Jack's instructions. We had a very difficult time convincing them to carry out work as we requested, even though we had been brought onto the project to provide our expertise.

In July, a trip was planned for the Korean client team and some of the Korean consulting team to visit other project sites in North America. The trip would permit the Koreans to find out more about the capabilities of WSI and to discuss issues with other clients involved with similar projects. Jack was sent on the trip, leaving Ellen in charge of the SI project team in Korea. While Jack was away on the North American trip, Ellen had her first opportunity to work with and to lead the Korean consultants on a daily basis. She was very pleased that she was able to coach them directly, without interference, and advise them on how to best carry out the required work. Ellen felt that everyone worked together in a very positive manner, in complete alignment. When Jack returned, he saw that Ellen was leading the team and that they were accepting Ellen's directions. Ellen recalled the tensions that arose as a result:

> On the first day he returned, Jack instructed someone to do some work for him, and the person responded, "I cannot because I am doing something for Ellen." Jack did not say anything, but he looked very angry. He could not understand why anyone on the team would refuse his orders.

The Marketing Research Project

A few days after Jack returned from the North American trip, the project team realized they did not have sufficient information about their client's customer. Jack decided a market research study should be conducted to determine the market requirements. However, this type of study, which is generally a large undertaking on a project, was not within the scope of the contracted work. Ellen found out about the proposed market research project at a meeting held on a Saturday, which involved everyone from the entire project – about 40 people. The only person not at the meeting was Mr. Park. Jack was presenting the current work plans for SI, and he continued to describe a market research study:

> I thought to myself, "What market research study is he talking about?" I asked him to put aside his presentation of the proposed study until he and I had an opportunity to discuss the plans. I did not want to interrupt his presentation or disagree with him publicly, but I felt I had no choice.

Dinner with Jack

Two hours following the presentation, Ellen's translator, Susan Lim, informed her that there was a dinner planned for that evening and Jack wanted everyone on the SI team to attend. Ellen was surprised that Jack would want her present at the dinner. However, Susan insisted that Jack specifically said Ellen must be there. They went to a small

Korean restaurant, where everyone talked about a variety of subjects in English and Korean, with Susan translating for Ellen as needed. After about one hour, Jack began a speech to the team, speaking solely in Korean. Ellen thought it was unusual for him to speak Korean when she was present, as everyone at the dinner also spoke English:

> Through the limited translations I received, I understood he was humbling himself to the team, saying, "I am very disappointed in my performance. I have clearly not been the project leader needed for this team." The team members were responding "No, no, don't say that." While Jack was talking to the team, he was consuming large quantities of beer. The pitchers were coming and coming. He was quite clearly becoming intoxicated. All at once, Susan stopped translating. I asked her what was wrong. She whispered that she would tell me later. Five minutes went by and I turned to her and spoke emphatically, "Susan, what is going on? I want to know now." She realized I was getting angry. She told me, "Jack asked me to stop translating. Please don't say anything, I will lose my job."
>
> I waited a couple of minutes before speaking, then I interrupted Jack's speech. I said, "Susan is having difficulty hearing you and isn't able to translate for me. I guess it is too noisy in this restaurant. Would it be possible for you to speak in English?" Jack did not say anything for about 30 seconds and then he started speaking in English. His first words were, "Ellen, I would like to apologize. I didn't realize you couldn't understand what I was saying."

Another 30 minutes of his speech and drinking continued. The Korean team members appeared to be consoling Jack, by saying: "Jack, we do respect you and the work you have done for our team. You have done your best." While they were talking, Jack leaned back, and appeared to pass out. Ellen turned to Susan and asked if they should help him to a taxi. Susan insisted it would not be appropriate. During the next hour, Jack appeared to be passed out or sleeping. Finally, one of the team members left to go home. Ellen asked Susan, "Is it important for me to stay, or is it important for me to go?" She said Ellen should go.

When Ellen returned to her hotel, it was approximately 11 p.m. on Saturday night. She felt the situation had reached a point where it was necessary to request assistance from senior management in North America. Andrew was on a wilderness camping vacation in the United States with his family, and could not be reached. Ellen decided to call the North American project sponsor, the Senior Vice President, George Peterson:

> I called George that Saturday night at his house and said: "We have a problem. They're trying to change the scope of the project. We don't have the available time, and we don't have the resources. It is impossible to do a market research study in conjunction with all the contracted work to be completed with the same limited resources. The proposed plan is to use our project team to handle this additional work. Our team is already falling behind the schedule, but due to their inexperience they don't realize it yet." George said he would find Andrew and send him to Korea to further assess the situation.

The Meeting with the Director

When Andrew arrived in August, he conducted a very quick assessment of the situation. The project was a month behind schedule. It appeared to Andrew that the SI team had made limited progress since his previous visit:

It was clear to me that the Korean team members weren't taking direction from Ellen. Ellen was a seasoned consultant and knew what to do. However, Jack was giving direction to the team which was leading them down different paths. Jack was requesting that the team work on tasks which were not required for the project deliverables, and he was not appropriately managing the client's expectations.

Andrew held several discussions with Mr. Park concerning these issues. Mr. Park insisted the problem was Ellen. He argued that Ellen was not effective, she did not assign work properly, and she did not give credible instructions to the team. However, Andrew believed the Korean consultants' lack of experience was the main problem.

Initially, we were told the Korean team consisted of experienced consultants, although they had not completed any SI projects. I felt we could work around it. I had previously taught consultants to do SI. We were also told that one of the Korean consultants had taught SI. This consultant was actually the most junior person on the team. She had researched SI by reading some texts and had given a presentation on her understanding of SI to a group of consultants.

Meanwhile, Andrew solicited advice from the WSI Co-Managing Director, Robert Brown, who had over ten years experience working in Korea. Robert suggested that Andrew approach Mr. Park's superior, Mr. Song, directly. He further directed Andrew to present his case to the Joint Venture committee if an agreement was not reached with Mr. Song. Andrew had discussed the issues with George Peterson and Robert Brown, and they agreed that there was no reason for Ellen to leave the project:

However, Robert's message to me was that I had been too compliant with the Koreans. It was very important for the project to be completed on time, and that I would be the one held accountable for any delays. Addressing issues before the Joint Venture committee was the accepted dispute resolution process at JVI when an internal conflict could not be resolved. However, in most cases, the last thing a manager wants is to be defending his position before the Joint Venture committee. Mr. Song was in line to move into senior executive management. Taking the problem to the Joint Venture committee would be a way to force the issue with him.

Andrew attempted to come to a resolution with Mr. Park once again, but he refused to compromise. Andrew then tried to contact Mr. Song and was told he was out of the office. Coincidentally, Mr. Song visited the project site to see Mr. Park just as Ellen and Andrew were completing a meeting. Ellen recalls Mr. Song's arrival:

Mr. Song walked into the project office expecting to find Mr. Park. However, Mr. Park was out visiting another project that morning. Mr. Song looked around the project office for a senior manager, and he saw Andrew. Mr. Song approached Andrew and asked if Mr. Park was in the office. Andrew responded that he was not. Mr. Song proceeded to comment that he understood there were some concerns about the project work, and suggested that perhaps, sometime, they could talk about it. Andrew replied that they needed to talk about it immediately.

Andrew met with Mr. Song in Mr. Park's office, a makeshift set of thin walls that enclosed a small office area in one corner of the large open project office. Ellen was working in an area just outside the office when she heard Andrew's voice rise. She heard him shout, "Well, I don't think you're listening to what I am saying." Ellen was surprised to hear Andrew shouting. She knew Andrew was very sensitive to what should and should not be done in the Korean environment:

> Andrew's behavior seemed so confrontational. I believed this behavior was unacceptable in Korea. For a while, I heard a lot of murmuring, after which I heard Andrew speak adamantly, "No, I'm very serious. It doesn't matter what has been agreed and what has not been agreed because most of our agreements were based on inaccurate information. We can start from scratch." Mr. Song insisted that I was the problem.

Notes

1. For an account of Ellen's experience in Bahrain, see Ellen Moore (A): Living and Working in Bahrain, 9A90C019, and Ellen Moore (B), 9A90C020; Ivey Publishing, Ivey Management Services, c/o Richard Ivey School of Business, University of Western Ontario, London, Ontario, Canada, N6A 3K7.
2. Some of the information in the "About Korea" and "Women in Korea" sections was obtained from *Fodor's Korea*, 1993, Fodor's Travel Publications, Inc.: NY; and Chris Taylor, *Seoul – city guide*, 1993, Lonely Planet Publications: Colorcraft Ltd., Hong Kong.

CASE **16**

Marconi Telecommunications Mexico

Henry W. Lane, Daniel D. Campbell and David T. A. Wesley

On January 12, 1997, Marconi Telecommunications Corporation (Martel) signed a letter of intent to purchase control of Lerida Telecom of Mexico, a leading telecommunications provider in Mexico with approximately 2,300 employees. Lerida operated 85 customer service centers throughout the country and had a full-time staff of 92 corporate sales representatives. It also had agreements with 39 distributors, including one majority-owned subsidiary of Lerida, which operated over 125 distribution locations. One year later, 14 Martel managers had been moved to Mexico.

On June 21, 1997, Martel announced that it had signed a letter of intent to purchase an interest in Communicaciones Carmona in Chile from the controlling shareholder. Two weeks later the company announced that it had signed a non-binding letter of intent to purchase a minority stake in Panamanian Cable Provider, RadioTelevisivo Panama, subject to the completion of a due diligence review and regulatory approval. The company also had minority interests in Colombia and Martel representatives were pursuing opportunities in Brazil, Venezuela, and Bolivia.

Senior executives knew that one of their most pressing issues would be finding the right people to manage their Latin American operations. The plan was to build a team at Lerida and use these managers in other Latin American countries. Martel had traditionally enjoyed success when placing managers in foreign countries, but executives wondered what had been learned from the recent experience in selecting and preparing managers for Mexico, and whether the current systems and plans would support the anticipated expansion.

Daniel D. Campbell and David T. A. Wesley prepared this case under the supervision of Professor Henry W. Lane solely to provide material for class discussion. The authors do not intend to illustrate either effective or ineffective handling of a managerial situation. The authors may have disguised certain names and other identifying information to protect confidentiality.

Background

Marconi Telecommunications Corporation was one of Canada's most international telecommunications providers. Although Martel owned minority positions in a few companies in Europe, it primarily focused on high growth opportunities in emerging markets, principally in Latin America and in Asia. Martel's expansion into emerging markets was fuelled by opportunities and by a need for growth. The Canadian market was very competitive with a lot of domestic competition as well as competition from giant American firms like AT&T and Sprint.

In 1997, Martel operated in 12 countries with approximately 3,700 employees. It owned, developed, and operated telecommunication systems such as cellular networks, PCS, paging systems, cable television, local telephone networks, long distance and fixed wireless.

Minority Interests

Martel began by purchasing minority equity interests in Latin American companies. Often, a single family controlled these institutions. However, an opportunity usually came to take a majority position. This was particularly true in times of financial crisis when the companies and their principal shareholders became strapped for cash.

Another reason for taking a minority interest was the company's lack of personnel to staff the operations. Few managers were familiar with Latin America or spoke Spanish. It was Martel's practice to send a small number of managers to the companies in which it held a minority interest.

Building a Competency

In 1990, anticipating Latin American expansion, Frank Kelly, who had just become the head of Latin America for Martel, each year began hiring recent graduates with appropriate backgrounds from MBA programs. In addition to their technical education and MBAs, they also had substantial Latin American backgrounds and spoke Spanish. These managers then began a four- to six-year tour of duty within the Canadian operations that exposed them to many aspects of the company's core businesses. Once they were familiar with the company's practices in Canada, it was expected that they would form the nucleus of a team that could manage a Latin American operation on behalf of Martel. By 1996, the company had hired about 12 managers with a Latin American background and had retained 10 of them.

Opportunity Knocks

Mexico's Secretariat of Communications and Transportation (SCT) began to deregulate telecommunications services in Mexico in 1990 with the privatization of Telefonos de

Mexico (Telmex), the national phone company. Telmex was granted protection from competition in local service until the year 2026, but all other services, such as data communications, satellite, cellular, and long distance, were opened to domestic and foreign competition. However, the SCT still maintained strict regulatory control on pricing. In 1997, Telmex faced a significant backlog in requests for new telephone line installations. By 1998, a number of multinational providers had entered the Mexican market, such as Bell Atlantic, Southwestern Bell, MCI, and France Telecom.

The currency crisis that began in late 1994 destabilized the Mexican economy and created an opportunity to purchase Lerida at an attractive price. Management believed that they could administer the operation and, after a period of difficult negotiations, bought Lerida.

"It's a great opportunity," said John Dolan, Chairman of Martel, shortly after completing the deal. "We're really into this for the very, very, long run. It's a part of our international telecommunications network." Separately, Dolan said: "I view Mexico as having enormous opportunity. It has 100 million people and it's part of NAFTA." Although the level of penetration with respect to the number of installed lines per capita was relatively low in Mexico, the demand for new services was very strong. Demand was expected to continue growing at a much higher rate than in the United States or Canada.

Martel and Lerida finally agreed that no more than 14 managers would be sent to Mexico at any one time. Kelly felt that 14 was ideal, in part because there were not more qualified staff to send, but also because more than 14 might appear too much like a conquest. Instead, management sought to create an atmosphere of partnership. This philosophy differed from that of some of the other foreign companies that chose to transfer more expatriate managers to the companies they had purchased.

As part of the due diligence to evaluate the investment in Lerida, approximately 25 managers were sent to Mexico. The group was made up of functional teams chosen by their team leaders. Virtually all of the Canadian company's employees with Spanish language competence were included on the various teams. The remainder of the team was selected for their technical skills.

Staffing the New Operation

In the normal process of selecting candidates for international placement, recruiting was done both internally and externally as the company tried to identify individuals with the skills required for an overseas assignment. Internally, a system of job postings called International Opportunities was used that listed the position and the requirements. This system was designed to provide an internal source of managers for a training pool. Martel also recruited at universities and searched for external candidates.

People who had been identified through these processes were then interviewed by a panel of four managers including three from line functions and one from International Human Resources. The successful applicants were streamed according to function (network, commercial sales) and regional pools (Latin America, Asia) and their development needs were identified. At the time seven slots were available in the management training program.

Language was a priority, but often other technical skills were major concerns as well. Most often, the external hires were individuals with limited telecommunications experience but who had an ability to function in Latin America, whereas internal hires often resulted from searches for skill requirements.

Those selected began an international orientation, based in Ottawa, that provided increased contact with international offices. Martel used a variety of methods including assignments on project teams and three-month "test" postings. Orientation lasted between three months and two years after which employees had a better sense of whether or not they were prepared for an international assignment. Some backed out at that point, but many could not wait to leave.

Sudden Demand For Managers

During negotiations, it did not appear that an agreement was possible and no one at Martel was expecting to complete the deal. However, at the last minute, the industrial group that owned Lerida agreed to additional concessions and a deal was reached. This sudden reversal created an unexpected and immediate demand for managers. Martel's International Human Resources (IHR) department was charged with the extremely difficult task of identifying and relocating a management team for the new company in a very short period of time. The 14 managers to be sent to Mexico were double the numbers then being prepared for that type of assignment.

Frank Kelly became president of the Mexican operations. A veteran in the telecommunications industry was selected to head up Lerida's residential services division. Two other senior, experienced Canadians were chosen to coordinate the cellular network and information systems and to be in charge of all commercial sales. These three executives then chose their respective teams to accompany them to Mexico.

Aside from those that had been originally hired specifically for their ability to speak Spanish and their knowledge of Latin America, individuals were chosen based on their technical expertise in areas deemed critical to the success of Lerida.

The expatriate managers assigned to Mexico fell into three broad categories: a) "traditional" managers with little or no previous international experience; b) the young "international" managers with a previous background in Latin America but without significant telecommunications experience; and c) a group that combined the traditional and the international. This latter group comprised experienced telecommunications professionals with previous international experience and/or who had emigrated from Latin America.

The "traditional" managers (six) ranged in age from 46 to 65 (average age approximately 54 years), were married with a family, Canadian, and had never worked outside of Canada before. This group comprised the senior managers with strong technical skills. The "traditional and international" group (four) were between 34 and 59 years of age (average age approximately 45 years), spoke Spanish and had previous international experience.

In contrast, the "international" managers (four) were in their early thirties, most were single, spoke Spanish fluently and had lived and worked in Latin America. Frank Kelly characterized them as world citizens who "were comfortable everywhere." They were

MBAs who had completed the basic training programs through the Head Office and also held degrees in engineering.

Human Resources: Process of Expatriation

It was Martel's policy[1] to provide a compensation package for managers undertaking international assignments that was competitive with other major international telecommunications providers. It would allow managers to maintain, to the extent local conditions permitted, a standard of living comparable to that available in their home countries.

The policy was designed to be equal to or superior to the average of other telecommunications companies from Canada, the United States, and Europe. The total compensation (salary plus benefits and allowances) was competitive. However, Jeff York, director of IHR, believed that the base salaries alone might have been less than those of competitors and this made Martel somewhat vulnerable.

The standard package of benefits covered housing, schools, compensation, relocation, automobiles, taxation and all other issues associated with the assignment. This package applied to all managers and their families. It included some additional benefits specifically for the executives being transferred to Mexico. The housing allowance was higher than normal; a security allowance was included as well as a pollution relief allowance. To claim benefits under this latter allowance, an executive and his family had to physically leave Mexico City one weekend each month during the seven worst months for pollution (November–May). An upper limit for expenses had been established and executives had to file an expense report to claim the allowance.

Although IHR was the principal point of support for employees beginning an international assignment, many other areas of the company provided services during the process. These included Relocation Services (moving, travel, hotels, selling house), Health (counselling employees and families about health risks, detailed discussions as necessary), Security (one-on-one meeting with employee to discuss country risk), and Finance (financial planning). In addition to these standard services, Martel's finance department arranged for an investment consultant to make a presentation on offshore investment opportunities not available in Canada and Martel provided an expense-paid trip to visit Mexico to see housing and schools.

It was also the general practice of the company to appoint a relationship manager for areas like Latin America to interact with the company's expatriates and to use a subsidiary company to provide on-site support. However, Martel was not able to use the services of Lerida, because the company relocated managers before it took formal control. Instead it relied on a senior manager with many years' experience in Latin America and a local relocation company. The relocation office arranged local real estate services. However, because of the large number of managers and families moving at the same time, it was impossible to provide the same level of on-site support that had been customary with prior international transfers within the company.

To avoid unnecessary travel, employees were asked to complete a list of requirements they needed to have satisfied before they would move in order to identify potential "deal breakers." IHR had a firm view about not negotiating individual packages, according to York.

We want to make sure there is a serious intent to go and that it is not just a vacation or fishing trip. If a person's spouse has a career and is making a big salary, we can't replace that, so let's not fool ourselves.

Our policies are flexible to handle differences between countries. We can't do 200 different, individual contracts. That would be unfair, particularly if one person were a better negotiator. Occasionally, exceptions are made, but only in very rare cases.

When employees felt comfortable with the provisions being made, IHR provided them the opportunity to visit the country with their spouses to see where they would be living and to know what schools were available.

Reactions by executives and their spouses to IHR policies generally varied by age, family status, and group ("traditional", "traditional and international", "international"). Similarly, ease of adaptation to Mexico varied by group.

To Go or Not to Go?

Generally, after being asked, managers reserved the final decision about accepting the position until they discussed it with their spouses and families. Most of the managers who were asked to move already had spent up to a month in Mexico during the due diligence. However, most of the spouses had never been to Mexico City:

My husband came home and said that they had offered him this great job. Our daughter could go to private school and they are going to pay for the residence fees of our two other children while they studied at university. It all sounded wonderful. I think I said yes without really knowing what we were headed for.

Some managers were unhappy with the process used by IHR. Some wanted guarantees about what would be provided for them once they arrived in Mexico. Many were frustrated by what they perceived as rigidity on the part of IHR and felt that there should have been more ability to negotiate with reference to personal circumstances.

There also was some concern about the lack of career planning regarding jobs for managers when the time came for them to return to Canada. Managers cynically commented that those returning from an overseas position often found themselves regarded as surplus employees with no plan for their re-integration into the domestic organization.

The decision was more complicated for dual-career families. The company's position was clear. Its obligation was to secure a work permit for the employee. The spouse might or might not be able to work. Several spouses had careers and these families had to think about whether or not the spouse would be able to find work in Mexico or even receive permission to work under Mexican immigration laws. There were concerns expressed about the loss of a second income and what the spouse could do to occupy spare time.

Among the young, "international" managers, the feeling was that the package of benefits was good, but their perception was that other companies' salaries were higher.

IHR eventually resolved most of the major obstacles. One by one, after they had found homes and suitable schools, the managers informed the company that they were prepared to move to Mexico. Most of the employees were excited by the prospect – a change, a new challenge. As one executive stated,

> I thought working in Mexico would be a wonderful opportunity. Canadian companies have a bureaucracy and hierarchy that has been built up over many years. The opportunity to advance and try something more challenging was certainly there on the international side. That was the main motivating factor.

Although most managers embraced the new job opportunity with a high level of excitement, the families shared varying levels of concern about leaving behind their communities, good friends, relatives, and children who would remain in school in Canada. Those who did not speak Spanish shared additional anxiety.

Preparation

Everyone agreed that they received very little formal preparation before going to Mexico. Managers with previous experience in Mexico or other Latin American countries were not concerned by the lack of preparation. The "traditional" executives had mixed feelings about the level of preparation that they had received. Martel sponsored a one-day program offered in Ottawa. Many felt that was not sufficient. One commented,

> There just wasn't enough preparation done for moving a group this size. The program in Ottawa wasn't sufficient. We probably needed two to three days and we needed to talk with people from Mexico. There needed to be more done for the wives and children.

However, another manager viewed it differently.

> Preparation was basically nothing. I don't necessarily think that was a bad thing. You could spend five years preparing, or five days. From my standpoint, there were so many things that I wasn't prepared for that jumping into the deep end was probably as good as anything.

A manager with previous international and Mexican experience added,

> There was really no preparation by the company. Some Mexican gentleman did a one-day seminar. It was interesting but not very useful.

The spouses of the traditional managers felt a strong need for more preparation and more information. One went to the library for articles or books on living in Mexico but could not find anything recent. She talked with a friend at work who had lived there and talked about all the good times.

Another spouse commented:

> The company employees had some kind of meeting to talk about houses and salaries, but the spouses were excluded from any sort of formal "orientation" that may have been done by the company.

After arrival, these spouses discovered the *New Arrival Survival Guide* published by the Newcomers Club of Mexico City:

> This book had a couple of hundred pages of good information. We never had this information. I also met the wife of a P & G executive who said that they had had an appointment with the US Embassy first thing to talk about what to expect and the dangers of the country.

Language

> We had planned to begin taking Spanish lessons when we arrived. Looking back on it, we should have started the day we said "yes."

Prior to the transfer, the company hired Spanish teachers in Ottawa for employees who had the time and motivation to study the language. Employees and their families were also informed about a language school in Cuernavaca, near Mexico City. Some Martel executives, as well as their spouses, took advantage of this opportunity and spent several weeks studying at this language and cultural training centre. The centre offered intensive eight-hour days of Spanish language instruction, both one-on-one and in small groups. Classes on Mexican culture were also available.

Most of the managers attending the centre arrived with limited Spanish skills and were overwhelmed by the amount of information they were trying to absorb:

> It was very difficult to learn. There was only so much new information I could absorb. It probably would have been better if I had started the school with a base to begin with. I should have started language training in Ottawa. In Cuernavaca, I was too much in awe of everything.

After being in Mexico for a while, most of the traditional managers and their families realized that, although there were often people available that spoke both English and Spanish, if they were going to integrate themselves into their living and working environments, they had to learn Spanish. They also began to learn that speaking only with Mexicans that spoke both English and Spanish had severe limitations. One manager commented:

> I find that I spend a lot more time with employees who are bilingual. I wasn't able to communicate directly with employees that only spoke Spanish. I often had to speak through someone who spoke both languages, but I never knew if my message was getting through the way that I intended it. I think often, it didn't.

Others had similar feelings:

> The language was the biggest issue. Anyone that tries to work down here without the language will fail or at least be frustrated for a very long time.

Some managers found themselves in situations where most, or at least key, subordinates spoke only Spanish and, therefore, had to speak Spanish immediately. At Santa Fe (the administrative center) nearly all of the employees were unilingual. Others had numerous English speakers in their departments but chose to conduct meetings in Spanish, despite the initial inconvenience. These managers learned the language quickly. Still others found the expediency of the tasks at hand too important to be slowed by a new language and often worked more closely with their English-speaking subordinates or through an interpreter. It was apparent that this practice, however, could not last:

> Over the past several months, I've noticed a change in the tolerance level of the Mexicans to work or think in a different language (English). I think their expectations are now "you have been here a year, you should know more than three words" and I can understand that perfectly.

Other managers observed:

> You are paid to manage a company. It is not possible if you don't speak the language.
> You can't ask them to write project reports in English or to translate all their documents.
> One of my strengths in Ottawa was an ability to communicate with people. That's gone.

Outside of the work environment, language was also a barrier when trying to meet Mexicans socially.

Arriving in Mexico

The majority of expatriates and their families went to Mexico City. The Mexico City metropolitan area was estimated to have about 22 million inhabitants making it one of the world's largest cities, maybe the largest. Although it was a fascinating city, rich in culture, history, and social activities, it also had a reputation for being a very difficult place to live, due to serious pollution and crime problems.

For the executives and their spouses who had previous experience in Latin America the move was not difficult. One person had gone to Latin America 20 years earlier and had learned the language. His wife was Mexican and they had family and friends in the city. They received no preparation, got on an airplane and found a house on their own. A second spouse rented a car the day after arriving and drove outside the city to the home in which she was going to live and started preparing it for possession.

Another manager commented,

> When I moved to Mexico City I spoke the language and I had one suitcase so it was easy. The biggest problem was learning my way around the city.

He added that since both he and his wife spoke Spanish, had minored in Latin American studies, had worked in Latin America, neither had required much preparation or support. They found their own house in an old colonial section of the city.

However, the situation was very different for the traditional managers and their spouses. During the initial visits to look for housing and schools, the company hired a firm to help families as well as to look after other aspects of their relocation when they arrived in Mexico. Executives and their spouses were shuttled from place to place by representatives from the relocation company and were sheltered from many of the challenges of getting around in a new city. Even so, what they did see and experience was often a shock. One manager recalled:

> A lot of places had big security gates. That was a brand new feeling for those of us who were not accustomed to it. The least safe area in Ottawa didn't have barbed wire or guards. That was a real shock to my wife. When she saw where I was going to work and two guys with machine guns standing out front, that was a big shock.

His wife commented:

> The armed guards in front of people's driveways, in front of stores, in front of the schools that we went to look at were pretty scary. The representative from the relocation company kept saying that those people must have a lot of money or be politicians and that's why they needed armed guards. What I didn't understand was that we were going to be one of those people. In Ottawa, relatively speaking, we were just average "Joes" with a three-bedroom house and a yard.

One spouse remembered:

> We had someone holding us by the hand, driving us around most of the time. We had been to restaurants and a nice hotel that I'm sure had experience with English-speaking foreigners. Then we went to the airport to go home. We were on our own and there were so many people. We had been dropped right in the middle of Mexico. It seemed like nobody wanted to help us, and we didn't know how to ask anyway.

In the early days after moving permanently, the families of traditional managers began encountering new challenges. None felt they had a strong enough grasp of the language to live and function in Mexico on their own. The problems began the first day when they began setting up their homes, and later continued into the workplace. Not speaking Spanish and being unfamiliar with their surroundings, some of the routine activities associated with moving a household became almost insurmountable obstacles. This manager's experience was not atypical:

> My dryer had a three-pronged plug but the wall socket had only two. I needed to hire a plumber and an electrician. We had no idea how to do that at first, especially without speaking the language. I wish there could have been someone assigned to us for the first couple of days after we moved in to help with the little things.

Many of the Canadians expected the relocation company to look after a lot of the small details. Very few people were happy with the service provided to them in the early days after arrival. This manager was an exception:

> A lot of people were unhappy with the relocation company, but that really depended on what their expectations were. I wanted to know what schools were available and I wanted a house with three bedrooms in a good area. They met those expectations. Anyone who had a bad experience had unrealistic expectations about what someone else was going to do for them.

Some managers chose to live outside Mexico City in a private, gated community to avoid the crime and pollution. However, they had a long commute early in the morning and late at night and their children attended school in the city, which negated some of the benefits.

Pollution was on the minds of the executives who lived in the city. One said that pollution was more of an issue for him than security. Another commented,

> Some days it's bad. You have to wonder what you are doing to your health. If I had little children I wouldn't be here.

A few of the "traditional and international" expatriates and their families went to live in cities other than Mexico City. Guadalajara, Mexico's second largest city, was easier to adapt to than the capital, but it had many of the problems associated with large population centers. Monterrey, on the other hand, was characterized as a "piece of cake," especially in a section called Garza Garcia:

> Everything worked. The police were not corrupt and you could call the telephone company in the morning and have your phone installed in the afternoon.

Even for executives who had prior Latin American experience and spoke the language, moving to Mexico did not always go smoothly. One family had their flight canceled in Montreal and did not arrive in Guadalajara until midnight.

> We were met by a chauffeur in a new Suburban that the company bought for us and we went to a hotel. The next morning the real estate agent met us and accompanied us to our house that, like all the homes, was surrounded by high walls. The agent forgot the garage door opener and went back to the office to get it. When she returned she asked us where our car was. It had been stolen from in front of our house on our first day in Mexico. My wife just looked at me and said, "Where have you brought us? I want to go home!"

Dual-Career Families

Generally, under Mexican law, spouses who were not Mexican citizens were not able to work during their stay in the country. Giving up jobs at home had been hard for some. Unable to work, and alone while their partners were at the company, the spouses took golfing lessons at the local country club and the majority studied Spanish throughout the week, but there were still a lot of hours left in the day:

> You can find lots of things to keep you busy, but finding a new purpose is difficult. I feel like my brain is becoming mush.

One executive commented that his wife always reminded him that she gave up a job and career to move to Mexico.

Even if they could work, most felt that they did not have a strong enough command of the language to function in a job. The same was true for volunteer work. In fact, several were turned down when they offered to work for a charity organization.

In one instance, IHR agreed to secure the services of an employment agency to find a position for one of the spouses. It also assisted in the process of changing her immigration status to allow her to work in Mexico. Even so, after one year, she had been unable to find employment, in part, due to a lack of Spanish language skills:

> I now know what my work really meant to me. At first, I felt like I lost my identity when I lost my job. I haven't replaced it with anything yet but now, what I first saw as a loss, I now see as an opportunity. There are probably a million things I can do, once I know Spanish a little better. It's changed from something pretty awful to something that has a lot of potential.

An ability to speak Spanish and prior experience in Latin America made a big difference in securing employment. One spouse, an American fluent in Spanish, had been a Latin American Officer in the US Peace Corps. She was hired by a US government agency in Mexico City and then went to an international foundation.

Isolation: Feeling Alone Among 22 Million People

The young managers, and those with previous Latin American experience, loved their life-styles. They had Mexican friends and adapted easily. One view was that "Socially, it's a blast."

On the other hand, the traditional managers and their spouses often had a more difficult time. One noted, "I'm not experiencing Mexico."

Outside of work-related activities, many of the Canadians found it difficult to form friendships with Mexicans. Generally, their social activities revolved around other families in the Martel team or other Canadian or American expatriates they met. The social contact they had with Mexicans was the occasional event with subordinates and their families.

Occasionally, their partner's unhappiness had an impact on the performance of some of the managers. Contributing to this unhappiness was a growing security risk, both real and perceived, that distanced the expatriates from Mexico.

Even after a year of living in Mexico, some of the families felt no more integrated into the country and culture than when they had first arrived. The spouse of one of the managers commented:

> There is a definite sense of not belonging. This isn't our home. Even just walking around, sometimes there is a sense of people looking at you like you are a foreigner. We're the minority here. Another spouse asked me 'We are never going to belong here, are we? We are always going to be "extranjeros."' (foreigners).

However, some individuals had a different reaction:

> We were told before we came down here that it was hard to make friends with the Mexicans. I don't know if that's true. My husband has made friends with several Mexicans at work. I just don't come into contact with Mexicans as much as the others.

Many of the managers chose to live in an exclusive development outside of Mexico City called Valle de Ayora in an upscale suburb of the city known as Desierto de Leones.

Desierto de Leones was the residence of Spanish aristocrats when Mexico was a colony of Spain. Walls and security gates surrounded the Valle de Ayora enclave. Armed guards at another set of gates also controlled the entrance into the general area. Because many of the families had chosen to live there, Valle de Ayora soon came to be referred to as Fort Marconi among Martel employees.

Families living there enjoyed many benefits associated with living outside of Mexico City, not the least of which were cleaner air, increased security, and quiet. However, it also increased the feelings of isolation and separation. The feeling of isolation was intensified for the spouses of Martel managers because they lacked the regular contact with other people from whom their partners benefited at work.

> A couple of weeks after I got here, I remember thinking "there's 22 million people in this city and not one of them is my friend."

Some managers rejected Valle de Ayora and chose to live in upscale neighborhoods within Mexico City. One spouse, referring to the level of isolation, commented, "I think I would go mad living in Fort Marconi."

For the traditional managers and their families, adaptation was slow but usually came:

> Even though things are getting better, some days are awful. I don't know if there will ever come a time where there won't be ups and downs, but it seems to be evening out a bit.
>
> You have to get on with living. A major milestone is adapting.

Security and Safety

> These people have no money. They are getting desperate and it's only going to get worse.

One thing everyone agreed upon and on which they shared the same viewpoint was security. Following the currency crisis in December 1994, the Mexican economy deteriorated rapidly. Inflation initially soared to more than 100 percent while wages were held relatively constant. As economic conditions grew worse, Mexico City began to experience a sharp increase in street crime. Tourists, expatriates, and Mexicans were all targets for armed robbery, pick pocketing, and purse snatching.

Mexico City police offered little relief and, in fact, were often reported as the perpetrators of crime. Police routinely stopped vehicles with illegitimate charges of traffic violations in order to demand money. Most of the Martel team had been forced to pay police for alleged traffic violations, often on more than one occasion. Police would even accompany them to an automated teller machine to withdraw funds. According to one manager experienced in Mexico, "The police in Mexico City are not your friends. I go to great lengths to stay away from them."

Another executive who had previously lived in Mexico said,

> Mexico is quite dangerous in some places. It is a much more dangerous place now than it was 15 years ago. If you go around the city and engage in lots of activities, you have more exposure. Some people isolate themselves.

Some of the expatriates, regardless of experience or language ability, had frightening experiences. One of the older, traditional managers had a friend murdered in another city and one of the young "international" managers was robbed at gunpoint. Another executive survived an attempted kidnapping:

> I was driving home from work about 8 p.m. A car was stopped in traffic in front of me and I noticed another on an angle behind me, blocking me in. The next thing I knew, there was a noise like something was hitting the window of the car. I thought it was kids throwing stones. I looked over my shoulder and saw a gun pointed at me. I looked out the passenger window and saw another gun. When I opened the door, I was hit on the head with a gun as they tried to force me to move over and allow them into the car. I tried to move over but couldn't because my car had a center console in the front seat. Then, realizing I didn't want to go anywhere with these guys, I pushed the door open, jumped out, and then dove over the car next to mine. A shot was fired as I jumped and I heard another shot as I ran. When I finally looked back, my car was still there with the doors wide open, but the attackers were gone.

The spouse and son of one of the Canadian managers were stopped by police, dragged from the car and searched for drugs.

The company, in its country and security allowances, had taken steps to compensate employees for the level of country hardship and risk. IHR used an external consulting service to conduct an independent hardship evaluation of the countries in which the company operated. This evaluation had three components, 1) threat (personal), 2) discomfort (availability of medical services), and 3) inconvenience (availability of goods and services). It was updated twice a year. Mexico ranked 26 of 51 countries and IHR checked this ranking against other sources. Martel managers received twice the percentage allowance for Mexico compared to the US State Department. Because of the number of expatriates sent to Mexico there was an increased risk of something happening.

The company's security consultant was sent to Mexico to evaluate the situation. The consultant had travelled to most of the countries where the company had offices, and commented to employees that he had never seen anything as bad as the situation in Mexico.

On the Martel team were some very senior executives, as well as middle to upper level managers. The different ranks received different levels of security such as drivers and alarms for their houses. Many families became upset at the differences. One manager commented:

> Security should not be a perk. Basic common safety should be for everybody; it shouldn't depend on rank. Some of the lower level managers had to ask "Why is that person's life more important than mine?"

The expatriates felt that they were experiencing random crime. There was no pattern of kidnapping or assaulting senior managers of multinational corporations. Employees realized, however, that managers with drivers had not had a single incident; those without drivers all had problems.

There was an internal debate at headquarters whether to provide additional money and let the employees purchase their own security services and hire a driver or to reimburse them for the actual expenses incurred. The company decided to provide additional funds that were distributed to individual employees to use as they saw fit (for example, hire a driver). The Security Department promised to hire security consultants to advise each family on their particular security risks, but three months later that had not happened. Jeff York commented that those services were supposed to come directly from Lerida, which made it more difficult for them to control.

> A Mexican firm represented itself as being able to deliver security services in English, but it couldn't.

Company employees became more sensitive after the attempted kidnapping. Although they were upset at the security situation, they were more upset by the manner in which the situation was handled:

> If we had known about the security risks before we had come, we would probably still be here, but we would be better prepared emotionally.
>
> After blaming the company for all of the problems on earth, at one point I had to ask myself "if I was in their shoes, what could I realistically do"? Other than being on the other end of the phone and being a little more understanding, there was little more I could realistically do. Just a kind word once in awhile would mean a lot.

Monterrey was felt to be a safer city than either Mexico or Guadalajara. An executive who lived in Guadalajara had multi-level security – a security system in the house, a 10,000-volt electric fence, and a neighborhood security guard.

Work and Compensation

Martel had lost three employees with previous Latin American experience to companies that offered more money. Team leaders believed there was a risk of additional losses among the younger managers.

Frank Kelly felt that one of the biggest problems was the compensation system. He explained:

> It's very competitive here. The European salaries are higher than the American salaries, which are higher than the Canadians' salaries. A person could be transferred from the Miami office of the company and earn more than his Canadian boss. That's wrong.
>
> We've lost three good young executives in the last couple of months. Other companies just buy them out.

The company based its international compensation on salaries of similar managers of other Canadian multinationals with expatriate managers, but a situation had developed where there were differences between the Canadian and international market for telecommunications professionals.

In the international marketplace for managers, competition for talented professionals had driven salaries higher. This effect was multiplied in Latin America as international companies continued to expand rapidly throughout the region. Demand for experienced managers with Latin American experience drove salaries well beyond what a typical manager working in Canada with similar experience could expect.

They can go work for any company in the world that does business in Latin America and double their salary.

One year of experience here is worth 10 years anywhere else. You see so many problems that you have to solve.

Some of the Martel managers working in Latin America did not think that the compensation packages were competitive with the marketplace. The company had begun to offer additional benefits, and some came in the form of salary increases:

The company seems to be very careful about what they will give you because they want to make sure that when you go back to Canada, they can take it all away. Additional benefits always seemed to be directly associated with working in Mexico such as athletic club memberships.

The work hours were long and there was not a lot of opportunity to take advantage of clubs:

I've never worked harder in my life. I leave the house at 6:30. Two nights ago I got home at 11:30 and last night at 10:30. And this was not cocktail circuit stuff. Everybody is working hard. The rewards are high but the costs are high also.

However, managers felt that the challenging work was an important motivating factor. Interesting work compensated for lower salaries, at least in the short term. One of the most attractive aspects of the jobs in Mexico for the Canadian managers was the perception that they could make a difference. This was true regardless of their age, seniority or experience. Their high level of autonomy, coupled with the challenge of modernizing Lerida in this competitive market provided a level of satisfaction that many managers believed was the greatest reward for their efforts.

A senior executive thought the company did well in recognizing that it could not run Lerida from Ottawa.

We have a lot of autonomy. It is not necessary to clear everything with Ottawa. It's my plan and I'm committed.

And it was not just the senior executives that experienced that satisfaction. One of the young managers worked with 12 people on his immediate team and had over 200 people reporting to him:

The strength of the company is its strategy. That's what interests us. We want to implement change – that's fun. We want to be involved in decision making regarding the strategy. We are doing real value-added stuff and making a difference that you don't get back in Canada being one of thousands.

Another echoed this sentiment,

I would love to live in Ottawa for the quality of life, but not for the job. We are living on the edge here. Home is a bureaucracy.

A Rewarding Experience

Along with the many challenges that Mexico provided, many of the expatriates found a plenitude of new and rewarding experiences. The families enjoyed travelling, new friends, food, and culture:

> Mexico has a rich culture. We've tried to appreciate the history and culture as much as possible. The first Christmas we spent in Mexico, our children came to stay with us and we were invited for Christmas with a Mexican family which was really a highlight. We had a piñata and later enjoyed the Mexican tradition asking for *posada*.[2]

Mexican hospitality, however, was not the only benefit bestowed upon the Canadians. Martel managers began to relate to their Mexican counterparts in new ways. At one point, a group of Mexicans provided a senior Canadian manager with a comic sculpture with the caption: *To the Mexicanised Canadians from your Canadianised Mexicans.*

Many felt they had learned a great deal from their Mexican counterparts:

> I have a subordinate who really helped me in many ways. Some were attitudinal things like how to approach Mexicans in various situations. I think he realized that I had a yearning to understand the Mexican way of doing things, so he openly offered suggestions.
>
> I have a tremendous respect now for most Mexicans. They work hard. They aren't afraid to work at all. They lack some management skills and some infrastructure, yes; but hard work is never a problem.

And, of course, the expatriates realized they had learned a great deal about themselves and their homes:

> At one point, I had to address all the pros and cons and make a personal decision to go or stay. On questions like security, I had to ask myself if I was really angry with the company or just frustrated as I adjusted. I finally had to identify which issues I could control and which ones I couldn't. You can't walk around unhappy all the time. I decided to stay, and things started to get better from that point.
>
> Little things don't bother me as much now.
>
> My self-definition has changed. I'm proud of Canada but I can see both sides. I'm also more self-confident and willing and prepared to tackle difficult decisions.
>
> You glamorize things back home – everything is good. But it isn't.

The Future

There was also agreement across the groups of expatriates that more development of executives was necessary:

> We need to have people in the pipeline – junior and senior people. We need to identify 25 to 30 promising people at all levels and develop them to run our Latin American operations.
>
> We need a structured, publicized development program like some of the top American companies like P&G.

The purchase of Latin American companies meant that soon Spanish would be the first language of almost one-half of Martel employees. Executives were wondering what they could learn from the Mexican experience to develop managers to run the expanding Latin American operations?

Notes

1. Expatriate Human Resource Policies, Marconi Telecommunications Corporation, February, 1997.
2. In Spanish, Posada means guest house or inn. The traditional celebration of asking for posada represents the search for an inn by Mary and Joseph on Christmas Eve. Guests stand outside the home and sing by candlelight, asking for lodging for the night.

PART **3**

Corporate Social Behavior in a Global Economy: Competing with Integrity[1]

Overview

In Part 2 of this book we presented selected strategic and operating issues that international managers experience. In this part we present situations involving decisions in areas of corporate social responsibility and ethical behavior that managers are likely to encounter in their careers. Our intention is to challenge you to consider your current or future responsibilities to society as a business leader more broadly than simply from an economic perspective. We have separated this topic from the discussion of strategic and operating issues for pedagogical purposes because we felt that issues of corporate social action do not always receive the attention that they deserve. In reality, there are social consequences that are linked to or result from firms' business decisions. Impact on people and society should be considered at the time the decisions are being made. Highlighting and emphasizing social behavior as a global concern for corporations allows more detailed analytical treatment of the issues and, hopefully, encourages development of a way of thinking about them that managers can use.

Corporate Social Responsibility

The concept of corporate social responsibility is not new, nor is it universally interpreted in the same way. One writer has suggested that serious discussion of the topic in North America started in 1953 with the publication of *Social Responsibilities of the Businessman*.[2] That discussion turned into a debate nine years later when Milton Friedman asserted that a company's only social responsibility was to make as much money as possible for its stockholders.[3]

The concern with social responsibility in an international context usually has arisen when companies have been linked to activities such as bribery, purchasing products from companies in other countries that use child or prison labor, or abandoning countries with strict legislation regarding environmental protection or employment practices for less strict jurisdictions. These latter issues became the topic of corporate social responsibility discussions during the debate about the North American Free Trade Agreement (NAFTA) and raised important questions about to whom and for what a corporation is responsible. The result was the eventual negotiation of side agreements covering labor and environmental matters.

Opponents of NAFTA claimed that firms from Canada and the United States would flock to Mexico because of its less stringent environmental and labor regulations. They would be able to reduce costs and increase profits by taking advantage of lower-paid Mexican workers at the expense of displaced Americans and Canadians. Opponents of NAFTA also claimed that companies would reduce costs by polluting the environment, since they would not have the expenses associated with compliance with environmental laws in Canada and the United States. In reality, it was not the laws that were the problem. Mexican environmental and labor laws and regulations were comparable to those in the United States and Canada, but the enforcement of them was not up to Canadian or American standards.[4] One can find examples of firms that have taken advantage of the lax enforcement of regulations, as opponents of NAFTA predicted, but it has not been true of all companies.

Corporate social responsibility has been thought of in many ways, but the concept usually describes a progression from narrowly prescribed responsibilities to more broadly conceived ones. For example, one such scheme would include the following:

- *social obligation*, or a responsibility limited to shareholders and compliance with laws;
- *social responsibility*, or a reactive approach to other organizational stakeholders (for example, customers, employees, suppliers);
- *social responsiveness*, a proactive approach to external societal interests, including environmental issues and social values.[5]

This range also could be thought of as a continuum of responsibility from solely maximizing profits now at one extreme, to trusteeship of the quality of life for present and future generations at the other.[6] Where should a company be positioned on this continuum? There is no easy or obvious answer to that question because the factors to be considered are complex and it represents a value judgment that executives of each corporation will have to decide for themselves.

A useful way of thinking and talking about corporate social behavior has been proposed by Carroll.[7] His social-performance model combines a delineation of categories (or *types*) of responsibility, *issues* for which responsibility exists, and the *philosophical orientation* of the enterprise toward action on the issues. Although this framework was developed in the United States with domestic concerns in mind, we believe that it can be applied in international settings. Many of the issues addressed by the framework exist in other cultures, and executives should develop guidelines for approaching them. However, this is not always straightforward because of differences in values, beliefs, and practices across cultures.

Types of Responsibility

Carroll defines expected corporate social behavior in the following way: "The social responsibility of business encompasses the economic, legal, ethical and discretionary expectations that society has of organizations at a given point in time."[8] The first two categories, *economic* and *legal*, receive the most attention in business schools and in business. These include the responsibility to produce goods and services that society wants, make a profit, and obey the laws and regulations that govern society and business. However, companies are expected to do business and to make profits in an ethical, as well as legal, fashion. Since all of society's desired behaviors are not necessarily written down, *ethical* responsibilities include those behaviors, not embodied in laws, that also are expected of businesses. A later section deals with ethical behavior in more detail. Finally, there is the area of *discretionary* responsibility "about which society has no clear cut message for business." As the name suggests, activities in this area are voluntary and left to individual choice and judgment. Some common discretionary activities might include charitable contributions or providing employee-assistance programs for substance abusers.

In an interview with the *New York Times Magazine*, Ben Cohen of Ben & Jerry's Homemade Inc. defined a socially responsible business as one that "seeks to use its power to improve the quality of life within society."[9] Rather than focus only on profitability and quality like many companies, Cohen said, Ben & Jerry's tried to make an "impact on the community, on the consumer, on our employees." For example, the company bought its coffee from a "rural cooperative in Mexico, helping to raise the standard of living there."

Ben & Jerry's is a company that devotes significant attention to discretionary responsibilities by providing a paid family-leave plan and child care facilities among other benefits, donating 7.5 percent of pretax profits to non-profit groups, and, in 1992, signing the Valdez Principles.[10] The Valdez Principles comprise a voluntary code of corporate conduct toward the environment, covering ten areas: protection of the biosphere; sustainable use of natural resources; reduction and disposal of waste (particularly hazardous waste); wise use of energy; reduction of environmental, health, and safety risks; marketing of safe products and services; environmental damage compensation; disclosure of hazards to workers and the public; commitment of management resources to implement, monitor, and report on implementation of the principles; and an annual audit.[11] The Ben & Jerry's cases (Cases 17 and 18) in Part 3 discuss the company's philosophy toward social responsiveness and illustrate its implementation in operations in Russia.

Another illustration of discretionary responsibility is provided by Procter & Gamble.[12] P&G promoted a program in Mexico called *Una Escuela en Cada Rincon* (A School in Every Corner), which would create 20 new elementary and preschools in rural areas of four Mexican states. The program had the support of the state governments, which granted P&G the necessary land, as well as the Secretariat of Public Education, which would accredit the schools. Consumers deposited wrappers or containers from 13 different P&G products in specially designated receptacles. Each wrapper or container, which represented a brick in a school, was recycled. Although discretionary, this activity appears to be a creative approach to societal needs in which everyone benefited. The consumers had their products; P&G had its sales and profits; Mexico acquired more schools which it needed; and the program promoted conservation and the environment.

Issues

Frederick has suggested that several international accords adopted in the past 50 years provide a base for the development of a transcultural standard of corporate social behavior in a global economy.[13] These accords[14,15] address the following issues:

* Employment practices and policies. For example, multinationals should develop non-discriminatory employment practices, provide equal pay for equal work, respect the right of employees to join unions and to bargain collectively, give advance notice of plant closings and mitigate their adverse effects, respect local host-country job standards, provide favorable work conditions and limited working hours, adopt adequate health and safety standards, and inform employees about health hazards.
* Consumer protection. MNCs should respect host-country laws regarding consumer protection, safeguard the health and safety of consumers through proper labeling, disclosures and advertising, and provide safe packaging.
* Environmental protection. MNCs should preserve ecological balance, protect the environment, rehabilitate environments damaged by them, and respect host-country laws, goals, and priorities regarding protection of the environment.
* Political payments and involvement. As examples. MNCs should not pay bribes to public officials and should avoid illegal involvement or interference in internal politics.
* Basic human rights and fundamental freedoms. Multinationals should respect the rights of people to life, liberty, security of person, and privacy; and freedom of religion, peaceful assembly, and opinion.

This may not be a comprehensive listing of all the issues to be encountered, but it is a good start in thinking about them.[16]

Orientation

The previous P&G example demonstrates another element of the social performance model – orientation toward social responsiveness. The range of orientations include *react* (resist), *defend* (do the minimum required), *accommodate* (be progressive), and *proact* (lead the way). In this example, P&G probably should be classified as proactive. The approach chosen by a company will most likely depend on the executives' view of the relationship between business and society. Managers with a view of society's moral values and business objectives as being inherently in conflict, or at best being totally separate domains of activity, are probably apt to favor a stance that resists doing more than the minimum.[17] A paradigm in which business objectives and societal values are in harmony or are complementary will more likely lead to actions deemed as progressive or as leading the way.

Northern Telecom is another example of a company leading the way in showing that society's values and business objectives can be complementary. Its "Free in Three" program was aimed at eliminating CFC solvents in its operations within a three-year period and being the first major electronics company to do so.[18] The goal was met in January 1992. Although the program cost $1 million, it saved $4 million on unpurchased CFCs during the three years, and the total projected savings is estimated to be $50 million.[19] In Mexico, in a joint venture with the Mexican government (SEDUE), the US Environmental Protection Agency (EPA), and industry associations from Mexico and the United States, Northern Telecom managed a training and demonstration project, sharing its experience with Mexican companies.[20]

Social responsiveness may be viewed as a naive ideal or as good business practice that produces a positive public image, creates a competitive advantage in selling environmentally-friendly products, and possibly assists in recruiting high-caliber staff looking for companies with whom they can identify.[21] Decisions about whether to be a leader, follower, or resister of socially responsive initiatives are not simple or easy ones.

Ethical Issues

The least clear aspect of social responsibility for managers may be in the domain of ethics, which is the "moral thinking and analysis by corporate decision makers regarding the motives and consequences of their decisions and actions."[22] Ethics is the study of morals and systems of morality, or principles of conduct. The study of ethics is concerned with the right or wrong and the shoulds or should nots of human decisions and actions. This does not mean that all questions of right and wrong are ethical issues, however. There is right and wrong associated with rules of etiquette – for example, in which hand to hold your knife and fork, in the use of language and rules of grammar, and in making a computer work. Holding a fork in the wrong hand or speaking ungrammatically does not constitute unethical behavior.

The ethical, or moral, frame of reference is concerned with human behavior in society and with the relationships, duties, and obligations between people, groups, and organizations. It is concerned with human consequences associated with decisions and actions, not solely profits, more sophisticated technology, or larger market share. In this concern for human outcomes, it differs from other perspectives such as financial, marketing, accounting, or legal. An ethical perspective requires that you extend consideration beyond your own self-interest (or that of your company) to consider the interests of a wider community of people, including employees, customers, suppliers, the general public, or even foreign governments. It also advocates behaving according to what would be considered better or higher standards of conduct, not necessarily the minimum acceptable by law, for example.

The separation of strategic or operating decisions and ethical decisions is artificial because problems in the real world do not come with neat labels attached: here is a finance problem; here is a marketing problem; and now, an ethical problem. Managers may categorize the issues by functional area or break up a complex problem into components such as those mentioned. Usually policy issues and decisions are multifaceted and simultaneously may have financial, marketing, and production components. They also may have ethical dimensions that managers should consider. However, in considering a typical complex problem with more than one dimension, the ethical dimension may be overlooked.

If situations did come with labels on them, a person could apply the techniques and concepts he or she had learned, such as net present value or market segmentation, to arrive at a decision. What would happen if a problem labeled "ethical dilemma" arrived? A manager probably would be in a quandary because he or she most likely would not have a way of analyzing, let alone resolving, this type of problem. The decision-making tools for this type of situation probably would be missing. Business schools, traditionally, have not emphasized the teaching of ethics as rigorously as they have the teaching of finance or marketing, for example. Business students and managers generally have not been trained to think about ethical issues as they have been trained in the frameworks and techniques for functional areas of specialization.

Some Examples

Ethical questions can arise in many areas of operations: the type of products produced; marketing and advertising practices; business conduct in countries where physical security is a consideration; hiring and promotion practices in countries where discrimination and racism exist; requests for payments to secure contracts or sales; and payments to prevent damage to plants and equipment or injury to employees. As an example, one could look at attempts by the US government to open up markets in Southeast Asia for cigarette manufacturers. Should the government spend money to combat smoking in the United States while also spending it to promote cigarette exports to other countries?

One side argues that the United States is exporting death and disease to the developing world.[23] Third-world tobacco consumption was extimated to be 35 percent higher in 1995 than a decade earlier. In 1994, almost one-half of all US cigarette exports were going to East Asia and the value of shipments had doubled since 1987. An epidemiologist from Oxford University suggested that the results of the increased smoking could be a potential lung-cancer epidemic in Asia, Latin America, the Middle East, and parts of Africa early in the twenty-first century.[24]

The other side counters that cigarettes are manufactured and sold in countries such as Thailand; therefore American manufacturers would not be introducing these items for the first time. Manufacturing and selling cigarettes is not illegal in Thailand, and American companies should have equal access to the market.[25] But, what about the US government's attempts to try to change Thai laws that restrict or ban cigarette advertising?[26] Is this acceptable or is it going too far?

At the company level, what obligations should a corporation have regarding advertising in other countries? Should the company follow the local laws even if they are less restrictive than at home, or would there be a responsibility to advertise that cigarette smoking is hazardous to your health and include all warnings required in the United States? And what if the laws in other countries are stricter than in the United States? For example, in Hong Kong the requirement is to insert large, boldface type on all cigarette ads that says, "Smoking Causes Cancer" or "Smoking Can Kill." There is no pussyfooting around! Should the US adopt these tougher messages? What about the problem that many people in developing countries cannot read? All these questions regarding exporting and advertising cigarettes could be treated simply as issues in international trade, or marketing and advertising, if one chose. To do so, however, is to address only part of the question.

Another example of a product-safety/consumer-protection dilemma involves RU486, the so-called abortion pill. Roussel Uclaf in France developed RU486 as an alternative to surgical abortions. Clearly, there are at least two sides to this issue. One position is that RU486 would help women who chose to have an abortion and who might be at risk in unsafe surgical abortions; another point of view is that its use would be murder – killing unborn children. Against a backdrop of vehement disagreement about the morality of abortions and the pill, and a threatened international boycott, was the fact that China wanted RU486 as part of its population control program and had approved the marketing of it. Should the company market RU486 in China? Further complicating the decision is the fact that Hoechst Chemical was Roussel UCLAF's largest shareholder. In addition, Hoechst has a corporate creed emphasizing support for life, which had been developed in reaction to its previous role as a supplier of cyanide gas for the Nazi gas chambers, and it thought that China did not have an adequate medical infrastructure to handle the product safely.[27]

Eventually, in April 1997, when it faced a boycott by the Christian Coalition, the National Right to Life Committee and other organizations in the United States, Hoechst Marion Roussel (HMR) decided to stop producing and distributing RU486. It gave the rights to Edouard Sakiz, former President of Roussel UCLAF and a member of the team that discovered the drug.[28] Although HMR removed itself from the controversy surrounding RU486, the debate about abortion and RU486 continued between the pro-life and pro-choice sides.

France, like some other countries, had a tainted blood scandal in which officials at the National Blood Transfusion Center permitted the distribution of blood products that might have been infected with the AIDS virus and which had not been heat-treated to destroy the virus. The decision was apparently made in order to use up inventory and stay within budget.[29] At the time, scientists reportedly knew that six donations per 1,000 were likely to be infected with HIV. Sadly, it is now known that thousands of hemophiliacs were infected. Blood testing was required starting in August 1985 and heat-treatment in October 1985. The situation became a public scandal in 1991. During legal proceedings in France, it became known that a pharmaceutical company had continued to sell untested plasma and products that were not heat-treated to 11 countries in Europe and Africa.[30] *LeMonde* reported that Institut Merieux continued to export "unheated and potentially fatal blood products" for over a month after such products were banned in France on October 1, 1985.[31]

Former French Prime Minister, Laurent Fabius, the former Social Affairs Minister and a former junior health minister were charged with manslaughter in the "tainted blood" scandal and faced three years in jail and heavy fines. In March 1999, Fabius and the former Social Affairs Minister were acquitted. The former junior health minister, who had been characterized as displaying "strangely apathetic behavior" in keeping unsterilized blood products in stock after the possibility of contamination became known, was found guilty but the court ruled he should not be punished. And two blood transfusion service doctors who had already served jail terms were facing yet another trial along with other scientific advisors to the Ministers.[32]

There is the issue of purchasing products from countries that have been found to abuse human rights. For example, Levi Strauss stopped purchasing from subcontractors in Myanmar and China because of practices such as using child and prison labor to manufacture products.[33] The company also has developed a set of standards called the "Global Sourcing Guidelines," which address workplace issues for its partners and subcontractors, and the selection countries for sourcing products.[34] IKEA, the Swedish furniture manufacturer and retailer, will not sell carpets unless they are certified as having been made without child labor, and some German rug importers have launched the first "human rights label," Rugmark, which signifies that children were not used to make the rugs.[35] An article in *The Economist* lists other retailers that also are tackling the human rights issue: Wal-Mart, Sears, Reebok, The Gap, Nike, Nordstrom, Liz Claiborne, and Eddie Bauer.[36]

Human rights and fundamental freedoms were issues in Nigeria in November 1995 when Ken Saro-Wiwa was executed by the military government. In 1994, General Sani Abacha had declared the death penalty for "anyone who interferes with the government's efforts to 'revitalize' the oil industry."[37] The declaration was his response to striking oil workers and demands for increased revenue sharing by local communities. Saro-Wiwa was a political activist who was campaigning on behalf of his people, the Ogoni, and against the degradation of the environment by oil spills and pollution caused by Royal Dutch/Shell.[38] In 1995, Saro-Wiwa's activities were construed as "interference" and he was executed.

Initially, Shell responded defensively with full-page advertisements in major newspapers around the world explaining its position.[39] Later, under pressure from shareholders who filed a resolution at its annual meeting in 1997, it changed the tone of its response dramatically. It specifically named the Chairman of Royal Dutch (the Dutch half of the company), Cor Herkstroter, as being responsible for human rights and environmental issues. Mr. Herkstroter has accepted the criticism that Nigeria Shell should have been more proactive in improving its environmental performance.[40] He also conducted a review of the company's business principles and added commitments to support human rights and sustainable development.

Situations in which physical security could be a problem may present ethical issues for managers and employees. Consider a situation in which British expatriate women working in the Middle East training center of a North American-based bank found themselves. They were en route to conduct a training program in Lagos, Nigeria, and were supposed to be met by one of the bank's local staff who would assist them through difficulties in customs at the airport. When the local staff member failed to appear, the women felt forced to pay bribes to bring legitimate training materials and equipment into the country. Soon after paying the money, their taxi was stopped at the darkened perimeter of the airport and machine guns were jabbed at them through the windows by uniformed men. The women were "shaken down" again and felt very vulnerable, particularly with no foreign currency left. After repeatedly showing their documents, denying that they were violating any laws, and playing dumb about the purpose of the delay, the accusing questions, and the threatening gestures, they were finally permitted to pass.

The women were deeply shaken by the experience and vowed never to travel into that country alone again. What responsibility did the local management bear for abandoning them? And what was the ethical responsibility of the experienced managers for whom the women worked who sent them into such a situation so ill-prepared? What is a manager's responsibility regarding the implementation of his or her decisions, particularly when the specific action has to be taken by another person?

Discrimination or racism may be deeply rooted in the history and cultures of a country and may be firmly ensconced in a country's laws, as they were in South Africa. The policies of many multinational corporations operating there lagged behind the views of the broader society where their headquarters were located. However, as public consciousness was raised and pressure for changes in multinational behavior in South Africa increased, some of the larger companies did become more assertive in providing changes in their subsidiaries in South Africa.

The primary pressure for this action was external, however. One force was the emergence of pressure groups that used proxies at annual meetings to confront the issue. These were often church groups that invested in the companies in order to apply such pressure. The second was a code of acceptable behavior, the Sullivan Principles, named for the black minister who led their development. The idea was that, if companies agreed to operate in South Africa in accordance with these principles, they would earn the right to be exempt from the pressure-group tactics.

In hindsight, these steps alone were not sufficient to bring substantial change. But unpopular policies of the South African government, political unrest, sanctions of Western countries, and an eroding economic climate finally influenced the multinationals' decisions. Many major corporations left. Some, such as Kodak, even decided not to sell their products in the country. It may well have been the case that no corporate policies directed at making change from within the system, no matter when instituted, would have been enough to end apartheid and that only by disinvesting and leaving the country did multinationals finally make a difference.[41] There still are countries where discrimination against indigenous ethnic and racial groups exists but is not as obvious to the outside world as was the situation in South Africa. This removes a significant external pressure for change from a corporation, but it does not remove the ethical responsibility for executives to diligently address such issues and to take action.

The discrimination may also be based on gender. For example, people in Japan or Saudi Arabia have beliefs about the appropriate roles for women that may discourage gender equality in the workplace.[42] This creates a problem for companies that actively promote workplace equality in their home countries. In 1991, the US Congress decided that Title VII of the Civil Rights Act of 1991 protected US citizens from employment discrimination by US multinationals in their overseas operations.[43] Companies are caught in a dilemma: violate a principle and possibly a law or risk offending people in another culture. The dilemma will not disappear by ignoring it, and corporations need to develop operating policies for managing in these environments. The Ellen Moore case in Part 2 shows that different perceptions of women in managerial roles complicate choices for individuals as well as challenge corporate operations.

Situations in which a country applies its laws outside its own territory may cause ethical dilemmas. Extraterritoriality is the unilateral application of laws by a nation to the conduct of persons or corporations beyond the borders of that nation. This creates conflict with a second nation that is trying to enforce its laws over people or corporations residing within its territory. More simply stated, two governments claim jurisdiction over the same corporation and issue conflicting and mutually exclusive demands. Management faces a real dilemma! Which law should it break, since it cannot obey both? Beyond the legal question may be some ethical ones. Who will be asked or required to actually break the law and, thus, be subject to possible criminal charges and a jail sentence? How can anyone be expected to manage in such a no-win situation?

Although the United States is, perhaps, the country that most visibly applies its laws extraterritorially, it is not the only one. However, the size and importance of the United States consumer and financial markets attract corporations from all over the world and, thus, provide greater opportunity for such action. In mid-1990, the US Senate attached a trade-ban amendment (the Mack Amendment) to a bill attempting to control the spread of chemical and biological weapons. The amendment would have made it illegal for any subsidiary of a United States company, including subsidiaries in Canada, to do business with Cuba. Canada did not have the same restriction or concern with trade with Cuba as the United States did, and Canadian companies could do business there. The Canadian government called this amendment an intrusion into Canadian sovereignty that it found "clearly unacceptable" and issued an order forcing these Canadian firms (Canadian because they are incorporated in and resident in Canada) to ignore the United States legislation.[44]

Ultimately, President Bush "pocket-vetoed" the bill and the amendment died with it.[45] The issue only disappeared temporarily, however. In 1995, two Republican-introduced bills (by Senator Jesse Helms and Representative Dan Burton) were before the US Senate and the House of Representatives. These bills prohibited sugar, syrup, and molasses exports from Canada to the United States or from any other country that bought sugar cane from Cuba; and they would make it illegal for foreign financial institutions with US operations to lend money to Cuba.[46] The bills were characterized by Canada and the European Union as an "assault on their sovereign right to forge an independent policy with Cuba."[47] It also was reported that the US Treasury Department was going to add some Canadian firms, like mining company Sherrit Inc., to a list of companies with Cuban ties, which would restrict them from dealing with US citizens or businesses.[48]

In 1996, after Cuban jet fighters shot down unarmed civilian aircraft from the United States, Helms and Burton were successful in getting their bill approved by Congress and signed into law by President Clinton. This law made it possible for US citizens to sue foreign firms that were profiting from facilities and land that were once US-owned and then expropriated by Fidel Castro. It also prohibited those foreigners from visiting the United States. In fact, Sherritt's senior corporate officers and directors, and their families, were barred from entering the United States. Canada, the European Union, Mexico, India, Chile, and other countries objected to the law and its extraterritorial reach before the World Trade Organization. In Mexico, President Ernesto Zedillo signed legislation imposing a $300,000 fine on Mexican business people who obeyed another country's law directed at reducing Mexican trade or foreign investment with a third country.[49] At least two Mexican companies, Cemex and Grupo Domos terminated their operations in Cuba to avoid US sanctions.[50] You can see the dilemma created for business people when governments act in this fashion.

Other dilemmas that executives may encounter are requests for bribes or even extortion. For example, mobsters threatened Otis Elevator that they would firebomb its operation in Russia if it did not pay protection money.[51] How should this situation be handled? Otis has a code that delineates its view of right and wrong behavior that all executives sign each year. Its response was not to give in to the extortion, but to pay more for security.[52] Situations involving extortion and bribery have many facets and usually are not resolved simply. The Valley Farms International case (Case 19) requires you to address these types of problems. A more detailed discussion of how to manage in the face of pressure for bribes can be found in the reading, "Bribery in International Business: Whose Problem Is It?" There are many myths surrounding the issue of bribery, and this reading sheds light on the issue from different perspectives. The authors of the reading suggest that there are acceptable alternatives.

Responding to Ethical Problems

One of the first things managers often do when they encounter an ethical problem is avoid it through the process of rationalization. They may focus on some other aspect of the problem. They may transform the ethical problem into some other type of problem – a legal or accounting problem, for instance. The reasoning seems to be that, so long as one is behaving legally or in accordance with accepted accounting practices, for example, nothing else is required. As is discussed later, compliance with laws and professional regulations is probably a minimum requirement for responsible managers.

Another kind of avoidance behavior is to see the problem as only one small piece of a larger puzzle and to assume that someone higher up in the organization must be looking after any unusual aspects, such as ethical considerations. Alternatively, the decision maker might turn it into someone else's problem – perhaps a customer, supplier, or person in higher authority – with the comment: "I am following my boss's orders" or "my customer's instructions." When a customer asks for a falsified invoice on imported goods for his or her records, with the difference deposited in a bank outside his or her country, and you provide this "service," is it only the customer's behavior that is questionable?

Rationalizing one's behavior by transforming an ethical problem into another type of problem, or assuming responsibility for only one specific, technical component of the issue, or claiming it is someone else's problem gives one the feeling of being absolved from culpability by putting the burden of responsibility elsewhere.

Who is responsible for ensuring ethical behavior? We believe that corporations have a responsibility to make it clear to their employees what sort of behavior is expected. This means that executives in headquarters have a responsibility, not just for their own behavior, but also for providing guidance to subordinates. A number of companies have corporate codes to do just this. For example, GE has a policy book entitled, *Integrity: The Spirit & Letter of Our Commitment* that covers, among other issues, ethical business practices, health safety and environmental protection, and equal employment opportunity. Employees sign a statement that they have received the book and that they understand that they are required to comply with the policies described in the guide. Jack Welch, in his statement printed at the front of the manual, explains:

> If you have a concern about what is proper conduct for you or anyone else, promptly raise that concern to your manager or through one of the other channels the company makes available to you. Nothing – not customer service, competitiveness, direct orders from a superior or "making the numbers" – is more important than integrity.
>
> GE leaders have the additional responsibility to make compliance a vital part of our business activities. Adherence to GE policy and applicable laws is the foundation of our competitiveness. Concerns about appropriate conduct must be promptly addressed with care and respect.

However, the person on the spot facing the decision is ultimately responsible for his or her own behavior, with or without guidance from headquarters. In all the cases in this part of the book, you will be asked to develop your own stance on the issues. We encourage you to think carefully about the problems depicted in the cases and to develop reasoned positions. You may find yourself in a similar situation some day, and you will have to make a critical decision. We hope that, by working through the decisions in these cases now, you will be better able to deal with similar decisions later.

As we encountered ethical dilemmas or heard about others who had experienced them, they wrote cases and developed a managerial framework for thinking about and analyzing the problems. We make no claim that the framework to be presented is a complete or definitive treatment of the topic of ethics. Nor are the cases an exhaustive set of issues that you may face in international business. Together, however, they provide a practical and useful way to start addressing the topic.

Ethical versus Legal Behavior

The question always arises as to the distinction between legal and ethical behavior. If one acts legally, in accordance with laws, is that not sufficient? Not all of society's norms regarding moral behavior have been codified or made into law. There can, therefore, be many instances of questionable behavior that are not illegal.[53] It would seem that acting legally is the minimum required behavior for executives. However, society relies on more than laws to function effectively in many spheres of endeavor. In business, trust is essential also. Finally, it should also be recognized that not all laws are moral.

Henderson has provided a useful way to think about the relationship between ethical and legal behavior.[54] He created a matrix based on whether an action was legal or illegal and ethical or unethical, similar to that shown in Figure 1. Assuming that executives want to act legally and ethically (quadrant 4) and avoid making decisions (or acting in ways) that are illegal and unethical (quadrant 2), the decisions that create dilemmas are the ones that fall into quadrants 1 and 3. For example, consider the decision of a

FIGURE 1 Framework for Classifying Behavior

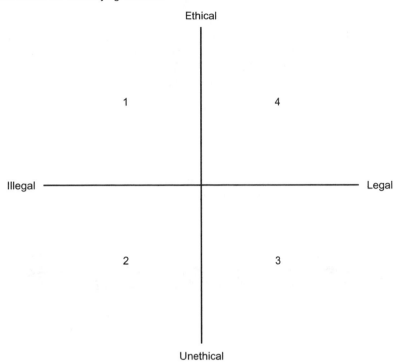

chemical company manager who refuses to promote a pregnant woman to an area of the company where she would be exposed to toxic chemicals that could damage her child. The manager probably would be acting ethically, but illegally. Maybe he could solve the problem by delaying the promotion, if that was possible. This simple example illustrates that a decision can be ethical but not legal; there also may be solutions that allow a win-win outcome in which the decision is legal and ethical because of the way it is made.

In quadrant 3, there will be situations like the marketing of infant formula in developing countries. Infant formula, which was misused in many countries with poor sanitation and polluted water and where people were illiterate and could not read directions, was blamed for the deaths of hundreds of thousands of babies each year. This activity was not illegal, but a vote of the United Nations regarding infant formula declared it unethical.[55] In an interesting twist to this story, studies now have shown that AIDS virus can be transmitted through breast-feeding and the UN has estimated that one-third of all infants with HIV got it through their mother's milk.[56] Infant formula may now be a way to combat the transmission of HIV. This example also points out that society's notions of ethical behavior may change with the times, and new conditions and knowledge. Another example in quadrant 3 would be apartheid, which might have been legal in South Africa, but it was not ethical. Similarly, selling unheated blood in Africa might not have been illegal, but was it ethical?

The last two examples raise the question about whose laws and values should be followed when there are conflicts. Although it might seem that we are avoiding answers, we believe that these are questions each person and company need to answer for themselves. The challenge is to find ways of operating that are consistent with local laws and high standards of conduct. We believe that this goal is attainable with thorough analysis and carefully considered action. In those situations where such a win-win outcome is not possible, there is always the option of choosing not to operate in that environment. The decision to walk away and lose the business may seem naive, but we have met and interviewed a number of executives of very successful companies that have done just that. One described how his company turned down a $50 million contract in a Latin American country because there was no way to avoid paying a bribe to a government official. Another explained that, in his experience, if a company developed a reputation for acting ethically it was not usually subjected to unethical demands. Each person has to make his or her own decision and live with the consequences of his or her actions. The information in the following sections is designed to help you in the decision-making process.

Ethical Framework[57]

Moral philosophers have developed frameworks for thinking about moral issues and for analyzing ethical problems, but those frameworks generally have not been included in international business curricula. We investigated various frameworks for analyzing ethical problems and quickly learned that there are conflicting positions and prescriptions among them. In classes we observed that people advocated actions that represented some of the major frameworks, but without understanding the foundations or the strengths and weaknesses of their positions. Consider the following discussion.

Person X: "If we don't pay what he is asking we will lose the contract and people back home will lose jobs. Is that ethical when people can't feed their families?"

Person Y: "I don't care. What you are suggesting is absolutely wrong."

Person Z: "Now hold on, it doesn't seem to be against the rules there. It is different in that culture. Everyone is doing it. They need the extra money to support their families. Besides, we should not impose our system of morality on other cultures."

You may have heard or have taken part in similar exchanges. The people in the conversation above may not realize it, but they are engaged in a discussion of moral philosophy. However, it is the type of discussion that tends to excite emotions and generate heat and argument, rather than provide insight and a thoughtful course of action.

Since you may likely take part in similar discussions (or arguments) at some time in your career, we think that knowledge of these three frameworks will be useful. The intent is to help you link some everyday reasoning and the positions you might espouse to the ethical frameworks underlying them. In the brief exchange above, one sees elements of Kant's categorical imperative, utilitarianism, and cultural relativism. These are commonly used frameworks, which is why they were chosen. Each represents a different moral calculus, a different ethical map. Thus, the MBI model from Part 1 can be applied using these frameworks as components of the map portion of the model.

The main categories of ethical theories can be divided into: consequential (or teleological) theories, which focus on the consequences, outcomes, or results of decisions and behavior; rule-based (or deontological) theories, which focus on moral obligations, duties, and rights; and cultural theories, which emphasize cultural differences in standards of behavior. These are discussed briefly here.

Consequential Theories

Consequential theories focus on the goals, end results, and/or consequences of decisions and actions. They are concerned with doing the maximum amount of "good" and the minimum amount of "harm." Utilitarianism is the most widely used example of this type of moral framework. It suggests doing the best for the greatest number of people. Another example is acting in a way that provides more net utility than an alternative act. It essentially is an economic, cost–benefit approach to ethical decision making. If the benefits outweigh the costs, then that course of action is indicated. The limitations of this approach are that it is difficult or impossible to identify and account for all the costs and benefits, and, since people have different utility curves, it is difficult to decide whose curve should be used. In real life, how do you compute this utility curve? Finally, in an effort to weigh the costs and benefits, one relies on quantitative data, usually economic data, and many important variables that should be considered are not quantifiable and, therefore, often ignored.

Rule-based Theories

Rule-based theories include both absolute (or universal) theories and conditional theories. The emphasis of these theories is on duty, obligations, and rights. For example, if an employee follows orders or performs a certain task, management has an obligation to ensure that the task is not illegal or harmful to that person's health. People in power have a responsibility to protect the rights of the less powerful. These theories are concerned with the universal shoulds and oughts of human existence – the rules that should guide all people's decision making and behavior wherever they are.

One of the best-known absolute theories is the categorical imperative of Immanuel Kant. Whereas utilitarianism takes a group or societal perspective, the categorical imperative has a more individualistic focus: individuals should be treated with respect and dignity as an end in itself; they should not be used simply as a means to an end. A person should not be done harm, even if the ultimate end is good. The criteria should be applied consistently to everyone. One of the questions to ask is: "If I were in the other person's (or group's or organization's) position, would I be willing for them to make the same decision for the same reasons that I am going to make?"

A variation on absolute theories is fundamentalism. In this case, the rules may come from a book like the Bible, Koran, or Torah. In these systems, one is dealing with an authoritative, divine wisdom that has been revealed through prophets. The Golden Rule (do unto others as you would have them do unto you) would fall into this category. Difficult questions arise when considering which book or prophet to follow and whose interpretation of the chosen book to use. Priests, mullahs, or rabbis who may reflect the views of an elite segment of society or possibly an isolated group usually interpret the books. There can be conflicting interpretations within the same religion as well. Also, the interpretations may be inconsistent with current social and environmental circumstances, as well as large segments of a society. The rules that people choose to follow can also be secular as well as religious, as in the case of Nazi Germany.

One potential shortcoming of these types of prescriptions is that they allow you to claim that you are not responsible for your own behavior: "I was just following orders" is a common excuse. The end result may be the same – you do not have to think for yourself or make a moral judgment, but rather you can avoid it by claiming to be following a higher authority. As far as secular orders are concerned, the war crimes trials after World War II established that following orders is not an acceptable legal defense for committing atrocities.

Cultural Theories

With cultural theories, local standards prevail. Cultural relativism is interpreted to mean that there is no single right way; in other words, people should not impose their values and standards on others. The reasoning behind the argument usually is that we should behave as the locals behave. The familiar expression tells us: "When in Rome, do as the Romans do." One problem, however, comes from the fact that the local people we are encouraged to emulate may not necessarily be the most exemplary. In your own culture, you know that people exhibit different standards of behavior. Does that mean we should advocate that business people coming to the United States act like the people convicted in Wall Street trading scandals, just because those people are Americans? Adopting this philosophy can encourage denial of accountability and the avoidance of moral choice. Using arguments based on this philosophy, the morality of bribes or actions of repressive regimes, for example, does not have to be examined very closely. These theories are summarized in Figure 2.

How does one choose among these conflicting approaches? There is no simple answer to this question. But we think that it is important for managers to recognize the basis for their moral and ethical decisions and to be aware, for example, if they are shifting from one theory to another as a way of avoiding tough decisions. And, if they are dealing with people who use a different moral calculus, maps (M) of these differences provide the basis for the bridging (B) and integration (I) components of the MBI model to communicate across the differences and to manage them.

Perry describes another perspective that managers may find useful – a process of intellectual and ethical development.[58] Although we should recognize that Perry's ideas reflect a cultural bias towards individualism and were derived from a narrow part of the US population, the ideas can help managers think about their positions on these issues.[59] The first category is *dualism*, in which a bipolar structure of the world is assumed or taken for granted. According to this world-view there is a clear right and wrong, good and bad, we and they. These positions are defined from one's own perspective based on

FIGURE 2 Analytical Frameworks

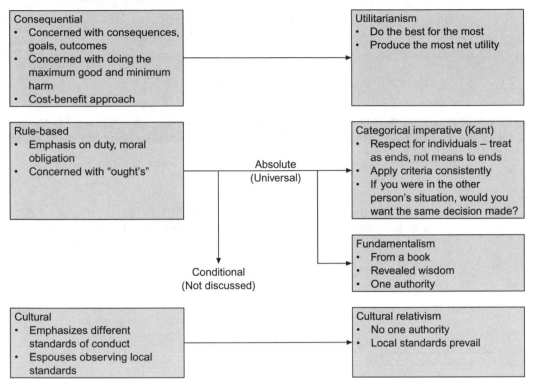

membership in a group and belief in or adherence to a common set of traditional beliefs.

The next category, posited by Perry as a "more developed" perspective, is *relativism* in which the dualistic world-view is moderated by an understanding of the importance of context, which helps a person to see that knowledge and values are relative. As we have seen through earlier parts of this book, different people in different parts of the world think and believe differently, and a relativistic mode of making ethical judgments recognizes this fact. As originally observed by Blaise Pascal, Hofstede notes in the preface to his book, *Culture's Consequences*: "There are truths on this side of the Pyrénées which are falsehoods on the other."[60]

In Perry's scheme, the third "level" of development is *commitment in relativism*, in which a person understands the relativistic nature of the world, but makes a commitment to a set of values, beliefs, and a way of behaving within this expanded world-view. The goal, implicitly reflecting the individualism and mastery orientations described in Part 1, is to arrive at the point where you assume responsibility for your own actions and decisions based upon careful consideration and the application of the "essential tools of moral reasoning – deliberation and justification."[61]

Perry suggests that progression to this stage is not automatic or guaranteed and that people may become "delayed" in their development or even "stuck" in the earlier stages.

People who adhere to a set of absolute rules, however, may reject this notion of a hierarchy of development. Our inclusion of Perry's ideas is not meant to judge others' choices in this regard, but rather to encourage self-awareness. Underlying our perspective throughout this book are (1) the assumption that you are interested in developing a relativistic understanding of the world, and (2) the encouragement for you to decide about your own commitments within this relativistic framework. We recognize that taking this position is a reflection of our own values.

Integrity and Ethical Behavior

De George suggests that executives should act and compete with integrity in international business.[62] Acting with integrity is the same as acting ethically, but the word integrity does not have the negative connotation, the moralizing tone, or the sense of naiveté that the word ethics carries for many people. What is integrity and how does one compete with integrity? According to De George: "Acting with integrity means both acting in accordance with one's highest self-accepted norms of behavior and imposing on oneself the norms demanded by ethics and morality."[63]

Competing with integrity means that executives of multinational corporations should compete against others in a way that is consistent with their own highest values and norms of behavior. Although these values and norms are self-imposed and self-accepted, they cannot be simply arbitrary and self-serving; but neither is there a requirement to be perfect. "The imperative to act with integrity cannot insist on moral perfection. It can and does demand taking ethical considerations seriously."[64]

Managers have multiple interests that they must consider because they are embedded in a complex network of relationships as depicted in Figure 3. The interests, goals, and values of the various actors in any situation can potentially conflict. Identifying these relationships helps in structuring one's analysis. Gandz and Hayes[65] have suggested some objectives for teaching business ethics: creating an awareness of the ethical components of the decision; legitimizing the consideration of ethical issues in the decision process; analyzing

FIGURE 3 A Manager's Context

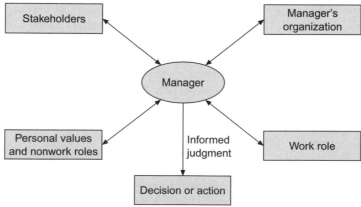

the ethical components with some framework; and applying this technique of ethical analysis to decision situations. To provide a framework for analysis, a series of diagnostic questions and some recommendations are presented. These can be applied to the case situations in the book and, we hope, can serve as a guide for you in the future.

Some Guidelines to Consider

1.   Who are the stakeholders that have an interest in or will be affected by the decision: shareholders; the home-country government; host-country governments; customers; suppliers; employees; unions? There are probably others that could be added to that list, but the point is to comprehensively identify the stakeholders and their interests.

2.   What are the responsibilities and obligations to these stakeholders? Identify the responsibilities that your organization has, but do not overlook the ones that you, personally, may have to external stakeholders and/or to your own organization. For example, a decision about whether or not to shut down operations in a country may involve ethical issues. Take the situation of an insurance company selling life insurance in Uganda during a period of civil war.[66] The company had been told years earlier that its operation was nationalized and now was having its ownership restored. The branch in Uganda was not profitable. The decision to shut down, from a profit-and-loss perspective, may have been easy to make. But what were the company's responsibilities to their managers who ran the company in their interest after it had been nationalized and who were concerned about possible violence to field personnel and to themselves if the company closed its operations? And what were its obligations to its policyholders? The issue may not be whether the company should shut down, but how it should handle its responsibilities, obligations, and commitments to its employees and customers, as well as to its shareholders.

It is important to remember that a company has multiple groups of stakeholders in addition to the investors in the business, and executives need to be clear about their responsibilities and obligations to all these groups. It is easy to ignore some of them, particularly when they are thousands of miles away and probably cannot exert any pressure on the company to behave in their interests. The ethical perspective advocates giving careful consideration to these types of issues and not avoiding them or pretending that they do not exist.

3.   In addition to the economic, managerial, and legal decisions, are there any ethical issues that need to be considered? Be careful not to fall into the trap of transforming ethical decisions into decisions of some other type.

4.   Do you have the best information possible and the facts? Take the time to get the facts, all of them. Avoid fuzzy thinking. Avoid using or being swayed by hearsay or unsubstantiated assertions. These are statements that have no specifics to go with them: "Everybody is doing it," "We'll lose business if we don't do it," or "It's a normal practice." When you hear statements like these, push for the analysis and details. Often, you may find that they are unsubstantiated assertions parading as analysis.

5.   What assumptions are being made? What ethical framework is being invoked? Whose utility is being maximized? Whose values are being used? Consider multiple (including opposing) viewpoints, but examine them carefully. Weigh the costs and benefits to all stakeholders.

6. Are there options that have not been identified? In trying to identify possible action, avoid characterizing decisions using false dichotomies – either/or characterizations that do not have to be win/lose positions. For example, the statement "We need to pay the bribe or lose the business" portrays the situation as win-lose, but it may not be. These positions often develop because the initial analysis was not as complete as it could have been. This mind-set can limit the action possibilities open to the manager. Strive for a win-win situation. Is there a way to solve the problem that satisfies all parties and allows you to fulfill your obligations?

7. How should you, as an individual, act? Is this different from your role as a manager? If there is a conflict, try to resolve it. (Remember the MBI model as a tool to help you.) Ask yourself if you are making a decision and will be acting in accordance with your own highest set of values and norms.

8. Do not let people put the monkey on your back. Do not accept responsibility for decisions that are not your responsibility. Some people will try to find a scapegoat to make a particularly difficult, possibly illegal or unethical decision. Do not let them use you. How do you protect yourself? You can ask for it in writing or suggest an open meeting with other people present to discuss it.

9. Do not avoid making ethical decisions on issues that are your responsibility.

10. Enter into dependent relationships with care. If you increase dependency on a particular customer or supplier, be certain about the relationship and make certain you retain enough power to maintain your standards.

11. Do not use "culture" as an excuse for not trying to do things the proper way. Just because the local company does not treat its toxic waste properly does not mean that it is acting as a model of behavior for that culture. Also, beware of confusing culture and an individual's personality and character. If a person is asking for something that is illegal or unethical, that tells you something about that person's character, not necessarily about his or her culture.

12. Some decision criteria to consider include: do the best for all involved stakeholders; fulfill obligations; observe laws and contracts; do not use deception; and avoid knowingly doing harm (physical, psychological, economic, or social).

13. Remember that there can be personal consequences associated with your decision. People have lost their jobs because someone higher in the organization needed a scapegoat, and others have gone to jail for their actions. Look after the interests of your company in your role as manager, but look after your own interests also. You may be the only one that does!

14. Consider the "billboard" or the "light-of-day" tests. When you drive to work in the morning would you be happy to see your decision or action prominently announced on a large billboard for everyone to read and to know about? Or alternatively, would you be willing to discuss your actions in a meeting where you would be subject to questions and scrutiny and have to justify them? Would your actions look as reasonable in the light of day as they did when the decision was made behind closed doors?

15. Maintain high standards! When in Rome do as the better Romans do.

16. Finally, ask yourself, and answer honestly, if you are leading the way in the area of global social responsiveness, doing the minimum required, or resisting. Are you happy with your answer? If not, you know what to do!

We wish you an interesting, rewarding, and enjoyable journey in your international activities and career.

Notes

1. The subtitle of this part has been adopted from Richard T. De George, *Competing with Integrity in International Business* (Oxford: Oxford University Press, 1993).
2. Howard R. Bowen, *Social Responsibilities of the Businessman* (New York: Harper & Row, 1953).
3. Archie B. Carroll, "A Three Dimensional Model of Corporate Performance," *Academy of Management Review*, 4, no. 4, 1979: 497–505.
4. Susan W. Liebeler, "The Politics of NAFTA," in *Foreign Investment and NAFTA*, Alan M. Rugman (ed.) (Columbia: University of South Carolina Press, 1994).
5. See Sita C. Amba-Rao, "Multinational Corporate Social Responsibility, Ethics, Interactions, and Third World Governments: An Agenda for the 1990s," *Journal of Business Ethics*, 12 (1993): 553–572. This article discusses conceptualizations of corporate social responsibility from a number of sources including the following, which is the primary source for the three-stage framework presented in the text, S. P. Sethi, "Dimensions of Corporate Social Performance: An Analytical Framework," *California Management Review*, 12 (1975): 58–64.
6. Amba-Rao, "Multinational Corporate Social Responsibilities."
7. Carroll, "Three-Dimensional Model."
8. Ibid., 500.
9. Claudia Dreifus, "Passing the Scoop: Ben & Jerry," *The New York Times Magazine*, December 18, 1994: pp. 38–41.
10. *Ben & Jerry's 1992 Annual Report.*
11. Rajib N. Sanyal and Joao S. Neves, "The Valdez Principles: Implications for Corporate Social Responsibility," *Journal of Business Ethics*, 10 (1991): 883–890.
12. Sandy Ornelas, "P&G Helps Build Schools With Promotional Program," *The News*, Mexico City, November 16, 1994.
13. William C. Frederick, "The Moral Authority of Transnational Corporate Codes," *Journal of Business Ethics* 10 (1991): 165–177.
14. These documents include: *The United Nations Universal Declaration of Human Rights* (1948); *The European Convention on Human Rights* (1950); *The Helsinki Final Act* (1975); *The OECD Guidelines for Multinational Enterprises* (1976); *The International Labor Office Tripartite Declaration of Principles Concerning Multinational Enterprises and Social Policy* (1977); *The United Nations Code of Conduct for Transnational Corporations*.
15. Frederick, "The Moral Authority of Transnational Corporate Codes," 166–167.
16. See also Kathleen A. Getz, "International Codes of Conduct: An Analysis of Ethical Reasoning," *Journal of Business Ethics*, 9 (1990): 567–577, for a discussion of these issues.
17. See John H. Barnett, "The American Executive and Colombian Violence: Social Relatedness and Business Ethics," *Journal of Business Ethics*, 10 (1991): 853–861, for a description of the three models: conflict, compartment, and complementarity.
18. A. G. Marcil, "Environmentally Friendly Development: Can the Private Sector Succeed Where Others Have Failed?," *Columbia Journal of World Business*, 27 (1992): 200.
19. Ibid.
20. Ibid., 198.
21. Kathleen Decant and Barbara Alumna, "Environmental Leadership: From Compliance to Competitive Advantage," *Academy of Management Executive*, 8, no. 3 (1994): 7–27.
22. Amba-Rao, "Multinational Corporate Social Responsibility," 555.
23. Philip Smucker, "U.S. Sending Marlboro Man to Rope in Asian Smokers," *The Globe & Mail*, May 29, 1990. This statement was attributed to Senator Edward Kennedy.

24. John Stackhouse, "Third World Lung-Cancer Epidemic Feared," *The Globe & Mail*, November 2, 1994: A1.

25. Smucker, "Marlborough Man."

26. Ibid.

27. Joseph L. Badaracco, Jr., "Business Ethics: Four Spheres of Executive Responsibility," *California Management Review*, Spring, 7 (1992): 64–79. See also the Harvard Business School Case 9-391-050, RU486 (A).

28. "Abort, Retry, Sell?," *The Economist*, April 12, 1997: 59.

29. Andre Picard, "France Makes an Example of Misdeeds," *The Globe & Mail*, September 7, 1993: A4.

30. "Plight of Hemophiliacs Worse in Third World," *The Globe & Mail*, September 7, 1993: A4.

31. "French Laboratory Sold Untreated Blood," *Independent*, November 3, 1992: 12.

32. "Fabius cleared in HIV trial. Not guilty verdicts in 'tainted blood' trial has caused widespread anger," Julian Nunday, *The Daily Telegraph* (London), March 10, 1999 and "Tainted blood scandal PM is cleared," *Birmingham Post*, March 10, 1999.

33. See "Human Rights," *The Economist*, June 3, 1995: 58–59; and William Beaver, "Levi's Is Leaving China," *Business Horizons*, March–April, 1995: 35–40.

34. Beaver, "Levi's Is Leaving China."

35. "Human Rights," *The Economist*.

36. Ibid.

37. "In Nigeria, the Price of Oil Is Blood," Nadine Gordimer, *New York Times*, May 25, 1997: E11.

38. "Shellman says sorry," *The Economist*, May 10, 1997: 65.

39. For example in the *Globe & Mail* in Canada on November 21, 1995.

40. "Shellman says sorry."

41. Mzamo P. Mangaliso, "The Corporate Social Challenge for the Multinational Corporation," *Journal of Business Ethics*, 11 (1992): 491–500.

42. Don Mayer and Anita Cava, "Ethics and the Gender Equality Dilemma for U.S. Multinationals," *Journal of Business Ethics*, 12 (1993): 701–708.

43. Ibid., 701.

44. Ross Howard, "Branch Plants Ordered to Ignore U.S. Bill Banning Trade with Cuba," *The Globe & Mail*, November 1, 1990: A1.

45. "Bush's Sanctions Veto Snubs Foreign Relations Leaders," *Congressional Quarterly*, November 24, 1990: 3932.

46. Drew Fagan, "Canadians Face U.S. Blacklist," *The Globe & Mail*, June 13, 1995: B1.

47. Drew Fagan, "Sherrit Assailed for Cuban Ties," *The Globe & Mail*, June 15, 1995: B1.

48. Fagan, "Blacklist."

49. "Return of the Yanqui," Jeffery Ryser, *Global Finance*, November 1996.

50. "Mexican Conglomerate Pulls Out of Cuba," Larry Rother, *CubaNet News*, July 1997 and "Don't Fret Over Anti-Cuba Law, White House Tells Mexico," *The Globe & Mail*, May 8, 1996.

51. Madelaine Drohan, "To Bribe or Not to Bribe," *The Globe & Mail*, February 14, 1994.

52. Ibid.

53. To see examples of this distinction in action in a large Wall Street firm in the 1980s, read Michael Lewis, *Liar's Poker* (New York: Penguin Books, 1989).

54. Verne E. Henderson, "The Ethical Side of Enterprise," *Sloan Management Review*, 23 (1982): 37–47.

55. Ibid.

56. "Breast-feeding wisdom in question," Barry Meier, *New York Times*, June 8, 1997.

57. This section draws on the following works: Jeffrey Gandz and Nadine Hayes, "Teaching Business Ethics," Working Paper No. 86-17R, October, 1986, School of Business Administration, The University of Western Ontario; Tad Tuleja, *Beyond the Bottom Line* (New York:

Penguin Books, 1985); John B. Matthews, Kenneth E. Goodpaster, and Laura Nash, *Policies and Persons: A Casebook in Business Ethics* (New York: McGraw-Hill, 1985).

58. William G. Perry, Jr., *Forms of Intellectual and Ethical Development in the College Years: A Scheme* (New York: Holt, Rinehart & Winston, 1970).

59. In Perry's full scheme there are nine stages. The authors have chosen to use only the three major positions in the scheme.

60. Geert Hofstede, *Culture's Consequences* (Beverly Hills: Sage Publications, 1980).

61. Jeffrey Gandz and Nadine Hayes, "Teaching Business Ethics," *Journal of Business Ethics*, 7 (1988): 659.

62. Richard T. De George, *Competing with Integrity in International Business* (Oxford: Oxford University Press, 1993).

63. Ibid., 6.

64. Ibid., 41.

65. Ibid.

66. David Burgoyne and Henry Lane, "The Europa Insurance Company," Case 9-84-C049 (London: The University of Western Ontario, School of Business Administration, 1984).

○ ○

Exporting Mental Models: Global Capitalism in the Twenty-First Century

Patricia H. Werhane

When one is asked to enumerate the most challenging ethical issues business will face in this century, the list is long. Environmental sustainability, international trade, exploitation, corruption, unemployment, poverty, technology transfer, cultural diversity (and thus relativism) are a few obvious candidates. Underlying these and other issues is a more serious global phenomenon: the exportation of Western capitalism.

There is a mental model of free enterprise, a model primarily created in the United States, that is being exported, albeit unconsciously, as industrialized nations expand commerce through the globalization of capitalism. This model is not one of greedy self-interested cowboy capitalists eagerly competing to take advantage of resources, low-priced employment, or offshore regulatory laxity. Rather I am referring to another model, one that has worked and worked well in most of North America and Western Europe for some time. This model contends that industrialized free enterprise in a free trade global economy, where businesses and entrepreneurs can pursue their interests competitively without undue regulations or labor restrictions, will produce growth and well-being, that is, economic good, in every country or community where this phenomenon is allowed to operate. The results of global free enterprise, if adapting itself to an American style, "can be compared to the strongest hand in poker: the royal flush, of all five of the most valuable cards of the same suit..." (Uchitelle, 1999, 16).

What is wrong with adapting a model for global capitalism out of the highly successful American model for free enterprise? What is wrong with economic growth and improved standards of living, particularly in developing countries? Isn't reduction of poverty a universally desirable outcome? The tempting answer is that there is nothing wrong with this model. In this paper I shall suggest that a more thoughtful reply requires some qualifications.

To begin, let me explain the notion of mental models. Although the term is not always clearly defined, "mental model" connotes the idea that human beings have mental representations, cognitive frames, or mental pictures of their experiences, representations that model the stimuli or data with which they are interacting, and these are frameworks that set up parameters though which experience, or a certain set of experiences, is organized or filtered (Gentner and Whitley, 1997, 210–11; Senge, 1990, Chapter 10; Werhane, 1991, 1998, 1999).

> Mental models are the mechanisms whereby humans are able to generate descriptions of system purpose and form, explanations of system functioning and observed system states, and predictions of future system states. (Rouse and Morris, 1986, 351)

Mental models might be hypothetical constructs of the experience in question or scientific theories, they might be schema that frame the experience, through which individuals process information, conduct experiments, and formulate theories, or mental models may simply refer to human knowledge about a particular set of events or a system. Mental models account for our ability to describe, explain, and predict, and may function as protocols to account for human expectations that are often formulated in accordance to these models (Gorman, 1992, 192–235).

Mental models function as selective mechanisms and filters for dealing with experience. In focusing, framing, organizing, and ordering what we experience, mental models bracket and leave out data, and emotional and motivational foci taint or color experience. Nevertheless, because schema we employ are socially learned and altered through religion, socialization, culture, educational upbringing, and other experiences, they are shared ways of perceiving, organizing, and learning.

Because of the variety and diversity of mental models, none is complete, and "there are multiple possible framings of any given situation" (Johnson, 1993, 9). By that I mean that each of us can frame any situation, event, or phenomenon in more than one way, and that same phenomenon can also be socially constructed in a variety of ways. It will turn out that the way one frames a situation is critical to its outcome, because "[t]here are . . . different moral consequences depending on the way we frame the situation" (Johnson, 1993, 9).

Why is the notion of mental models of concern for business, and in particular, for global business? Let me explain by using some illustrations. One of the presuppositions of Western free enterprise, a supposition that fueled and made possible the industrial revolution, is that feudalism, at least as it is exhibited through most forms of serfdom, is humiliating, it demeans laborers, and worse, it does not allow serfs, in particular, to create or experience any sense of what it would mean to be free, free to live and work where one pleases (or to be lazy), to own property, and choose how one lives. Adam Smith even argued that feudalism is inefficient as well (Smith, 1776, Book III). It is commonly, although not universally, argued that individual property ownership is a social good. In agriculturally-based economies, in particular, owning one's own farmland is considered a necessary step toward freedom and self-reliance. The industrial revolution coupled with free commerce, wage labor, and property ownership changes the feudal mental model, and, it is commonly argued, improves the lives of serfs, farm workers, and tenant farmers, in particular.

However, as Akiro Takahashi points out in a recent article in *Business Ethics Quarterly*, even twentieth-century feudal arrangements are complex social institutions. One cannot simply free the serfs or sharecroppers, engage in redistributive land reform, and hope that a new economic arrangement will work out. Takahashi's example is from a 1960s rice-growing community in Luzon in the Philippines. From as long as anyone can remember until land reforms in the 1970s the village had operated as a fiefdom. There were a few landholders and the rest of the villagers were tenant farmers. In order to work the land, each year the tenant farmers paid rents equal to half the net production of their farms. But because the tenant farmers were always in debt to the landlords, they usually owed all the net production to the landlords. The tenant farmers, in fact, never paid their debts, but because of high interest rates, as much as 200 percent, their debt increased each year so that they really could never leave the property. Since in fact what was owed the landlord was the *net* produce, each sharecropper was allowed to hire workers to farm the land they rented. So tenant farmers hired workers from other landlords or from other communities to till and harvest. Each sharecropper, in turn, went to work for another landlord's sharecropper. In addition, it was common practice for the harvesters not to do a perfect job, leaving often as much as 20–25 percent of the rice unharvested. Gleaning was not allowed by tenant farmers or their families on the land they rented. But the wives of the farm workers and the rest of the community "gleaned" the rest of the rice for themselves. In this way the poor were supported by the landlord and tenant farmers got some rice. The landlords pretended none of this occurred, still demanding the net product from each of its tenant farmers[1] (Takahaski, 1997, 39–40).

The value of private ownership (as linked to personal freedom) is a perfectly fine idea in principle. But abstracting that idea and universalizing it as a mental model for all reform has severe negative moral consequences, as the following example illustrates.

> Seven years ago, the prayers of 39 families were answered when the government [of Mexico] gave them this 1,000 acres communal farm in southern Mexico to raise livestock. Today the exhausted pastures are a moonscape of dust and rock. Cattle here don't graze quietly; they root like pigs as they yank rare blades of grass from the parched earth. . . . All arable land has been split into five-acre patches of corn per family. To stay alive, the men earn 21 cents an hour cutting sugar cane in nearby fields.
>
> Farms like this one, known as ejidos, have helped the government win political support in the countryside by answering peasant demands for "land and liberty" that date back to the revolution of 1910. Unfortunately, this continuing land-redistribution plan has done a better job of carving farmland into small, barren plots than it has of growing food or providing a decent living for farmers.
>
> . . . Farmers tend to split their parcels among their sons, and with two-thirds of farms already smaller than 12.5 acres, there isn't any room in the countryside for the next generations. (Frazier, 1984, 1, 18)

Another example: the Neem tree is a wild scraggly tree that grows well throughout India. For thousands of years, in hundreds of villages throughout that country the Neem tree has had a special place in the community. The tree has special religious meaning in some Hindu sects. Its leaves are used as pesticides, spread on plants to protect them from insects. Various herbal medicines are made from Neem leaves and bark, its products are used as contraceptives and for skin ailments, and many Indians brush their teeth with small Neem branches. Because of its effectiveness as a pesticide, recently the W. R. Grace Company began studying the tree, and in 1992 they developed a pesticide, Neemix. Neemix works as effectively as Neem leaves and has a long shelf life, thus making it more desirable as a pesticide than the leaves. Following the guidelines of the Indian government regarding patenting, Grace patented Neemix, opened a plant in India, and manufactured the product.

However, there have been mass protests against this patenting, both from Indians and from the Foundation on Economic Trends, a biotechnology watchdog organization. The argument is that Grace committed "biopiracy" because the Neem tree belongs to Indians, and products from the tree cannot be patented. Moreover, such patenting and manufacture of Neemix and other products drives up prices of Neem such that the indigenous poor, to whom the tree belongs, can no longer have access to the trees (Severence et al., 1999; Vijayalakshmi, Radha and Shiva, 1995).

A fourth illustration: SELF, the Solar Electric Light Fund, a United States-based NGO, for some time has been developing a project aimed at electrifying rural communities in China. SELF has promoted a small photovoltaic solar unit that produces about 20 to 60 watts of energy. SELF has a policy of not giving away its photovoltaic units. This is because, it argues, if people have to pay something, even a small amount, for this service, they will value it more. So SELF has set up complex, long-term lending schemes so that some poor rural people in China can afford electricity and own their own units as well (Sonenshein et al., 1997a).

SELF has been highly successful in some rural communities in China, so it decided to export that project to South Africa, concentrating on small Zulu villages. Working with village leaders in one community, SELF tried a pilot project, with the aim of providing electricity for 75 homes in a small village of Maphephethe. Six units were installed and were well received, and those receiving the units were delighted to have reliable power. However, one serious problem developed. Previous to the introduction of PV technology all the villagers lived modest but similar lives in a fairly egalitarian community. Now, those who have PV units are able to improve their social and economic status by operating manual sewing machines at night. The distribution of PV technology has upset a very delicate social balance by creating social stratification within this community (Sonenshein et al., 1997b).

What do these examples tell us? They tell us something very simple, something we should have learned years ago from the Nestlé infant formula cases. American (or in Nestlé's case, Western European) mental models of property and free enterprise cannot be exported uniformly to every part of the world without sometimes producing untoward consequences. This is because, as Michael Walzer reminds us, the notion of what is good or a social good is a socially constructed idea that is contextually and culturally relative. Abstract ideas, such as autonomy, equality, private property, ownership, and community create mental models that take on different meanings depending on the social and situational context. Differing notions of community, ownership, intellectual property, exchange, competition, equality, and fairness, what Walzer calls social goods, create cultural anomalies that cannot be overcome simply by globalizing private free enterprise and operating in the same way everywhere (see Walzer, 1983, Chapter One).

Land reform based on the notion of private ownership will not be successful in every community without making drastic social changes that alter communal relationships, family traditions, and ancient practices. This does not mean that land reform is wrongheaded; it suggests that it must be reconceived in each situation, so that what falls under the rubric of "reform" is contextually relevant such that change does not destroy the cultural fabric underlying what is to be changed.

It is tempting to argue that what is needed in remote communities or in some developing countries is a rule of law, similar to Anglo-Saxon law, that respects rights and property ownership, enforces contracts, protects equal opportunity, etc., along with adequate mechanisms for enforcement. Indeed, it has been argued, I think with some merit, that one of the difficulties in Russia today is inadequate commercial laws or means to enforce them. But this argument, too, needs qualification. For example, intellectual property rights, already under siege with the electronic revolution, cannot merely be spelled out in every instance using a Western notion of ownership without infringing on some deeply-rooted traditions and customs. An Anglo-Saxon model of patent protection, adapted in Indian law, may not be appropriate in many parts of rural India.

Do these examples, and there are thousands of others, point to the conclusion that because of the relativity of custom and culture, we should either abandon the ideal of global economic well-being, or, alternately, simply continue to convert the world into versions of Dallas? Is the aim a television in every village? Or is John Gray correct when he declares in his recent book that "the global economy system [based on Western *laissez-faire* free enterprise] is immoral, inequitable, unworkable, and unstable?" (Zakaria, 1999, 16).

These two alternatives, as I have crudely stated them, present us with unnecessary dilemmas as if there were only two sorts of responses to problems of globalizing free enterprise. I want to suggest that there are other ways to deal with these issues.

The existence of widespread complex cultural, social, community and even religious differences along with differing social goods does not imply that we can neither operate in those settings if they are alien to our own nor merely export Western versions of capitalism. To appeal again to Michael Walzer, despite the plurality and incommensurability of cross-cultural social goods, there is a thin thread of agreement, across cultures and religious difference, about the "bads," what cannot be tolerated or should not be permitted in any community. Walzer also calls these thin threads of agreement "moral minimums" (Walzer, 1994). Human suffering, abject poverty, preventable disease, high mortality, and violence are abhorred wherever they occur. We are uncertain about the constitution of the "good life," but there is widespread agreement about deficient or despicable living conditions, indecencies, violations of human rights, mistreatment, and other harms.

Given that perspective, almost everyone will agree that poverty, however contextually defined, disease, high infant mortality, and violence are bads. Alleviating suffering of these sorts is surely a good. Improving economic conditions, in most cases, alleviates poverty and human suffering, if not violence. Then, is not economic value-added in the form of economic growth the proper solution to those evils?

We must cautiously reach that conclusion. Economic growth is not a "bad." Indeed, in most cultures it is considered a social good. But the notion cannot be identified without qualification with a Western idea of free enterprise. The model of economic growth in each context has to be framed in terms of each particular culture and its social goods.

Free enterprise and private ownership, as practiced in most industrialized nations can be, in many contexts, viable options, but only if they are modified so as not to destroy the fabric of a particular set of social goods, or replace that fabric with a new "good" that destroys, without replacing, all the elements of that culture. For example, land reform and the redistribution of property, apparently worthwhile projects to free tenant farmers from feudal bonds, will only be successful if the new landholders have means to function as economically viable farmers and in ways that do not threaten age-old traditions. As the Philippines example demonstrates, the fragile distributive system in the feudal community cannot be dismantled merely for the sake of independence and private ownership without harming the complex communal relationships that maintained this system for centuries.

As purveyors of free enterprise, when moving into new communities and alien cultures corporate managers need to test their business mental models, *especially* if a particular system, service, or product has been successful in a number of markets. One needs to examine one's own mental models and try to fathom which models are operating in the community in which a company is planning to operate. In particular, it is important to find out what operative social structures and community relationships exist, what it is that this community values as its social goods, and try to imagine how those might be different given the introduction of a new kind of economic system. Because it is *not* just "the economy, stupid." What matters are social relationships, family, religious, and community traditions, and values – deeply held values about what is important and treasured – that is, those social goods a community cannot give up without sacrificing more than its lack of material well-being. If endemic poverty is an evil, we must create new ways to engage in free enterprise that takes into account, and even celebrates cultural difference.

All of this is rather vague, and one might well contend, has more to do with public policy than the operations of transnational corporations. Yet as Richard Rorty and Cornell West (hardly hearty libertarians) argue, it is not the state, but the multinational corporation that is probably the most viable and creative social institution today. Many multinational corporations are more stable than the cultures of many developing countries, and according to Rorty, their leaders often have "a more perspicuous view of globalizing trends" (Rorty, 1999, 3) than our political leaders.

As a philosopher, I want to conclude, then, that given their economic power and stability, MNCs have moral responsibilities not to produce economic changes that result in negative cultural harm in any of the countries or cultures in which they operate. But that, too, is oversimplistic and didactic, and repeats the mistake of exporting mental models by universalizing a negative harm principle without contextualizing the meaning of harms and benefits. Interestingly, John Gray suggests that attempts at economic colonization of free enterprise will not produce world homogenization and the destruction of indigenous cultures that I have suggested. Rather, he argues, "[w]hen new technologies enter economies from which in the past they were shut out . . . they will interact with indigenous cultures to generate types of capitalism that have hitherto not existed anywhere" (Gray, 1998, 58). Although Gray finds the expansion and fragmentation of Western-style free enterprise frightening, one might think of these changes as part of what Joseph Schumpeter thought of as the positive process of "creative destruction" (Schumpeter, 1976, 83).

In a new article in the *Harvard Business Review,* Stuart Hart and C. K. Prahalad make a different kind of argument for this same point. Hart and Prahalad contend that it happens to be in the long-term self-interest of global multinational companies to tread cautiously and with respect in alien cultural contexts. This is because, in brief, developing countries represent 80 percent of the population of the world and thus are a yet untapped source of growth and development. If that growth is done carefully through working within indigenous constraints, the result could be the creation of exciting new products and services that enhance rather than destroy communities while at the same time benefiting the companies in question (Hart and Prahalad, 1999).

The challenge is to create new mental models for global business that achieve the aims Hart and Prahalad propose. There is at least one such attempt by a large transnational corporation to do exactly this. Unilever is a multibillion-dollar global company with over 300,000 employees operating in almost 100 countries. Its main products are foods, fish, chemicals, and household products. Because it was founded in the Netherlands, a country one-third of which is reclaimed from the seas, Unilever has always been concerned with questions of environmental sustainability. In addition, the more recent expansion of its agricultural and fishing operations in remote communities has made Unilever increasingly aware of cultural difference. Beginning in 1993, Unilever began a process that resulted in a corporate-wide initiative that they call The Triple Bottom Line (Vis, 1997). The rationale for this initiative is that if Unilever is going to continue to be successful in the next century, its success depends on its worldwide financial, ecological, and social assets. So Unilever changed the definition of "economic value-added" to an expanded triple bottom line that measures economic, ecological and community assets, liabilities, profits (or benefits), and losses. According to Unilever in its statement of corporate purpose and practice, each of these assets is of equal importance, and its aim is to be able to quantify the corporate contributions to each of these three areas. This may sound Pollyannaish, but Unilever's defense of this initiative could have been written by Milton Friedman.

> Each type of asset represents a source of value to the company and its shareholders. The sustained development of each of these sources of value ensures that the overall value accruing to shareholders is built up sustainably over the long term. This is in essence the significance of sustainable development to a company that aims at sustainable profit growth and long-term value creation for its shareholders, [customers], and employees. (Vis, 1997, 3)

As part of this Triple Bottom Line initiative, Unilever is currently engaged in a series of small enterprises in a few small villages in India to develop new products aimed at the rural poor. These are microdevelopment projects, because the products they are supporting require little capital, they are locally produced, and of only indigenous interest. Unilever's goal, however, is to make those villages and their inhabitants economically viable managers, entrepreneurs, and customers as those notions are defined and make sense within a particular village culture and in ways that are not environmentally threatening (Hart and Prahalad, 1999). Whether this example will be a success story remains to be seen. There is to date no outcomes data, since the case events are still unfolding, and it will be some years before one can determine whether these projects are successes.

Is this stretching the limits of what we should expect from global corporations? Not according to Unilever. It argues that human flourishing in diverse settings creates needs for a diversity of products and services, products and services that Unilever will be able to provide. At the same time human well-being creates long-term economic value-added, both for Unilever and for the cultures and communities in which it operates.

Note

1. According to Takahashi, agrarian reforms designed to break up large land holdings and feudal practices were instituted in the Philippines in the 1970s. However, lax enforcement and political unrest has left villages such as the ones he describes with pretty much the same arrangement.

References

Frazier, S. 1984: Peasant Politics: Mexican Farmers Get Grants of Small Plots, But Output is Meager. *Wall Street Journal*, June 4: 1, 18.

Gentner, Dedre and Whitley, Eric W. 1997: Mental Models of Population Growth. In M. H. Bazerman, D. M. Messick, A. E. Tenbrunsel and K. A. Wade-Benzoni (eds), *Environment, Ethics, and Behavior*. San Francisco, CA: The New Lexington Press.

Gorman, Michael 1992: *Simulating Science*. Bloomington, IN: Indiana University Press.

Gray, John 1998: *False Dawn: The Delusions of Global Capitalism*. New York: The New Press.

Hart, Stuart and Prahalad, C. K. 1999: Strategies for the Bottom of the Pyramid: Creating Sustainable Development. *Harvard Business Review*. Forthcoming.

Johnson, Mark 1993: *Moral Imagination*. Chicago: University of Chicago Press.

Rorty, Richard 1999: Can American Egalitarianism Survive a Globalized Economy? *Business Ethics Quarterly*, 8, Special Issue no. 1: 1–6.

Rouse, William B. and Morris, Nancy M. 1986: On Looking Into the Black Box: Prospects and Limits in the Search for Mental Models. *Psychological Bulletin*, 100: 349–63.

Schumpeter, Joseph 1976: *Capitalism, Socialism, and Democracy*. New York: Harper & Row.

Senge, Peter 1990: *The Fifth Discipline*. New York: Doubleday & Co.

Severence, Kristi, Spiro, Lisa, Werhane, and Patricia H. 1999: W. R. Grace Co. and the Neemix Patent. Charlottesville: Darden Case Bibliography: UVA-E-0157.

Sonenshein, Scott, Gorman, Michael E. and Werhane, Patricia H. 1997a: SELF. Charlottesville: Darden Case Bibliography: UVA-E-0112.

—— 1997b: Solar Energy in South Africa. Charlottesville: Darden Case Bibliography: UVA-E-0145.

Standish, Miles, Gorman, Michael E., Venkataraman, S., and Werhane, Patricia H. 1999: Unilever. Charlottesville: Darden Case Bibliography: UVA-E-0152, 0153.

Takahashi, Akiro 1997: Ethics in Developing Economies of Asia. *Business Ethics Quarterly*, 7, 33–45.

Uchitelle, Louis 1999: The Stronger It Gets, the Sweatier the Palms. *New York Times: Week in Review*, May 21: 1, 16.

Vijayalakshmi, K., Radha, K. S., and Shiva, Vandana 1995: *Neem: A User's Manual*. Madras: Centre for Indian Knowledge Systems.

Vis, Jan-Kees 1997: *Unilever: Putting Corporate Purpose Into Action*. Unilever Publication.

Walzer, Michael 1983: *Spheres of Justice*. New York: Basic Books.

—— 1994: *Thick and Thin*. Notre Dame: Notre Dame University Press.

Werhane, Patricia H. 1991: Engineers and Management: The Challenge of the Challenger Incident. *Journal of Business Ethics*, 10, 605–16.

—— 1998: Moral Imagination and Management Decision-Making. *Business Ethics Quarterly*. 8, Special Issue no. 1: 75–98.

—— 1999: *Moral Imagination and Management Decision-Making*. New York: Oxford University Press.

West, Cornell 1993: *Race Matters*. Boston, MA: Beacon Press.

Zakaria, Fareed 1999: Passing the Bucks [a review of Gray's *False Dawn*]. *New York Times Book Review*, April 25: 16, 18.

○ ○

In Search of the Moral Manager

Archie B. Carroll

Ethics and morality are back on the front page as a result of the Ivan Boesky, General Dynamics, General Electric, E. F. Hutton, and Bank of Boston scandals. A June 1985 *New York Times* survey confirmed what earlier studies have shown repeatedly – the public gives business managers low marks for honesty.

In this era of searching for excellence, perhaps an appropriate way to phrase the theme of this article is "Searching for the Moral Manager." Pertinent questions then become:

- Are there any?
- How many are there?
- Where are they?
- Why are they so difficult to find?

Immoral, Amoral, and Moral Management in Action

The thesis of this discussion is that moral managers are hard to find because the business landscape is cluttered with *amoral* as well as *immoral* managers. It is easy to discuss immorality among the managerial ranks, and we'll look at some immoral managerial behavior. The real focus here, however, is on a kind of ethics – *amorality* – that has been less explored.

To lay a foundation for our discussion, let us look at examples of the three major types of more or less ethical management: immoral, amoral, and moral.

Reprinted from *Business Horizons*, March–April, 1987, by the Foundation for the School of Business at Indiana University. Used with permission.

Immoral Management

Three plant managers at a big GM Chevrolet truck plant in Flint, Michigan, installed a secret control box in a supervisor's office so they could increase production by over-riding the control panel that governed the speed of the assembly line. Their action was a serious violation of the company's contract with the UAW. One plant manager explained that the bosses were putting on the pressure because of constantly missed production targets. The bosses' reaction? "I don't care *how* you do it – just do it."

Thus, with the aid of the hidden controls, the managers soon began meeting their goals and winning praise from their superiors. Once the speeding up was exposed, the UAW won $1 million in back pay.[1]

Amoral Management

To advertise its Mr. PiB soft drink, Coca-Cola U.S.A. planned a promotional scheme designed to identify the "PiB girl." The contest focused on a nationwide search for a girl who most closely resembled a composite picture of five white American actresses. The composite girl would have the eyes of Susan Anton (NBC's "Golden Girl"), the mouth of Debby Boone (the singer), the hair of Pam Dawber ("Mork and Mindy"), the face shape of Melissa Sue Anderson ("Little House on the Prairie"), and the nose of Kristy McNichol (Buddy on the TV series "Family").

The contest became controversial when the principal of a black school in Chicago saw a contest entry blank. His response was not surprising: "It is immediately apparent to any sensitive person that non-Anglo contestants need not apply."

The company decided on the promotional scheme with no evil intention. The decision makers simply did not see the moral issue of fairness to all races that was implicit in the choice of actresses. Fortunately, at least one major group of bottlers, the Atlanta Coke Bottlers, were quick to note that the national contest contained racial bias. By deciding not to participate, the Atlanta Bottlers engaged in moral management.[2]

Moral Management

Polaroid's program in environmental auditing is one example of putting to work the principles of moral management. According to the corporation's director of health, safety, and environmental affairs, "For Polaroid, the *spirit* of environmental law, not just the letter, must be reflected in all of its environmental policies."[3]

Polaroid systematically searches out environmental weaknesses and strengths through company-wide audits that yield a "report card." Since 1981 the audits have helped the company to identify problems early and to prepare timely solutions. In conjunction with this, a public-issues policy committee serves as a corporate lookout, scouting dangers and opportunities that lie ahead.

FIGURE 1   Three Types of Management Ethics

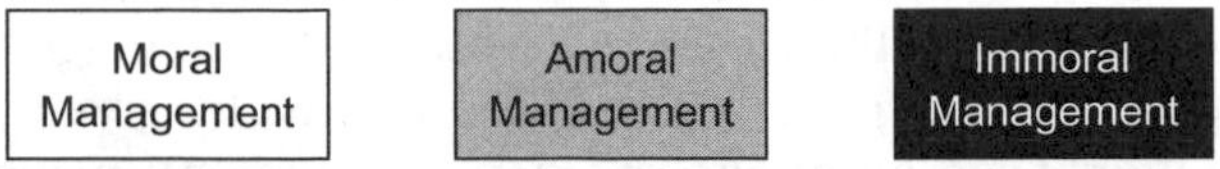

Moral Management	Amoral Management	Immoral Management

Black and White and Gray all Over

In the past ten years, newspapers, television, and magazines have chronicled case after case of immoral or unethical business activity. Though some of these cases have reached scandal proportions, many have been examples of routine, garden-variety immorality. As often as not, these accounts have referred to the actions, decisions, or behavior of managers or employees as "questionable practices," a euphemism for unethical or immoral activity.

Scant attention has been given to the subtle distinctions that may be made between activities that are *immoral* and those that are *amoral*. Similarly, little attention has been given to contrasting these two forms of behavior with ethical or *moral* management. In its preoccupation with malfeasant behavior, the media may have ignored the gamut of moral management styles.

What can happen when these styles come to life through description and example? Managers will be better able to assess their own ethical styles and those of other organizational members – their supervisors, subordinates, and peers. The presumption is, of course, that managers desire a heightened ethical awareness, particularly in light of the increasingly important role that ethics plays in business, the professions, and other organizations.[4]

Another central objective is to identify more accurately the amoral management style, a style often overlooked in the rush to classify things as good or bad, moral or immoral. Finally, looking at different styles enables us to define the elements of moral judgment that must be developed if the transition to moral management is to succeed.

Figure 1 positions these three styles along a continuum, but in reality, because of the unusual nature of the amoral approach, they do not reside on a continuum. Amoral management is, in a sense, neutral and therefore is placed in between. It is no accident that moral management has a white background, immoral management a black background, and amoral management a gray background. These colors capture the tendency, in discussions of ethics, to speak of black (clearly wrong), white (clearly right), and gray (uncertain, but somewhere in between).

Let us first consider the two extremes of management style – immoral and moral management – before looking at amoral management.

Immoral Management

If "immoral" and "unethical" are synonymous, then immoral management is not only devoid of ethical principles or precepts but also positively and actively opposed to what is ethical. Management decisions, behavior, or actions do not accord with ethical principles.

This view holds that management's motives are selfish and that it cares only (or principally) about the company's gains. If management is actively opposed to what is regarded as ethical, the clear implication is that management knows right from wrong and chooses to do wrong. Thus, it is motivated by greed. Its goals are profitability and organizational success at almost any price. Immoral management does not care about others' claims to be treated fairly or justly.

What about management's orientation toward the law, considering that law is often regarded as an embodiment of minimal ethics? Immoral management regards legal standards as barriers to be overcome in accomplishing what it wants. Immoral managers will do what they can to circumvent the law.

The operating strategy of immoral management is focused on exploiting opportunities for corporate or personal gain. Corners are cut anywhere and everywhere it appears useful. Thus, the key operating question guiding management is: "Can we make money with this action, decision, or behavior?" Implicit in this question is that nothing else matters – or matters very much.

Examples of immoral management abound. The Frigitemp Corporation, manufacturers of refrigerated mortuary boxes, illustrates immoral management at the highest levels of the corporate hierarchy. In litigation, criminal trials, and federal investigations, corporate officials, including the president and chairman, admit to making millions of dollars of payoffs to get business. They took kickbacks from suppliers, provided prostitutes to customers, exaggerated earnings in reports to shareholders, and embezzled corporate funds. One corporate official said that greed was their undoing. They were so busy stealing that they got caught. Records indicate that Frigitemp's executives permitted a corporate culture of chicanery to flourish. The company eventually went bankrupt because of management's misconduct.[5]

Brown & Root, Inc., which had been building a nuclear power plant for Texas Utilities, fired a quality control inspector in 1982. It fired two other inspectors the next year. Evidence gathered by the government suggests that the employees may have been doing their jobs too well. The inspectors claim that they were discharged after resisting orders from management to overlook flaws in the plant. The Nuclear Regulatory Commission (NRC) is now conducting inquiries into the cases of dozens of inspectors who maintain that managers pressured them to ignore defects because repairs might delay construction, causing added costs and delays.[6]

The Securities and Exchange Commission (SEC) has accused Southland Corporation, a convenience-store operator and independent gasoline retailer, of paying kickbacks to big buyers of its dairy products. According to the accusation, the company disregarded minimum pricing laws in about eight states and dispensed almost $2 million in what it called "dairy discounts." A number of the major customers received monthly kickback checks in the form of anonymous cashier's checks from a bank in Utah.[7]

These are clear cases of immoral management. Executive decisions or orders are self-centered, actively opposed to what is right, focused on organizational success at whatever the cost, and cutting corners where it is useful. Such concerns as safety or fairness are disregarded.

Moral Management

At the opposite extreme from immoral management is moral management. Moral management strives to be ethical in its focus on ethical norms, professional standards of conduct, motives, goals, orientation toward the law, and general operating strategy.

In contrast with the selfish motives discussed earlier, moral management aspires to succeed, but only within the confines of sound ethical precepts – that is, standards predicated upon such ideals as fairness, justice, and due process. Management's motives, therefore, might be termed fair, balanced, or unselfish. Organizational goals continue to stress profitability, but only within the confines of obeying the law and being sensitive to ethical standards. Management, therefore, pursues its objectives while simultaneously requiring and desiring profitability, legality, and morality. Moral management would not pursue profits at the expense of the law and sound ethics. Indeed, the focus here is not on the letter of the law but on the spirit as well. The law is viewed as a minimal standard of ethical behavior, and moral management strives to operate well above what the law mandates.

Moral management lives by sound ethical standards, seeking out only those economic opportunities that can be pursued within the confines of ethical behavior. When ethical dilemmas arise, the company assumes a leadership position. The central question guiding management actions, decisions, and behavior is: "Is this action, decision, or behavior fair to us and all parties involved?"

Companies in the toy industry illustrate moral management when they thoroughly test toys before releasing them for commercial production and sales. The toy industry has adopted strict standards for flammability. Other standards have been set for toxicity, safety, and durability. The safety testing process at Hasbro-Bradley, Inc., for example, eliminated nearly 2,000 toy concepts in one year before the company chose the 100 toys it planned to produce. Toys also undergo psychological testing as companies attempt to screen out toys that might have a lasting negative emotional impact on children.[8]

Organizations that engage in moral management have not done so all along. These companies – and that includes the toy industry – arrived at this posture after years or decades of rising consumer expectations, increased government regulations, lawsuits, and pressures from social and consumer activists. In many instances moral management is a pragmatic posture that evolved over time. If we hold management to a 100% historical moral purity test, then no management will fill the bill. But moral managements now see the enlightened self-interest of responding in an ethical way.

An excellent example of moral management in which the organization took the initiative in displaying ethical leadership is provided by the actions of McCulloch Corporation, a manufacturer of chain saws. Chain saws are notoriously dangerous. The Consumer Product Safety Commission estimated that in 1981 there were 123,000 medically attended injuries involving chain saws, up from 71,000 in 1976. In spite of these statistics, the Chain Saw Manufacturers Association, in what appears to be a knee-jerk, self-interested reaction against government regulations, has fought mandatory safety standards. The association claims that the accident statistics are inflated and do not offer any justification for mandatory regulations. Manufacturers support voluntary standards. However, some manufacturers say that when chain brakes, which are a major safety device, are offered as an option, they do not sell. Apparently, consumers do not have adequate knowledge of the risks inherent in using chain saws.

McCulloch became dissatisfied with the Chain Saw Manufacturers Association's refusal to support higher standards of safety and withdrew from the association in 1978. The chain brakes, which have been standard on McCulloch saws since 1975, are also mandatory for most saws produced in Finland, Britain, and Australia. The Swedish Company, Husqvarna Inc., now installs chain brakes on saws it sells in the United States. Statistics from the Quebec Logging Association and from Sweden demonstrate that kickback-related accidents fell by about 80% after the mandatory installation of safety standards, including chain brakes.[9]

McCulloch is an example of moral management. It attempted to persuade its association to adopt the higher standard that, based upon statistical evidence and sound, sensitive judgment, would greatly reduce injuries. When its attempts at persuasion failed, McCulloch took a courageous action and withdrew from the association.

Amoral Management

In some respects amoral management appears to be a hybrid between the other two. However, it is not just a middle position on a continuum. Although conceptually positioned between the other two, it is different in kind. Actually there are two types of amoral management: intentional and unintentional.

Because they believe business activity resides outside the sphere to which moral judgments apply, intentional amoral managers do not factor ethical considerations into their decision making, actions, or behavior. These managers are neither moral nor immoral; they simply think that different rules of the game apply in business than in other realms of life.

Unintentional amoral managers do not think about business activity in ethical terms either, but for a different reason. These managers are simply morally casual, careless, or inattentive to the fact that their decisions and actions may have negative or deleterious effects on others. These managers lack ethical perception and moral awareness; that is, they blithely go through their organizational lives not thinking that what they are doing has an ethical dimension to it. They may be well intentioned, but they are either too insensitive or egocentric to consider the impacts of their behavior on others.

Amoral management pursues profitability as its goal, but it does not cognitively attend to moral issues that may be intertwined with that pursuit. If there is an ethical guide to amoral management, it is the marketplace as constrained by law – the letter of the law, not the spirit. The amoral manager sees the law as the boundary that marks off the playing field where business pursuits take place.

Amoral management does not bridle managers with excessive ethical structure. It permits free reign within the unspoken but understood tenets of the free enterprise system. Personal ethics may periodically or unintentionally enter into managerial decisions, but they do not preoccupy management. Furthermore, the impact of decisions on others is an afterthought – if it ever gets considered at all. To the extent that they are present, the managers' ethical mental gears are in neutral. The key management question guiding decision making is: "Can we make money with this action, decision, or behavior?" This question does not imply an active or implicit intent to be either moral or immoral.

Some Examples

There are perhaps more examples of amoral management than of any other kind.

- When police departments stipulated that candidates must be at least 5 ft 10 in and weigh 180 pounds to qualify, the decision was amoral. No consideration was given that women – and men of some ethnic groups – do not, on average, attain that height and weight.
- When companies decided to use scantily clad young women to advertise autos, men's cologne, and other such products, they did not think of the degrading and demeaning characterization that eventually would come from their ethically neutral decision.
- When firms determined to do business in South Africa, their decision was neither moral or immoral. But a major unanticipated consequence has been the appearance that capitalism – and the United States – approve of apartheid.
- Nestlé's decision to market infant formula in underdeveloped, Third World countries was an amoral decision. Nestlé simply did not consider the detrimental effects of such a seemingly innocent business decision on mothers and babies in areas with impure water, poverty, and illiteracy.
- The liquor, beer, and cigarette industries have not been immoral, according to generally accepted standards, in making, advertising, and distributing their products. But they did not think about – at least not to an extent that altered their decisions – some serious moral issues: alcoholism, drunk-driving deaths, lung cancer, deteriorating health, and offensive secondary smoke.
- When Pepsico promoted corn chips on television with its "Frito-Bandito" theme, it greatly offended a group of Mexican-Americans, who put such pressure on the company that the ad campaign was dropped. Surely Pepsico did not enter into this campaign with the idea of perpetuating a stereotype. It just didn't think through the ethical consequences of its promotional campaign.

A Distribution Curve for Management Morality?

Figure 2 summarizes the major characteristics of amoral, immoral, and moral managements. Data are not available to indicate precisely what proportions of managers each represents in the total management population, but we can hypothesize a normal distribution such as that depicted in Figure 3. Based on reports of management behavior, studies of ethics, and experience in teaching ethics in executive development programs, we believe that this distribution, though the percentages are not specified, captures fairly accurately the actual proportions. However, although our hypothesis has received support in discussions with managers, for now this distribution remains untested.

To the extent that these approximate numbers capture even generally the proportion of manager types, this hypothesis is disturbing, for it suggests that the vast majority of

FIGURE 2　Approaches to Management Ethics

		Immoral Management	Amoral Management	Moral Management
Organizational Characteristics	Ethical Norms	Management decisions, actions, and behavior imply a positive and active opposition to what is moral (ethical). Decisions are discordant with accepted ethical principles. An active negation of what is moral is implied.	Management is neither moral nor immoral, but decisions lie outside the sphere to which moral judgments apply. Management activity is outside or beyond the moral order of a particular code. May imply lack of ethical perception and moral awareness.	Management activity conforms to a standard of ethical, or right, behavior. Conforms to accepted professional standards of conduct. Ethical leadership is commonplace on the part of management.
	Motives	Selfish. Management cares only about it or the company gains.	Well-intentioned but selfish in the sense that impact on others is not considered.	Good. Management wants to succeed but only within the confines of sound ethical precepts (fairness, justice, due process).
	Goals	Profitability and organizational success at any price.	Profitability. Other goals are not considered.	Profitability within the confines of legal obedience and ethical standards.
	Orientation Toward Law	Legal standards are barriers that management must overcome to accomplish what it wants.	Law is the ethical guide, preferably the letter of the law. The central question is what we can do legally.	Obedience toward letter and spirit of the law. Law is a minimal ethical behavior. Prefer to operate well above what law mandates.
	Strategy	Exploit opportunities for corporate gain. Cut corners when it appears useful.	Give managers free rein. Personal ethics may apply but only if managers choose. Respond to legal mandates if caught and required to do so.	Live by sound ethical standards. Assume leadership position when ethical dilemmas arise. Enlightened self-interest.

managers are amoral. It suggests that, in general, ethical considerations do not get factored into management decisions, even though there is no active intent to be unethical.

It is disturbing to think that the amoral management style predominates in organizations today. Equally disturbing is an alternative hypothesis – that, for the average manager, these three styles all operate at various times under various circumstances. That is, the average manager is amoral most of the time but, because of a variety of impinging factors, slips into a moral or immoral style on occasion. Like the first hypothesis, this view cannot be empirically supported at this time, but it resembles the situational ethics argument that has been in vogue for some years.

A serious social problem in organizations today is this large middle group of well-intentioned managers who, for one reason or other, subscribe to or live out the amoral

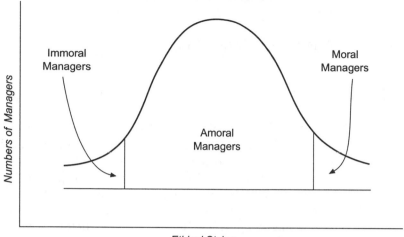

FIGURE 3   Immoral, Amoral, and Moral Managers: A Hypothesized Population Distribution

ethic. These managers are driven primarily by the profitability or bottom-line ethos that makes economic success almost the sole barometer of organizational and personal achievement. They are basically good people, but they see the competitive business world as ethically neutral. Until this group of managers moves toward the moral ethic, we will continue to see American business and organizations criticized as severely as they have been in the past two decades.

Developing Moral Judgment

At this point one might rightly ask, "What can or should be done about the prevalence of amoral management in business?" The question is easier to ask than to answer, but the direction must be toward developing moral judgment among managers.

First, managers must undergo a paradigm shift from looking at the organization as a purely economic or legal entity to one in which a multitude of responsibilities reside. Principal among these other responsibilities or perspectives is an ethical one. It is becoming increasingly obvious that society expects business to be responsive to claimants other than just the shareholders. And many of these claimant groups, whether they be employees, consumers, or community members, expect to be dealt with fairly and justly.

Second, managers must come to appreciate the key elements in making moral judgments. Powers and Vogel argue that there are six major elements or capacities that are essential in making moral judgments:[10]

1. Moral imagination;
2. Moral identification and ordering;
3. Moral evaluation;

4. Tolerance of moral disagreement and ambiguity;
5. Integration of managerial and moral competence; and
6. A sense of moral obligation.

Let us examine each of these in turn.

Moral Imagination

Moral imagination refers to the ability to perceive that a web of competing economic relationships is, at the same time, a web of moral or ethical relationships. Developing moral imagination means becoming sensitive to ethical issues in business decision making, but it also means searching out places where people are likely to be hurt by decision making or behavior of managers. This moral imagination is a necessary first step, but because of prevailing methods of evaluating managers on bottom-line results, it is extremely challenging. It is essential, however, before anything else can happen.

Moral Identification and Ordering

Moral identification and ordering means being able to discern the relevance or non-relevance of moral factors that are introduced into a decision-making situation. Are the moral issues real or just rhetorical? The ability to see moral issues as issues that can be dealt with is at stake here. In addition to their identification, moral issues in a decision must be ranked or ordered just as economic or technological issues are. Not only must this skill be developed through experience, but it also must be finely honed through repetition. Only through repetition can it be developed.

Several decision environments in which moral identification and ordering have become important in recent years include the future of affirmative action programs, the status of employees' "right to know" what toxic chemicals they are being exposed to, the question of how to deal with whistle-blowers, and the issue of business or plant closings.[11] In each of these instances, the ability to identify and order moral issues is a key to their effective handling. To decide wrongly opens the firm up to extensive public criticism and the threat of endless lawsuits.

Moral Evaluation

Once issues have been identified and ordered, the question of making evaluations or judgments enters in. This practical phase entails minimal skills – such as coherence and consistency – that have proven effective in other contexts. What managers need to develop here are:

• The importance of clear principles;
• Processes for weighting ethical factors; and

- The ability to identify what are likely to be the moral as well as economic outcomes of a decision.

The real challenge in moral evaluation is in integrating concerns for others into organizational goals and purposes. In the final analysis, the manager will not know what is the "right" answer or solution but only that moral sensitivity has been introduced into the process. There are multiple right and wrong decisions, but the important point is that amorality has not prevailed or driven the decision process.

Tolerating Moral Disagreement and Ambiguity

One of the principal objections managers often have to discussions of ethics is the amount of disagreement generated by the volume of ambiguity that must be tolerated in thinking ethically. This disagreement and ambiguity must be accepted, however, for there is no other way.

To be sure, managers need closure and they need precision in their decisions. But the situation is never clear in moral discussions any more than it is in many traditional but more familiar decision contexts of managers – such as introducing a new product based upon limited test marketing, choosing a new executive for a key role, deciding which of a number of excellent computer systems to install, or making a strategic decision based upon instincts. All of these are precarious decisions, but managers have become accustomed to making them in spite of the disagreement and ambiguity that prevail among those involved in the decision or even within the individual.

In a real sense the toleration of moral disagreement and ambiguity is just an extension of a managerial talent or facility that is present in practically all decision situations managers face. But managers are more unfamiliar with this area because they have not had practice in it.

Integrating Managerial and Moral Competence

Integrating managerial and moral competence underlies all we have been discussing. Few kinds of decision making are exempt from moral or social factors. The issue is whether the manager has chosen to deal with the factors.

Moral issues in management are not isolated and distinct from traditional business decision making but right smack in the middle of it. The scandals major corporations face today did not grow up apart from the companies' economic activities but were embedded in a series of decisions that were made at various times and are only the culmination of these earlier decisions. Therefore, *moral* competence is an integral part of *managerial* competence.

Managers are learning – some the hard way – that there is a significant corporate – and, in many instances, a personal – price to pay for their amorality. The amoral manager sees ethical decisions as isolated and independent of managerial decisions and competence, but the moral manager sees every evolving decision as one in which an ethical perspective must be integrated. This view to the future is an essential executive skill.

A Sense of Moral Obligation

The foundation for all the capacities we have discussed is a sense of moral obligation and integrity. This sense is the key to the process, but is the most difficult to acquire. This sense requires the intuitive or learned understanding that moral fibers – a concern for fairness, justice, and due process to people, groups, and communities – are woven into the fabric of managerial decision making and hold the systems together. These qualities are perfectly consistent with – indeed, are essential requisites to – the free enterprise system as we know it today.

One can go all the way back to Adam Smith and the foundation of our system and find no reference to immoral or unethical practices as elements that are needed for the system to work. Our modern-day Adam Smith, Milton Friedman, has even alluded to the importance of ethics when he stated that the purpose of business is "to make as much money as possible while conforming to the basic rules of society, both those embodied in the law and *those embodied in ethical custom.*"[12]

The moral manager, then, has a sense of moral obligation and integrity that is the glue that holds together the decision-making process in which human welfare is inevitably at stake.

Figure 4 summarizes the elements of moral judgment as seen in amoral and moral managers.

Making Moral Management Actionable

These characterizations of moral, immoral, and amoral management should provide a useful basis for managerial self-analysis. For self-analysis and introspection will be the way that managers move from the immoral or amoral ethic to the moral ethic. Numerous people have suggested management training for business ethics, a prescription with great potential. However, until senior management fully embraces the concepts of moral management, the transformation in organizational culture that is essential for moral management to blossom, thrive, and flourish will not take place.

Ultimately, senior management has the leadership responsibility to show the way to an ethical organizational environment by leading the transition from amoral to moral management, whether that is done by:

- Business ethics training and workshops;
- Codes of conduct;
- Corporate ombudsmen;
- Tighter financial controls;
- More ethically sensitive decision processes; or
- Leadership by example.

Underlying all these efforts, however, needs to be the fundamental recognition that amoral management exists and that it can be certainly, if not easily, remedied. We have outlined the symptoms and characteristics of amoral management, a morally vacuous

FIGURE 4 Moral Judgment in Amoral and Moral Managers

Amoral Managers	Moral Managers
Moral Imagination	
See a web of competing economic claims as just that and nothing more. Are insensitive to and unaware of the hidden dimensions of where people are likely to get hurt.	Perceive that a web of competing economic claims is, simultaneously, a web of moral relationships. Are sensitive to and hunt out the hidden dimensions where people are likely to get hurt.
Moral Identification and Ordering	
See moral claims as squishy, not definite enough to order into hierarchies with other claims.	See which moral claims are relevant or irrelevant; order moral factors just as economic factors are ordered.
Moral Evaluation	
Are erratic in their application of ethics, if it gets applied at all.	Are coherent and consistent in their normative reasoning.
Tolerance of Moral Disagreement and Ambiguity	
Cite ethical disagreement and ambiguity as reason for forgetting ethics altogether.	Tolerate ethical disagreement and ambiguity while honestly acknowledging that decisions are not precise but must be made nevertheless.
Integration of Managerial and Moral Competence	
See ethical decisions as isolated and independent of managerial decisions and managerial competence.	See every evolving decision as one in which a moral perspective must be integrated with a managerial one.
A Sense of Moral Obligation	
Have no sense of moral obligation and integrity that extends beyond normal managerial responsibility.	Have a sense of moral obligation and integrity that directs and holds together the decision-making process in which human welfare is at stake.

condition that can be disguised as an innocent, practical, bottom-line philosophy – something to take pride in.

Amoral management is – and will continue to be – the bane of American management until it is recognized for what it is and managers take steps to overcome it. American managers are not all "bad guys," as so frequently portrayed, but the idea that managerial decision making can be ethically neutral is bankrupt. It is no longer tenable in the society of the 1980s and beyond.

Notes

1. George Getschow, "Some Middle Managers Cut Corners to Achieve High Corporate Goals," *Wall Street Journal*, November 8, 1979: 1, 34.
2. Evan Kossoff, "Coke Bottlers Here Noticed Bias, Rejected PiB Contest," *Atlanta Journal and Constitution*, April 20, 1980: B-1.
3. "Environmental Auditing: Putting Principles to Work," *Ethics Resource Center Report*, Spring 1985: 5.

4. In a study of performance factors considered important by various levels of management, integrity is a critical factor for senior executives, while entry-level managers assign it a lower priority. The author concludes, "It may be that as managers rise to the top, they become increasingly concerned with the way they are looked up to by their peers and subordinates in the area of moral values" (Richard A. Johnson, James P. Neelankavil, and Arvind Jadhav, "Developing the Executive Resource," *Business Horizons*, 29 (1986): 32.

5. Edward T. Pound and Bruce Ingersoll, "How Frigitemp Sank After It Was Looted by Top Management," *Wall Street Journal*, September 20, 1984, p. 1.

6. Ron Winslow, "Regulators Investigate Harassing of Inspectors at New Nuclear Plants," *Wall Street Journal*, November 7, 1984, p. 1.

7. Bruce Ingersoll and Edward T. Pound, "SEC Says Southland Was Involved in Questionable Payoffs in the 1970s," *Wall Street Journal*, November 9, 1984, p. 1.

8. Pamela Hollie, "Seeking Safe Toys That Sell," *New York Times*, February 10, 1985, p. 4F.

9. Ray Vicker, "Rise in Chain-Saw Injuries Spurs Demand for Safety Standards, but Industry Resists," *Wall Street Journal*, August 23, 1982, p. 17.

10. Charles W. Powers and David Vogel, *Ethics in the Education of Business Managers* (Hastings-on-Hudson, NY: The Hastings Center, 1980): 40–45.

11. As outlined . . . by Kenneth A. Kovach and Peter E. Millspaugh, "Plant Closings: Is the American Industrial System Failing?," *Business Horizons* (March–April 1987).

12. Milton Friedman, "The Social Responsibility of Business Is to Increase Its Profits," *New York Times Magazine*, September 12, 1970: 32 (emphasis added).

Bribery in International Business: Whose Problem Is It?

Henry W. Lane and Donald G. Simpson

Introduction

No discussion of problems in international business seems complete without reference to familiar complaints about the questionable business practices North American executives encounter in foreign countries, particularly developing nations. Beliefs about the pervasiveness of dishonesty and the necessity of engaging in such practices as bribery vary widely, however, and these differences often lead to vigorous discussions that generate more heat than light. Pragmatists or "realists" may take the attitude that "international business is a rough game and no place for the naive idealist or the fainthearted. Your competitors use bribes and unless you are willing to meet this standard competitive practice you will lose business and ultimately, jobs for workers at home. Besides, it is an accepted business practice in those countries, and when you are in Rome you have to do as the Romans do." "Moralists," on the other hand, believe that cultural relativity is no excuse for unethical behavior. "As Canadians or Americans we should uphold our legal and ethical standards anywhere in the world; and any good American or Canadian knows that bribery, by any euphemism, is unethical and wrong. Bribery increases a product's cost and often is used to secure import licenses for products that no longer can be sold in the developed world. Such corrupting practices also contribute to the moral disintegration of individuals and eventually societies."

The foregoing comments represent extreme polar positions but we are not using these stereotypes to create a "straw man" or false dichotomy about attitudes toward practices such as bribery. These extreme viewpoints, or minor variations of them, will be encountered frequently as one meets executives who have experience in developing countries. Some "realists" and "moralists" undoubtedly are firm believers in their positions, but many other executives probably gravitate toward one of the poles because they have not found a realistic alternative approach to thinking about the issue of bribery, never mind finding an answer to the problem.

The impetus for this article came from discussions with executives and government officials in Canada and in some developing nations about whether a North American company could conduct business successfully in developing countries without engaging in what would be considered unethical or illegal practices. It was apparent from these talks that the question was an important one and of concern to business executives, but not much practical, relevant information existed on the issue. There was consensus on two points: first, there are a lot of myths surrounding the issue of payoffs; and second, if anyone had some insights into the problem, executives would appreciate hearing them.

In this article, we would like to share what we have learned about the issue during the two years we have been promoting business (licensing agreements, management contracts, joint ventures) between Canadian and African companies. Our intention is not to present a comprehensive treatment of the subject of bribery or a treatise on ethical behavior. Our intention is to present a practical discussion of some dimensions of the problem based on our experience, discussions, and, in some cases, investigation of specific incidents.

The Problem is Multifaceted

It can be misleading to talk about bribery in global terms without considering some situational specifics, such as country, type of business, and company. Our discussions with managers indicate that the payoff problem is more prevalent in some countries than in others. Executives with extensive experience probably could rank countries on a scale reflecting the seriousness of the problem. Also, some industries are probably more susceptible to payoff requests than others. Large construction projects, turnkey capital projects, and large commodity or equipment contracts are likely to be most vulnerable because the scale of the venture may permit the easy disguise of payoffs, and because an individual, or small group of people, may be in a strategic position to approve or disapprove the project. These projects or contracts are undoubtedly obvious targets also because the stakes are high, the competition vigorous, and the possibility that some competitors may engage in payoffs increased. Finally, some companies may be more vulnerable due to a relative lack of bargaining power or because they have no policies to guide them in these situations. If the product or technology is unique, or clearly superior, and it is needed, the company is in a relatively strong position to resist the pressure. Similarly, those firms with effective operational policies against payoffs are in a position of strength. Many senior executives have stated, with pride, that their companies have reputations for not making payoffs and, therefore, are not asked for them. These were executives of large, successful firms that also had chosen not to work in some countries where they could not operate comfortably. These executives often backed up their claims with specific examples in which they walked away from apparently lucrative deals where a payoff was a requirement.

Two other elements of the situational context of a payoff situation that vary are the subtlety of the demand and the amount of money involved. All payoff situations are not straightforward and unambiguous, which may make a clear response more difficult. Consider, for example, the case of a company that was encouraged to change its evaluation of bids for a large construction project. Some host-country agencies were embarrassed by the evaluation results since Company X, from the country providing significant financing for the project, was ranked a distant third. The agencies sought a re-evaluation on questionable technicalities. The changes were considered but the ranking remained the same. At this point pressure began to build. Phone calls were made berating the firm for delaying the project and hinting that the large follow-on contract, for which it had the inside track, was in jeopardy. No one ever said make Company X the winner or you lose the follow-on.

Although no money was to change hands, this situation was similar to a payoff request in that the company was being asked to alter its standard for acceptable business practices for an implied future benefit. The interpretation of the "request," the response, and the consequences, were left entirely to the company's management. Refusal to change may mean losing a big contract, but giving in does not guarantee the follow-on and you leave the company vulnerable to further demands. In ambiguous situations factors such as corporate policies and the company's financial strength and its need for the contract enter into the decision. In this case the company had firm beliefs about what constituted professional standards and did not desperately need the follow-on contract. Although it refused to change, another company might find itself in a dilemma, give in to the pressure, and rationalize its behavior.

Finally, payoffs range in size from the small payments that may help getting through customs without a hassle up to the multimillion dollar bribes that make headlines and embarrass governments. The payoff situations we discuss in this article are more significant than the former, but much smaller and far less dramatic than the latter. These middle-range payoffs (tens of thousands of dollars) may pose a problem for corporations. They are too big to be ignored but possibly not big enough to be referred to corporate headquarters unless the firm has clear guidelines on the subject. Regional executives or lower-level managers may be deciding whether or not these "facilitating payments" are just another cost of doing business in the developing world.

On the Outside Looking In (The North American Perspective)

"It's a corrupt, payoff society. The problem has spread to all levels. On the face it looks good, but underneath it's rotten." Comments such as these are often made by expatriate business people and government officials alike. The North American executive may arrive in a Third World country with a stereotype of corrupt officials and is presented with the foregoing analysis by people-on-the-spot who, he or she feels, should know the situation best. His or her fears are confirmed.

This scenario may be familiar to some readers. It is very real to us because we have gone through that process. Two cases provide examples of the stories a businessperson may likely be told in support of the dismal analysis.

The "New Venture": Company Y, a wholly owned subsidiary of a European multinational, wished to manufacture a new product for export. Government permission was required and Company Y submitted the necessary applications. Sometime later one of Company Y's executives (a local national) informed the Managing Director that the application was approved and the consultant's fee must be paid. The Managing Director knew nothing about a consultant or such a fee. The executive took his boss to a meeting with the consultant – a government official who sat on the application review committee. Both the consultant and the executive claimed to remember the initial meeting at which agreement was reached on the $10,000 fee. A few days later the Managing Director attended a cocktail party at the home of a high-ranking official in the same agency. This official recommended that the fee be paid. The Managing Director decided against paying the fee and the project ran into unexpected delays. At this point the Managing Director asked the parent company's legal department for help. Besides the delay, the situation was creating a problem between the Managing Director and his executives as well as affecting the rest of the company. He initially advised against payment but after watching the company suffer, acquiesced with the approval of the parent company. The fee was renegotiated downward and the consultant paid. What was the result? Nothing! The project was not approved.

The "Big Sale": Company Z, which sold expensive equipment, established a relationship with a well-placed government official on the first trip to the country. This official, and some other nationals, assured Company Z representatives that they would have no trouble getting the contract. On leaving the country, Company Z representatives had a letter of intent to purchase the equipment. On the second trip Company Z representatives brought the detailed technical specifications for a certain department head to approve. The department head refused to approve the specifications and further efforts to have the government honor its promise failed. The deal fell through. Company Z's analysis of the situation, which became common knowledge in business and government circles, was that a competitor paid the department head to approve its equipment and that the government reneged on its obligation to purchase Company Z equipment.

While in the country, the visiting executive may even have met Company Z's agent in the "Big Sale," who confirms the story. Corruption is rampant, and in the particular case of the "Big Sale" he claims to know that the department head received the money and from whom. The case is closed! An honest North American company cannot function in this environment – or so it seems.

On the Inside Looking Out (The Developing Country's Perspective)

During his visit the executive may have met only a few nationals selected by his company or government representatives. He probably has not discussed bribery with them because of its sensitive nature. If the business people and the officials he met were dishonest, they would not admit it; if they were honest he probably felt they would resent the discussion. Also, he may not have had enough time to establish the type of relationship in which the subject could be discussed frankly. It is almost certain that he did not speak with the people in the government agencies who allegedly took the payoffs. What would he say if he did meet them? And more than likely he would not be able to get an appointment with them if he did want to pursue the matter further. So the executive is convinced that corruption is widespread having heard only one side of the horror stories.

Had the visitor been able to investigate the viewpoints of the nationals what might he have heard? "I would like to find a person from the developed world that I can trust.

You people brought corruption here. We learned the concept from you. You want to win all the time, and you are impatient so you bribe. You offer bribes to the local people and complain that business is impossible without bribing."

Comments like these are made by local business people and government officials alike. If the visiting executive heard these comments he would be confused and would wonder whether or not these people were talking about the same country. Although skeptical, his confidence in the accuracy of his initial assessment would have been called into question. Had he been able to stay longer in the country, he might have met an old friend who knew the department head who allegedly was paid off in the "Big Sale." His friend would have made arrangements for the visitor to hear the other side of the story.

> *The "Big Sale" Revisited:* After the representatives of Company Z received what they described as a letter of intent to purchase the equipment they returned home. On the second visit they had to deal with the department head to receive his approval for the technical specifications.
>
> At the meeting they told the department head that he need not worry about the details and just sign off on the necessary documents. If he had any questions regarding the equipment he could inspect it in two weeks' time in their home country. The department head's initial responses were: (1) he would not rubber stamp anything, and (2) how could this complex equipment which was supposedly being custom made for his country's needs be inspected in two weeks when he had not yet approved the specifications.
>
> As he reviewed the specifications he noticed a significant technical error and brought it to the attention of Company Z's representatives. They became upset with his "interference" and inferred that they would use their connections in high places to ensure his compliance. When asked again to sign the documents he refused, and the company reps left saying they would have him removed from his job.
>
> After this meeting the premier of the country became involved and asked the company officials to appear before him. They arrived with the premier's nephew for a meeting with the premier and his top advisors.
>
> The premier told his nephew that he had no business being there and directed him to leave. The company officials then had to face the premier and his advisors alone. The premier asked if the company had a contract and that if it had, it would be honored. The company had to admit that it had no contract. As far as the premier was concerned, the issue was settled.
>
> However, the case was not closed for Company Z representatives. They felt they had been promised the deal and that the department had reneged. They felt that someone had paid off the department head and they were quite bitter. In discussions with their local embassy officials and with government officials at home they presented their analysis of the situation. The result was strained relations and the department head got a reputation for being dishonest.

Well, the other side of the story certainly has different implications about whose behavior may be considered questionable. The situation is now very confusing. Is the department head honest or not? The executive's friend has known the department head for a long time and strongly believes he is honest; and some other expatriate government officials have basically corroborated the department head's perception of the matter. But the business people and the government officials who first told the story seemed reputable and honest. Who should be believed? As the visiting executive has learned, you have to decide the truth for yourself.

Patterns of Behavior

The preceding vignettes illustrate our position that bribery and corruption is a problem for North American and Third World business people alike. We also have observed two recurring behavioral patterns in these real, but disguised, situations. The first is the predisposition of the North American businessperson to accept the premise that bribery is the way of life in the developing world and a necessity in business transactions. The second behavioral pattern occurs in situations where payments are requested and made.

We believe that many executives visit Third World countries with an expectation to learn that bribery is a problem. This attitude likely stems from a number of sources. First, in many cases it may be true. In some countries it may be impossible to complete a transaction without a bribe and the horror stories about the widespread disappearance of honesty are valid. However, in some instances the expectations are conditioned by the "conventional wisdom" available in international business circles. This conventional wisdom develops from situations like the ones we have described. As these situations are passed from individual to individual, accuracy may diminish and facts be forgotten. This is not done intentionally but happens since it is rare that the story tellers have the complete story or all the facts. Unverified stories of bribery and corruption circulate through the business and government communities and often become accepted as true and factual. The obvious solution, and difficulty, is learning how to distinguish fact from fiction.

Another factor influencing initial expectations are the unfavorable impressions of developing countries and their citizens that are picked up from the media. Often only the sensational, and negative, news items from these countries are reported in North America. We learn of bombings, attacks on journalists and tourists, alleged (and real) *coup d'états*, and major scandals. These "current events" and the "conventional wisdom" combined with an executive's probable lack of knowledge of the history, culture, legal systems, or economic conditions of a country all contribute to the development of unfavorable stereotypes that predispose the executive toward readily accepting reports that confirm his already drawn conclusions: all Latin American or African countries, for example, are all the same and corruption is to be expected.

The stories that constitute "evidence" of corruption may be tales of bribery like the "New Venture" or the "Big Sale," or they may take other forms. The story we have heard most often has the "protect yourself from your local partner" theme. It goes like this: "If you are going to invest in this country, particularly in a joint venture, you have to find a way to protect yourself from your partner. He is likely to strip all the company's assets and leave you nothing but a skeleton. Just look what happened to Company A."

On hearing the "evidence," particularly from expatriates in the foreign country, a visiting businessperson most likely accepts it without further investigation. He has forgotten the old adage about there being two sides to every story. His conclusion and conviction are most likely based on incomplete and biased data.

Is there another viewpoint? Certainly! Many nationals have expressed it to us: "The Europeans and North Americans have been taking advantage of us for decades, even centuries. The multinationals establish a joint venture and then strip the local company bare through transfer pricing, management fees, and royalties based on a percentage of sales rather than profits. They have no interest in the profitability of the company or its long-term development."

The situation is ironic. Some local investors are desperately looking for an honest North American executive whom they can trust at the same time the North American is searching for them. Our experience indicates that this search process is neither straightforward nor easy. And while the search continues, if it does, it is difficult for the North American to maintain a perspective on the situation and remember that there are locals who may share his values and who are equally concerned about unethical and illegal practices.

In summary, we would characterize the first observed pattern of behavior as a preparedness to accept "evidence" of corruption and the simultaneous failure to examine critically the "evidence" or its source.

The second behavioral pattern appears in the actual payoff process. The request very likely comes from a low- or middle-level bureaucrat who says that his boss must be paid for the project to be approved or for the sale to be finalized. Alternatively, it may be your agent who is providing similar counsel. In either case you are really not certain who is making the demand.

Next, the payoff is made. You give your contact the money, but you never really know where it goes.

Your expectations are obvious. You have approached this transaction from a perspective of economic rationality. You have provided a benefit and expect one in return. The project will be approved or the sale consummated.

The results, however, may be very different than expected. As in the case of the "New Venture," nothing may happen. The only outcome is indignation, anger, and perhaps the loss of a significant amount of money. Now is the time for action, but what recourse do you have? Can you complain? You may be guilty of bribing a government official. And, you certainly are reluctant to admit that you have been duped. Since your direct options are limited, your primary action may be to spread the word: "This is a corrupt, payoff society."

Why Does it Happen?

There are numerous explanations for corruption in developing nations. First, and most obvious, is that some people are simply dishonest. A less pejorative explanation is that the cost of living in these countries may be high and salaries low. Very often a wage earner must provide for a large extended family. The businessperson is viewed opportunistically as a potential source of income to improve the standard of living. Finally, some nationals may believe strongly that they have a right to share some of the wealth controlled by multinational corporations.

Besides being familiar to many readers, these explanations all share another common characteristic. They all focus on "the other person" – the local national. Accepting that there may be some truth in previous explanations, let us, however, turn our focus to the visiting North American to see what we find. We could find a greedy, dishonest expatriate hoping to make a killing. But, let us give this person the same benefit of the doubt we have accorded the local nationals so far.

On closer examination we may find a situation in which the North American executives are vulnerable. They have entered an action vacuum and are at a serious disadvantage. Their lack of knowledge of systems and procedures, laws, institutions, and the people can put them in a dependent position. Unfamiliarity with the system and/or the people makes effective, alternative action such as they could take at home difficult. A strong relationship with a reputable national could help significantly in this situation. Quite often the national knows how to fight the system and who to call in order to put pressure on the corrupt individual. This potential resource should not be dismissed lightly. Although the most powerful and experienced MNCs may also be able to apply this pressure, most of us must be realistic and recognize that no matter how important we think we are, we may not be among those handful of foreigners that can shake the local institutions.

Time can also be a factor. Often the lack of time spent in the country either to establish relationships, or to give the executive the opportunity to fight the system contributes to the problem. Because North American businesspeople believe that time is money and that their time, in particular, is very valuable, they operate on a tight schedule with little leeway for unanticipated delays. The payoff appears to be a cost-effective solution. In summary, the executive might not have the time, knowledge, or contacts to fight back and sees no alternative other than pay or lose the deal.

Some Real Barriers

If, as we think, there are many honest business people in North America and in the developing world looking for mutually profitable arrangements and for reliable, honest partners, why is it difficult for them to find each other? We believe a significant reason is the inability of both sides to overcome two interrelated barriers – time and trust.

Trust is a critical commodity for business success in developing countries. North Americans going to invest in a country far from home need to believe they will not be cheated out of their assets. Nationals have to believe that a joint venture, for example, will be more than a mechanism for the North American to get rich at their expense. But, even before the venture is established trust may be essential if the prospective partners are ever to meet. This may require the recommendation of a third party respected by both sides.

Establishing good relationships with the right people requires an investment of time, money, and energy. An unwillingness of either party to make this investment is often interpreted as a lack of sincerity or interest. The executive trying to do business in four countries in a week (the "five-day wonder") is still all too common a sight. Similarly the successful local businessperson may have an equally hectic international travel schedule. Both complain that if the other was really serious he would find time to meet. Who should give in? In our opinion the onus is on whichever party is visiting to build into the schedule the necessary time to work on building a relationship or to find a trusted intermediary. Also both parties must be realistic about the elapsed time required to establish a good relationship and negotiate a mutually satisfactory deal. This will involve multiple trips by each party to the other's country and could easily take twelve to eighteen months.

The Cost of Bribery

The most quantifiable costs are the financial ones. The cost of the "service" is known. The costs of not bribing are also quantifiable: the time and money that must be invested in long-term business development in the country, or the value of the lost business. However, there are other costs that must be considered.

1. You may set a precedent and establish that you and/or your company are susceptible to payoff demands.
2. You may create an element in your organization that believes payoffs are standard operating procedure and over which you may eventually lose control.
3. You or your agents may begin using bribery and corruption as a personally non-threatening, convenient excuse to dismiss failure. You may not address some organizational problems of adapting to doing business in the developing world.
4. There are also personal costs. Ultimately you will have to accept responsibility for your decisions and actions, and those of your subordinates. At a minimum it may involve embarrassment, psychological suffering, and a loss of reputation. More extreme consequences include the loss of your job and jail sentences.

Conclusion

It is clear that bribery can be a problem for the international executive. Assuming you do not want to participate in the practice, how can you cope with the problem?

1. Do not ignore the issue. Do as many North American companies have done. Spend time thinking about tradeoffs and your position prior to the situation arising.
2. After thinking through the issue establish a corporate policy. We would caution, however, that for any policy to be effective, it must reflect values that are important to the company's senior executives. The policy must also be used. Window dressing will not work.
3. Do not be too quick to accept the "conventional wisdom." Examine critically the stories of bribery and the sources of the stories. Ask for details. Try to find out the other side of the story and make enquiries of a variety of sources.
4. Protect yourself by learning about the local culture and by establishing trusting relationships with well-respected local business people and government officials.
5. Do not contribute to the enlargement of myths by circulating unsubstantiated stories.

Finally, we would offer the advice that when in Rome do as the better Romans do. But, we would add, do not underestimate the time, effort, and expense it may take to find the better Romans and establish a relationship with them.

Case 17

○ ○

Ben & Jerry's Homemade Inc.: Background Note

Henry W. Lane and Iris Berdrow

Introduction

Ben Cohen and Jerry Greenfield, good friends since their 7th grade gym class, started their ice cream business in May 1978 after taking a $5 correspondence course on the art of ice cream making. Each invested $4,000, with the intent of engaging in a temporary endeavor until a real career opportunity came along. From one small ice cream parlor in a converted gas station in Burlington, Vermont, they sold their homemade, chunk-intensive ice cream. The original idea, as Jerry said, was to make ice cream that "was dense, solid and heavy – like us."

In 1992, the company had sales of over $130 million and produced more than ten million gallons of ice cream.[1] Ben managed company relationships with external groups, while Jerry managed product distribution. Although successful businessmen, their appearance keeps this fact a secret. "Ben does not own a suit, although he does have a sports jacket. Jerry recently bought a $30 suit, his first he claims, but he's waiting for an occasion to wear it."[2]

Jeff Furman, an accountant and an attorney, met Ben when they were both counsellors at a working farm for emotionally disturbed adolescents in the Adirondack Mountains. Their friendship led Jeff to handle legal and accounting matters informally for the partners during the early days of the business. Jeff joined the company in 1982 and was vice president for ten years. He was also appointed to the board of directors. Jeff's primary involvement in recent years has been managing special projects. His job

Iris Berdrow prepared this case under the supervision of Professor Henry W. Lane solely to provide material for class discussion. The author does not intend to illustrate either effective or ineffective handling of a managerial situation. The author may have disguised certain names and other identifying information to protect confidentiality.

description reads "To do good." Jeff stated, "We have always tried to use our company to do good in the community."

The Company's Missions

The company had three Mission Statements which were displayed in every office and retail outlet – one each for Product, Social, and Economic activities:

Product – To make, distribute and sell the finest quality all-natural ice cream and related products in a wide variety of innovative flavors made from Vermont dairy products.

Social – To operate the company in a way that actively recognizes the central role that business plays in the structure of society by initiating innovative ways to improve the quality of life of a broad community: local, national, and international.

Economic – To operate the company on a sound financial basis of profitable growth, increasing value for our shareholders and creating career opportunities and financial rewards for our employees.

Products

Ben & Jerry's principal product was super-premium ice cream made from natural ingredients. This high butterfat ice cream represented less than 10 percent of the total ice cream market by gallonage or dollars.[3] Ben & Jerry's also produced low-fat frozen yogurt, other frozen dessert products and the waffle cones in which the ice cream and yogurt are served. The 1992 total sales of $131 million were comprised of 83 percent ice cream pint sales, 8 percent 2.5 gallon ice cream tub sales, 7 percent novelty products, and 2 percent retail products.

In addition to standard flavors, Ben & Jerry's produced some novel ones such as Cherry Garcia, Chunkey Monkey, Heath Bar Crunch, Peanut Butter Cup, New York Super Fudge Chunk, White Russian, Pistachio Pistachio, Chocolate Chip Cookie Dough, Chocolate Fudge Brownie and Rainforest Crunch.

New flavors were developed by highly skilled research and development experts but the final taste tester was Ben Cohen. In 1993, about six to eight new products were to be introduced. Products were discontinued if they did not sell well.

Twenty-five percent of 1992 sales came from Chocolate Chip Cookie Dough which used a real cookie dough recipe, leaving out only the baking soda. In 1992, 3,478,219 pounds of cookie dough were used in ice cream production.

Facilities

The head office was in Waterbury, Vermont and over 500 people were employed at the company's five principal manufacturing and warehousing sites. Production facilities had expanded from the back of the gas station in 1978 to three modern ice cream production plants in Vermont – Waterbury, Springfield and St. Albans. The first plant was built in Waterbury in 1985 and the more complicated flavors were produced there. Frozen yogurt was produced at St. Albans. A video conferencing system was used to coordinate production between the sites. A small percentage of total production was awarded to a co-packing company which produced, packaged and shipped ice cream under the supervision of on-site Ben & Jerry's employees.

In the spring of 1993, the Waterbury plant was operating without a plant manager. The seven-to-one salary ratio between scoopers and top executives was not attractive to managers with the technical skills required to run the plant. Finding the right "cultural" fit was not a problem, but attracting a person who also had the expertise and experience was.

Ben & Jerry's products were sold mostly through franchised "scoop shops", although the company did own some scoop shops in Vermont and distributed to other private retail outlets. The franchises ensured a uniform standard in marketing efforts, cost analysis, site improvements, and product offerings. Many franchised shops made community and social issues part of their business plan. Ben & Jerry's had 95 franchised scoop shops in 17 states plus the District of Columbia, as well as four in Canada and eight in Israel.[4]

The Production Process

Making ice cream is a simple process, but making super-premium chunk-intensive ice cream is highly technical. According to Dave Morse, a production supervisor at the Waterbury plant, the highest skilled position in the company was the mix-maker. A technically skilled person could become a good mix-maker within six months, but to be great took at least a year. In his opinion: "If a company is going to sink or swim, it's around the mix-maker." The challenge was in the process, and in the ingredients.

The two key ingredients were milk and cream which had to be fresh for each batch. They were combined with liquid cane sugar and egg yolks in six 5,000 gallon tanks. This sweet mix was then pumped through pipes in hot and cold water vats to homogenize and pasteurize it and distributed into the flavor vats on each of the four processing lines.

Fruit and other flavorings were added to the sweet mix in the vats. All fruit was cleaned and inspected by hand before being added. The flavored mix was cooled to a soft consistency, after which the chunks and crunches were added. The mix was then packaged into pint containers. In the early days, pints were filled by hand until a filler machine was developed which could handle the large chunks used by Ben & Jerry's. The new fillers could handle 70 to 90 pints per minute. The filled containers were shrink-wrapped in groups of eight, using a different color wrapping for each line. This color coding enabled quality control to trace imperfections back to the source. Conveyors moved the packages from the filling machine to the wrappers and then into the freezer room.

Employees in the factory were allowed to eat as much ice cream as they wanted while working on the production line. All employees were allowed to take home up to three pints of ice cream per day.

The final freezing took three hours, during which time the containers travel upwards through a spiral hardener located inside the freezer room. At the bottom of the spiral hardener, the temperature of the pints was 22 degrees F; at the top, the temperature was −5 degrees F. The air temperature inside the hardener was −35 degrees F; the air velocity 900 cubic feet per minute; and the wind chill factor −60 degrees F. The capacity of the spiral hardener was 25,000 pints of ice cream. When the pints reached the top of the spiral, they were stacked on pallets and moved to storage shelves for shipping. The pallets of ice cream were sent to an independent shipping company for distribution.

The plant operated three shifts per day but was closed Sundays. The Wednesday and Saturday afternoon shifts cleaned the tanks and equipment. The flavor vats were also flushed between each flavor batch, which meant that changing a flavor required a 30 to 45 minute shutdown of the production line. The capacity of each batch was 720 gallons of sweet mix and the plant produced 170,000 to 200,000 pints per day, with each pint weighing 350 grams. About 30 tons of ice cream were produced daily at the Waterbury plant. Visitors to Waterbury could see the production process by taking one of the numerous daily plant tours.

Jerry, with a sharp intuition for people's concerns, had noticed at one point that some of the production people were becoming complacent and the general cheerfulness level was dropping. His solution was the "Joy Gang." He posted a notice in the Waterbury plant asking that any employee who wanted to help him boost morale to contact him. The "Joy Gang" then met twice a month to initiate ideas that would make working in the plant more fun. Some of the ideas that have been implemented were a stereo system for the production floor, a hot chocolate machine in the freezer, and a weekly visit from a massage therapist.

The Waterbury plant also employed a group called the "Wiz Kids." These physically challenged people put the "seconds" stickers on pint containers and did other tasks such as spring cleaning.

Quality

Each production site had its own quality improvement and R&D departments. The quality improvement technicians conducted 16 different tests on raw materials during the production process, and on final products. The production staff took five pints off the line randomly every 15 minutes to be tested. Tests included cutting a pint in half to check chunk distribution; melting a pint down, sifting the chunks out and weighing them; and weighing the whole pint.

About 4 to 5 percent of the ice cream was rejected because it was not hard enough or the mix was not right. This waste was sent to local farmers to be used as pig feed. Ice cream that had the right taste, but not the right amount of chunks was sold as seconds in "seconds freezers" at retail shops, or donated to local community groups.

Social Citizenship

Supplier Relationships

Suppliers were carefully chosen to foster alliances with businesses that shared the Ben & Jerry's social vision. Efforts were made to influence other businesses to use their own resources to address social concerns. Many of the unique flavors of ice cream were based on these alliances.

All the milk and cream for the Waterbury plant was supplied by the St. Albans Co operative. The yogurt cultures were supplied by Cabot Creamery, a subsidiary of a dairy cooperative Agri-Mark. The chunks and flavoring were often purchased from local suppliers, which varied by location.

Chocolate Fudge Brownie was made from brownies supplied by the Greyston Bakery in Yonkers, NY. The bakery provided employment and training to the homeless. Its profits were reinvested in housing programs, child care and counselling. The supply contract with Ben & Jerry's allowed it to provide full-time employment for approximately 15 people.

Rainforest Crunch candy was made by Community Products, Inc. (CPI) from a combination of Brazil and cashew nuts. These nuts were harvested from the Amazon rainforest and purchased directly from native rainforest peoples. CPI supported tropical rainforest preservation. Ben & Jerry's purchases from CPI totalled 1 million in 1990. Sixty percent of CPI's profits were donated to environmental and peace organizations.

Wild Maine Blueberry ice cream was made with fresh berries purchased from the Passamaquoddy Indians of Maine. The company also was working with a group of African-American farmers on a plan to purchase pecans.

Partnershops

Partnershops were Jeff Furman's initiative. The first one opened in Ithaca, New York. The shops were retail franchises which were donated to not-for-profit agencies. The partners who formed these agencies would manage all the operations themselves, including hiring, firing, payroll, inventory and accounting. Ben & Jerry's would then redistribute the franchise profits to help those in need. In Ithaca, the partners were young teenagers aged 14 to 20. In Harlem, the partner was HARKhomes, a group which provided housing, work, and training to homeless men. The partner in Baltimore was People Encouraging People, a non-profit organization that hired and trained developmentally challenged people. The operations of each of the Partnershops were managed through committee decisions made jointly by members of the partner agency. The initiative did not prove to be a simple process, however; it took two years for the Harlem partnershop to become a reality.

Community-Oriented Marketing

Ben & Jerry's 1991 annual report made the following statement:

> Ben & Jerry's does very little media advertising, nor does it use an outside advertising agency. But that doesn't mean it doesn't promote. In 1991, in a throwback to Woodstock and other jamborees of the 1960s, it sponsored four big outdoor festivals at Stowe, Vermont (in conjunction with the annual shareholder's meeting), Navy Pier in Chicago, Golden Gate Park in San Francisco and Newport, Rhode Island (the annual Newport Folk Music Festival). And each of these events was used to rally support for various campaigns the company has adopted, including Save the Family Farm, Pass A Peace Dividend (by cutting the defense budget) and Enact the Bryan Bill (to force car makers to improve the fuel efficiency of their cars). The Golden Gate Park festival, attended by an estimated 100,000 people, resulted in 22,000 postcards dispatched to Congress to urge a diversion of weapons spending into peacetime programs.

Marketing resources were generally directed towards community-oriented efforts, such as The Giraffe Project which sought out, acknowledged, and encouraged people who stuck out their necks by doing extraordinary work in their communities. Each winner and his or her community were awarded a thousand pints of Light ice milk.[5] In June 1990, a group of 30 student "giraffes" was sent on a two-week journey to the Soviet Union. Other community-oriented efforts included a solar-powered scoop truck which travelled around Vermont selling ice cream; using product packaging to support social and environmental issues; and providing inner-city children with free tickets to the Big Apple Circus.

Corporate Citizenship

Caring Capitalism

Ben and Jerry maintain a philosophy of Caring Capitalism: serving the community was just as important as generating a profit or producing super-premium ice cream. The prevailing attitude was always to fulfil the missions in a way that was different and fun: "weird" was a favorite criterion. Once Ben and Jerry decided to build the world's largest sundae – it was 20 feet tall. On another occasion, during a bad Vermont winter when spirits were particularly down, Ben and Jerry started a "Penny Off Per Celsius Degree Below Zero" campaign.

The company was listed on the stock exchange in 1985 when Ben and Jerry took advantage of an obscure stock regulation allowing companies in Vermont to become listed with minimum shares being offered. The Annual General Meeting has traditionally involved a two-day music festival to which all shareholders are invited.

In 1985, Jerry Greenfield and Jeff Furman formed the Ben & Jerry's Foundation. The mandate of the Foundation was to help small, not-for-profit, grassroots organizations in the United States by donating 7.5 percent of Ben & Jerry's pre-tax profits to families, disadvantaged groups, social change organizations and environmentalists. Although the company had always donated to social causes, the Foundation sent the message to shareholders that this was a formal practice. The Foundation was the agency-owner that supported the Partnershops. It also held Vermont Festivals every summer to provide food, music, and ice cream to local residents.

In 1988, Ben & Jerry's charitable donations earned them one of ten America's Corporate Conscience Awards presented by the Council on Economic Priorities to recognize remarkable examples of corporate good citizenship.

Employees at the Waterbury and Springfield plants participated in Caring Capitalism through the Employee Community Funds. Cash donations of as much as $60,000 per year were sent to non-profit community and statewide groups in Vermont.

One employee found her own way of being a Caring Capitalist. Gail Mayville, a manager at Ben & Jerry's, received The Business Enterprise Trust's Award in 1991 for "helping society while turning a profit." Gail had cut costs by introducing new recycling methods such as selling waste products as pig feed and reusing plastic ice cream containers for fertilizers.[6]

Employees

Ben & Jerry's also had a strong concern for its employees. The social assessment report in the 1992 Annual Report stated that "the quality of work life at Ben & Jerry's is clearly an area where the Company has done so many things right, above and beyond what other companies do . . ." It indicated that the company provided employees with "generous starting wages and a benefits package that may be second to none." Some of the benefits included health and dental coverage (also available for dependants and same sex partners), life insurance, paid family leave, an Employee Assistance Plan, a bonus and profit sharing plan, and a childcare facility in Waterbury.

Performance

The company operated on a double bottom line principle – profit and community service. Two audits were conducted every year: a financial audit and a social audit. The purpose of the social audit, conducted by an independent expert, was to determine whether Ben & Jerry's improved the lives of the people it touched. Exhibits 1 and 2 provide excerpts from addresses by Ben Cohen, chairperson of Ben & Jerry's and Jerry Greenfield, president of Ben & Jerry's Foundation, Inc. describing the company's philosophy. The results of the social assessment were published in the Annual Reports.

The financial performance of the company exceeded the expectations of the board members, achieving a 62 percent growth rate from 1988 to 1990. Chuck Lacy, president and COO, made the following statement in the 1990 Annual Report:

> Our sales growth surged from 23% in 1989 to 32% in 1990. Ben & Jerry's Light accounted for about one third of this growth. Most of the rest of the growth was due to the acceptance of Ben & Jerry's by the last few major supermarket chains in our targeted markets, increased sales per store in many existing markets and substantial sales gains of our novelties

EXHIBIT 1   Ben & Jerry's 1990 Annual Report, Chairperson's Letter

The most amazing thing is that our social values – that part of our company mission statement that calls us to use our power as a business to improve the quality of life in our local, national and international communities – have actually helped us to become a stable, profitable, high growth company.

This is especially interesting because it flies in the face of those business theorists who state that publicly held corporations cannot make a profit and help the community at the same time, and moreover that such companies have no business trying to do so.

The issues here are heart, soul, love and spirituality.

Corporations which exist solely to maximize profit become disconnected from their soul – the spiritual interconnectedness of humanity. Like individuals, businesses can conduct themselves with the knowledge that the hearts, souls and spirits of all people are interconnected; so that as we help others, we cannot help helping ourselves.

It makes no sense to compartmentalize our lives – to be cutthroat in business, and then volunteer some time or donate some money to charity. For it is business that is the most powerful force in our society. Multinational corporations are the most powerful force in the world – stronger even than nation states.

So, if business is the most powerful force in the world, it stands to reason that business sets the tone for our society. Nonprofits and charities cannot possibly accomplish their objectives if business does not use its power to help people.

The wonderful thing is that despite Ben & Jerry's avowedly and unabashedly populist leanings, you, our shareholders, continue to support us. I am proud to say that the employees of Ben & Jerry's are finding ways to help make money and help people at the same time. Once you start figuring out how to put these things together, the old way just doesn't make sense anymore.

We are grateful that you have invested your money in us, and we will do our best to make that investment a profitable one for all of us.

Ben Cohen
Chairperson

(primarily the Peace Pops). A long awaited shake out in the super-premium ice cream category took place in 1990. Two of our three biggest competitors lost supermarket distribution in many major markets.

He added:

We are pleased to be named to the Forbes list of top 200 small companies for return on stockholder's equity. It reaffirms our commitment to staying focused on our mission, to doing things our way, and steering clear of the corporate excesses of the 1980s.

In 1992, sales increased 36 percent over the previous year and national market share increased to 36 percent, up from 23 percent in 1989.

Global Citizenship

Russia

In the mid-1980s, changes were taking place in Eastern Europe as Mikhail Gorbachev moved the Soviet Union towards democracy and free enterprise. This situation raised the question at Ben & Jerry's, "How can we help?" Ben talked a lot about Russia at

EXHIBIT 2   Ben & Jerry's 1990 Annual Report, Excerpts from the Ben & Jerry's Foundation, Inc. Letter

---

Dear Shareholders and Friends of Ben & Jerry's:

The Ben & Jerry's Foundation has, from its beginnings, sought to share the successes of Ben & Jerry's Homemade, Inc., in a way that expresses our hope for a better world. As Ben & Jerry's has grown, the resources the foundation has to share have grown as well. This growth makes our potential effect greater, and thus requires us to be much clearer about our focus, our review process, and our follow-up with organizations to whom we hope to make grants.

We have always sought to fund less traditional organizations than do many foundations; now, with better follow-up, we can improve our assessment of the effectiveness of the efforts we fund. We are committed to funding imaginative models for social change, not simple social service maintenance efforts. The need for such services is tremendous, but is one that could quickly overwhelm the resources of our foundation. We want to know what kinds of models for change really work.

We currently have an ongoing commitment to the 1% for Peace organization, and we are encouraged by that group's progress toward building a positive peace agenda. The question of whether other organizations can best be helped by a similar commitment over time is one we need to resolve. This summer, the Ben & Jerry's Foundation board will host a conference of social activities and foundation professionals to raise these and other issues that affect the future of foundation giving.

We find ourselves more excited by the proposals we hear and the groups we fund each time we meet. Notable among 1990 grants are:

* The Devastators, an all children's Afro-Latin percussion band that performs at parades, community events and celebrations. Their music is focused on combatting drug abuse, AIDS and homelessness, and promoting world peace and environmental protection.
* The Heifer Project, which provides agricultural animals to impoverished communities to promote economic self-sufficiency.
* The Women's Institute for Housing and Economic Development, in Boston, which provides technical assistance to housing and economic development projects for women.
* The Worker Owned Network of Athens, Ohio. This network seeks to mobilize community resources for worker cooperatives and develop the area's cooperative economy.

As all of us grow in knowledge and experience, we begin to make decisions about how we will focus our energies. For a time, we may feel some regret for the things we set aside, but the satisfaction in doing well and properly those things for which we choose to work and care is the reward for making difficult choices. The Ben & Jerry's Foundation is making the choices that our growth requires. We celebrate the success that gives us what we have to share, and we look forward to planting the fruit of that success in fertile ground, and to watching it grow.

In peace and hope,

Jerry Greenfield
President,
Ben & Jerry's Foundation, Inc.

---

employee meetings which were held to discuss current thoughts and ideas. As a result of his interest three initiatives were started: (1) Peace Pops, chocolate-covered ice cream on a stick with a message on the wrapper questioning the amount of money going to defense spending; (2) One percent for Peace, an organization dedicated to convincing the American government to donate 1 percent of its defense budget towards peace through understanding; and (3) People to People, a social exchange initiative which would provide people from other countries with an opportunity to visit North America. In 1987, Ben envisioned opening a scoop shop in Russia and using the profits to fund cultural exchanges between Russia and the United States.

EXHIBIT 3 Five-Year Financial Highlights (In thousands except per share data)

Income Statement	12/28/92	12/28/91	12/29/90	12/30/89	12/31/88
Net sales	$131,968	$96,997	$77,024	$58,464	$47,561
Cost of sales	94,389	68,500	54,203	41,660	33,935
Gross profit	37,579	28,497	22,821	16,804	13,627
Selling, delivery, admin. expenses	26,242	21,264	17,639	13,009	10,655
Operating income	11,337	7,233	5,182	3,795	2,972
Other income (expenses)	(23)	(729)	(709)	(362)	(274)
Income before taxes	11,314	6,504	4,473	3,433	2,698
Income taxes	4,639	2,765	1,864	1,380	1,079
Net income	6,675	3,739	2,609	2,053	1,618
Net income per common share*	$1.07	$0.67	$0.50		
Weighted average common shares outstanding	6,253,825	5,572,368	5,224,667		
Balance Sheet Data	12/28/92	12/28/91	12/29/90	12/30/89	12/31/88
Working capital	$18,054	$11,035	$8,202	$5,829	$5,614
Total assets	88,207	43,056	34,299	28,139	26,307
Long-term debt	2,641	2,787	8,948	9,328	9,670
Stockholder equity**	66,759	26,269	16,101	13,405	11,245

* The per share amounts and average shares outstanding have been adjusted for the effects of all stock splits, including stock splits in the form of stock dividends.

** No cash dividends have been declared or paid by the Company on its capital stock since the Company's organization. The Company intends to reinvest earnings for use in its business and to finance future growth. Accordingly, the Board of Directors does not anticipate declaring any cash dividends in the foreseeable future.

Notes

1. See Exhibit 3 for five-year financial summary.
2. Christy, Marian. 1991. Ben & Jerry: Here's the Scoop. *Boston Globe* 239/177 (June 26): P77.
3. Ben & Jerry's *1991 Annual Report.*
4. The rights to Canada have since been bought back by Ben & Jerry's. The shops in Israel were owned and managed by a friend of Ben's cousin.
5. This is a play on words of President George Bush's reference to "a thousand points of light."
6. McCartney, Robert J. (1991) 5 Who Blended Business, Beneficence Are Saluted. *The Washington Post.* 114/107 (March 22): P1.

CASE **18**

Iceverks (A): Ben & Jerry's in Russia

Henry W. Lane and Iris Berdrow

Introduction

In early 1993, Jeff Furman was rereading Dave Morse's report for 1992. It was hard to believe, but the first few months of Iceverks' operations had been profitable.[1] The joint venture partners wanted to expand and offers were coming in from all over the Commonwealth of Independent States (C.I.S.). It seemed that Dave Morse, the general director, was of the same opinion. Jeff was less excited about expansion however. He wondered whether Ben & Jerry's should stick to its original plan or take advantage of the apparent opportunity. What would it mean for Iceverks and the partners? He knew he would have to deal with the issue on his upcoming trip to Russia.

History

Ben Cohen had an interest in starting an initiative in Russia and first travelled there with Jeff in 1986. Jeff's grandparents had been born and raised in Russia so he also was interested. They visited both Moscow and Karelia, a beautiful resort region in Russia near the border with Finland.

In 1988, the Governor of Vermont declared Karelia the sister state of Vermont. In honor of the occasion, the Governor visited Karelia with a delegation including Ben.

Iris Berdrow prepared this case under the supervision of Professor Henry W. Lane solely to provide material for class discussion. The author does not intend to illustrate either effective or ineffective handling of a managerial situation. The author may have disguised certain names and other identifying information to protect confidentiality.

Representatives of the Karelian government encouraged Ben to start a business in their region and even proposed potential land sites. At that time, he was not ready to commit to the scale of business proposed, so he declined the offer.

In 1988, Ben and Jeff again travelled to Russia to seek opportunities. The Academy of Sciences arranged several meetings in Moscow with members of the Knowledge Society which had expressed an interest in a joint venture to produce ice cream in Moscow. They even suggested a suitable location. Ben and Jeff made several attempts to see the potential site, to start drawing up a joint venture document and to discuss available equipment and supply sources, but never seemed to get very far in the process. They finally thought they might be making progress when arrangements were made to see a plant; but instead of visiting an ice cream plant to view equipment and processes, they visited a museum in the Georgia region. Several meetings were held but nothing was ever accomplished. They again visited Karelia and found a potential site for a plant. Although they were no further ahead on a partnership, they went home with a potential location and insights into doing business in Russia.

The following year, Ben received a letter from Serge Lukin, a translator for the 1988 Vermont delegation. Serge introduced himself as a member of a Karelian cooperative consisting of four businessmen. Serge and one of his partners, Vasili Mikheev, had been involved in producing a television series depicting the creative endeavors of young Russians. During an interview with a government official, they saw an empty Ben & Jerry's ice cream container in the office. Reading the label, they concluded that Ben & Jerry's was the type of company with which they had been hoping to collaborate in opening a communications center aiding American/Russian partnerships. They wrote to Ben asking if he would be interested in sponsoring an information center in Karelia. Serge also mentioned that perhaps in the future he and Vasili would be interested in a partnership with Ben & Jerry's. Ben responded quickly with a long letter stating that they would be very interested in an ice cream plant in Karelia and that all equipment could be shipped from the United States; no mention was made of the information center.

Management Selection

While seeking out opportunities in Russia, Ben and Jeff were also searching for an American manager for the project. They initially focused on applicants who spoke Russian and had a business background. Interviewing mostly graduates from top business schools, they found that the character of these applicants did not fit the Ben & Jerry's culture. So, they posted the position internally.

Dave Morse was a production supervisor who had worked at Ben & Jerry's for five years. He felt he had reached the limit of his growth potential in production and had been interested in the Russia project since he first heard about it at employee meetings. He had read about Russia and its history and felt that he was suited to such an adventure. However, because of the initial selection criteria, he had not applied for the position.

When the job was posted internally, Dave encouraged Ben and Jeff to reconsider the type of person for whom they were looking. He argued that it was harder to learn how to make ice cream than to learn anything else that the job would require, including learning Russian. At least a year was required to learn the basics let alone to be a trouble-shooter or to teach others the process. There were issues of ensuring sanitary conditions, adapting recipes and finding ingredients. Dave had contacts in the industry from which to source materials and equipment; he had the technical knowledge needed to maintain and operate the equipment; and he had the skill to make super-premium ice cream.

Although he had no business training, was not able to speak Russian and had never lived overseas, Dave's energy and "can do" attitude impressed Jeff enough to name him the first manager of the Russian venture.

Partner Selection

In March 1990, Jeff and Dave went to Russia to choose a joint venture partner and to initiate an agreement. In Moscow they met with a representative of one cooperative which owned several restaurants and other businesses. They stayed in one of the two apartments owned by a member of the cooperative. This Russian businessman also owned two cars, nine televisions, two refrigerators, two washing machines and 3,000 coffee-table books. The cooperative members were enthusiastic about a partnership and asked Dave to open U.S. bank accounts for them in order to get started, yet they had no potential sites and little understanding of what was needed to get the project going. Their attitude was, "We don't care if we are doing it right, we just want to do it – we want to get rich."

Before leaving Vermont, Jeff had arranged to meet Serge Lukin and his cooperative as well. Serge met them in Moscow and took them to Petrozavodsk, a small city in the Karelia region. It turned out that this cooperative was just a group of entrepreneurial friends, but despite the facade they made the impression of being intelligent, friendly, enthusiastic, and "regular" Russians. Serge did not own a car, had only one small television, and when the Americans visited his apartment, his wife served borscht. Serge had graduated from the Leadership Institute in Moscow and came from a respectable family. His partner, Vasili, graduated from the department of foreign languages at the Petrozavodsk University and had been a director in a military factory managing 500 people by the time he was 25. Since they knew little about Ben & Jerry's, they had gathered all the articles and information they could find. They liked what they read and heard.

The decision was made to locate in Petrozavodsk. Dave felt uncomfortable with Moscow. Even with trusting partners, he would have felt uncomfortable living in the city and dealing with the bureaucracy. Jeff was impressed by the enthusiasm and initiative of Serge and Vasili. They realized this choice would mean travel and communications difficulties as well as less publicity, but they liked the parallel to their own start in small-town Vermont.

Jeff and Dave returned to Vermont with a potential partnership. In June, Ben and Dave visited Petrozavodsk to choose a suitable location for the production facility and scoop shop. Of several options, they chose an existing building known as the Pioneer Palace, a Russian equivalent to the "YMCA." The owners agreed to provide the space in return for ice cream in the future. Renovations were planned to accommodate a production capacity sufficient to supply three or four scoop shops.

The partnership agreement was signed in September 1990 while Serge and Vasili were in Vermont learning how to make ice cream. It was important to Jeff that the partnership be 50/50 between Russians and the Americans, although the contributions made by each were not important. The joint venture would be called Ben & Jerry's Vermont-Karelia Ice Cream, Iceverks for short, and would consist of the following principals: Ben & Jerry's Homemade Inc. with 50 percent ownership; the Intercentre Cooperative (Vasili Mikheev and Serge Lukin) with 27 percent; the Petro Bank with 20 percent; and Pioneer Palace with 3 percent. Half of all profits would stay in the company and the other half would be split among the partners. The Board consisted of one representative from the Intercentre Cooperative, one from the Petro Bank, Ben Cohen and Jeff Furman.

Dave Morse was appointed general director and Vasili Mikheev was appointed commercial director. Under Russian law, the general director had full authority over everyone, including the commercial director. However, the partners agreed that the directors would make all decisions jointly. Conflicts would be resolved to the directors' mutual satisfaction or no action would be taken. This agreement resulted in a lot of give and take and the development of an informal working relationship between Dave and Vasili.

Getting Started

Renovations to the Pioneer Palace site were to start immediately under Vasili's supervision. Serge was to register the partnership in Moscow and in Petrozavodsk. Dave was to gather the necessary equipment and supplies in Vermont to be shipped to Petrozavodsk.

Dave already had spent about a year gathering all the necessary equipment and supplies, developing recipes based on available Russian ingredients, and testing equipment for Russian voltages. A lot of the equipment was borrowed from, or donated by, companies in Vermont. During this time, Dave worked on a business plan which in hindsight he realized was far from realistic, but it was a good business exercise for him. He also engaged a private Russian tutor.

In December 1990, Dave went to Karelia to check progress. He was disappointed to find that the partnership had not yet been registered and that the construction had only reached the point of adapting the architectural drawings to Russian building codes. Dave made it clear that progress was needed or Ben and Jeff would lose interest. He and Jeff had decided that progress was necessary in at least one of three areas within six months: the architectural drawings had to be approved; the business had to be registered; or suppliers had to be established. Serge's response was that an American was needed at the meetings in Karelia and Moscow to prove that this was a legitimate venture.

Dave moved to Petrozavodsk in January 1991. His wife and two children joined him in March. They lived in Russia until March 1993, during which time his wife taught English and the children attended a Russian school.

While Iceverks was struggling to get started, Gorbachev was struggling to decentralize government control and the country was moving into chaos. No one knew where to register a business, or who had the authority to sign government contracts such as those required to guarantee supplies. Documents were coming from everywhere, proving that authority lay with whomever decided they had it. A contract could be signed by one government department and another bureaucrat could come up with a different document that proved the contract void.

Not the least of the problems for Iceverks was enduring the 1991 attempted overthrow of Gorbachev's government. The coup attempt in Moscow scared the Iceverks crew, although it did not directly affect progress. There were large demonstrations in Karelia. Throughout this time, the Iceverk's family held together and an e-mail network was used to keep head office in Vermont updated on their situation and progress.

Registration

Because of the political and bureaucratic chaos, registration was a difficult process. Dave and Serge had a list of people to contact for assistance, but each one led to a dead end. Jeff hired an American consultant, a lawyer experienced with the Russian system. The consultant travelled to Moscow, made initial changes to the registration documents although the documents had been checked and approved by several Russian authorities, and then attempted to proceed with the registration.

The consultant suggested that a Russian lawyer be hired and, with Dave's consent, initiated contact with a lawyer he knew in Moscow. The lawyer worked for the Russian government in the joint venture registration department and had a private practice as a registration consultant for joint ventures. The American lawyer reported back to Dave and Serge that the company could be registered within two weeks but it would cost U.S.$20,000 in consulting fees. For this fee, the Russian lawyer would stand in the appropriate queues to get the registration processed and approved.

Dave and Jeff knew from the start that they would be working in a different system and they had decided not to pay bribes. Ben & Jerry's had a policy against paying bribes. If this consulting fee were paid, there would probably be a continuing series of consulting fees and registration would drag on indefinitely. Dave was sure they could succeed without giving in to the corruption. He said:

> Finding the honest people is just a matter of patience. There will be honest people who will like you and those that don't. The ones that don't will tell you. There are honest bureaucrats who just do their job. You have to find the ones who really care, that will be on your side and make things happen. It's frustrating, but once you find the honest people it's simple.

Dave turned down the offer from the lawyers and he and Serge took on the task with a renewed burst of energy. Finally things moved. They were able to arrange meetings with the right people, the lawyers for the city council read the charter documents and agreed to help, calls were made, and the documents were approved. The joint venture company was finally registered in Moscow in April, 1991 and in Petrozavodsk in May, 1991. Iceverks was the first joint venture to be registered in Petrozavodsk under the new decentralized system, an endeavor that took about eight months and cost the normal registration fee of 8000 rubles or about US$50.

Construction

Construction was another nightmare. Although the drawings had been completed, the state architects had to redraft them. Every week these architects would ask Dave for information, but they always asked the same questions and no progress was evident. Even though there were no other construction projects, they were always too busy to work on the Iceverks drawings. Finally, after six months of delayed meetings and unresolved problems, Dave and Vasili bypassed the general director and met with each director personally. They asked each one to complete the drawings specific to his area of responsibility – the electrical schematics director, the concrete specialist, etc. Finally, in June 1991 a stamped set of drawings were produced that looked remarkably close to Dave's original version.

Dave returned to Vermont to supervise the packing of the container of equipment and supplies. There were tanks, batch freezers, mix tanks, water-jacket cooled holding tanks, piping, laboratory equipment, seven tons of coca, duct tape, skis, and lots of toilet paper. A construction crew had been hired and they were to have the freezer finished by the time the container arrived in Petrozavodsk.

The container was ready to ship in July but Dave had not yet received a progress report from the construction crew. In Petrozavodsk he found that none of the work had been done on the list he had left. He fired the crew and another company contracted. Unfortunately, when the first crew cleared out their equipment in the middle of the night, they took all the construction materials with them. Retrieving the materials would have been a lengthy, involved process with slim chance of success, so new materials had to be found. Dave had doubts about the second company also. However, he felt that it was small enough to need the work, but big enough to have the people to put on the job. By December, that company was fired as well.

At this point, it was decided that the Iceverks employees would complete the renovations themselves. Dave had experience building his own home and working in the steel industry for a time, and he found that many Russians had a broad base of survival skills among which construction was one. Dave hired two workers from the previous crews who had proven to be reliable and the Iceverks construction crew of ten went to work. They had managed to acquire more building materials and knew people who would sell them cement. Some of the work, such as the electrical installations, was contracted.

Job descriptions of the crew members included, "Get stuff," so every few days, the crew would update the materials list and assign the acquisition of items. Iceverks had employed a driver with a car; he also had a radio so that when an item was found, a crew member would call the driver and tell him where to pick the item up. Most of the materials were found through private contacts and obtained by bartering. It took about four months, but they gathered all the materials they needed to complete the renovations.

When the container finally arrived in Petrozavodsk, most of the essential equipment had to be rebuilt due to damage in transit.[2]

Suppliers

The government controlled 70 percent of the production of state farms, which meant that the output, selling price, and distribution were decided for the farmers by state planners. The other 30 percent could be sold privately. Iceverks had to secure a cream supply through the agriculture minister for the Karelia region. The Karelian council of ministers directed the agriculture minister to provide Iceverks with the supplies it needed. Even then, it was not clear that the ministers had the authority to sign a deal for cream supplies since regulations were constantly changing. The support of the politicians in Petrozavodsk also helped in getting other supplies such as sugar. Vasili and Dave tried to secure as much of the private sector output as they could in case the government supplies did not materialize. They visited all the collective farms to determine what supplies might be available. At one point, they considered buying land and pasturing cows themselves.

Dave and Vasili had developed a relationship with the director of the milk plant in Petrozavodsk. Her cooperation was fuelled by her desire to work for Iceverks. Dave and Vasili did not disagree with this even though they knew she would not leave a job in which she managed 300 to 400 people to work in a production facility of about 10 people.

Operations

According to the joint venture agreement, the general director was responsible for production, administration, marketing, and other operational factors, and the commercial director was responsible for growth – the development of business and trade. However, Dave trained Vasili to run the ice cream equipment and then Vasili assumed the job of managing the production staff.

Jeff left the implementation and operations of the joint venture to the directors. His involvement was to provide a sense of reality and to keep them focused on ice cream rather than other opportunities. In December 1991, Jeff visited Petrozavodsk. The e-mail he sent home read as follows:

> The plant is well on its way to being finished. The walls are up and tiled, the floor is in, the freezer door is ready to be installed and more importantly, all the needed building materials are in hand and secure. This is a major accomplishment. Typically, renovations here can take 40 years. The most amazing part of our progress is it has been done without the traditional "Russian bribes." We don't flaunt our dollars there. Dave and his family live on a typical Russian salary and only use their hard currency for souvenirs. They wait on line and search the shelves for food but there's always something available. Of course, there was no milk for two weeks and there had been a meatless period previously. When I was there, we managed to dine on something called "mystery meat" – which Dave and Katie's son Dan liked to eat raw.
>
> Dave and his family are truly pioneers out in the frontier – geographically, socially, and economically. People live day-to-day with real, concrete problems. They have, however, an upbeat position and are excited about our project. We are the main event there besides the larger political scene. The dedication and caring of the people mirrors that of our staff here.

Production

The recipes had to be adapted to accommodate the ingredients available while maintaining the flavor and quality standards. There were differences in the milk, the cream and the sugar used. Although some of the best separators were built in Russia, the milk was only separated to 25 percent cream instead of to 40 percent as in Vermont. During the summer months the milk was adequate for ice cream production, but in the winter the cows were not fed properly, causing the milk to taste differently. Condensed milk was not available, so dry milk powder was used. The milk powder had to be fresh, used within one month of processing. However, it was a difficult ingredient to acquire. Granulated sugar was used instead of liquid cane sugar. The stabilizer and cocoa were shipped from the United States.

The production area at the Pioneer Palace was 2,260 square feet, the freezer 2,649 cubic feet, the engine room 1,942 cubic feet, the store 1,076 square feet and the office and dry storage area 1,184 square feet. The total production capacity was 21 tons of ice cream per week, although to keep the machinery in good repair, real capacity was 12 tons per week. In the Spring of 1993, production was at seven to eight tons per week.

The production schedules were planned months in advance because of the lead time needed to get supplies. A year's supply of ingredients such as flavoring and stabilizer, as well as paper goods were purchased simultaneously from American suppliers. Shipments were often delayed in customs and would take months to get to Karelia.

The plant operated 19 to 20 hours per day, three days per week. Sanitary conditions and quality standards were closely observed. The containers, either pints or tubs, were filled by hand. The containers were seconds shipped from Vermont and relabelled indicating a Karelian product. All the scoop shops were supplied from the stock kept in the plant's freezer.

Products

When Dave was originally adapting recipes in Vermont, he had decided to start with the basic flavors of vanilla, chocolate and coffee. Once these flavors gained acceptance, they would produce more exotic ones. Large quantities of vanilla, chocolate and coffee flavoring were shipped to Petrozavodsk and only a small quantity of fruit flavors. They soon found that the demand for exotic flavors was much greater than for the basic ones. Orange, mango, maple, and other fruit flavors proved to be the most popular. Some flavorings were purchased from an American company with an office in Moscow. Local produce was used whenever possible, although most of the fruits were shipped from Israel. For example, blueberries were purchased from local residents; and one day, two elderly women, each carrying a 100-pound basket of walnuts on their backs, arrived by train from the Ukraine. They had heard that Iceverks purchased produce for its ice cream.

The flavors produced began to resemble those in the United States such as Melon, Banana with Walnuts, Fudge Chocolate Brownie, Karelia Crunch, Blueberry, and Black Currant. One of the more popular flavors was a cookie ice cream made from Finnish sandwich cookies similar to Oreo Cookies. Fudge Chocolate Brownie (another favorite), Oatmeal Cookie and Apple Pie ice cream were all made from goods baked at Iceverks. Sometimes the employees or even the general director and his wife would spend their evenings baking goods for the next day's production.

Iceverks had not been able to find a reliable supplier of chocolate, so the vanilla-chocolate chunk was sometimes made from Swiss, sometimes French, and sometimes Soviet chocolate which was by far the best according to Dave. The Soviet chocolate was hard to get, but sometimes he negotiated for factory second chunks.

Staffing

Finding highly educated, intelligent people to hire was not a problem. A university-educated Russian would be happy to get a good paying job as an ice cream scooper with an American company. Employee backgrounds could easily be reviewed since Russians carried a Work Book stamped by each employer. In it, a record was kept of training received, specializations, qualifications, employment history, merits and disciplinary actions. Andre Ichenko, the assistant bookkeeper, located potential applicants and Vasili interviewed them. The first characteristic he looked for was honesty. Next was a willingness to work hard.

In 1993, there were just under 100 employees in Karelia in production, administration, three scoop shops, and transportation (Exhibit 1 is a listing of positions). All employees were paid in cash. In March 1993, a good scooper would earn 10 to 12,000 rubles per month for a 24-hour week. The directors were earning 30,000 per month and the production workers 36,000 per month. Wages were increased monthly because of the inflation rate, so that by May 1993 the scoopers were making 30,000 rubles per month.

Benefits included health insurance for procedures not available through state care, free ice cream, and one month vacation per year. As yet, no one had been able to take the vacation time so they took the pay instead.

The production, maintenance, and supervisory employees tended to remain with Iceverks. Scoopers had a high turnover rate, although not as high as scoopers in the United States. Great efforts were made to prevent turnover of production and maintenance people because of the importance of those functions. Vasili felt that the maintenance people were the most important of all employees; they were capable of fixing anything.[3]

Training

Training these highly educated employees for production, maintenance or service positions was just a matter of laying out the details of the job, and the problems inherent in it. By providing good guidelines, such as being efficient and paying attention to cleanliness, they would develop their own solutions to problems that arose.

One skill that needed more specific training was providing friendly service and smiling at the customers. During construction employees were instructed not to be rude to people who came by asking about the project because they were potential customers.

EXHIBIT 1   Iceverks Personnel Listing, 1993

Petrozavodsk:
Co-Director Joint Venture
General Director Joint Venture
Production Manager, Freezer Equipment Supervisor
Chief Bookkeeper
Assistant Bookkeeper
Accountant
Assistant to General Director
Cafe Director
Attorney
Sales & Marketing Director
Lab Technician
Ice Cream and Ingredients Stock Manager
Assistant to Co-Director
Five Production Workers

Pioneer Palace Cafe Personnel:
8 two-shift scoopers including 2 shift administrators
6 three-shift waffle cone makers
2 cashiers
2 dishwashers
2 floorwashers

Dverlanka Cafe Personnel:
5 two-shift scoopers including 1 chief administrator
5 three-shift waffle cone makers
3 cashiers
2 dishwashers-floorwashers

Kondopoga:
Director
Assistant-Director
Scoop Shop Manager
1 Production Manager, Ice Cream and Ingredients Stock Manager
3 scoopers
2 cashiers
2 dishwashers
3 waffle cone makers
1 driver
1 electrician
1 cleaner

The employees started to recognize that it was useful to be nice and that nothing was gained by being rude. In Russian culture, the norm seemed to be to act exactly as one felt; otherwise a person was thought of as deceptive. It was hard to convince the employees that if they acted happy they would eventually feel happy, but after experimenting with smiling they found that they did feel better. By the time the shop opened, the scoopers understood the philosophy of friendliness. The new scoopers would still say "What do you want?" or "Hurry up," but they soon overcame this urge through peer-training. Being rough or rude with customers was justification for immediate release.

Dave's management style was hands-off: he expected employees to try to solve problems themselves first. The Russian expectation was to have a strong manager who was very directive. After half a year of steady encouragement, the employees came to favor Dave's approach. At first, they would not make decisions or admit to problems or mistakes for fear of losing their jobs. Eventually, they found things got done faster if they each took some responsibility themselves and that this behavior was acceptable, even encouraged.

Distribution

Retail

When the first scoop shop opened in Petrozavodsk on July 9, 1992, a Russian Orthodox priest blessed the grand opening ceremony and free ice cream was scooped for the entire day. The ceremony, attended by American visitors as well as the Russian media, attracted a lot of publicity.

A second shop was opened several days later in Kondopoga. Situated 40 kilometers north of Petrozavodsk on the border with Finland, Kondopoga had a population of 35,000 people and was the location of Russia's second largest paper mill. The mill's annual export sales were in the hundreds of millions of dollars and it supplied most of the newsprint used in Russia. The plant occupied half the territory of Kondopoga and employed half of the residents.

The director of the mill knew Mikhail Vasiljev who had been a local hero because he had constructed apartment buildings for the city that actually were completed. Mikhail told the director about his friends who had opened an ice cream shop in Petrozavodsk. When the director was introduced to Dave and Vasili in the spring of 1991, he was thrilled to discover that Vasili was the son of one of the labor heroes of the mill 20 years earlier.

The director wanted a scoop shop in Kondopoga so that his workers could enjoy super-premium ice cream. Dave told the director and Mikhail that he could not accommodate them because of administrative difficulties in getting two shops and a production facility operational, as well as the fact that Iceverks was financially strained. It already needed money to replace a damaged refrigeration unit in Petrozavodsk. Mikhail convinced Dave that he could get the facilities in order. The director offered to loan the shop U.S.$40,000, as well as to donate U.S.$40,000 for the refrigeration equipment and supplies. Dave trusted them and an agreement was signed in June, 1991. It took until December, 1991, but Iceverks did receive the $80,000, Mikhail found the location, made the necessary renovations, and the residents of Kondopoga got super-premium ice cream. At the grand opening of the scoop shop, Jeff asked the director, "Now what?" The reply was, "I want pizza!" The director later provided space at the mill for an additional retail counter which was supplied and staffed by the scoop shop in Kondopoga.

Russia was still basically a feudal society with each city being its own duchy. Kondopoga was run by the director of the mill and Petrozavodsk was run by politicians. For Iceverks to enter Kondopoga would have been an intrusion; therefore the scoop shop was operated autonomously. Mikhail Vasiljev was director of the Kondopoga scoop shop, and he answered to the director of the paper mill if any problems arose with the shop's service. He also answered to Dave and Vasili regarding the shop's operations. The scoop shop had its own bank account into which all deposits were made and from which all bills were paid. The Kondopoga ledgers and bank accounts were separate from the Petrozavodsk ledgers since the tax systems and the banks were different in the two cities. Both the ledgers and the bank account of the Kondopoga scoop shop were in Mikhail's name. The scoop shop was registered as a department of another business owned by Mikhail, but operated as a department of Iceverks in Petrozavodsk.

Without Mikhail, the scoop shop would not have been a possibility. A local person ensured that the interests of the town were met. Relationships with the paper mill director and other officials were maintained by keeping prices in the store low and occasionally delivering free ice cream to the orphanage or to the official's offices. Dave commented:

> The mill director is an old communist idealist. His idea of the ice cream shop was purely as a gift to his workers. He did not want his money to go to Moscow.

Mikhail hired Irina Vasiljeva as the manager of the scoop shop. A graduate of a medical institute, she quit her job in a drug store to join Iceverks. The shop served about 2,000 people per day, although in summer months this number increased. Scoopers earned 65 rubles per hour or about 26,000 per month; a mill worker would earn 40,000 rubles on average.[4]

The scoopers in Kondopoga received the same smile-training as the scoopers in Petrozavodsk. They were also taught to encourage their customers to be friendly and to clean up after themselves. Even though the price was higher than for ice cream sold on the streets, there were many repeat customers. From street vendors, a brick of ice cream could be purchased for 60 rubles and an eskimo sandwich (a brick of ice cream sandwiched between two wafers) for 110 rubles. A large serving in the scoop shop was 120 rubles.[5]

Wholesale

Pints and tubs were shipped from Petrozavodsk to Moscow and St. Petersburg, and sold for hard currency to restaurants and hard currency outlets. The client base in 1993 consisted of about 10 to 12 hard currency stores[6] which purchased pints, and several restaurants which purchased tubs. Two of the most stable restaurant customers were the Radisson Hotel and Pizza Hut. Stores generally had a freezer capacity of 50 to 80 pints, a supply which lasted about one week. Iceverk's main competitors in Moscow were Yarnells, Baskin Robbins, and Haagen Daz. These products were imported and suppliers usually made weekly deliveries.

Iceverks would have preferred to sell their ice cream for rubles but shipments would have had to be either prepaid or C.O.D.; granting credit would be difficult because of the inflation rate. The hard currency outlets had difficulty selling goods in rubles because of money transfer regulations, but also because the consumer belief was that if something was sold for rubles it was not a foreign product and hence not of good quality or worth a premium price. Hard currency shipments were paid whenever the customer was able, although all payments were received within 30 days.

In October 1992, 70 to 90 percent of hard currency sales had been to expatriate-based clientele. In 1993, this dropped to 50 percent and the partners predicted it to drop even lower. Over the same period, pint sales had grown from about 200 per month to 5,000.

Shipments were made every two weeks according to specific orders received ten days in advance of delivery either by phone or direct contact. The trip took about 24 hours and there was always at least one breakdown of either the truck or the refrigeration unit.

Difficulties with delivery trucks and drivers prompted Iceverks to purchase its own transportation equipment. The delivery company Iceverks had been using often delivered melted ice cream because the refrigeration unit would break down en route. Two delivery trucks had been purchased by Iceverks. The first had no refrigeration unit, but the necessary parts to install one had been ordered from Finland. It took two and a half months to register the truck and even longer to get the parts. In the meantime, a second truck was acquired; it had a refrigeration unit which needed repairs.

Marketing

James Flynn was a student at the University of New Hampshire when he spent the summer of 1992 in St. Petersburg. After finishing his degree, he returned to Moscow in March, 1993 to seek a job. He saw a notice at the American Embassy that Iceverks was looking for a marketing sales representative in Moscow. Although the directors were looking for a Russian, they decided to hire James. His goal was to get Ben & Jerry's ice cream into all the hard currency stores in Moscow.

The first shipment of ice cream received by James from Petrozavodsk arrived several hours later than scheduled with half of the ice cream melted because of a mechanical failure and the refrigeration unit had broken down. When he brought the unmelted orders to the customers, the managers had already purchased from the competition. The customer's freezers were full, so the Iceverks' deliveries were refused. The ice cream was sent back to Petrozavodsk and given away. James met with each customer to assure them of consistent deliveries in the future.

James loved his job and found it very challenging. In his words: "You can't plan beyond three days here." He had more authority and responsibility than he could have hoped for at home.

Performance

The first four months of operations proved to be profitable for Iceverks and the American partners' share had been transferred successfully to Vermont. From the time of opening to the end of October 1992, sales from the Petrozavodsk store were 8.1 million rubles, and from Kondopoga 4.3 million rubles. Wholesale sales totalled 700,000 rubles and hard currency sales totalled U.S.$2,442. The net profit before taxes for this period totalled 6.4 million rubles plus U.S.$334.[7]

In keeping with the intent of the joint venture to use Ben & Jerry's as a model for operating a business in Russia, Iceverks prices were not raised frequently. In May 1993, Baskin Robbins was selling cones for 1,000 rubles each, while Iceverks' price for two scoops was 130 rubles. Jeff called this model "Linked Prosperity," caring capitalism without any exploitive nature. The local residents recognized these efforts and voted Ben & Jerry's one of the top three ethical businesses in Karelia.

Iceverks shipped souvenirs from Russia to Vermont for sale in the Waterbury outlet. These included Matrushka dolls, tops, tee-shirts with Ben & Jerry's logo in cyrillic, and whatever else they could find that might be of interest to Americans. The goods could be made in Russia at a very low ruble cost and sold in the United States at a large markup to a guaranteed distributor – Ben & Jerry's Homemade Inc. One of the contentious issues between the American and Russian partners was that the money made on souvenir sales was debited to the cost of the equipment containers shipped from Vermont to Petrozavodsk. The Russian partners felt this prevented them from taking advantage of opportunities such as cheap sugar for which they needed cash.

Social Citizenship

Maintaining relationships with local politicians was important to the continuing survival of Iceverks, but this involved more than just supplying free ice cream. One of Iceverks endeavors was providing communication links and references for businesses and professionals involved in Project Harmony, a program established in Vermont to provide exchange opportunities between Karelia and Vermont through the sister-state relationship.

Iceverks was fostering relationships with Finland because it seemed that Karelia would one day become a major trading partner with Finland. Finland was to join the European Economic Community by 1997 and could potentially become a back door into Russia for foreign businesses.

One of Iceverks initiatives was an exchange program started by Jeff and funded by Iceverks' profits to promote cross-cultural experiences. Two Russian children and two American children were the first to be involved in the summer of 1993. The exchanges were three weeks long, during which time the children would live with a host family, work in the scoop shops as paid apprentices and sit on committees as observers to learn about the problem-solving and decision-making processes. The two Russian children were chosen by the Petrozavodsk staff. One was Serge Lukin's daughter Sasha. Sasha was very enthusiastic about visiting Vermont, and since she could speak English and was liked by everyone, she was an easy choice. The other was also a unanimous decision; he was Misha, a young Russian who was hired to crack walnuts during the summer of 1992. Misha was a smart child and a hard worker. Dave described him as "an adult in kids clothing." Sasha and Misha were to travel to Vermont in June of 1993 with the general director.

When Jeff first developed the exchange program, he suggested that the scoopers be the ones selected since they were the youngest and would benefit the most. However, to Russians this represented a major opportunity and the older staff were saying, "You are sending kids who are just scooping ice cream, why not send me?" So, Jeff had to consider amending the program to include all staff in the program. The difficulty was whether to choose participants by seniority or by position. Some employees, such as bookkeepers, production workers, and laboratory workers would really benefit from understanding the American business environment better. But the prestige of being selected suggested that choosing senior employees would be more appropriate.

In September 1993, groups of Ben & Jerry's franchise owners were to travel from the United States to Petrozavodsk to learn more about Russians. In a similar effort, satellite exchanges had been envisioned which would provide a social benefit for people in both countries in that they could see what Ben & Jerry's was like in the other country. Jeff's intent was, "You can see people eating ice cream in both countries."

Management Transition

The relatively short tenure of the American general director was problematic for the Iceverks operations and for the Russian partners, particularly since decision making was shared equally. It took time for the directors to learn about each other, especially with a language barrier. Yet finding an American who would be willing and capable of making a long-term commitment while still fitting the Ben & Jerry's culture was even more difficult.

Jeff Furman preferred continuing with someone who understood the Ben & Jerry's culture and could be trusted, over choosing someone who could speak Russian and had a business background. Jeff chose Greg Quinn, who had been working in the tour department of Ben & Jerry's in Waterbury for a few months. Before joining Ben & Jerry's, Greg had spent two years in Niger with the Peace Corps. Jeff felt Greg's experiences would help him adapt quickly even though he did not have a lot of technical knowledge about making ice cream and spoke no Russian. At this point, the production crew in Petrozavodsk were skilled enough to operate without an American expert.

Greg spent three months in training in Vermont in the finance, research and development, quality control, production, and maintenance departments as well as taking Russian lessons before he moved to Petrozavodsk in September 1992. He knew the basics of the production process because he, as all employees who start at Ben & Jerry's, spent time on the production floor and in the freezer learning the operations. Greg spent time after his regular shifts learning more about the making of ice cream. Ben & Jerry's would sometimes hire people for the weekends to work on the production line and Greg often volunteered. Although he did not know as much as Dave Morse, he knew enough to help the Russian production crew when needed.

Originally, Dave was to return to Vermont in September 1992 after the grand opening of the Petrozavodsk scoop shop, but when Greg had been there a few weeks, Dave decided he should stay until 1993 to ease the transition. This was Greg's first time in Russia and he was very excited about the opportunity. He was accompanied by his wife Ellen and their newborn son. The first winter was difficult for Ellen, but she stayed busy by teaching English. After several months, they still had not been able to hire a regular babysitter as the local residents were reluctant to look after a foreign child; a trusting relationship had to be developed first.

Greg committed to staying until December 1993. However, by May he realized it would be difficult to leave at the end of the year. "I am starting to become really close to these folks and close to this project, so I don't know what will happen."

One of the benefits of having Dave back in Vermont was that communications between the two partner companies improved. When Dave was in Russia there was no one in Vermont who could answer questions or provide needed information, especially since Jeff was in Ithaca, New York and the communication lines ran between Petrozavodsk and Waterbury, Vermont. Upon his return to Vermont, Dave was given the new position of Iceverks coordinator. His functions were to source financing and funding programs as well as provide other administrative support. Jeff still held the position of director and coordinator of Iceverks.

East Meets West

Jeff was in the project for the adventure; he never really thought that they would be successfully producing and selling Ben & Jerry's ice cream in Russia. As he says even now: "This is one of the few successful, small company joint ventures in Russia that actually makes something, but it could disappear tomorrow. We have been in this from the beginning because it's an adventure." He saw his role as that of a coach. "The biggest input I offered from here was making the place stay focused on this opportunity as opposed to other opportunities, because there are so many potential opportunities and you have no sense of what is real and what is not real."

Greg also felt it was important for Iceverks to stay focused on the ice cream operations. One of the joint venture's commitments was to provide inexpensive ice cream, so when choices came up like buying ten tons of sugar from the Karelian government or buying souvenirs to ship to the United States, the sugar won. In the first year of Iceverks, Dave had tried a diversity of money-making endeavors, but Greg felt that since the joint venture was profitable through scoop shops and hard currency sales, it could stay more focused on just making ice cream in 1993.

The general and commercial directors had different opinions about issues such as marketing, promotion, and business diplomacy. There were some Russian laws and customs of which the Americans had no concept. Issues such as these were sometimes heavily debated by both parties.

According to Vasili, Ben & Jerry's had maintained the strategy from the beginning of investing as little as possible and allowing the people who committed themselves to Iceverks to find opportunities to survive. Vasili agreed that 1 percent of profits should be allocated to promoting peace, and he understood about ecological problems such as the Brazilian rainforest. He accepted these philosophies and respected the company for them. He also accepted the Ben & Jerry's practice of creating an image through word of mouth and social activities rather than allocating profits to advertising.

However, he did not agree that Iceverks should focus solely on ice cream production. He felt there were some projects which, although not immediately feasible, would ensure their future. One such project was in agriculture – milk production. This would solve their milk supply problem in Karelia. Without the cream, they would not be able to survive as a company. In Vermont, Ben & Jerry's did not face the same problem, so

Vasili felt the American partners did not understand the importance of such a project. His vision was to develop a small farming cooperative in Karelia, but Iceverks needed funding to achieve this. The Karelian politicians were also anxious to develop a small farm program and they envisioned a model similar to one developed in Finland. This would break down the monopoly held in Karelia by the large state-owned production farms. The farms had been privatized, so the state no longer provided the distribution channels; the initial investments made by the previous administration now had to be repaid by the new owners of the farms. The state did not have the funds required to start smaller farming enterprises unless these investments were repaid. There was a program in Vermont funded by businesses such as Ben & Jerry's to support small farming cooperatives such as Cabot Creamery. The funds were also used for exchanges of agricultural businesspeople and industry specialists between Vermont and Karelia. Vasili, Greg and Dave had been facilitating the arrangements for these exchanges. Vasili felt this program should also fund Karelian cooperatives.

Both Greg and Vasili felt that Ben & Jerry's had been sluggish in responding and reacting to issues in Russia such as the milk supply problems. The support – financial, managerial, and administrative – was getting better but was still slow. The Russians felt that the venture could fail as a result of sluggish decision making; there were many other companies gaining a presence in Russia at a rapid pace. Competition in ice cream production, both foreign and Russian, was going to grow quickly. Greg commented:

> It seems that Ben & Jerry's does not have a strategy for Russia. Perhaps now that Dave has been put into the position of full-time management of the project in Vermont, things will be better. Also, the joint venture is now making money and will perhaps gain more attention.

Serge wanted the business to grow; he was aggressive and entrepreneurial and eager to earn a profit. Vasili was methodical and cautious, he wanted the partnership to grow so that he could provide housing for the employees – his vision was a company town. Vasili really believed the employees were part of a family. This was an old Russian attitude but he took it to heart.

Jeff understood that the partners wanted to grow, that they wanted to expand the distribution of ice cream in Moscow and St. Petersburg. Yet, he was reluctant because of the corruption and the political situation in these large cities. He also believed in getting things right first before expanding. One of the dangers of not growing was that the Russian partners and the skilled Iceverks labor force would probably start their own business. Hence, Ben & Jerry's had potentially created their own competitors and Jeff had to decide how to deal with this. In the United States, Ben & Jerry's had made a big impact with the Iceverks project, creating a push from home to continue the growth as well. Jeff recognized that Ben & Jerry's small start and slow growth was a different approach from the Russians' preference for large endeavor and rapid growth and that this was a major source of tension between the parties.

On Jeff's upcoming trip to Russia, he planned to review the joint venture agreement with the partners to determine which objectives (see Exhibit 2) were being met and what improvements could be made. His view was that the joint venture should not expand further. For now he had to consider Dave's report and formulate an action plan.

EXHIBIT 2   Joint Venture Agreement Excerpts

Purpose and Goals

1.1   In keeping with the stated purposes . . . ICEVERKS is organized to:

A.   Produce, market and sell Ben & Jerry's superpremium ice cream in Karelia, U.S.S.R., and in other areas only with the express written consent of Ben & Jerry's, in its sole discretion.

B.   Establish retail outlets designed by Ben & Jerry's to sell ice cream and other products of the Joint Venture in Karelia, U.S.S.R. and in Leningrad [St. Petersburg] subject to paragraph 3.13.

C.   Produce, market and sell souvenirs, advertising articles, tee-shirts and other similar goods, which will help to promote the ice cream business and Soviet-American, mainly Karelia-Vermont, friendly relations.

D.   Trade with foreign countries, or in areas of the Soviet Union for hard currency, only with the express written consent of Ben & Jerry's, in accordance with applicable Soviet law.

E.   Trade agricultural and other products and goods, including nuts, honey, berries, mushrooms, bananas, chocolate, to promote the high quality of Ben & Jerry's ice cream produced in Karelia, U.S.S.R., in accordance with applicable Soviet law.

F.   Produce confectionary from ingredients used in Ben & Jerry's ice cream and other similar products, the quality of which must be approved by Ben & Jerry's.

G.   Organize its own dairy farms, or in cooperation with other dairy farms for self-supplying of milk and cream.

H.   Organize foreign tourism to help promote sister-state relations between Karelia and Vermont and advertising of the Joint Venture.

I.   Organize public affairs such as exhibition performances and others to help to promote the ice cream business and other activity of the Joint Venture.

J.   The Joint Venture may have a building construction affiliate that will be a separate business, and financially independent. They may perform construction work for the Joint Venture, as well as construction for other enterprises or private persons.

The Legal Status of the Joint Venture

3.13   Nothing herein shall prevent Ben & Jerry's from establishing additional manufacturing and retail outlets in the Soviet Union except that the Joint Venture will have exclusive rights in Karelia as long as the Joint Venture is operating the facilities correctly, producing Ben & Jerry's superpremium ice cream on a daily basis, and adhering to all aspects of this agreement. In addition, Ben & Jerry's grants the Joint Venture a two year option of opening additional retail scoop shop outlets in Leningrad [St. Petersburg] on terms mutually agreed to in writing by both parties.

Notes

1.   See Exhibit 3 for excerpts from the General Director's report.

2.   Dave Morse, "Report on Joint Venture activities," 1992.

3.   In early 1993, the City Council members in Karelia offered to lease a large grocery store to any tenant that would repair all the refrigeration equipment and other machinery. Serge rented the store and took Iceverks' maintenance crew of four to fix the equipment. They had everything repaired and running within one week.

4.   May 1993 rates which were 1 ruble = $.0014 Cdn. or $.0011 US.

5.   May 1993 prices.

6.   There were about 40 hard currency stores established in Moscow in May 1993.

7.   These figures include 1.8 million rubles in expenses for the purchase of a truck.

EXHIBIT 3   Excerpts from Report on Joint Venture Activities by Dave Morse, 1992

The Board of Directors of Iceverks has set the following goals for Iceverks.

1. To create an on-going concern which is flexible enough in its structure and methods of operation to remain profitable under the destabilizing influence of the current socio-political revolution occurring in the former Soviet Union.
2. To operate the business as a model of corporate social responsibility in terms of ecological impact, human relations, and community involvement.
3. To operate the business along the theme of furthering good will and friendship between the people of the C.I.S. and the U.S.A.
4. To maintain or exceed minimum standards of quality established by Ben & Jerry's Homemade Inc., i.e. to provide consistently high standards of excellence in terms of quality of products and of service rendered.
5. To sell super-premium ice cream at prices which are within the reach of average citizens.

Iceverks had a very difficult formative period, often requiring blind faith on the part of both sides for progress to be facilitated, and at times seen by one side or the other as a hopeless cause. The faith and efforts of the partners and employees of the business have begun to pay off with consistently positive financial and social results.

Plan for Growth in 1993

Summer demand in Petrozavodski for Iceverks's ice cream far exceeds our ability to service through our Palace store. Also, transportation to the store in Petrozavodsk is a serious problem for many residents. It may take a resident of outlying neighbourhoods over 40 minutes to come into town for a cone, and then another 40 minutes to get back home. This travel time becomes even more of a discouragement in winter given the cold, icy streets and long periods of darkness.

"Neighborhoods" tend to be laid out to accommodate about 35,000 to 50,000 people each. Petrozavodsk has five distinct neighborhoods outside its central city area. The report went on to map out potential expansion plans within the city and in St. Petersburg.

Operating Plan – Goals and Objectives for 1993

A. *Goal* – To establish a formal, fair process for the expenditure of ten percent of pre-tax profits in the sphere of charitable activities in Karelia.
   Problem – Iceverks's charitable activities are willy-nilly, often at the sole discretion of the co-directors or upon the informal advice of various employees. Thus we have a system of charitable activities which are sporadic and in which company members feel little formal involvement.
   Solution – There are several steps to be enacted in solving this problem. They are: (the report explained the need to declare profits on a quarterly basis; to formally authorize opening a special charitable activities sub-account; to develop a formal application process and locate organizations to assist; and to develop a process whereby the employee voted on which applications would be granted funds).
B. *Goal* – To develop a reliable delivery system for distribution of Iceverks products to Moscow and St. Petersburg.
   Problem – Intercity telephone communications are unreliable. Roads are in poor condition, especially in winter, making transportation difficult to obtain and subject to very high rates if outside trucking firms are employed. Iceverks representatives are needed in both the Moscow and St. Petersburg markets in order to maintain accounts, obtain new accounts, and assure proper handling of Iceverks products.

EXHIBIT 3 *(cont'd)*

Solution – This problem has a multistep solution, and many of the objectives to reach the goal have been accomplished. The objectives are: (the report indicated that an e-mail link had been established with the sales rep in Moscow; a system of controls, invoicing and reporting had been instituted; a truck purchased; 100,000 pint containers had been ordered; hard currency accounts had been opened by Iceverks in Petrobank, and in its corresponding account with Okobank in Helsinki for the receipt of billed accounts in Moscow and St. Petersburg; point of sale displays were being developed; and distribution sites being sought in Moscow and St. Petersburg).

Measure of success will be the steady increase of hard currency sales up to maintainable limits, and the long-term maintenance of accounts.

C. *Goal* – To develop a system of financial reporting to the American partners which is timely, reliable and accurate. (The report explained the incompatibility between Russian and American accounting practices and recommended some solutions.)
D. *Goal* – To work toward improving and tightening the relationship between Ben & Jerry's and Iceverks.
    Problem – Personnel at the two locations do not have an understanding of each other. Mutual respect and friendship between employees of Ben & Jerry's and Iceverks should be encouraged, as should mutual understanding of each other's culture and economy.
    Solution – Iceverks will lobby with upper management at Ben & Jerry's for the establishment of a system whereby two employees from each company are traded for periods of from one to two months. Each side would pay for air travel of its own employees (host family system), as well as reasonable salary for the guest employees. This would mean entry level pay for Russian guest employees, and average administrative salary for U.S. guest employees.

Iceverks is prepared to begin this program at any time, and can see no real negative financial considerations to stall the start-up of this program for the U.S. side. Costs for the program, providing that guest employees are given the real opportunity to work and contribute to the efforts of the host company and that host families are used, would be the cost of travel.

Measure of success will be largely subjective: improved understanding and respect between the two companies. Some objective results may be observed through the cross-seeding of innovations between the two companies, especially if we are able to work out a system whereby employees are traded according to their specialties.

E. *Goal* – To establish a formal, reliable and answerable support network for Iceverks (and possibly for other international filials) at Ben & Jerry's.
    Problem – At several critical junctures in its history, Iceverks has stood in danger of failure due to a lack of timely response or reliable action on the part of Ben & Jerry's. This is a sensitive issue, and difficult to broach diplomatically, but is of considerable importance, and must not be ignored if Iceverks is to continue as a good example of Ben & Jerry's positive commitment to improving international relations, and of Ben & Jerry's ability to function well and maintain its image and standards in international markets.
    Solution – It is proposed by the outgoing General Director and the incoming General Director in agreement with the U.S. Chairman of the Board of Iceverks, that a permanent 1/2 to full-time position be created at Ben & Jerry's. Responsibilities of this position would include liaison in the areas of timely communication, the organizing and expediting of materials ordered by Iceverks, the expediting of souvenirs (and potentially ingredients) imported to the U.S., and general oversight of Iceverks in the interest of Ben & Jerry's. The position would also oversee employee exchanges and any other matters of mutual concern between the two companies.

Costs would include salary, benefits, travel expenses and office expenses for the international liaison person.

EXHIBIT 3   (cont'd)

Measure of success would be improved response times, decreased frustrations for the upper management of both partners, decreased lag time between placement of orders and delivery of goods to Iceverks, and potentially, purchase by Ben & Jerry's of food ingredients for Russian theme ice cream flavours in quantities and at prices which would allow Iceverks to maintain profitable pint production.

Depending upon level of investment by Ben & Jerry's, measures of success could also include improved levels of understanding and liaison with its Israeli filial, as well as the possible turnaround of its Canadian operation.

Summary

The joint venture, Ben & Jerry's Vermont-Karelia Ice Cream, has established itself as a positive and welcomed presence in its chosen markets. The company has achieved its goals of providing fantastic ice cream at affordable prices for the citizens of Petrozavodsk and Kondopoga, Karelia. By its honest and respectful approach to the Karelian market, Ben & Jerry's has developed a reputation as an excellent American partner for Russian business.

Offers for partnerships with businesses in other republics of the C.I.S. have come from: Khirgizia, Lithuania, Azerbijan, Tatarstan; and from Moscow, St. Petersburg and Vladivostock. Iceverks has gone from a business which was quietly chuckled at by local businessmen during its initial stages, to a company which is widely renowned and respected as a model of development during its first five months of active production and sales.

Iceverks is serving not only as a possible paradigm for foreign businesses coming into the C.I.S., but also as an example to businessmen within the C.I.S. that honest incomes can be generated by the *production* of new goods, as opposed to the mere brokering of already produced items. Iceverks is in a fairly visible position, and its continued success will play a real, if small role in the successful transformation from command to market economy in the C.I.S.

As with any business, Iceverks has its areas of strength and critical areas for improvement. By drawing on available assets, and by continuing the development of an attitude of excellence in all aspects of its functioning, from the brewing of morning coffee up to the critical phases of its operations, Iceverks expects to keep improving as a business and to keep growing as an influence in Russia.

I feel that Ben & Jerry's has accomplished something very important here in Karelia. Everyone has learned a lot, and hopefully we'll be able to make the adjustments necessary to guarantee a solid future for Ben & Jerry's in Russia. With the continued commitment and involvement of all parties in this business, I believe that we can maintain a successful, two-part bottom line, Ben & Jerry's presence in Karelia.

At present, Russia is long on challenges and short on rewards for foreign businesses, but as time goes on I believe that the challenges will lessen and the rewards will increase. There are basic historical processes in motion which are practically irreversible, and these processes will lead to a democratic free market society in which these companies properly poised will be able to take advantage of opportunities for growth. With its human and material resources, shedding its shackles of militarism and participating in the world market, Russia stands to become one of the wealthiest nations on earth, and will constitute a market that should be considered as a component of Ben & Jerry's future.

CASE 19

○ ○

Valley Farms International (A)

Donald G. Simpson and Henry W. Lane

John Roberts, a university professor of finance, was trying to decide whether to change careers when he took a six-month leave of absence to see if he had an aptitude for international business. He accepted a short-term consulting job to conduct a feasibility study for a milk-processing plant in a country in the Middle East (which will be referred to as the "Republic").

At the time, the country's Regent was still in control, although opposition to his regime was becoming more open. When Roberts made his first trip in August, optimism for the Regent's regime was still high among Westerners and the local middle class. However, by his second trip in November, the situation was changing. There were uprisings and demonstrations, but it was considered only "temporary unrest."

Valley Farms, which was to be the supplier of cattle for the milk-processing plant project, was also supplying a small number of cattle for a demonstration farm. It had shipped 80 cattle in November, which arrived during Roberts' visit and during violent demonstrations against the Regent. The airport authorities would not allow the plane to be off-loaded, nor would they connect the power for the air conditioning. By morning, half the cattle had died before Roberts could free them. Crowds, out of control, were frantically attacking the Regent's military as well as women in Western clothing. Roberts was caught in the demonstration in a taxi. It was a frightening environment, and John commented that it was one of the few times he had been truly scared.

IVEY Professors Donald G. Simpson and Henry W. Lane prepared this case solely to provide material for class discussion. The authors do not intend to illustrate either effective or ineffective handling of a managerial situation. The authors may have disguised certain names and other identifying information to protect confidentiality.

The feasibility study concluded that the project was economically viable, but not feasible due to the deteriorating political conditions. During the course of the study, Roberts had made the acquaintance of the owner of Valley Farms, a dairy farm and cattle auction operation that was selling a lot of cattle to countries in South America. Since the milk plant project was not going to go forward, Roberts was easily persuaded to complete his leave of absence with Valley Farms and to take on the task of organizing its burgeoning domestic and international operation.

Roberts never returned to his life as a teacher. He remained with Valley Farms as Export Manager and assumed the responsibility of arranging financing for the export sales. Eventually, a decision was made to split the export and domestic operations, and Valley Farms International (VFI) was incorporated with Roberts as one of the partners. The export operations were driven by three aspects: demand by clients for cattle, which was cyclical; the ability of the client to obtain hard currency; and the ability of Valley Farms International to find successful local agents to represent its interests. Although Roberts was prepared to travel widely to close a deal, the operation depended to a significant degree on the work of local agents. Within a short time of the incorporation, VFI had withdrawn from the South American market as Brazil's holdings of foreign currency declined rapidly. Attention turned to North Africa and the Far East. Small sales were concluded with Morocco and for three years VFI made extensive sales to South Korea. This market was saturated by 1984 and sales ended quickly.

Amazingly, however, Roberts' attention had been drawn back to the Republic. One of his old contacts in that country advised him that the Ministry of Agriculture was in the market for cattle. Yogurt, a staple in the diet of the people of the Republic, requires substantial milk supplies, and the cattle population had been reduced during the worst days of the revolution. Supply sources were limited mainly to Western Europe or Canada.

In spite of the bad memories of his last involvement in the Republic, Roberts saw a good commercial opportunity. With only a general lead from his contact in the Republic as to where he might find the Ministry of Agriculture delegation, John headed off to Europe. He eventually found them in Holland and learned quickly that he was having to match wits with a group of committed young revolutionaries who behaved as if, and no doubt believed that, they were running the show and shaping the rules of the game now. Roberts' intuition, however, was that someone higher up behind the scenes was probably still pulling the strings. Two members of the group had been students in the United States and understood North Americans reasonably well; the others had not been to the United States. The leader of the group spoke no English and was a hardened revolutionary.

Following their discussions in the Netherlands, Roberts offered to fly the group of six to visit VFI and to pay their expenses while they surveyed the VFI operation. They accepted and came for a week. Roberts was kept busy showing them the dairy operation, the auction barns, and some of the farms from which cattle would be obtained and discussing the technical details of cattle selection, in which these people were not highly experienced. He also found himself discussing social responsibilities and the role of morality in one's life.

A deal was reached by the strangest of events. Throughout the week, Roberts had spent almost every waking hour touring, dining, and talking with the group in order to build trust. On Sunday, he told them he was going to church, and they were welcome to wait until his return or to go with him. To his surprise, they went and sat through the service and the informal coffee time discussion following. Rather than being offended by their exposure to a Christian service, these religious fundamentalists were pleased to know they were dealing with a religious person.

Shortly afterward, a $6 million contract was signed with the Ministry of Agriculture. Obtaining the contract had been much easier than Roberts had expected, but no doubt implementing the contract would provide some challenges. A four-person delegation from the Republic arrived to inspect the cattle, which were to be shipped in planeloads of 200 cattle each. Roberts arranged for them to inspect the cattle, which at this point, were being held at different farms in the area. They did not want to see the cattle, only the papers on the cattle. To Roberts, this was not a good sign. It suggested that they were going to be more concerned with all the paper technicalities than with viewing the animals to judge their quality.

On the first morning after a cursory examination of the papers, they rejected half the available cattle. Of the half tentatively approved, they visited one small group and rejected almost all of them. One of Roberts' partners, who had been viewing the behavior incredulously, finally lambasted them for their incompetence. The members of the delegation were deeply offended and said that they were leaving for home. It took Roberts three days to calm them down. Although they agreed to stay, the following days with them seriously tested Roberts' patience. Their behavior was wildly erratic. One day they seemed to be happy with the way things were going, and the next day they would be angry. Afterwards, Roberts reflected that part of the problem was that they were not confident in the job they were assigned. They took seriously the responsibility that had been given to them, but they were not sure how much to trust the word of this North American stranger.

The first shipment was made in June. A major problem developed when the cattle were tested upon arrival in the Republic. Inspectors claimed that most of the animals in the first shipment had TB and slaughtered them. Almost immediately, Roberts flew to the Republic with a veterinary doctor from the federal Department of Agriculture. Part of the problem was the manner in which the cattle were tested. Also, the cattle were being tested for a TB strain for which North Americans did not test. The testing had to be changed for future shipments. This was done and the shipments were completed to the satisfaction of both the customer and VFI, which made a good profit on the sales.

Two years later, Roberts was back in the Republic to sign a contract to deliver 10,000 cattle. As Roberts described it, negotiating in a revolutionary country was different from anything he had experienced before. The young revolutionaries who had taken over the bureaucracies were working hard to get the best deal for the government. With their bazaar-mentality upbringing, they were prepared to bargain for days at a time. Although these young bureaucrats seemed to believe honestly that they were in charge, Roberts realized that another system was at work. He needed information to understand what was going on. This information came from a contact he had made in pre-revolutionary times, a person with earlier Canadian connections who was Westernized, capitalistic, and motivated by money.

To get negotiations started, Roberts needed his help. For a price, this man claimed he would open the gate to the powerful force behind the scenes in the Republic, that Westerners came to call "the Invisible Hand." Although Roberts knew that according to law of the Republic, agents were forbidden, he understood also that all serious Western companies doing business in the country had a "contact." This man had had previous contacts with Canada and knew something about how North American firms operated. The first information he had offered Roberts was accurate and useful. He had informed VFI that the Ministry of Agriculture was back in the market for cattle, and that the purchasing team was in Europe. From that time on, their conversations had been sprinkled with references to the need for some payment. These discussions were confusing to Roberts, for it was never clear exactly for what he might be paying or even to whom the money would be going.

In convoluted discussions, spread over time, he had been led to believe that "the invisible hand needed to be fed." The inference was that these were powerful people who, of course, could not be identified. However, the clear message was that without their approval Roberts' negotiations would never be treated seriously. Eventually, a figure of $300 a head (approximately 10 percent of the contract price per head) was suggested as an appropriate fee. Payment would be made upon delivery.

Thus, Roberts found himself carrying on two sets of negotiations simultaneously . . . one with the buyer and one with his contact. With the latter, he kept asking himself: "What am I buying?" As he saw it, the payment might be necessary "to get into the game . . . to begin serious negotiations with the buyers." It would be an expensive admission fee and he wondered whether or not it would be worthwhile.

CASE **20**

○ ○

Building Products International – A Crisis Management Strategy (A)

Donna Everatt and Joe DiStefano

It was Friday, May 15 and Nick Alanzo, director of human resources, Asia-Pacific for Building Products International, had let his dinner grow cold during the closing banquet of the company's regional annual meeting in Korea. His mind was elsewhere, and he was exhausted with keeping up his attendance at various meetings and events during the three-day conference, while concurrently monitoring the situation in Jakarta, where BPI had extensive operations. In the preceding three days, Jakarta had erupted in "an orgy of violence," as the *Washington Post* referred to it. Hourly updates on CNN showed coverage of the violence as it unfolded and its aftermath – streets littered with the smoldering, burned-out carcasses of cars and buildings, plumes of black smoke emanating from the hardest-hit areas of the city, and frightened victims and residents panicking and fleeing from danger. These and other disturbing images were splashed on the front pages of the *Asian Wall Street Journal* and the *International Herald Tribune*.

Alanzo had lost his appetite as a result of several difficult decisions, including not only the myriad of issues involved in the logistics of a probable evacuation of BPI employees from Jakarta, but also the question of which employees to evacuate. BPI's three senior managers were expatriates (expats) whereas BPI's four middle managers were Indonesian citizens of Chinese origin. BPI's 15 supervisors were a mixture of Chinese and indigenous Indonesians (or 'Prebumi'). The remaining 228 employees were exclusively Prebumi (see Exhibit 3). Experts believed that expats and Indonesians of Chinese origin would be exposed to greater risk during the social strife in Indonesia than the Prebumi. Alanzo

IVEY
Donna Everatt prepared this case under the supervision of Professor Joe DiStefano solely to provide material for class discussion. The authors do not intend to illustrate either effective or ineffective handling of a managerial situation. The authors may have disguised certain names and other identifying information to protect confidentiality.

also had to decide whether to authorize the return to Jakarta of those managers attending to the conference who were demanding to return to Indonesia to protect their families. Complicating his decision was the fact that he was receiving inconsistent information as he scrambled to piece together an assessment of the situation in Jakarta. Alanzo had overseen the development of a crisis management strategy for Jakarta, and he knew that in its implementation, time was of the essence. He had to act fast if he wanted to protect BPI employees and their families during the worst rioting Asia had seen for decades.

Building Products International

Headquartered in Detroit, Building Products International (BPI) was a multinational conglomerate, operating in over 100 countries, with significant investments in multiple businesses in Indonesia, throughout Asia and the world. BPI's market strengths were its advanced technology and process knowledge, combined with its global manufacturing, service and marketing capabilities. In 1997, its bi-centennial year of operations, BPI saw a double-digit increase over its 1996 sales to US$2.7 billion, and an after-tax income of over US$175 million. A good portion of these revenues was generated from its Asian operations, of which Indonesia represented one of the top three divisions, in terms of revenues as well as size and scope of operations.

BPI's Indonesian operations consisted of the manufacture and distribution of tools and machinery for the construction industry. Manufacturing operations were concentrated in Indonesia's large urban centers, with the largest site located in the outskirts of Jakarta, where the vast majority of BPI's 250 employees worked. Over the years, an extensive sales and marketing network had been established in Indonesia, which distributed BPI products and after-sales service to far-flung regions throughout Indonesia's expansive area.

Given that its global operations were widely dispersed throughout so many countries, the company developed a highly decentralized organizational structure which became an integral part of the culture of the company. This decentralized structure allowed a high degree of local autonomy, which, in turn, resulted in increased operating flexibility and customer responsiveness throughout the many diverse regions where BPI operated (see Exhibit 1). However, this type of organizational structure posed certain challenges, which Alanzo explained:

> Sometimes, it's very hard to get people to work together – to coalesce. By and large, managers will not follow central mandates unless they originate from the top one or two executives in the organization. Thus, it takes a lot to get "buy-in" and to have everyone move together in the same direction unless you are clearly aligned with their local interests. Often, department heads can be myopic.

Regional Crisis Management at BPI

Responsibility for the development of a regional crisis management program fell under the jurisdiction of the human resources (HR) department. Alanzo had been BPI's director of human resources for the Asia-Pacific region for the last two years, after

EXHIBIT 1 BPI Organizational Chart

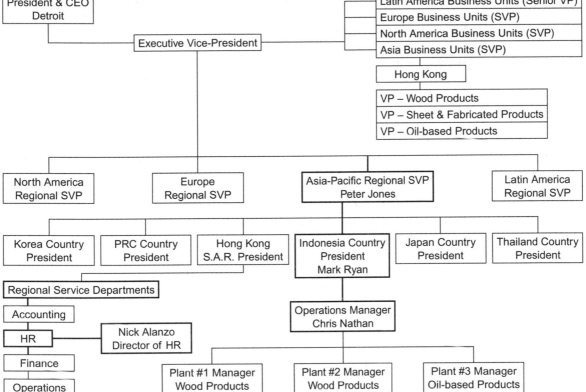

having held a similar position in the U.S. for several years. He had joined BPI directly after obtaining his MBA from an American university almost 15 years ago.

Alanzo explained that the development of a crisis management policy typically fell under the umbrella of HR responsibilities for several reasons. First, the HR division would be the most effective within the organization to coordinate a multi-divisional strategy. Moreover, much of the information that would be required during an emergency resided in HR files. Finally, it was necessary for someone at the regional office to take responsibility for the development of a crisis management program and it seemed, almost by default, that HR ended up with the responsibility. Alanzo had attended and spoken at several crisis management seminars over the past couple of years and had more knowledge on the subject than anyone else at BPI.

In the development of a regional crisis management plan, Alanzo recognized that, as part of doing business in Asia, it was necessary for BPI to assess country risk in the region on an annual basis. Alanzo described his analysis of the situation in Jakarta:

> Our concern with Indonesia began about a year and a half to two years ago. There were signs on the horizon – relatively small-scale student uprisings had occurred and there was

some question as to how the military would react and whether they were the harbinger of more widespread social unrest. We did some scenario planning and asked ourselves "What if" in Indonesia. That scenario planning included the development of a template for an evacuation plan, and we sat down with security experts and talked through how we should deal with a crisis, should one occur.

BPI had initiated discussions with the global security firm, Aegis International, based in Washington and it was decided that in the event of a crisis in Indonesia, BPI would call upon Aegis' services. Aegis had agreed to commit a complement of eight staff to BPI on a 24-hour a day basis during the crisis period. Under normal circumstances, Aegis would also supply BPI with monthly updates on various Southeast Asian countries where BPI operated and would augment these reports with flash updates if a particular region began to heat up. Their duties during a crisis management phase would include: management of a crisis center in the U.S.; operation of a crisis center on-site; convoy support of employees; liaison with local authorities; collection of tactical intelligence in the region; management of evacuation flights; coordination with BPI staff, employees and dependants; coordination of immigration issues; liaison with airport authorities; escort services for movements within the city; inspection of and security for residents; liaison with BPI HR and executive personnel in Hong Kong and the U.S.; management of local problems; and coordination of exit formalities.

The plan which BPI and Aegis developed addressed many of the logistical issues which were expected to arise during a crisis situation. It also covered detailed elements of a crisis management and evacuation plan ranging from how local managers were to brief their employees, to how to coordinate the transfer of expatriate managers and their dependants and guests to safe-houses, to how to secure the manufacturing site and transfer important documentation off-site. Alanzo explained the local manager's roles and responsibilities in the context of BPI's crisis management program:

> The plan was communicated to each of the local managers throughout the region so that they could understand the actions of central control during the crisis and would know what to expect. Moreover, in the event of interruptions to communication, the managers could implement the plan to the best of their ability, take "appropriate action," and make decisions according to a range of options as laid out in the plan, using their best judgment. Nonetheless, during periods of normal communication, the plan dictated that a local manager should acquiesce to commands from the person in charge in regional office, most likely myself.
>
> We did not fully develop a contingency plan for every possibility, as that would have added several layers of detail, requiring vast amounts of time and resources. The development of the initial crisis management template had proven to be a very time-consuming process for me and my staff, as it was in addition to our regular responsibilities.

According to Alanzo, although BPI had forged an initial relationship with Aegis and developed a thorough template for an evacuation plan, it "pretty much sat on the shelf, although we dusted it off from time to time and reminded our country managers of their roles and responsibilities as they related to the plan."

The Evacuation Plan

As was common with many crisis management plans, one of the first major components of the plan was to sequester BPI's expatriate staff into large foreign hotels, designated as "safe-houses." This was a common practice during a crisis and it made sense to Alanzo for several reasons. First, the foreign hotels offered a degree of security through professionally trained staff – families were more vulnerable in individual houses with little or no security. Army personnel could often be found stationed outside of large international hotels, because the local governments were concerned with keeping foreign businessmen and tourists safe since the local economy would suffer acutely once foreigners were harmed. According to Alanzo, high-rise hotels also had the psychological advantage of being imposing, more so than individual homes. Importantly, by congregating employees in a few select locations, they could be evacuated at a moment's notice. Also, it was easier to monitor their employees if they were contained in one area. Finally, Alanzo had hoped that a sense of togetherness would help the employees feel more secure and comfortable knowing they were not alone. During this process, the services of Aegis would be called upon, and they would coordinate the evacuation through their field operations and their headquarters in the U.S., using their established network throughout Indonesia.

The question of which employees were to be evacuated was an issue that would be decided on an individual basis. However, BPI policy dictated that, generally speaking, all expatriate managers and their dependants were to be evacuated. When to evacuate was another issue, and it was generally agreed that discussions with managers in the field were to be the determining factor, augmented with media reports as well as advisories from the U.S. embassy based in the city in question. Alanzo was fairly certain that under the terms of BPI's insurance contract, embassy advisories issued from each employee's embassy (that is, the American embassy for American employees) would justify BPI's evacuation of expatriate employees from Jakarta. Further, such advisories would activate coverage for the evacuation costs of the employees and their dependants and guests (see Exhibit 2). BPI, however, had a policy that allowed greater flexibility. Alanzo explained:

EXHIBIT 2 Endorsement – Emergency Repatriation and Relocation Extension

---

Issued to: Building Products International, Co.

This endorsement effective on 08/12/95 at 12:01 a.m. standard time for part of Certificate No. A91 – 298933352

It is agreed that Section IV – Item 4 (Additional Coverage) shall be amended to include Insured Losses hereinafter defined and sustained by the Named Insured or an Insured Person (RELATIVE or GUEST) in connection with EMERGENCY REPATRIATION and RELOCATION necessitated by:

I.   The officials of the RESIDENT COUNTRY issuing, for reasons other than medical, a recommendation that categories of persons which include insured persons, RELATIVES or GUESTS should leave the country in which such persons are temporarily resident and/or;

EXHIBIT **2** *(cont'd)*

II.   An insured person, RELATIVE or GUEST being expelled or declared "persona non grata" on the written authority of the recognized government of the country of temporary residence, and/or;

III. The wholesale seizure, confiscation or expropriation of the property, plant and equipment of the Named Insured.

For the purposes of this endorsement, Insured Losses shall be deemed to mean:

I.   Costs incurred by the Named Insured or an Insured Person, RELATIVE or GUEST for passage to the nearest place of safety or to the RESIDENT COUNTRY;

II.   Reasonable accommodation costs incurred by the Named Insured or an Insured Person, RELATIVE or GUEST;

III. Economy class fares on any licensed common carrier operating from a published timetable incurred by the Named Insured or an Insured Person, RELATIVE or GUEST for the RELOCATION of said individuals;

IV.   The SALARY paid by the Named Insured to an Insured Person at the rate in effect immediately prior to the INSURED EVENT. Said SALARY to be reimbursable for a maximum of three months following the EMERGENCY REPATRIATION, or until the date of RELOCATION, whichever comes first.

CONDITIONS

It is agreed that, as respects coverage provided hereunder for EMERGENCY REPATRIATION, the Named Insured and/or Insured Persons, RELATIVES or GUESTS shall be indemnified solely for the costs of transportation by economy fares unless unavailable, clearly impractical or unless travel by any other class of service is essential to ensure the safety of an Insured Person, RELATIVE or GUEST.

DEFINITIONS

For the purposes of this endorsement, the following definitions should apply:

I.   INSURED EVENT means the Emergency Repatriation and Relocation of an Insured Person, RELATIVE or GUEST.

II.   RELOCATION means the return of the Insured Person, RELATIVE or GUEST who has been the subject of an EMERGENCY REPATRIATION to the country from which he/she had been repatriated.

III. EMERGENCY REPATRIATION means the return of an Insured Person, RELATIVE or GUEST to his/her resident country.

IV.   RESIDENT COUNTRY means the country of which an Insured Person, RELATIVE or GUEST is a national.

EXCLUSIONS

It is further agreed that coverage shall not apply to Insured Losses sustained by the Named Insured or an Insured Person, RELATIVE or GUEST by the Named Insurer or an Insured Person, RELATIVE or GUEST attributable to:

I.   Violation by the Named Insured or an Insured Person, RELATIVE or GUEST of the laws and regulations of the country in which the EMERGENCY REPATRIATION and RELOCATION takes place.

II.   The failure of the Named Insured or Insured Person, RELATIVE or GUEST to properly procure and maintain immigration, work, residence or similar type visas, permits or documents.

III. A debt, insolvency, commercial failure or repossession of any property by a title-holder or any other financial cause.

IV.   The failure of the Named Insurer or Insured Person, RELATIVE or GUEST to honor any contractual obligations or bond or to adhere to any condition(s) in a license.

At any point, if an expatriate or members of his or her family stated their desire to depart prior to a perceived need on the part of regional headquarters in Hong Kong, company policy dictated that their wish was to be respected – without question.

In order to facilitate an emergency evacuation, the senior expatriate managers in each country had an emergency fund of several thousand U.S. dollars, kept in a safe place in their homes. However, Alanzo had concerns regarding travel documentation. BPI lacked specific details, such as passport numbers, for employees or any visiting relatives and friends, which might be required in an emergency to ensure a hassle-free exit from Indonesia.

Moreover, Alanzo had no way of knowing for certain whether the employees, their visiting friends or relatives had kept their visas current (which required renewal on a two-month basis). Generally, expats in Indonesia traveled outside the country on a regular basis (i.e., to BPI headquarters or to Hong Kong), permitting an additional two-month stay upon their return to Indonesia. If they had not kept their visas up to date, it could delay the departure of the entire group, or at the very least, result in increased stress for those having problems with immigration authorities – and for Alanzo.

By May, Alanzo's staff had begun the process of updating BPI employee's HR files with passport, immigration and visa information as well as emergency contact numbers. The impetus for Alanzo to begin this process was several flash reports from Aegis that a crisis in Indonesia could erupt given enough provocation. In 1997, the regional financial crisis provided just that. However, by the time the crisis erupted in Indonesia and the country became unstable, the employee files were far from complete.

The political and social climate in Indonesia began to heat up and Alanzo had been alerted by several flash reports from Aegis that a crisis could erupt given enough provocation. In 1997, the regional financial crisis provided just that.

The Political, Economic, and Social Situation in Indonesia – A Historical View

The shape of Indonesian politics last took a cataclysmic turn over 30 years ago in October 1965, following a leftist coup attempt against President Sukarno, the republic's first leader. This insurrection sparked the killing of tens of thousands of alleged communists by rightist gangs, reportedly encouraged by military commanders. By 1966, an estimated 500,000 people had been killed and President Sukarno was forced to transfer key political and military power to then General Suharto, who had led the military defeat of the leftist coup.

With the crucial backing of the military, Suharto advocated policies of economic rehabilitation and development, transforming Indonesia into highly diversified manufacturing and export-driven economy, from an inefficiently operating agricultural base. Per capita income rose from U.S.$70 in 1966, to almost U.S.$1,000 in 1996, with an accompanying decline in poverty rates to an estimated 11 percent, from 60 percent over the same period.

The 1980s saw further economic reforms and the liberalizing of trade and finance sectors in Indonesia, expanding foreign investment and deregulation. The resultant boom in trade and investment was reflected in the growth of Indonesia's economy, averaging 7 percent from 1985 to 1996. Suharto, his friends and family benefited greatly from this impressive economic expansion, controlling an empire estimated in the range of U.S.$20 billion, covering many industries including hotels, transportation, banks, and automobiles by 1998.

The country's economic prosperity, however, did little to improve the political freedoms of the average Indonesian. Over the '60s, Suharto's security forces routinely crushed uprisings by jailing activists for speaking out against the government, and rumors of torture and murder were substantiated with gruesome facts. Despite the corruption and human rights abuses, Suharto maintained his power for over three decades.

However, the President's grip began to loosen with Thailand's devaluation of the baht in July 1997, causing the value of the rupiah to drop precipitously – almost 80 percent. Foreign investors fled and the domestic bankruptcy rate increased dramatically. As with many other regional economies, weaknesses in Indonesia's banks were exposed, and 16 had their operations suspended. Indonesia's food distribution system was inefficient, meaning that the majority of food had to be imported, and even then it was difficult and expensive to get food to outlying areas or avoid the black market activities in the urban centers.

As the country negotiated with the International Monetary Fund (IMF) over the terms of its U.S.$43 billion bailout package in early 1998, riots began to erupt over rising food and basic commodity prices, gradually intensifying despite police efforts to quell them.

In March 1998, Suharto was re-elected to a seventh term by the People's Consultative Assembly, a legislative body largely assembled by the President himself, spiked with key military figures. Student protests ensued and calls for Suharto to relinquish his post grew louder by the day. By May, the situation had turned violent. No longer were the gatherings comprised of students calling for reform; by that time, starving Indonesians, with nothing to lose, began a wave of rioting and looting which reached levels of violence not seen in Indonesia for several decades. The ethnic Chinese in Indonesia were the primary targets of the looting and violence.

The Ethnic Chinese in Indonesia

Although the ethnic Chinese comprised only 3 percent of Indonesia's population, they were a key driver of the Indonesia economy. The Chinese had been a part of Indonesia's history for several centuries, as they fled China to escape persecution and established a niche for themselves as traders and entrepreneurs. When the Dutch arrived in Indonesia 400 years ago, they established a semi-apartheid state that segregated the population into three groups – the Europeans, the foreign Orientals, and the indigenous. The Dutch employed a selected group of Chinese as trading partners, creating the foundation of patronage that many believed still existed in 1998. The few wealthy Chinese who had become extremely rich through their close association and system of patronage with the Suharto government, his ministers and generals, were often accused by indigenous Indonesians of using Indonesia to get rich while investing their capital abroad. Indonesians did not always make a distinction between this select group of wealthy Chinese owners, and the shopkeepers on the streets of Jakarta who held a commanding control of the retail sector. Although the ethnic Chinese were a minority in Indonesia, their business activities were an integral part of Indonesia's middle class.

This economic dominance continued despite affirmative action and various government programs which had restricted the rights of the Chinese minority for decades. Chinese-language reading materials and characters were banned in Indonesia, as were public celebrations of the Chinese New Year. Moreover, Chinese were not permitted to be involved in politics in Indonesia. Their employment in the civil service was restricted, as was their entrance to Indonesian universities. Although they were free to practice their religion – Christianity or Buddhism – religion acted to further separate the ethnic Chinese from Prebumis (or native Indonesians). Indonesia was the largest Muslim nation in the world – almost 90 percent of Indonesians were Muslim.

The dominance of a few dozen ethnic Chinese families who had amassed incredible wealth through the system of patronage with the Suharto government had resulted in a public image of the ethnic Chinese as rich opportunists. Moreover, by 1998, the ethnic Chinese were Indonesia's most powerful economic group, controlling about 70 percent of Indonesia's private wealth and much of its retail and banking sectors. With ever-increasing ranks of Indonesians continuing to fall below the poverty line and several thousand losing their jobs each day, the temptation to use the Chinese as scapegoats was growing to ever more dangerous levels.

The First Signs of Trouble

By early May, Alanzo was receiving weekly updates, augmented with flash reports from Aegis, regarding the situation in Indonesia and had discussed the information with several managers in the field. By May 6, Alanzo became aware of the most dramatic wave of violence seen in the past few months, with riots and looting breaking out in Medan, in Northern Indonesia, and tens of thousands of students demonstrating throughout the country. According to the news reports Alanzo was receiving, IMF-dictated price increases – part of a recovery program which ended subsidies for basic commodities mandated as a condition of the bailout funds – were the impetus for the protests. Indonesians saw the price of gasoline rise 70 percent in one day, accompanied by dramatic increases in the price of electricity and transportation. These austerity measures, which harshly affected the average Indonesian, were not the type of "economic reform" that the students had been calling for – they considered the abolishing of the corruption, collusion, and nepotism which characterized the Suharto regime a more appropriate response to the country's woes. Alanzo believed at this point that the economic hardship imposed by these measures meant that the protests would swiftly gain momentum. Nonetheless, he was assured by his managers in the field that the media were "over-reacting" and that the demonstrations that day, although on a larger scale, were similar to many seen in the past in Indonesia. Alanzo was nonetheless concerned about the situation and questioned whether the field managers had a sense of false confidence due to their experience in Jakarta, resulting in a sense of complacency. By mid-May, Alanzo's fears seemed much more justified.

Three Days in May

Wednesday May 13 – 2:40 p.m.

Alanzo had just arrived in Korea for BPI's annual regional meeting. The meeting was attended by all heads of business units and regional senior executives, including the president and the CFO of Asia-Pacific, as well as a number of executives from the U.S. headquarters, including BPI's COO.

Over lunch, Alanzo had heard rumors from other attendees at the conference that Jakarta was in a state of emergency. Although over recent weeks police had fired rubber bullets and tear gas into crowds, apparently live rounds of ammunition were now being used in a more heavy-handed crack-down by Suharto's security forces and the military. This resulted in the first student deaths in nearly three months of demonstrations on campuses across the country. Alanzo heard that this bloody outbreak of violence resulted in the death of at least six students and the wounding of dozens more. He also heard reports that the demonstrations had involved crowds of over 5,000 but when he contacted managers in the field, he was still reassured that there was no clear and present danger to BPI employees who avoided the "isolated insurrections."

Given Alanzo's familiarity with operations throughout Indonesia, as well as his exposure to crisis management planning, BPI's executive group in Korea came to the consensus that Alanzo should be responsible during the crisis for closely monitoring the situation, and responding as he felt the situation warranted. This was a contentious issue as Mark Ryan, the country president for Indonesia, as well as his direct subordinate, Chris Nathan, reported to Peter Jones, the Asia-Pacific regional SVP (see Exhibit 1). Alanzo understood the need to show a great degree of diplomacy and protect the established and entrenched normal reporting lines. Therefore, although he was in charge, he was very careful to solicit opinions and encourage the participation of other managers in the decision-making process.

Alanzo's first step was to initiate communications with Chuck Conrad, his contact at Aegis. Conrad and Alanzo immediately began planning for an operations control center in Jakarta, to be staffed 24 hours a day by several Aegis employees.

Although the afternoon business reviews at the conference were conducted as planned, Alanzo was outside the conference rooms on his cell phone for the majority of the meetings, attempting to gather information from managers in the field, the U.S. Embassy and Conrad, with a view to piecing together an understanding of the events as they unfolded. Alanzo formally disseminated a summary of this information immediately to the management complement still within Indonesia, to the managers that had gathered at the conference, and to BPI's head office in Detroit.

Alanzo noted that "the informal communications were the most complicated and time-consuming." Later that night, Alanzo's room in the hotel had become an operation control center. He fielded calls from every stakeholder in each region, including the regional managers in Korea, the regional president, the manager on-site in Jakarta, the wives in Jakarta of the managers in Korea who wanted to get in touch with their husbands (and vice versa), the U.S. head office, Aegis' staff, and the U.S. embassy in Jakarta.

EXHIBIT 3   Personnel profiles

Name	Ethnicity	Nationality	Position
Indonesian Senior Managers*:			
Mark Ryan	N/A	American	Country Manager
Chris Nathan	British	British	Operations Manager
Christopher Wright	Australian	Australian	Purchasing Manager
Field Managers:			
Stan Lin	Chinese	Indonesian	Personnel Manager
Yang Chan	Chinese	Indonesian	Head of Forestry Division
2 Plant Managers	Chinese	Indonesian	Plant managers, Plants A & B
Supervisors:			
Wei Fong	Chinese	People's Republic of China	Supervisor
Alan Li	Chinese	Indonesian	Supervisor
4 supervisors	Chinese	Indonesian	Various supervisory capacities throughout BPI Indonesian operations
9 supervisors	Indonesian	Indonesian	Various supervisory capacities throughout BPI Indonesian operations
Workers:			
228 employees	Indonesian	Indonesian	Factory and forestry workers crews, support services, ground workers, maintenance crews, and assistants to supervisors and managers

* (all in attendance at the annual global conference in Singapore)

As his research uncovered the serious and swift nature of the unfolding events in Jakarta and the speed with which they could deteriorate, Alanzo began to appreciate the magnitude of the situation. As he retired for evening, he found it difficult to sleep as his mind kept running to the myriad of organizational details that would be required over the next few days with the prospect of evacuation of several BPI employees and their families.

Thursday, May 14 – 6:00 a.m.

After a disturbed night of half-sleep, Alanzo awoke to a call from Conrad alerting him of a U.S. Embassy advisory indicating that the 8,000 Americans living in Jakarta, as well as those in Surabaya, Indonesia's second-largest city, should "depart the country as soon as possible" and that the U.S. Pacific Command had begun making plans for an emergency military evacuation of U.S. citizens which they were prepared to invoke should the situation further deteriorate. According to Conrad, a flotilla of U.S. warships was positioned off the coast of Thailand and was standing by to assist. According to Conrad, this meant that the situation in Jakarta had deteriorated significantly. He explained:

Aegis developed evacuation plans separate from the Embassy evacuation plan. This is because the Embassy must take into consideration the political implications and potential to further destabilize the region by ordering an evacuation. An evacuation of the U.S. Embassy signals that the current government is no longer viable, or can't handle the situation. Therefore, an Embassy will delay the decision to evacuate as long as possible. We generally use the Embassy plan for contingency purposes only.

While drinking several cups of strong black coffee, Alanzo poured over Associated Press reports which reported that major U.S. companies in Indonesia had begun moving their expatriate employees into downtown hotels for possible evacuation. This prompted Alanzo to make similar arrangements for expatriate employees and their families (see Exhibit 3). Aegis' team in Jakarta planned to escort them to an internationally managed hotel in downtown Jakarta.

Alanzo was somewhat relieved that he had taken this step. Throughout the day, he heard steady reports from Conrad and various media sources that Jakarta had erupted in a series of violent riots, resulting in the destruction of hundreds of stores, malls, and offices, sending panic-stricken residents fleeing for the airport or the relative safety of downtown hotels.

To augment the media reports, Alanzo was on the phone all day with Ryan and Aegis control center. He also attempted to contact field managers, although he often was very frustrated by his efforts to reach them because they were busy attempting to operate their business units in an environment of anarchy. When he did reach them, he was somewhat surprised by their complacency in the face of what Alanzo considered to be a clear and present danger – they were not overly concerned with the events in Jakarta, and felt that they were at a safe distance outside Jakarta, sufficient to avoid the worst of the chaos. Thus, they stayed on-site and prepared to suspend and secure operations should the need arise, while reassuring Alanzo that there was little to be overly concerned with. They did, however, concede that the Chinese staff members would be wise to adopt a low profile over the next few days.

In the meantime, some of the spouses who were sharing hotel rooms had been discussing the situation in Jakarta. These discussions, augmented by various disturbing rumors circulating throughout expatriate informal communication networks in Jakarta, had increased their sense of urgency for evacuation. They were conveying these concerns to their husbands in Korea, which meant that the pressure to act was increasing and Alanzo felt pressed from every direction.

Although no one was able at that point to establish the death toll in Jakarta, Alanzo had heard reports from witnesses that the Chinatown section in North Jakarta was particularly devastated. This prompted businesses in other parts of the city to erect signs outside of their businesses reading "Prebumi" to avoid being mistaken for a Chinese business. Alanzo watched the news that night with great anxiety as he listened to reports of closure of schools and businesses, disrupted transportation services, and delays and cancellations at the airport due to mass rioting along the main artery to the airport. Alanzo had heard reports of victims, whose cars had been stopped by the rioting crowds on the way to the airport, pulled from their vehicles and beaten and robbed. Chinese and expatriates were the primary targets as they were the wealthy segments of the population and the most likely to be fleeing. In newscasts from Jakarta, plumes of black

EXHIBIT **4** Initial Aegis Estimate of Indonesian Repatriation Project

Expense	Amount (US$)
Fees incurred to activate Jakarta evacuation plan	4,600
Professional services fee*	35,000
Hotel (safe-house accommodation)	6,790
Air tickets	12,750
Meals	690
Land travel	372
Security patrols at residence	980
Exit fees and immigration facilitation	900
Air travel incurred by Aegis staff	2,530
Telephone, fax (local and international)	874
Miscellaneous	2,500
Total	**67,986**

* professional services including: management and staffing of regional crisis center and U.S.-based coordination; convoy support of employees within Jakarta; liaison with local authorities; coordination of evacuation flight services; security escorts; liaison with BPI employees in the field, at the regional and head offices; local emergency supplies coordination; etc.

N.B. Insurance coverage was "first dollar" coverage (i.e., not deductible), with the expectation that most expenses as listed would be covered fully.

smoke could be seen rising from several sections of the city which looked as if it was being shelled.

By Thursday night, all expatriate BPI employees and their families had been moved from their respective homes, and were ensconced in the hotel. However, this gave Alanzo only partial relief. As he watched CNN's coverage of Thursday's events on the nightly news, Alanzo became aware that the prospect of evacuating these, and perhaps other BPI employees, was quickly becoming a reality. This kept him up late into the night, but by 3:00 a.m., he lay down to try to get some rest.

Friday May 16 – 11:50 a.m.

Friday morning, with the annual meeting coming to an end, Alanzo made his return booking for the first flight to Hong Kong the next morning. By this point, he had made the decision to begin with the evacuation of various BPI staff, but some difficult issues remained.

Beyond the challenging logistical decisions such as how exactly the employees should be evacuated, Alanzo felt the burden of making other difficult decisions, such as whom to evacuate, and whether to facilitate the re-entry of the managers who wished to return to Jakarta to aid their families. During the past several days, several of the expatriates and Chinese management with Alanzo in Korea who had family in Jakarta made requests of Alanzo to arrange for their return to their families. It was clear that those in Indonesia were in great danger and naturally the managers wanted to return, regardless of the personal danger they would face. Alanzo could certainly understand their desire to return – he himself had a wife and two young children. However, in his opinion, logic was against authorizing their return. First, personal danger to the managers would be great and likely increasing. Moreover, their return would compound the organizational logistics of the evacuation exponentially, further adding to the risks to their families. However, many of the managers had been in contact with their Indonesian managers, and the field reports they were receiving portrayed a much less serious perspective than that conveyed through the media. Thus, they were clamoring to be let back in.

Alanzo also faced other difficult decisions, such as to whom to provide emergency assistance. He thought to himself:

> Should I offer safe refuge for all of BPI's 250 employees in Indonesia? If so, the cost could be enormous. And who would end up paying those costs? Would it come from the unit's budget, regional expense budget, or even that of BPI general emergency fund? Moreover, the ramifications of offering refuge to some employees and not others could be enormous, both in terms of morale and morality.
>
> Even if I were to decide that only certain employees were to be offered refuge, which factors should serve as the basis for my decision? An employee's years of service? Their service record? Their ethnicity? Their position seemed like a good place to start but where do I draw the line? Should I evacuate only those who explicitly stated their desire to leave? My own moral perspective impacts my decision, of course, but I also have to consider my actions and their implications as a director of BPI. I'm caught between a rock and hard place, but someone has to make the difficult decisions in this situation. I've taken on that responsibility and I accept that. The most important thing at this point is the safety of BPI employees. The other stuff I can work out later.

The events of the past few days had so consumed Alanzo that he was exhausted by the time Friday's closing banquet started. He excused himself right after dinner, and returned to his hotel room to pack for his return to Hong Kong the following day. He knew he would need a good night's sleep to get the strength to face several difficult decisions which he had to make. During the night, Alanzo slept fitfully, as he woke up and jotted down more notes in preparation for the next day.

CASE **21**

○ ○

Citibank Mexico Team: The Salinas Accounts[1]

Henry W. Lane and David T. A. Wesley

Mexico was . . . a country of smoke and mirrors, where yesterday's heroes are today's villains and today's champions of justice may be tomorrow's crooks.

Andres Oppenheimer – Senior Correspondent, *Miami Herald*[2]

On July 4, 1995, Amy Elliott, head of Citibank's Mexico Team, had just returned from Switzerland, where Swiss narcotics agents were encouraging her to lay a trap for the wife of one of her clients,[3] Raul Salinas, who had been arrested in Mexico a few months earlier on charges of murder, illegal enrichment and laundering money for the Mexican drug cartel.

The fate of one of her former employees, who had recently been sentenced to ten years imprisonment for managing the account of a convicted money launderer, provided food for thought. If she cooperated with narcotics agents, perhaps she could avoid the same fate. On the other hand, she had to consider her obligation to her client, who, as the brother of Mexico's most popular president in recent history, was believed by some to have been falsely accused by his political enemies. Another consideration was whether, by cooperating with authorities, Citibank could be liable for violating Swiss bank secrecy laws.[4]

Company Profile

Citibank was established in 1812, and by the end of the nineteenth century had grown to become the largest bank in the United States, and the first to establish a foreign

David T. A. Wesley prepared this case under the supervision of Professor Henry W. Lane solely to provide material for class discussion. The authors do not intend to illustrate either effective or ineffective handling of a managerial situation. The authors may have disguised certain names and other identifying information to protect confidentiality.

trading department. In 1914 the bank established its first overseas office in Buenos Aires, Argentina, and shortly thereafter began to aggressively expand across South America and Asia. In 1929, Citibank became the largest bank in the world.

By the early 1990s, Citibank had grown to more than 3,400 branches in 100 countries, and was considered the world's most global bank. Of the company's 90,000 employees, more than 50,000 resided outside the United States.

In Mexico, Citibank had more than 65 years of history, and was the only foreign bank permitted to operate in that country following the nationalization of Mexico's banks in 1982. In the 1990s, more than 20 percent of the bank's revenues came from Latin America.

The Mexico Team

Amelia Grovas Elliott, a Cuban American, began working for Citibank in 1967. In 1983 she became head of the bank's Mexico Team, consisting of ten private bankers, at Citibank's New York office. The Mexico Team specifically sought out clients with a net worth of at least $5 million and at least $1 million of available liquid assets to invest with the bank. In the early 1990s, the Team managed accounts for about 250 Mexican clients.

Private banking services included deposit taking, mutual fund investing, personal trust, estate administration, funds transfers, and establishing offshore accounts and trusts. Service was very personal. Bankers typically knew their clients well and understood their specific needs. Elliott explained:

> We visit our clients 10 to 12 times a year in their country. They come back three or four times to New York. We see our clients a lot. It's obviously a growing kind of thing and not just in knowing your customer, but making sure you know what's going on. Because the relationship can grow deeper the more you know the person, we go to their homes, visit their family, go to their business, and remember birthdays. It just increases the depth.[5]

Raul Salinas

On May 11, 1992, Elliott received a phone call from the Mexican Minister of Agriculture, Carlos Hank Rhon, one of the wealthiest men in Mexico and a long-standing client of Citibank. He wished to arrange a meeting between Elliott and Raul Salinas, brother of Mexican President and Harvard educated economist, Carlos Salinas. Salinas was in need of private banking services, and the agriculture minister had recommended Citibank.

John Reed, CEO of Citibank, was a personal friend of President Carlos Salinas, and Citibank had been working for some time to further its Mexican operations.[6] Securing the account of the president's brother could only serve to advance the Mexico Team's profile and possibly Elliott's career.

Later in the week, Salinas flew to New York to discuss his financial needs. There, Salinas stated that he had recently sold a construction company and needed a bank to provide confidential investment of the proceeds. Salinas explained:

> I do not want anyone in Mexico to know that I am moving large amounts of money out of the country. If the public finds out that I am not reinvesting the money in Mexico, it could harm my brother's political career.[7]

As such, confidentiality was a prime consideration. Rhon told Salinas that he believed Citibank could provide the type of confidentiality that Salinas was seeking. Apparently, Salinas was assured that indeed it could.

Normally when new accounts were opened, the bank followed strict procedures that made the process somewhat bureaucratic. Elliott explained:

> The relationship manager would be discussing the prospective client with his or her supervisor throughout the entire process. It's a complex kind of sale, so it has a fairly long lead-time, especially if you're not physically located in Mexico.[8]

In order to smooth the way as much as possible for Salinas, bank references and background checks were waived. Citibank policy allowed for such exceptions. In Salinas' case the waiver was allowed on grounds that he was a "known client and referred by a very valuable client of long standing." In most cases bank references did not provide useful information anyway and were viewed as a mere formality. Furthermore, this was the president's brother. Elliott noted:

> You can trust some Mexican officials, some not. If you get to know them, it's fairly obvious if they can be trusted. Public figures in Mexico are talked about a great deal. Generally speaking, it's a fairly small and tight upper crust.[9]

On May 26, 1992, Salinas was approved as a Citibank client. A chequing account was opened at the New York office under the name of his accountant, Juan Guillermo Gomez Gutierrez.

The Salinas Accounts

An "investment optimization" strategy had to be devised that would both conceal the identity of the account holder and produce a superior return on investment. In order to avoid a potential information leak, nobody at Citibank Mexico would be advised about the accounts.

Deposits made in Mexico would be done in the name of Salinas' fiancée, Patricia Rios Castañon. Rios delivered cheques, denominated in pesos, of between US$3 million and $5 million. The teller delivered the cheques, which were made payable to Citibank, to a manager at the branch, who then wired the money to New York.

Five corporations were opened in the Cayman Islands on behalf of Salinas. The main corporation was Trocca Private Investment Company, and the others were created to act as shareholders and directors of Trocca (see Exhibit 1). The principal shareholder, Tyler Ltd., received the transferred funds in a concentration account in New York where they were converted from Mexican pesos to U.S. dollars. The concentration account was designed as a transfer point of funds wired from Mexico to offshore corporations, and allowed the holder to mix both personal and business deposits in one

EXHIBIT 1 Trocca and Related Companies

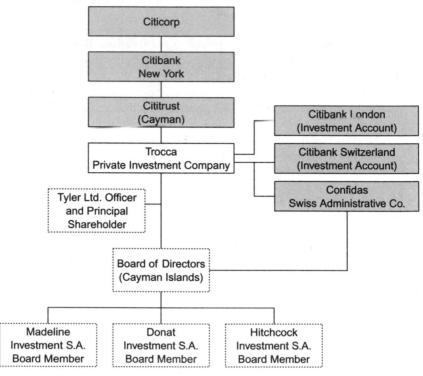

Source: U.S. General Accounting Office.

account. The only record that showed Salinas as the owner of the company was held in Cayman where bank secrecy laws could protect his identity.

From Trocca, funds were transferred to Citibank Switzerland. Salinas was assured that, while the scheme was complicated, it provided the best protection of his identity. She explained:

> By using a corporation in Cayman as the account holder, the source of ownership will be concealed from people who have no reason to know.
>
> The reason for the account in Switzerland is their very strict secrecy laws. A Swiss banker can be put in jail if they divulge the confidentiality of the name of an account.[10]

Salinas understood the value of the Swiss accounts. He had visited Switzerland on many occasions to take part in equestrian competitions in Lucerne, and to visit his two nephews who were attending school there. Salinas was well aware of Switzerland's international reputation for secrecy, and since his identity would be held in confidence, he could have direct contact with the banks and bankers involved.

In Switzerland, funds were deposited at various banks, including Citibank Zurich, Banque Pictet and Julius Baer Bank. Trocca, not Salinas, officially held the funds at Citibank Zurich. Funds were transferred back and forth between Zurich and London in order to take advantage of higher money market rates in the United Kingdom. Citibank London was not made aware that Salinas was the beneficial owner of the account.

Over the next two years, a total of $100 million was transferred through Citibank to accounts in Switzerland. Patricia Rios Castañon, who, in 1993, became Salinas' third wife, handled most of the transactions. A large portion was transferred on November 30, 1994, the last day of Carlos Salinas' presidency.

Offshore Banking Secrecy

While the United States had its own bank secrecy laws, these laws provided less protection than most offshore jurisdictions (see Exhibit 2). Federal law required that banks report all financial transactions above $10,000 to the Internal Revenue Service (IRS). If the bank deemed any transaction to be suspicious in nature, the bank was also required to contact the Criminal Investigation Unit of the IRS. As a result of these reporting requirements, banks operating in the United States were exempted from liability to their customers for reporting account information, even without customer consent.[11]

Investors have used the services of offshore banking in jurisdictions that provided greater protection of privacy, as well as tax advantages and limited legal liability. U.S.

EXHIBIT 2   Relevant Bank Secrecy Laws: United States*

The Right to Financial Privacy Act of 1978

. . . as amended, the Privacy Act provides that it shall not preclude any financial institution, or any officer, employee, or agent of a financial institution from notifying a government authority that such institution, or officer, or employee, or agent has information that may be relevant to a possible violation of any statute or regulation. Such information may include only the name or other identifying information concerning any individual or account and the nature of any suspected illegal activity.

The Bank Secrecy Act and the Currency and Foreign Transactions Reporting Act, 1970

. . . all domestic and foreign currency transactions of more than US$10,000 must be reported within 15 days.

. . . Financial institutions must file a Currency Transaction Report (CTR) for each deposit, withdrawal, exchange of currency, or other payment of transfer, by, through, or to such financial institution which involves a transaction of currency of more than $10,000.

. . . the Report of International Transportation of Currency or Monetary Instruments (CMIR). Every person or entity must file a CMIR who physically transports, mails, or ships, or causes to be physically transported, mailed, or shipped, currency or other monetary instruments in an aggregate amount exceeding $10,000 on any one occasion.

. . . financial institutions are required to maintain for a five-year period, a variety of records, such as copies of signature cards, bank statements, and checks drawn for more than US$100.

Violation of the Bank Secrecy Act provides for jail terms up to 10 years and fines from US$1,000 to US$500,000.

---

* Campbell, D., *International Bank Secrecy*, Sweet and Maxwell, London, 1992.

banks used offshore branches to hold information about the beneficial owner of accounts, where bank secrecy laws protected the client from disclosure. This provided a competitive advantage that allowed banks with offshore branches to attract clients who did not wish banking regulators and others to know about their substantial wealth. While such accounts were usually used for legitimate and legal purposes such as estate planning, tax shelters and reduced legal liability, they have also attracted those engaged in illegal activity, such as money laundering, investment fraud and tax evasion.

The main instrument for concealing wealth was the Private Investment Company (PIC). These were shell companies registered by banks in the offshore jurisdictions and used solely to hold the funds of clients. PICs, since they were not in the client's name, could be used to transfer funds in any country of the world without drawing the attention of regulators or others to the beneficial owner. Information about the beneficial owner was held secretly and safely in the offshore branch.

While many offshore jurisdictions provided the aforementioned benefits, the U.S. General Accounting Office[12] identified nine where U.S. bank subsidiaries and branches held substantial accounts (in excess of $1 billion). These were the Bahamas, Bahrain, the Cayman Islands, the Channel Islands, Hong Kong, Luxembourg, Panama, Singapore and Switzerland.

All of these locations, with the exception of Bahrain, had regulations that required the reporting of suspicious transactions to local authorities. And, in most jurisdictions, U.S. law enforcement could gain access to individual accounts to investigate certain criminal acts. Only Bahrain, Luxembourg and Singapore did not allow access for these purposes. On the other side, without a legal mandate to provide information, bankers could face fines or imprisonment for violating secrecy laws in several jurisdictions, including the Cayman Islands and Switzerland (see Exhibits 3 and 4). Furthermore, Switzerland allowed for third parties to take civil action against banks, and as a result, many bank officials expressed concern over the liability to their banks of breaching confidentiality in these jurisdictions.[13]

A Swiss judge had the power to overturn secrecy obligations for the purpose of criminal investigations conducted in Switzerland. Under most conditions, the same was true for crimes committed outside of Switzerland, provided that international law enforcement officials formally requested assistance, and the crime was also considered illegal in Switzerland (such as drug trafficking). A 1977 treaty signed between Switzerland and the United States allowed for co-operation between these countries, even when the crime was not considered illegal in Switzerland.[14]

U.S. banking regulators relied heavily on self-monitoring by banks to prevent offshore accounts from being used for illegal purposes. A "know your customer" (KYC) policy was considered the most effective of the self-monitoring measures implemented by the banks. Most banks stipulated under KYC policy that clients had to submit bank references and other information related to the origin of their wealth. Banks also monitored accounts for unusual or large transactions that could be a sign of illegal activity. However, a study by the Federal Reserve Bank of New York concluded that "in general . . . client profiles contained little or no documentation on the client's background, source of wealth, expected account activity, and client contacts and visits by bank representatives,"[15] even though such information was believed to be critical in preventing the illegal use of offshore accounts.

EXHIBIT 3 Relevant Bank Secrecy Laws: Cayman Islands*

Banks and Trusts Companies Law, 1989

. . . provides for the preservation of secrecy on the part of the Inspector of Banks and Trust Companies and any person authorized to assist him in his functions.

It prohibits the disclosure of any information, by the Inspector or his staff, of the affairs of a licensee or any customer of a licensee and provides a penalty of a fine not exceeding CI $10,000, or a term of imprisonment not exceeding one year, or both for contravention of this law.

Confidential Relationships Law, 1976

. . . as amended, provides that, if any person in possession of confidential information, however obtained, divulges it or attempts, offers, or threatens to divulge it to any person not entitled to possession, or who willfully obtains or attempts to obtain confidential information is guilty of an offense and is liable on summary conviction to a fine not exceeding CI $5,000, or for imprisonment of a term not exceeding two years, or both.

In addition, where such person solicits such information for himself or another for reward or being a professional person entrusted with such information, the above mentioned penalties are doubled.

Section 3(2)(b) of the Law provides a number of cases in which the law has no application. These are as follows:

1. Any professional person acting in the normal course of business or with consent, express or implied, of the relevant principal;
2. A constable of the rank of Inspector or above investigating an offense committed or alleged to have been committed within the jurisdiction;
3. A constable of the rank of Inspector or above, specifically authorized by the Governor in that regard, investigating an offense committed or alleged to have been committed outside the Islands which offense, if committed in the Islands, would be an offense against its laws; or
4. The Financial Secretary, the Inspector, or in relation to particular information specified by the Governor, such other person as the Governor may authorize;
5. A bank in any proceedings, cause, or matter when and to the extent to which it is reasonably necessary for the protection of the bank's interest, either as against its customers or against third parties in respect of transactions of the bank for, or with, its customer, and
6. The relevant professional person with the approval of the Financial Secretary when necessary for the protection of himself or any other person against crime.

. . . as amended, provides in section 3A that, where it applies, the following provisions shall apply: Whenever a person intends or is required to give in evidence in, or in connection with, any proceeding been tried, inquired into, or determined by any court, tribunal, or other authority, any confidential information within the meaning of the Law, he shall, before doing so, apply for directions . . . Upon hearing an application under subsection (2), a judge shall direct:

1. That evidence be given; or
2. That evidence shall not be given; or
3. That the evidence be given subject to conditions which he may specify whereby the confidentiality of the information is safeguarded . . .

. . . a bank should disclose information . . . Where disclosure is under compulsion by . . . the Mutual Legal Assistance Treaty (signed by the United Kingdom, United States, and Cayman Islands), or the Misuse of Drugs Law (of the Cayman Islands).

* Campbell, D., *International Bank Secrecy*, Sweet and Maxwell, London, 1992.

EXHIBIT 4   Relevant Swiss Bank Secrecy Laws and Regulations*

... the right to privacy refers to a person's right to protection of his or her person in the sense referred to by article 28(1) of the Swiss Civil Code ... Violation of the right to privacy is also tantamount to a tort under articles 41 *et seq.* of the Code of Obligations. Thus a bank can not only be held liable on contractual grounds but also toward third parties.

Article 47 of the Federal Law on Banks and Savings Banks of November 8, 1934

As amended,
1. Whoever divulges a secret entrusted to him or of which he has become aware in his capacity as officer, employee, mandatory, liquidator, or commissioner of a bank, as representative of the banking commission, officer, or employee of a recognized auditing company and whoever tries to induce others to violate professional secrecy, shall be punished by imprisonment for not more than 6 months or by a fine of not more than 50,000 Swiss francs.
2. If the act was committed by negligence, the penalty shall be a fine not exceeding 30,000 Swiss francs.
3. The violation of secrecy remains punishable even after termination of the official or employment relationship or the exercise of the profession.
4. Remaining reserved are federal and cantonal provisions concerning the duty to testify in court to give information to a government authority.

Swiss Penal Code, Article 305 bis

1. Whosoever undertakes actions which lend themselves to defeat the ascertainment of origin, the discovery or collection of assets which, as he knows or must assume, emanate from crime, will be subject to punishment by imprisonment or a fine.
2. In severe cases punishment is penal servitude up to five years or imprisonment. Added to this penalty of detention is a fine of up to 1 million francs. A severe case is if the perpetrator:
    a) acts as a member of a criminal organization;
    b) acts as a member of a criminal organization whose purpose is the continued practice of money laundering;
    c) realizes a large turnover or considerable profit from professional money laundering activities.
3. The perpetrator will also be subject to sentencing if he commits the principal act of violation abroad and such act is also punishable in the place of perpetration.

Lack of Due Diligence in Financial Transactions

Whosoever professionally accepts, keeps in safe custody, assists in the investment or transfer of assets which are the property of others and fails to apply the relative due diligence called for in establishing the identity of the economic beneficiary, is subject to punishment by imprisonment of up to one year or a fine.

* Campbell, D., *International Bank Secrecy*, Sweet and Maxwell, London, 1992.

The Hobbs Act

The Hobbs Act was a federal law enacted in the United States in 1951 to allow prosecution of corrupt American government officials. Specific unlawful activities under the Hobbs Act included extortion, fraud against a foreign bank, kidnapping, narcotics, and robbery. The law could be used against foreign nationals and institutions if any aspect of illegal activity occurred in the United States. Therefore, if the proceeds of drug trafficking were either held in the United States or transferred through the United States, the law's jurisdiction would become extra-territorial.[16]

In 1994 Antonio Giraldi, a former banker in Elliott's Mexico Team, was arrested and tried for violations of the Hobbs Act. At the time, Giraldi was employed by American Express Bank International. In 1989, Giraldi secured a client who deposited $21 million over a very short period and was later discovered by U.S. federal agents to be laundering money for the Mexican drug cartel. Elliott was asked to testify against her former employee.

Elliott explained to the federal court that it was a banker's responsibility to know the client, and that an experienced banker should be able to spot irregularities in an account. Citibank had specific guidelines used to protect the bank from becoming an instrument for drug money laundering:

> "Know your client," at least in our bank, is part of the culture. It's part of the way you do things. It's part of the way you conduct yourself. If you come in with a prospect or the name of a prospect, you will be sure to be asked, "Who is this person, what do they do, who introduced them to you," by at least three or four people higher than you. It's just the way it is . . . It's too risky to not do the due diligence, not to know who you are dealing with.[17]

No direct evidence was provided that proved Giraldi knew of the illicit origins of the money. Nevertheless, the court convicted Giraldi and sentenced him to ten years imprisonment on the grounds that he had been negligent in not determining the source of his client's wealth. In Giraldi's case, "willful blindness" was deemed the same as having knowledge.[18] A female colleague who helped Giraldi with the accounts was also sentenced to three years in prison.[19]

The Murder Investigation

On February 13, 1995, the lead story in the Mexican news briefs that were delivered daily to Elliott's office by e-mail reported that Raul Salinas was under investigation for the murder of his brother-in-law, José Ruiz Massieu. As Salinas was one of Elliott's most important clients, she called him. Salinas claimed:

> Those allegations are absolutely false. They are lies made up by my brother's enemies. He made some unpopular decisions in order to modernize Mexico and this attack against me and my family is a result of that.[20]

Although it seemed unlikely that the former president's brother could be formally charged, she decided to prepare a profile which, under bank policy, should have been completed when Salinas first became a client. Filling out the form, it became apparent that she had very little information about Salinas and the sale of his construction company. She had never visited the company, and did not even know its name.

On February 27, Salinas was arrested and formally charged with murder by Mexican authorities. A few days later, Mario Ruiz Massieu, the victim's brother and former chief investigator in the case, was arrested by U.S. Customs agents at the Newark Airport, also in connection with the murder. Ruiz Massieu, a professional civil servant, had somehow amassed millions of dollars, which had recently been deposited in a Texas bank. Within days allegations began to surface that both men had developed close ties with the Mexican drug cartel.[21]

In early March, Citibank's vice-president of legal affairs was contacted by a senior official at the bank and asked to investigate the Salinas accounts. Elliott was instructed to immediately report any activity on Salinas' accounts to the vice-president of legal affairs.

During the summer, the Swiss federal prosecutor and agents of the Swiss Central Narcotics Division contacted the executive vice-president of Citibank's office in Switzerland. They reported that at one of Salinas' residences in Mexico City, Mexican authorities had discovered phony identification which linked Salinas to a safety deposit box at Citibank Switzerland. The safety deposit box was believed to contain documentation valuable to the investigation that was being conducted by Mexican authorities.

Citibank Switzerland referred the matter to Elliott, who met with Swiss narcotics agents shortly thereafter. A senior agent asked Elliott to make arrangements with Patricia Rios de Salinas to remove any documents that were being held in the safety deposit box. She was to use the pretext that they were no longer secure due to an internal investigation by the bank. Since the agents, under Swiss law, were not permitted to enter the bank in order to seize the contents of the box, they planned to arrest Rios, documents in hand, while she was leaving the bank. The Swiss federal prosecutor asked Elliot to not discuss the matter with Citibank's vice-presdient of legal affairs, among others.

An article in the June 24 *New York Times*, "Score One for Salinas,"[22] revived doubts about Salinas' guilt. "We will get Mario!" began the fifth paragraph, which quoted a Mexican government official. The article continued:

> The [June 22] ruling of the U.S. magistrate in Newark, Ronald J. Hedges, also revived broader questions about the case against Raul Salinas. . . . Most of the witnesses whose credibility Hedges challenged in New Jersey when they implicated Mario Ruiz Massieu are lined up in Mexico to testify against Raul Salinas. . . . Hedges sharpened the public focus on doubts that have long existed about changes, gaps and contradictions in the testimony. . . . The most important witness left against Salinas is a congressional aide . . . [who] was probably the first person Hedges had in mind when he complained of being handed testimony from witnesses who changed their stories, contradicted themselves and said they had been tortured into confessing.

The U.S. magistrate further criticized Mexican prosecutors for having "picked and chosen" from testimony given against Salinas, and for having "glossed over" testimony that called into question the credibility of the witnesses.

Perhaps Salinas had been telling the truth. Perhaps this was a ploy by his family's enemies to undo the reforms begun by Raul's brother. Furthermore, neither Mexican nor Swiss authorities could offer any evidence linking Raul, or anyone in his family, to drug trafficking.

However, any feelings of vindication had to be balanced with knowledge of the fate of Giraldi and Elliott's testimony against him. The court, when passing sentence, had declared:

> A rational jury could have found it incredible that carelessness and honest mistakes could account for the complexity required to give the transactions the appearance of legitimacy.

The court's opinion was largely based on Elliott's testimony about Citibank's meticulous "Know Your Customer" policy, a policy that she herself may have violated.

Notes

1. This case has been written on the basis of published sources only. Consequently, the interpretation and perspectives presented in this case are not necessarily those of Citibank or any of its employees. Many of the events documented in this case were adapted from "Private Banking: Raul Salinas, Citibank, and Alleged Money Laundering", *United States General Accounting Office*, October 1998.
2. Oppenheimer, A., *Bordering on Chaos*, Little Brown & Co., New York, 1996.
3. Raul Salinas', Testimony, "Murder, Money, and Mexico: The rise and fall of the Salinas Brothers," *The Corporation for Public Broadcasting*, 1998. Also see "How a Mover and Shaker Manoeuvred His Millions", *The New York Times News Service*, June 2, 1996.
4. Under article 28(1) of the Swiss Civil Code, a bank could be held liable, both on contractual grounds and by third parties, for violating a client's right to privacy.
5. Amelia Elliott quotations throughout this case were adapted from official testimony given by Amelia Elliott in United States vs. Antonio Giraldi, May 12, 1994, cited in "Murder, Money, and Mexico: The rise and fall of the Salinas Brothers", *The Corporation for Public Broadcasting*, 1998.
6. "How a Mover and Shaker Manoeuvred His Millions", *The New York Times News Service*, June 2, 1996.
7. Raul Salinas quotations throughout this case were adapted from official testimony given by Raul Salinas to Swiss prosecutors on December 6, 1995, cited in "Murder, Money, and Mexico: The rise and fall of the Salinas Brothers", *The Corporation for Public Broadcasting*, 1998.
8. United States vs Antonio Giraldi, May 12, 1994, cited in "Murder, Money, and Mexico: The rise and fall of the Salinas Brothers", *The Corporation for Public Broadcasting*, 1998.
9. Ibid.
10. Ibid.
11. Campbell, D., *International Bank Secrecy*, Sweet and Maxwell, London, 1992.
12. The General Accounting Office is the investigative arm of the U.S. House of Representatives.
13. "Money Laundering: Regulatory Oversight of Offshore Private Banking Activities", *United States General Accounting Office*, June 1998.
14. EWJ Newsletters, Grendelmeier, Jenny, and Partners, Switzerland, 1998.
15. "Money Laundering: Regulatory Oversight of Offshore Private Banking Activities", *United States General Accounting Office*, June 1998.
16. "U.S. Laundering Law Applies in Salinas, other Corruption Case", *Money Laundering Alert*, January 1996.
17. United States vs Antonio Giraldi, May 12, 1994, cited in "Murder, Money and Mexico: The rise and fall of the Salinas Brothers", *The Corporation for Public Broadcasting*, 1998.
18. "Business crime: Appeals court thumps money-launderer", *International Commercial Litigation*, London, November 1996.
19. "Legal Guide to White Collar Crime", *International Financial Law Review*, London, July 1995.
20. Official testimony given by Raul Salinas to Swiss prosecutors on December 6, 1995, cited in "Murder, Money and Mexico: The rise and fall of the Salinas Brothers", The Corporation for Public Broadcasting, 1998.
21. Real-life soap opera, *Time*, March 20, 1995.
22. "Score One For Salinas", *The New York Times News Service*, June 24, 1995.

Index